# THE GOOD SOLDIER

# GARY MEAD

# THE GOOD SOLDIER

The Biography of Douglas Haig

Atlantic Books

LONDON

First published in hardback in Great Britain in 2007 by Atlantic Books,
an imprint of Grove Atlantic, Inc.

Copyright © Gary Mead 2007

The moral right of Gary Mead to be identified as the author of this work has
been asserted in accordance with the Copyright, Designs and Patents Act of 1988.

Maps © Jeff Edwards 2007

The moral right of Jeff Edwards to be identified as
the illustrator of this work has been asserted in accordance
with the Copyright, Designs and Patents Act of 1988.

Every effort has been made to trace or contact all copyright-holders.
The publishers will be pleased to make good any omissions or rectify any
mistakes brought to their attention at the earliest opportunity.

9 8 7 6 5 4 3 2 1

A CIP catalogue record for this book is available from the British Library.

ISBN 978 1 84354 280 3

Typeset by Avon DataSet Ltd, Bidford on Avon, Warwickshire

Printed in Great Britain

Atlantic Books
An imprint of Grove Atlantic Ltd.
Ormond House
26–27 Boswell Street
London WC1N 3JZ

# CONTENTS

This book is dedicated to the memory of Charles Hemming – teacher and friend, and the finest example of the impossibility of ever really knowing anyone.

# ACKNOWLEDGEMENTS

It is one of the pleasures of writing a book that one is frequently reminded of the innate kindness of strangers, who respond with generosity and warmth to a query for help that arrives out of the blue. Another is the process of discovery and acquiring greater understanding, and through that having one's prejudices demolished. I owe considerable debts to a number of people who have been very supportive of my writing this book. At Atlantic Books, Toby Mundy, publisher, has been very patient and encouraging; Angus MacKinnon, who commissioned the book, has been a tower of calm strength and has been unflagging in his intellectual engagement in the project – no author could wish for a better editor; Emma Grove has taken a keen interest and helped in numerous ways to steer it into print. Barry Holmes and Polly Lis gave unparalleled professional service in the editing process. My literary agent, Christopher Sinclair-Stevenson, has shown his usual unswerving confidence and extended unfailingly kind and regular morale-boosting. Colm McLaughlin, curator of the Haig Archive, and other staff at the National Library of Scotland (hereafter NLS), pointed me in fruitful and previously unexplored directions. Writers on the First World War and Douglas Haig owe a large debt to the 2nd Earl Haig for enabling access to the Haig archive at the NLS; I additionally owe a personal one for his agreeing to meet me and talk about his father, Field Marshal Earl Haig. Professor Hew Strachan of All Soul's College, Oxford University, whose grasp of the events and personalities of the First World War is unrivalled, read the manuscript and placed some episodes in a wider, more complex context than I had previously considered, as well as ensuring that some mistakes were suffocated before print. Those that may inadvertently remain are entirely my responsibility.

Denise Brace at the Museum of Edinburgh was inordinately helpful in photographic research, as were Dr A. R. Morton at the Royal Military Academy Sandhurst and David Fletcher, historian at the Tank Museum, Bovington, and archivists at the Imperial War Museum in London. Michael Orr provided much useful material from the records of the Douglas Haig Fellowship. Andrew Jefford gave me new insights into the Scottish whisky business. Matthew Turner helped me understand more of the difficulties of trying to measure the relative value of money over time. Martin Hornby of the Western Front Association provided me with useful background research materials. Colonel John Wilson, editor of the *British Army Review*, generously provided me with archive resources. Elizabeth Boardman, Archivist at Brasenose College, Oxford University, yielded fresh insights into the shifting perceptions of Haig.

The London Library is a remarkable entity, having under one roof so many of the essential materials that would otherwise be almost impossible to consult. The literature on Douglas Haig, the British army he spent his life serving, and the First World War is staggeringly vast and daily added to; a book of this kind could not exist without the work of many previous scholars and writers. The bibliography should be understood not as claiming a spurious authority but rather as a gesture of appreciation to some of those who have toiled before. Last but far from least, it would have been impossible to get this far without the support of my wife Jane and our daughters Freya, Theodora, and Odette, who bore this lengthy enterprise with fortitude, fun and frankness – they stoically endured a lot of absent fatherhood.

# LIST OF MAPS

# LIST OF ILLUSTRATIONS

**Section 1**
Young Haig
Haig family at Cameronbridge
BNC Wine Club, 1882
Sandhurst
7th Hussars, Secunderabad
Kitchener in the Sudan
Haig and Henrietta
Douglas and Dorothy Haig on their wedding day

**Section 2**
Boer Commandos
1912 aircraft
Haig with King George V
Cavalry at Mons
Haig with Lloyd George, General Joffre and Albert Thomas in France
Haig with Sassoon at GHQ
Passchendaele
Mark V tanks

**Section 3**

# The Anglo-Egyptian Sudan, 1898

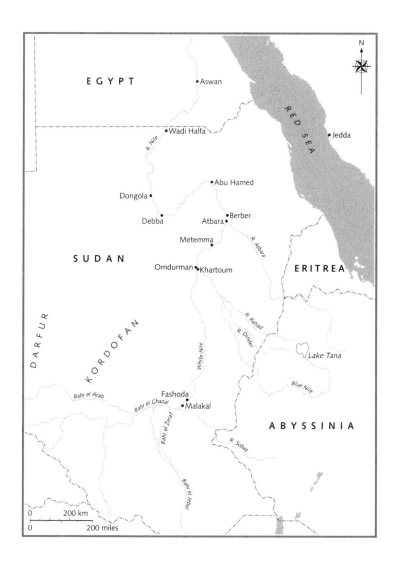

# South Africa, 1899

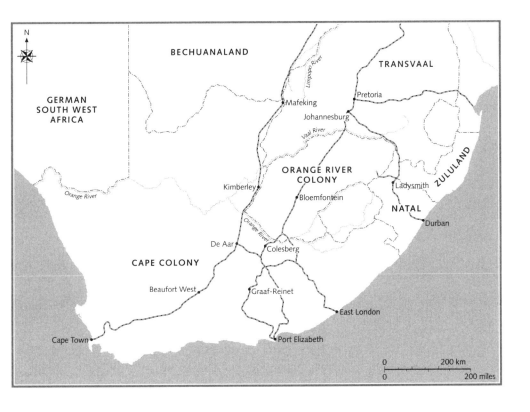

# The Western Front, 1914–1918

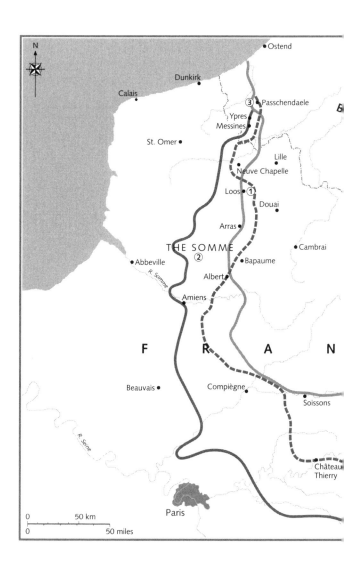

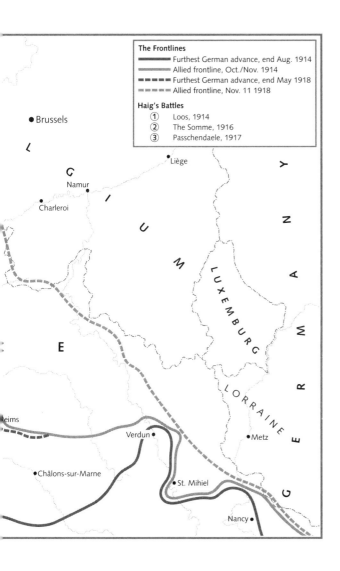

**The Frontlines**
— Furthest German advance, end Aug. 1914
— Allied frontline, Oct./Nov. 1914
--- Furthest German advance, end May 1918
··· Allied frontline, Nov. 11 1918

**Haig's Battles**
① Loos, 1914
② The Somme, 1916
③ Passchendaele, 1917

• Brussels

L

G
• Liège

Namur
•

• Charleroi

I

U

M

LUXEMBURG

N

A

M

E

LORRAINE

R

Reims

Verdun •
• Metz

E

• Châlons-sur-Marne

• St. Mihiel

G

Nancy •

# Neither Butcher nor Saint

There is little doubt that Haig was an idiot.

> The unofficial Australian view; see *www.diggerhistory.info*

Arguably he killed as many of his own men as Stalin and Hitler put together.

> Andrew Grimes, *Manchester Evening News*, November 1998

As any historian who has tried even mildly to be revisionist about Field Marshal Sir Douglas Haig on television will acknowledge, there is a corpus of opinion which is not overly interested in the facts because it has already made up its mind.

> Richard Holmes, foreword to *Blindfold and Alone*,
> Cathryn Corns & John Hughes-Wilson, Cassell, 2001

Douglas Haig's misfortune as a British general is that he was born and schooled in one era but had to fight his most important battles in another. His Victorian upbringing could not prepare Haig, nor anyone, for the stalemate of the Western Front's trenches and the incremental technological improvements which gradually made possible the grudging victory of November 1918. Haig was a cavalryman by profession and faith, who never felt comfortable using the telephone and never travelled in an aeroplane. His experiences in Sudan and South Africa had more in common with that of the Duke of Wellington – who died less than a decade before Haig's birth – than the battlefields of 1914–18, which saw the tank supersede the horse in attack, radio communications displace the telegraph, and aircraft come into their own as the eyes of command. Haig's inexorable rise to the highest reaches of the British army coincided with a remarkable social, political and technological change in human affairs. This wider social revolution affected all aspects of life, including the military. Perhaps the greatest advantage officers of Haig's era had over those in Wellington's time was simply that, unlike their predecessors, they had access to a professional education. The training available at the Royal Military College at Sandhurst (established in 1800) and the Staff College at Camberley (revived in 1857) was perhaps not ideal, but at least it was a schooling of sorts in their chosen profession; that in itself draws Haig closer to Montgomery's era rather than Wellington's. Although the popular view of Haig is that he was little more than a snobbish and ignorant opponent of all such change, this innately conservative man proved himself remarkably flexible in using and getting others to use new technology, once he was convinced it offered greater chance of success on the battlefield.

Haig was an ardent and lifelong believer in the virtues of the British empire, regarding it, as Lytton Strachey put it, as 'a faith as well as a business'; he would have shared Strachey's conviction that the monarchy was 'a symbol of England's might, of England's worth, of England's extraordinary and mysterious destiny.'1 Haig's unquestioning devotion to the British monarchy and the empire it crowned seems today anachronistic; yet to understand Haig requires a comprehension of this. While Haig never questioned the sovereignty of Parliament, he early acquired an unwavering contempt for politics and politicians. They were, for him, ephemeral; apart from God, with whom Haig enjoyed almost the same taciturn relationship as he did with his fellow humans, only the monarchy was eternal and beyond questioning.

In the popular imagination today Haig enjoys low esteem. Few associate him with the Scotch whisky, whose famous slogan went 'Don't be vague, ask for Haig', although he was a son of the founder of John Haig & Sons Distillers.2 If he is remembered at all, he is fixed in our minds as an incompetent Great War general, yet that conflict occupied only a fraction of Haig's total military service. His dedicated professionalism preceding the Great War and his unpaid devotion to the welfare of ex-servicemen afterwards are both now largely forgotten. The argument that Haig can no longer be casually written off as a nincompoop has been advanced in a small but growing range of more thoughtful studies of the Great War, yet he is still seen as a sort of cack-handed butcher, the result largely of the prevailing view of the Great War as one vast, awful mistake.[3] As Commander-in-Chief of the British Expeditionary Force (BEF) in Belgium and France between mid-December 1915 and the Armistice of 11 November 1918, a war in which almost nine and a half million men from the British empire enlisted in the armed forces and 947,023 died,[4] Haig stood at the peak of a vast termite-like social, military and technological organization, with almost two million men under his overall command. The complexity of administering the BEF was such that Haig's position was that of *primus inter pares* among the BEF's most senior generals – most of whom jockeyed for power and influence and few of whom emerge from the conflict with any glory, personal or military – rather than that of an absolute autocrat.

Another conventional black mark against Haig is that he lacked the gift of social badinage possessed by contemporaries; his taciturnity meant that, even for those who worked closely with him, he was an enigma. As so often with quiet people, condemnation is easier than comprehension. A former mistress of King Edward VII and, according to contemporary gossip, of Haig also, remarked on the striking contrast between Haig and Sir John French, his predecessor as C-in-C:

> Sir John French was very sociable, and, save where his work was concerned, frivolous, whereas Douglas Haig, a Scot, was chary of words and cautious as only a Scot can be. I once chafed him by declaring that he solemnly counted five before answering any question, including his opinion about the weather. 'Now that you call my attention to it, perhaps five is not enough. I will consider making it ten,' Haig replied, unmoved.[5]

Haig was modest and preternaturally calm. He neither courted publicity nor sought personal self-aggrandizement either before, during or after the Great War. His inability to coin a pithy phrase and reluctance to strike grand postures, in a context in which all his political masters and most of his military peers engaged in a bitterly conducted struggle against one another for position, power and promotion, has made it easier for Haig to become the focal point for our horror at how the Great War was conducted. Even on his death, the leader writer of *The Times* struggled to construct an appropriate elegy, the best that could be mustered being 'Haig's great characteristic was thoroughness.'[6] A more recent historian described Haig's methods as 'plodding professionalism.'[7] As adjectives go, 'thoroughness' and 'plodding' do not set the blood racing. Yet Haig's great virtues – gritty determination and a refusal to indulge in melodramatics – were and are precisely the qualities necessary in a general. This is true even if we acknowledge that his ambition for the battles he managed was inappropriately large for the tools at hand, leading him into grotesque errors of judgement at Loos (1915), the Somme (1916) and Third Ypres or Passchendaele (1917).

By the 1960s, when public opinion of the Great War had crystallized into its dismissal as futile, pointless, and mismanaged, the considered academic position was to damn Haig by faint praise:

Haig's career before 1914 was that of an efficient officer enjoying the advantages of wealth, high social position, and the important 'connexions' which had always been of considerable help in securing military promotion. He might not have obtained this promotion if he had been a fool; the fact that he obtained it did not necessarily mark him out as possessing outstanding qualities of mind or imagination. His knowledge of his profession was sound and solid; he was a man of strong nerve, resolute, patient, somewhat cold and reserved in temper, unlikely to be thrown off his balance either by calamity or success. He reached opinions slowly, and held to them. He made up his mind in 1915 that the war could be won on the Western Front, and only on the Western Front. He acted on this view, and, at last, he was right, though it is open to argument not only that victory could have been won sooner elsewhere but that Haig's method of winning it was clumsy, tragically expensive of life, and based for too long on a misreading of the facts.[8]

Haig's once high reputation thus degenerated so that, until quite recently, he was little more than an Aunt Sally. As John Terraine put it: 'A lot of people don't really hate Haig; they hate the War. Haig became the scapegoat.'[9] He was rich; he was a conservative; he was a committed cavalryman; he had a stereotypical Colonel Blimp moustache; and as for his rise to the top, even within the army his nickname was 'Lucky' Haig.[10] Haig's detractors accuse him of being incompetent, stubborn and callous; they have, from David Lloyd George (the Prime Minister during Haig's time as C-in-C) on, demonized him. This dehumanization is now popular received wisdom, even sweeping up professional historians who purport to write objectively:

> Unlike Kitchener, Wolseley, Roberts, Allenby and others, Haig never captured the imagination of his country. At a time when pictures of famous generals were passed among schoolboys like football cards are today, one suspects that Haig's was the least coveted and the most often traded away. His fame came not through the impression he made on his Army or his time, but rather via association – through his connection with the worst losses in British military history.[11]

There is ample evidence, however, to show that Haig certainly *did* capture the imagination of his country, and in a positive way, ranging from flattering contemporary full-page drawings in *Punch* to lavish newspaper coverage for his actions and person, through to a vast outpouring of national grief upon his death. The puzzle is not that Haig was never popular, but how his wartime and post-war popularity declined so rapidly after his death. Complex truths, messy and difficult to grasp, are rarely the victor in any struggle with that much wilier opponent, satire, and its brother-in-arms, myth. One of British television's most successful comedies, *Blackadder Goes Forth*, successfully satirized Haig as a dunderhead, building on the broad-brush attacks on Haig in Joan Littlewood's 1969 *Oh! What A Lovely War*, whose antecedents in turn are traceable to A. J. P. Taylor's enormously influential 1966 Penguin book, *The First World War: An Illustrated History*, which en passant poked fun at Haig's religious faith:

> Though he had no more idea than [Sir John] French how to win the war, he was sure that he could win it. Divine help would make up for any

deficiencies on his part. [...] His strategical judgements were sound within the framework of the Western Front, though he lacked the technical means for carrying them to success until almost the end of the war. [...] Haig had to do what he did; and though he did not succeed, no one better was found to take his place.[12]

Taylor's book, which was dedicated to Joan Littlewood, sold some 250,000 copies by 1989, an astonishing success for a work of history.[13] Contemporaneously with Taylor's work, Field Marshal Viscount Bernard Montgomery of Alamein, no slouch at massaging his own public image, was busily undermining Haig's reputation in public and in letters such as this, from 1969:[14]

> I served on the Western Front during the 1914/18 war, as a platoon commander in 1914 and rising to GSO1 of a Division by 1918. I never once saw Haig, nor did I ever see him after the war [...] I can never forgive a general who intrigues, as did Haig – against his C-in-C, and against his political chief [...] There was a tremendous gulf between the staff and the fighting army; the former lived in large chateaux miles behind the front. [...] Kiggell,[15] who was in my regiment, had no idea of the conditions under which the soldiers lived and fought.[16]

By 1998, even Haig's statue[17] in Whitehall was fair game for those casting around for someone to blame for the ghastliness of the Great War. During the Armistice commemoration that year the *Daily Express* carried a photograph of the statue under the headline 'Why do we let this man cast a shadow over our war dead?'[18] The newspaper gained the support of Alan Clark MP – taught at Oxford University by A. J. P. Taylor, and whose own 1961 anti-Haig book, *The Donkeys*, shamelessly wrenched Haig's words out of context – in its campaign to have the statue removed. In 2000, the writer A. N. Wilson called for the statue to be vandalized, as Haig was 'arguably a mass murderer [who should] never have been honoured by a statue in the first instance.'[19] In 2004, the anti-Haig cliché was aired at the National Theatre in London, in Alan Bennett's play *The History Boys*. A history master, Irwin, grooms schoolboys for entry to Oxbridge:

IRWIN: So we arrive eventually at the less-than-startling discovery that so far as the poets are concerned, the First World War gets the thumbs-down. We have the mountains of dead on both sides, right . . . 'hecatombs', as you all seem to have read somewhere . . . Anybody know what it means?

POSNER: 'Great public sacrifice of many victims, originally of oxen.'

DAKIN: Which, sir, since Wilfred Owen says men were dying like cattle, is the appropriate word.

IRWIN: True, but no need to look so smug about it. What else? Come on, tick them all off.

CROWTHER: Trench warfare.

LOCKWOOD: Barrenness of the strategy.

TIMMS: On both sides.

AKTHAR: Stupidity of the generals.

TIMMS: Donkeys, sir.

DAKIN: Haig particularly.[20]

Haig's name today is still synonymous with pointless expenditure of life in conditions of ghastly filth.[21] Yet many of his contemporaries saw Haig quite differently. In his 1958 novel *Love and the Loveless*, set in October 1916 on the Western Front, Henry Williamson (who met Haig) depicts his central character, Philip Maddison, reporting to Haig: '[. . .] a feeling of calm came over him [Maddison]. Dissolved was the figment of the great Field-Marshal. This man beside him was *safe*. It might almost have been Father, without the life-narrowing that Father had suffered. This father-like man was simple, and good like Father.'[22]

Williamson's allusion is clearly not just to Maddison's father, but to God-as-Father, a deification of Haig impossible to reconcile with the *Blackadder* version. Yet both misrepresent the truth about Haig, who was neither butcher nor saint but a man who, with human foibles and strengths, struggled with the demands of a vast army, variably supportive allies, back-stabbing politicians, a ferociously determined enemy, and the painfully slow arrival and erratic performance of unknown and previously untried new technology. His top intelligence staff officer in France for most of the Great War, John Charteris, thought Haig 'rarely erred but like all human beings he erred at times.'[23] It is a fair judgement. That Haig rose to a position of such eminence was, as so often, a matter of serendipity, personal effort and canniness. There were times when he succeeded; there were times when he failed. There are aspects to his personality which are shadowy; there are others which are in clear focus. As we approach the centenary of the outbreak of the Great War it is time to re-humanize Haig. For what emerges from any reasonably balanced view of Haig's life is that he strived to be a good professional soldier, and that he tried to live by a set of ideals which, while we may no longer share them, were nevertheless commonly regarded as virtues in Haig's day. Haig was a good soldier because he assiduously devoted himself to improving the professional competence of an army which, when he joined it, had been guided by a spirit of corrosive amateurism.

But he was also a good soldier in a more profound sense, demonstrating as much in the way he coped with adversity, adhered to principles in the face of pressure, and constantly applied his conscience. Leading a good life by definition involves *struggle*; those who do not struggle are unaware of the existence of ethical choice. Although he was born to privilege, at times in his life Haig none the less had to struggle almost daily with personal and professional dilemmas, the two often overlapping. His most severe personal crisis obviously came during the Great War, when he was regularly presented with the outer extremity of ethical trial as he deliberated the fate of large numbers of human lives; his way of coping with this was not to ignore the test but to embrace it wholeheartedly, and convert it into an intense devotion to what he saw as his primary ethical imperative: winning the war. That he was obsessed with victory was, in his time, regarded as a mark of his inestimable dedication. It is more than a little odd that he has since been denigrated for precisely this dedication. By the beginning of the twenty-first century Haig has been tarred, feathered and run out of town – lynch-mob justice borne aloft by TV and cinema satire:

Haig is absolutely central to the popular view of the war. His 'stupidity' and 'indifference' to the sufferings of his men provide an explanation for the

war's horrors which people can readily grasp [. . .] popular opinion holds
Haig responsible for the British Expeditionary Force's bloody failures but
academic revisionist history has not credited him with responsibility for
its bloody successes.[24]

A more balanced examination suggests that Haig is deserving of
neither simple condemnation nor rapt adulation. In January 2006 a
magazine article described how, within France, the 1789 Revolution is
now seen as much as a merchandising opportunity as a bloodbath, and
posed the possibility that 'The time may come, too, when General [sic]
Haig is reduced to a cuddly toy and Siegfried Sassoon's fine features
decorate a mud-pack in a beauty parlour.'[25] There is, perhaps fortunately,
not much likelihood of that happening. The popular view of Haig is still
irredeemably – and mistakenly – negative.[26]

'We need no more books devoted exclusively to Sir Douglas Haig.'[27] This
is rather like saying we need no more books devoted to Napoleon. Key
moments in history will always be explored and as long as that is the case,
the central characters will also exercise a perennial fascination. John
Buchan, who knew and admired Haig, correctly anticipated that 'Lord
Haig was so rich in character and talents that many books will be written
about him, for in the words of the German philosopher, "the compulsion
which a great man lays upon the world is to try to understand him".'[28]

The historian John Bourne has commented that, for him, writing
about Haig is 'always'[29] a depressing experience because it is difficult to
avoid controversy; yet this controversy gives extra piquancy to any biographer, who invariably goes through differing stages in relation to their
subject, the final and most serene perhaps being acceptance, which is
what I now feel for Haig. That serenity will probably not be shared by
many others. Haig's family may find this biography too intrusive, too
lukewarm, and too irreverent, while those for whom Haig is a monster
will find its understanding strays too far into forgiveness. Those yearning
for yet another history of the Great War will lose patience with the lack of
intricate battlefield details. Anyone engaged in a search for Haig the

philanderer, Haig the wit, or Haig the self-tortured soul, is destined for frustration; the archive materials (and only Haig's long-dead wife can have known to what extent they may have been 'weeded' of any potentially embarrassing materials) contain nothing of these. While he left a mountain of military papers, sporadically kept a diary, and wrote innumerable letters, Haig thought little of his papers from before the Great War, instructing his wife in early 1914 to destroy them; she ignored his request.[30] Those of his personal writings that remain offer next to no self-revelation and are completely lacking in self-analysis.[31]

Nor do I believe it sensible to try to psychoanalyse Haig at a distance.[32] My original intention was to try to understand Haig, who, for me as for many others of my generation, weaned in adolescence on A. J. P. Taylor's *The Great War*, was simply a 'donkey' general. At the end of my work on this iconic figure, I now believe that he was incorrigibly private, and that not only did he never fully unburden himself to anyone, he may not have even considered that he had an inner self that might be unburdened – perhaps the biggest mystery of his life. Yet I also have grown to realize that he is a fellow human being who exemplified numerous of the petty weaknesses we all share, but whose intimidating stiffness was his only salvation at times of great crisis. Haig's life reveals how a man lacking exceptional innate talent, possessing a substantial private income, fortunate enough to become noticed and favoured by the monarchy, and whose main professional skill was an ability to supervise and administer the work of others, could mount to the summit of the British army. Haig's moment in the harsh spotlight of history – the Great War – required him to bring to bear, when most needed, the perhaps minor but nevertheless vital virtues of stability, determination, dedication and personal authority. It is irrational to criticize him for being incapable of bringing that conflict to a swifter ending, for that was beyond the capacity of any individual.

In common with his age, Haig was often indifferent to the rules of grammar. He sprinkled capital letters with abandon, using them for emphasis ('Cavalry' was always thus, with upper case C). He peppered his private correspondence with exclamation marks, using them as a written tic equivalent to a kind of verbal harrumph. Where this book quotes directly from his personal papers, it reproduces his spelling, punctuation and grammar without alteration. The most important primary resource is the Haig Archive at the National Library of Scotland (NLS) in Edinburgh, on which much of this book is based; bibliographical details are sourced in the footnotes. The most comprehensive previous biography remains Alfred Duff Cooper's elegantly written, if overly deferential two-volume *Haig*.[33] The memoir by his widow, the Countess Haig,[34] is fascinatingly stilted and ultimately an exercise in devoted uncritical adulation. John Terraine's magisterial vindication of Haig[35] devotes itself almost entirely to Haig's Great War experiences, skipping across what preceded and followed. Philip Warner's *Field Marshal Earl Haig*[36] is an excellent study in many respects, despite shaking the reader's confidence when the opening sentence gives an incorrect date for Haig's birth. The academic historian Gerard de Groot's *Douglas Haig, 1861–1928*[37] makes diligent use of source materials but its author so clearly loathed Haig that his claim to objectivity is questionable. The most recent biography, by Walter Reid,[38] advances the sympathetic case for Haig more robustly than any since Duff Cooper, but tends to reinforce the notion that the success of the Allies in the final days of the Great War was a vindication of Haig's management of the war, rather than – as is my view – that by mid-1918 a conjunction of events had overtaken any single individual commander's understanding or control of events on the Western Front. While not a biography, the 2005 edition of Haig's Great War diaries and letters by Gary Sheffield and John Bourne has rendered considerable service to all those interested in Haig, by providing a modern scholarly edition – to which I refer frequently, not least because unlike archive materials this source is available to general readers.

All previous biographers of Haig have skirted around the subject of money, an unusual omission given that Haig himself kept a watchful eye on his financial position. Haig's private income – which meant he did not *have* to work – freed him from financial anxiety, yet was not grand enough to render him indifferent to his army pay. He was thrifty and the subject of money crops up regularly in his papers; it therefore seems pertinent to give, wherever possible, equivalent contemporary values.[39] If Douglas Haig's financial position seems by our standards enviably comfortable, we should recall that he lived at a time when the gap between rich and poor was much more extreme. In 1873 (twelve years after Haig was born), mill-hands at the silk factory in Halstead, Essex, complained to their employer Samuel Courtauld that they were unable to keep themselves 'respectable' on their wages of eight shillings a week; Courtauld, meanwhile, was taking an average of £46,000 a year from the business, almost completely tax-free.[40] To be moderately wealthy in 1861 or even 1914 was to be very comfortable indeed; to be poor meant continual fear of penury.

# CHAPTER ONE

# Whisky Gentleman

I am really, sir, the English public schoolboy. That's an eighteenth-century product. What with the love of truth that – God help me! – they rammed into me at Clifton and the belief Arnold forced upon Rugby that the vilest of sins – the vilest of all sins – is to peach to the head master! That's me, sir. Other men get over their schooling. I never have. I remain adolescent. These things are obsessions with me. Complexes, sir!

Ford Madox Ford, *Parade's End*

Douglas Haig was the eleventh child of one of Scotland's most successful members of the nineteenth century's rapidly growing middle class. His father, John Haig, had established in 1824 – and was sole owner of – the Haig distillery at Cameron Bridge, in Fife, the first to produce grain whisky.[1]

John Haig's family was enviably wealthy. The Haigs had been distilling whisky in Scotland for centuries; Robert Haig was one of the first to establish a distillery in Scotland, in 1627. In 1928 one of Douglas Haig's older brothers wrote: 'My father was a Distiller and large Farmer and was making £10,000 a year[2] when he married my mother in 1839. The Distillery Cameronbridge [sic] was sold to the Distillers Company in 1876; he remained on as a Director till his death. He was not connected with any business except his own, but I can remember him as a hunting man & taking an interest in County Affairs. He was first & last Chairman of the Leven & East of Fife Railway. Took a great interest in the Volunteers & Freemasonry.'[3]

Douglas Haig's paternal grandfather, William Haig of Seggie, died in 1847 and left a considerable fortune to his sons John – father of Douglas – and Robert. Shortly after Douglas was born, eight Lowland distilleries formed the Scotch Distillers Association, in 1865. The prime mover in establishing this venture was John Haig, whose John Haig & Co was by 1878 selling more than a million gallons of whisky a year.[4] The possession of a substantial private income was essential to carving out a career as an officer in the fashionable regiments of the army. Until the Cardwell army reforms of 1871 the British army permitted the purchase of commissions, although this was not the only way of getting one. In the field, officers could be promoted without purchase if a vacancy arose through death, and they could also receive brevet (temporary acting) promotions without purchasing them. There was no purchase mechanism at all for ranks beyond lieutenant-colonel. Nevertheless, Haig's early years were spent in a strictly class-conscious society, in which, as David Cannadine has observed, 'For good or ill, with enthusiasm or regret, most Victorians believed that theirs was a viable hierarchical society, that individual identities based on superiority and subordination were a better guide than collective identities based on conflict or accommodation.'[5]

This notion of hierarchy could be taken to ridiculous extremes, as Field Marshal Sir Evelyn Wood VC, one of Douglas Haig's earliest and strongest proponents, recalled. Wood remembered as a young boy visiting a rich female relative in her large Jacobean mansion. One morning the household's cook, Elizabeth, hanged herself from the rafters of the hall. The body dangled for a few hours while awaiting official investigation. A servant begged her mistress to use the servants' stairs, but she declined: 'I shall not use the servants' stairs because Elizabeth has been so rude as to hang herself in sight of my front hall.'[6]

Douglas Haig was born on 19 June 1861 into a strict although loving, close-knit lowland Scots Presbyterian household. Exactly one month after his birth at 24 Charlotte Square in Edinburgh, the baby was baptised into the Church of Scotland by the Reverend James Grant at the family home in Edinburgh.[7] By some oversight, Douglas's first name was not entered on the birth certificate, which merely carried as his name 'Haig'.

His elder brother John recalled his birth: 'I remember distinctly being told that a new baby had arrived in place of Georgie. I remember, too, his being christened by Dr Grant in the drawing room of 24, Charlotte Square. The reverend gentleman douced [sic] him heavily with cold water, which the infant resisted strongly by screaming loudly [. . .] Douglas was then a strong healthy child. After the birth of Douglas, our mother was in indifferent health [. . .] It was at Cameron House that Douglas spent most of his childhood. As a baby, Douglas was carried, or put in a kind of chair on a pony's back. We never had a perambulator.'

It was a world on the cusp of radical change, shifting towards a consumer-oriented, scientifically adventurous and politically more uncertain era. Some other births in 1861 indicate the kind of multifarious world in which Haig was to grow up. That year saw the birth in the USA of William Wrigley Jnr, founder of the eponymous chewing gum company, and of James Naismith, inventor of basketball; in Britain, that of Morgan Robertson, who invented the periscope in 1905, and Frederick Gowland Hopkins, winner of the Nobel Prize for medicine in 1929 for his joint discovery of vitamins; in Russia, that of Nikolai Rysakov, who in 1881 threw the first bomb at Tsar Alexander II; in France, of Georges Méliès, film-maker and special effects innovator. That year, 1861, was in many respects the high tide of Victorianism, halfway through Victoria's life and twenty-four years into her reign; the world was, in intellectual, cultural and technical terms, far more remote from the twentieth century than the simple chronological gap of thirty-nine years might suggest. The first major battle of the American Civil War, Bull Run at Manassas, Virginia, where the most advanced artillery piece was a muzzle-loading smoothbore cannon which would have been familiar to those fighting at Waterloo, took place a month after Douglas's birth. In China, British and French troops had recently concluded the second Opium War, and for the British the Indian Mutiny of 1857 was a fresh memory. The Suez Canal would not open for another eight years. British society was also tentatively shifting from unthinking brutality – the last public execution in England took place in 1868 – towards modest social reforms; the first compulsory schooling legislation was passed by

Parliament in 1870. Douglas Haig thus grew up when some of the contradictions at the heart of Victorian Britain were at their most extreme. As the historian G. R. Searle has observed, '. . . the apogee of Imperialism, with its idealization of war, occurred alongside the belated advent of democracy, the start of the Labour Party, a socialist renaissance, welfare politics, and a challenging of traditional gender stereotypes in the face of the prevailing cult of "masculinity".'[8]

Yet this social ferment naturally left some pockets of British society untouched, and the Haig household was thoroughly conventional in its distrust of change. Haig's formative years comprised a strict diet of unquestioning Presbyterianism, an inculcation of the virtues of manliness and dutiful deference to authorities, be they God, parents, schoolmasters, senior officers or the royal family, as well as a distaste for unseemly displays of extreme personal emotion. The moral code he early imbibed emphasized self-reliance and determination, endowing him with a system of beliefs that prized independence, stubbornness, fortitude and feigned indifference to ill fortune. This array of loosely interconnected principles provided him with a moral and spiritual compass until his death. Others similarly brought up may have rejected these values in adult life; for Haig they were eternal verities. His upbringing also instilled in him an awareness that superior social status was precarious, threatened by political radicalism and social upheaval; the whiff of anarchy was always around the corner.

Fortunately for Douglas Haig, a gritty slogger rather than a gifted intellect, the aspiring middle classes prized hard graft above genius. Samuel Smiles, the Victorian bourgeoisie's greatest exponent of success through individual endeavour, extolled the virtues of diligent labour in *Self-Help*, published two years before Haig was born. For Smiles, 'It is not eminent talent that is required to insure [sic] success in any pursuit, so much as purpose – not merely the power to achieve, but the will to labour energetically and perseveringly. Hence energy of will may be defined to be the very central power of character in a man – in a word, it is the man himself.' Smiles' creed was a comfort to those who, like Douglas Haig, lacked the spark of exceptional mental agility.

Though he spent his early childhood in lowland Scotland, Haig always talked of England when he spoke about his country, and in this he was firmly of his time. Almost two thirds of the United Kingdom's population lived in England and there was a widespread habit of using 'England' when what was meant was 'Britain'. Yet while Edinburgh's culture was strongly anglophone, several of Haig's abiding traits owed much to his Scottish ancestry. His whisky-distilling Scottish forbears had proved obdurate in the face of a harsh climate and the politically rigged competition they faced from English brewers and distillers, and, like them, Haig was remarkably strong-willed. This obstinacy was further honed by his being the last to arrive in a large family with a distant, elderly, crotchety father, and a devoted but ceaselessly preoccupied mother, to whom Haig had little choice but to clamour loudly to make himself heard above the demands of his siblings. Rachel, Haig's mother, doted on him, as on all her children, and for Douglas she became the rock upon which he built his life.[9] In prophecy as well as blood and parenting, Douglas Haig was born to be immoveable. The name Haig in the Scottish border country can be traced back as far as the thirteenth century, when Thomas the Rhymer (Thomas of Ercildoune) reputedly witnessed the charter granting Petrus de Haga, from whom the Haigs where descended, a modest castle and estate at Bemersyde, some fifty miles south-east of Edinburgh, about which he supposedly uttered his famous prophecy: 'Tide what may, whate'er betide, Haig shall be Haig of Bemersyde.'[10]

Douglas Haig's father was sixth in descent from Robert Haig, the second son of the seventeenth Laird of Bemersyde. The direct line of Bemersyde Haigs expired on 14 January 1854, when the unmarried James Haig, the twenty-fifth Laird of Bemersyde, died after a brief illness. His three surviving sisters, also unmarried, then leased the mansion-house to Lord Jerviswoode while they settled permanently near Rome. In 1866 they conveyed the whole estate and lands of Bemersyde to Lieutenant-Colonel Arthur Balfour Haig, another descendant of Robert Haig,[11] who took possession of the ancestral home at Bemersyde upon the death on 8 November 1878 of the final surviving sister, Sophia. The old stone house, much altered and added to by its various owners, was bought in 1919 by a number of private subscribers – including Winston Churchill, who during the Great War was a frequent critic of Douglas Haig – and freely given to the now Field Marshal Earl Douglas Haig, who finally took up residence there in early 1924.

Following a path fairly familiar in Victorian Britain, the wealthy John Haig married in 1839 at a relatively advanced age, thirty-seven, and took a young bride, nineteen-year-old Rachel Veitch. Just as her husband traced his family back through generations of Scots, so too did Rachel, whose ancestors, the Veitchs of Eliock, were reputed to have rustled cattle and smuggled contraband back in the early eighteenth century. John Haig remains an enigma, from whose hand there are scant surviving words. Of Douglas's mother we know much more, both because she wrote many more surviving letters than her husband and, tellingly, her children clearly adored her and carefully preserved her in their memories and their own correspondence. In a letter to Douglas Haig after the Great War, one of his sisters, Janet, then aged 72, recalled their mother; she made no mention of their father.[12] Rachel was born

at Stewartfield House, near Edinburgh, on Feb 29 1820 – married when she was 19 – and died when she was 59 – The Veitchs were a notably handsome race – tall, fair, with fine features, & well-shaped heads, and Rachael was worthy of her race. [. . .] I have heard it said she was 'the most beautiful woman in Scotland.' [. . .] She was shy and sensitive, & quick to <u>understand</u>, & sympathize (with others), somewhat silent and reticent, well-read, fond of poetry, and in her artistic discrimination, & appreciation of everything beautiful, she was before her time – yet she was no dreamer, but a capable, sensible, clearheaded woman, absolutely unworldly, & with a deep & reverent sense of Duty. [. . .] Selflessly devoted to her children she loved her youngest above them all, for, with the fine insight of great love she knew herself to be specially blessed in her quiet, worshipping but wordless, little son – Douglas.

Rachel strived to see her children well-educated by the standards of the day, as well as resilient in their Christian faith. As an adolescent she tried her hand at poetry and, despite the surviving examples being entirely conventional – on topics such as love, friendship, and fond memories – her literary efforts testify that she felt emotional self-expression was a vital part of life. This is an extract from a poem entitled 'What is Love', dated 1837, when she was sixteen:

Love is the passion which endureth
Which neither time nor absence cureth;
Which nought of earthly change can sever;
Love is the light which shines for ever.
What cold and selfish breasts deem madness
Lives in its depths of joy and sadness:
In hearts, on lips of flame it burneth;
One is its world – to one it turneth.
Its chain of gold – which hand can break it?
Its deathless hold – what force can shake it?
These passions nought of earth may sever,
But Souls that love – love on for ever.

Even the Haigs' wealth could not diminish the sorrows typical enough of Victorian times; three of Rachel's eleven children died before their first birthday.[13] Such large families were then unusual but not unknown.[14] According to Douglas's elder brother John: 'After her first son (William) was born, she withdrew almost entirely from the outside world and devoted her life to her children. She heard our prayers night and morning till she died in 1879. Every morning, in winter or summer, came to the nursery at 4 am to see if we were all right! Her devotion to us shortened her life by many years, as she died a comparatively young woman at the age of 58 (one year after my father).'[15]

Rachel's love for her children had a severely practical edge. In a letter of 4 April 1859 she discussed her wish for William, her first-born, to go to Oxford University, and artlessly revealed her pragmatic ambitions: 'Our object is not to make Willie a Distiller or anything in particular, we desire to develop in him to the utmost such gifts as he has received from God – to improve those intellectual qualities in which he may be deficient, & to cultivate his moral powers: to see him grow up a humble & honest

Christian – an accomplished well informed liberal <u>Gentleman</u> – with these qualifications be his lot in life what it may, he will command respect, & be in a position to desire happiness in whatever position of life God may place him [. . .] As for myself, I attach so much importance to scholarship – especially as an antidote to the vulgarity and narrowness of mind which active commercial pursuits are apt to engender in the best [. . .]'[16]

For families such as the Haigs the possession of wealth did not guarantee social status; the final necessary stamp in the passport marked 'gentleman' was attendance at a good public school, followed by a stint at Oxford or Cambridge.[17] Douglas and his brothers embodied a peculiarly Victorian contradiction. They owed their wealth to commerce and were thus of a class which was only just beginning to be accorded the status of gentlemen; yet their freedom from the necessity of earning their living clearly qualified them to be recognized as such. This self-doubt about their social status troubled their mother and, through her, some of her children. As a relatively belated entrant to the ranks of socially confirmed gentlemen, Haig always took great pains to conform to what he early learned were the outward marks of such status. Given that it was so important for Victorian males to regard themselves – and be regarded – as gentlemen, the lack of a conclusively shared definition of what it meant to be one must have been inordinately frustrating. As David Cannadine has remarked, when Douglas Haig was born it was 'still not clear who was a gentleman and who was not [. . .] by the middle of the nineteenth century, virtually anyone with a public-school education might be described as a gentleman, regardless of his parents' social background. The only sure way of knowing you were a gentleman was to be treated as such.'[18]

By pushing her sons towards the best available public schools and then Oxbridge, Rachel did no more than any other socially anxious parent of the day, trying to ensure that when they were adults they would be freed of the social disability of being considered not *quite* a gentleman. This preoccupation – who was, who was not, and what constituted being a gentleman – permeated Douglas Haig's life. His voluminous correspondence is littered with *ad hoc* snap judgements about men he met and dealt with; the highest acclamation he could bestow was to call someone a gentleman. It might seem as though in her letters to Douglas his mother was too preoccupied with his intellectual attainments – and his failures – but she was acutely aware that to succeed in Victorian England money was not in itself enough; attendance at the right educational establishments provided an additional guarantee of social status.

While the financially comfortable Haigs could easily afford all the servants they required, the sheer size and complexities involved in managing such a large group, together with the relative elderliness of John Haig, meant there was inevitably an emotional distance between Douglas and his father, already in his fifty-ninth year when Douglas arrived. Rachel took charge of all matters relating to the children and frequently consulted William, twenty years senior to Douglas, about the education and career plans for the younger boys. Douglas's splenetic father suffered from asthma and gout and shunned society, yet in the few accounts of John Haig by his children he is recalled as a loyal and affectionate husband and devoted father. According to his son John: 'Our father too was a good, liberal minded gentleman. He may have been a little quick-tempered and used bad language, but then swearing in those days was considered an attribute to many. And we did not mind it as it was all over as soon as said!'

Rachel's love of Douglas gave him security and self-confidence. This motherly worship occasionally, however, sparked jealousies: 'Due to the fact that he was his mother's favourite there were occasions when his brothers and sisters were overcome with resentment. One day they [John and George] seized him, cut off his curls and ordered him to carry them in his pinafore to his mother, who with sadness put them carefully in a parcel.'[19] George and John used horse shears to crop Douglas's hair. Some of the curls, still very blond, can be found in the National Library of Scotland archive, carefully tucked inside a small, age-grubby Victorian envelope.

The family indulged in a wide use of nicknames. One of Douglas's early childhood pet names was 'Paulie', which Rachel intensely disliked, though she tolerated another, 'Dougal'.[20] Even during the Great War his sister Henrietta would still write to him on occasion using yet another nickname, 'Dockey' or 'Docky'. His brother John explained its origin: 'In the family circle Douglas was generally called "Doctor". The name came about like this. He was first called Dougal, then there was a friend called Dougal Paul. From him Douglas, from being called Dougal, came to be called "Paul" or "Paulie". At that time there was a famous Scotch Divine called Dr. Paul, Minister of St Cuthberts. From him we called Douglas "Dr. Paul" and finally this was shortened to "Doctor" and more familiarly "Dockey", by which name my sister Henrietta always addressed him and in her letters too – to the end.'[21]

The main family home when Douglas was born was Cameron House, in Fife, near the distillery, while the family-owned Charlotte Square residence in Edinburgh was used as a convenient place to house the older children who were attending Edinburgh schools. Although he was never employed in the day-to-day running of the family whisky business, as an adult Douglas Haig became a director of the company and took an active interest its affairs. Whisky not only gave him financial security but also through his elder sister Henrietta brought him a crucial piece of good luck, an entrée into the entourage of Edward Prince of Wales (the future King Edward VII). This ensured that Haig's undoubted merits as an officer were not, unlike those of some of his contemporaries, to be overlooked by the monarchy. This proximity to the monarchy is a key facet of Haig's rise. Queen Victoria had reintroduced personal approval of all commissions in the British army by the monarchy, and Edward VII perpetuated this habit. In 1869 Henrietta married William Jameson – of the Jameson Irish whiskey family – a close personal friend and yachting companion of Prince Edward's. Jameson had an eye for the ladies and one dalliance caused Henrietta unhappiness even in her old age, when she turned to her younger brother for solace.[22]

In his later life Jameson was considered 'frightening' by his nephew George Haig, Viscount Dawyck, Douglas's son: 'He always looked to us as though he had a sour plum in his mouth.'[23] But Jameson's royal connections provided Douglas, via Henrietta, with a smooth entry into an incalculably useful milieu which might otherwise have remained forever closed. Henrietta exercised considerable influence over her younger brother and was a point of stability throughout his life, the elder sister who, after the death of Rachel, was clearly a maternal surrogate. According to Brigadier-General John Charteris, who probably knew Haig as well as anyone outside his family: 'Between these two – brother and sister – there existed throughout the whole of Haig's life a very remarkable bond of comradeship and affection. Henrietta was much more than a sister; until his marriage, she was the only woman to whom Haig ever gave a thought; she was his confidante and adviser.'[24] Henrietta, locked into marriage to a wealthy rogue and herself childless, gave to Douglas her maternal devotion and love.

The Haigs were a peripatetic family, regularly frequenting seaside towns on the south coast of England and travelling to continental European spas, often on the pretext of John Haig's needing to take the waters to ease his over-burdened liver. Rachel would also move the family to be closer to those elder children she felt might need her support, as in 1864, when the family relocated temporarily at Blackheath, on the edge of London, to be with Hugo, then employed in a stockbroker's office in the City. At Blackheath Rachel gave Douglas a toy drum on which she wrote: 'Douglas Haig, 1 Lee Park, Blackheath. Sometimes a good boy.' She also gave him a handkerchief on which were embroidered the words 'Douglas Haig. A good boy.' Rachel's labelling of Douglas as 'good' was wishful thinking; he was a passionately determined and recalcitrant child, as Haig's widow commented: 'very self-willed, extremely difficult to manage and subject to occasional fits of violent temper. Even his mother, whose love for him was quite exceptional, and, perhaps the most abiding and powerful influence on his whole life, was, at times, then quite unable to manage him.'[25]

On one occasion, when the family visited a photographic studio for a group portrait, the infant Douglas refused to sit still; he kicked and yelled so much the sitting was abandoned. Next day he was taken back, alone, and this time was well-behaved, after being bribed by the promise that he could hold his favourite pistol, as well as being given peppermints and confectionery called 'black balls'. On another occasion the child Douglas refused to cross a small bridge across a ditch. He 'simply lay down and kicked, and made a scene! And he was strong! The nurse could hardly carry him over, and one kindly old gentleman, thinking he was being hurt, remonstrated with the nurse, but he suddenly discovered it was only temper, said so and went away.'[26]

What is interesting, however, is how *little* evidence of bad temper there is in his adulthood, though he clearly disliked having his opinion and authority challenged once his mind was made up. Today we would not be so inclined to judge the infant Douglas as naughty; he seems to have been entirely normal in the vociferous expression of his then ungovernable emotions. This is what normal children aged three are often like.

It was a practical necessity, given the family's size, that Douglas was brought up in a household where order was imposed. When he was nearly four his mother wrote out some rules for the nursery. The nurse 'must rise every morning at 6. The nurse must devote her time & thoughts to the Comfort, and well being of the 3 little boys under her charge – <u>cheerily</u> – and <u>happily, always being beside them</u>. <u>Perfect Regularity Necessary</u>:- children's porridge at 8 o'clock – dinner at ½p. one – tea at 6. Lights out, and nursery quiet at 10. Children bathed every night – their hair washed once a week – their socks changed twice a day [. . .] Good fire, and everything comfortable for the children on rising – when out to walk they are not to go to people's houses [. . .] All children's tempers must be studied – the treatment which is good for one child may not suit another – Cameron House, 21st April 1865.'

It would take a particularly perverse reading of this to regard it as anything but a fairly basic and, for the time, relatively liberal requirement for the orderly running of a bustling group of boisterous children. The young boys, who were 'not worried very much by lessons and allowed to run, more or less, wild', enjoyed considerable freedom, spending much of their time riding old ponies called The General, Bismarck and The Doctor. No serious childhood illnesses afflicted Douglas, except for an early tendency to asthma, which troubled him into adolescence; his lifelong adoration of horses and riding is partly explained by the contemporary belief that horse-riding and outdoor exercise were helpful for asthmatics. His asthma and the willpower he applied to try to conquer it speak volumes about Haig's inner strength. Coping with chronic asthma often induces in young people an early resilience and boundless energy as part of their efforts to resist such attacks; other famous, equally driven asthmatics include Charles Dickens, Benjamin Disraeli, Theodore Roosevelt, and General William Tecumseh Sherman, each of whom had enough energy for several ordinary men. Douglas Haig refused to be cowed by his asthma and in this lies a key to understanding his adulthood. He had fewer attacks as he grew older, but his childhood experiences of fighting to breathe remained powerful memories, and meant that he early on developed the habit of being scrupulously careful of his own health.

There is nothing to suggest, however, as some[27] have alleged, that Haig was a hypochondriac, which, strictly speaking, implies an unbalanced anxiety about one's health.[28] Haig coped with asthma by developing as a boy a careful regime to keep fit, active, and avoid exacerbating a congenital weakness. According to his brother John, he 'was always careful about his diet because he knew how much he would suffer if he took things that brought the asthma on, refusing dainty dishes, saying, "Don't you think I should be very foolish to eat anything that I knew might bring on another attack, merely for momentary selfish gratification of eating something I liked." '

Patience, deferred gratification, self-discipline – these facets of Haig's early development can be seen in his adulthood. His mother's letters to the young Douglas are littered with exhortations that he should keep warm and dry, wear sufficient clothes, and her prayers that his asthma is being kept at bay. Douglas reciprocated his mother's adoration; even after the Great War he kept her portrait over his bed at his Bemersyde home. Yet, according to Douglas Haig's niece he 'never spoke of her – one doesn't often mention sacred things. I asked him if his mother was a clever woman, "Yes," he replied, "she was clever but she was not educated . . . women were not taught lessons in her day." '[29]

Some have made the charge that Rachel's influence was detrimental:

'His early development presents the picture of an unusually sullen and aggressive child being pushed resolutely forwards and upwards by a strict and puritanical mother [. . .] Under the circumstances it is hardly surprising that, though remaining devoted to his mother, he became somewhat ambivalent towards women, and uneasy, to say the least, about the whole subject of sex.'[30]

This contains a grain of truth perched on a hill of exaggeration. Haig was not 'unusually' sullen or difficult, nor does this depiction of Rachel tally with the evidence of her maternal kindliness. But it is true that Haig's diaries and papers are remarkably silent on the matter of sexuality and emotions; in his surviving papers there are only one or two general and usually disparaging remarks about women, and before his late marriage he had acquired the reputation of being a misogynist.

As she grew more elderly, Rachel became increasingly religious and strongly encouraged her children to adopt her own very conventional piety, which they did not always appreciate. His elder brother George, then aged sixteen, wrote to fourteen-year-old Douglas from Biarritz on 17 June 1875 that 'Mamma is getting vy pious she reads prayers two times a day at which I have to say my prayers too. The drinks nothing but vin de table d'hote its doing penance with the salt water cure.'[31]

Rachel's Presbyterian devotion lived happily alongside her belief that it was possible to contact the spirits of the dead; she and Douglas's sisters frequently tried to make contact with beings in the after-life. Henrietta engaged in 'automatic writing' throughout her life, while right up to her death Rachel participated in seances. One of Rachel's final letters to Douglas, when he was seventeen, describes the efforts of his sister Janet, then aged thirty-two: 'Jenty is busy waiting for the Spirits to write but they won't answer to day is the anniversary of my Father's death & I thought perhaps we might address him: but it is of no use.'[32]

The possibility of spirits living beyond the grave and reappearing when summoned by a sympathetic medium was not then regarded as absurd. The Society for Psychical Research, established in 1882, was dedicated to imposing scientific rigour on the investigation of the paranormal. It gained the support of William Gladstone, two bishops of the

Church of England, eight fellows of the Royal Society, John Ruskin, Alfred Tennyson, the Cambridge philosopher Henry Sidgwick, the first president of the Society, the physicist Oliver Lodge, the first person to transmit a radio signal (a year before Marconi), Alfred Russel Wallace, co-discoverer with Charles Darwin of the principles of evolution, and Arthur Balfour, whose presidency of the Society in 1894 was no handicap to his becoming Britain's Prime Minister in 1902.[33]

The absence of any surviving signs of warmth between Douglas and his elderly father, who had too great a fondness for his own product, suggests something other than the conventional middle-class Victorian mores which imposed a distance between father and children. Through regular heavy drinking, copious eating and little exercise, John Haig was already fast approaching his dotage when Douglas arrived. There is little surviving correspondence from John Haig senior to Douglas; he added a postscript to a letter from Rachel to Douglas dated 5 March 1878, when Haig was sixteen and at school. Appropriately enough, John Haig talked about guns: 'PS Your Mother wishes me to draw your attention to the sad accident which took place in your rifle corps a week ago & to draw your attention to the absolute need there is in managing fire arms. As a rule I never allow any friend of mine to bring loaded fire arms into the house or carriage or have a loaded gun in charge of any one – Now that the Breetch [sic] loaders are in universal use no one should even sit down to lunch without first removing the cartrages [sic] from every gun in the party. In our Volunteer Corps the Officer Commanding had strict orders to see this done & to allow no one to get into any train or carriage of any kind until the charges were drawn or fired off.

Yr Afft Father

John Haig.'[34]

Douglas's early education was typical for the middle classes of his day, involving the employment of a private tutor whose main task was to get the boy into one of the better public schools. Such an education was relatively expensive, with the total cost of educating a son and fitting him to enter a profession as much as £2,000, spread over ten years.[35] Tutoring Douglas was an uphill struggle: 'Like Wellington before him,

[Douglas] was considered the dunce of the family [. . .] Douglas Haig gave no precocious evidence of intellectual ability.'[36]

At the age of eight he was sent, along with brother John, to be tutored by Mr Olliphant at 33 Charlotte Square, Edinburgh. He spent a brief period there before going to the Edinburgh Collegiate, under Dr Bryce, during 1869–1871. He then went to Orwell House, a preparatory school at Rugby, where he was prepared for public school under the tutelage of Dr Hanbury. At Orwell House he showed a marked lack of concentration and, according to a contemporary school report, was 'very backward in Latin; spelling very poor and writing careless; rather tiresome at times; as he is backward he ought to be more attentive.'[37]

Rachel dearly wanted Douglas to attend Rugby, one of the most renowned public schools at the time. There was no hint at this stage of his life that Douglas was destined for the army, but attendance at an esteemed public school was almost de rigueur for any boy who wished to make a career in one of the socially fashionable regiments. As Sir John Keegan has remarked: 'Public school was a perfect preparation for a military career, an observation none the less true for being hackneyed. For late nineteenth-century public schools inculcated many of the military qualities – physical fitness, skill at games, toughness, love of the outdoors – and taught most of the military virtues – obedience, companionability, leadership, concern for the welfare of subordinates.'[38]

On 9 June 1875 Rachel wrote to Douglas's elder brother John, who had attended Clifton College in Bristol, to congratulate him on his decision to try for Cambridge University: '[. . .] It is God's doing! & I desire to acknowledge His loving Hand in this as in every event of my past life! [. . .] You must write to Douglas about your prospects – & it will be an immense spur to him in his Greek which he dislikes so much – when my brothers were at school, it was considered that a boy who did not learn Greek was uneducated – & to my idea an Oxford & Cambridge University man is of a higher stamp than those who are not.

'Of course you must mix with men in college who, in the course of a few years, will be the Great Men of the day – Statesmen lawyers etc & the training makes a Gentleman!'[39]

Despite her regular exhortations, Douglas struggled at school. Rachel again wrote about this disappointment to his brother John on 24 September 1875: 'Dr Hanbury tells Douglas, but I hope he is wrong, it is hardly worthwhile his going up to Rugby as he wd be kicked out in a year or so [. . .] I am dreadfully vexed at this, but I hope he may be allowed to try & he may come off better than he expects – Meantime write & advise the poor Laddie to do all he can to get in to big school – Rugby suits his health & were it for no other reason I do most anxiously hope he may not leave the place.'[40]

Dr Hanbury informed Rachel that, as his abysmal grasp of Greek would let him down if he sat Rugby's entrance examinations, Douglas should be steered towards Clifton College, where entry was not dependent upon passing an exam in Greek, but whose new headmaster, who had taught at Rugby, nevertheless maintained high academic and moral standards. Haig attended Clifton between 1875–1879, until he was eighteen. Established in 1862, Clifton College was a newcomer among public schools. Under its second[41] headmaster, the Reverend John Percival – who went on to help establish Somerville College, Oxford, one of the university's first women's colleges, and ended up as a somewhat free-thinking Bishop of Hereford – Clifton was, for the period, a relatively open-minded institution; Percival established Polack's House, the first Jewish boarding house at an English public school.[42] Conditions at Clifton were not unusually harsh, though the school was – and is today – unique in employing a master with the title 'Marshal', whose sole responsibility was to enforce discipline, class attendance and school rules. Percival, a high-minded Christian Socialist sympathizer, made school uniform and games compulsory and instilled in the boys an ethos of public-school chivalry, in which patriotism and group loyalty were cardinal virtues. It was a school ideally suited to the needs of the Haigs, its original prospectus stating that its main purpose was to provide 'for the sons of gentlemen a thoroughly good and liberal education at moderate cost.' It catered, in the words of a more recent headmaster, for the 'needs of a class newly enriched by the profits of industrial and commercial growth.'[43]

The timetable of the older public schools was largely preoccupied with training in the reading and writing of Latin and Greek prose and verse, and, while Percival introduced more French, history and some sciences, by the time Haig left Clifton those boys who were unable to make the grade in the Classics and who spent more time on the Moderns found themselves lumped in a category which Percival's successor described as 'a refuge for the less cultivated and the less capable [. . .] the home of the unambitious, the unliterary, the stagnant.'[44] Percival insisted that intellectual achievement was a guide to superiority of moral character, and entry to the school's sixth (and highest) form was by academic merit alone; Haig did not make the grade. According to his brother John: 'I fear Douglas was not a success at Clifton, with difficulty he reached the fifth form!' Clifton stood out in one other respect, as being one of a handful of public schools which had 'the nurturing of future army officers [as] almost their principal function.'[45] At Clifton, despite his loathing for Greek, Douglas persisted with the language as it was a necessary torture if he were to enter Oxford or Cambridge. Henrietta, who never had to tackle Greek but felt justified in giving advice, cajoled him into trying harder, as in a letter she sent from Biarritz in 1875:[46] 'Of course you know Bee [John] has to begin Greek again if he goes to Cambridge for he cant get in without it – don't you think it wd have been much better if he had stuck to it instead of giving it up at Clifton? It wd have saved him a lot of hard work & drudgery now.'[47]

Haig left little mark on his contemporaries at Clifton – perhaps the most famous of whom, Sir Henry Newbolt, arrived there in 1876 – and, happy or not, he would have realized and accepted that stoic endurance was expected. At Clifton a pattern was set, whereby Haig co-existed with his fellows without forming intense associations. Public schools were places of notoriously whimsical but harsh punishment – beatings by both masters and older boys were commonplace and regarded as an essential part of discipline – and also of a nebulous homoeroticism. The nineteenth-century revival of interest in chivalric codes and behaviour, traceable to Sir Walter Scott, fed into the muscular Christianity that suffused public schools at the time and provided a useful cloak for those whose homoerotic interests strayed into overt homosexuality, as in the case of John Addington Symonds, a poet and critic who periodically taught at Clifton during Haig's time. After Douglas's death, his widow wrote to Clifton's headmaster, Mr N. Whatley, in her desire to learn more about her deceased husband's early life. Whatley was of little help: 'Oddly enough it is very difficult to find anyone who knew him at all intimately. Last year [1928] we were trying to find someone who had known him intimately at School to give us more detailed information than we possessed. Everyone who was at School with him remembered him, but none of them said they had known him at all intimately. Of those I wrote to, Sir Francis Younghusband [the Central Asian explorer] knew him better than any, but he does not claim to have known him well.'[48]

But Clifton clearly left its mark on Haig and, in his lifelong quest to find and loyally serve a higher authority (mother, headmaster, king, God), Clifton provided him with a permanent reference point as to the idealized behaviour of a gentleman. In later life he recalled Clifton fondly and the school's motto – *Spiritus intus alit*, the spirit that quickeneth – was frequently on his lips in adulthood.[49]

The humdrum regularity of life at Clifton was interrupted by the death of John Haig senior, at the age of seventy-six at the family home in Edinburgh on 22 March 1878, when Douglas was sixteen. It was an agonizing and, no doubt, horrifying death through haematemesis, probably induced by chronic alcoholism, in which he vomited blood for some part of the sixteen hours between the onset of his fatal attack and his death.[50] In the Haig archives there is nothing to show that Haig senior's passing was deeply mourned by his children, although Rachel evidently suffered something like a stroke shortly after. Douglas learned from the example of his father the dangers of self-indulgence; throughout his life he ate simply and moderately, did not smoke, not even cigars, and his consumption of alcohol was very low by contemporary standards.

By the spring of 1879, then approaching his eighteenth birthday, Douglas was being prodded by his eldest brother William into leaving Clifton so that he could attend a crammer to help him achieve sufficient knowledge of Greek to pass Oxbridge entrance exams. William Haig had investigated the possibility of Douglas receiving coaching from a Mr Rhoades, at Rugby, who had performed the same service for John junior. But Mr Rhoades could not assist. William forwarded Rhoades' letter to Douglas, accompanied by his own suggestion as to what Douglas should do.

Rugby March 14 1879

My dear Sir,

I have given up taking pupils; but my brother James Rhoades, Haileybury, Banksome Park, Bournemouth, is a better Tutor than I ever was [. . .]'

Edin 15 March '79

My Dear Douglas,

You see what Mr Rhoades says. Please let me know if you will go to his brother to read & prepare yourself for college in October. If you will, please go at once & give notice that you will not return to Clifton after Easter, & if it is necessary I will send written notice. If you decide on going to James Rhoades wire me over night & I will put matters in trim for you.

There is however no time to be lost if you are going to a Tutor & to Oxford in October. You ought to go to him at once & take no holidays at Easter. Bournemouth wd be a nice place for Mama to go to but if she were there, you wd do no work at all.

Yours affct

W.H.H

Douglas took William's advice. Soon after William's letter to Douglas, Rachel, who by this time was scarcely able to speak or write, was taken to Ramsgate, where she swiftly declined and died on 21 March 1879; she was subsequently buried next to her husband at Markinch, Fife. After the funeral Douglas joined his elder brother Hugo, then aged thirty-four, on a brief excursion to California, before returning to be crammed full of Greek grammar. The loss of his mother removed the most important figure of his formative years. For future guidance and support Douglas depended on Henrietta. Of Rachel's death, Douglas's son, Dawyck, wrote: '[W]hen she died at the early age of fifty-eight in 1879 my father was heartbroken.'[51] This may well have been true, but to what degree did this upbringing manifest itself in Haig's adulthood? Given Douglas Haig's strangulated emotional nature, his unquestioned grief at Rachel's death was in all probability deeply internalized. Certainly in the voluminous Haig archives at the NLS there is nothing in Douglas Haig's own hand which refers to his feelings concerning his mother's death.

Despite this, given that he did have a formidably affectionate mother and emotionally distant father, some have been tempted to interpret his conduct as a general through the prism of his childhood. Such efforts, however, can lead to triteness: 'From research into the nature and aetiology of authoritarianism it was concluded that the condition derives from the impact on the child of status-anxious parents. Subsequent research has confirmed a relationship between sexual repression, militarism, religiosity, aggression and having a restrictive mother. Haig fits this pattern pretty well.'[52]

This kind of theorizing cannot really explain why Haig became the kind of general he did or the actions he took, for the simple reason that his own brothers experienced the same upbringing by their parents and yet went on to lead very different and rather unexceptional lives. While Rachel was 'status-anxious' – and in this respect completely typical of her class and epoch – John Haig appears to have possessed none of these worries, simply assuming his sons would naturally follow him into the distilling business. And while Rachel was clearly ambitious for Douglas, she did not single him out for her especial attention; she was ambitious for *all* her sons. More important, her letters reveal her to have been remarkably kindly, even indulgent, to her children. Had she been the fierce Calvinist of the clichéd picture, it is unlikely that her children would have recalled her, many years after her death, with such loving affection. There is no 'pattern' into which Haig can be straitjacketed without being remarkably indifferent to the individual complexities of his family background and social environment. Such *post hoc* lobotomizing of historical figures can lead to nonsense, such this interpretation of the reasons why Haig chose to fight the battles of Passchendaele: 'Whether by accident or by design, the events of Third Ypres [also known as Passchendaele] – the enormous release of destructive energy, the churning up of ground until the overlapping craters coalesced into one great reeking swamp, and the expulsion into this morass of more and yet more "faecal" bodies – constitute the acting-out of an anal fantasy of impressive proportions [. . .] the conclusion [is] that acting-out was not so much coincidental as deliberately, if unconsciously, motivated.'[53]

Haig's 'real' motive for staging the battle of Passchendaele was, on this reading, because it enabled him to express the long repressed fantasy of dabbling in the biggest pile of excrement ever imagined. This crass interpretation, like all quasi-Freudian analysis, defies challenge. If we search for clues in Haig's upbringing as to his future actions, behaviour and success, then the facts are that he was fortunate in having a rich father, an indulgent and loving mother, and a network of strong sibling support, particularly that of Henrietta. These positive influences counterbalanced his own rather limited innate intellectual abilities, by inculcating in him a determination to work hard and master his own weaknesses. By the time he left Clifton to go to Oxford University, having crammed enough Classics to matriculate, Haig was an undistinguished, thoroughly conventional, parentless young Victorian. There was nothing in his life thus far which hinted at a rise to eminence – except, perhaps, the useful social connections of Henrietta, his devoted sister.

CHAPTER TWO

# Polo Field and Parade Ground

It is not that the Englishman can't feel – it is that he is afraid to feel. He has been taught at his public school that feeling is bad form. He must not express great joy or sorrow, or even open his mouth too wide when he talks – his pipe might fall out if he did.

E. M. Forster (Tonbridge School)

In October 1880, the nineteen-year-old Douglas Haig arrived at one of Oxford University's least intellectually eminent colleges, Brasenose (BNC), where he was one of eighty-nine 'commoners' or ordinary entrants; there were also twenty-nine scholars and exhibitioners. His student days were clearly happy, if academically undistinguished, and in later life he always recalled them with affection. On the day of his marriage he even took a detour to show his bride his old college rooms. Such was Haig's high regard for Brasenose that although his busy life forced him to turn down many invitations to college dinners after he left the university, he nevertheless maintained a close relationship with BNC to the end of his life. After the Great War, BNC's governing body erected in 1920, as one part of a three-fold war memorial, a heavy Doulting stone tablet in the entrance to the college, on which were engraved the words:[1]

THIS RECORD IS HERE SET THAT THOSE
WHO PASS MAY BE PUT IN MIND OF
FIELD MARSHAL EARL HAIG & ALL
THE OTHER BRASENOSE MEN WHO

DEVOTED THEMSELVES AT HOME OR ABROAD
TO THE SERVICE OF THEIR COUNTRY
IN THE TIME OF PERIL
1914 ~ 1918

In 1969, when Haig's reputation had perhaps reached its nadir, the BNC governing body used the pretext of refurbishing the Lodge to remove this memorial. Today it languishes unnoticed in a hidden corner of the college in the open air, under a rusting radiator and other detritus, its face symbolically turned to the wall, testimony to how far Haig's name and his achievements have been not just forgotten, but now represent an embarrassment to the place he so revered.[2]

Haig and BNC were a perfect match. The college's solid reputation as a bibulous, hearty, sporty and convivially unacademic place ideally suited his intellectual abilities and social interests. In the second half of the nineteenth century BNC was particularly attractive to sons of the squirearchy; it fulfilled the task of getting an Oxford education without demanding strenuous application to books. Its entrance standards were less demanding than more intellectually prestigious colleges such as Balliol, and it could not afford to turn down many applicants; shortly before Haig arrived, it had, for financial reasons, considered amalgamating with another small college, Lincoln.[3] Haig matriculated to study for a Pass degree in French literature, Elements of Political Economy, and Classical History; at that date there were no Honours degrees in modern European languages. University Pass degree examinations in French were then 'less demanding than the modern A-level and could be taken without ever speaking a word of the language in question.'[4] Studying for a Pass degree was something which a BNC man (there were no women) could easily fit around the more important activities of drinking and dining clubs, fox-hunting, rowing, horse racing, cricket or – in Haig's case – polo. The tone of BNC was set by its long-standing principal, the Reverend Dr Edward Hartopp Cradock, head of the college since 1853 and husband of Harriet Lister, a former maid of honour to Queen Victoria. Cradock[5] informed the young Haig on his arrival: 'Ride, sir, ride

– I like to see the gentlemen of Brasenose in top boots.' To another undergraduate of Haig's intake he exclaimed: 'Drink plenty of port, sir. You want port in this damp climate.'[6]

It was, in other words, an ideal college for a reasonably intelligent but unscholarly son of a distiller, whose natural inclination was to be off at a gallop rather than hunch over textbooks; the perfect finishing place to reassure someone that they were, after all, a gentleman. Haig was never intent on academic prowess at Oxford; he always 'cherished the deepest contempt for examinations as a test of ability',[7] possibly because he did not shine at such tests. As someone whose relationship with books was generally adversarial rather than amiable, Haig embarked on one of the least strenuous routes up the academic mountain.

Despite, or perhaps because of, its reputation as one of Oxford's leading colleges for youthful male athleticism, BNC was also the adopted home of Walter Pater, the leading figure of the Aesthetic Movement. Pater arrived at the college in 1864 and stayed until his death in 1894, and for a period was Haig's tutor. It is one of the quirks of Haig's story that someone without much interest in the creative arts should be drawn into such close proximity to one of the Victorian age's greatest exponents of art for art's sake. There is a regularly repeated story that Haig later claimed Pater taught him how to write clear English,[8] but this is wrong. Pater did not teach Haig to write, but to read, as Haig revealed at a BNC dinner held in London on 16 December 1927:[9]

> Walter Pater had the (for him) uncongenial task of expounding the beauties of Homer to me alone. How often I used to go to him ready dressed for hunting with my boots and breeches concealed under a pair of trousers. I used simply to long for the hour to pass. But as I had not much to do for my first two years, before Mods. he told me what to read, Thackeray, Dickens &c., and now I know that I have to thank him for showing me what good English prose really is.

Haig's personality was instinctively inclined towards a longing for certainty rather than ambiguity, for action rather than passivity, and was diametrically opposed to the solipsistic aestheticism of Pater. There were other distinctions. Pater's homoerotic temperament was thinly disguised and although he, like Haig, left no written account of his sexual activities, the assumption today is that he was a repressed homosexual: '[Pater's] lyrical outbursts on the subject of naked male beauty seem positive indications of homosexual feeling, however repressed in his daily existence, and have been widely taken as such in our day.'[10]

Pater was an admirer of handsome, physically active and wealthy young men – John Buchan recalled him once saying, 'It is so beautiful to see young men leaping over bars like panthers'[11] – and Douglas Haig at nineteen was a fine example of the breed. At BNC Haig could hardly have missed gossip concerning Pater's personal proclivities, garbed though they were in philosophizing about the nature of Art and Beauty. Pater's book *Renaissance*, published in 1873, had outraged English conservative public opinion by its anti-Christian paganism and its endorsement of the views of the eighteenth-century German classical scholar Johann Winckelmann, who was murdered by a male lover. In 1874 it became known that Pater had formed an intense friendship with a Balliol undergraduate, which was enough to ensure Pater was passed over for a proctorship[12] at BNC – despite being the most eligible senior fellow for the position – and in 1877 he withdrew, under pressure, his candidacy for the university's prestigious poetry professorship.

Men with same-sex desires (the term 'homosexual' did not gain currency in Britain before 1892)[13] who wished to avoid social disapprobation and possible criminal prosecution, as Oscar Wilde – who graduated from Magdalen two years before Haig arrived at BNC – painfully discovered, had little choice but to live a repressed existence.[14] John Addington Symonds, who had taught Greek poetry part-time at Clifton College during Haig's time there, popped up again during Haig's years at BNC, forming a passionate friendship with Walter Pater.[15] Fear of social opprobrium dictated silence and hypocrisy concerning all sexual activity for anyone who aspired to be considered a gentleman. This contradictory age was, at least nominally, resolutely sexually repressive, despite the notorious sexual voraciousness of Edward, Prince of Wales, who, in a period of widespread prurience, was the exception that proved the rule. Just seven years after Haig was born, Dr Henry Maudsley published an article in his *Journal of Mental Science* on 'self-abuse', asserting that the 'masturbator is a moral pervert whose insanity is disagreeable in the extreme; it makes him morbid, egotistical, self-centred, downright amoral. Should he marry, he will be impotent or cruel and inevitably become insane, haunted by delusions and megalomania. The sooner he sinks to his degraded rest the better for himself, and the better for the world which is well rid of him.'[16]

Given such prevailing mores, it is little wonder that a young man such as Haig, raised in dogmatic and God-fearing Christian conservatism, kept any sexual thoughts or deeds well concealed, for fear not only of eternal hellfire but also of unpleasant gossip and social damnation. There is nothing in the Haig archives to show that he endured inner turmoil regarding his sexuality; indeed, there is no evidence – even after marriage – that he had any sexual feelings whatsoever, apart from the existence of his four children, for whom he evinced a greater paternal affection than he received from his own father.

Alfred Duff Cooper wrote that Haig 'learnt more at Oxford than to ride and to play polo' but failed to specify what that 'more' might have been. If he meant Haig learned the importance of social connections, he was right. Oxford represented a social interlude as well as a vital step towards establishing Haig's credentials as a gentleman, a word which today has lost the intangible yet palpable indication of social standing it possessed in Victorian Britain. 'Gentleman' was an unquestioned term of praise, implying honesty, loyalty, self-discipline and moral integrity. It was not thought that *only* a gentleman could embody and demonstrate such virtues; but the possession and display of such virtues were the marks of a gentleman. One might be a gentleman in terms of wealth, manner and social standing, but it still might not be enough to overcome all barriers, such as that of being Jewish.

In 1910 Lewis Namier, later to become a distinguished historian, was refused an All Souls Fellowship because he was Jewish.[17] It might not have been the dominant reason he was declined, but it was a factor in the minds of some college fellows. Douglas Haig and his wife, along with most of their class, shared the ubiquitous assumption that Jews were not quite part of 'proper' society, despite Edward, Prince of Wales, having not just Jewish friends but even a Jewish banker, the German-born Sir Ernest Cassel, who became Edward VII's private financial adviser and treasurer in 1902.[18] A former mistress of Edward, the Countess of Warwick, explained this apparent contradiction: 'We resented the introduction of the Jews into the social set of the Prince of Wales; not because we disliked them individually, for some of them were charming as well as brilliant, but because they had brains and understood finance. As a class, we did not like brains. As for money, our only understanding of it lay in the spending, not in the making of it.'[19]

During the Great War, Lord Northcliffe, the British press baron, was given to making wild accusations about alleged Jewish pacifism, as was David Lloyd George.[20] For the upper echelons of Victorian and Edwardian society, in Britain, France, Germany and elsewhere in Europe, casual anti-Semitism was a fact of life,[21] although extreme expressions of it, such as that of Kaiser Wilhelm II at a banquet held in his honour at Windsor Castle on 15 November 1906 – 'There are far too many of them [Jews] in my country. They want stamping out. If I did not restrain my people there would be a Jew-baiting'[22] – were considered distressingly vulgar. For people of Haig's class it was axiomatic that Jews were irritating, as he betrayed in a letter to Henrietta dated 23 June 1895 from the Railway Hotel, Haywards Heath, when he was attending an army staff tour: 'We rode from here towards the Coast, over the Downs towards Shoreham, then to Brighton. We got there about 3p.m and lunched at "The Old Ship" which seems a capital hotel, and preferable to these new semi-continental Hostelries, as there are fewer Jews about the place.'[23] Haig was thirty-four at the time. These were the words neither of callow youth nor callous maturity but simply a reflection of his uncritical absorption of the prejudices of the time. An individual Jew *might* be a gentleman; Jews in general were not.

Yet the concept of a gentleman was terribly slippery, and Victorian writers spilled much ink deliberating its definition. Haig's birth was bracketed by two of the key Victorian texts on this thorny topic. In 1852 John Henry Newman published *The Idea of a University*, in which he explored the definition of a gentleman, and his portrait of a stoical, silent person is in many respects a good depiction of what Haig tried to emulate. For Newman, a true gentleman 'never speaks of himself except when compelled, never defends himself by a mere retort, he has no ears for slander or gossip, is scrupulous in imputing motives to those who interfere with him, and interprets every thing for the best. He is never mean or little in his disputes, never takes unfair advantage, never mistakes personalities or sharp sayings for arguments, or insinuates evil [. . .] he observes the maxim of the ancient sage, that we should ever conduct ourselves towards our enemy as if he were one day to be our friend. He has too much good sense to be affronted at insults, he is too well employed to remember injuries, and too indolent to bear malice. He is patient, forbearing, and resigned, on philosophical principles; he submits to pain, because it is inevitable, to bereavement, because it is irreparable, and to death, because it is his destiny.'

Two months after Haig's birth, the concluding episode of Dickens's *Great Expectations* was published. It is arguably the most important literary depiction of the struggle to become and be accepted as a gentleman, in which Pip learns it means much more than simply possessing an unearned income; it also implies loyalty and personal humility. Certainly, Haig, along with myriad others, fell short of Newman's ideal: he could be mean-spirited and penny-pinching; he listened to and indulged in gossip; he never admitted mistakes; and he appeared sometimes to be disloyal to his superiors. Perhaps the closest Haig ever got to defining for himself what he understood by the term 'gentleman' came in the final days of the Great War. He found time to write to the Earl of Dartmouth on 23 August 1918 to accept the offer of being granted the Freedom of the I. Zingari cricket club, formed in the mid nineteenth century by a group of old Harrovians. 'I shall wear no decoration with greater pleasure,' wrote Haig, 'than the one your distinguished Club has given me,' adding that he prized the 'three Zingaric principles to "keep your temper, keep your promise, keep your wicket up." '[24]

There were, however, countervailing attitudes towards the highly amorphous state of grace that was gentlemanliness. Neville Lytton, the Eton- and École des Beaux Arts-educated grandson of the Victorian novelist Edward Bulwer-Lytton, is a good touchstone in this respect. Lytton served as a major at the BEF's GHQ in France for part of the Great War, in charge of newspaper reporters and press censorship, and he was thus often in close contact with Haig. His private income afforded him the opportunity to become a champion tennis player as well as an accomplished artist; he was by any standards of the day a gentleman. Yet sometimes, he felt, there could be too much of a good thing: 'Personally I hate the word "gentleman"; you may take it as the highest term of praise that can be given to a human being, embodying all the aristocratic qualities of body, mind, and soul, but in the Army and in English life generally it is applied to those who dress conventionally, and who are lacking in all power of thought, imagination, or initiative. I always used to say "give me Jews and not gentlemen, and we will win the war." Certain it is that we had many magnificent officers who, by no flight of the imagination, could be described as gentlemen.'[25]

Douglas Haig aspired to the positive qualities Lytton depicts, yet his intellectual narrowness meant he was also prone, at Oxford and in later life, to judge others by Lytton's lesser, conventional definition. How was a gentleman to know what his duties were, beyond those superficialities? In 1876, when Haig was fifteen, the quintessentially Victorian Oxford philosophy don F. H. Bradley published *Ethical Studies*, giving formal elaboration to what he believed were the fibres that knitted individual self-realization into society. While Bradley's argument was very abstract, it nevertheless provided the epoch with a rationale for its pragmatic conservatism. In the essay 'My Station and its Duties' Bradley argued that the ethical priority for an individual was first to understand his self and how that self fitted into the world; from that, it followed that the highest moral aspiration was to perform the duties allotted by this station. This deeply conservative philosophy imposed a broad imperative peculiarly appropriate to the age, one that resonated with those already conservatively inclined, such as Haig.

For Bradley, 'political philosophy has not to play tricks with the state, but to understand it; and ethics has not to make the world moral, but to reduce to theory the morality current in the world. If we want it to do anything more, so much the worse for us; for it cannot possibly construct new morality [. . .] That which tells us what in particular is right and wrong is not reflection but intuition. [. . .] there is nothing better than my station and its duties, nor anything higher or more truly beautiful. It holds and will hold its own against the worship of the "individual", whatever form that may take.'[26]

Bradley's views played to the unquestioned assumption of the public schools that the highest form of morality was a form of stoicism, one in which the individual's public duty was, in the words of Sir Henry Newbolt's 1897 poem *Vitai Lampada*, to 'play the game'. Bradley instructed that the true realization of the self was to grasp that 'I am what I am by being one of a people, by being born in a family, by living in a certain society, in a certain state; accordingly my role is determined by my function in that large social system; and so my duties are derived from reflection upon the station that I occupy within it.'[27]

Haig was no theoretician and could not have articulated this position so succinctly; yet he perfectly embodies Bradley's assertions as to what the true moral life was, and the ethos of the British army Haig was to enter was a practical exemplification of Bradley's argument. Of course, it was also a deeply hypocritical age, one in which the worst crime for carefree sybarites, on the fringes of whose ranks Haig was to tarry a while, was, as Countess Warwick suggested, to be found out: 'What a man or woman might feel or do in private was their own affair, but our rule was No Scandal!'[28]

In this respect the Victorian period was no different from any other, proselytizing high-minded ideals yet practising low-minded indulgences. Nevertheless, the strongly held belief of Victorians was that a true gentleman could be relied upon intuitively to do the right thing in a crisis. For Haig, in some of the worst days of the Great War, this meant he yearned to have more former public schoolboys and Oxbridge graduates, like himself, to guide and lead the army. In November 1914 he informed

General Sir Henry Crichton Sclater, then adjutant-general to the army, that the reservists being sent to France at that time:

> had neither the will, nor the physique for fighting. I said we wanted patriots who knew the importance of the cause for which we are fighting. The whole German people have been impregnated from youth up with an intense patriotic feeling, so that they die willingly for their country. There are not many of our men who will do this unless well led. Now we are short of officers to lead them. I said send out young Oxford and Cambridge men as officers; they understand the crisis in which the British Empire is involved.[29]

Having arrived at Oxford University, the final staging-post for gentlemen, Haig ineluctably gravitated towards the social – inescapably synonymous with wealthy – elite of his college and the university, getting himself elected to some of the most fashionable clubs including the Vampyres, a BNC Sunday lunch club; the Bullingdon, then as now a byword for wealthily carefree drunken rowdiness; the Phoenix, a BNC society and Oxford's oldest dining club; and Vincent's, the university club for Blues and sportsmen. He tried his hand at rowing but found it monotonous. Instead, he quickly returned to his boyhood passion of horse-riding and took up polo, the expenses of which necessarily restricted it to the richer members of the university. According to a contemporary, Haig was socially restrained:

'While courteous to everyone, he did not spread himself, and stuck to his College and the House.[30] The only outside persons [. . .] whom he ever introduced to Oxford were brothers, and he never (as far as I am aware) entertained any woman except his sister, though I have seen his face set, in a silent but obstinate protest, against any loose talk about women. My impression was and is that he disliked any remarks derogatory to women, and showed it, without speaking, so clearly that any would-be raconteur "dried up". His principal friend was "Tommy" Hitchcock,[31] of BNC, from America, himself a great polo player, and father of a great polo player; and by him Haig was started on "polo", worked hard at the game with strenuous energy, and with Hitchcock played polo for the University of 1882 and 1883. [. . .] He loved also a quiet joke, but I never heard him make one. To Hall he seldom, if ever, went; but dined out, always returning early, and hating to sit up at night.'[32]

The larger international events of the time passed Haig by at Oxford; it is unrecorded, for example, what this future field marshal thought of the military disaster on 27 February 1881 on Majuba Hill, a bitter catastrophe for the jingoists of the day, where a small force of Boer commandos ambushed and killed Sir George Colley, Governor of Natal, and killed, wounded or took prisoner another 266 of his force of 554 soldiers. Only in his final year at Oxford did Haig begin erratically to keep a diary. His diary-writing ebbed and flowed in later years and he never used the pages as a means of self-exploration; on the contrary, they are relentlessly dedicated to externalities. Even during the Great War, when he wrote a daily entry, he neither generated profound insights nor memorable phrases and most entries, particularly in the early years, are Pooterishly conventional. Indeed, Duff Cooper dryly commented that Haig's Oxford diaries were 'a cheerful chronicle of Oxford life from the point of view of one whose principal interests are hunting and polo, who enjoys the club life of the University and plays his part in club politics, but who is determined to combine with this easy-going existence that modicum of work which will enable him to satisfy the examiners.'[33]

It would be more honest to say that Haig's early diaries reveal a mind lacking in profundity, a character which judges so-and-so a 'nice fellow' and which is completely absorbed in the minutiae of insignificant under-graduate dining clubs. Their general flavour is captured in the first entry of the first volume, from February 1883:

Having oftentimes heard of the advantages to be derived from keeping a diary I determine to keep one. The difficulty is to have a good day to begin upon.

I think it is as well to start from the 19th day of last June upon which day I was twenty one, and put down as many events as I can remember with accuracy which happened from then until this day.

Haig's good intention of keeping his personal records up to date petered out almost immediately. His Oxford diaries depict a life consisting of club meetings, hunting, dining, polo, and an occasional drawing class at Ruskin School of Art.[34] Haig encountered several undergraduates who later gained prominence, such as Edward Grey, Foreign Secretary at the start of the Great War, and Lord William Cecil, the future Bishop of Exeter and second son of the Marquess of Salisbury, who was himself soon to become Conservative Prime Minister. William Cecil, known as 'The Fish', was considered an eccentric[35] and quite unlike anyone in Haig's previous experience: he confided to his diary that the future bishop's clothes were 'very seedy resembling the garb of a scholar!' Scholars, by definition, were poor, and possibly not gentlemen.

In the meantime, the visits to continental European spas by his parents had ingrained the habit in their children, and Haig spent part of March 1883 in France with his brother Hugo and his family, and their sister Janet, in the Pyrenean spa town of Pau, where Douglas was irritated with brother Hugo's genuine hypochondria and selfishness. 'Sat 17th: Hugo expects everyone to give way to him; he is indeed most annoying and rubs one up terrible but I manage to say nothing – Archie [Hugo's wife] seems more delicate than he as he eats and drinks well while she can only do the latter – Henrietta expected tomorrow.'

Haig longed for the arrival of Henrietta, who was accompanied by her sister-in-law, Agnes Jameson, whom he snobbishly dismissed. 'Sun 18th: Train due at 1.22 but was a few minutes late – at last the train came in Hentta, Mary Morisson and Agnes Jameson in same carriage, this latter with a Cook's ticket! not able to speak a word of french [sic]; coin indeed cannot replace want of education! We arrive at the Villa and find Hugo at lunch – He did not come down to the door and seemed to receive Hentta coldly, Hugo & Archie angry because she had delayed coming for so long.'

On 3 April he and Henrietta visited Lourdes, which prompted a rush of Presbyterian revulsion at religious idolatry. At the grotto he found 'innumerable ends of burnt candles, some people praying and thousands of well worn crutches! What credulity! What superstition! The road from our hotel to the Grotte is simply nothing but booths where are sold religious ornaments, crucifixes [. . .]'[36]

On 8 April the group travelled to Paris, where Haig saw Sarah Bernhardt take the lead role in Victorien Sardou's play *Fedora* at the Vaudeville Theatre and, on Tuesday 10th, after riding in the Bois de Boulogne, they saw Racine and Molière pieces at the Théâtre Français, where Pater's training failed him; he merely recorded that 'The acting at this Theatre is splendid!' By Saturday 14 April he was once again in Oxford, back amid the dining clubs that were his staple preoccupation. His diary entry for Wednesday 18 April 1883 is unusually long:

'Dinner at 7 o'c with Noll – Macdonnell and Ld Henry Bentinck dined with us – after dinner we have great argument on the present evils of the church, notably the narrow-minded views of clergymen and their hypocracy [sic]. Mac. talked loudly but did not listen to our arguments, he was all in favour of the "good work done by the Church" – Jumbo (Bentinck) listened but said little; Noll stammered out his views on "Charity" which, he said, "was never preached to the people." I must say I thght he had right on his side tho' he cd not explain his feelings. [. . .] At dinner we had discussed the meanness of some fathers to their sons up here, in the hopes of making them acquire the knowledge of the value of money – such as the Duke of Westminster to Henry Grosvenor who is obliged to bet a little in order to get some money.[37] And "Puppy" Weymouth who is allowed £300[38] by Marquess of Bath, his father. Chas. Trefusis is also kept a bit strict – To bed about 11.30.'

Complaints about the supposed meanness of parents is a perennial undergraduate gripe, but £300 a year in 1880 was ample for a single man; Joseph Wells, who studied at Wadham College, Oxford, during the same decade Haig was at BNC, reckoned the annual cost of living for a careful undergraduate was around £160; tuition fees were an additional £20 or so a year. An Oxbridge education was, however, still a luxury which only the few could afford, when most of the working population were subsisting on less than thirty shillings a week.[39] The novelist E. M. Forster managed to live very comfortably at Cambridge University a decade later (1897–1901) on £320 a year, from 4 per cent interest on an £8,000 legacy from his aunt Marianne Thornton.

The buying of ponies, polo matches, the stinginess of parents, the elections to clubs now mostly long forgotten and of importance only for the future social connections they bestowed – while these were his daily round, somewhere in Haig's mind was also forming a determination to enter the army. Indeed, he became so motivated by this that his inattentiveness to academic work evolved into complete indifference to the acquisition of a degree. One of Haig's contemporaries at Oxford later revealed his response when his choice of profession was questioned: 'I said I thought the Army did not shew much of an opening. His chin went out squarer and more determined than ever as he replied: "It all depends on a man himself how he gets on in any profession. If I went into the Church I'd be a Bishop." '[40]

During the summer term – then officially classed as two terms, running from Easter to Whitsun, and from Trinity Sunday for a further three to four weeks – of 1881, Haig's congenital bronchial weakness had forced his temporary absence from the university, so that the college authorities deemed he had not 'kept' the full term.[41] Twelve terms of residence were required for the BA degree at this date, and because of this absence – a technicality but one that was strictly enforced[42] – Haig failed to qualify for a degree. He could easily have returned to Oxford for Michaelmas (autumn) term in 1883 to fulfil this requirement, but by then he had already decided to join the army via the Royal Military Academy at Sandhurst, and needed to devote himself exclusively to cramming for its entry examinations.[43] At that time the latest a university candidate could take Sandhurst entry tests was in their twenty-second year. Haig was twenty-two in June 1883 and thus, if he wished to get into Sandhurst, he had only one chance. He left Oxford and employed another crammer, Mr Litchfield at Hampton Court, with whom he boarded from 21 July 1883.

Litchfield charged £6 a week for his services; shortly after beginning his studies, Haig 'found that I had forgotten Latin greatly.' One of his fellow pupils at Litchfield's recalled Haig as a serious student: 'We were the usual careless lot of youngsters but Haig did not join freely in our frivolities. He plodded on steadily with his own work. That he had made up his mind to a serious career in the Army is proven by the following incident. We were playing Roulette [sic] in my bedroom when Haig came in. We at once tried to make him play too. He refused, saying abruptly, "It is all very well for you fellows, you are going into the Army to play at soldiering. I am going into it as a profession." '[44]

Getting a place at Sandhurst was not difficult for a gentleman with a private income so long as a candidate had been well tutored by experienced crammers. The compulsory papers in maths and English, together with three options, including Classics, were all familiar for anyone with a public school background. Haig naturally sat the optional Classics test, as it carried three times as many possible marks as any other optional paper. It has been suggested this method of entry was 'ill-suited to selecting officers'[45], but it is difficult to know what other method would have been both possible and also an improvement. The suggestion that the acquisition of short-term memory-based knowledge was of little use to future soldiers is questionable; at least it demonstrated that the cadet could absorb, retain and regurgitate relatively complicated information, a necessary if not sufficient skill for any officer. Haig entered Sandhurst on 12 February 1884, slightly older than most of his contemporaries, who largely came straight from public schools.

The possession of a private income was vital for any young man who aspired to join a socially prestigious regiment of the British army in the 1880s. In 1900 Captain W. E. Cairnes published an essay, 'Social Life in the British Army', in which he pithily remarked: 'Officers have lived in the 10th (Hussars) [one of the elite regiments of the day] with an allowance of only £500 a year but they have rarely lasted long.'[46] Douglas Haig at Sandhurst was well-off. His father had left him a substantial capital sum of £6,000 which had been placed in trust, paying interest of £300 a year. This does not take account of benefits he may have gained on the death of his mother, who had been granted an annuity of £700 under the will of her husband. Nor does it include Douglas's inherited interests in the family's whisky business. At Sandhurst he therefore probably had an income in the region of £400 a year; not inordinate riches but enough for him not to work and certainly sufficient to ensure that he could without embarrassment seek a place in an elite regiment. At Sandhurst he was 'envied rather than admired. He was appreciated but not popular. His determination to excel had intensified his "aloneness". [. . .] He was not apt in conversation, and his shyness, carefully concealed, was mistaken for conceit. He left Sandhurst as he entered it, without any close friendship for any of his contemporaries: but Sandhurst taught him complete self-control.'[47]

Haig had acquired his capacity for self-control far earlier, but the Academy certainly honed and channelled his innate character. Little prior military experience was expected of Sandhurst's 'gentleman cadets', as its students were known, apart from the assumption that they could ride and shoot. Where Sandhurst did perhaps fail its students – and their country – was in its neglect of a more practical curriculum once they had arrived. The core subjects were maths, fortification, and surveying; optional subjects included French, German, Latin, siege operations, landscape and military drawing, as well as drill, gymnastics and riding. Haig nevertheless here discovered something that personally and intellectually engaged his attention; the schoolboy duffer and university dilettante found reserves of enormous self-discipline. He passed out from the College on 21 December 1884 in first place out of a total of 129,[48] with 2,557 marks out of a possible 3,350, and he received the Anson Memorial Sword[59] (named in honour of Lieutenant-Colonel the Honourable A. H. A. Anson VC) as his right. It has been suggested that Haig owed this award to his social status, but it was in fact a competition open to all the intake; Haig simply was the best of his year. He was duly promoted Senior Underofficer, the highest honour then available for a Sandhurst cadet, giving him responsibility for the maintenance of discipline among the intake.

Gerard de Groot has asserted that Sandhurst was generally a damaging influence. It 'constrained the young officer's intellect, encouraging him to be unimaginative and accepting. [. . .] Due to his social background, his education and his pedantic nature, Haig's intellectual horizons were limited even before he entered Sandhurst. Unfortunately, the Academy did nothing to broaden them. He became, at a very early age, a guardian of tradition.'[50] This misreads both the aim of Sandhurst and the nature of

Haig, who, like the majority of England's public schoolboys of his era, was a guardian of tradition long before his days at the Academy. Sandhurst in the late 1880s could do no more than instil a modicum of military discipline and physical prowess in its cadets, hoping to bridge the gap between their school and the more serious business of the army, in the short space of just two academic terms. The broadening of intellectual horizons, whatever that might mean, was not its purpose. The place where its cadet officers would truly learn soldiering would be in their new family, the regiment they joined as subalterns. That might be regarded as a hopelessly amateurish method; it can equally be seen as entirely pragmatic, espousing the belief that the best way of learning is by doing.[51]

Sandhurst was not a typical experience for the average soldier. Another cavalryman, who also ended his career as a field marshal, Sir William Robertson, joined the 16th Lancers as a private at Aldershot in November 1877, at the age of seventeen and three quarters, when Haig himself was sixteen. Robertson's career is one of the most unusual in the annals of the British army, as he rose from an extremely poor background – definitely *not* a gentleman to begin with – to become Chief of the Imperial General Staff (CIGS) and one of Haig's most ardent supporters in the Great War. Robertson recalled the start of his army life in Aldershot barracks:

> The barrack-room arrangements for sleeping and eating could not be classed as luxurious. The brown bed-blankets were seldom or ever washed; clean sheets were issued once a month; and clean straw for the mattresses once every three months [. . .] The food provided free consisted of one pound of bread and three-quarters of a pound of meat, [a day] and nothing more of any kind. Groceries, vegetables, and all other requirements were paid for by the men, who had a daily deduction of 3½d made from their pay of 1s. 2d for that purpose. The regulation meals were coffee and bread for breakfast; meat and potatoes for dinner, with soup or puddings once or twice a week; tea and bread for tea. If a man wished to have supper or something besides dry bread for breakfast and tea he had to purchase it from the barrack hawkers or canteen. Putting the cost of this at

4½d a day, he thus had to expend a total of eight pence a day on his food, besides which he was subjected to a further daily charge of a penny for washing.[52]

Robertson's lack of a private income plagued his whole career; as a junior officer, he drank water in the mess while his fellow officers quaffed champagne, and he would leave the room to smoke his pipe – only cigars were permitted – as pipe tobacco was all he could afford. By contrast, Haig's private wealth and education meant that from Sandhurst he could have his pick of any regiment. This discrepancy between the highs and lows of army life did not begin to break down until Britain was forced to recruit a citizen army during the Great War.

The requisite qualities of a Sandhurst cadet in the late nineteenth century were not intellectual ability, nor even practical skills such as map-reading or experience of battle, but those 'valued by the country gentry: courage, physical toughness, a determination to stand up for one's rights, a touchy sense of honour. Almost the only acquired skill highly regarded was horsemanship, and that was taken for granted. The notion that an officer should be a professional soldier, qualified by technical as well as by the traditional virtues of a gentleman, was derided and looked down upon, except in the engineers and artillery, two corps which were only rather doubtfully fit for gentlemen to serve in.'[53]

Yet there were soldiers and teachers of soldiers who later aspired to mould the army along very different lines, creating from the raw materials of courage and high-spiritedness a professional officer corps to rival those of continental Europe. Haig was to prove himself one of those, as, at the opposite end of the social spectrum, was Robertson. By 1885, when Haig was commanding men much older and more experienced than himself, Robertson was a sergeant-major, his poverty a real obstacle to obtaining a commission: 'I had no private means, and without some £300 a year in addition to army pay [£120 a year for a subaltern] it was impossible to live as an officer in a cavalry regiment at home. The infantry was less expensive, but I could not entertain the idea of leaving my old arm, the cavalry. [ . . . ] The true ranker, having no influence behind him, had to toil for several years before receiving a commission, and even then the chances were that he would, owing to the want of private means, be miserable in himself and a nuisance to his brother officers.'[54]

Both Haig and Robertson would have been acutely aware that the Second Duke of Cambridge, 'The Great German Sausage' who had been present at the Crimea and was first cousin to Queen Victoria and Commander-in-Chief between 1856 and 1895, had decreed that British officers should be gentlemen first and officers second.[55] The only units of the army which dispensed with purchased commissions prior to their general abolition in 1871 were the engineers and the artillery, and these had inevitably tended to attract the technically minded and professionally committed soldier, who was generally of a higher intellectual calibre but lacked the private income to attempt the army's social heights. In 1821 a young man who wished to become a cornet in the Royal Horse Guards required £1,200 to purchase the privilege of being the lowliest officer in the most fashionable regiment of the day.[56] To become the same regiment's lieutenant-colonel required £7,250. These 'list' prices of a commission were usually less than the actual prices paid; Sir Evelyn Wood VC claimed to have paid the government £1,000, the stipulated regulation price and a further £1,500 to the officer he replaced as a captain in 1861 in the 17th Lancers, the regiment Haig later joined.[57] Little wonder, in view of how much they paid to join, that British soldiers were so keen on taking 'booty' from those they defeated.

By 1884 this widely abused system had gone, but the network of attitudes from which it evolved were still embedded in the military psyche. Army pay scales remained unaltered between 1806 and 1 January 1914, and the heavy costs involved in mess bills, subsidizing the regimental band, stabling a horse and so on meant that only those with a private income could contemplate the life of an army officer without financial distress.[58] A further black mark against the army was the widespread social opprobrium in which it was held. When William Robertson told his mother in 1877 he was leaving his post as a servant in the household of the Earl of Cardigan to enlist in the army, her angry response expressed the widely held view of the time: 'You know you are the Great Hope of the Family . . . if you do not like Service you can do something else . . . there are plenty of things Steady Young Men can do when they can write and read as you can . . . [the Army] is a refuge for all Idle people . . . I shall name it to no one for I am ashamed to think of it . . . I would rather Bury you than see you in a red coat.'[59]

The general disapprobation which shrouded the army in late Victorian Britain was largely prompted by the general belief that the rank and file was an uncivilized rabble, ill-paid and even more ill-mannered, and that the officer class was indolent and unprofessional in equal measure. When civilians brushed up against the army they were often shocked by its bureaucratic ineptitude. On 8 February 1886 there were serious riots in Trafalgar Square and along Pall Mall, the heart of London's aristocratic clubland and home to the War Office, when unemployed demonstrators smashed windows and caused mayhem. The War Office was asked to mobilize troops to safeguard the capital. Sir Sam Fay – who was later, in December 1916, to leave his civilian job as manager of the Great Central Railway to take over as Director of Movements at the War Office – was then Superintendent of the London and South-Western Railway, the line serving Aldershot and thus the main route along which troops would be ferried to London. The L & S-W Railway duly provided an emergency troop train; but the regiment failed to turn up and the train went missing. Sir Sam visited the War Office to ask what happened: 'I found the military anything but helpful; it looked above and beyond me; it passed me on from one office to another. [. . .] Troop records prove defective – if the regiment was not at Portsmouth, where was it? I came away with instructions to cancel the train until further orders. The War Office may have found the regiment, but the railway never did. My experience of the old War Office is emphasised by a military writer who, referring to a former epoch, stated that "The officers of the War Department led an administrative life of exquisite confusion." '[60]

A year before this debacle, on 7 February 1885, Haig, fresh from his Sandhurst triumph, was gazetted into the 7th Hussars, long known as 'the Saucy Seventh' and, together with the 10th Hussars, one of the most fashionably elite regiments in the British army, joining the regiment at

Aldershot. Originally an exclusively Scottish regiment, the 7th Hussars traced their history back to the late seventeenth century; in succeeding years they had established themselves at the forefront of British military snobberies, courting princes and the aristocracy, and accepting as officers only those who were unquestionably gentlemen. It was natural that Haig, who loved riding and polo and who was anxious to prove himself a gentleman, should choose the cavalry, the most socially prestigious branch of the army. But in electing to join the 7th Hussars Haig also ensured that he would stand a good chance of rubbing shoulders with royalty, influential members of the upper class, and the top echelons of the army. Any young man in the fortunate position of possessing private wealth would have been foolish not to have joined such a regiment. Any regimental mess would have been delighted to have Haig: handsome, quiet but self-confident, reserved yet amiable, he dressed well, was utterly conservative in his opinions and outlook, had perfect manners, and enough money to ensure that he was no embarrassment to his brother officers.

# CHAPTER THREE

# 'The Long Long Indian Day'

If your officer's dead and the sergeants look white,
Remember it's ruin to run from a fight:
So take open order, lie down, and sit tight,
And wait for supports like a soldier.
Wait, wait, wait like a soldier . . .

Rudyard Kipling, 'The Young British Soldier',
*Barrack Room Ballads First Series* (1892)

The duties of a young officer in the British army in 1886 were not particularly onerous. He was not expected to exert himself on behalf of his men's welfare, nor trouble too greatly about training. His task was to lead by example and, if sufficiently junior, to die gallantly if required. The daily work of the regiment was largely conducted by experienced non-commissioned officers or NCOs. The languorous routine of a cavalry officer provided plenty of time for riding, hunting, and other sporting pursuits; study of the art – never mind the science – of war was regarded as rather common, the kind of thing to be left to engineers and possibly artillerymen. At Aldershot with the 7th Hussars Haig quickly gained 'the title of "von Haig," the cognomen being a friendly recognition of his punctilious attention to duty. When he was appointed president to the regimental coffee-shop, he promptly went down to the markets to make new contracts, with the result that prices were reduced by 50 per cent.'[1]

In November 1886 the regiment was briefly stationed at Shorncliffe Camp, near Folkestone in Kent, preparatory to sailing for India. Haig found conditions at Shorncliffe rather grim: '[. . .] the Officers huts have been condemned years ago as unfit, yet they are still standing. My quarters consisted of two small rooms about 8 feet square each, the roof let in the water when it rained, there was no lock on the doors and the wind came whistling through the cracks. At Shorncliffe it is always blowing half a gale and one is perished with cold. The men's huts are of concrete and are most comfortable.'[2]

On the bitterly cold, snowy morning of 25 November, the 7th Hussars marched to the local railway station and entrained for Portsmouth, where they boarded the troopship *Euphrates*. Haig handed over his Irish terrier to the ship's cook, 'a fine big fat fellow, who promised to look after him well, as I must say he did', and settled himself into a cramped cabin shared with two other officers, before heading off to dine at the Pier Hotel in Southsea with Henrietta and his brother George, who had come to bid farewell. The next day the *Euphrates* steamed away for India, the regimental band giving an indifferent rendition of 'Auld Lang Syne' as the ship narrowly avoided running aground in Portsmouth harbour. The 601 men of the 7th Hussars, including twenty-one officers, along with 525 horses and assorted women and children, endured an uneventful twenty-seven-day voyage.[3] Inevitably, in such cramped conditions and with scant amusement, there were frictions. One diary entry Haig made during this voyage is fascinating because, unusually, it contains a brief, throwaway comment about women:

> The passengers are as a whole an uninteresting lot. Several newly married couples, greatly taken up with each other. [. . .] 5 or 6 Doctors on board, mostly married. One, styled 'the dirty Dr' a German looking creature, excites the jealousy of an infantry Captain: both have just lately entered the matrimonial state, and both men's wives are in the same cabin. The Dr has the pull over the other, he can visit his wife's cabin to administer physic. The other feels annoyed no doubt, there are words, and recourse is had to the Captain of the ship! But women are at the bottom of all quarrels.[4]

This casual remark of a young, twenty-five-year-old officer heading for his first real foreign adventure is not easily interpreted. Haig had already acquired a reputation for misogyny, and this glib comment might be no more than an expression of this. But equally plausibly it can be seen as venting a rather heartfelt sadness; it is a phrase that might easily come to the mind of a young man jilted or thwarted in love. Whatever the cause, it is even more piquant that his widow later added, in pencil: '(poor women! Dorothy Haig)'.

On 22 December 1886, the *Euphrates* arrived in Bombay, where Haig was delegated to organise a celebratory dinner: 'I am the first to get off from the ship as I am sent to order dinner at Watson's Hotel: we are to entertain the officers of HMS Euphrates. We all enjoy our dinner, our first in India, though I thought Bombay ought to have better cooks! We brought our own Champagne from the ship with us, the Hotel could not supply us with anything really good! Such are Bombay Hotels!'

A lengthy train journey then took the regiment to the cramped, hot, and dusty Secunderabad camp, the largest military station in southern India at the time, near Hyderabad, where life was harsh and entertainment limited. Anthrax plagued the horses and, disappointingly for Haig, the polo prospects were poor: 'The polo ground at Secunderabad is very hard as the sub soil is rock. The players and their ponies are vy 3rd rate.'

For any soldier fresh out from England, India presented a gruelling test, demanding mental and physical fortitude to cope with the boredom of limited social life and the difficulties of living within but separate from a very different culture. Since 1773 the chief British civil power in the country was the governor-general, who from 1858 also enjoyed the title of viceroy, symbolizing that his authority was delegated from the British monarchy; Victoria took the title Empress of India in 1876. The viceroy's rule was, to all intents and purposes, autocratic, although during the 7th Hussars' posting the viceroy of the time, the First Earl of Dufferin, Frederick Temple Hamilton-Temple-Blackwood, helped advance the cause of Indian nationalists. A posting to India as one of the empire's policemen carried 60 per cent higher pay than a soldier could earn back in Britain and at a much lower cost of living, but the temptations of drink and sex – licensed brothels reserved for British soldiers were tolerated – meant that alcoholism and sexually transmitted diseases were commonplace within the British Indian Army.

Haig, who nowhere betrays personal doubt or misery in his diaries, bore India's trials without obvious complaint, while the almost equally buttoned-up William Robertson wrote to his father from India 'it is so miserable out here – *you don't know*.'[5] At this early stage of his career, Haig embodied a paradox of the British army at the time and since; although he had never previously commanded anything other than the attention of his family, he was deemed qualified to travel to the most distant and important outpost of the empire to take charge of men who had, in many cases, seen years of toughening active service. He immediately set to his tasks with gusto. Unlike some brother officers who were posted to India around this time – men such as Robertson and Ian Hamilton – and who also later rose to the highest ranks of the British army, Haig appears to have made no effort to learn any of the indigenous Indian languages, although his job would have required a basic vocabulary, sufficient to issue commands.[6]

In March 1887 Secunderabad was ravaged by typhoid, which killed an officer, twelve men and two women. Until the discovery of suitable antibiotics, typhoid was a potentially fatal disease, with chronic effects for survivors. Haig contracted typhoid on 2 March and was seriously ill for a month, his temperature peaking at 105.6°F.[7] He recovered and proved sufficiently diligent to be promoted regimental adjutant in 1888, above more senior officers, taking on much of the administrative burden of the regiment. Haig rapidly acquired a reputation for his unswerving attention to duty.[8] His diaries of this time graduate to recording and passing judgement upon cavalry manoeuvres and the skills – more often their lack – of fellow officers. He also considered how better to occupy the troops, as he contemplated in a letter of 17 April 1889 to his brother Hugo:

The people who get seedy are those who do nothing. Some of our Temperance Generals Roberts & Co., talk about amusements for the soldiers during the heat of the day such as Troop clubs where they can read the papers and play cards (not for money of course) and drink 'aerated waters' – keeps the men from that vile place, the Canteen, don't yer know!!

My idea is this that people won't play dominoes for nothing, or read papers or drink plain water <u>all day</u>. I recommend workshops with tools, turning lathes for wood & iron etc. etc. I am sure that is the proper principle to go on: if men find they can make money they will work: here it is impossible to get a good carpenter & joiner. Anyone who could make picture frames or do odd jobs wd. make a fortune.

They asked for our suggestions the other day on this subject so I hope the Govt. will do something and not waste money.

Some troopers, such as former Sergeant Stancel Griffiths, found Haig to be a sympathetic officer. Haig, he wrote, 'was always Kind and Considerate to his men. [. . .] I had a breakdown in health and was in Hospital with Interic fever [typhoid] off and on for 12 months around the time Haig was made Adjutant in mid 1888. [. . .] He would come down to the hospital and talk to the serious cases, ask if he could do anything for you, he would write to your friends in England if you was not well enough, he was most kind to me.'[9] Others, such as H. J. Harrison, who claimed[10] to be a sergeant-major in the 7th Hussars, found him a stern disciplinarian, although his views were coloured perhaps by his claim that Haig, out of prejudice against Harrison's role as a signaller, declined to recommend him for promotion. Whatever the facts, Harrison's first encounter with Haig left a lasting impression which rings true: 'Lieutenant Haig in plain soldierly language made it clear to every member of that draft that a soldier in the famous regiment must be a man, and that effeminate or sentimental qualifications would prove a menace, and a detriment to promotion, which in after years proved correct. Exactitude, Promptitude, Smartness and strict veracity, were a few of the virtues our Adjutant tenaciously adhered to, and sympathy for a technical error was unknown. [. . .] At all times and in all weathers, Haig went about "Soldiering", and Haig's soldiering was admitted by all who mattered, to be unrelated to ordinary military drills and tactics, but was embellished with a kind of finishing off process exclusively Haig.

[. . .] A good soldier was Haig's delight, but a bad one gave him a liver, which resulted in a rough time for the "bad un".[11]

India in the late 1880s and early 1890s experienced a period of relative calm, although fear of the Russian threat was omnipresent and the Afghan hinterland was, as always, a dangerous place. Haig passed his Indian days in training, tiger-shooting, polo-playing and regimental dinners, occasionally as one of numerous guests of His Exalted Highness the Nizam of Secunderabad, then the wealthiest of all Indian princes. In 1889 he further established his reliability by assisting in the resolution of a minor scandal involving Major Creighton, the regimental paymaster. In January Creighton was interviewed by the commanding officer over allegations that some men had not been paid for almost a year. On Monday 4 March 1889 Creighton was given twenty-four hours to produce the outstanding pay; failing that, 'very serious notice will be taken of the matter.' Creighton was unable to comply; Haig was ordered to place him under house arrest and was appointed acting paymaster. He took pity on Creighton, sending some ice to his home and joking in his diary: 'Mrs C. asked leave to remove the piano: will C go away inside it?'

In August Creighton was court-martialled and found guilty of misappropriation of the money. In the meantime Haig had sailed for England, leaving Secunderabad on 28 April; by Wednesday 22 May he arrived in Dover, where he was met by his brothers John and George and, of course, Henrietta. He spent some of this brief respite socializing in London and having a broken tooth (damaged in a polo match) repaired. On 14 June, five days before his thirtieth birthday, he travelled to France and from there to Brindisi, where he joined the P&O ship SS *Thames* to Bombay, arriving on 30 June. He again found some of his fellow passengers lacking; Monday 17th June: 'Not a very classy lot of passengers: most are in the cotton "line"! After dinner in the smoking room there are several orations – The Dr of the ship being most ignorant but quite self satisfied and brazen faced – let us hope he is better informed about his profession!' By 4 July, he was back in the dust of Secunderabad.

Despite his self-discipline, these were trying days for Haig. Well regarded in his regiment, he was nevertheless a minnow in a very large lake. In a letter in October 1890 to his brother Hugo, then active in the volunteer yeomanry, he betrayed both his class consciousness and his sense that the cavalry required a higher calibre of officer than did the mounted infantry: 'There is one, Capt. Col Hamilton of this regt. anxious to go to the Yeomanry he says to the Fife Lt. Horse! He came from the mounted Infantry and doubtless was sharp for that, but his mind moves too slow for Cavalry. He is a good <u>creature</u>, with a very 2nd rate wife of the barmaid stamp; he has been with us about 2 years. He is a clean, smart, gentlemanly fellow to look at, <u>very well meaning</u> but I am afraid he has mistaken his calling in attempting to become a <u>leader</u> of Cavalry. His intentions are of the best, and doubtless you would find him superior as an Adjt. to a good many of the half hearted devils found in similar positions, because if you want a thing done, he will take a very great deal of trouble to carry out one's wishes. But as I say above, he is stupid, slow and deaf; all of which are two [sic] inconsiderable drawbacks in the line of life he has lately chosen [. . .]'

Haig was promoted captain on 23 January 1891, a relatively straight-forward step for any young officer who had proved himself eager and able, but Haig was five years older than many of his contemporaries. He may have begun to wonder where his life was headed and there are indi-cations that the weariness of the exhausting climate and some personal loneliness may have affected him more than he explicitly acknowledged. In his 1891 diary (on paper headed Ramornie, Ladybank[12]), is a Kiplingesque ballad, in Haig's handwriting, the first and last verse of which read:

> The long long Indian day,
> So slow to pass away,
> Longing for the day
> When home we'll sail away,
> In heat and anguish,
> I'm nearly dying,
> E'en there's no rest at night,
> The cursed mosquito's bite,

Around the morning,
As I lie groaning–

Thus drags the long long day
From year to year away
Until we've earned our pay
One paltry pound a day
Then struggle home to die in England
A worthy recompense
For loss of health and sense
So ends my story
Of India's glory.[13]

A certain poignancy breaks through the clichéd imagery; the fact that Haig bothered to copy it out suggests these verses had some resonance for him. For relief, he paid a tourist visit to Australia and Ceylon, writing to Henrietta from Melbourne on 2 May 1891: 'The Australians [. . .] are extraordinarily hospitable; we only arrived last Tuesday and each day we have had invitations for lunch and dinner & theatre:- the moment one is introduced to anyone, there is sure to be an invitation for some amusement or meal of sorts! The climate is fine and fresh here, and the eating and drinking is of the best: I only mention this because you are always so afraid I don't take proper "nourishment"!! With best love and hoping to get a line from you some day soon, I am, your affect Brother, DH.'

In Colombo he stayed at the Mount Lavinia Hotel, which he noted was 'famous for its "fish tiffin" on Sunday. Certainly today's lunch menu contained curious dishes of fish, and among them "Fresh Turbot from England".' He was again laid low with fever on 3 June but by 10 June, a blustery day, he was well enough to start learning a new game, one which became a lifelong passion and, indirectly, helped him find a wife – golf: 'There are 9 holes here. Rather a nice course tho' one crosses & re-crosses the ground over and over. The head of the Ceylon P.W.D [Public Works Department] gave me a lesson in driving in the Billiard room before starting – I found I got on v. well, much better than I expected.'

By the beginning of July he was back at his temporary base in Quetta, and, once more laid up with fever, spent the month recuperating. The harshness of Secunderabad was left behind when, in October 1891, the 7th Hussars moved to Mhow, more than 300 miles north-east of Bombay, high up in the Vindhya range of hills and with a much healthier climate. His reputation had by now brought Haig to the notice of Major-General Sir George Luck, then Inspector-General of Cavalry in India, who recruited Haig to be his brigade major during a cavalry training exercise at Aligarh, near Delhi. In January 1892 Haig was attached to the HQ of the Bombay Army during further exercises near Poona, and in July was given command of his own cavalry squadron.

These incremental promotions were all very well but, for a man in a hurry, as Haig was, frustratingly slow. He began to consider applying for a posting to the army Staff College at Camberley in England, to acquire the increasingly sought-after letters 'psc' (passed staff college) after his name. Although the British army, unlike continental European counter-parts, had no General Staff at the time, an informal system had evolved whereby Staff College graduates were increasingly regarded as being most qualified for staff duties. An officer with 'psc' had a better – although not guaranteed – chance of rapid promotion than one who stayed put with his chosen regiment. Prior to this period, attendance at the Staff College had not been widely regarded as a vital step towards achieving the highest rank; indeed, it was generally seen as a place where the sport was good and the work light.[14] And some able officers of Haig's generation, such as Ian Hamilton, turned down the chance of taking Staff College entry exams when an attractive field posting came up. But by the time Haig sat its exams the College was developing a more professionally minded ethos, thanks in good part to Colonel Henry J. T. Hildyard, Commandant of the College between 1893–8, whose motto – 'We want officers to absorb, not to cram' – signified a radically beneficial new intention, and also to the inspirational teaching of Colonel George F. R. Henderson, who expected students to think for themselves and apply their knowledge in a practical fashion.[15]

Haig thus wrote to Henrietta from India on 1 September 1892 that he would return to England to be tutored by an experienced Staff College crammer named Mr James: 'as the examn for the Staff College is very hard, I think the sooner I come home the better and arrange what I can do. I have therefore engaged a passage in the "Peninsular" which leaves Bombay on 9th September. [. . .] Everyone goes to James or some coach for the Staff Coll. as he saves one so much trouble and knows whether one can pass or not.'

On 9 September Haig left India. Among those of his comrades who came to see him off was regimental Sergeant-Major Humphries: 'Humphries wrung my hand and said I was "the best sort he had ever had to do with". They go down the ladder into a small boat, the tide running very strong towards the lighthouse. I watched them with my glasses till they were quite a small speck, [. . .] I feel quite sorry at leaving them all.'[16]

Haig journeyed home in a relaxed fashion, via Brindisi, to Naples, visiting Pompeii – about which his diary is jarringly silent – on Saturday 24 September. He was under no pressure to arrive back in England but was anxious to see Henrietta: '[. . .] you might drop me a line and tell me what you are doing because if you are paying visits I'll just take it easy on the continent till you are free.'

In Naples he received a telegram from Henrietta, quickly changed his plans and travelled to Paris to meet her. Back in London, he stayed at Henrietta's flat at 45 Albert Gate, close to Hyde Park. On 30 October Haig reassured his sister that he was in good shape: '[. . .] In order to set your mind at rest regarding my health[17], I went and saw Dr after leaving James Enright at 5p.m – the Hamilton Brown of a certain fame and certainly a most careful and painstaking Physician. He looked at me all over! My tongue of course, chalked with a pencil the size of my liver on my skin, put things in his ears, and listened to my lungs and heart and so forth. – He said he would pass me as "a thoroughly sound man" but a little below par. So I hope you will be satisfied now. All I want is plain food and a certain amt of exercise. This I am getting and I'll be as fit as ever in a short time. Don't forget to let me know the exact hour at which your train will arrive on Saturday in order that I may meet you. – I'll take two stalls for the Haymarket tomorrow so that we can get good places for Saty night. With much love, Your vy Afft Brother D.H.'

Prior to sitting the Staff College exams, Haig travelled to stay with a family in Düsseldorf with the intention of improving his German, although he clearly felt homesick, writing to Henrietta in March 1893: 'I thought you were looking very nice last night and I was real sorry to leave you. But I fancy it is the best thing to do to come away by oneself in order to read up for this beastly exam. [. . .] It is no pleasure coming to these foreign parts I can tell you, and you don't know how sorry I was to leave you last night, With kindest love, I am, your vy Affct Brother DH'.

He returned to England in May. The Staff College entry exams were spread across the week of 29 May – 7 June 1893, requiring candidates to write two three-hour papers each day. Twenty-eight places were annually offered by examination, eighteen reserved for the cavalry and infantry, with the C-in-C of the army having the right to nominate four more places to candidates who were permitted slightly lower pass marks.[18] The examinations were not onerous for the well-tutored; passes were obligatory in mathematics, French or German, fortification, military topography and tactics, with the pass mark being 50 per cent in each. Optional subjects included second and third languages (no candidate could offer more than three languages), military history and geography, and military law; additional languages had a 50 per cent pass mark, the rest 25 per cent.

The regulations also stipulated that officers should be passed physically fit. Haig notionally fell at this first hurdle; his medical examination at Horse Guards in London in January 1893 found him to be colour-blind as, in Haig's own words later, he could not 'match certain pale green and pale pink wools, on a foggy day in January.'[19] He nevertheless obtained official clearance in February, which stated that his medical report was satisfactory and that therefore he would be allowed to sit the exams. In Düsseldorf he consulted an eminent ophthalmologist, Professor Alfred Mooren, as his eyesight had never previously been questioned nor given him trouble. In September 1894 Mooren was called upon by Haig to provide a formal opinion, in which the ophthalmologist stated: 'Captain Douglas Haig from the 7th Hussars consulted me on 7th April 1893 on account of his eyes. The acuteness of vision was exact and Captain

Douglas capable to read without any difficulty the smallest print. There existed only a slight degree of myopia. [. . .] The retina and the optic nerve were on both eyes in the best condition and Captain Douglas was capable to distinguish all sorts of colours may they have been fundamental or complimental [sic].'[20]

Haig did well in most of the compulsory papers: military topography 86.6 per cent; tactics 80 per cent; fortification 72 per cent; French 70.4 per cent. But in maths he scored just 45.5 per cent, 18 marks below a pass. He also passed his optional papers – military law 60.5 per cent, German 57 per cent, military history and geography 52.25 per cent. His aggregate total was 2,642 marks, against the minimum pass requirement of 1,600 marks, placing him twenty-seventh out of sixty-seven candidates. He thus found himself in an anomalous position; there were positions for twenty-eight new entrants to the College, and on that basis he should immediately have been invited to join. But his maths result meant that, according to the rules, he had failed. Haig's efforts to enter the Staff College have provided his critics, who accuse him of pulling strings to get in, with plentiful ammunition. The truth is more complicated; he *did* pull strings, via Henrietta, but her influence was of no immediate avail.

This apparent disaster with the maths paper has been put into context by John Hussey, who has pointed out that Haig was one of twenty-one of the 1893 candidates who failed, an astonishingly high failure rate of 31 per cent, a rate so abnormally high – the previous three years' maths failure rate averaged 10 per cent annually – that the Director General of Military Education gave special consideration to it in his published report on the examination results; the matter was even raised in the House of Commons.[21] What seems to have happened is that the 1893 maths papers were set and examined by a new examiner, the previous having died – and the students of 1893, who had been encouraged to cram according to one type of maths paper, were wrong-footed. Hussey invited a Cambridge maths don to compare the 1893 maths exam with previous years; it was discovered that the 1893 paper was 'much harder' than previous years and that 'even strong candidates would be unable to do much with this paper if presented with it without warning. The weaker candidates might well be unable to do anything at all.'[22]

Haig was nevertheless informed he could not attend Staff College and on 10 August Sir Redvers Buller, Adjutant-General of the army, furthermore told him that, as a result of the medical examination in London classifying him as colour-blind, he was in any case 'not fit for Staff work.'[23] This was especially galling for Haig, as not only had he been ruled physically fit to sit the examinations, but the thirteen candidates from overseas, who had not been required to attend the Medical Board in London, had not been so tested. Haig wrote a strong appeal in which he emphasized that, as far as the maths papers were concerned, the Staff College's own reports called 'the attention of intending candidates [. . .] to the papers previously set, and they are directed to take them as guides as to what is required of them.'[24] He asked to be considered by the C-in-C for a nominated place, for which he was certainly eligible as he sensibly had, prior to the exams, taken the precaution of obtaining written confirmation from the C-in-C's office that his name would be submitted for approval. Haig also resorted to Henrietta, whose powerful social connections enabled her to intervene at a higher army level than could Haig himself. She appealed to the Inspector-General of Cavalry, Lieutenant-General Sir Keith Fraser, asking him to recommend her brother for a nominated place at the College. Fraser in turn wrote to the Acting Military Secretary of State, but ultimately had to report to Henrietta on 19 August 1893 that the final decision as to whom should be recommended for nomination was in the hands of Sir Redvers Buller – who had already turned Haig down.

What is remarkable about this episode is not that Haig should try to use all means at his disposal to secure what he thought was a just result – which of us would not do the same? – but how *little* influence Henrietta could exert. All avenues exhausted, Haig had no option but to return to his regiment or leave the army. Had he evinced any bitterness at this frustrating injustice it would have been entirely normal, yet he displayed no chagrin.[25] On balance only a prejudiced mind would argue that Haig did not deserve a nominated place. Eventually, in 1896, he was permitted to take up a nominated place, but he obviously did not imagine that possibility in 1893.

It must have been deeply humiliating to return to Mhow, where regimental gossip would not have bothered with the complexities of the process but merely muttered about Haig's 'failure'. Moreover, on his return to India he found another officer had, naturally, replaced him in command of his squadron, and Haig found himself merely second-in-command.

His remaining months in India pass without any surviving diary record, perhaps an indication of the blackness which must have descended. That he bore this disappointment stoically is apparent from a letter from the regiment's commanding officer, Colonel Hamish Reid, in April 1894, when Haig was about to return to England to act as aide-de-camp to General Fraser, who had decided that Haig's ambition and abilities merited his being pulled out of India and given a consolation prize back in England. Fraser's move – which may have also been prompted by consideration for Henrietta's powerful friends – was the lucky break Haig needed, as it lifted him into a general staff role and thus circumvented the obstacle presented by his Staff College rebuff. Reid's farewell letter reveals genuine warmth:

> My dear Douglas,
> I cannot let you go without saying how I have appreciated what you have done for the Regiment. You came back to a position that a great many people would have disliked extremely, second fiddle in a squadron. Instead of making a grievance of it all, I know what a lot of pains you have taken and how much the improvement in that squadron has been owing to you; and up to the last moment when you knew you were off, you have taken just as much interest in the preliminary musketry in the squadron as if you would be here to see the results. I cannot say how much you will be missed by all of us, officers, NCOs and men. Your example in the regiment has been worth everything to the boys. You know I wish you every luck. You are, I think, bound to succeed because you mean to. I hate saying 'goodbye' as I am sadly afraid I shall never soldier with you again, but only hope I may.
> Yours very sincerely,
> Hamish Reid[26]

Haig spent autumn 1894 with Sir Keith Fraser in organizing and training cavalry in England, and part of October in France, observing French cavalry manoeuvres at Limoges. In January 1895 he worked with Fraser on writing a report on the previous autumn's manoeuvres and spent his spare time hunting in Warwickshire, staying at Henrietta's home in Radway. In the spring of 1895, still attached to Sir Keith's entourage, he visited Berlin to observe German cavalry training and organization. Before he left for Germany he again consulted a doctor, once more at the insistence of Henrietta. At this point Haig weighed eleven stones and six pounds and was, despite the repercussions of typhoid and malaria, in good physical shape. Nevertheless there was anxiety about an enlarged liver and he always had at the back of his mind the discouraging example of his father. He wrote reassuringly to Henrietta on 23 April 1895: '[. . .] saw Weber M.D just to please you. He examined me with the greatest care, compared his present with the last notes [from 1891] also the Govnr's & Mamma's constitution was enquired into with the help of his books. – He says that I must live carefully – meat only once a day and ½ Bott of Claret as a maximum allowance for <u>a whole day</u>!! Etc. If I attend to this he says that my constitution is similar to a large number of people who live to great ages! So you and I will be both useless together it seems! His present recommendation is Kissingen [a spa town in Germany] for a month, say after 4 or 5 weeks at Potsdam.'[27]

In the same letter Haig told Henrietta he had recently received a letter from Colonel John French, who was to have considerable influence in Haig's life and whom Haig eventually replaced as C-in-C of the British Expeditionary Force (BEF) in 1915: 'He [French] writes at the end of his letter "Rely on it I have done and will do my utmost for De Pree." I therefore feel sure that everything has been done to get Tito a commission.' 'Tito' was the nickname of Haig's nephew, Cecil George De Pree, the son of his elder sister Mary, who had married George Charles De Pree, of the Royal Bengal Artillery and who became Surveyor General of India. Douglas Haig and John French had known each other since Haig's time in India, where in 1891 French had been a staff officer to Sir George Luck.

Their friendship got onto a firmer footing during the autumn 1894 cavalry manoeuvres in Berkshire, when French commanded a cavalry brigade, from which he emerged with considerable credit.[28] In 1895 Sir George Luck, newly appointed Inspector General of Cavalry in Britain as replacement for Sir Keith Fraser, asked French to serve with him at the War Office, bringing French closer to the circle of power and influence in army affairs, and making him a useful contact if seeking a favour. That Haig approached French for his personal intervention on behalf of a family member's desire for an army commission may seem reproachable today, in our nominally meritocratic era, but in the British army of 1895 this was normal behaviour. Personal recommendations had always been custom and practice and, ironically, the abolition of the commission-purchase system in 1871 reinforced this widely used lubrication. French, Haig and many other rising officers benefited from mentor-protégé relationships early in their career; it was a necessary – if not sufficient – condition of rapid and continued promotion that an influential senior officer would work on one's behalf. In the absence of an objective and rational system of army appointments, such an informal network of string-pulling was ubiquitous, right up to and through the First World War.[29]

This hierarchical, deferential, network mirrored Victorian society generally: 'Socially the army, like early Victorian society, was held together by the bonds of deference. [. . .] The military code of obedience was supplemented by a complex pattern of social relationships which mirrored those of the parent society in an earlier period. In turn, junior officers normally deferred to their more seniors, not because of the latter's professional expertise but because the considerable self-confidence and authoritarian style of general officers reflected their upper-class assumption of an inborn right and duty to lead others.'[30]

On 24 April 1895 Haig sailed from Southampton to Bremerhaven; by 26 April he was booked into the Hotel Bristol in Berlin, eager to watch the German cavalry at Potsdam. On Monday 29 April, he visited the 1st Dragoon Guard Regiment at 8.30am, and spent the rest of the day observing cavalry and artillery drilling on Tempelhof Plain. He was impressed with what he saw, noting on Friday 17 May that a unit from the

1st Uhlan Guards was '[. . .] the finest squadron I have ever seen – pace direction all perfect and cohesion always maintained [. . .]'.

Haig found his German peers hospitable and the only obstacle he encountered in Berlin derived from the resentment of the British military attaché: 'I am getting on very well here – all the German officers I have met do everything to make my stay agreeable and show me anything I want. The only officer who does not go out of his way to assist is Col. Swaine, our own military attaché. – He has been here for nine years is a friend of the Emperor's and can do pretty well anything he likes. [. . .] I fancy he does not want one there [at the manoeuvres] as he being an infantry man has never said much about Cavalry matters in his reports home. However I am independent of him: outwardly he pretends to be best friends to me offers to assist in anything I want, but when I ask a thing he throws obstacles in the way.'[31]

With a reasonable grasp of the language and an introduction from 'old Keith' (Sir Keith Fraser) Haig could confidently circumnavigate Swaine, whose uncooperativeness, if such it was, may have stemmed not just from the old infantry-cavalry rivalries, as Haig assumed, but from simple personal jealousy. Haig was a popular guest of his German hosts, the height of his visit being a grand dinner on 30 May in honour of the first grandchild of Queen Victoria, Wilhelm II, Emperor of Germany, whose mother, Princess Victoria, was sister to Edward, Prince of Wales.

Wilhelm II, who in 1894 had been implicitly accused of megalomania by the German pacifist Ludwig Quidde,[32] was already deeply embroiled in diplomatic tensions with Britain. In July 1895, shortly after Haig's brief tour in Germany,[33] the Boer Republic of Transvaal in South Africa opened a new rail route between Delagoa Bay and Pretoria, largely built with German money. This connection deprived the British-owned Cape Colony of its monopoly of traffic to the Rand, by now an important gold-mining area within the Transvaal, and thus enabled German citizens to reach the Boer republic without the need to cross British territory. Wilhelm celebrated the railway's opening by sending a congratulatory telegram to Paul Kruger, president of the Transvaal. Haig's diaries betray no sense of this simmering Anglo-German clash of interest. Instead, he was delighted when halfway through the dinner the Emperor toasted his health and 'came and shook me by the hand and asked about the regt, what I was doing and how long leave I had – Hoped to see me again soon – and again shook me by the hand and said Goodnight.'[34]

Before he left Berlin, he wrote to Henrietta and asked her to spend up to £30 on presents for nine[35] German officers who had befriended him: 'They have all been so kind here that I would like just to give a few of them a little present. – I enclose a list in order of the way I would like the money spent [. . .] I must have genuine articles that will last: for of course it would never do to say to me next time I come back "that rubbishy things are made in England." Get whatever you like: but you know they always wear uniform so pins and that sort of things are no use, but of course they smoke considerably.'[36]

In June 1895, Colonel French informed Haig that Sir Evelyn Wood had offered French the command of the cavalry in a staff tour between 21–26 June on the South Downs in England; French hoped Haig would join him as staff officer. He accepted with alacrity. This staff tour, which involved senior officers on horseback in civilian clothes preparing plans for the disposition of forces (these were not real, but existed only on paper) over a pre-ordained area, was another key turning point for Haig, as it brought him to the personal attention of General Sir Evelyn Wood, who was the army's adjutant-general and one of the umpires of the exercise along with, notably, General Sir Redvers Buller. No doubt Haig did his best to impress on Buller that it had been a serious mistake to have blocked his Staff College entry two years earlier.

After the staff tour, Haig returned to Germany to take the waters at Kïssingen, where he followed a strict diet which precluded tea, butter, coffee and milk. While there he had a 'civil letter' from Sir Evelyn, who requested from Haig more details about the duties of NCOs in the German army. More gratifying for Haig was Wood's personal praise: 'His last sentence was as follows: "It gave me great pleasure to meet you and have a talk with you and the more so because I knew you pretty well on paper before – I think I may honestly say of you, what we cannot always alas say, that the expectation, though great, was even less than the pleasure you gave me by your conversation." I told you that we got on very well together – Sir E.W is a capital fellow to have upon one's side as he always gets his own way!'[37]

To have a full general and, moreover, a gallant hero – Wood had won the VC in India in 1858 – as one's mentor was invaluable, and Haig can be forgiven for regarding Wood as a 'capital fellow'; to have felt anything else would have been folly. Until his death in 1919 Wood remained an ardent admirer of Haig, and his unflagging support from 1895 onwards is another instance of how Haig succeeded in attracting senior figures who were prepared to aid his career. In the autumn of 1895, Haig attended manoeuvres at Aldershot in the capacity of brigade major and completed work on a new *Cavalry Drill Book*, which French had begun but abandoned on being promoted to assistant adjutant-general, Wood's closest aide.

With these new, influential figures overseeing Haig's prospects, and his own determination to develop a reputation for professionalism and be noticed, it is not surprising that Haig's entrance tests for the Staff College were reconsidered and finally deemed good enough to permit him a nominated place for the following year, 1896. Yet another rule appears to have been bent here, although this time in Haig's favour. A candidate's examination results for a place nominated by the C-in-C were, according to the regulations, only to be 'allowed to hold good for the examinations of the following year.'[38] Haig had sat the exams in 1893; but in Army Order 184 of November 1895, one of the last to which the Duke of Cambridge put his name (he retired on 31 October 1895), Captain Douglas Haig was one of nine officers[39] nominated by the C-in-C to report to Camberley on 15 January 1896. Rules are made to be broken and ultimately in this instance justice was done; the subsequent year rule had in any case been waived before in the case of other officers who had received the C-in-C's nomination. As John Hussey argues: 'Although Haig had been only one of the victims of a serious blunder by the examiners – as the Secretary of State had admitted – he had also suffered from some very severe rulings and subsequent shilly-shallyings by the Medical Boards, had been the object of bureaucratic obstruction within the

Adjutant-General's department, and had not been granted the remedy promised by the Secretary of State. [. . .] Sir Evelyn and the Duke may have stretched the rules a little, but they were in reality merely applying good sense in the administration of natural justice.'[40] Upon arriving at Camberley Haig discovered that the ever thoughtful Henrietta had arranged to have some curtains put up in his quarters.

There are no surviving diaries from his two years at the Staff College, and few letters, but there are some reminiscences from Haig's contemporaries, who collectively represented a 'galaxy of future stars,'[41] including Edmund Allenby, James Edmonds, Richard Haking, George Macdonogh, and Thompson Capper.[42] Of 1896's intake of thirty-two, two became field marshals and peers – Haig and Allenby – and fifteen became generals. Edmonds in particular has great relevance to Haig's later reputation, as Haig appointed him to a staff job at GHQ in the Great War after he appears to have had a breakdown. Edmonds was later commissioned to write the official history of the Great War and evidently had very mixed feelings about Haig, towards whom he felt both gratitude and resentment.

Edmonds had joined the Royal Engineers partly because, unlike the cavalry, there was no need to possess a large private income, and partly because he realized his intellectual ability could be better employed solving problems than sitting on a charger. Attending Camberley involved significant financial sacrifice; officers had their pay stopped on the absurd grounds that they were not engaged on regular regimental or corps work. Thus while at Camberley Captain Edmonds lost his £750 annual salary but had to find about £400 a year to sustain himself and his family. This was obviously not a difficulty for wealthy officers such as Haig, but for Edmonds and others it involved real hardship. Edmonds complained many years later that the first year at Camberley was largely wasted although the second, more practically oriented year, was an improvement. He reflected on his time there with some bitterness: 'I shall never consider the Government returned me value for the two years of my life, the engineer pay I gave up, and the additional £400 I had to spend. [. . .] [In the first year] What actually happened was that we sat at a few lectures – the good boys in the front row, the idle asleep in the back row – and heard what amounted to no more than the reading of some paragraphs of the regulation books (mostly out of date) and some pages of military history. [. . .] There was a written marked examination at the end of the first year, but nobody regarded it seriously.'[43]

A more balanced, if less sensational, view is to be had from Robertson, who attended Camberley in 1897–1898: 'The Staff College does not aspire to make wise men out of fools, or to achieve any other impossibilities, and, like other educational institutions, it has had its failures. It can, however, and does, make good men better, broaden their views, strengthen their power of reasoning, improve their judgment, and in general lay the foundations of a useful military career. Further, the benefits of the course are by no means confined to the lectures the students are given [. . .] for in addition there is a smartening friction with others of their own standing with whom they may have to work later in life.'[44]

That 'smartening friction' neatly captures the way in which many of his Staff College peers rubbed along with Haig, whom Edmonds initially found rather supercilious. He recalled Haig at Camberley as diligent, private, and seldom in the mess apart from mealtimes. On his first day, Haig requested three days' leave to go shooting with the Prince of Wales, which Edmonds regarded as ostentatious name-dropping although for Haig it was nothing of the sort; nevertheless it did nothing to enhance Haig's image in the eyes of the penurious Edmonds. One can sympathize with Edmonds, a man whose brain was bigger than his wallet, who felt his talents were disregarded because he lacked the right connections. The army in 1896 was still top-heavy with those who would have regarded Edmonds as a parvenu; within two decades the army had little choice but, reluctantly, to embrace a degree of social change: 'By 1912 three out of every five British army officers came from a middle-class environment but this did not signify a democratisation of the recruitment process because the elite regiments were still largely controlled by the aristocracy [. . .] in 1870 when there were seventy-six generals in the army, 43 per cent could be identified as the sons of land-owners, while in 1897, as the Victorian military establishment was coming to an end, 40 per cent of the generals and lieutenant-generals were from this group.'[45]

While Haig was alive, Edmonds was always publicly loyal, but after Haig's death he became significantly less so; his later view that he found Haig 'terribly slow on the uptake' at Camberley may be just sour grapes. After Haig's death Edmonds wrote a brief memoir of Haig[46] in which he conveyed some flavour of Haig at Camberley: 'He did not, however, become "popular" in the year. As a captain he had a brusqueness of manner, an abruptness, almost ruthlessness in speech which cut all conversations short. [. . .] Haig made not the slightest attempt to "play up to" the instructors. If a scheme interested him he took tremendous pains with it; if he thought there was no profit in working it out, he sent in a perfunctory minimum. I remember a road reconnaissance sketch on which most of us lavished extreme care, marking all the letter-boxes, pumps, gateways into fields and such-like. Haig handed in a sheet with a single brown chalk line down the centre, the cross roads shown and the endorsement, "20 miles long, good surface, wide enough for two columns with orderlies both ways." '

The final outdoor examination at Camberley saw temporary Lieutenant-Colonel (later Field Marshal Viscount) Herbert Plumer observe Edmonds, Haig and Arthur Blair, who formed a firm and lasting friendship with Haig, conduct a four-day mounted reconnaissance. Haig 'chose the line of country to take, and said that I might provide the "jargon" that the examiner expected.'[47] This kind of insouciance did not hinder Haig's prospects, however, for, as Edmonds also recalled, he was one day 'somewhat taken aback' when Colonel Henderson made a prophecy: ' "There is a fellow in your batch who will be C-in-C one of these days." And when we asked, "Any of us?" he replied, "No, none of you, Haig." ' [48]

CHAPTER FOUR

# 'Hard Work in Hot Sun'

These news [sic] from Khartoum are frightful, and to think that all this might have been prevented and many precious lives saved by earlier action is too frightful.

Queen Victoria to William Gladstone

By January 1898 Haig, at the relatively advanced age of thirty-six and still only a captain, was newly graduated from the Staff College. This carried no guarantee of rapid promotion but merely boosted his chances. Energy and determination were not enough; without luck and connections his prospects might still have been no better than those of his future biographer John Charteris – to end up a brigadier-general at best. At this point, however, Haig set about exploiting his new influential social and military contacts to gain some practical fighting experience. Sudan was the ideal spot, the focal point of British imperialism at the time, as encapsulated by Haig's fellow Old Cliftonian, Sir Henry Newbolt, in his 1898 poem *Vitai Lampada*,[1] the second verse of which epitomised what it meant to be an Englishman in pursuit of an empire:

> The sand of the desert is sodden red,–
> Red with the wreck of a square that broke;–
> The Gatling's jammed and the colonel dead,
> And the regiment blind with dust and smoke.
> The river of death has brimmed his banks,
> And England's far, and Honour a name,

But the voice of a schoolboy rallies the ranks,
'Play up! Play up! And play the game!'

The massive African territory of Sudan, largely unpopulated desert, had been a political and military embarrassment for the British political establishment since the Mahdi, the Islamic religious leader, cut off the head of General Charles Gordon in Khartoum, Sudan's capital, on 26 January 1885. That the great imperial power of Queen Victoria had been humiliated by a motley collection of ill-equipped and fractious indigenous rebels known to the British as dervishes, who pledged allegiance – frequently under duress – to an Islamic fanaticism, outraged British jingoists. At the same time the traditional enemy, France, was salivating at the prospect of feasting at the table in place of Britain. In March 1895 Haig's Oxford contemporary, Edward Grey, now the Liberal Party's Under-Secretary of State at the Foreign Office, warned Paris from the floor of the House of Commons that any French expedition to the upper Nile would be regarded by Britain as an 'unfriendly act', a speech that further inflamed British public opinion.

The stage was thus set for a classic piece of British imperialist adventurism, which came to be known as the River War. This episode brought fame, glory and wealth to the previously somewhat obscure Horatio Herbert Kitchener, gave Winston Churchill his first opportunity to prove himself both courageous and a skilled writer, and presented Haig with his first taste of battle. The River War was presented by its proponents as a justified campaign to topple a cruel despotic tyranny, thereby extirpating the regional Arabic slave trade. It was also a perfect example of imperialist rhetoric in the service of hard-headed British practical interests. Sudan in itself offered no immediate advantage for the expanding British empire, other than the sheer possession of land. But Sudan's disorderliness threatened to spread Islamic nationalist rebelliousness across the border into the much more vital territory of Egypt, under British military occupation since 1882, the protection of whose vital sea link, provided by the Suez Canal, was a central tenet of British foreign policy.

The River War was fought along very extended lines close to the lower reaches of the Nile in Sudan, where the harsh climate tested the Anglo-Egyptian army under its commander-in-chief or Sirdar, Major-General Sir Horatio Kitchener, to the utmost. Kitchener and Haig, whose paths were to cross again in India and during the Great War, shared many characteristics. Both were physically tough, abstemious, fearless, stubborn, outwardly self-confident, hard-working and extremely fastidious in their personal habits. Neither liked ostentatious displays of emotion. Kitchener was also, like Haig, handsome and dashing, attractive to women (although apparently impervious to their blandishments), uncomfortable in most social circumstances, lacking in polished eloquence, deeply suspicious of politicians and journalists and, as his biographer remarked, 'preternaturally reserved'.[2] Above all, Haig and Kitchener shared a determination to be thoroughly professional in an army where ostentatious amateurism was encouraged. In one respect, however, they differed markedly; while Kitchener remained a determined bachelor to the end, Haig was eventually to marry.[3] Although Kitchener was only eleven years older than Haig he had become a major-general at an enviably youthful age. His dictatorial style and brusque demeanour made him many enemies, but he was recognized as a soldier of exceptional quality, as both his predecessors as Sirdar, Sir Evelyn Wood and Sir Francis Grenfell, reported to the War Office. The latter in 1890 judged Kitchener to be: 'A good brigadier, very ambitious. His rapid promotion has placed him in a somewhat difficult position. He is not popular, but has of late greatly improved in tact and manner; and any defects in his character will, in my opinion, disappear as he gets on in the service. He is a fine, gallant soldier, and a great linguist, and very successful in dealing with orientals.'[4] Grenfell's hopes that Kitchener's defects would mellow proved vain.

Haig's Sudan adventures were both character-forming and professionally pivotal, giving him his first experience of real combat. They also reveal the intricate backroom manoeuvring officers were forced to resort to in order to advance their careers. Many serving British officers wanted to go to Sudan to fight alongside Kitchener but few were invited; among the spurned was the young Churchill, whom Kitchener distrusted, although Churchill eventually managed to wangle his way into the Sudan campaign. In January 1898 Kitchener asked the Adjutant-General, Sir Evelyn Wood, to recommend three men from the graduating year at the Staff College to serve under him as special staff officers. Captains Arthur Blair, Thompson Capper and Douglas Haig were the fortunate three. Wood's motives for recommending Haig, whom Wood asked to write privately and frankly his opinion of the Sudan campaign's progress, have been judged biased. In this view, Wood 'was suspicious of Kitchener, and was therefore eager to keep a close eye on him'[5] and he used Haig as his eyes and ears. Yet Sir Evelyn was a highly professional soldier who would not have jeopardized his own reputation by recommending an incompetent. Haig was delighted at being selected, though it meant he had to suspend his British army career and take a temporary commission in the Anglo-Egyptian army. The gamble paid off handsomely.

By 1896, in the final stages of the River War, Kitchener had moved south to the Sudanese province of Dongola at the head of an army of assorted British, Egyptian and Sudanese troops. This force spent much of 1897 building a long railway across a desert between Wadi Halfa, a straggly three-mile-long mud-built settlement garrisoned by 3,000 men, and, ultimately, Abu Hamed, an even smaller town 230 miles to the south. This railway link was a key element in Kitchener's careful preparations for the final assault on Khartoum, and its construction, in one of the world's harshest climates where all manner of tropical diseases steadily depleted the ranks, was a tremendous feat of engineering, human endurance, and logistical resourcefulness. Yet the railway was not merely a demonstration of British industrial prowess; it was also of immense practical importance, ensuring that Kitchener's forces would be properly equipped and supplied. Even with the railway, the lines of communication were stretched. In a characteristic conceit, Churchill described the tortuous journey a simple box of biscuits had to take between Cairo and the front line, at Berber: 'From Cairo to Nagh Hamadi (340 miles) by rail; from Nagh Hamadi to Assuan (205 miles) by boat; from Assuan to Shellal (6 miles) by rail; from Shellal to Halfa (226 miles) by boat; from Halfa to

Dakhesh (Railhead) – 248 miles – by military railway; from Dakhesh to Shereik (45 miles) by boat; from Shereik by camel (13 miles) round a cataract to Bashtinab; from Bashtinab by boat (25 miles) to Omsheyo; from Omsheyo round another impracticable reach (11 miles) by camel to Geneinetti, and thence (22 miles) to Berber by boat. The road taken by this box of biscuits was followed by every ton of supplies required by 10,000 men in the field.'[6]

By 1898 Kitchener's army was ready for an all-out assault to eliminate the dervishes, now situated in and around Omdurman; Khartoum had become, since Gordon's death, largely a ghost city. Kitchener's force numbered 8,200 British and 17,600 Egyptian soldiers, with forty-four guns and twenty Maxim machine-guns on land, thirty-six guns and twenty-four Maxims on the river, together with 2,469 horses, 896 mules, 3,524 camels, and 229 donkeys. Churchill considered some of the indigenous troops recruited to fight alongside the British to be of dubious value: 'The black soldier was of a very different type from the fellahin. The Egyptian was strong, patient, healthy, and docile. The negro was in all these respects his inferior. His delicate lungs, slim legs, and loosely knit figure contrasted unfavourably with the massive frame and iron constitution of the peasant of the Delta. Always excitable and often insubordinate, he required the strictest discipline. At once slovenly and uxorious, he detested his drills and loved his wives with equal earnestness; and altogether "Sambo" – for such is the Soudanese [sic] equivalent of "Tommy" – was a lazy, fierce, disreputable child. But he possessed two tremendous military virtues. To the faithful loyalty of a dog he added the heart of a lion. He loved his officer, and feared nothing in the world. With the introduction of this element the Egyptian army became a formidable military machine.'[7]

This final phase of the River War provided a perfect opportunity for an aggressive young British officer to make his mark. The rather remote risk of a spear through the ribs, blood poisoning from an antiquated musket bullet, or, more likely, a grisly death from disease, were thought by many to be worth it. Simply existing in the harsh conditions of the Sudanese desert was an endurance test for, as Haig wrote in his diary on 16 August 1898, it was 'hard work in hot sun all day.'[8] Any British officer at the time reckoned that the dervishes under the Mahdi, and his nominated successor, the Khalifa[9] Abdullah, were no real match for well-disciplined professional British soldiers and the local Egyptian and Sudanese regiments they had trained. The possession of artillery and Maxim machine-guns heavily weighed the odds of success in their favour, even though the Khalifa could count upon an estimated 50,000 cavalry, as well as masses of press-ganged infantry as cannon fodder.

Intriguingly, the hagiography written by Haig's widow Dorothy – always known to Haig as Doris – does not deal with his Sudanese experiences, when Henrietta was the only woman of significance in his life. Of his time in Sudan, Doris simply wrote: 'During this period he wrote constantly to his sister Henrietta. His letters were very full of descriptions of his activities and were all very carefully preserved by Henrietta. [. . .] The letters are written in a very intimate way. Douglas kept nothing back from her and expressed his opinions on many matters and personalities quite freely. Between Douglas and his sister [. . .] there was a deep affection and understanding which lasted all their lives, and in writing very fully to Henrietta Douglas knew that he could trust her implicitly. These letters, so carefully kept and jealously guarded by a devoted sister, form a most important part of my husband's writings, and it has always been my intention to publish them just as they are. I propose therefore in this book to omit all references to the years that Douglas spent in the Sudan and South African campaigns.'[10]

This does not quite add up. After Haig's death, Doris regarded herself as the keeper of the flame; her biography, at more than 320 pages, could easily have accommodated his time in Sudan. She was also the guardian, at the time, of the massive archive of materials which Haig and his family had carefully maintained. It is conceivable that Doris – who had initially, at least, a slightly barbed relationship with Henrietta – skipped over this important episode not least because she was disinclined posthumously to award Henrietta any greater significance in Haig's life than absolutely necessary.

On Friday 14 January 1898 Haig, then on leave in Scotland, received the longed-for telegram from Sir Evelyn Wood, which simply said: 'Will be selected for Egyptian Army. Call here (War Office) at 11 am Tuesday.' He travelled south the same day. On the 15th he was medically examined and passed fit for active duty. He reported to the War Office on 18 January as instructed, where he met Sir Evelyn, who ordered him to leave for Cairo the following week. On Wednesday 19 January Haig travelled to Enfield, where he was instructed in the use of the Maxim automatic machine-gun.

It is wrong, incidentally, to assume that the British army at this time, and right into the Great War itself, was contemptuous of machine-guns. Along with all major continental European armies it had already trialled the Gatling, Gardner and Nordenfelt machine-guns, with the twin-barrelled Gardner gun being recommended for use by the War Office in 1881 because it was light and had a relatively simple mechanism. Very few machine-guns were purchased by the army in the late nineteenth century, not simply because their potential was underestimated, but to avoid wasting money: technology was constantly improving and some senior officers thought it misguided to invest heavily in a machine-gun that was possibly destined for swift obsolescence. Even the reactionary Duke of Cambridge was quoted in a War Office memo of 1886 as being 'greatly impressed with the value of machine-guns, and feels confident they will, ere long, be used generally in all armies, [but] he does not think it advisable to buy any just yet. When we require them we can purchase the most recent patterns, and their manipulation can be learnt by intelligent men in a few hours.'[11] Haig did not record his first impression of the Maxim gun, but it is absurd to imagine that such an enthusiastic professional army officer would fail to be persuaded of the potential battlefield usefulness of a robust, relatively lightweight single-barrelled machine-gun which could fire more than 600 rounds a minute.

Haig then spent a couple of days at Henrietta's London home, before travelling on Saturday 22 January to a social occasion that symbolized Haig's deepening intimacy, thanks to Henrietta, with the royal family. He journeyed to Sandringham, the weekend residence of Edward, Prince of

Wales, at Edward's invitation, joining a party of guests including Princess Victoria, the Duke (and future King George V) and Duchess of York, the Bishop of Ripon and the ubiquitous Sir Evelyn Wood. The Prince of Wales, then fifty-seven, possessed a restless, easily frustrated mind and an incorrigibly trivial soul; he could not abide being alone. Parties at Sandringham were convivial, hearty, lavish and, above all, personal affairs, with little standing on ceremony, and during them Edward, whose prodigious bedroom and table appetites were legendary, denied himself nothing. His dinners usually consisted of twelve courses, normally starting with caviar, of which he was extremely fond.[12] The flavour of Edward's parties was captured by Hilaire Belloc:

> There will be bridge and booze 'till after three,
> And, after that, a lot of them will grope
> Along the corridors in *robes de nuit*,
> Pyjamas, or some other kind of dope.
> A sturdy matron will be set to cope
> With Lord——, who isn't 'quite the thing',
> And give his wife the leisure to elope,
> And Mrs James will entertain the King![13]

While the ascetic thirty-seven-year-old Haig undoubtedly found some of Edward's proclivities unpalatable, he also relaxed into the undemanding superficial conventionalities of this set, where he could play the part of the upright, thrusting young officer in surroundings that did not make great conversational or intellectual demands. It is largely forgotten today just how influential the monarchy was in the appointment and support of senior military figures, and this early direct connection with his future king was of incalculable use to Haig. Certainly, when Haig was C-in-C on the Western Front, his main political enemy, David Lloyd George, was perpetually conscious that Haig had the devoted backing of George V, who as a young prince had sat down to supper at Sandringham with Haig in late January 1898.

On this, Haig's first visit to Sandringham, Edward was on the verge of forming his enduring liaison with Alice Keppel, then twenty-nine and married to George Keppel, having recently ended his affair with Frances Maynard, the beautiful if rather vacuous Countess of Warwick, universally known as 'Daisy', then thirty-six. In his biography of Haig, Walter Reid asserts that Daisy Warwick and 'the dashing young general [Haig] . . . became lovers'.[14] There have long been tantalizing suggestions[15] that Haig picked up where Prince Edward left off as regards Daisy Warwick's favours, but although the two were evidently on close terms, there is no evidence of a sexual liaison.[16] In her sixty-seventh year – the year after Haig died – Daisy published a disingenuous autobiography in which she hinted that she and Haig had been unusually close:[17]

> I note in our old visitors' book the often recurring name of Douglas Haig, of Bemersyde, then a Captain in the Seventh Hussars. He lived at Radway with his devoted sister, dear Mrs W. Jameson. He took his soldiering earnestly and even in those early days gave little time to play, though none was better company than he. [. . .] He sent me once a copy of Bacon's Essay on Friendship with the following cryptic sentence inscribed in the fly leaf:
> On Monday 30th December 1895
> The Warwickshire [hunt] met at Binton Bridges
> D from D
> [. . .] My friendship with Douglas Haig continued during his life, but I rarely met him after the War lifted him among popular heroes.[18]

As for Edward and Haig, they had been introduced prior to this Sandringham party but the prince was keen to see the captain before he left for Sudan, not least because he had once aspired to make the same journey. When in August 1884 Gladstone had belatedly given way to enormous public pressure and finally authorized the dispatch of an army to Khartoum to save Gordon's skin, Edward had pleaded to be allowed to join, though he was, naturally, refused. Haig was to be Edward's River War surrogate; during the Sandringham weekend, as Haig confided to his diary, Edward desired 'me to "write regularly" to him from Egypt.' Haig was thus given an opportunity to form a direct, discreet line of communication with his future monarch, a perfect opportunity to gain and retain Edward's attention.

On Monday 24 January Haig left Sandringham and returned to London where, three days later, he dined with Henrietta, and his brothers Hugo, George and John and their families. Next morning he started out for Cairo, taking the boat train from Charing Cross station to Paris, where he was irritated by officious customs officers: 'Customs at Gare du Nord most inquisitive. Certainly they do nothing which encourages travellers to pass thro' France!'

He had a similar experience in Rome, where Italian customs officials made him open most of his packages, though they were 'not so bad as Paris!' He arrived in Naples at 1.36 pm on Sunday 30 January, where he found an agent from the Orient Company, who assisted him to get his baggage aboard the SS *Ormuz*, which lay quite close to the pier. Haig, always careful with money, was outraged at the cost for the ferry to the *Ormuz*: 'Charge 2½ frcs (sic) each passenger on tender! a most exorbitant extortion! Return to shore after writing to Henrietta. Send telegram to War Office Egyptian Army Cairo reporting my departure and also notify War Office London in official form. Ormuz sails at midnight.'

An uneventful passage to Cairo ended on 3 February. The next day, Haig met Sir Francis Grenfell, commanding the Egyptian Army of Occupation, from whom he learned that the contract to serve with the Anglo-Egyptian army was 'not very binding' and that 'one can always get out of it without a great deal of difficulty.' He signed up for two years on 7 February 1898, three years to the day after he was gazetted to the 7th Hussars, and bought two supposedly sand-proof watches, which next day he had to return as they failed to keep accurate time.

Haig's diaries and correspondence from this period show he enjoyed himself immensely during the River War, his description of his escapades a perfect model for a John Buchan adventure. He was inordinately proud to be one of Kitchener's chosen few, as he wrote to Henrietta on 6 February:

The longer I stay here the more lucky I seem to be in having got into this Egyptian Army. The crowds of fellows that have asked to be taken & refused is very great. You would like Cairo I think. Parts are like a bad Paris or Brussels, but the native town is full of bazaars & places where you can bargain & spend money!

How it will really end up I don't know, but Kitchener will only take the best now & picks & chooses from the 100s who are anxious to come.[19]

Haig then made his way from Cairo to Wadi Halfa, staying overnight on 9 February at Keneh, a 'town of about 28,000 a mile from river [Nile] on east bank. Many pilgrims concentrate here for pilgrimage to Mecca. Scores of well built houses, a couple of hotels, numerous coffee houses & dancing girls.'

He took a steamer for part of the journey and described to Henrietta, in a heavy-handed manner reminiscent of *Punch*, an episode involving fellow passengers: 'There was rather an amazing incident the first night on board this steamer. There are about 7 or 8 Germans out of the 32 passengers on board. At dinner one of them sent to have the cabin door shut. Some non-Germans insisted on its remaining open. The Germans at first retaliated by putting up their coat collars and the lady sent for a jacket which she flung vigorously around her expansive shoulders! Many of us laughed and the Germans no doubt felt uncomfortable and got up en masse and left the table, like so many petted children – No doubt they felt as if they had withdrawn from the concert of the Great Powers. So in due course they will receive a telegram from "Wilhelm" to congratulate them in their spirited conduct in supporting his Kolonial Politik & "mailed hand" theory on the banks even of the Nile!'.

Less than three years after he had been toasted by the German Kaiser in Berlin, Haig had clearly acquired some contemporary British antagonism towards Germany's own imperial ambitions. He arrived at Wadi Halfa on the afternoon of 15 February and immediately reported to Colonel Maxwell, the Commander in Nubia. There Haig met Kitchener for the first time and found him 'very cordial.' That night he left for Berber for a month's tour, though without any specific duties. Kitchener '[. . .] could not say exactly what I wd do but wd telegraph – Probably I will go to Debbeh & take over Squadron in bad order now commanded by native officer.' He comforted himself by believing that 'If anything doing Debbeh will be the direction of attack.'

This was an erroneous assessment; Debbeh was almost 200 miles west of Berber and roughly the same distance north-west of Omdurman, where the final action of campaign was to be fought. Fortunately for Haig, Kitchener telegraphed on 20 February and instructed him to go to Berber. Haig wrote again to Henrietta on 17 February with news that he had purchased a couple of horses, two camels, and hired 'a cook at £3 a month, and the black fellow "Suleiman" (whom I got in Cairo from a Major Bourke) as body servant.' Haig depended heavily on Henrietta during his days in Sudan and later, both emotionally and logistically; until his marriage she was his base camp, organizing his personal supplies and providing him with a home and support when not on active service. In the same letter he asked her to send him some of life's essentials. Here, and elsewhere in other lists of supplies he made in other fields of operation, there is an element of a *Boy's Own* adventure, as if he were about to embark on a splendid escapade:

> You might however when you get this send me out 2 or 3 boxes of supplies, each box not to exceed 150 lbs in weight and to be <u>about</u> 3 ft long by 1½ ft wide and 1' deep [. . .] the object of the shape & weight is to go on the side of the camel without difficulty. The sort of things I wd like would be jam, tinned fruits, cocoa, vegetables, haddocks in tin, tongue, biscuits, some hock, and a bottle or 2 of brandy or any other sort of drink – whisky I get here all right – But you know better than I do what sort of things to send. Spend whatever you like on these things, £50 or more, which please get from the Royal Bank Leven [. . .] I don't expect them before August and can get on well enough with the supplies I can buy here, but things come better from England. Put a little soap (shaving) in, & a few odds & ends & by the way a <u>small</u> mincing machine wd be useful for the meat is usually real tough.

An officer in Kitchener's Egyptian Army had no limit set to the quantity of kit he could take with him, and so was at a distinct advantage over his British counterpart, who was permitted a maximum of thirty pounds, supposedly because of transport pressures. By the end of February, Captain Haig thus arrived magisterially in Berber, three days in advance of the British army contingent, trailing behind him seven camels burdened with just his personal gear and supplies. When the British Brigade finally arrived at Berber on Thursday 3 March, Kitchener called for three cheers for the queen; the exhausted British soldiers would probably have preferred three beers. If Haig relished his privileges, he was also generous in sharing them with less fortunate British army officers, informing Henrietta on 2 March that 'Well we fed 17 or more at breakfast, many more at lunch and there are a heap coming to dinner [. . .] We have 6 champagnes for tonight!'

At Berber, Haig was daily engaged in scouting forays with his Egyptian cavalry squadron, chasing dervishes and becoming acquainted with the surrounding countryside. Berber was bleak, according to Churchill:

> The Berber of Egyptian days lies in ruins at the southern end of the main roads. The new town built by the Dervishes stands at the north. Both are foul and unhealthy; and if Old Berber is the more dilapidated, New Berber seemed to the British officers who visited it to be in a more active state of decay. [. . .] The houses were constructed by a simple method. A hole was dug in the ground. The excavated mud formed the walls of the building. The roof consisted of palm-leaves and thorn bushes. The hole became a convenient cesspool. Such was Berber, and this 'emporium of Soudan trade,' as it has been called by enthusiasts, contained at the time of its recapture by the Egyptian forces a miserable population of 5,000 males and 7,000 females, as destitute of property as their dwellings were of elegance.[20]

Yet for Haig the ghastliness of Berber's filthy poverty did not detract from his delight in the well-fed and active outdoor military life. He wrote to Henrietta in the middle of March that, while in camp at least, he was 'living in luxury. [. . .] For instance we breakfast about 8 or 8.30 and usually commence with crushed oatmeal porridge (which I asked you to send me in my last letter) and milk – the latter excellent from the goat. Then we have eggs from the hens [. . .] Bacon (in tins) and sausages –

sometimes fish from the Nile – & other food, and finish up with Jam or marmalade. We lunch about 1 o'c and every man does himself well – soup, 2 meats, puddings etc with tinned fruits. Dinner abt 7.30. So you see we are very well off at present.'

Haig diligently recorded the dishevelled appearance of the British regulars:

Saturday 12 March: Egyptian troops lined the road thro' camp at 7.30 am while the British Bde marched between them to Darmali 2½ miles distant! The Egyptian troops cheered louder: Sambo rather bad at it, the sounds sent forth resembled the hoots of a crowd of Apes! The British v. dirty: this no doubt impossible to avoid, but a pity to show them to the 'allies' in this condition! Still the <u>intention</u> was good.[21]

On 21 March Haig was part of a small reconnaissance in the vicinity of the banks of the Atbara river, a tributary of the Nile, when he came under hostile fire for the first time in his life. In what was 'little more than a disorderly scuffle'[22] Haig, who was accompanying 'as a sort of odd man'[23] a cavalry squadron under the command of Captain Le Gallais, showed that he could keep cool under attack when, in the early afternoon, a hundred or so dervishes ambushed the squadron in the riverbed. The dervishes killed ten of the Egyptian cavalry and wounded eight more, for the loss of half a dozen of their own. The cavalry gave chase but eventually relinquished the pursuit and arrived back at camp at 11.30pm. It had been a busy and risky afternoon's fighting and Haig wrote a full report to Sir Evelyn, including the observation that his party 'felt the want of machine guns when working along outside of scrub for searching some of the tracks.' On 25 March Haig was appointed a staff officer with the Cavalry Brigade and on 30 March the Brigade – a battalion of Horse Artillery, a company of the Camel Corps and two Maxim batteries – moved to a position about one mile from a dervish camp at Nakleia, in front of the river Atbara. Haig recorded that the enemy trenches 'seemed filled with infantry. Fired 10 common shell & 19 shrapnel at 1000 yards from B and 2000 rounds from maxims. Fire <u>not</u> returned. Difficult to observe fire but enemy did not leave trenches!'

With these first tastes of action, Haig felt competent to vent his criticism of some of his superiors. He wrote to Henrietta from the Hudi Camp on the Atbara on Friday 1 April, detailing the tribulations faced by the British army's contingents, which he found inexplicable, and even questioned Kitchener's style of command:

> Although we (the Egyptian Army) live in comparative luxury with our baths, cooking pots, beds etc the British Brigade (ie General Gatacre's lot) live in the greatest discomfort – In fact the officers only have what they stand in! & a blanket [. . .] It is quite unnecessary in my opinion that the English should be in such discomfort. For the last 2 or 3 months they all, stout elderly parties of Majors and Colonels, have gone to sleep in the dust with one rug apiece rolled round them – I felt sorry for them with their ration of bully beef & maybe a sardine as a luxury [. . .] I see that you imagine that I am with the Sirdar [. . .] He is a man that does everything himself and in fact has no Head Qrs Staff at all! Indeed General Hunter, who has hitherto commanded the troops in the field, cannot get the Sirdar to tell him what his position in this Army is! In addition the Sirdar is most silent & no one has ever the slightest notion what is going to be done until he gives his orders! [. . .] Please send me out (by parcel post) a big white umbrella lined with spike to stick in the ground – Briggs keeps them. Also half a dozen white silk neck cloths. I wear an ordinary shooting jacket with turned down collar.[24]

His letter to Henrietta was pertinent; if Haig could have delivered to him everything from champagne to white umbrellas, it was surely a serious indictment of the British army and its political masters that its own soldiers were on semi-starvation rations and without adequate sleeping gear for the cold desert nights.

On 5 April, during what was intended to be no more than a reconnoitre of the dervish positions, the Egyptian cavalry to which Haig was attached stumbled into a serious combined infantry and cavalry force. At 5am the Cavalry Brigade, a Horse Artillery battalion, a company of the Camel Corps and two Maxim gun batteries moved off to conduct a forceful probe of the enemy's lines. Unusually, the dervishes decided to lift themselves from what Churchill contemptuously referred to as their 'idiotic apathy' and sought to engage the Anglo-Egyptian contingent. Major-General Hunter, in command of the Egyptian Division, accompanied the foray, as did the commander of the 1st Brigade of the Division, Lieutenant-Colonel Maxwell. According to Haig the 'management of the whole force rested with [Lieutenant-Colonel] Broadwood of course, Commanding Cavalry.' At walking pace they approached the dervish lines to within some 1,200 yards and tried to gauge the strength of the enemy. Under a helpful cloak of dust, massed groups of dervish cavalry threatened to outflank Broadwood's force. At one point Broadwood took personal command of two cavalry squadrons and charged the dervish lines. According to Churchill's account, 'Thus headed by Broadwood himself, and with their British officers several horse-lengths in front, the Egyptians broke into a gallop and encountered the Baggara line, which numbered not fewer than 400 men but was in loose order, with firmness. They struck them obliquely and perhaps a third of the way down their line, and, breaking through, routed them utterly.'

Haig informed Henrietta that he gave orders to other cavalry squadrons to act in rear support of Broadwood's charge, as well as directing the Maxims to give covering fire once Broadwood's cavalry had cleared the field:

This saved us for the moment, and the squadron again being steadied, we were able to fight our way out of the reach of infantry fire. Had the Dervish horsemen been all the papers say of them, we would never have got away. Fortunately they ran away the moment we showed a bold front, and only came on when we turned our backs. Our casualties were pretty severe, 30 and 10 killed.[25] [...] Broadwood was much obliged to me for my assistance, and told the Sirdar so. He, Broadwood, was wrong to charge as he did with the first line, for the whole Brigade then passed from his control. But he is a very sound fellow, and is excellent at running this show.

Kitchener rewarded Haig for his services here by appointing him to the acting rank of major. At this distance it is impossible to know precisely how vital a role Haig played in this scrap; he certainly gave

Henrietta to understand that he had performed vitally useful service. What it *did* demonstrate was his sheer gusto for the fray; he loved the smell, the noise, the sights of battle. He had courage, enormous self-confidence, and made sure that his superiors were well aware of him and his efforts.

The penultimate act of the River War was now imminent. On 8 April there occurred a larger and more decisive clash, known as the battle of Atbara, at which Kitchener decided the time was ripe to attack the forces of Mahmud, the Khalifa's deputy. After marching almost twelve miles through the night, briefly resting in pitch darkness close to Mahmud's encampment, the Anglo-Egyptian force started its artillery bombardment of the dervish trenches and buildings at 6.15am. The Mahmud's forces had constructed a *zareba*, a protective enclosure of prickly thorns, behind which were trenches in which many of the hapless dervish soldiers were later discovered to have been chained to their positions, to prevent them fleeing. The cavalry, Haig included, were briefly deployed chasing some dervish cavalry, but otherwise spent the time as onlookers. It was during this minor fracas that Haig rescued an Egyptian army soldier from possible capture, a spirited though actually not particularly dangerous effort for which his future wife (though not Haig himself) would always insist, when the subject came up, that he deserved the Victoria Cross.[26] After an hour's bombardment, and with some of the buildings now ablaze, the Anglo-Egyptian infantry formed up in columns behind a double firing line of men abreast, preparatory to an assault on the dervish lines. At 7.40am Kitchener ordered the advance and some 11,000 men began to walk towards the *zareba*, advancing down a gentle slope. Churchill described the scene: 'Large solid columns of men, preceded by a long double line, with the sunlight flashing on their bayonets and displaying their ensigns, marched to the assault in regular and precise array. The pipes of the Highlanders, the bands of the Soudanese, and the drums and fifes of the English regiments added a wild and thrilling accompaniment.'

The dervishes put up a ragged but occasionally heroic resistance, particularly around the innermost defences, where the Mahmud was eventually captured. By 8.25am, when the ceasefire was sounded, the British and Sudanese infantry had rapidly moved through the encampment and its fortifications, shooting and bayoneting all those who resisted. According to Churchill, eighteen British and sixteen Sudanese officers as well as 525 other ranks had been killed and wounded; several thousands of the Mahmud's soldiers lost their lives, were wounded or taken prisoner. There was also plenty of loot to be had. In a letter to Henrietta (dated 21 April 1898) Douglas wrote:

> I have a lot of odds and ends to send you. 'Gibbers' (dervish coats), spears, flags, knives, etc. The post won't take anything away by parcel post, so I must wait till someone I know goes to Cairo. I did not take anything myself, excepting one knife, out on patrol, when we captured 7 or 8 prisoners. I had not time to take 'Loot' so I bought this from some of these 'Sambo' soldiers, who are devils to loot and now want money to pay their lady friends in Berber.[27]

Haig sent an account of the battle to Sir Evelyn Wood on 29 April, in which he queried if the severe casualties of the Anglo-Sudanese infantry – which he put at 603[28] – could perhaps have been avoided, had Kitchener deployed his forces differently, and that the large numbers of the enemy who had managed to flee the battlefield might have been trapped. He also ridiculed British press reports of the battle, evincing a contempt for journalism and journalists which was a consistent thread throughout his life: 'We have just received the London papers of 9th April with accounts of the Battle of the Atbara. What rubbish the British public delights to read. The exaggeration of some of the reports almost makes a good day's work appear ridiculous. The headings of the D.T [*Daily Telegraph*] are so overdrawn that instinctively one says, "Waterloo Eclipsed".'

He was also irritated that Kitchener had not made greater use of the cavalry during the battle: 'By this time, however, you will have had an official account of the battle with plans, etc. I wonder what your opinion of the whole thing is. I had a good view of what took place, because we Cavalry did all that the Sirdar would allow us to do, quite early; namely, we drove the enemy's cavalry across the river and halted on the bank.'

Haig questioned Kitchener's frontal attack, and also disparaged the use and effectiveness of the artillery: 'Distant fire was not required; in fact, the 1st and only range was some 700 yards. Our side says the guns did tremendous damage. Mahmud and over 300 (enemy) questioned by Fitton (who is a sort of intelligence officer here) say, "We did not mind the guns, they only hurt camels and donkeys. The infantry fire was what destroyed us." As far as I can make out, the artillery preparation frightened a good many of the spearsmen, and they bolted. The deep nature of the trenches prevented shrapnel searching it.'

There are at least two points worth noting about this correspondence with Wood, not the least of which is Haig's early introduction to the value of trenches as a defence against shrapnel. Another is his boundless self-confidence; Haig not only criticized Kitchener's conduct of this minor skirmish but proffered his own views about how it could have been better handled. Whether Haig's proposed modifications of Kitchener's attack, suggested with hindsight, would have resulted in fewer casualties is impossible to say. Of greater note is that Haig writes as if he were no mere acting major but was fully confident of the backing of very powerful forces within the army. A typical officer of such lowly rank would have trembled in his boots at the thought of going behind the back of the notoriously irascible Kitchener. Not Haig. Whether this back-door channel of communication was honest, honourable, or even useful, is debatable. Some of his views might have been designed to show himself in a good light to his superiors, and there is nothing particularly objectionable in that; but it is also true that Haig's professionalism was such that he enjoyed trying to articulate, in great detail, the course of a military engagement. He rounded up his view of the Atbara incident by drawing back somewhat from his initial criticism of Kitchener, acknowledging to Wood that 'The weak point in my plan is that I calculated as if I had troops that can shoot and manoeuvre. It would be unwise to rely upon the Blacks doing either well. So all the more credit is due to the Sirdar for limiting himself to a moderate victory instead of going for annihilating Mahmud's army.'

A few days after Atbara, Haig wrote to an anxious Henrietta, reassuring her that he felt perfectly safe. He also told her to stop worrying about his finances: '[. . .] neither the Dervish horsemen nor the bullets of their infantry worry me in the least. [. . .] I am sorry you should take so much trouble about my investments; for they will only worry you, and I never want for money. My pay here moreover is good (£500 a year) & will keep me going more or less. So just let my investments slide, as £1,000[29] more or less capital does not disturb me. All the same I am greatly obliged to you for having gone into the question.'

Kitchener showed after Atbara that he would not be hurried into committing any errors through over-confidence; he carefully reconstructed his forces between April and late August, avoiding battle in the worst heat of the year, and prepared for the final assault against the Khalifa on the plains of Omdurman, four miles outside Khartoum. On Sunday 8 May Lieutenant-Colonel Broadwood left Berber via a steamer for Dakhila and Haig took command of the Cavalry Brigade in the interim. Another of Sir Evelyn Wood's protégés popped up in Haig's diary on Tuesday 12 July, when Haig and Captain Le Gallais were 'sent for by Sirdar at 12 noon. He told us that he was much bothered by people with influence forcing useless officers on him. Asked if I thought that young Churchill suitable. Said I did not want him in my squadron.'

Churchill was then just twenty-three and already a noted young thruster. Despite being initially spurned by Kitchener, he had secured himself a temporary attachment as a lieutenant with the 21st Lancers in Sudan, leaving his regular regiment, the 4th Hussars, so that he could be part of the Sudanese campaign.[30] Churchill owed his chance to participate in the River War to a network of string-pullers no less powerful than those who worked behind the scenes on behalf of Haig. Churchill's mother lobbied Kitchener, and, after he refused her, she turned to the Prime Minister, Lord Salisbury, and Sir Evelyn Wood, the latter browbeating Kitchener into granting Churchill's requests. Kitchener's disdain for Churchill was thus partly due to being forced against his better judgement into accepting this young maverick, and partly because Churchill's alter ego was that of a journalist; Churchill was keen to be in Sudan partly to write as a war correspondent for the *Morning Post* newspaper.[31] For Kitchener – and for Haig – someone stooping to write a newspaper column for £15 a time should not be an officer, and could not be a gentleman.[32]

Haig had another reason for his reluctance to see Churchill advanced: rivalry. He had hardly gained a toehold in circles of power and influence himself and was not magnanimous enough to tolerate the close proximity of a much younger, equally ambitious and highly gifted man. At that stage of his life Churchill was evidently not intent on becoming a career professional soldier, as was Haig, but his powerful connection with Sir Evelyn Wood was one which Haig himself wished to cultivate as fully as possible. Haig's casual 'blackballing' of Churchill in this fashion – which, given the gossipy nature of Kitchener's entourage, would certainly have reached Churchill's ears – cost him dearly in later life, when Churchill, as a minister in Lloyd George's administration during the Great War, became an occasional thorn in Haig's side by arguing strongly for an 'eastern' front (the Dardanelles) against Haig's firm support for the Western Front.

Haig's thirty-seventh birthday, in 1898, passed unremarked by him; while many other officers after Atbara chose to return to the fleshpots of Cairo, Haig preferred to stay in camp in the brief interlude before the decisive battle at Omdurman at the beginning of September. From 4 August he was almost continually on the march, harrying dervishes and moving his unit ever closer to Khartoum. His day would usually start with reveille at 2.45am, followed by breakfast at 3.15am, and on the march by 4am. On Monday 8 August his cavalry squadron reached Metemma, a grisly place. He confided to his diary that 'The dervishes massacred several thousand of Jaalin tribe here over a year ago – many human skulls & bones on the road, & carcasses of donkeys passed on our way. Metemma deserted & houses still unwholesome with human remains.'

On Saturday 13 August, in a revealing diary entry, he noted that 'Last night a deserter from one of the Sudanese Battalions was caught & at once shot. They have been deserting in some numbers of late, 12 in a week, 25 to 30 in all from 6 Battn, so an example had to be made – still it seems a bit hard to make men who are prisoners of war soldiers, who don't want to do so, and then shoot them if they desert.'

It is worth emphasizing that Haig here was talking about a black African soldier, not a British white regular. Haig mouthed the conventionally dismissive remarks about black Africans, common to his day and class, but that did not preclude human feelings where he thought an injustice was done.

If Haig was irritated by the young whipper-snapper Churchill following Atbara, he was to be positively livid after the concluding engagement of the war, at Omdurman. While Omdurman finally removed a seventeen-year regime of horrible brutality, it lives on in history as an invidious example of technology in the service of slaughter. As Churchill wrote, 'it was a matter of machinery.' In the early hours of the morning of Thursday 1 September a terrific thunderstorm and a heavy downpour drenched the assembling Anglo-Egyptian army, which at 5am moved out of its camp to approach Omdurman. The cavalry reached the west end of Kerreri ridge, overlooking Omdurman at a distance of some six miles. Haig led a patrol that afternoon to a nearby round topped hill to the south west of the city, from where he observed that 'our approach had evidently been perceived, because on reaching the round hill a most wonderful sight presented itself to us – A huge force of men with flags, drums & bugles was being assembled to the west of the city.'

Haig estimated this force to be some 30,000 strong. He was itching for action and some dervish horsemen gladly obliged by galloping towards and engaging some of his squadron: 'two Dervishes were disabled: my fellows still all right and full of pluck.' He received a report that one of his squadron had been brought down and chased by dervishes, and he galloped to within 250 yards of the enemy lines: 'They commenced firing briskly but, as usual, high. [. . .] I saw that there was no man to be rescued, and galloped back. We caught the horse and found it belonged to the <u>maxim</u> battery.'

Kitchener finally gave battle on Friday 2 September, with the left flank of his army on the river Nile, protected by a gunboat flotilla. The right flank was taken by the cavalry brigade, now back under the command of Broadwood, assisted by Haig as staff officer. At one point the cavalry, including Haig's squadron, was halted behind the artillery which was in action – a position which, he wrote in his diary on the day of the battle, was unsuitable: 'I had scarcely made the remark, before my trumpeter was shot above the right temple, the bullet remaining embedded at the back of his head, he was still quite cheerful, his horse was also wounded – my leading troop leader standing next was hit, and the guide behind him was hit in the thigh – 2 other horses were also hit – all in less time than it takes to write.'

Meanwhile the bulk of the dervish ranks mounted suicidal assaults against the artillery shrapnel, machine-guns and massed rifle fire of Kitchener's main army; as many as 20,000 dervishes were killed or wounded in a very short time. While Haig's day was exciting but thin on action, that of Lieutenant Churchill and the 21st Lancers would go down in history as one of the last great massed cavalry charges – precisely the kind of blood-tingling episode Haig had fruitlessly yearned for since he first joined the 7th Hussars.[33] The Lancers were ordered by Kitchener to cut off the line of the dervishes' retreat back into Omdurman, towards which hundreds of scattered dervishes were now headed. It was thought, from a quick estimate of the situation, that the Lancers would face little or no opposition.

Yet as they advanced they came under scattered gunfire from what they judged was a body of a few hundred dervish skirmishers. At 250 yards from the enemy the order was given to charge and, lances lowered and horses galloping, the regiment was about to hit the skirmishers square-on when its ragged ranks scattered to reveal that behind the enemy was a dry river bed, packed with several thousand more dervishes. Unable to halt their momentum the Lancers plunged into the thick ranks of dervishes and, aghast at their predicament, immediately started hacking and shooting their way free, eventually succeeding in getting a sufficient distance beyond the dervishes to dismount and fire their carbines.

A blunder by any reckoning, the charge of the 21st Lancers, who that day out of almost 400 troopers lost twenty-one killed and fifty wounded, was the stuff of schoolboy yarns; it saw the bestowal of three Victoria Crosses, each for the rescue of a fallen comrade. It irked Haig enormously.

His calm, collected bearing and inspirational self-control with the Egyptian cavalry, while entirely sensible, was far removed in spirit and outcome from the heroically glorious charge a mile or so away; VCs did not (and do not) necessarily go to the competent professional who, without flamboyant gestures, does a good job. That the dilettante Churchill was forever afterwards associated with such a grand episode, and Haig, the professional cavalryman, was not, only further disinclined Haig towards a favourable view of the youthful interloper. Haig's chagrin did not, however, prevent him from asking Churchill, when he left Sudan on 9 September, to carry back to England letters to Henrietta and, of course, Sir Evelyn, both being fully informed of how Haig would have fought a much better battle than the Sirdar.

Omdurman duly fell, though the Khalifa eluded capture, dying in a skirmish against Anglo-Egyptian troops in November 1899. On the afternoon of Sunday 11 September Haig rode into Khartoum, where he learned that the Mahdi's body had been disinterred. Kitchener, by now a national hero in Britain popularly known as 'the conqueror of the Sudan', had left the city the day before together with a flotilla of five gunboats, headed for Fashoda to confront a tiny and impertinent French contingent under Major Marchand. Haig heard rumours that the Mahdi's skull had been removed and sent to England, the torso burned and the ashes thrown into the Nile.[34] He witnessed 'boxes of loot going to HM & the P. of Wales. Nothing much worth having!' On Monday he recorded that Kitchener had been made a peer and remarked in his diary, alluding to the battlefield slaughter, that 'Baron Khartoum & Viscount Bury shld suffice!' A grateful British Parliament was to vote the forty-eight-year-old Kitchener a grant of £30,000 in June 1899.[35] Part of the gratitude of British politicians was that Kitchener had avenged Gordon on the cheap; Kitchener was given to boasting after the fall of Khartoum that he had conquered Sudan, a country of about one million square miles, at a cost of just £2,354,000 (of which the British contribution was a mere £800,000), the equivalent of only two pounds, six shillings and sixpence a square mile.[36]

The River War was over and there was nothing left for Haig to do in

Sudan; on 13 September he sent a letter to Broadwood requesting that he be allowed to resign from the Anglo-Egyptian army. By 5 October he was back in London, where he was met by his brother John and Henrietta at Victoria Station. His Sudan escapade had lasted just eight months, but in this brief period the personal and military lessons he learned, the habits he acquired, and, not least, the insight he gained into the importance of personal connections in fostering a career, would always remain with him. Sudan was a marked success for Haig, even if he had not displayed the possibly foolhardy bravado of Churchill. He had cemented relations with Wood and the Prince of Wales and forged a lasting bond with Kitchener, three figures who were to exert enormous beneficial influence over his future. He had conducted himself professionally and proved utterly reliable and cool under fire. He was shortly able to parade these attributes on an even grander stage, that of South Africa.

# CHAPTER FIVE

# Chasing Boers

I only hope that if I reach the age of decrepitude that I'll have the sense to go and grow cabbages, or do anything but clog the military machine with the antiquated fads of a past generation.

Douglas Haig, letter to Henrietta, 26 October 1901

Let us admit it fairly, as a business people should,
We have had no end of a lesson: it will do us no end of good.

Rudyard Kipling, 'The Lesson'

By the beginning of October 1898 Haig was once more back in England with the 7th Hussars, then stationed at Norwich, although he did not have to kick his heels in Norfolk for very long. In May 1899 he received a summons to join Major-General French as brigade major. French, aged forty-seven, had by now established himself as the army's leading cavalry officer, in command of the 1st Cavalry Brigade at Aldershot, where General Sir Redvers Buller was commandant. Yet according to Charteris even the prestige of a posting to Aldershot failed to alleviate a gloom that descended upon Haig, following his return from Sudan:

Neither the brevet rank [acting major] nor the new appointment satisfied him. He felt that the Egyptian Campaign had been a failure as far as he was concerned. He was thirty-eight years of age and still a regimental captain. There was no prospect of swift promotion. The goal of his ambition was still dim and distant. [. . .] His work at Aldershot did not absorb him, and the amusements of London entirely failed to attract him. He fell a victim to discontented ambition. Even his studies were in arrears, and he became morose and brusque in manner. This was perhaps the least satisfactory year of Haig's military life; but it proved only a brief interval.[1]

Was Haig really so deeply in the doldrums in the first half of 1899? He may have missed the adrenalin of the Sudan but by proving himself to the army's rising star, Kitchener, Haig had considerably improved his long-term prospects. To return from the escapades of the Sudan to the spit-and-polish of Aldershot parades and dinners was, no doubt, difficult; but of all the officers of his generation Haig had by now sufficiently established his reputation and connections such that there was every chance of swift promotion. By seeking out Haig as his brigade major, French had taken note of the esteem in which Haig was held by French's own seniors. Moreover, a secret pact closely bound French and Haig together. A charmer, roguishly witty and socially adept, the Irish-descended John French was also notoriously profligate.[2] As a young officer, French had made 'a hasty and ill-advised marriage'[3] only to divorce within a year. He managed to keep both the marriage and its break-up hidden from his brother officers in first the 19th Hussars[4] and then later the Northumberland Yeomanry, the unit to which he transferred in order to gain promotion. At a time when divorce was disreputable, French was fortunate that his career was not finished before it had really begun. In 1880, at the age of twenty-eight, he married for a second time, and despite this being a much happier relationship he 'began pursuing women with the mad passion of a Casanova. Over the years he had a succession of beautiful and well-connected mistresses and was cited as correspondent in at least one divorce action.'[5]

French expended almost as much energy in his sexual conquests as he did on his peacetime military duties, although, like Haig, he possessed ample bravery on the battlefield. While divorce was socially unacceptable, the open secret of his womanizing posed no threat to his career. His other serious weakness – financial improvidence – was a different matter, for a bankrupt could never be considered a gentleman and would certainly find it impossible to remain an officer. Throughout his life

French borrowed money unscrupulously and failed to repay his debts to, among others, his brother-in-law. French's background was relatively poor, yet he could never control his expenses. The lack of a private income, as we have seen, was potentially a serious handicap for anyone wishing to make a career in the cavalry, but despite his fecklessness French contrived, through a careful cultivation of the popular press, an innate skill as a courtier, and a charmed life, to elude public scandal. However, by the time French appointed Haig as his brigade major he had 'suffered serious financial reverses through unwise speculation in the South African gold market. In May 1899 his creditors were so pressing that he would have been obliged to leave the service if Haig, who was a man of substance, had not provided him with a loan of £2,000.'[6]

In fact, the loan was probably even bigger, perhaps £2,500.[7] Haig sensibly took the precaution of having his solicitors assign to him a life insurance policy on French to the value of £2,500, with the British Natural Premium Life Association Limited, from 31 August 1899.[8] This was a considerable sum. What should we make of this incident? Haig did not readily lend money nor make charitable handouts.[9] The loan to French could be viewed as a purely practical arrangement; Haig's personal wealth was well-known and French perhaps sought a loan from him because he knew Haig could easily afford it and would be discreet. For his part, Haig could easily justify it as helping a brother officer in need, someone he knew and valued and who quite probably might otherwise have been forced to leave the army in disgrace. Nor can we discount the fact that, as both were Freemasons, this placed an obligation, of sorts, on Haig to assist French. Moreover, it seems that the pair got on well, at least at the start. Haig was a regular visitor to French's home, where they discussed military matters and the developing unrest in Transvaal.[10]

They were certainly very different characters, French loquacious, self-dramatizing and a bon viveur, Haig silent, introspective and anti-social. Haig was excruciatingly buttoned up about women; French never disguised his priapic tendencies. French had no patience for the necessary intellectual effort involved in planning, organizing and running a campaign; Haig was almost obsessively interested in the minutiae of military organization. Yet by the standards of the time, French's financial scrapes undermined his claim to be a gentleman, a matter which Haig outwardly took most seriously. Would a gentleman ask for such a large loan – and would another gentleman agree to lend the money, especially to a known bounder? Were Haig's motives entirely honourable? French and Haig both knew around the time the loan was being negotiated that French was to be given command of the British cavalry in Natal in mid-September 1899, preparatory to a resumption of the war against the independent-minded Boer farmers of Transvaal. The loan therefore takes on greater significance, as it coincided with French formally appointing Haig as his principal staff officer for the South African campaign. The least that can be said is that, rather than enjoying a close friendship – Haig's circle of friends was always very limited, that of French very wide – they found one another mutually useful in professional terms; Haig's money enabled French to continue his thriftless ways, while French in turn nurtured Haig's promotion prospects.

During the Anglo-Boer War French did all he could to promote Haig's reputation, while Haig provided French with administrative competence. According to one of Haig's god-children, whose father was on Haig's staff during the Boer War, Haig's usefulness to French was well-known at the time: 'My father was then 25 and farming in the Karoo: he volunteered and raised a troop of Scouts. In his diary he wrote of your father (Haig): "He is a man of great self-control and foresight; careful; courteous; thoughtful and, in my amateur opinion, a first rate soldier. I can believe the common report that General French was ¾ Haig, all the time the latter was his C.S.O." '[11]

The fact of the matter is that Haig lent a superior officer a great deal of money; it would not have been necessary for either to have spelled out precisely the mutual obligation this created. It was a potentially corrosive act which nevertheless provided Haig with another means of career advancement, beyond his own unquestionable abilities.

As the political tensions between London and Pretoria intensified, the Aldershot command prepared to embark for the Cape Colony. As French's deputy assistant adjutant-general and chief of staff, Haig was entitled to two servants. Together with French's entourage, they set sail from Southampton in the SS *Norman* on the windswept afternoon of 23 September 1899. They left to fight a war whose origins today are little recalled[12] and would do so under the command of Haig's old Staff College bugbear, Sir Redvers Buller, 'a red-faced Devon squire.'[13] From the time Buller's force of 47,000 arrived in Africa it lurched from crisis to crisis, continuously wrong-footed by a part-time army of Old Testament-inspired farmers.

On 26 September Haig wrote to Henrietta the kind of letter one might expect of a husband saying farewell to a wife of several years' standing, after the initial throes of passion have ebbed: 'You and I always seem to be saying "Good-Bye" to each other, and yet practice in this does not seem to make the process easier, but rather more trying. However, you must not allow yourself to feel low-spirited, but arrange to enjoy yourself in a quiet sort of way.'[14]

By this date Henrietta, childless and approaching her fifties, had been married for thirty years to a man whose affections roamed; it is understandable that she was so downcast at the departure of probably the only man she truly loved. In the evenings on board the *Norman* Haig and French enjoyed some port Henrietta had given him as a parting gift, while they pored over War Office confidential reports about the situation in South Africa. For Haig, the shipboard company was hardly congenial: along with two nephews of Paul Kruger, the wily President of the Transvaal Republic and bitter foe of the British empire, were a gaggle of newspaper correspondents. Arriving in Cape Town on 10 October, he and French took rooms at the Mount Nelson, still today one of South Africa's most fashionable hotels. The city was tense with a palpable sense of the imminence of war; the previous day, Kruger had given the British an ultimatum to withdraw their troops and cease their interference in Transvaal's affairs, a threat which Haig regarded as 'Boer swagger'. Haig never departed from the conventional British view of the war, that the Boers were a troublesome people who should recognize and accept British sovereignty, although he grew to respect certain individual Boer commanders, notably Jan Smuts and Louis Botha. The politics of the war's antecedents, its rights and wrongs, never troubled him; his mind was entirely given over to professional duty and his career's progress.

On 12 October Lord Milner, Britain's Governor of Cape Colony and High Commissioner to South Africa, issued a proclamation of war between Britain and Transvaal; the Orange Free State, another Boer Republic, joined Transvaal in its fight. That same day Haig and French investigated the local market for suitable horses: 'General French and I went with Moses Heilbron [. . .], a Jew, but a most knowledgeable and pleasant fellow, to look at a pony which was for sale at Newlands. [. . .] The pony, tho' well-bred, lacked a rib; price also too high – £50.'[15]

The pair of British officers then took a tram out to Sea Point, on the outskirts of Cape Town, where they strolled along the sea front and had tea at a small hotel. It was a civilized, leisurely start to what was to be, for Haig, three trying years of almost continuous active service, a period in which he learned many important lessons, both military and political. On 14 October they re-boarded the *Norman* and arrived in the port of Durban five days later. They immediately headed the cavalry north for Ladysmith, which they reached at dawn on 20 October. This was a busy day; upon reaching Ladysmith they moved on to Elandslaagte, a moderate ride north-east, where they stealthily observed the camp of an estimated 200 Boers who had previously occupied the town, stopped a train and broken up the railway line, a crucial communication route. At 9pm, back in Ladysmith, they received orders to return to Elandslaagte early next morning, attack the Boers and re-take and repair the railway line.

In the chilly, drizzling dawn of 21 October, French led out of Ladysmith five squadrons of the Imperial Light Horse together with the Natal Field (Artillery) Battalion. The drizzle turned into a downpour and swiftly made the ground muddy, slowing the column's pace to a crawl. By 5.30am, when they halted for fifteen minutes' rest, the column had covered just seven miles, less than half the distance to Elandslaagte. As the British column slowly closed on Elandslaagte, scouts reported that the Boers were in trenches occupying a hill overlooking Elandslaagte railway station, about 1,800 yards to the south of the town. The British artillery opened fire on the railway station but the Boers were out of range of the 7-pounder guns. The Boers returned artillery fire and landed some shells very close. By about 7.45am an armoured train carrying infantry was approaching Elandslaagte, from which disembarked re-inforcements for French's column – half a battalion of the Manchester Regiment, more field artillery, a squadron of the 5th Lancers and a squadron of Dragoons. At 1.20pm French issued orders to attack the Boers, now thought to be between 800–1,000 strong. A desultory exchange of fire took place until finally, at 6pm, it was apparent that the Boers had slid away, leaving the British free to occupy the position and the Lancers to capture surrendering stragglers and spear those who resis-ted. Yet this minor success at Elandslaagte was overshadowed by events elsewhere. The British forces at Ladysmith were about to be surrounded by Boer commandos, and on 22 October French and Haig were ordered to return there at all speed.

As in Sudan, Haig immensely enjoyed this sort of military adventure – the open air, tracking down supposed renegades, no moral scruples about the war itself, plenty of manoeuvre and the possibility of action and personal military glory. The occasionally close-quarter combat was sometimes brutal, though Haig was as always indifferent to his personal safety. To Henrietta he wrote on 26 October with great relish about his daily life:

> I have not had much sleep, but the climate here is so good that I feel very fit indeed. [. . .] We were very lucky to have the fight at Elandslaagte, General F in command and self Chief Staff Officer. The Boers fought to the end with extraordinary courage. [. . .] They are wild at the way the fugitives were killed with the lance! They say it is butchery, not war. But as they use express rifle bullets[16], I don't quite see where the difference comes in. [. . .] Best love, and hoping that you are not anxious; for _if_ I am meant to be shot, no amount of care will prevent it.[17]

For Haig the South African campaign was both a protracted stint of active duty and also a frustrating lesson in how the army was badly led by incompetent older generals who, he felt, should have been retired long ago. More contentiously for later historians, the South African war re-inforced Haig's view that cavalry was a key battlefield weapon. In the South African context, where rapid movement and defence of isolated slow-moving infantry columns were vital, his belief in the usefulness of cavalry was justifiable, and provides the context for understanding why he cherished cavalry throughout the Great War. Haig's professional education had taught him that to succeed in battle it was necessary to achieve both superior firepower *and* mobility; until late in the Great War, despite the invention of the tank, that meant cavalry. The South African war was predominantly a campaign where there was a real need for swift mobility and long-range firepower; while the British cavalry gave the former, the British infantry and artillery were singularly poor at provid-ing the latter.

On 31 October disastrous news arrived in Ladysmith, where French and Haig were now situated. The previous day, four companies of the Gloucester Regiment and six of the Royal Irish Fusiliers, both experi-enced regiments from India and comprising about 1,000 men, together with a battery of six 7-pounder guns, had been surrounded and forced to surrender on Nicholson's Nek, a long ridge about six miles north of Ladysmith. These troops, some of the best in Buller's force, had run out of ammunition, their pack-mules having been stampeded by Boers in a brief, surprise raid in the dark. Haig commented wryly in his diary: 'It should be noticed that this detachment moved without any Cavalry. As well let a blind man out without a dog, as Infantry without some horse-men to attend and reconnoitre for it.'

The Boers were then able quickly to surround and lay siege to Lady-smith, positioned as it was on the far right of the over-extended British lines. On 2 November French and Haig were ordered by Buller to leave Ladysmith and return to Cape Town to take charge of the Cavalry Division, then en route from Britain. The last train to leave Ladysmith, before the noose tightened around the town, was due to depart at midday. They got their kit and ten horses on board the train, which headed south for Durban under shell and rifle fire from the Boers. There were no other passengers and the two hid under the seats for the first part

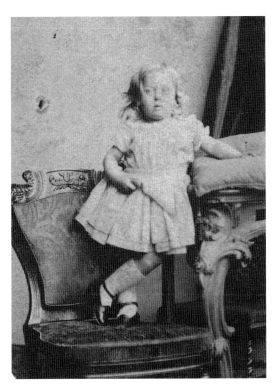

Douglas Haig, aged about three, holding a toy pistol – a reward for 'good' behaviour – in Edinburgh, *c*.1864. (*Museum of Edinburgh*)

The Haig family at Cameronbridge, *c*.1868. Douglas sits at his mother's feet; Henrietta is standing, far left. (*Museum of Edinburgh*)

Haig (seated, middle row, looking to his left) with the members of the BNC wine club at Oxford University, 1882. On the wall is carved 'Vampyres' – a social club he favoured. (*Museum of Edinburgh*)

The Underofficers – senior Gentlemen Cadets – at Sandhurst, 1884. Haig is standing to the far right. (*Sandhurst*)

A group of the 7th Hussars at Secunderabad, India, *c*.1889; Lieutenant Haig is seated in the middle, facing his right. (*Museum of Edinburgh*)

Major-General Kitchener (facing camera, centre), Sirdar of the Anglo-Egyptian Army, Sudan, *c*.1898. Haig felt himself privileged to be on the campaign. (*Imperial War Museum*)

Haig and his sister Henrietta, 1909. A lifelong devotee of spiritualism, she encouraged Haig to attend séances. (*Museum of Edinburgh*)

11 July 1905, Buckingham Palace: Queen Alexandra supervises the weddings of two maids of honour, Dorothy Vivian to Douglas Haig (left), and Mary Hart Dyke to Captain Bell of the Rifle Brigade. (*Museum of Edinburgh*)

of their potentially perilous journey, trying to avoid being seen by their attackers. A 3-inch shell, which blasted a hole through one of the trucks, was among the ordnance which peppered the train; but they arrived unscathed back in Durban early next morning. By 8 November they were back in the Mount Nelson at Cape Town, though as the town was now teeming with British reinforcements they were forced to share a room.

Over the next two days Haig and French met Buller and, among other things, drew him maps of the Ladysmith area. Haig also reflected upon his experiences in the field, composing some tactical notes, a sort of *aide-mémoire* in which he explored the use of cavalry. There has evolved in writings about Haig a distracting and ultimately dead-end debate as to his unquestioned support of cavalry. He always favoured the use of cavalry as opposed to mounted infantry and it is important to understand why. It does him an injustice to suggest that he blindly adhered to the idea that men riding horses at the charge into battle was always and forever the ultimate offensive weapon. In the notes he made in Cape Town in 1899 he sensibly considered that 'these operations have shown clearly the greatly increased power of action possessed by Cavalry, now that it is armed with a good carbine.'[18]

This is entirely in line with Haig's view which he had developed while in India, that what the cavalry required was a good rifle, so that its firepower while dismounted would be more effective. Haig's assessment in South Africa was that the cavalry's most useful function was its mobility, to get to a place fast and dismount, fire its weapons and then to be off again. In these same notes he also considered it imperative to 'pay more attention to' musketry training, and questioned whether 'the Dragoon-lancer is not a mistake! His lance hampers him.' It was a matter he felt very strongly about, as can be seen from a letter he wrote to Henrietta late in 1899:

The one thing required here is 'Cavalry'! I think the country ought to be alive now to the fact (which we have always pointed out) that we don't keep up enough of this arm in peace time. This Mounted Infantry craze is now I trust exploded. So far they have proved useless, and are not likely to be of use until they learn to ride. You had better not give these views to Sir Evelyn, for both he and Lord Wolseley [Commander-in Chief] are the parents of the Mounted Infantry.

Wolseley, Wood and others correctly saw the need for greater infantry mobility and their inescapable solution was the horse; Haig's complaint against the mounted infantry of the British was that, unlike the Boer farmers, who were also mounted infantry, they were usually less mobile than was ideal, because they were all too often very poor horsemen. The inability to handle their main advantage effectively – the horse and the mobility it granted – rendered them, in Haig's view, less useful than well-trained cavalry which could also act, when needed, as infantry. To prefer mounted infantry to cavalry was, for Haig, like suggesting that an armed motorcyclist who lacked the ability to balance was a useful battle-field weapon.[19] He shared Kipling's view that:

We have spent two hundred million pounds to prove the fact once more,
That horses are quicker than men afoot, since two and two make four.[20]

Against Haig's pragmatic readiness to adapt, however, must be set another, less sensible conclusion from his 1899 tactical notes, that 'the effect of Artillery fire is chiefly moral [sic]! The teachings of peace manoeuvres and text-books require to be considerably modified. Briefly, in our Army many have over-estimated the power of shrapnel fire.'[21]

This was, in hindsight, clearly a false conclusion to draw from the relative ineffectiveness of British artillery fire on the Boer troops, who were adept at using trenches and other cover, and who were skilled exponents of the hit-and-run methods which militated against the success of artillery. The most serious criticism to be made of Haig during his South African venture is not that he failed to draw lessons from his experience, nor that he was ignorantly fixed to preconceived notions of warfare, but rather that, from his own observation of the relative uselessness of the British artillery at killing Boers, he misjudged artillery's usefulness, believing that it was in general limited only to intimidation and terror.

He suffered not from hopeless rigidity in his thinking, but a tendency, as in South Africa, to not go far enough in his probing of how changed conditions of warfare should translate into changed training, equipment and methods. This was a serious weakness, but not the one he is usually accused of, a failure to grapple with changing circumstances.[22] Contemporaries of Haig who served in South Africa and who were later to serve with him in the Great War were also provoked into considering the failings of the British army, and some of them proved themselves rather more profound in their conclusions.[23]

On 18 November Buller ordered French, Haig and the Cavalry Division to proceed to the important railway junction of De Aar and thence to Colesberg, where there were reports of a gathering force of some 2,000 Boers. By 26 November Haig had been given the acting local rank of lieutenant-colonel and was assistant adjutant-general with the Cavalry Division. Haig's local colonelcy was a money-saving device as well as recognition, as such temporary field promotions did not accrue additional salary and their holders could be reduced to their permanent rank without fuss. French's orders from Buller were to maintain an active defence, without running any risks. By the end of the year Haig's life had settled into a routine, as he reported to Henrietta:

> Our usual day's work is to go out about 4.30 am to one or other flank of the Boers' position and have a look to see if they are going on all right. For this we take out usually some dozen or so men as escort to the General and to look out when we halt. There is quite a large plain on three sides of the enemy's position, so we feel quite safe, as the Boers won't venture into the open with us near them. It is very satisfactory to have kept so many (about 5,000) of the enemy to their positions near Colesberg.[24]

This sanguine attitude was not reflected in the fortunes of the British army overall, which during the Black Week of 10–15 December 1899 suffered three devastating defeats at Magersfontein, Stormberg, and Colenso, where Buller's attempt to cross the Tugela River to relieve Ladysmith was repulsed, with more than 1,000 casualties and the loss of much of his artillery. Buller was swiftly relieved as C-in-C, to be replaced by an even older general, Lord Roberts, known more familiarly throughout the army and the British nation as 'Bobs'. Even at the age of sixty-eight, however, 'Bobs' was a better general than Buller and, more importantly, he brought with him as his chief of staff Major-General Kitchener. Buller remained in command of the attempt to relieve Ladysmith and suffered yet another devastating humiliation when, on 24 January 1900, British troops were caught exposed on a small hill called Spion Kop, suffering casualties of some 1,500 killed and wounded. This disastrous effort to relieve Ladysmith did not involve French's Cavalry Division, which had so far conducted itself successfully whenever called upon. Haig's performance was recognized by French, who mentioned him in his dispatch of 2 February as having shown 'the same zeal, untiring energy, and consummate ability as have characterized his conduct and bearing since the very commencement of the campaign.'

This official acclamation was quite justified, but it was also coincidentally useful and timely, as Haig's career had just suffered another minor setback; in January 1900 Haig had been removed from his position as French's chief of staff and replaced by a full colonel, the Earl of Erroll, who had recently landed at Cape Town as part of a contingent of reinforcements. French fought hard to retain Haig but was overruled on the basis that a full colonel must take precedence over a local temporary, even though this adherence to protocol failed to take account of the fact that Erroll knew nothing of local conditions, while Haig was by now well acclimatized. The gentlemanly code dictated that Haig should feign indifference to this snub but he was actually 'very annoyed' according to a fellow officer.[25] In a letter to Henrietta from Cape Town he displayed his usual irrepressible self-certainty:

> Everyone I meet down here condoles with me on being superseded by Erroll, so I expect the Field Marshal has discovered that he has done the wrong thing. As a matter of fact I think less about this appointment than my friends. But of course it is gratifying to find that one's work has been appreciated in the Division. [...] People at home seem to be excited

without due cause. I would disband the politicians for 10 years. We would all be the better without them!

The start of 1900 saw a turning point in the balance between British and Boer forces, but Haig's role in one of the few British triumphs, the relief of the 103-day blockade of Kimberley in February 1900, was reduced to that of deputy assistant adjutant-general, though to all intents and purposes he remained French's right-hand man. The march on Kimberley from the Modder River, led by French, was a pivotal moment in the campaign, demonstrating that caution and due respect paid to the enemy, plus a healthy numerical superiority, could defeat the less formally organized Boers. Some 3,700 British veterans and local Cape militia marched from the Modder River on 11 February. In the tremendous heat and dust of the height of the South African summer, and covering about one hundred miles in four days, they swept aside what was occasionally tough resistance until, on the morning of 15 February, they reached the outskirts of Kimberley, the centre of the country's diamond mining. By this stage they had acquired further reinforcements and now totalled about 5,000 cavalry and mounted infantry and seven batteries of Royal Horse Artillery.

In front of the British forces lay a plain, bracketed by two ridges which were occupied by about 1,000 Boers and a handful of artillery pieces, and beyond which lay Kimberley. French ordered his artillery to lay a covering fire on the Boer positions and then set the 9th and 16th Lancers to gallop across the plain, through the gap between the ridges and into Kimberley. It was a classic cavalry charge and, with just seven men killed, could be acclaimed a great success. As such, it further reinforced Haig's belief in the battlefield usefulness of cavalry. But it was rather a lucky stroke; had the Boer positions been better prepared – Haig himself wrote to Colonel Lonsdale Hale after the skirmish that the 'ground rose from the river, so we could not see whether there were wire fences or not, but there seemed to be only a few Boers at the end of the rise' – or had they been greater in number, neither of which French could have known before he issued his order to charge, it could have been a disaster. At

6.30pm French and his staff marched triumphantly into the centre of the liberated Kimberley. For Haig, the biggest surprise after the battle was that, despite being surrounded by hostile Boer forces since the beginning of November 1899, the citizens looked 'fat and well. It was the relieving force which needed food! For in the gallop many nosebags were lost and 7lb tins of bully beef are an unsuitable adjunct to one's saddle in a charge.'[26]

That night he and French dined with Cecil Rhodes, the swashbuckling entrepreneur whose De Beers diamond company's ruthless exploitation of the country's mineral wealth had done much to bring about the war in the first place; they dined off horsemeat, together with copious quantities of champagne. As reward for his efforts in the relief of Kimberley, on 21 February Haig was given command of the 3rd Cavalry Brigade, which meant a local rank of brigadier-general and promotion over the heads of others. He was also formally returned to his post as chief of staff to the now newly promoted Lieutenant-General French, with Erroll being moved to Lord Roberts' staff to take charge of the mounted infantry. As he wrote, with considerable understatement, to Henrietta: 'This will suit me very well.'[27]

The pace of events quickened after the symbolically important success at Kimberley, and Mafeking was relieved in May. On 31 May 1900, with President Kruger having fled for the Portuguese colony of Mozambique and thence to Holland, Lord Roberts placed an army of occupation in Pretoria, where French's Cavalry Division, Haig included, arrived on 8 June. On 3 July Haig wrote to Henrietta thanking her for some small luxuries:

> Some fine warm things from Jaeger's – socks, muffler, gloves etc etc received today! Also soap and scent from Floris! Many thanks for thinking of all these nice things. The drawers however are a bit too much of the hair-cloth style, for you know Pvt Miles 7th Hrs does the washing as a rule, so flannels don't last long. For this reason I prefer silk ones like what you sent me before. I got the three sleeping bags all safe which Mary sent me [. . .] One I gave to General French who is badly supplied with bed kit, another I gave to John Vaughan who is in the same condition and I have the third for myself.

For most of the British army it seemed as though the war was over, and many, Haig included, started making plans for the future, though the British rejoicing which accompanied these advances was premature; the war was to become more bitter as it dragged on for two more years, during which Haig, in his own words, was almost 'continually on the move', chasing Boer guerillas and fugitives around Bloemfontein and Thabanchu. The war moved from its formal, semi-chivalrous phase, where mutual respect was usually accorded by both British and Boer, to a messier, more sordid conflict, with Boer civilians interned in concentration camps, their farms burned to the ground, and Boer resisters unceremoniously hanged if captured. Throughout this later period of the conflict Haig's correspondence is replete with reflections on the nature of the combat and the army's dismal organization, as he saw it, such as this in a letter dated Sunday 2 March 1900, to an unnamed colonel:[28]

Roberts is surrounded by a lot of old Simla warriors, grey with the experience of years of office work in India. (I don't refer of course to the many lordlings and social lights of the Field Marshal's personal staff of course these are of all ages) [. . .] The H.Q's staff don't know what is going on in front or what the enemy is doing, (though we tell them) or the state of the country [. . .] I see by a telegram that Army Reform is again to the fore. I trust to you to insist on a large and efficient Cavalry being kept up in time of peace. At least two Divisions complete. All that is wanted is that our Cavalry should pay more attention to shooting. The idea of M.I [mounted infantry] alone is to my mind exploded. Why have we, cavalry, had success against the Boers? Because we can charge in the open as well as act dismounted. The Boers can only do the latter. You must rub this fact into those wretched individuals who pretend to rule the Empire! And in any case, before they decide on reorganising the Army let them get the experience of those who have seen the effect of modern firearms and have learnt to realise that the old story is true, viz. that 'moral' [morale] is everything, and not merely guns but men who can use them is what is wanted to defend the Empire.

Gerard de Groot has criticized Haig for letting the dust of Kimberley 'blur his vision for the rest of his career'[29] but the points Haig makes in this letter are quite innocuous if viewed without prejudice. His essential argument is a perennial fact of warfare; superior numbers, morale and mobility *as well as* firepower are required for military success, and these were the crucial ingredients for victory on the Western Front in 1918, just as they have been on battlefields since time immemorial.

By now Haig had acquired the services of Thomas Secrett,[30] a master-servant relationship that endured for twenty-five years. Secrett's ghost-written memoir of the field marshal, published soon after Haig died in 1928, is gossipy and unreliable but it casts some light on a man about whom he clearly nursed ambivalent feelings. Secrett, a poorly educated and scarcely literate lifetime soldier given to full-blast swearing, had been a dispatch rider at French's HQ. He recalled his first encounter with Haig:

> Haig met me and, from the first moment, I knew that I should like him. He handed over his keys, made one or two remarks about what he required done, smiled, and left me. Most other officers would have gone into a lot of detail, asked a lot of questions, directed minutely how they wanted things done. Haig was not a bit like that. He trusted his staff implicitly, from the lowest to the highest rank. He said what he wanted done, and he left it to the staff to get it done. He trusted to their intelligence to do the job in the best manner possible, but he never worried them in the process. He went by results.[31]

On 7 August 1900, Haig informed Henrietta that Sir Evelyn Wood had recommended that he should be given a regiment of his own as soon as possible. French was working assiduously on behalf of his protégé: 'French is anxious to have me made an A.D.C to the Queen because that at once gives me the rank of full Colonel. At present I am a Lieut. Colonel in South Africa. Personally I don't care much what happens to me in the way of reward, for I despise those who only work when they hope to get something in return!'

This is a revealing thought process; Haig feigns indifference to reward but muddles that by then saying something slightly different, that he despises those who work *only* because they hope for a reward. Promotion and the prospects of advancement were never far from Haig's mind; his apparent indifference here masks just how much they preoccupied his and his sister's thinking. The same subject cropped up in a letter to Henrietta dated 14 December 1900:

> Of course it is a necessary thing to command a regiment and I should like to do so if I was given command of a good one in a good station. French is only too anxious to help me on, but I think in remaining on as his Chief Staff Officer I did the best for the Cavalry Division, for him and for myself. One did not foresee this war lasting so long, otherwise I might have taken some skallywag corps or other. So don't make a fuss about my being now in the same position as I started in. Recollect also many have gone lower down! And as to rewards, if you only knew what duffers will get and do get H.M's decorations and are promoted, you would realise how little I value them. Everything comes in time, and decorations come in abundance with declining years and imbecility. No one yet on this Staff, fortunately, has got a decoration of any kind, otherwise we might have achieved disaster like the other <u>decores</u>.

It has been claimed[32] that Haig was conspicuously insincere in protesting so much, but it seems rather as though he was here, as so often, tussling over what he *knew* he wanted – promotion, recognition, advancement – with what he knew he *ought* to feel – indifference to personal reward in the cause of serving his country as it deemed fit. Haig's letter to Henrietta was self-contradictory; he dismissed promotions and decorations as being for duffers, yet he was always delighted when they came his way. Nevertheless it reveals inner conflict as much as hypocrisy. In any case, it would be absurd to expect Haig *not* to seek preferment; his contemporaries in South Africa, such as Henry Wilson and Henry Rawlinson, both senior generals in the Great War, reveal in their own diaries and letters from South Africa at the time that they were equally ambitious for promotion and recognition. While they pinned their hopes on being plucked from among the shoal of attentive sprats swimming in the wake of Lord Roberts, who returned to England a popular hero for having clawed back victory from ignominy, Haig assiduously cultivated Generals French and Wood.

For the remainder of his time in South Africa Haig had a semi-independent role, with as many as six columns of cavalry under his command, attempting to round up recalcitrant Boers and trying to force them into submission. Kitchener had sent Haig a telegram with his orders, which were to take command 'of all columns now operating in the Midland area of Cape Colony. Act vigorously with the object of clearing Cape Colony of the enemy as soon as possible.' Haig told Henrietta on 11 April 1901 that he had also been ordered to

> 'Consult with General Jones and Settle.' – Old Inigo Bones is the man meant. He is here and has been here for the last 5 or 6 months living in a railway carriage. He is a nice old man and feels quite sure that 'things will be all right once General Settle is sent back to De Aar.' I am practically relieving Settle who is at Graaf Reinet and seems to have commanded merely by writing long telegrams. Old Jones can't give me much information as to where the parts of my army are, or what they consist of! So I am off at once to Graaf Reinet to see Settle [. . .]
>
> It is more difficult hunting Boers in this Colony when all farmers are secretly their friends, and the Government almost seems to assist the invader, than in the Free State where one can treat everyone as an enemy. However it is very satisfactory to be again chosen for this job when things have got into a mess.

Haig expressed no qualms about the harsh treatment meted out to the Boers; but neither did anyone else in the British establishment. What few critical voices were raised back in England were widely regarded as mad or traitorous.

In June 1901 Haig finally got his (non-scallywag) regiment when he was appointed commanding officer of the 17th Lancers. This appointment, at the behest of Kitchener, caused the angry resignation of an officer more senior than Haig who was already with the Lancers, Herbert Lawrence, who quite understandably believed himself to have been cheated of his greater claim to be made CO. Lawrence was the same age as Haig but had joined the army earlier. He resigned his commission and went into the City, where he made a fortune. He was to encounter Haig again, when he first succeeded Brigadier-General John Charteris as Haig's intelligence chief in December 1917, before eventually taking over from Sir Launcelot Kiggell as Haig's chief of staff in January 1918.

Soon after Haig took over command of the Lancers, its C Squadron was badly beaten up in an ambush on 17 September, while in camp at Modderfontein. They were attacked by a Boer commando garbed in captured British khaki uniforms; out of 130 men, twenty-nine were killed and forty-one wounded. This was a blow to the new regimental colonel, though he himself was unscathed. On 25 October 1901 French ordered Haig to take three weeks' rest at Cape Town. Despite his duties, Haig found time to monitor his personal financial affairs. In a letter to Henrietta on 6 January 1902 he revealed he had taken financial advice from the South African-born, British-educated mining tycoon Abe Bailey, who

> has been of great assistance to me, not only in getting these people [pro-Boer sympathisers in the Cape] out of Govt., but in helping me to get men for Intelligence work ever since I came to this Colony a year ago. He went up to Johannesburg today to reopen his office there. I gather from him that things are booming. I bought 200 South African Gold Mines [shares] for £4 [each] a year ago. He tells me they will go to £20 in a year! Anyhow you cannot lose over them, so possibly you might buy a few! He also bought me last week 200 Lace Diamonds for 84/-. He is a Director and tells me they will pay 80% for the next 3 years.[33]

Haig also had to contend with a perennial feature of military life – envy. The British army in South Africa was a gossipy place; just as Haig was reporting to his mentors back in London, so too were other officers, such as Ian Hamilton, by now appointed Kitchener's chief of staff in South Africa but also still holding the post of military secretary to Earl Roberts, who was back in London as C-in-C. While Hamilton informed Roberts in February 1902 that Haig was 'one of the most thoughtful, educated and large-minded of our staff officers', he also suggested that Sir John French had surrounded himself with personal friends rather than good staff, and could not find much to say of Haig's command because he did so little with his troops and appeared reluctant to use them in action.[34]

Throughout his career, Haig had been encouraged by superior officers, and indeed the Prince of Wales, to report his military experiences privately to them. In this respect, Haig was again unexceptional: others of his generation, such as Henry Wilson and Henry Rawlinson as well as Ian Hamilton, were also placed in this sometimes invidious position by the prince or Wood, Roberts, Kitchener and their like. The young officers may have enjoyed a sense of power and prestige as a result, but they were forced to tread a narrow line and could sometimes be rapped across the knuckles for overstepping unmarked boundaries. Towards the end of his stint in South Africa, Haig received word from Henrietta via her husband that the Prince of Wales thought Haig should tone down his criticism of his superiors. In a letter to a friend, Haig gave a good insight into his thinking in this regard, and inadvertently provided an explanation of his future public reticence and his general disinclination to express an opinion outside very tight circles:

> My 'criticisms' says H.R.H 'may be correct, but it does not do.' Now I never criticise people except privately, and what a stupid letter it would be if I did not express an opinion. Besides, I think we would have better generals in the higher ranks and the country would not have had to pass through such a period of anxiety had honest criticism, based on sound reasoning, been more general in reference to military affairs during the last twenty years. But whether I am right or wrong, I like to let my pen have a free run when I write to you, so I trust you won't give me away and say I consider our worthy authorities are old stupids, ignorant even of the first principles of the game of war. Still I never go as far as that and make general statements of such a sweeping nature; I always give particular instances – chapter and verse in fact.[35]

Eventually, the majority of the Boers, harassed and corralled into submission, conceded defeat. At the end of May 1902 the Treaty of

Vereeniging concluded an unsatisfactory peace, with some of the British regarding the commitment to eventual self-government too generous, while some Boers bridled under the knowledge that their previously independent republics were once again colonies of the British empire. Haig's responsibility under the new peace treaty was to take charge of a sub-district of Cape Colony, with a mandate to maintain law and order, which included granting Boer families access to food stocks in return for the surrender of their weapons. French left the country in June, the 'little man', as Haig referred to him, 'almost in tears bidding goodbye, and I was sorry to part with him.' He informed Henrietta on 25 August that French, back in England and now Commandant at Aldershot, was once more working on his behalf:

> I see General French told you that I could have either the Aldershot Cav. Bde. or the Inspector Generalship of Cavalry in India – which one I preferred! He did not write that to me, but said that Lord K. wished me to become the latter and French the former. However, I have already told you all my views on those matters, but I fancy the excellent house at Aldershot in which the General Officer commanding Cav. Bde. lives will oblige Lord Roberts to select the husband of dear Mrs So-and-So because the nursery rooms will exactly suit the family – and I'll be given the Indian appointment.

Haig did not wish to return to the unattractive climate of India, nor did he wish to be physically so distant from the army's centre of power. But there was only so much French could do, and for the time being Colonel Douglas Haig was required to serve a stint as a simple, albeit rather elevated, regimental commanding officer. On 23 September 1902 he sailed from Cape Town, accompanying the fourteen officers and 527 men of the 17th Lancers, headed for Piershill Barracks in Edinburgh. Three years previously to the day he had left England a mere captain. He was now one of a handful of rising stars in the British army, known to be favoured by the new King Edward VII, and also Lord Kitchener, the hero of Sudan. Thanks partly to Sir John French's goodwill, purchased or not, his own diligence and sheer good fortune, as well as his professional dedication, Haig was one of the few British officers to emerge from the messy and frequently humiliating South African war with an enhanced image. His reputation for luckiness was becoming more firmly established, even though he – and Henrietta – yearned for still greater things.

# CHAPTER SIX

# 'One of the Most Fortunate Officers'

He had told me very little of what he had done before I married him.

Dorothy, Lady Haig

All I require is people of *average* intelligence who are keen to do their work properly.

Douglas Haig

Haig arrived in Southampton from Cape Town on 19 October 1902, more than three months after Kitchener, who, now more than ever a national darling, had been greeted on his arrival in London by a massive crowd, a royal reception, a viscountcy, promotion to full general, a gratuity of £50,000[1] from a grateful Parliament, and the news that he was to be the first to be invested with the Order of Merit, a new title created by King Edward VII.

Haig's return was altogether more humdrum, although he now had the coveted position of aide-de-camp to Edward VII. He was delighted to be back with Henrietta, family and friends after such long overseas service, but the prestige of commanding one of the army's leading regiments, based in Edinburgh, was not enough. To Henrietta he glumly wrote: 'Edinburgh is a bad place for cavalry, no drill ground and half the regiment on detachment – so I wired to General French and asked him to try and get the station altered to York or Aldershot. Indeed, any place is better as a cavalry station than Edinburgh.'

French could do nothing immediately to improve Haig's lot. The

British army's pyrrhic victory in South Africa had revealed its many shortcomings, not least the serious command and control deficiencies disclosed by the lack of a general staff. The possession of a world-dominating navy was clearly insufficient protection against all possible threats. Britain's army had shown itself scarcely able to fight a colonial war. What if it had to fight a war in Europe? The late German Chancellor Bismarck had had no doubts, having dismissively threatened that if ever a British army landed on the continent, he would 'have it arrested' by his police force. The French staff view of the British army in 1904 was scarcely more flattering. In a European land war it would be 'almost without value, worth much less, for example, than an alliance with a much smaller country such as Switzerland.'[2] While the disasters in South Africa were the impetus for army reform, there was also a fast-developing rivalry against Germany. Germany had a standing army of almost 750,000 troops in 1903, plus a potential reserve of up to five million; Britain's professional regular force was less than 150,000, one third of which was stationed outside the country, in colonial outposts.

In September 1902 Prime Minister Arthur Balfour established the Elgin Commission, charged with reflecting on the army's performance during the Boer War. In November 1903 he also created the War Office Reconstitution Committee, under the chairmanship of a civilian, Reginald Brett, the second Viscount Esher, with the brief to consider how to reform the army's senior management, then the responsibility of Hugh Oakley Arnold-Forster as Secretary of State for War.[3] Esher demanded and was given an entirely free hand to make the reform he thought necessary.

A psychologically complex character, while a young man at Eton Esher had formed a string of romantic attachments with younger pupils; this practice of falling in love with younger men he maintained until his death.[4] During the Great War Esher befriended Sir Philip Sassoon MP, an even more sexually ambiguous figure who was to become Haig's military secretary. Esher's own career epitomizes how finely tuned obsequiousness could be instrumental in gaining social status and political power in Edwardian England. Possessed of a modest inheritance from his father, a prominent lawyer, Esher diligently cultivated the social connections he formed at Eton and Cambridge University to create for himself an informal and constitutionally nebulous position of backroom influence over the monarchy and military affairs – an influence which ultimately extended to taking a hand in the career of Douglas Haig. It is one of the enduring peculiarities of Edwardian politics that from such an unlikely person, occupying an amorphous position close to the heart of the British establishment, there emerged a clear and practical vision to prepare the army for the terrible task of war with Germany.

Esher presciently observed in 1906: 'There is a very bad time coming for soldiers; for the laws of historical and ethnographical evolution (it sounds rather priggish) require that we shall fight one of the most powerful military empires that has ever existed. This is certain, and we have a very short period of preparation. I fear that proficiency in games, or in the hunting-field, will not help our poor lads much when they have to face the carefully trained and highly educated German officers.'[5]

The Elgin Commission concluded that almost every aspect of the army's management in South Africa had been badly handled. Under-investment, lack of maps, insufficient quantities of ammunition, the collapse of the Royal Army Medical Corps, a deficit of khaki uniforms, and a failure to anticipate both the length and nature of the campaign were the most egregious mistakes it identified. Partly the problem was money; British governments gave financial priority to sea power to guard the empire, while the army was always forced to scrabble around for funds. Raising army budgets was politically difficult not least because the War Office was notoriously bureaucratic and wasteful.

Esher informed King Edward VII, whom Esher wanted to see restore the monarchy's erstwhile close involvement in army matters (lamentably, in Esher's opinion, in decline under Queen Victoria because of her sex), that: 'The War Office was inefficient, obfuscated and interfering; that the Army was never given its head; and that the situation of the Commander-in-Chief was nebulous and anachronistic. "As Your Majesty can well imagine, it is difficult to thread the way through the mazes of the War Office system. At every turn the road appears blocked by some

Board or Committee, designed apparently to conceal the place where such responsibility should lie." [6] Few critically minded senior officers wanted to set foot in the War Office; it stifled innovation and creativity. [7]

Haig began to be noticed by Esher and other army reformers around the time he gave evidence to the Elgin Commission in early 1903. The Commission's final report, published 28 March 1903, said:

> It is refreshing to read the very practical suggestion put forward by Colonel D. Haig CB, [Companion of the Order of the Bath] 17th Lancers, concerning the equipment of cavalrymen. He advocates the provision of light regimental transport to carry the daily requirements of men and horses. Colonel Haig's suggestion strikes at the root of our immobility during the recent Boer campaign. Equipped as he was with an unnecessarily heavy saddle and wallets, a nosebag of horse food, rifle, sword, lance, great coat, blankets and other paraphernalia, the cavalryman looked more like a travelling showman than a death dealing soldier. [8]

The following year posed a conundrum for cavalry officers. The brief 1904–1905 Russo-Japanese land war in Manchuria saw the combined use of artillery and machine-guns widen the zone of deadly fire on the battlefield, without necessarily improving the efficiency of killing. [9] For some of the twenty-seven British observers accredited to the Japanese, along with the Japanese army itself, this technological revolution on the battlefield did not dislodge their faith in cavalry. [10] Those few British military observers who thought that the events in Manchuria meant the end of cavalry were distrusted by an army hierarchy in which, socially, cavalry officers still held sway.

The infantryman Sir Ian Hamilton, [11] whose antagonism towards cavalry was well-known, submitted a report on the Manchurian conflict in which, with his customary elegance, he dismissed the notion that cavalry had anything significant to contribute on a battlefield dominated by firepower: 'I maintain that it would be as reasonable to introduce the elephants of Porus onto a modern battlefield as regiments of lancers and dragoons who are too much imbued with the true cavalry spirit to use fire-arms and too sensible, when it comes to the pinch, to employ their

boasted *arme blanche* [a hand-held weapon such as a sword or lance] –
willing to wound and yet afraid to strike. The role they are condemned
to play in 20th century battles is one deserving of the most profound
commiseration.'[12]

Hamilton had been on the ground in Manchuria and seen part of the
future; Haig, whose battlefield experience prior to 1914 was limited to
Sudan and South Africa, had not.[13] The endemic rivalry between
cavalry and infantry in the nineteenth and early twentieth centuries
invariably led to any criticism from the likes of openly antagonistic
infantrymen such as Hamilton being dismissed. The fact that Hamilton
was also a successful writer, both on military subjects and of poetry and
fiction, was only further confirmation of his unsteadiness. In Haig's
eyes no *proper* soldier would have been able to say, as did Hamilton: 'I'd
rather write one really sweet and famous sonnet than be QMG in India,
or even C-in-C himself.'[14] It is also true that the pace of change was not
immediately obvious. The horse was and would remain for some time
the main form of transport, and was only gradually being displaced
by the combustion engine: in 1908, only 142,000 motorized vehicles
cruised the roads of Europe and North America, and while by 1913 this
had increased to one and a half million,[15] it was still a tiny percentage
of the horse population in Europe and the USA. In the first decade
of the twentieth century it was inconceivable for Haig – and many
other military thinkers, in all branches of the army – that the days
of cavalry attacks were over. For him the debate was what *kind* of
mounted soldier was preferable, as he had informed the War Office on
2 April 1903:

> [. . .] our regiments of Cavalry should be armed in equal proportions viz.
> half the Cavalry should have swords; the other lances – but I believe that a
> good hog spear would be better than the existing long lance – there is no
> doubt that the latter is an impediment when scouting and when acting
> dismounted – but I don't think it is wise to abolish the lance. Strategical
> reconnaissance must culminate in a tactical collision if the enemy
> possesses Cavalry; we want the lance for this. I have expressed my opinion

to the War Comt. very strongly that I consider Cavalry (properly trained) should fulfil all the requirements of mounted troops, and that Mounted Infantry should be abolished.

Yet the lessons of the Russo-Japanese war were not entirely ignored by some British cavalry officers, who were becoming increasingly aware that old-fashioned cavalry tactics no longer served. Captain D. I. Macaulay of the 1st Lancers (Duke of York's Own) wrote in *The Cavalry Journal* in 1908: 'That modern improvements in firearms have seriously curtailed the possibilities of Cavalry action with cold steel cannot be denied. Shock action, nevertheless, retains its supreme importance. [. . .] Owing to the modern formations and the extent of modern battlefields, the effect of even successful shock action can only be very local. It can certainly never be as decisive as when masses were crowded into a space so small that the effect of a successful charge on a part was immediately felt throughout the whole.'[16]

Whatever the rights and wrong of the cavalry versus mounted infantry debate, overall British military performance in South Africa had been lamentable. The failures identified by the Elgin Commission provided Esher with the justification he sought for a root-and-branch re-organisation of the army's senior command structure. He formed a triumvirate of himself, Admiral Fisher, the great moderniser of the Victorian navy, and Colonel Sir George Sydenham Clarke to formulate proposals. Esher insisted they should work from first principles, as he outlined to Balfour on 15 December 1903:

What is the minimum regular army we require?
On what terms can it be enlisted?
What will it cost?
It is not a problem of Home Defence. The Navy can deal with home defence. It is a problem of foreign defence.[17]

With the approval of the king and Balfour, Esher's triumvirate enthusiastically lopped dead wood from the army's hierarchy, even abolishing the office of Commander-in-Chief, despite the fact that its incumbent,

Field Marshal Lord Roberts, was a popular national hero. They peremptorily sacked all senior officials at the War Office, notifying them that in place of a C-in-C, the army's affairs would in future be controlled by an Army Council, comprising four military and three civilian figures, the most senior military member designated chief of the general staff (CGS). A permanent Committee of Imperial Defence (CID) was set up, chaired by the Prime Minister and including the chiefs of the army and navy and charged with strategic military policy, although it had no official status and its establishment was never submitted for Parliamentary approval. By the time the Esher Committee dissolved in May 1904 it had arrogated to itself tremendous executive power. Above all, it focused attention on the increasingly important question as to what Britain's commitment could and should be in the event of a European land war. From its deliberations arose an enduring framework for the construction of something which had hitherto been lacking in the British army – a general staff.

Esher galvanised thinking but also ruffled feathers. General Sir Horace Smith-Dorrien, a contemporary of Haig, later described what he felt was the triumvirate's brusqueness: 'At first chaos was the result, and this was well described by a War Office official in a letter to me as follows: "It is just as if the authorities had taken a motor-car and smashed it up and then called in people entirely ignorant of motor-cars to repair the damages."'[18] For Colonel (later Field Marshal Sir) Henry Wilson, then at the War Office, 'Our days pass like nightmares. The Triumvirate are carrying on like madmen.'[19] Yet even Smith-Dorrien conceded the reforms that followed were 'excellent'. Haig approved of Esher's work, writing to him on 23 March 1904:

> You must be overwhelmed with congratulations on the success of your labours, but I feel sure that no one appreciates what you have done for the Army more than I do. I never believed it possible to get such a thorough reorganisation without undergoing first of all some military disaster! At the time it seemed impossible to get the country and the politicians to interest themselves in the condition of the Army. Now, thanks to your energy, things seem on the right road for efficiency.[20]

No doubt Haig was sincere, and disasters in South Africa there had been, but it was nevertheless politically astute to demonstrate his backing so fulsomely. It certainly helped consolidate Esher's view that Haig was part of the cohort of younger officers who could be depended upon for future support.

As Esher plotted a new type of army command structure, Haig idled his days in polo chukkas at Murrayfield and regular Sunday rounds of golf at Muirfield. His polo-playing at this date led to a distant early sighting of his future wife, the Honourable Dorothy Maud Vivian, a maid of honour to Queen Alexandra. At Hurlingham on 11 July 1903 Haig's 17th Lancers polo team beat the Royal Horse Guards (The Blues) 5–1; Dorothy's brother, Lord Vivian, was an officer in The Blues. The queen presented Haig with the winners' cup, filled to the brim with champagne by the victors, while Dorothy observed the scene from a short distance; later that evening Haig hosted a celebratory supper at the Savoy in London for his team and their supporters.

Haig's fear that command of the Cavalry Brigade at Aldershot would go elsewhere proved accurate; in July 1903 he was appointed Inspector-General of Cavalry of India, succeeding General Sir E. Locke Elliott. It was not Haig's first choice but, in the eyes of many fellow officers, he had again struck lucky; it was a plum post for one still relatively young, and normally went to a major-general, while Haig was still only a colonel. In the eighteen years since graduating from Sandhurst, Haig had by now not only caught up with but overtaken some younger contemporaries. *The Times* noted: 'By the time he arrives in India, Colonel Haig will have entered upon his forty-third year. No case is recorded in the annals of the British Army in India of an Officer being appointed to a post of such distinction and importance at anything like so early a period in his career. In Colonel Haig's case the exception is thoroughly well merited.'

The news of his return to India prompted one old sweat from the 7th Hussars, his former regiment, to write on 25 July 1903 to Haig, thanking him '[. . .] for all your great kindness to me. You perhaps do not know, sir, how much I have to thank you for, but there was a time in India when I (a young fool) was being rapidly led away by bad companions, when suddenly the thought struck me "what would Capt. Haig think of me if he saw me now", and I put down the glass and said "I have done with drink". That was 15 years ago, and I have touched none since.' Given his family's business, Haig might perhaps have wished that the trooper at least had the occasional glass of whisky.

In early October 1903, prior to setting off for India, Haig stayed at Balmoral, where, on 4 October, 'His Majesty presents me with the C.V.O [Commander of the Royal Victorian Order] in recognition of services which I had rendered in the past and would render in the future as I.G of Cavalry in India, and also as a "mark of personal esteem".'

From South Africa, a frustrated Haig had, less than two years previously, denigrated such distinctions as being only for 'duffers'; when they came his way it was a different matter. The honour gave him inordinate satisfaction not least because it was a public demonstration of his close association with the king, and marked his rising status. That Edward also on this occasion privately gave Haig a walking stick as a memento was no less valuable a statement of the personal patronage of the sixty-three-year-old king. At dinner that night Haig sat next to Edward, who informed him that Henrietta would shortly be receiving a haunch of venison from the king's estate. Of such apparently small gestures, a stick and a slab of deer, was the nexus of power reconfirmed and were the social stratifications carefully groomed.

Haig left London on 15 October 1903 and arrived in Bombay fifteen days later, from where he went straight to Simla, where the two most powerful authorities in India, Lord Curzon, Viceroy, and the now Lord Kitchener, C-in-C of the Indian Army, had their residencies. Curzon and Kitchener were engaged in a bitter feud: nominally it was over who controlled the Indian Army, but in reality it had as much to do with their mutual personal detestation. On 5 November Haig proudly informed Henrietta he had joined Kitchener for a dinner prepared by the C-in-C's personal French chef, after which the two officers sat up late over whisky and soda: 'The Chief [Kitchener] is looking very fit and well, and is in the best of spirits. I think that already K. has done a vast amount of good. Lord K. wired home "Haig has taken over." "Has he been made Major

General yet." "I hope this will be done." In any case I wear the uniform and am called M.G.'

Kitchener had sought out Haig because he had great need of a capable and competent administrator, someone who would free him of routine burdens while he devoted himself to the struggle with Curzon. Prior to his arrival in India, Kitchener had no practical experience of the country nor its army, though he made up for it in early 1903, travelling to the North-West Frontier to see conditions there at first hand. Haig had built a justified reputation for discretion, willing subordination and managerial competence, qualities Kitchener prized in his staff. Kitchener and Haig shared another interest; both were Freemasons, the rituals of which greatly appealed to Kitchener, while Haig's interest in this closed global club appears to have been passive to the point of indifference. In his struggle with Curzon, Kitchener enjoyed a crucial advantage – a certain plausibility that belied a streak of ruthless mendacity. According to David Gilmour, Curzon's biographer, Kitchener 'looked hearty, direct and honest, but was in fact artistic, devious and unscrupulous',[21] although the size of their egos was well-matched.[22] Curzon had been appointed Viceroy in August 1898 at the exceptionally young age of thirty-nine, full of confidence in his ability to handle the complex task of governing an ethnically and socially diverse nation of almost 235 million people. Winston Churchill considered that Curzon had right on his side in his struggle with Kitchener but 'in craft, in slow intrigue, in strength of personality, in doubtful-dangerous manoeuvres, the soldier beat the politician every time.'[23]

Curzon, against the advice of numerous Foreign Office officials, had sought Kitchener's appointment as C-in-C of the Indian Army, a subordinate power to the Viceroy. Kitchener, however, one of the few men impervious to Curzon's formidably intimidating temperament and intellect, had fervidly worked behind the scenes to obtain the post of Military Member of the Viceroy's Council before being appointed C-in-C.[24] Those favourable to Kitchener correctly point out that the presence on the Viceroy's council of a Military Member effectively paralysed reform of the Indian Army. However, Kitchener used devious means to achieve his end, employing the services of two disreputable scandal-mongering journalists, H. A. Gwynne, editor of the *Standard*, who had grown to know and admire Kitchener in Sudan, and Colonel Charles À Court Repington,[25] military correspondent of *The Times*. Curzon in turn used his friendship with Valentine Chirol, *The Times'* leading commentator on India, to bolster his position.

Kitchener and Haig shared a lofty contempt for journalists but, whereas Haig never learned how to manipulate newspaper reporters for his own ends, Kitchener exploited the possibilities to the full. Once in India, he devoted his attention to this conspiracy against Curzon, seeking to accumulate to himself control over *all* India's military matters, thus ending the constitutionally enshrined dominance of civil imperial power over the military in India. A casual remark by Curzon, who had a string of heterosexual affairs before his marriage, that Kitchener should spend his holiday in England in the summer of 1902 looking for a wife,[26] did little to endear him to Kitchener who, as their power struggle dragged on, once remarked that he would have enjoyed shooting the Viceroy 'like a dog'.[27] Kitchener's ultimate ambition was to become Viceroy himself, the failure to achieve which he blamed on the death on 6 May 1910 of Edward VII, who had previously led Kitchener to believe he would get the position.

Understandably, Haig took Kitchener's side in the dispute. In November 1904, Haig loyally touted Kitchener's line to Henrietta: 'The C in C in India really has very little power. All the Supply, Transport and Finance are under an individual called "The Military Member of Council". That is to say that Lord K. may order men to Thibet [sic] but he does not know whether they will starve or not because he has nothing to do with the supply arrangements. Such a system is obviously ridiculous. It is like a pair of horses in double harness without a coachman.'

This was true, but there were sound constitutional considerations why the civilian authorities maintained authority over the Indian Army, not the least of which was preventing figures such as Kitchener from trying to exercise a personal satrapy. Moreover, when Haig wrote to Henrietta, Esher had already led him to believe that Curzon's days were numbered:

'In India, you will have great changes, for I doubt George Curzon returning. He is such an uncertain subject for prophecy that one cannot be sure
[. . .] Anyway, his successor has already been designated.'[28]

Under Kitchener, Haig enjoyed a very free hand in his supervision of
the country's cavalry regiments. There were four army commands in
India – Punjab, Bengal, Bombay and Madras – and Haig's duties included
a tour of each at regular intervals, as well as wider excursions to outlying
areas. He would normally spend three days with each outpost he visited,
travelling in quasi-regal splendour, as he revealed to Henrietta on 26
November 1904:

> You would be surprised at the amount of baggage and stuff I have to go
> about with – horses and clerks and office boxes and orderlies. I am half
> ashamed at the number of bullock wagons [seven] required to convey all
> this stuff to and from the station. Then they fire a salute of guns when I
> come and go at each station, so 'l'arrive' is most impressive at times –
> especially for the regiments, for they are not quite certain what to expect.

Haig insisted on intense physical training and fitness in both officers
and men, and, with painstaking attention to detail, scrutinized all aspects
of the administration of the regiments he inspected. He was paternalistic
to more able younger officers but delivered blunt warnings to those who
fell short of expected standards. He believed that his visits gave positive
support, writing to Henrietta that 'I am most considerate, as it is better to
carry people with one than to stifle keenness by mere criticisms, without
explaining what improvements and in what direction changes are
required.'

He introduced to India the practice known as staff rides, later to
become an established form of general staff instruction in the British
army (and since known as TEWTS, Tactical Exercises Without Troops).[29]
He helped establish the cavalry officers' training school at Saugor, and
was instrumental in pushing through a proposal for a Staff College at
Quetta. He also explained to Henrietta the kind of people he felt most
comfortable working with, revealing in a letter his suspicion of cleverness, unconsciously echoing Thomas Carlyle's epigram that 'clever men

are good, but they are not the best': 'The so called sharp people very often disappoint us or cheat or have some other drawback such as being disagreeable, bad-tempered, etc. All I require is people of <u>average</u> intelligence who are keen to do their work properly.'

What Haig sought, in other words, was more people like himself. Haig's suspicion of intellectuality was in stark contrast to the serpentine Kitchener; one of Haig's most attractive characteristics, his dogged honesty, was the obverse of Kitchener's delight in duplicitous dealing. Where Kitchener was mercurial and despotic, Haig was artlessly self-controlled and much more collegiate. Yet at this period Haig was also clearly in a state of some personal agitation; the arch-conservative could also deliver a breathtaking surprise.

On 5 May 1905 he arrived back in England on leave. A little more than two months later, Henrietta found herself displaced from the centre of his affections by the same Dorothy Vivian who had watched Haig win a polo match two years previously. Dorothy was a physically attractive yet highly strung woman, eighteen years younger than Haig – coincidentally, the same age gap that had existed between Haig's own father and mother.[30] In June 1905, after an acquaintance of just thirty-six hours, Haig proposed marriage to Dorothy and was accepted, a shock to all concerned except, apparently, Haig himself. He dismissed the suggestion that this hasty marriage was out of character by remarking he had often "made up my own mind on more important problems than that of my own marriage in much less time", but this sounds as much an attempt to prevent further scrutiny than anything else. That he became engaged to a twenty-six-year-old, apparently plucked from thin air, astonished all who knew him; yet the marriage was clearly mutually happy and grew into one of loving devotion on both sides, producing four children.[31]

Superficially, this proposal might seem a rare – for Haig – moment of impetuous passion, but impetuosity and Haig were strangers. Typically, Haig privately deliberated at great length before making any decision; the more momentous the act, the longer Haig took to consider it. But once he had made his mind up, he saw no reason to delay implementing his decision; in the case of his marriage, it was perhaps merely a matter of finding someone suitable.[32] His decision to find a wife was a matter that Haig may have been privately contemplating for some time, although the particular choice of Dorothy may indeed have been fairly spontaneous – rather like, having decided he needed a horse, then moving swiftly to purchase one at a reliable auction. Not even Henrietta, whose feelings were bruised by this whirlwind affair,[33] was taken into his confidence. Haig's tongue-tied embarrassment would have prevented him from discussing the matter beforehand with anyone, even his sister. At least he could afford to marry. The army had a long-standing if contradictory attitude towards marriage: while it might prevent young officers from temptation, it was to be discouraged unless the officer was wealthy. The army's view had altered little since this warning was carried by the *British Army Review* in April 1864 (later reprinted under the title 'Should Officers Marry?' in the same periodical in April 1956): 'We need hardly point out the miseries of those unfortunate girls who marry subalterns with nothing, or perhaps an allowance of £100 a year, beside their pay. Squalid lodgings, miserable food, and the worst of all annoyances, the striving to keep up an air of gentility upon their pitiful monthly receipts. Of all forms of poverty none is so distressing as this.'

Haig's bride was the daughter of Hussey Crespigny, third Baron Vivian, who had died in 1893 while British ambassador to Rome, and Louisa Alice Duff. Dorothy's beautiful mother had suffered a nervous breakdown in Rome, and was nursed to better health by Axel Munthe, the physician and psychiatrist whose autobiography, *The Story of San Michele*, became a bestseller in 1929.[34] Dorothy's brother, George Crespigny Brabazon, fourth Baron Vivian, an old Etonian with a reputation for being an eccentric bully,[35] had been in the 17th Lancers in South Africa during Haig's command of the regiment and, after Baron Vivian was seriously wounded at Tarkstad, Haig contacted the family with news of Baron Vivian's health:

> Colonel Haig had most kindly sent a wire to my family telling us of my brother's exact condition, which wire had been most opportune because we had received one just before, unofficially, that my brother had been

killed, and it was many hours after that the correct official telegram reached us from the War Office. It was not known at that time by us that it was Douglas who had taken the trouble to let us know.

Haig's reputation as a misogynist had reached Dorothy's notice before they first met: 'It is a curious thing that neither my sister, Violet Vivian, nor I knew Colonel Haig, although he commanded my brother's regiment, but we were given to understand that he was rather a woman-hater.'[36]

Douglas and Dorothy's fate hinged – as so much in Haig's adulthood – on his close proximity to the monarchy. While on leave in England, Haig had been invited to stay with the king at Windsor Castle. By now Haig was so fixed a member of the royal entourage that such invitations were quite normal. Court Circulars meant he would probably have been aware of the names of maids of honour who were to be in attendance on Queen Alexandra during this visit in June 1905. On the first evening of his stay, Haig accompanied another maid of honour, not Dorothy, into dinner. They were not even formally introduced until the evening of the second day of his stay, a Thursday, as they had been paired to play in a round of golf on Friday; Dorothy was a keen golfer as, by now, was Douglas. The Duke of Devonshire played in the pair against them and kept getting stuck in the bunkers, leaving Haig and Dorothy with time to chat, although romance was not initially in the air:

> I naturally questioned him about his life and work in India, but he seemed rather impatient because time was getting on, and kept pulling out a beautiful gold watch which I noticed particularly and about which I made some remark. This watch was given to him by his mother to give to his future wife. I thought that Douglas had not really enjoyed his game, for the long wait had been trying, but as we walked back to the castle he asked me to play a single with him next morning.[37]

Haig had found a suitable partner; and not just for golf. On Saturday morning 'as arranged, we met to play golf before breakfast, but to my surprise, Douglas did not wish to play and paid off the caddies. We looked for a quiet seat but, not finding one, he blurted out "I must propose to you standing!" This was very abrupt, and I must own quite unexpected, but I accepted him.'[38]

The couple then took General Brocklehurst, an equerry to King Edward, into their confidence. Brocklehurst was initially confused: 'He could not help expressing his surprise at such a quick engagement and thought at first that it was my [twin] sister to whom Douglas was referring.'[39]

Once the intended was correctly identified, Brocklehurst informed Queen Alexandra. The king met the couple later that day, congratulated Dorothy and 'spoke many appreciative words about Douglas, both as a man and a soldier. The king, however, became very serious, and asked me to promise him that I would do my utmost not to interfere with the military work of his "best and most capable General".'[40]

They were married on 11 July 1905 in the Chapel Royal of Buckingham Palace in a joint service with another maid of honour, Mary Hart-Dyke, who was irked that her more long-standing plans to wed Captain Bell of the Rifle Brigade were thus overshadowed. Dorothy was tall, at five foot eight inches. She had bronze-coloured eyes, a strong nose and mouth, and dark brown hair. In contemporary photographs she appears calm, intelligent and attractive.[41] One newspaper report of the marriage alluded to what was now an established cliché in press mentions of Haig – his good luck:

> General Douglas Haig, who today marries the Hon. Dorothy Vivian, is one of the most fortunate officers in the British Army. He is only forty-four years of age, and has seen plenty of active service, while his bride has long enjoyed the intimate confidence of the Royal Family as a Maid-of-Honour to the Queen, and has been the recipient of some handsome presents from their Majesties. General Haig, who is a very soldierly-looking fellow, and almost rivals General Baden-Powell as a cavalry expert, was in the famous battles of Atbara and at Khartoum, and subsequently achieved no small distinction in South Africa, where he was Deputy-Assistant-Adjutant-General of Cavalry. He was made a major-general last year, and few officers have such a promising future as he.[42]

The king and queen gave a wedding party lunch and, as their gift to Dorothy, a pearl and diamond tiara; later that day the Haigs drove to Henrietta's home, Radway Grange in Warwickshire. A few days later Charlotte Knollys, private secretary to Queen Alexandra, wrote to Haig: 'I do feel so glad to think that she [Doris] has such a good husband to take care of her – for her young life has been beset with difficulties & she had not one who could <u>really</u> help her – now that is all of the past & I do not know which is the luckiest individual of you two . . .'[43]

Charlotte Knollys was seventy and had long been part of the royal household. Her brother, Francis, Viscount Knollys, aged sixty-eight, was King Edward's private secretary and a personal friend of Esher. It was through Viscount Knollys that Esher maintained his close relationship with the king, and thus was forged another link in Haig's chain of useful contacts. Charlotte Knollys' note to Haig contains a hint of why the lonely maid of honour might have accepted Haig with such alacrity. It is also an indication of why Dorothy came to rely on Haig so absolutely after her marriage, and an explanation of why, after his death, she felt so utterly bereft, and defended Haig's posthumous reputation with growing imbalance. Haig gave Dorothy the granite-like emotional stability her own family could not provide her with; Dorothy in turn gave Haig the close emotional warmth he had lacked, save from Henrietta, since the death of his mother.

Haig arranged a marriage settlement worth slightly more than £600 a year (after tax) for his new wife in the form of dividends from a thousand shares in John Haig and Company, placed in trust for his new wife. These shares were valued at £10,000 at that date.[44] That he could afford this without any hardship is a clear indication of his relative affluence.[45] A typical skilled factory worker at this time had an annual wage of some £40 while average household income (based on the husband's wages and that of one elder child) was about forty-five shillings a week.[46] Dorothy also received one third of £10,000 from a trust her parents had set up for their children, to be allocated upon their marriage. She also stood to receive £6,000 upon the death of her mother. They were a wealthy couple by standards of the day. After their marriage, Douglas had two more weeks' leave and, stifling her pangs, Henrietta joined them at Radway before seeing them off from Paris to Marseilles. It was obviously a strange and difficult time for Dorothy, whisked away from the claustrophobic certainties of the court and plunged into a new life, one in which an unhappily married woman twice her age regarded her as an interloper, taking the affections of her brother.

It was equally unsettling for Henrietta. As Dorothy later said of her about this period, 'She felt her brother's marriage keenly, but Douglas tried to tell and show her that things between them would be unaltered. Poor devoted sister, I was too young then to appreciate what my husband's marriage meant to her, and sadly she stood waving good-bye as the train took us off.'[47] Not that Douglas obviously changed his behaviour towards Henrietta; he immediately set about writing a lengthy letter to her as soon as they sailed from Marseilles on 30 August, as though nothing had altered. The world had been turned upside down for Henrietta and Doris, but not for the imperturbable Haig.

When they arrived at a stiflingly hot Bombay on 13 September 1905, the Haigs stayed briefly at the Taj Mahal hotel on the waterfront, where one of Douglas's oldest Indian friends, Sir Pertab Singh, called on them and insisted on paying their bill. On 15 September they travelled by rail to Simla where, four days later, they were entertained at lunch by Kitchener, now certain of his victory over Curzon. In June 1905 St John Brodrick, Secretary of State for India, had abolished the Military Member post on the Viceroy's Council, thus betraying his old friendship with Curzon although all the while protesting otherwise.[48] This was seen by Curzon as a final stab in the back and on 16 August his resignation was accepted by the king. Doris found Kitchener to be 'most human and considerate during the whole of our visit. At that time the Kitchener-Curzon trouble was in full swing, but Lord Kitchener did not mention anything about it before me. He had, however, got what he wanted and therefore there was no reason for him to feel aggrieved. We played billiards when not out in the evenings and it was amusing to see how Lord Kitchener liked to be on the winning side!'[49]

While the struggle between Kitchener and Curzon played out, the radical reform of the army in London initiated by Esher's triumvirate had received fresh impetus with the appointment in December 1905 by the Prime Minister, Sir Henry Campbell-Bannerman, of Viscount Richard Burdon Haldane as Secretary of State for War. Haldane was an eminent legal figure and a respected academic philosopher. He had no prior experience of ministerial office, yet he proved himself one of Britain's ablest war ministers, his greatest political gift being his willingness to listen to all professional advice, distil the best, and facilitate its implementation. Haldane held the post during the crucial years of 1905–1912, during which time he assembled a team to build on the intellectual groundwork laid by Esher and create an expeditionary army designed for deployment in far-flung outposts of the empire, so that the catastrophe of the early part of the recent war in South Africa should not be repeated. Haldane's team also welded together a systematically organized auxiliary home defence force, and constructed a general staff. Haldane early on looked to Esher for guidance as to where he might find the kind of hard-working, young but experienced officer who would be useful in further army reforms; Haig's name inevitably cropped up. On Esher's advice, Haldane set about bringing Haig back to London from India, to become first Director of Military Training and later Director of Staff Duties at the War Office.

Haig first learned of Haldane's interest when Esher wrote to him on 15 February 1906 that 'I think that very shortly – i.e in April or May – there will be a shift here. It is absolutely necessary, the King says, for you to come back. [. . .] It will be a godsend to get you here.'[50] On 2 March Esher wrote again to Haig: 'Between ourselves, and the King feels this most strongly, Lyttleton[51] requires guidance. He is a most excellent good fellow, but Providence did not endow him with a clear brain. "Defence questions", as they are called, are in a hopeless muddle: and the creation of a G.S [General Staff] makes slow progress, and what progress it makes, is not in the right direction. So you can imagine how desperately you are required.'[52]

In promoting to Haldane the return of Haig to a position of backroom power at the War Office, Esher was well aware of the close tie between

King Edward VII and Haig, recently consolidated by his marriage, as well as Haig's own merits. Haig was delighted to be drawn back to London. On 28 March 1906, he wrote to Henrietta from Peshawar:

About a week ago I got 2 letters from Esher and one from General Lyttelton offering me the Directorate of Training. The former said Mr Haldane was very anxious for me to come home and assist in his schemes of reorganisation, and both he and the King were desirous that I should accept the billet. Although called 'Training' the department also deals with 'War Organisation' and 'Home Defence' so that it is the most important Directorate in the General Staff at the present time [. . .] Mr Haldane wishes me to come home as soon as I have finished my winter's work here.

By 1 June 1906, Douglas and Doris were back in London; on 6 June they travelled to Windsor Castle to stay for three days with King Edward and Queen Alexandra. Shortly thereafter they rented Coombe Farm, near Farnborough in Hampshire,[53] from where Haig would commute into London to the War Office most days. Many years later Frederick Carpenter contacted Doris with his boyhood recollection of encounters with Haig, near Farnborough railway station:[54] 'The General was in the habit of walking to the Farnborough Railway Stn on fine mornings on his way to the War Office, and would often come suddenly upon my brothers and I playing at fencing. I can still see the General with his walking stick showing us the correct position etc and laughing at us, and finally he told his man Hall to hunt up some foils for us.'

On 9 June, Haig drove to Aldershot and stayed with Sir John French[55] at Government House, where for the first time he met Haldane, whom he found to be 'a big fat man but with a kind genial face. One seems to like the man at once [. . .] a most clear headed and practical man – very ready to listen and weigh carefully all that is said to him.'

Haldane, born in Edinburgh almost three years before Haig, immediately won over the cautious soldier, despite their very different characters. While the abstemious, practical Haig, congenitally suspicious of intellectuals, liked to be in bed early, Haldane, an authority on Hegelian metaphysics, delighted in sitting up to the early hours over cigars and brandy. Unlike Haldane, Haig was never comfortable with the political manoeuvrings that were intrinsic to life at the War Office, and its procedural bureaucracy taxed his patience. Moreover, this new turn in his professional life, with an almost ceaseless round of committee meetings and protracted deliberations to be undergone, called for a greater verbal dexterity than Haig possessed. Even Esher, whose admiration for Haig was unequalled at this date, found that while 'on paper he is hard to beat [. . .] he is so obscure in speech.'[56]

Haig was quickly introduced to the numbing nature of War Office life. On 10 June 1906 he attended a conference on the disposition of the eight battalions of Guards. Next day he was back at the War Office where a forty-strong committee of civilians and assorted yeomanry, militia and regular army personnel – known as the 'Duma' and presided over by Esher – considered how to create a unified civilian reserve army from Britain's disparate auxiliary forces. The Duma comprised very divergent entrenched factions, few of which were prepared to cede their authority and social standing to a new national reserve army as envisaged by Haldane. Reactionary opposition to army reform was still deeply embedded; one senior regular officer remarked to Haldane's military secretary: 'If you organise the British Army, you'll ruin it.'[57] On 12 June 1906, Haig acerbically recorded in his diary that one of the firmest opponents of the creation of a Territorial Force (as it was initially referred to) was Jack Seely,[58] 'a Yeoman, [who] seems to think that the country requires no Army as long as the Volunteers and Yeomanry are kept up.'[59]

While the officers commanding auxiliary reserve units strove to preserve their independence out of a fear of loss of social position, senior regular army officers dug their heels in against Haldane's mission to tighten the army's financial laxity by slimming its budget to below £28 million a year, which Haldane nevertheless achieved in the Army Estimates for 1907–08. Haig's duty at this period was not to consider the cost of the regular and auxiliary armies, but to produce a scheme whereby Britain would be able to put an army of 900,000 men in the field within twelve months and maintain it there for five years. By October 1906 Esher and others were already referring to it as 'the Douglas Haig

T.A.' (Territorial Army).[60] Besides fighting the rearguard defence conducted by county dignitaries anxious not to see their amateur soldier status undermined, Haig had his own personal skirmishes with War Office bureaucracy. He received a letter on 13 June informing him he would be paid less than he expected when he accepted the job. The Army Council 'had decided that my pay is to be £1200 instead of £1500. Write to [Colonel Gerald] Ellison[61] and ask if this has been done with Mr Haldane's knowledge, because if so, I would like to reconsider my acceptance of the appointment.' On 15 June, Haldane met Haig and assured him the reduction had been done without his approval and the lost £300 would be immediately reinstated.

Haig's diary entries for this period are replete with complaints about commanding officers of auxiliary units resisting the amalgamation of reserve units to create a single, more streamlined reserve army. He was exasperated at what he felt was their failure to recognize the national crisis he was certain would shortly erupt. On 26 June 1906 twenty colonels of militia regiments attended a sub-committee of the Duma, to debate how best they could reinforce the regular army when it was overseas. On 27 June Haig confided to his diary that it was 'Impossible to get Militia Officers to agree to wishes of War Office Council, namely to provide <u>drafts</u> for Army in the Field, instead of <u>expanding</u> the Regular Army. Some are willing to supply "companies" when required. So these sign paper to that effect, remainder sign to go abroad as "Battalions".'

During his War Office days Haig maintained his strict routine of horse rides before breakfast, followed by an early train for London, normally arriving home late into the evening. His personal life was also changing. By early July 1906 Doris realised she was pregnant and on doctor's orders gave up cycling, motoring and playing golf. And his own health was still troublesome: shortly after news of his wife's pregnancy, Haig, now aged forty-six, was again laid low with malaria while attending meetings at Aldershot. Throughout their married life Doris was, like Henrietta, concerned for Douglas's health, and with reasonable cause, given his chronic illnesses. His doctor – the sixty-three-year old Scot, Sir Lauder Brunton, famous for his use of amyl nitrate in treating angina and digitalis for heart conditions – diagnosed an 'enlarged liver' and recommended a period of rest at a continental spa. On 20 July a physically weakened Haig, putting off his doctor's advice to rest, attended a meeting of the Duma at the War Office, where it was agreed to start organizing seventeen divisions (about 450,000 men) for a Territorial Army, a term which gained currency as the weeks went by.[62] Next day he travelled (without Doris) to Tarasp, in Switzerland, as part of his recuperation, where he struck up a lasting and close friendship with the Jewish banker Leopold Rothschild, who during the Great War kept Haig's staff well-supplied with champagne, brandy, cigars and choice delicacies from Fortnum and Mason.[63]

The ways of the War Office – its procedural dilatoriness especially – annoyed Haig, who was accustomed to issuing commands and having them obeyed. Haig was no diplomat. He also resented its penny-pinching. While in Switzerland, Haig was annoyed to receive a letter from the finance department of the War Office, informing him that the pay he might otherwise have expected to receive for his new post, at which he had already been working for almost two months, would not start until 11 August, the date which his predecessor, General Stopford, formally vacated the post of Director of Training. He returned to London on 24 August and that day officially took up his duties as Director of Military Training, and also shouldered the task of advising Haldane on the selection and appointment of the seventy-two officers for the new general staff. Next day Haldane told Haig that he had a free hand to form a committee and to call into it anyone he thought necessary, just so long as the plan to form a Territorial Army got off the ground. On 11 September 1906 Haig wrote to Colonel Ellison setting out his aim:

Our object, in my opinion, should be to start a system of finance suited to the 'supposed situation', ie a great war requiring the whole resources of the nation to bring it to a successful end. Even if the proposed system cost more in peace, it should be inaugurated provided that it is more practical in war. The Swiss system seemed to me to be exactly what is wanted to 'root the Army in the people' [. . .] The Germans seem to be going ahead in every direction with the utmost self-assurance and energy, so that the crisis is sure of coming before many years are over.

Haig's suggestion that Britain should emulate the Swiss system, under which all adult males were professionally trained and deemed part of the country's auxiliary army in times of need, rather than adopt a policy of national full-time conscription, was a subtle shift from his previous thinking and was shared by Haldane, who regarded conscription as politically unworkable except during war. On this they diverged from Esher, a committed advocate of compulsory military service, as was Henry Wilson, also then at the War Office and about to take over as commandant at the Staff College with the rank of brigadier-general.[64] This ambition, of subtending the whole resources of the nation to achieve proper military preparedness, was one of Haig's abiding and most prescient insights.

Yet while he encountered high drama at the War Office, low farce occasionally interrupted the routine, in the form of attendance at seances at the behest of Henrietta. Dorothy later rebutted the suggestion that Haig actually believed it was possible to summon up the dead: 'My personal idea of spiritualism and mediums is that the latter usually reflect what those who approach them are thinking about. Douglas did not really believe in seances, but attended some to please his sister Henrietta.'

One seance he attended was on 20 September 1906 when, after lunch with Doris and Henrietta, Haig and his fifty-five-year-old sister (but not Doris) went to 6 Bloomfield Road, Maida Hill, where a medium, Miss McCreadie, welcomed them at 3pm. They talked about Haig family affairs and, in response to a question from Haig about army reorganization, Miss McCreadie pronounced that a company basis was better than a battalion basis for the expansion of the Territorial Army. Then, according to his diary entry for the day, she 'went under control' of

a little native girl 'Sunshine', said that I was influenced by several spirits – notably a small man named Napoleon aided me. That it was in my power to be helped by him for good affairs but I might repel him if his influence was for bad tho' he had become changed for better in the spirit world. I was destined to do much good & to benefit my country. Asked by me how to ensure the Territorial Army Scheme being a success, she said <u>thought governed the world</u>. Think out the scheme thoroughly, one's thoughts would then be put in so convincing a manner that the people would respond (<u>without any compulsion</u>) and the National Army would be a reality. She cd not bring Napoleon to me when I wanted but I must think of him & try & get his aid as he was always near me. My mother too was close to me and a sister Lally. My mother threw a light round me, and Henrietta, & placed on my breast a star which illuminated all about me. Hugo also sent me a message. So did George but latter feeble.[65]

John Hussey has pointed out that Haig had three days prior to this decided to propose to the War Office that territorial forces should be expanded on a company basis, should war break out, and had on the morning of 20 September written a memo to Ellison informing him of such; the suggestion that Haig's decision as to the formation for the Territorial Army units to go overseas was swayed by a north London woman in a trance is therefore groundless.[66] Haig was to attend another seance with Henrietta on 24 November 1908. He recorded in his diary this particular meeting, which was clearly not to his taste: 'At 5 o'clock Henrietta calls at War Office for me. We drive to Peckham Rye and attend a spiritualistic seance. Mr Husk, medium. The whole is a great fraud. Dine with Sir J. French. We have a happy evening together and settle many things.' Even if we accept that Haig did not believe in the possibility of conjuring up dead spirits, it is an abiding curiosity that this forty-seven-year-old major-general was so under the sway of his older sister that he felt compelled to take time out of his extremely busy schedule simply to please her.

With Douglas so often absent, Doris was occasionally lonely. He once invited her to visit him on manoeuvres near Leighton Buzzard, where she stayed with the Rothschilds, but it was not a success: 'He had purposely taken a horse for me to ride, but when I met him out with the troops and dared to go and speak to him, he just looked at me as if he had never seen me before. His blue eyes, which were usually so kind, took on a steely, hard look which quite alarmed me. He was altogether too military!'[67] That look and the impenetrable silence was a technique Haig had long used to good effect and would do so again on the Western Front, crushing those he felt had overstepped the mark.

During this visit to the Rothschilds one of a party of German officers, there at the invitation of the War Office to attend the manoeuvres, became rowdily inebriated and over-familiar with Dorothy, calling her 'Süsse Doris' and placing Haig in a difficult position, although – according to her – he maintained a frosty politeness to the offending German. Doris later claimed to have brushed the incident off as nothing more than the ramblings of a drunk, but she complained to the German attaché. The drunk officer, incomprehensibly, later sent his photograph to Haig.

The Haldane-Haig plan for a single territorial force, carved from the reorganised yeomanry and the volunteers, which by now had been formed into County Associations under the leadership of Lords Lieutenant, finally gained Cabinet backing on 21 December 1906. On 25 February 1907 at 3.50pm Haldane introduced his second Army Estimates to Parliament, speaking without pause until 7.10pm, Haig observing the scene. Haldane used the occasion to detail the shortcomings, both financial and military, of the auxiliaries and to outline the efficiencies to be gained by uniting these part-time soldiers into a national Territorial Army which would, on the outbreak of war, he emphasized, be trained to serve overseas in support of the regulars.

The Territorial and Reserve Forces Act of 1907 was introduced by Haldane on 4 March 1907 and given its final reading by the House of Commons on 19 June, though by that stage one important change had been made by Haldane, under intense pressure from some auxiliary officers – the Territorial Army would be restricted to home defence and not used as support for any expeditionary force, unless individual units expressed a willingness to serve overseas. On 2 August 1907 it received the Royal Assent, the first Bill passed by the Liberal government. At long last, the administration, training and conditions of service for Britain's system of auxiliary forces could be placed on a centralized basis. Shortly afterwards that same year, the Colonial Conference in London gave rise to the Imperial General Staff, which was given the task of combining the autonomous armies of the empire into a single military entity to be used in times of imperial crisis.[68]

Even those who later expressed an ambivalence about Haig's abilities acknowledged his pivotal role in assisting Haldane to formulate and then carry through these vital reforms. Brigadier-General Edmonds commented after Haig's death that: 'Without his persistent advocacy the General Staff and the Territorial Army would have gone the way of many another military innovation, and we should never have heard of the Imperial General Staff, or of the Dominion Forces coming into line with the Home Army.'[69]

However, although the Territorial Army now existed in principle, giving it substance, persuading the Lords Lieutenant to lend the new force their support, obtaining the goodwill of employers in giving their workers leave to attend annual training, and bringing the part-time soldiers to the requisite professional standards, were all to tax Haldane's and Haig's energies and dedication still further.

# CHAPTER SEVEN

# An Army Equipped to Think

I felt that the incapacity of the whole of the people in defending
their homes was disgusting.

Douglas Haig

Haig's congenital loathing of political as opposed to actual warfare was
reinforced during his days at the War Office, when he was required
patiently to wait upon the opinions of brother officers and auxiliary
soldiers who, often motivated by vested personal or political interests,
were disinclined to make the Territorial Army a reality. The reluctance of
these 'sharp' men to sink their differences on behalf of what he saw as the
wider interests of national defence was deeply irritating to Haig. His
health was poorly and his family responsibilities growing; on 9 March
1907 Doris gave birth to Alexandra, their first child, while Haig was playing golf at Sunningdale. The new baby was baptized on 17 April at the
Chapel Royal, with Queen Alexandra (represented by Lady Emily Kings-
cote) and Henrietta among the godparents. In July of this year Doris and
Douglas travelled to the Swiss spa towns of Tarasp and Pontresina for
some rest and recuperation, leaving the four-month-old baby in the
capable hands of a quarrelsome nurse; on their return, all three of their
domestic servants gave notice, leaving the nurse and Secrett, Haig's military servant, to run the busy household.

Towards end of 1907, Haldane arranged for Haig to exchange titles at
the War Office – from that of Director of Military Training to Director of
Staff – as, now that the legislative basis for the Territorial Army was laid,

Haldane wanted Haig's assistance with the creation of the Imperial General Staff, an idea born out of the same year's Colonial Conference in April.[1] In this new post Haig was in charge of military affairs and war organisation, and second only to Haldane in developing army policy. By now Haig had firmly decided that the urgent need was, as he wrote to Haldane on 18 March 1908, the creation of 'a 2nd-line Army complete in all arms and services,' the full realization of which was still incomplete when war broke out in August 1914.

A second daughter, Victoria Doris Rachel, was born on 7 November 1908; Haig's family was disappointed she was not a boy. Despite personal exhaustion and professional duties, he found time to squeeze in bits and pieces of a social life, including a visit on 3 February 1909 to Wyndham's Theatre in Drury Lane, where he, Doris and her mother watched one of the season's popular hits, *An Englishman's Home*,[2] then enjoying an eighteenth-month run. This dramatized what might happen to an England invaded by German forces, a possibility that was Haig's daily preoccupation.[3] He was unable to suspend disbelief: 'It is extraordinary how the play draws crowded houses every night and how impressed the audience seem to be with the gravity of the scenes. I trust that good may result and "universal training" may become the law of the land, but for myself, the performance was not an interesting sight. I felt that the incapacity of the whole of the people in defending their homes was disgusting.'[4]

Haig spent the first week of March 1909 conducting a staff ride around Oxfordshire and the Cotswolds; as a major-general, he was by now senior enough to be looked upon as a potential mentor himself, and on his staff during this exercise Haig employed Colonel Hubert Gough, another cavalryman. Haig promoted Gough's career throughout the Great War, often to the disbelief of some generals, who found Gough's vigorous, attack-minded spirit a poor compensation for his weak planning ability. In his reports on this ride,[5] Haig reaffirmed his belief that cavalry would always have a useful battlefield role:

Compare the results of even the most skilfully managed dismounted action, and the results will be insignificant in comparison. Occasions for charging will be few, but they occur – and the results from such action will be immense. The mounted attack, therefore, must always be our ideal, our final objective. At the same time, dismounted tactics are an absolute necessity. [. . .] There is no period in the actual operations when Cavalry may not intervene with success, but the greatest energy should be reserved for the decisive battle. [. . .] Hunger, heat, cold will have had their effect on the hostile troops, who are inevitably more exhausted after the modern battle, whilst their moral [morale] has probably been shaken by rapid fire of modern guns. Another point in favour of the attacking Cavalry is that the small bore bullet does not stop a horse, whilst accidents of ground, mist, dust and rain all favour the stealthy approach and rapid dash of Cavalry. In carrying out its role Cavalry will make use of guns, rifles, swords and lances.

That Haig felt confident in regarding the mounted attack as the cavalry's 'final objective' five years after the Russo-Japanese war suggests that he either dismissed or was ignorant of the opinions of such as Major-General Sir Ian Hamilton. More seriously, in five years' time, when Britain itself was at war, Haig's loyalty to his own branch of the army and his continuing faith in its value would commit him to the enduring hope that a breakthrough battle on the Western Front would see the cavalry come into its own. In this he was, however, to be greatly disappointed.

Fatigued by life at the War Office,[6] Haig decided to take up an offer which came out of the blue to return to active duties. His experience at the War Office had placed Haig at the centre of the contradictions prevailing at the heart of Britain's evolving military culture. Haig, himself a beneficiary of what has been described as the 'personalized' nature of the British army, had – along with Esher, Haldane and some other senior officers – sought to bring about a more professional ethos, but with limited success.[7] Throughout his career Haig embodied this contradiction – schooled in one type of army ethos, that of the Victorian amateur, he nevertheless recognized that this would not suffice in future wars and that greater professionalism was called for. That he could not completely slough off the skin of his own experience is not surprising;

the full implication of his drive towards higher professional standards would, ultimately, threaten the kind of army he had grown up in.

The offer came on 15 April 1909, when General Sir Garrett O'Moore Creagh VC, recently appointed Commander-in-Chief in India in succession to Kitchener, invited Haig to go to India as his chief of staff. Haig initially declined, but pondered and finally accepted on 3 May. There is no discussion of this decision in Haig's diary and prima facie it was an odd move. Kitchener regarded Creagh personally as an amiable and amusing Irishman, but professionally 'undoubtedly second-rate'.[8] Kitchener would have regarded any successor as inadequate, but it is certainly true that Creagh, an old Indian Army man, was not the kind of powerful, up-and-coming mentor that Haig normally sought. It was a sideways step politically, away from the army centre of gravity in London, and, moreover, returning to India inevitably meant incurring health risks and the enforced socializing he found so tedious. Honours still came his way and, in recognition of his work at the War Office, on 23 June 1909 Haig learned that the king had created him a Knight Commander of the Royal Victorian Order (KCVO) in the Birthday Honours. As to why he chose to return to India, neither Haig nor Doris left a full explanation. Perhaps most incomprehensible for us today is their decision to leave their two small children behind in England, in the nominal care of Henrietta but really in the charge of a nursemaid. The eldest child was then less than two and the youngest under a year. Although Dorothy later wrote it was 'a great wrench' to leave them behind, she gave an odd explanation as to why they did so: 'We did not like taking them because of the difficulties of getting good milk and food in India.'[9]

The children would have been at risk of typhoid, malaria and other tropical diseases – although some officers and their wives nevertheless did take their children with them – but there was certainly no shortage of good food in India, as the Haigs' position ensured them the best of local cooks, as well as plentiful imported supplies from Britain. Even more peculiar is the idea that the lack of 'good milk' was a reason to leave them behind. Pasteurized milk was far from guaranteed even in England at that time.[10] The Haigs may have been dutiful parents by the standards of the time, but the ever conventional Douglas always left the practical responsibilities of parenting to his wife.

On 6 October 1909, Haig bade farewell to Haldane and handed over to his successor as Director of Staff, Major-General Sir Launcelot Kiggell, who was a year younger than Haig. Kiggell was later to join Haig as his chief of staff at General Headquarters (GHQ) when Haig was appointed C-in-C of the British Expeditionary Force (BEF). He had a reputation of being a conventional officer who had failed to grasp the full implications of the Russo-Japanese war.[11] Two days later, the Haigs sailed from Marseilles for India aboard the newly completed P&O passenger liner *Mantua*. On board ship he wrote self-deprecatingly to Esher: 'Personally I felt that I had done but little and that the thanks were really due to those who were working under me at that time, and to yourself more than anyone else. I shall never forget the many discussions which we had together and the careful way in which you used to revise our proposals, etc. etc., and helped me also to deal with opposition which existed even in the Gen. Staff. I wish you had been present and heard Haldane's praise, because it was you who suggested my name to him for the work and I was, consequently, brought back from India.'[12]

By the start of 1910, the basis had been laid for the raising of a British army sufficiently large to cope not just with imperial threats, but also those that might emerge from Europe, Germany in particular. That this progress was achieved, thanks in great part to the efforts of a Scottish Hegelian metaphysician who revered German culture, a half-French nepotist with pederastic inclinations, and of a tongue-tied Scots cavalry-man who had spent most of his career in India is, retrospectively, all the more astonishing. Ten years previously, Haig had been a relatively ordinary major in the 7th Hussars, without noticeably better career prospects than dozens of other middle-ranking officers; now he was returning to India a highly respected major-general laden with baubles from the monarchy. It had been an unusually rapid rise. As one anonymous officer commented to the press at the time, 'I would rather have Haig's luck than a licence to steal horses.'[13]

The Haigs' journey to India was uneventful, save for a brief interlude at Port Said, Egypt. Of all possible entertainments available on land, Haig chose to confer once more with the darker mysteries of life, this time in the guise of an Indian fortune-teller. Does this hint at how much his innate scepticism struggled with his curiosity, or was it simply passing the time? With her characteristic faux-naivety, Doris later averred that 'Indian fortune-tellers are generally known to be above the average.[14] We found a wonderful man at Port Said who foretold Douglas's future like reading a map. The Great War was described and the anxieties and responsibilities entailed. Douglas was to be successful in everything that he undertook, and would save his country. Honours would be showered on him, but he would be much concerned about the sufferings around him. At the time I did not realise properly the future that this man was unfolding.'[15]

How could she? We do not know if it was Douglas or Doris who suggested consulting the Indian fakir who, after all, revealed nothing of Haig's future but, like all such tricksters, engaged in generalities with this pair of somewhat gullible, wealthy tourists.[16] The fact that Haig agreed to consult a medium without Henrietta's encouragement casts a modicum of doubt over claims that his dallying with such jiggery-pokery was only ever at the behest of his sister.

From Port Said the couple arrived in Bombay on 22 October 1909 and quickly returned to Simla, where Haig went to his office the day after their arrival. By December that year they were stationed at Calcutta, much preferred by Doris to Simla, which was entirely focused on military affairs and lacked Calcutta's wider social life. Their Calcutta days were, for Doris, 'delightful; riding early, horse shows, golf at Tollygunge, and in addition Douglas was much less away than as Inspector-General of Cavalry.'[17]

This period in India was little more than an interregnum for Haig, for by May 1911 he knew that he was destined to return to England to take over at Aldershot, a clear sign he was being groomed for the highest command of the British army. The death of King Edward VII on 6 May 1910, a professional blow to Haig and a personal loss to both him and Doris, and the subsequent coronation of George V, were the greatest events that punctuated a routine of dinners, parties, golf, hunting, manoeuvres and inspections. He re-read texts such as Clausewitz's *On War*, which he found to be 'still the best guide on general principles.' Haig also proselytized what he had begun to formulate at the War Office in London: the new, imperially oriented nature of the army.

With the support of Sir O'Moore Creagh, Haig elaborated a plan under which the Indian Army would be mobilized and used outside India, in the event of a large-scale European land war. Lord Morley, then Secretary of State for India, regarded this as an unacceptable extension of the military authority of the C-in-C/India, despite the creation of the Committee of Imperial Defence, which might have been thought precisely designed to encourage such lateral thinking. Morley instructed Lord Minto, the Viceroy, an old Etonian and erstwhile private secretary to Lord Roberts, the former C-in-C, to order all such studies to be abandoned and any existing plans physically destroyed. Minto did as he was told, as did Haig, who instructed General Alexander Hamilton-Gordon[18], the senior officer involved in supervising the plans, to destroy them, but, said Hamilton-Gordon, Haig did so with 'a look in [his] eye which made me realise that he would not regard any deviation from rigid adherence to orders with undue severity.' The plan was surreptitiously preserved and dusted off in 1914, when it was used as the basis for the deployment of Indian regiments in France.[19] Haig did not forget this absurdity and, in his speech at Minto's farewell dinner at Simla in late 1910, used the occasion to emphasize that if he had anything to do with it, in any future European conflict the Indian Army would be fully deployed and used to fight, as indeed it was.

Haig kept in close touch with his friends, relations and colleagues back home in England, and in one letter to Haldane's military secretary, Ellison, revealed in early 1910 his distaste for Lloyd George. As Chancellor of the Exchequer, in his People's Budget of 1909, Lloyd George had proposed the introduction of a super-tax on incomes over £5,000 a year, at the rate of sixpence on every pound over £3,000, as well as raising the standard level of income tax from one shilling to one shilling and two pennies in the pound. This budget, and the Lords' refusal to pass it, dominated the January 1910 British general election. Haig, no lover of high taxation nor of Irish independence, wrote: 'I am sorry to see that Mr Haldane was so poorly during the winter, but conclude from his speeches in the Commons that he is quite fit again. What a pity it is that he has to associate with such a pack of rascals as Lloyd George & Co! They seem to be ruining the country in trade; and in reputation also by working at Redmond's bidding!'[20]

Lloyd George got his budget through with the support of the Irish nationalists, led by John Redmond MP, who made a new Home Rule Bill for Ireland a condition of their support for the budget. On 12 May 1911 Haig received a telegram from Haldane asking if he would be interested in the Aldershot command, currently in the hands of Major-General Sir Horace Smith-Dorrien. He immediately responded 'yes I would', despite being conscious not just of the onerous military nature of the position but also the financial burden it imposed, writing on 18 May to his nephew Oliver that he was 'delighted to hear such good accounts of J. H. & Co [John Haig and Co] – and I hope the dividends will be good as the exs [expenses] at Aldershot are great and the pay small for what one has to do – £3000 a year.'[21] This was more than double the salary he had received from the War Office just one year previously.

On 18 June he received a warm letter from Haldane, for whom it was 'a great satisfaction to me that you are coming home to take over Aldershot. This has been my own strong wish for some time past. You will find a good deal to do.' While flattering to Haig, this was hardly complimentary to Smith-Dorrien, an infantryman who in fact had done a fine job trying to render the Aldershot garrison much more proficient at musketry, while leaving the cavalry under his command in no doubt that they needed to adjust to new an entirely new type of warfare.[22]

While commandant at Aldershot, Smith-Dorrien, who was to command II Corps in France in 1914 and initially was a rival to Haig for the position of C-in-C of the BEF, had encouraged the cavalry to accept that its future role was more likely to be dismounted than at the gallop: 'It had for a long time been evident to many soldiers that, both in the mounted and dismounted services, rapid and accurate fire [. . .] might prove a decisive factor in war, and that the days of charges of cavalry in large formations were numbered, and that in a big action their horses would be chiefly valuable to get them to a position quickly, where they could dismount and fire. This had been admirably illustrated by the Japanese in pressing back the Russian Army on Mukden in 1904.'[23]

When he had first arrived at Aldershot, Smith-Dorrien had been shocked to find that the cavalry were hopeless shots and still spent most of their time practising 'perfectly carried out, though impossible, knee to knee charges against infantry in action.' On 21 August 1909 he had ordered all cavalry officers to improve their musketry and stop imagining that they would win future battles by charges against infantry.[24] Many cavalry officers bitterly resented this sensible intervention by Smith-Dorrien, an officer who was also fully aware of the likely future importance of the machine-gun; the Maxim machine-gun was reckoned to be able to deliver firepower equivalent to twenty-five rifles, while the Vickers machine-gun of 1912, with a flatter trajectory that made it potentially more lethal, was estimated to be worth forty rifles. Smith-Dorrien found opposition not just from hidebound cavalrymen, but politicians too. He recalled a lunch he attended with an (anonymous) Cabinet minister in 1909, where he "used the occasion to impress upon him, as a member of the Government, that it was most important we should be armed with the new Maxim Machine-gun, which was half the weight of the gun we then had, and much more efficient, and I urged that £100,000 would re-equip the six Divisions of the Expeditionary Force. Mr "—" jeered at me, saying I was afraid of the Germans, that he habitually attended the German Army at training, and was quite certain that if they ever went to war "the most monumental examples of crass cowardice the world had ever heard of would be witnessed." '[25]

Aldershot was the most important of the UK's District Commands, each of which was commanded by a major-general, being the only one composed entirely of regular troops. The post of Aldershot commandant brought with it political and social responsibilities; it was expected that he should regularly and splendidly entertain the men under his authority, as well as frequent visitors, both civilian and military, from the UK and abroad, yet the salary was scarcely commensurate with the expenses incurred. Smith-Dorrien had found the financial costs onerous: 'Taking up a command was financially a serious matter in those days – for one was provided with a bare house devoid even of fenders and curtain-poles.'[26] Smith-Dorrien had ultimately proved a popular commandant, despite his occasionally violent temper and the fact that he too had initially been an unknown quantity; when he took over at Aldershot, he had spent twenty-seven years in the army without doing a single day's duty in the UK.[27]

Haig's Aldershot appointment was first publicly announced by Reuters on 10 August 1911. His suitability for the job was not merely professional; he had also known the new king, George V, since 1898. Just as his father had done, George paid annual visits to Aldershot lasting up to ten days, visits that for senior officers were a professional strain and, for the commandant, a financial nuisance.

While he knew he was soon to leave India, Haig was none the less kept busy with helping to organize the forthcoming Delhi Durbar, the culminating ceremony of which took place on 12 December 1911. The Durbar, an enormously colourful extravaganza, was intended by George V to mark his accession to the throne and also to mark his desire to be recognized as the titular head of the empire. For those who cared to listen – and the king was not among them – even the Delhi Durbar's glittering pomp could barely stifle the increasingly vociferous grumbling of Indian nationalists while, closer to home, British Cabinet ministers openly and regularly complained that its costs were insupportable. George V, neither as politically astute nor as socially emollient as his father, initially insisted that the Durbar's climax should feature him crowning himself Emperor of India, with a specially commissioned crown costing £60,000.[28] He was sensibly counselled that, given India's politically sensitive condition,[29] this was inadvisable, so instead he chose to be wearing the crown as he arrived at the Durbar.

During the run-up to the Durbar, when Haig's specific responsibility was running the polo committee, he learned at first hand from Smith-Dorrien, a member of the extensive entourage the king had brought with him from England, what was involved in the Aldershot command. He was aghast to learn from Smith-Dorrien that the cost of simply equipping Government House at Aldershot, the C-in-C's residence, would be some £4,500.[30] Smith-Dorrien, three years Haig's senior and leaving Aldershot to take up the post of General Officer in Command (GOC), Southern Command, offered to sell the Haigs the fixtures and fittings he had himself installed. In the event, the Haigs managed to spend a little less than Smith-Dorrien estimated.[31]

The climax of the Durbar on 12 December 1911, amid blazing sunshine and stifling humidity, saw King George V and Queen Mary, in a resplendent open-topped coach and garbed in lavish purple regalia, sedately parade through the new capital of the empire's most prized possession. They traversed the temporary town of 40,000 tents housing the 300,000 Indians invited to attend the ceremony, all of whose expenses had been paid for by the Indian government. In contrast, the British soldiers and their families were required to pay to enjoy the privilege of a momentary glimpse of their new king and queen.

To the echoes of a 101-gun salute, the royal couple processed to the centrepiece of the Durbar, a three-tiered Royal Pavilion, supported by four columns and topped by a large golden dome, bedecked in red cloths. For the king, it was 'the most beautiful and wonderful sight I ever saw', although he later confided that he felt 'rather tired after wearing the Crown for 3½ hours, it hurt my head as it is pretty heavy.'[32] George, after duly reminding his subjects that he intended a seamless continuation of imperial rule, then departed for Nepal on 15 December, after scattering honours around him: Haig was made a Knight Commander of the Indian Empire (KCIE).

Now freed of his Indian responsibilities, Haig handed over to his successor, General Sir Percy Lake, and prepared to depart for England and Aldershot.[33] On 23 December 1911 the Haigs embarked from Bombay on the P&O liner *Oceana* along with 400 other passengers, leaving India forever, although any sadness was quickly displaced by Douglas's fears for the life of his fragile wife; Doris had dysentery, which she believed she had contracted through sleeping in the damp tents at the Durbar. The ship's doctor – not a breed for whom Haig had much respect – gloomily pronounced the end was nigh; but Doris regained her strength and, by the time they arrived at Charing Cross station in London on 11 January 1912, was almost completely better. On the 13th they travelled to Henrietta's house at Radway. At Kineton, the nearest railway station, they were met by their two daughters, who initially did not know what to make of these two strangers: 'The 2 children waiting for us on platform at Kineton. A very happy surprise. Two pretty little girls in red coats and green hats! Doris and the two children and I motor down to Radway and we have tea with the bairns. Doris telegraphs to Henrietta, to Cairo. "Arrived here. Children very well. So grateful for your motherly care of them. Doris." '

The children had suffered their own trials during their parents' absence, the elder, Alexandra – known to her parents as Xandra and still less than four – having undergone surgery for a glandular problem. It was a difficult time for parents and children, re-encountering one another after an absence of sixteen months, a lifetime for children so young. The following day Haig noted: 'Children come in to see us about 8 am. Cannot make their Mother and Daddy out. Doris and I go to Church. [. . .] We walk after lunch with the children.'

The children quickly proved themselves to be very much like the infant Douglas; they were wilful, disobedient, and destructive. Dorothy called them 'our two little monkeys . . . they were up to every conceivable trick they could think of!'[34] Recalcitrant children did not prevent the Haigs enjoying days on the golf course. Douglas also called on his bank, visiting William Shepherd of the Royal Bank of Scotland on 21 February to discuss his loan account, then totalling a substantial £9,300, though Shepherd was pleased to see that Haig had managed to reduce it 'so much. Fife Coal is a very sound investment . . .'

On 28 February, a by now ailing Sir Evelyn Wood congratulated Haig on taking command at Aldershot:

My dear Haig,

Tomorrow you begin where I did in 1889. I like to look back, and it is a real pleasure to think that you'll be helped in every way from the War Office – whereas I was bitterly opposed by the C-in-C [the Duke of Cambridge] in all I tried to do to make the Army a fighting machine. He reprimanded me before all O.C and D. [commanding and deputy] commanders for doing night operations 'I've never done them they are unnecessary and I strongly disapprove.' Poor man. Before a Royal Commission he declared – 'I will never concede to the British Army going into action except in full dress.' He really thought he was right![35]

The British army had certainly moved in the right direction since Wood's days at Aldershot, but not sufficiently far to cope easily with the world war which now lay just over two years away. Haig had done his bit to lay the right foundations while at the War Office; at Aldershot, where he finally took command on 1 March 1912, now in his fiftieth year, he sensibly tried to get his troops into fighting shape. He brought with him two others from his India days, Captain (and later Brigadier-General) John Charteris of the Royal Engineers, a clever man whose indifference to personal hygiene rendered him a standing joke in the Haig household, and Captain Harry Baird of the 12th Cavalry, as his ADC. At Aldershot, Charteris became Haig's Assistant Military Secretary and was to serve by his side for almost all the Great War, when he was placed by Haig in charge of intelligence gathering. Haig also appointed Captain Lord Worsley, Dorothy's brother-in-law and another Freemason, as an extra ADC; Worsley, of the Royal Horse Guards, was fatally wounded near Ypres on 30 October 1914, while manning a machine-gun. Baird and Charteris, neither of whom had any private income, were invited by Haig to live with him and Doris at Government House.

Aldershot's gossips regarded Haig initially as a privileged interloper, referring to him and his Indian cadre as the 'Hindoo Invasion', as Charteris later recalled. Haig was certainly a stranger to the expansive base, set in some 500 hectares of heathland, and which had originally been purchased by the War Office in 1854, home to some 20,000 troops. His reputation as 'Lucky' Haig, together with the suspicion that he owed his rapid rise to his social connections rather than talent, meant he was not warmly welcomed. The suspicion was mutual; Haig's first impressions of the condition of the Aldershot troops were not positive. On 14 March the Haigs visited the Army & Navy store to buy a new thirty-six-piece glass and dinner service for Government House. On the way he observed a company of the Bedford Regiment digging trenches, and inspected some artillery. He was shocked to see some of the infantry wearing coats as they dug, while 'many could not use pick and shovel.' As for the artillery, he found that a 'careful test of our Artillery ammunition shows that half our fuzes are bad!' Haig nevertheless gradually won the hearts and minds of those under his command at Aldershot, partly by holding weekly dinners for senior and junior officers at Government House, and partly by encouraging higher standards of discipline and setting his own good example.

He also became less casual about money than he had been in South Africa, when he could tell Henrietta that a loss of £1,000 of capital was of no great concern. On 26 July 1911, shortly after a visit to Aldershot by George V, he learned from the War Office that he had been selected for recommendation to the king for a 'Reward for Distinguished or Meritorious Service'. This carried an annuity of £100, a useful supplement to his regular salary. The War Office letter stated:

> In view of the fact that the enjoyment of the annuity of £100 is probably of greater moment to some officers than to others, it has been decided that, while all officers who by their service fulfil the conditions should equally be eligible for the honour of being recommended to His Majesty for the reward, an opportunity should be given to officers selected for such recommendation to waive their claim to the annuity, if they should feel that their circumstances were such as to render appropriate that course.

Given his earlier battles to get what he thought his due from the War Office, it is perhaps no surprise that Haig took the money.[36] Haig possessed that characteristic sometimes to be found in the wealthy, of being penny-wise but pound-indifferent. While he never worried about his finances in bigger terms, his petty thriftiness is occasionally surprising. On 31 January 1913 he wrote to his nephew Oliver Haig, who worked for the Haig distillery: 'Please tell me when you write if the jars of whiskey are "filled to the bung" or only with an exact 6 gallons. The reason I ask is that the last jar we received was left standing outside the cellar here before it was put into the cask for a few days as Baird was in Switzerland when it arrived! I noticed when they were about to empty the whiskey into our cask that there was a space of about 3 inches between the liquid & the cork. So I am not certain whether some of our thirsty friends might not have helped themselves before the whiskey was put under lock & key, or whether the jars are sent out <u>not</u> quite full.'[37]

Life at Aldershot was not all golf, dinners and ticking off trench-digging soldiers. One of the most embarrassing episodes of Haig's professional life occurred during long-planned manoeuvres, the first since he took over Aldershot, held in East Anglia in the autumn of 1912. The manoeuvres of 6–22 September 1912 – four days of which, the 16–20th, had been set aside for action by the ground forces – were for Haig a personal humiliation, one he felt particularly keenly as the exercises took place in the presence of the king, who observed the scene from horseback. Even Haig's most ardent recent admirer, John Terraine, reluctantly acknowledged that the 'manoeuvres of 1912 were not a shining hour for Haig.'[38] Yet a closer examination of these manoeuvres suggests that Haig learned from them an abiding lesson, one he carried with him during the Great War – the importance of aircraft.

The East Anglian operations were an opportunity to gauge how a combined regular and territorial British Expeditionary Force might function in practice. Under the direction of Sir John French, now a general, and who in March 1911 had been appointed Chief of the Imperial General Staff in place of Field Marshal Sir William Nicholson, Haig commanded Red Force, which had theoretically invaded England via a landing on the Norfolk coast, and which was intent upon marching on London. The opposing Blue Force, led by the portly but gifted Lieutenant-General Sir James Grierson, was to defend London from south of Cambridge.[39] Haig's force comprised the 1st and 2nd Divisions and the three brigades of the Cavalry Division, all from Aldershot. Grierson's force was numerically and qualitatively weaker, with two infantry divisions but only two cavalry brigades, one from the (volunteer) yeomanry. Each force also had the assistance of a Royal Flying Corps unit consisting of one airship and a squadron of seven aircraft.

Grierson made much better use of the reconnaissance possibilities of his aircraft and out-manoeuvred Haig, concealing his troops from aerial observation while Haig's troops were fully observed from the air. In mitigation, it should be pointed out that Haig was badly let down by the technological limitations of this still experimental air service. In the build-up to the manoeuvres, four aircraft had crashed, causing several fatalities among their pilots and observers, and this left Red Force without wireless contact with the aircraft that were hurriedly substituted. Such technical failures only reinforced the suspicion with which these novel aircraft were regarded by some senior army officers. Indeed, the seriousness of Haig's aerial handicap was quickly established when Blue Force aircraft carried out several early-morning sorties on 16 September and, possessing full air-to-ground wireless communication, rapidly reported back to Grierson the disposition of Red Force. Despite Haig establishing a ground wireless post to try to intercept messages from Blue Force's aircraft and airship, every Red Force action was easily observed by Blue Force aircraft and immediately communicated to the ground. Inevitably, Blue Force came to dominate the 'battlefield' completely, and a premature halt was called to the manoeuvres late in the day of 18 September.[40] Further embarrassment came with the post-manoeuvre conference held on 19 September in the Great Hall of Trinity College, Cambridge University, where the king sat among the audience.

Haig had prepared well beforehand a carefully written speech, having assumed his regulars would outshine the part-time soldiers opposing him. His carefully prepared statement was now rendered utterly irrelevant by events, and, lacking either sufficient time to prepare an appropriate response or any talent for improvisation, he floundered. He merely noted in his diary that: 'I am called upon first to explain my operations as C in C of Red Force. I think my remarks were well received. Grierson followed; then French. His criticisms especially on the strategical value of Cambridge were not generally agreed to.'

Charteris had a very different memory of the episode: 'Although Haig had written out a clear and convincing statement of his views, and held the paper in his hand throughout the Conference, he did not refer to it when he spoke, but to the dismay of his staff attempted to extemporize. In the effort he became totally unintelligible, and unbearably dull. The University dignitaries soon fell fast asleep. Haig's friends became more and more uncomfortable; only he himself seemed totally unconscious of his failure. A listener, without other and deeper knowledge of the ability and personality of the Aldershot Commander-in-Chief, could not but have left the conference with the impression that Haig had neither ability nor military learning. Fortunately the men in responsible positions knew better.'[41]

Grierson, meanwhile, previously sceptical about aircraft, drew in his speech the only sensible conclusion from the manoeuvres – that the aeroplane 'had revolutionised the art of war.' Haig took rather longer to come to the same conclusion – but come to it he did.

Haldane, himself an exceptionally dull public speaker, and the inarticulate George V did not regard Haig's verbal paralysis as a significant handicap, although the loquacious Lloyd George was later to take it as a fatal indication of Haig's stupidity. Haig had much in common with his sovereign. They shared the same dislike of rich food and public occasions, the same distaste for publicity-seeking, and the same devotion to the empire and distrust of politicians. Neither enjoyed travelling on the continent of Europe. They even physically resembled one another.

Haig was wrong-footed in September 1912 but, not for the last time, he had been let down by newfangled military machinery. He was, however, always ready to embrace technological innovations if they worked, and this early, bruising encounter with aircraft ensured he took a keen interest in the Royal Flying Corps during the Great War.

The relationships Haig developed at Aldershot were, as ever, distant, although characteristically he was to remain loyal through thick and thin to those who proved themselves useful and and supportive. This was especially true of Captain Charteris, who repaid Haig during his lifetime by demonstrating intense loyalty, even if after Haig's death Charteris felt no need to disguise his version of events, much to Doris's chagrin. A highly articulate and intelligent man as well as a loyal officer, Charteris, like many who grew to know Haig better over time, felt ambivalent about him.

Doris never disguised her dislike of Charteris and this, together with his servile status in the Haigs' household, sometimes rendered him the butt of foolish practical jokes at their hands. She intensely disliked Charteris's biography of her husband, published in 1929, which she felt was insufficiently reverent. She later took revenge in her own biography by relating how, during a minor blaze at Government House early one morning – which Haig, with the aid of servants, managed to put out before too much damage was done – Charteris was subject to a small but unkind jape. 'Captain Charteris, A.D.C, had appeared in rather dirty-looking pyjamas and, when the fire was extinguished, the flooring was all burnt and we could see anyone passing underneath. Douglas spied Charteris just below and, out of pure mischief, seized the largest jug he could find and poured the contents all over Charteris's head saying, "A very good shot, and," he whispered, "that will clean him!" Captain Baird and myself, who were looking on, could not help roaring with laughter, which ended our experience rather amusingly, and we all went back to our beds quite happy.'[42]

Charteris, who made no mention of this incident in his biography of Haig, no doubt returned to his bed without quite the same degree of hilarity. Such public-school humiliations must have rankled with Charteris and perhaps explain why his usually respectful biography occasionally gently mocks Haig's rigid dedication to trivialities, such as his account of Haig's golf-playing at Aldershot: 'His attack on the citadel of golf was characteristic. He spared no pains to conquer its difficulties. He was determined to succeed. He took lessons from a professional. He practised assiduously. Each stroke was treated as a separate and all-important problem. He was not content until he felt that he had acquired the utmost proficiency within his scope. His ball never left the fairway. His play was as consistent as that of Colonel Bogey himself. If his official handicap was never very low, he was a most difficult opponent to beat.'[43]

While Haig was playing golf and supervising the training of the flower of British regiments, Germany's relations with Britain and France were rapidly deteriorating. The signing of the Entente Cordiale on 8 April 1904 had created an Anglo-French pact of peaceful coexistence, while Britain and Germany were locked in an expensive struggle for naval supremacy, one in which the former had committed itself to a policy of constructing two capital fighting ships for every one built by Germany. Sir Edward Grey, Foreign Secretary, outlined the British position in a speech in the House of Commons on 29 March 1909: '[. . .] if the German navy were superior to ours, they maintaining the army which they do, for us it would not be a question of defeat. Our independence, our very existence would be at stake. [. . .] For us the navy is what the army is to them.'

The Anglo-German race to construct Dreadnoughts, the latest and most powerful type of battleship, was clearly unsustainable in the long term, and the British government sought a rapprochement with Berlin by initiating – ultimately unsuccessful – talks in 1910. By the time war broke out in August 1914, the British Admiralty's annual budget was a staggering £48,800,000.[44] The Agadir crisis in mid–1911, when Germany sent the gunboat *Panther* to the French-controlled Moroccan port of Agadir, came to symbolize the intensifying crisis, in which Britain had informally tied itself to France's fate; under the terms of the Entente Cordiale, Britain recognized France's right to exercise its influence in Morocco. Grey once more carefully summed up Britain's position at the height of the crisis: 'Although we cannot bind ourselves under all circumstances to go to war with France against Germany, we shall also certainly not bind ourselves to Germany not to assist France.'

Lloyd George, using the occasion of his speech at Mansion House as Chancellor of the Exchequer on 21 July 1911, warned Germany that 'if a situation were to be forced upon us in which peace could only be preserved by the surrender of the great and beneficent position Britain has won by centuries of heroism and achievement, by allowing Britain to be treated where her interests were vitally affected as if she were of no account in the Cabinet of nations, then I say emphatically that peace at that price would be a humiliation intolerable for a great country like ours to endure.'[45]

The *Panther* was reluctantly withdrawn, but Germany's determination to face down the Entente was, if anything, strengthened. In February 1912 Haldane, still Secretary of State for War, visited Berlin to discuss how to halt the Anglo-German naval race. He was briefed by Grey, Lloyd George, and Winston Churchill, now First Lord of the Admiralty. His instructions were:

1. Fundamental. Naval superiority recognised as essential to Great Britain. Present German naval programme and expenditure not to be increased, but if possible retarded and reduced.

2. England sincerely desires not to interfere with German Colonial expansion. To give effect to this she is prepared forthwith to discuss whatever the German aspirations in that direction may be. England will be glad to know that there is a field or special points where she can help Germany.

3. Proposals for reciprocal assurances debarring either power from joining in aggressive designs or combinations against the other would be welcome.[46]

Haldane's mission did not offer Germany what it sought: British neutrality in exchange for an agreed limitation to naval expansion. The most Grey could offer was an assurance that Britain would not attack Germany, or join any hostile alliance against it. On 7 February 1912, Kaiser Wilhelm told a tumultuous Reichstag that Germany's naval programme would continue unabated. That might have been bluster, but it was an inauspicious moment for rhetoric. Haldane's discussions were not helped by an inflammatory speech by Churchill in Glasgow on 9 February – when Haldane was still negotiating in Berlin – in which Churchill spoke of British naval strength as a 'necessity' while Germany's naval expansionism was a 'luxury'. The Berlin talks ran into the sand. By May that year Churchill had announced that Britain would build two new ships for every one that came down a German slipway.

Haig's preoccupations at Aldershot at this time were, as always, practical. He produced several reports which have been neglected by historians because, one suspects, they are highly detailed and written without sparkle.[47] They testify both to Haig's commitment to preparing his troops and to the limitations of his comprehension of how the nature of war had altered since the Russo-Japanese war. For example, in his *Review of the Work done during the Training Season, 1912*, Haig sensibly requested that more senior cavalry officers attend the musketry training course at Hythe, to learn 'the practical application of rifle fire to suit various tactical conditions.' He also exhorted that the cavalry should learn how to use machineguns more effectively: 'More attention should be paid to the handling of cavalry machine guns when brigaded. Their drill and manoeuvre should, before departure to practice camp, attain a high standard of efficiency.'

He also wrote a paper for a Staff College conference, posing the question: 'The regimental officer especially in the more junior ranks, is frequently accused of being wanting in what is called imagination. Is it possible to do anything to improve this state of things? Can the General Staff assist?'. His answer was mixed. He proposed a general education 'be given in the schools of the country; the nature of the test of this education for entrance into the military schools being regulated not by the views or requirements of some outside authority but by the General Staff,' followed by 'a general military education of all cadets at one military school designed to continue his [sic] general education.'

More radically, Haig also wanted a dramatic shift of emphasis away from the public-school intake system to one much more focused on university graduates: '. . . to get the greatest mental development at our military schools the system of education should be based more on that of our great universities and less on that of our public schools. The prime difference in the two methods seems to be that whereas in our public schools and also at present in our military colleges, knowledge is imparted in the form of hard facts, to be assimilated by an effort of memory, in the universities a constant series of problems are presented, and the mind of the student is induced to <u>think</u> these out. The reasoning power is thus developed and we get a really educated man – the man who can and does think for himself. Such a man will clearly be capable of taking most advantage of the experience and training which the work can and does afford him and, other things being equal, will himself undoubtedly prove the most efficient officer in war.'

This emphasis by Haig on training the British soldier to 'think for himself' was visionary, and contradicted the kind of schooling at Sandhurst – and even Camberley – that he himself had received. As it was, the business of training soldiers to develop independent thought – prepare them for the unexpected – was managed more successfully in the German army, which inculcated a greater degree of independence in its officers and NCOs. Nor is it incompatible with Haig's preference, expressed earlier, for 'men of good average intelligence'; what Haig always wanted was an army equipped to think, and therefore better able to fight. He also compiled some 'Notes On Infantry Tactics'; these emphasized the importance of not deploying attacking infantry in single lines of advance but instead as small squads rushing forward, taking advantages as they see them, a recommendation that sits uncomfortably with the clichéd (and mistaken) view that he instructed troops at the Somme, for instance, to walk slowly in neat lines over no man's land.

Although Haig made some progress, he was unable to jettison some of his more antiquated and increasingly irrelevant notions. He was, for example, still devoted to the cavalry's glory. In his *Comments on the Training Season for 1913* sits this rebuke to Aldershot's cavalry (and also, implicitly, to the infantryman Smith-Dorrien), for failing to charge in the 'correct' manner: 'The General Officer Commanding-in-Chief [i.e. Haig] had occasion to comment on the manner in which the charge is delivered. [. . .] There must be no depth, no hanging back of men in the rear rank, strict preservation of two ranks, troop leaders at their proper distances in front, the gallop must be quite uniform and even, and no restiveness of horses getting out of hand. All other charges, especially when the men open out, must be considered failures. The compactness and force of the charge depends on the good order and calm of the squadron during the gallop preceding the charge.'

To train cavalry to conduct gallop charges in 1913 seems somewhat absurd, but only in retrospect. If the cavalry was to be maintained, then logically it needed to be trained properly to perform one of its main functions, to charge in tight formation to thereby maximize its shock impact. That this was a pointless exercise can only be judged, despite the evidence of the Russo-Japanese war, in hindsight. Haig was by no means the only British commander who, in 1913, imagined that a continental war in Europe would be one in which swift movement would be a dominant feature of the battlefield. Haig's undying ambition was that the cavalry should be able both to charge properly *and* to be good shots when dismounted: he noted with some pride in 1913 that 77.8 per cent of Aldershot's rank and file cavalry were 'reliable shots (ie marksmen and 1st class shots)' compared with 62.9 per cent of the garrison's infantry.

Haig's busy professional life at Aldershot did not mean he neglected the family business, in which he remained attentively, although distantly, involved. On 21 January 1913 he wrote from Aldershot to his nephew Oliver, describing a meeting in London that morning with his brother John, who also worked for J. Haig & Co in a sales capacity, together with the firm's manager. At the meeting it had been agreed that John would get 10 per cent of profits of new accounts and 5 per cent where 'we already have an agent'. Haig discussed the firm's plans to open up exports to North America and Germany, and revealed he had written to the company auditor to ask if he was genuinely entitled to receive a salary as a director:[48] 'In my opinion the responsibilities of a Director of a Company were now so serious that we ought to be quite sure of our ground in every case and that I'd like to have Gourlay's [the company auditor] opinion sometime as to whether we the Directors cd. vote ourselves £50 apiece as salary! In fact I question whether I am legally correct in taking it, having regard to the amount of work which I do for the Company! I have not heard from him in reply – perhaps he is thinking over his own emoluments which he gives himself!'

He even found time to consider the firm's advertising. Oliver Haig had asked his views about putting up billboards. It was Haig's view that: 'It is a mistake to be in too great a hurry in putting up these big signs, because so much depends on the position in which each one is put; and a few days spent in selecting the best site for each one will repay you well [. . .] I suppose the whisky can be bought at every place where the advt. is shewn? [. . .] As regards the big signboards! I agree with your proposals for the North of England, but instead of Willesden and Grantham, I suggest Brighton, Birmingham, Bristol or Southampton as better for the South, with a couple in London if its possible to get 2 good sites!'[49]

Less than two months after Haig was considering advertising poster sites, the British army was thrown into fresh and completely unexpected turmoil, the reverberations of which affected some senior officers' career prospects far into the Great War. In what became known as the Curragh Incident,[50] in March 1914 a number of senior British officers based in Ireland – including Brigadier-General Sir Hubert de la Poer Gough, then in command of the 3rd Cavalry Brigade at the Curragh – threatened to resign their commissions rather than face the prospect, which they believed imminent, of being ordered to fight the Ulster Unionists, who had formed armed militias to resist the threatened introduction of Home Rule. Gough and Major-General Henry Wilson, then Director of Military Operations at the War Office, both staunch Anglo-Irish Protestants, showed themselves ready and willing to put personal political allegiances above duty and obedience in those tense weeks in March, with Wilson – of whom it was said he got into a state of sexual excitement whenever he saw a politician – duplicitously, and strictly against Army regulations, feeding gossip to Bonar Law, the leader of the opposition, about the mood of the army.

The Curragh Incident was a muddled mess of misunderstandings. The political reliability of a small number of senior army officers became questionable as a result, but Haig's role in the affair was minor. When his opinion was canvassed by Hubert Gough, whose brother, John Gough, was one of Haig's ADCs at Aldershot, Haig exhorted the dissident officers to keep calm, obey orders, and accept political authority. He sent a telegram to Hubert Gough: 'Hope you will not act precipitately I feel equally strongly on subject as you know there is no question of Army fighting against Protestants or against Catholics our duty is to keep the peace between them. Haig Beach Hotel Littlehampton.'

Given Haig's strong dislike of Roman Catholicism and distrust of its adherents, this was a remarkably balanced and apolitical telegram to send to Gough, whom Haig much admired. Haig genuinely always sought to keep himself, and the army that he adored, above politics. It was a commendable stance to take and one rather more decisive than that adopted by Sir John French.

French was exposed during the Curragh affair as a ditherer under pressure. In addition, his uneven temperament, an unfortunate cocktail of the sybaritic and the splenetic, his inability to speak French, a disinclination to grapple with the tedious but vital tasks of logistics, and his readiness to distort the truth to avoid personal responsibility all made him a poor choice for the task of C-in-C when war broke out in August 1914. Although after the Curragh debacle concluded French was all for coercing and disciplining the fractious officers, he nevertheless resigned as CIGS,[51] reluctantly accepting some responsibility for the fracas. Churchill's impression of French after the Curragh affair was that he was 'a heart-broken man'.[52]

In July 1914, approaching sixty, French was made Inspector-General of the Army, although he tacitly remained the British Expeditionary Force's (BEF) C-in-C designate. For Churchill, who had been snubbed by French during the South African War in 1900 and with whom he did not enjoy good relations until he became a government minister, French was nevertheless 'a natural soldier. Although he had not the intellectual capacity of Haig, nor perhaps his underlying endurance, he had a deeper military insight. He was not equal to Haig in precision of detail; but he had more imagination, and he would never have run the British Army into the same long drawn-out slaughters.'[53]

This does not accord with the facts. In 1914 and 1915 French proved himself both incompetent to manage a large, complex expeditionary force, and too weak to oppose his seniors, Kitchener especially, when commanded to carry out offensives he felt were unwise. Haig played a very straight bat during the Curragh affair and demonstrated that he did not wish to become professionally entangled in political matters, no matter that privately he was as much opposed to Irish Home Rule as Gough, Wilson or many other senior officers. Very shortly, however, the domestic imbroglio over Ireland was to be overshadowed by the global repercussions of a far more serious international incident, the assassination of the heir to the throne of the Austro-Hungarian empire. Haig was soon to find it impossible to stand aside from the world of political intrigue that he so loathed.

# CHAPTER EIGHT

# 'This War Will Last Many Months'

We have to make war as we must, and not as we should like to.

Lord Kitchener

Few saw the assassination by Gavrilo Princip of the Austrian Archduke Franz Ferdinand, heir-presumptive to the Austro-Hungarian throne, and his wife Sophie, at Sarajevo on 28 June 1914 as the spark that would set Europe ablaze. While Haig had, since before his days at the War Office, expected that Britain would eventually be forced to go to war with Germany, he always hoped his task was that of preparing the army for a conflict which might never come. At Aldershot, peacetime manoeuvres and territorial training carried on as usual during July 1914; on the day of the assassination itself, Haig was in France attending exercises with the French army.

According to Thomas Secrett, the French generals 'saw trouble' arising from the Sarajevo murders, while Haig 'always took rather an odd view about a great European war ever breaking out. He considered such an event possible, but thought it more probable that the politicians at the last minute would come to some sort of an arrangement, and perhaps be strong enough to stop the whole business. [. . .] he always took the view that if and when we became embroiled, the Navy would settle matters before the armies ever got an opportunity of coming to grips.'[1]

A full month elapsed following the assassination before Aldershot received the first official inkling that war was imminent, in the form of a War Office communiqué on 29 July instructing it to enter into a 'precautionary period', the preliminary to full mobilization. On 3 August, a public holiday in Britain, Germany declared war on France and reports reached London of Germany's ultimatum to Belgium, demanding free passage for its troops en route to France. When Belgium refused, Germany declared war on it, too. On 4 August at 5pm mobilization orders were issued for the British army and at midnight the War Office telegraphed Haig: 'War has broken out with Germany'.

That day Haig's sister Henrietta sent him a note written in pencil: 'Tell Douglas with my love and blessing to go forward without fear because God will watch over and guide him. And he will return covered with glory – He is not to feel anxious about Doris and the children as all will be well with them. Douglas must not forget to ask for the blessing of God on his great campaign because nothing happens by accident and God blesses those who ask Him for it. Now get ready & keep a brave face and a light heart for all the people at Aldershot are so dejected it will cheer those you meet if you can give out a happy atmosphere. I am not deceiving you or Douglas He will come back with honour.'[2]

This, Henrietta claimed, had been dictated to her by their dead brother George, and it was the first of numerous such communications she sent to Douglas during the war. Haig was the recipient – willing or otherwise – of many supposed spirit messages both from Henrietta and, occasionally, from complete strangers, during the Great War. Haig may have regarded all of them as nonsense but he never openly disparaged those he was sent by Henrietta. And of course, despite our rational scepticism, the dead George was ultimately proved right. On 4 August 1914 it was clear to all, to Haig more urgently than some, that the British Expeditionary Force (BEF) could initially play no more than a junior role in France and Belgium. Haig was by now one of Britain's most thoroughly professional soldiers, with a depth and range of practical field experience and War Office schooling that was unsurpassed. That victory would be achieved only at heavy cost very few, including Haig and Kitchener, immediately recognized; both anticipated from the outset that the struggle would be long and bitter. One of Haig's first actions after war was declared was to write to Haldane, who on 2 August had taken over as Secretary of State for War

– a post previously held by Herbert Asquith, the Liberal Prime Minister – while retaining his position as Lord Chancellor. That Haig possessed a clear vision of how the war would go, at least in the early stages, is evident from this letter, in which he expressed his anxiety that, in the rush to assist France, the regular army would be carelessly thrown into battle and thus lose experienced officers and NCOs who would be vital to train the future volunteer national army Haig expected would become necessary in the long term. This fear was to be proved fully justified by the end of 1914; the BEF, the bulk of Britain's regular army, was to be destroyed on the Western Front in the first five months of the war.

Haig therefore floated the idea to Haldane that the dispatch of the BEF should be delayed, so that the territorials and regulars could be put together to create an army sufficiently well-trained to survive the initial calamity:

[. . .] This war will last many months, possibly years, so I venture to hope that our only bolt (and that not a very big one) may not suddenly be shot on a project of which the success seems to me quite doubtful – I mean the checking of the German advance into France. Would it not be better to begin at once to enlarge our Expedy. Force by amalgamating less regular forces with it? In three months time we shd. have quite a considerable army so that when we do take the field we can act decisively and dictate terms which will ensure a lasting peace.

I presume of course that France can hold on (even though her forces have to fall back from the frontier) for the necessary time for us to create an army of say 300,000.[3]

In a prescient postscript Haig added:

I have dashed off this letter on reading the leader in today's Times on Lord K [Kitchener]. What I feel is that we have such a mass of undeveloped power which no one knows better than yourself how to organise and control. This will be impossible if the bulk of our highly trained regular officers are at once carted off to France and a Secretary of State is appointed who is new to the existing system.

As it was, Haldane held the post of Secretary of State for War for just four days; on 6 August, borne aloft on a torrent of newspaper acclamation, Kitchener took over. He had not wanted the job and was already on the boat train to Calais, returning to Egypt, on 4 August. Forced into accepting Kitchener against his better judgement – he later claimed to have considered it 'a hazardous experiment'[4] – Asquith would have preferred Haldane remained in this key position, but the virulently anti-German public mood would not have tolerated that. Haldane's political influence, once so unassailable, waned rapidly; by late 1915 there was no room in government for the man who had laid the basis for the British army's being able to endure to the end.

Much to the chagrin of the more junior Sir John French, who was duly appointed the BEF's C-in-C on the outbreak of war, Kitchener wore his field marshal's uniform throughout the war, despite his essentially civilian role. Kitchener's appointment was a mixed blessing. His inspirational energy and vision were vital in building the scale of army that was required; but his contempt for politicians, his autocratic and occasionally devious style, and his prickly relationship with Sir John created all manner of frictions that made management of the war more difficult than it might have been. But unlike Sir John, Kitchener had one great asset; his instincts were usually correct.

Kitchener and French, who had not seen each other since their time in South Africa, twelve years previously, were almost immediately at loggerheads, over both where the BEF should form up on the continent and the likely length of the conflict: Sir John was adamant that the war would be brief; Kitchener was equally convinced it would not. As for the deployment of the BEF, the Committee of Imperial Defence had decided on 24 July 1909 that, in a continental European war, Britain would send four infantry divisions in support of France; these plans envisaged that the BEF would be required to fight at most a six-month campaign. This scheme was largely the brainchild of Major-General Henry Wilson, an ardent Francophile, a fluent French speaker, a personal friend of senior French generals and, moreover, a long-standing rival of Haig's. As Director of Military Operations at the War Office in June 1910, Wilson had taken it on himself to steer pre-war contingency plans for any continental deployment of a British force to ensure that it would position itself on the left wing of the French army. France, meanwhile, would go to war according to Plan XVII, which had been drawn up by the French C-in-C, General Joseph Joffre.

Plan XVII, which became effective in May 1914, was the culmination of years of French preparations designed to prevent in any future conflict the kind of humiliating defeat the country had suffered at the hands of Prussia in 1870. It was drawn up partly on the basis of French knowledge of German map exercise plans from 1905, in which it appeared that German thinking was to contain the Belgian army to the north, while attacking Lorraine in the south, with Verdun, Nancy and St. Dié as possible objectives. A pre-determination to carry out an offensive through the Ardennes to counter the anticipated German attack there was a key element of Plan XVII, which was formally silent on the deployment of a British Expeditionary Force. As the historian Hew Strachan has put it, 'Britain's job was to prevent a quick German victory.' German plans, meanwhile, were elaborations of a very general scheme drawn up in 1905 by Alfred von Schlieffen, then German chief of staff, who insisted it was vital to achieve a quick surrender of the French army in order to avoid fighting a war on two fronts, against France in the west and Russia in the east. His successor, Helmuth von Moltke the younger, believed Schlieffen's hopes were too optimistic, based as they were on an assumption that the French would remain on the defensive and not leave themselves open to a sweeping northern envelopment. Both theories fairly rapidly foundered on the rocks of reality.[5]

On 5 August, Haig was passed by a medical board as fit for home and overseas service. Later that day he attended a meeting of the War Council at 10 Downing Street, chaired by Asquith,[6] where Sir John French insisted that, in view of the tardy mobilization – it was to be a further three weeks before the BEF was fully deployed on the continent – and the rapidly changing situation, the BEF should link up with the Belgian army at Antwerp rather than, as originally planned, join the left flank of the French army at Maubeuge. Haig strongly disagreed with his erstwhile mentor. He recommended instead that the BEF should abide by the original plan, adding that 'our best policy at the present time was to be ready to do as the French wished us.'[7] He also claimed to have made three general points, all of which proved valid in the years ahead:

1st. That Great Britain and Germany would be fighting for their existence. Therefore the war was bound to be a long war, and neither would acknowledge defeat after a short struggle. [. . .] I held that we must organise our resources for a War of several years. 2nd. Great Britain must at once take in hand the creation of an Army. I mentioned one million as the number to aim at immediately, remarking that this was the strength originally proposed for the Territorial Force by Lord Haldane. Above all, we ought to aim at having a strong and effective force when we came to discuss peace at a Conference of the Great Powers. 3rd. We only had a small number of trained Officers and N.C.Os. These must be economised. The need for efficient instructors would at once become apparent. I urged that a considerable proportion of Officers and N.C.Os should be withdrawn forthwith from the Expeditionary Force. (This latter suggestion met with much opposition from Sir J. French, with the result that only 3 Officers per Battalion were retained in England from the Battalions now ordered to France). Lastly, my advice was to send as strong an Expeditionary Force as possible, and as soon as possible, to join the French Forces and to arrange to increase that Force as rapidly as possible.[8]

Many of those gathered at this first session of the War Council were already at loggerheads, and remained so throughout the war. Henry Wilson described it as 'an historic meeting of men, mostly entirely ignorant of their subject'.[9] Privately, Haig had concluded that Sir John French would not be up to the job of commanding the BEF. If French was unfit, so too was the BEF, despite its professional ethos.

The British army's typical soldier was a hardy creature, accustomed to daily marches of twenty miles while carrying a forty-pound pack, as well as greatcoat, rifle and ammunition. The men who went to France in August 1914 were toughened by their working-class and rural labouring backgrounds and had been moulded into an impressively disciplined army. Six in every ten of them were reservists who had already spent up to nine years in the regular army before passing into the reserves. The BEF's biggest defect was that it was, by comparison with the enemy it was to face, pitiably small, consisting of some 160,000 men, out of a total army strength which, even if augmented by the part-time soldiers of the territorial divisions, was only about 400,000. At the start of the war it was not even clear how many of the Territorials would agree to serve overseas. In late 1913 the Territorials numbered slightly more than 245,000, of which less than 10 per cent volunteered to serve overseas on mobilisation. The conscript armies of France and Germany were much larger. When war broke out each could summon a full, mobilized army of almost four million. On the Western Front, two million Germans faced 1.7 million Frenchmen: it would be a close match.

The professional BEF was essentially Victorian in its outlook. One newly commissioned officer in the 2nd Cameronians recalled: 'We were, I suppose, very innocent by modern standards. [. . .] Right was right, and wrong was wrong and the Ten Commandments were an admirable guide. There was no obsession with sex, drink and drugs. The approach to sex was perfectly normal, whilst the horror of V.D was very real. A "homosexual" was a bugger and beyond the Pale. [. . .] Frugality, austerity and self-control were then perfectly acceptable. We believed [sic] honour, patriotism, self-sacrifice and duty, and we clearly understood what was meant by "being a gentleman." '[10]

This collection of convictions, characteristic of the pre-Great War British officer class, crumbled in later years as a massive influx of temporary officers from all walks of life – sometimes dubbed 'temporary gentlemen' by snobbish regular officers – gradually replaced the losses of the regular army. The walls that divided the various branches of the army – infantry, cavalry and artillery – in 1914, with each acting as an independent entity, were much greater obstacles to fighting efficiency, and crumbled much more slowly. And while the BEF's mobilization was conducted proficiently, it was also distressingly short of the two weapons which came to dominate the battlefield, machine-guns and heavy artillery.

Each battalion of 600–800 officers and men had two Maxim machine-guns[11] in 1914 (there were 150 for the whole BEF), and four by February 1915; the German army possessed more than 80 times as many Maxims in August 1914, an estimated 12,000. Haig had long known of the usefulness of machine-guns and reiterated his belief in the need for both more guns and more intelligent use of them.[12]

As for artillery, when the BEF arrived in France it had 490 guns, twenty-four of which were medium and the rest light field guns and howitzers, predominantly 18-pounders; there was no heavy artillery of the kind possessed by the Germans and which came to dominate the war.[13] The War Office had posited that the 18-pounder field gun – the British army's standard piece – would require 1,000 shells per gun; another 300 shells would be held in reserve, and an additional 500 shells serve as replenishment over the next six months. With a firing rate of 240 shells per hour, the British army's main artillery weapon could thus be used for a total of seven and a half hours during the first six months of any conflict.[14] There was no immediate shortage of rifles; Britain's arms manufacturers were capable of producing some 47,000 rifles annually in 1914, although wastage of this basic infantry weapon meant the require-ment by July 1915 was for 1.1 million a year.[15]

All armies on the Western Front in 1914 had cavalry, although the swiftly imposed stalemate condemned most cavalry to fight dismounted in support of hard-pressed infantrymen. The Germans assigned such importance to cavalry at the start of the war that of the eleven cavalry divisions they possessed, they placed ten on the Western Front. The British cavalry, however, was the most efficient and also the most readily prepared to dismount and fight. Moreover, unlike the French and German cavalry, it was equipped with rifles rather than carbines, mean-ing that its firepower when dismounted proved as effective as that of the infantry.

British military thinking at the start of the war, dominated by senior officers from the cavalry and infantry, still held that the most correct form of gunnery was direct fire at an enemy in plain view, using shrapnel at a maximum range of 1,200 yards. This was considered to be not only more effective but also more attuned to a war of movement; the guns needed to be close up to the infantry, both to boost their morale and also to be ready to move at a moment's notice, to take advantage of the capture of enemy positions. There were alternatives, and indirect fire at an unseen enemy had by 1914 become a well-established practice and earned its place in the British army's artillery manuals. But in the early stages of the Great War artillery officers, who were often subordinate to more senior commanders from the cavalry or infantry who understood little of the technical aspects of indirect fire, were usually directed to carry out direct-fire gunnery in close support of the infantry. The 18-pounder was certainly an ideal weapon for a war of movement and its range initially proved sufficient. When, however, the mobile phase of the war ended, and German troops began constructing ever deeper defences, this light artillery quickly proved ineffectual. The static warfare of late 1914 onwards dictated a much greater use of high-explosive shells, shortages of which were to plague the BEF right up to mid–1916. In any case, the 18-pounder's effectiveness was dependent on it being brought as close to the front lines as possible, which inevitably rendered it more vulnerable to counter-battery fire.

Battlefield communications at the start of the war were largely limited to what could be carried via a messenger or spoken down an all too vulnerable telephone line. Mobile wireless communications were in their infancy and signalling by flags, Morse code and pigeons was still commonplace. In the absence of instant and reliable communications, battle plans drawn up by commanders normally consisted of highly detailed timetables for movements of troops, supplies of ammunition and food, and sequences of attack. These plans were consequently highly inflexible and any junior officer on the ground who deviated from them risked his career. They were also thrown into confusion when the unexpected happened, as it almost always did. Things were eventually to change by mid–1918, when radio technology became more widely deployed, but essentially both the Allied and German armies fought the bulk of the war half-blinded by bad weather and intermittently deaf. These material shortcomings of the British army were bad enough, but they were compounded by the grotesque command and control structure of the BEF, with Kitchener in London believing and acting as though he were the sole strategic planner and Sir John French equally convinced that his experience of the daily practicalities in charge of the BEF meant he should exercise sole operational control. This uneasy tension between London and the field commander was never resolved.

The implications of static battlefield conditions had long been acknowledged in theory – but they were not expected in practice. In principle, French himself knew what was coming. In 1906 he had drawn some sensible lessons from the Russo-Japanese war, commenting that in the future, 'we shall have battles lasting for several days, troops probably perfectly stationary, and firing at one another in the hours of daylight, whilst all movements in attack, whether infantry or artillery, and all entrenching, whether in attack or defence, will have to be done under cover of darkness. This is a subject upon which we cannot spend too much time, or give too much attention to.'[16]

In 1897 a relatively obscure Polish banker named Ivan Stanislavovic Bloch[17] had argued that technological developments would produce a static battlefield in which no side would find victory. Translated into English in 1899, Bloch's massive *The War of the Future in its Technical, Economic and Political Aspects*[18] asserted that 'there will be increased slaughter on so terrible a scale as to render it impossible to get troops to push the battle to its decisive issue. They will try to, thinking that they are fighting under the old conditions, and they will learn such a lesson that they will abandon the attempt forever [. . .] Everyone will be entrenched in the next war.'[19]

The difficulty was that Bloch's work was far too long and detailed for easy digestion. Written by a civilian – another black mark against it – *The War of the Future* smelled rather like another contemporary dystopian fantasy, coming as it did just a year after H. G. Wells' *The War of the Worlds*. In June and July 1901, Bloch, who insisted his dense six-volume work was scientifically based and not in the least capricious, argued with British army officers at meetings of the Royal United Services Institute in London[20] that new technologies – among them smokeless gunpowder, which meant a soldier no longer betrayed his position every time he fired a shot, and improved long-range firearms – had altered the nature of battle. Bloch's opinions were respectfully listened to, yet they directly contradicted the military spirit of the age, which reasserted the dominance of the shock offensive, considered to be more likely to achieve victory.

It was axiomatic in military thinking of all combatant nations that what made the ultimate difference between victory and defeat was the quality and morale of the individual soldier. The emphasis given to the infantry's tactical attacks in the early days of the Great War has occasionally been depicted as a quasi-mystical assertion of the battle-winning superiority of well-trained soldiers, whose high morale would let nothing halt their charge. There was a severely practical edge to this, however; only through encouraging a sense of their invincibility could field commanders hope to convince infantry that they could win through against the terrifying improvements in firepower, such as breech-loading rifles, rapid-firing light artillery, and machine-guns. While all recognised that the massed-rank infantry charge of old was utterly suicidal, the occupation of the enemy's ground remained the one certain proof of victory – meaning that an attack was at some stage a necessity. The risk was that such an attack could result in the first waves being massacred, lowering morale among those succeeding. One historian, Anthony Clayton, has asserted that French offensive doctrine held that: 'The army would destroy its opponents by the sheer audacity and violence of attacks pushed to the limit, regardless of casualties. All that was needed was knowledge of the enemy positions, clear orders for an attack, and local superiority in numbers. Rigid unquestioning obedience to orders was heavily emphasized. Any other form of operational art was contrary to the true nature of warfare.'[21]

Such a doctrine had profound implications for the French army's use of artillery. Because overwhelming shock and speed were at the core of French infantry tactics, they had come to rely almost on a single type of gun, the 75-mm quick-firing field piece, designed to provide extremely high rates of fire over relatively short distances. The 75 was good at drenching the enemy's front lines with shrapnel, but when their offensives failed the French were left without the kind of accurate heavy artillery that the war soon demanded.[22] *Offense à la outrance* dominated the minds of both Allied and German[23] commanders in the first months of the war, although in practice it brought not victory but huge losses. By 29 August, French casualties were 260,000, including 75,000 killed.[24] By 6 September, German losses were equally horrendous – a total of 265,000 killed, wounded and missing.[25] Bloch had been proved right.

In London, the War Council resumed its deliberations on 6 August 1914, and decided to send four infantry (the 1st, 2nd, 3rd and 5th) and one cavalry division to France, to form up on the left wing of the seventy French divisions then opposing the seventy-two German divisions intent on driving through northern France to Paris. Haig had by now been appointed GOC of the BEF's I Corps, General Sir James Grierson GOC of II Corps.[26] On Tuesday 11 August King George V and Queen Mary visited Aldershot to bid farewell to its departing soldiers. Haig recorded in his diary a significant moment of the monarch's visit that day:

> The King seemed delighted that Sir John French had been appointed to the Chief Command of the Expeditionary Force. He asked me my opinion. I told him at once, as I felt it my duty to do so, that from my experience with Sir John in the South African War, he was certain to do his utmost loyally to carry out any orders which the Government might give him. I had my grave doubts, however, whether either his temper was sufficiently even, or his military knowledge sufficiently thorough to enable him to discharge properly the very difficult duties which will devolve upon him during the coming operations with the Allies on the Continent. In my own heart, I know that French is quite unfit for this great Command at a time of crisis in our Nation's History. But I thought it sufficient to tell the King that I had 'doubts' about the selection.[27]

Haig's private blackballing of French to George V in this manner has provoked ferocious criticism of him over the years, the suggestion being that Haig's supposed betrayal was motivated by his hope of replacing French. But it is not that simple. For one thing, Haig's written eloquence always excelled his verbal; he is unlikely to have expressed himself to the king in this carefully precise manner. We cannot know the exact tone of the conversation, nor the degree to which Haig saw this as an opportunity to undermine the king's confidence in French. Haig faced a difficult choice when asked such a direct question; he could either lie to his sovereign or speak his mind. George V sought the opinion of many senior army officers on a variety of military topics; he no doubt also asked Sir John French his opinion of Haig and Grierson. Moreover, at this stage of the war Haig was not the only or indeed the obvious choice to replace Sir John French as C-in-C. Generals Sir Horace Smith-Dorrien, Sir Herbert Plumer, Sir William Robertson and Sir Ian Hamilton[28] all enjoyed the king's esteem and, despite the backstabbing that was rife at the highest levels of the British army, were reasonable contenders.[29] Some were senior to Haig and each could have laid a serious claim to have been considered as a successor to Sir John French, with the possible exception of Robertson, whose lack of experience in field command told against him. Had he lived, Grierson would have been a particularly strong candidate.[30]

We know that Haig took every passing opportunity to boost his own chances of promotion, as did all his contemporaries, but in giving his honest answer to the king on 11 August 1914 all that can be said with certainty is that Haig had a variety of plausible motives, not all of them dishonourable. It is also true that, given the haste and confusion of the first few months of the war, the position of the BEF's C-in-C, who was often in the dark about the French high command's intentions and actions, and who lacked adequate resources to cope with a vastly superior enemy, was well nigh untenable. 'Lucky' Haig was fortunate *not* to be C-in-C at the start of the war; had he been so, he might have been ground down by Kitchener in precisely the same manner as was Sir John.

As he left Aldershot Haig's military manservant, Thomas Secrett, was handed a lunch basket by Doris, with the words: 'There you are, Sergeant, that will do for you to pack the General's meals in. I am sure it will bring you luck. I know you will look after him.'[31] Doris's lunch basket stayed with Haig throughout the war, and he invariably used it on his many visits to the forward lines. The Haigs' two young daughters meanwhile were, in the words of the rather unmaternal Dorothy, 'packed off' to

North Wales under the charge of her twin sister, where they remained – apart from a few brief visits home when their father was back on leave – until almost the end of the war.[32]

On 13 August, Haig was informed by Sir John French that a decision had been made to concentrate the BEF in the vicinity of Le Cateau and Wassigny, far too close to the German armies in Haig's opinion, given their rapid advance through Belgium and northern France. In the typed version of his diary for that day, Haig reiterated his unease about French's suitability as C-in-C, but averred he would not sabotage his former mentor: 'I am determined to behave as I did in the South African War, namely, to be thoroughly loyal and do my duty as a subordinate should, trying all the time to see Sir John's good qualities and not his weak ones.'[33]

Privately, however, in his diaries and in letters to Doris and others, Haig criticized not only the C-in-C, but also offered snap judgements on junior officers he encountered.[34] While strictly against Army Regulations,[35] which forbade personal correspondence on military matters, this laxity was common to all the BEF's senior commanders, not least French himself. Sir John French's attention was not entirely focused on the war: he juggled trench maps and artillery barrage schedules with Dover–London railway timetables, fitting in attendances at War Office meetings with visits to his latest – and lasting – mistress, Mrs Winifred Bennett. French wrote frequently to Mrs Bennett, revealing all manner of confidential matters: 'He laments the death of friends and the frightful losses in battle; makes frequent references, usually unflattering, about the French leaders; complains bitterly about Kitchener and the War Office; [. . .] He discusses, sometimes in surprising detail, his forthcoming plans and preparations for battle; reports on his own movements, troop deployments, and the itineraries of eminent visitors to the front.'[36]

Throughout the Great War Haig himself kept a detailed hand-written diary, a running commentary on and assessment of the situation on the Western Front, its key personalities and developments. He regularly sent a copy of this via King's Messengers[37] to Doris in England, which she diligently typed up. Haig's motive for keeping such a detailed account of his time in France is unclear.[38] He had always sporadically kept a diary and, as the war dragged on, he became more conscious of the momentousness of what he was caught up in and his diary became the main outlet for his view of events and personalities. As well as his daily diary, he also wrote and had sent on his behalf many letters, mostly to Doris (she received the first from him on 19 August 1914) but also to family, friends, and rich hangers-on who, through this correspondence with Haig, enjoyed the illusory sense of being closer to mighty affairs.[39]

Haig spent the night of 13 August 1914 at the Dolphin Hotel in South-ampton. Henrietta and William Jameson drove down from London the next day, and along with John Charteris, now in charge of intelligence in I Corps, John Gough, Haig's chief of general staff, and his ADC, Major Harry Baird, they enjoyed a farewell 'sumptuous' lunch with several bottles of champagne, brought by Henrietta. On the evening of 14 August, I Corps embarked from Southampton to France; Haig sailed on the SS *Comrie Castle* and, after an uncomfortably cramped night, reached Le Havre early next morning.[40]

On its arrival in France, the BEF was immediately caught up in a confusing turmoil. It lacked clear lines of deployment and was without reliable means of communication; these difficulties were compounded by an immediate and enduring mutual contempt between Sir John French and General Charles Lanrezac, commander of the French Fifth Army on the far left of the French line. Lanrezac's army faced the German Second Army and was outnumbered by more than two to one. French was also burdened with orders from Kitchener that contained an unhelpful but probably inescapable ambiguity. While Sir John's command was to be 'entirely independent', he was also to 'support and cooperate with the French Army against our common enemies'. This inherent contradiction at the heart of the Anglo-French alliance on the Western Front – where did independence end and cooperation begin? – lasted almost until the war's end, creating endless problems for both Sir John and, later, Haig, as well as providing fertile ground for disputatious historians ever since.[41]

In the first weeks of the war the German army's swoop through Belgium threatened the Channel ports, which were crucial for any rapid evacuation of the BEF, should that prove necessary. The French army, under General Joffre, initially persuaded that the German attack on Belgium was a feint, ignored intelligence reports of German dispositions and rolled out Plan XVII's offensive in the Ardennes. As the true nature of Germany's intentions became more apparent, Joffre ordered the French Fifth Army under Lanrezac, on the left wing, to attack at Charleroi, an industrial town on the River Sambre. On 21 August the German Second Army crossed the Sambre to attack Lanrezac's forces and, as the French retreated, the belatedly arriving BEF found itself fully exposed to the brunt of the German offensive, at Mons, with six German divisions threatening to envelop its left flank.

That same day, the BEF's II Corps, now under the command of Smith-Dorrien since the death of Grierson, came under heavy fire in the vicinity of Mons; they stood their ground, but by 23 August the French Fifth Army fell back in confusion along its whole front, as the Germans occupied the fortress town of Namur; Sir John French later claimed it was twenty-four hours before he was informed that the French offensive had been abandoned. The first contingents of the British 4th Division began arriving the next day and took their position on the extreme left of the BEF, coinciding with Sir John French's withdrawal of his GHQ from Le Cateau to Saint Quentin. By 24 August the British, now dangerously exposed, had no choice but to withdraw; I and II Corps were now separated by the Forest of Mormal, with Haig's I Corps, to the east of the forest, heading south to Landrecies.

In a fast-changing situation that threatened to turn into a rout, Sir John French ordered Smith-Dorrien to pull back still further his by now exhausted II Corps, but Smith-Dorrien pleaded that this was impossible; his troops were unable to move and must make a stand at Le Cateau, to the west of the Forest of Mormal. General Sir Edmund Allenby, GOC Cavalry Division, had informed Smith-Dorrien in the early hours of 26 August that his cavalry regiments were scattered across a wide area; they would not be able to cover the retreat of II Corps, as commanded of Smith-Dorrrien by the C-in-C.[42]

In the surrounding confusion, Haig's war almost came to an early end. In the hours before dawn on 24 August, he and Major Harry Baird drove forward along roads crowded with panic-stricken refugees, to the village of Givry. Haig was hunting for the HQ of 6 Brigade in order to give it instructions to withdraw, but soon discovered he was instead heading for the German lines. He and Baird rapidly reversed direction back to their own lines. Later that day, Haig made arrangements for I Corps to retire to the village of Landrecies.

On the evening of 24 August, at the village of Vieux Mesnil, Haig was struck down by a severe attack of diarrhoea and 'was at his worst, very rude' but took some medicine which, according to Charteris, 'must have been designed for elephants, for the result was immediate and volcanic!' Next day, Haig's entourage reached Landrecies late in the afternoon. In the evening, a company of Coldstream Guards, defending the road leading into the town, came under what at first appeared to be a heavy attack. Unaware of the true extent of the force in front of him, Haig asked for reinforcements from II Corps but Smith-Dorrien, who was facing an equally fierce onslaught, could not help. For once, says Charteris, 'Haig was quite jolted out of his usual placidity. He said, "If we are caught, by God, we'll sell our lives dearly." '[43] Landrecies was turned upside down by the Coldstreams, who rapidly built barricades with whatever was to hand, but the next morning their retreat continued unimpeded; they left behind their wounded to become prisoners of war.

While Smith-Dorrien's divisions were fighting for survival at Le Cateau, Haig ordered that I Corps should continue to retire south, having signalled first to Sir John's GHQ its willingness to go to the aid of II Corps. No reply was received and, between then and 1 September, when the relatively unscathed I Corps reached Villers-Cotterêts, southwest of Soissons, contact between the two corps was non-existent. By now relations between Sir John French and Haig had become severely strained; the C-in-C rebuked Haig for having 'promised' to assist General Lanrezac in an offensive at Guise without authorization from GHQ, a suggestion that irked Haig, as he had merely obeyed French's instructions to undertake no active operations and had simply sought French's permission to provide what little support could be given by I Corps. French apologized to Haig, but by now French had concluded that all was lost. On 30 August he informed Kitchener and Joffre that he intended withdrawing the whole BEF to south of Paris until he was satisfied it had regained sufficient strength and equipment to rejoin the struggle. He informed Kitchener: 'I think you had better trust me to watch the situation and act according to circumstances.'[44]

An infuriated and anxious Kitchener had no such intention. He travelled to Paris and met French at the British Embassy on 1 September, where, in what must have been a heated exchange, conducted in private, he insisted that Sir John stick by the French and not withdraw the BEF. Only French's version of what passed between the two men exists, and it misleadingly concludes that 'we finally came to an amicable understanding'.[45] Whatever passed between them, Sir John dropped his plan to withdraw. On 5 September Sir John issued orders that next day the BEF would cease its retreat and go over to the offensive. The French armies were ordered to do likewise, and the German advance was thus checked, just forty miles short of Paris, in what became known as the First Battle of the Marne.

For the previous thirteen days Haig's I Corps had been in continuous retreat, fighting a rearguard action over 160 miles and losing eighty-one officers and 2,180 other ranks in the process; overall, the BEF had so far suffered 20,000 men killed, wounded or missing in action. This loss of more than 20 per cent, in less than a month, was nothing less than a disaster; the heroism of individuals and some units could hardly compensate for the fact that Britain's army lacked sufficient men, artillery and machine-guns. Haig bitterly commented in his diary however that, for him, the 'actual fighting was the least of our difficulties'. Coping with the uncommunicative and whimsical Sir John French was more trying by far. On 14 September, I Corps was engaged in its fiercest fighting yet, on the northern banks of the Aisne river, where for the first time the BEF dug itself defensive trenches to withstand an anticipated German counter-attack.

In this position, the I Corps had to its right a contingent of French Moroccan troops; Haig noted that these 'Poor wretches were in cotton clothing and had nothing to eat but wet bread and raw meat for 4 or 5 days in the trenches on our right. It was to improve their fighting efficiency that I arranged to give them the tinned meat rations. [Haig sent them 10,000 British rations of tinned beef, cheese and other items.] General Maud'Huy [commanding the French XVIII Corps, which included the Moroccans] was delighted and so were the troops. They will do anything to help us now! The General Commanding the Moroccan Division had one eye on his line of retreat all the time, and his troops were constantly withdrawing, until we gave him a direct order to hold the trenches [. . .] This order, enlivened with a regular dose of rhum has kept the old boy up to the mark so far.'[46]

General de Maud'huy sent Haig a note of thanks and a crate of champagne, something which, it seems, could easily be supplied, even if proper rations were unavailable. Yet Haig's distrust of the fighting will of the French was growing. On 24 September, after I Corps had endured several days of intense German shelling and failed infantry attacks, Haig noted in his diary that: 'The 18th Corps [French] were supposed to attack Craonne today but did not progress far. They (the French) resemble somewhat the "Mikado". "Craonne is to be attacked" "Of course Craonne will be attacked" etc etc but nothing more than talking is done!'[47]

By 1 October, the front lines had barely altered since the first German successes. The BEF took advantage of a lull to move its position, which was almost in the centre of the front line, to the far left in Flanders, to be closer to the Channel ports and thus make its supply chain less complicated. By mid-October the BEF consisted of three corps, with III Corps under the command of Lieutenant-General Sir William Pulteney.

For much of the second half of October, Haig's I Corps was engaged in continuous hard fighting around the Belgian market town of Ypres. On 19 October, Sir John French ordered I Corps to advance from the Ypres sector and capture Bruges and Ghent, absurdly optimistic targets given the stiffening resistance of the Germans, who were by now in well-defended positions. On 29 October, the Germans attacked the village of Gheluvelt. Two days later, Haig received reports that Gheluvelt had been taken, despite fierce resistance. He set off on horseback along the Menin road from Ypres, heading towards Hooge, where that afternoon General

Lomax, commander of the 1st Division, and six staff officers had been fatally wounded by shellfire. The sight of Haig calmly riding towards the fighting at Gheluvelt heartened the troops; that afternoon, when Haig returned to his temporary HQ at White Château on the Menin Road, the 2nd Battalion of the Worcestershire Regiment, under the command of Brigadier-General Fitzclarence VC, an Irish Guards officer, surged into Gheluvelt and retook it in ferocious hand-to-hand fighting; Fitzclarence was to die soon afterwards, on 12 November. With support from a French cavalry brigade, the line before Ypres was held. On 2 November, as the BEF's Cavalry Corps were forced out of their positions at Messines and Wytschaete, which were joined by a ridge overlooking Ypres, White Château was shelled; three men were killed and a large chandelier was sent crashing down onto the desk of Haig's office. He moved his HQ back into Ypres, only to have that damaged by a direct hit the next day.

These were long days, full of confusing and contradictory reports, and none could have realized at the time that, by 12 November, the BEF had withstood the immediate worst of what was to become known as the First Battle of Ypres. By 21 November, when II Corps had managed to relieve the hard-pressed and by now severely battered I Corps, Haig felt that conditions were secure enough for him to take five days' leave back in England. On 22 November, he was met by his wife at Victoria station in London where, he wrote in his diary, he felt 'as if a hundred years had passed since I parted with Doris at Aldershot'. In this brief respite, he had audiences with the king, Asquith and Kitchener, and managed to spend an afternoon with his young children, brought to London especially to see their father, taking them to London Zoo. He then returned to France, where I Corps was now in reserve positions, and established his HQ at Hazebrouck, remaining there until just before Christmas.

The nature of the fighting around Ypres in October and November had shocked Haig; in December 1914 he informed George V, who was on his first visit to the BEF, of the 'crowds of fugitives who came back down the Menin road from time to time during the Ypres battle having thrown everything they could, including their rifles and packs, in order to escape, with a look of absolute terror on their faces, such as I have never before seen on any human being's face.'[48]

By the end of 1914 the BEF, which had expanded to nine infantry and three cavalry divisions in Flanders, had suffered 96,000 casualties. Territorial and New Army divisions – the latter the result of Kitchener's call for volunteers – were completing their training back in Britain, but very little of the old regular army was left. French losses had been even more terrible, at around one million casualties in five months. This represented an unprecedented scale of human destruction on a battlefield, one so vast as to be beyond the comprehension of individual participants. The gruelling nature of this static warfare was, for all combatants, something unique; how to break out of it into open warfare, with scope for movement and outflanking, was to be the central conundrum for most of the rest of the war.

By December 1914 Haig, who now had a breathing space in which to think a little more deeply, was beginning to formulate his own robust view of what this new form of warfare necessitated: 'In my opinion there are only 2 ways of gaining ground either, (a) a general offensive all along the front, with careful preparation of artillery in order to dominate the Enemy's artillery at specially chosen points, use of trench guns, mortars, hand grenades, etc. to occupy the Enemy's attention everywhere, and press home in force at certain points (where not expected.) The other method (b) is to sap up, as in siege warfare. This is a slow business especially in wet ground.'[49]

While the German soldiers could depend on plentiful supplies of hand grenades, the only close-combat bomb the BEF had at that time were 'jam pot' grenades – empty jam tins filled with gun cotton and nails, topped off with a small detonator and length of fuse, and sealed with mud. The Mills grenade did not reach the front until the spring of 1915 and was in any case in short supply to begin with. Haig's abiding interest in the possibilities yielded by new inventions is revealed by several diary entries in December 1914, including this from the 12th, describing the trench mortar, a new and increasingly useful weapon, again largely unavailable to the BEF at that time: 'They are made of steel piping about 2 feet long, with a movable support near the muzzle to alter the elevation. A kind of spade is fixed to the base to prevent the gun from sinking in to the ground. They fire a bomb of 2lb weight. This can be thrown up to 300 yards by means of gunpowder charges.'[50]

On Christmas Eve 1914, Haig held a meeting of I Corps' divisional GOCs, along with senior engineers and artillery officers, to 'consider best method of carrying on operations under the new conditions. We discussed:

(1)a) Trenches. [Size, depth and state, nature of revetment etc.]
   b) Care of men. Not to put into wet trenches up to their knees in water as has been done [in parts of this front.]
(2) Nature of Defence.
   It must be active, otherwise enemy will advance and blow in our trenches with "minen werfer" as he did to the Indians.
(3) Trench Mortars. Personnel to be gunners or specialists.
(4) Hand Grenades. Keep enemy at a distance as long as possible. Use outposts entrenched.
(5) Local Attack. As in the old days
   Bomb throwers
   Bayonet party
   Attacking body, with flank detachments etc.
(6) General attack. I asked GOCs to get to know the ground so as to be ready for a general advance when the time comes [. . .]

Tomorrow being Xmas day, I ordered no reliefs to be carried out, and troops to be given as easy a time as possible.'[51]

Back in Britain, the war had brought with it a drive to personal austerity. George V and his family determined they must set an example in this respect, partly out of a sense of duty and partly to stem occasional public grumbling about the hardships of wartime. The king gave away most of his civilian clothes and spent much of the time in uniform. Throughout the war he rarely dined out and never went to the theatre.

Balmoral was closed and some royal gardens were given over to the growing of vegetables. On the mischievous suggestion of Lloyd George, Chancellor of the Exchequer, the king, who was in any case quite abstemious, gave up wine for the duration and enforced this abstinence on all royal households, although he complained that it was 'a great bore'. It was, in his view, a black mark against Lloyd George, whom the king felt had made him look foolish by leaving him no choice but to give up alcohol. Later, when, as Prime Minister, Lloyd George sought to dislodge Haig as C-in-C, the king's adamant opposition might perhaps have been diminished had he been able to drink a glass of port or claret, and so mull over the decision in greater comfort.

Haig's first Christmas of the war was certainly not teetotal. The ever-attentive Leopold Rothschild sent Haig and his staff as a seasonal offering turtle soup and 1820 cognac, as well as fifty pairs of fur-lined gloves. Haig's gift from Sir John French was to be given command of a new military creation, the First Army; Horace Smith-Dorrien was appointed GOC of the Second. This novel expansion of the army's command structure was an indication of the anticipated growth in size and complexity of the BEF, as well as a rueful acknowledgement that the war would be much longer than French had first imagined. In a letter of thanks on 26 December, Haig told Rothschild of an alarming new weapon being used by the Germans: 'The turtle soup was quite excellent – tasted far better than anything does in London! The Germans have a marvellous "Mincer Werfer [sic]" which throws a bomb of some 120lbs of high explosive. It seems to be worked by compressed air and is difficult to locate. The effect on our trenches and on the poor fellows near is terrific and, as you can well understand, most demoralizing. I hope we'll soon have similar guns.'

Haig and the BEF were, however, shortly to learn that, as far as the Western Front was concerned, there were never to be enough guns, and for many months ahead, not enough shells either.

# CHAPTER NINE

# 'There are Spots on Every Sun'

Lithe and alert, Sir Douglas is known for his distinguished bearing and good looks. He has blue eyes and an unusual facial angle, delicately-chiselled features, and a chin to be reckoned with. There is a characteristic movement of the hands when explaining things.

Lord Northcliffe

If I can beat the French and the politicians, I will win the war.

Douglas Haig

In selecting his First Army staff, Haig followed his standard practice, by assembling a small group of those he had come to know and trust over the years, most of whom had served with him at Aldershot. His chief of staff was Brigadier-General John Gough VC, brother of Major-General Hubert Gough. Charteris headed Haig's intelligence staff, while Major Fletcher and Captain Straker were his senior ADCs, as at Aldershot. These formed the core of a staff which comprised some thirty-three personnel by the end of January 1915. There was also attached a French interpreter of whom Haig noted: 'M. Lazare (a financier of standing, with a splendid car) [. . .] but his real role is to go to Paris or elsewhere to buy the necessary food and drink to supplement rations for the whole of the Army Staff (a matter of some difficulty at times, as the country is getting eaten up near at hand.)'[1] Haig also supplemented his diet with a daily breakfast dose of Sanatogen, a milk-based vitamin-enriched food tonic produced by a company which, oddly enough, was owned by the Berlin-based Bauer Chemical Company.[2]

On 30 December 1914, Haig assembled First Army's corps commanders: Sir James Willcocks, Indian Corps; Sir Henry Rawlinson, IV Corps; Charles Carmichael Monro, I Corps, together with Gough and Henry Horne, First Army's CRA (Commanding Royal Artillery). Haig told them what he expected to encounter: close artillery support for front-line troops, and, while awaiting reinforcements from the New Army divisions training at home, 'we should follow a policy of quiet determination, and push on our saps steadily each night with a definite object in view.'

The corps commanders wanted guidance with coping with the water-logged condition of the trenches in the Flanders fields. Haig informed them that 'the men are on no account to be placed in flooded trenches, but points of support on high ground [are] to be held and our original front line by outposts.' His general advice concerning tactics was simple: 'Points with all round defence (as ordered) are to be organised in rear. Machine guns and guns [artillery] must be placed to cover intervening space; also guns to be trained on our trenches in case enemy should occupy them. Lastly, a detachment of troops must be kept ready at hand in Reserve to counter attack the moment the enemy pierces our line. The mistake usually made is to allow the enemy to pierce our line and to consolidate his hold on the captured trenches before any attempt to counter attack is made. The troops intended for counter attacking should be brought as close up as possible as soon as the enemy begins to bombard our front trenches and shows definite signs of attacking.'[3]

These defensive guiding principles scarcely altered for the rest of the war. Haig's instructions about not positioning troops in water-logged trenches was wishful thinking, given the low-lying positions the BEF occupied. Haig found on 12 January when he visited his old regiment, the 17th Lancers, at Rely, that they had just returned from frontline trenches where they had stood in water up to their hips for twenty-four hours. He immediately drove to Bethune, the HQ of the 1st Division (of which the 17th Lancers were a part), where he met Major-General Richard Haking, GOC 1st Division, and Major-General Monro: 'I gave them both a good talking to and ascertained that a second position about 2000 yards in rear was already prepared along a high road with houses etc prepared for defence; and in case of Lord Cavan's section further north (4th Brigade of 2nd Division) he has fallen back to a similar line, but keeps a few individual men (volunteers for the job) for four hours in tubs at certain points in the abandoned trenches. These men of course get very wet, but when they come out Lord Cavan has arranged for hot baths and warm blankets in a house near at hand.'[4]

Frontline conditions for the cold, water-logged, and already lice-ridden troops were indeed miserable. Haig was fully aware of the discomforts but there was little he or indeed anyone could do. He may never have had a louse himself but he certainly found out what they looked like. On 21 January 1915, he inspected temporary baths at the HQ of the 8th Division (GOC Major-General Francis Davies): 'The old woman in charge told me that she has 120 women at work washing, and the work is very difficult. She showed me a comforter simply covered with "beasts" [lice] all dead. I had no idea they were so large.'[5]

The next day he encountered Repington, who was still military correspondent of *The Times*, at Lillers, where he was a guest of his old friend, Sir John French. Haig learned that Repington 'thinks the German front is impregnable and much doubts whether we can ever get a General sufficiently fearless of public opinion to incur the losses which must be suffered in any attempt to pierce the enemy's fortified front. He thinks the British people will not stand heavy casualties. I replied that as soon as we are supplied with ample artillery ammunition of high explosive, I think we can walk through the German lines at several places. In my opinion, the reason we are here is primarily due to want of artillery ammunition, and secondly to our small numbers last November.'[6]

Haig wrote almost the same to Rothschild two days later: 'We are not making much progress – but that is not to be expected until we get an ample supply of high explosive ammunition for our guns, and a few more troops. Given lots of artillery ammunition I think there are several points at which we might advance as soon as the ground dries up a bit. At present, along most of our front, the ground is a swamp, and the only fellows who have any fun at all are a few picked shots in waders who, with telescopic sights on their rifles, pick off the unsuspecting German at long range!'[7]

By the end of January 1915, Sir Archibald Murray, who had collapsed under the strain of life at French's GHQ, was replaced as chief of staff by the BEF's quartermaster general, Sir William Robertson, who had managed almost miraculous supply work for the BEF in its frantic retreat from Mons in August and September 1914.[8] Murray went back to England to work as deputy chief of the Imperial General Staff under Kitchener, whom he found to be utterly secretive.[9] The working practices of Sir John's GHQ did not inspire confidence at lower reaches of the army; they seemed to replicate the cautious, buck-passing habits of the War Office. Major Christopher Baker-Carr, whose efforts to persuade GHQ to increase the number of machine-guns had proved fruitless, later considered: 'The chief trouble at G. H. Q. was that there was no one there who had time to listen to any new idea. Everybody was so busy writing "Passed to you," "Noted and returned," or "For your information," etc., etc., on piles and piles of "jackets" that no one had a moment to consider any proposal for altering the existing condition of affairs.'[10]

On 15 February 1915 the first naval shots were fired in the Dardanelles, the prelude to an attempt to force a backdoor invasion of Turkey and thus perhaps break the stalemate on the Western Front. This campaign was the brainchild of Winston Churchill, who, as First Lord of the Admiralty, had persuaded his Cabinet colleagues in November 1914 of the merits of this venture, much to the disgust of French, Haig, Robertson and other BEF generals. They regarded the Gallipoli campaign as a wasteful diversion of resources from the main theatre, the Western Front – a view which in Haig's case derived from his understanding of military history. In his *Cavalry Studies* in 1907 Haig had quoted a letter from Napoleon, his favourite example of a successful military strategist, to Robespierre in 1794:

War must be waged on the same principle as a siege: fire must concentrate on a single point. Once a breach is made, the equilibrium is broken, the other defences become valueless and the place is taken. Attacks must not be scattered but concentrated.

For Haig this became a cardinal principle, both in strategic and tactical terms on the Western Front. This occasionally brought him into serious conflict with the British government, which, when faced with the apparent intractability of the Western Front, sought to undermine the Central Powers by launching campaigns elsewhere. At the start of 1915 Kitchener informed Sir John French that the New Army divisions (Kitchener's Armies) currently being formed and trained in Britain might be deployed in Italy or Greece as well as in the Dardanelles against Turkey. Haig responded to this proposal by telling French on 4 January that 'we ought not to divide our military force [. . .] but <u>concentrate on the decisive front</u> which was on this frontier. With more guns and ammunition, and more troops, we are bound to break through.'[11]

The cry for more guns, troops and ammunition was one Haig repeated throughout the war; yet our judgement of the manner in which he disposed of those he possessed does not inspire confidence that a significant increase in men and materials would in themselves have produced earlier, more successful results. The year of 1915 put Haig's abilities as a general to the first real test, and the results do not flatter him.

By mid-February 1915, Sir John French had approved Haig's scheme for the BEF's first major offensive, an attack on a small German salient protruding into the British lines around the village of Neuve Chapelle, west of Lille, in north-west France. Some 40,000 men from four divisions along a two-mile front were to open the assault at 7.30am on 10 March. Haig had by this time also met Major (later Brigadier-General and Air-Marshal Sir) Hugh Trenchard, who commanded the Western Front detachment of the Royal Flying Corps (RFC) and for whom Haig developed a lasting and mutual respect.[12] On 22 February, as plans for the forthcoming battle were developing, John Gough, due to return to Britain to take command of a newly formed division, was hit by a stray rifle bullet; he died two days later.[13] Haig felt his loss keenly.[14] His diary reference to Gough's death also reveals his occasional impatience with less senior officers who disagreed with him, even those such as the devotedly loyal Gough:

Only once throughout the whole war did I have to say a sharp word to him. It was during the retreat, on the night after the action at Villers-Cotterêts. [...] he in his impetuous way grumbled at my going on retreating and retreating. As a number of the Staff were present I turned on him rather sharply and said 'That retreat was the only thing to save the Army, and that it was his duty to support me instead of criticising.' He was very sorry, poor fellow.[15]

While Haig's irritation, especially in such tense days as those of the retreat from Mons, is understandable, the fact that he was known not to be receptive to remarks he felt were personally critical did little to encourage useful deliberation in his presence. It is, of course, the job of a commander to command; but it is also the sign of a wise commander that he listens to and encourages the expression of opinion that diverges from his own.

The Battle of Neuve Chapelle, a minor engagement compared with many that followed, was seen from the start by Haig as possibly leading to greater things than simply pinching out a salient. It has been suggested that Haig's perspective was limited; he had never commanded infantry or artillery, and was predisposed to look 'at the ground between the ears of a horse.'[16] This need not, in itself, have been disadvantageous, yet Haig was none the less always tempted by the open vistas beyond the horizon. It was almost as if he believed that submitting to a battle plan which did not contemplate a lasting breakthrough was an acknowledgement of defeat. Haig's eternal belief that the stalemate would be broken was in itself virtuous; but his vice was that such optimism was too often ill-founded.

Thus, at the start of March, Haig informed Sir Henry Rawlinson,[17] whose IV Corps was to bear the brunt of Neuve Chapelle, that 'our objective was not merely the capture of Neuve Chapelle. Our existing line was just as satisfactory for me as if we were in Neuve Chapelle! [...] It seemed to me desirable to make our plans with the definitive objective of advancing rapidly, (and without any check) in the hope of starting a general advance.'[18] This was to be 'a serious offensive movement with the object of breaking the German line.' Accordingly, two cavalry divisions were to be held in close reserve to take advantage of the intended break-through.

The infantry advance at Neuve Chapelle was preceded by a concentrated thirty-five-minute artillery bombardment by 340 guns along a 2,000-yard line and, in a innovative touch, directed in part by eighty-five RFC reconnaissance aircraft. To Rothschild, Haig futilely complained that *The Times* had, after the battle, accurately published the duration of the preliminary bombardment: 'It will make surprise more difficult next time.'[19] By later standards this was both an exceptionally brief preliminary bombardment and unusually concentrated; the weight of high explosive per yard of enemy trenches was equivalent to 288 pounds.[20] Under such a surprise blizzard of fire, the BEF rapidly broke through a lightly defended section, and within four hours had crossed four lines of German trenches to capture Neuve Chapelle.

This was a key moment for Haig and other BEF commanders, who mistakenly deduced that an artillery bombardment in itself was always an effective means of terrifying the enemy and destroying resistance. The early success at Neuve Chapelle also presented Haig with a difficult counter-example to his previous experiences with artillery, in South Africa, where he judged its usefulness to be more intimidatory than destructive. On 12 March, however, German forces counter-attacked and ended British hopes of a lasting breakthrough; the battle was brought to an end on 13 March with more than 12,000 casualties.

Despite this relatively heavy cost, Neuve Chapelle was considered a success by Haig, even if it did demonstrate the need for more reserves to be brought up close to any attack and in sufficient numbers to push home the initial advantage and break out from captured positions. Indeed, this would become a mantra for Haig later in 1915 at the Battle of Loos. But Neuve Chapelle was misleading; henceforth, and through many of the battles to come, the BEF's commanders clung to the belief that longer bombardments by greater numbers of guns, over a wider front, would significantly increase the chances of a permanent breakthrough. What Neuve Chapelle did not, could not, tell the BEF was that the German response would simply be to construct stronger, deeper and wider defensive positions which were better able to withstand bombard-ments, however terrifying.

At the end of March Haig took five days' leave in England, his second trip home since the start of the war. He spent it at the coastal town of Folkestone, playing golf and dining alone with Doris. They stayed at lodgings under the names of 'Colonel and Mrs Brown', a subterfuge of Doris's designed to prevent Haig from being troubled. Sir Clive Wigram wrote and asked if Haig would consider going to London to see the king; Doris took it on herself to 'write firmly that I insisted that he stayed the few days at Folkestone, and I received a very kind letter in reply saying that the King quite understood.'[21]

Haig was always receptive to the chance of ingratiating himself with George V; his decision to remain in Folkestone hardly supports the suggestion that he was already at work on pouring poison against Sir John French into the king's ear. But relations between Haig and Sir John deteriorated further after he returned to France to discover that, in the official report on Neuve Chapelle, drawn up at his First Army HQ and submitted to French at GHQ, the original heading 'General Officer Commanding the First Army' (Haig) had been struck out and substi-tuted by 'Commander-in-Chief' (French). Haig, by now ready to inter-pret any move by Sir John negatively, took this to mean French was seeking to claim for himself the supposed success at Neuve Chapelle: 'Report now reads as if the action taken was on the orders of the GHQ! This is as it should be, but the actual orders received by me from GHQ were dated after the whole plan had been worked out by us in detail. The whole thing is so childish, that I could hardly have credited the truth of the story had I not seen the paper.'[22]

By 2 April, after another minor contretemps with French, Haig confided to his diary that 'something must have upset the balance of Sir John's mind.' His distrust deepened when French invited Henry Wilson, always a *bête noire* for Haig, to join his mess at GHQ: 'Wilson's face now looks so deceitful! By having Wilson in his Mess [. . .] the C-in-C is courting trouble. Billy Lambton (the Military Secretary) is weak, and quite under the influence of Wilson it seems. Luckily

Lambton is stupid, and more than once given away what Wilson has been scheming for.'[23]

Haig, rarely able to concede the possibility that other views might have something to be said for them, suspected stupidity and irresolution were uniting to conspire against the BEF. On 17 April 1915, shortly before the Germans used poison gas for the first time on the Western Front in an attack on Smith-Dorrien's Second Army in the Second Battle of Ypres,[24] he wrote to Rothschild complaining about the press coverage of the war and strikes in England:

> The 'Times Military Correspondent' [Repington] deduces military lessons (or tries to do so) from gossip: soldiers' letters are published: and Sir J. French's despatches sometimes also give away military information of value to the enemy. All this might be stopped by having military correspondents of the Bennet Burleigh[25] type – who will write highly coloured descriptions which are of no real military value, but would please 'Arriet and sell the newspaper! [. . .] I expect the effects of Alcohol on the output of ammunition have been greatly overstated. My idea is that the authorities have begun at the wrong end of the scale. They should have punished, or even shot a few of those who gave way to drink to such an extent that they became unfit for work. Why should the whole community suffer because of a small number of drunkards? Personally I believe in moderation, and have little confidence in the water-drinker! It is usually a sign of weakness in some respect.

Meanwhile Smith-Dorrien, GOC Second Army, was under considerable pressure from the German offensive at Ypres, and recommended to Sir John French a sensible orderly withdrawal to new and more easily defended positions. Relations between French and Smith-Dorrien, not very good even before the war started, now rapidly deteriorated. In a fit of pique, French refused to permit any withdrawal and on 6 May Smith-Dorrien offered his resignation, writing to French that 'my position as Army Commander has become impossible. Plenty of complicated situations have arisen in the last few months, and the difficulty of dealing with them has been greatly enhanced by the knowledge that unless I was successful, I and the 2nd Army would be blamed – in fact, *I have had more to fear from the rear than from the front* [original emphasis].'[26]

This letter went unanswered by French until, late that evening, Smith-Dorrien was abruptly sacked via a reply from French's adjutant-general, C. F. N. MacReady: 'The Commander-in-Chief directs me to inform you that the Secretary of State for War wishes to see you, and he requests that you will proceed to England tomorrow – 7th May. Lieutenant-General Sir H. Plumer has been instructed to assume command of the II Army and informed that you will communicate direct with him as to when you leave for England. Kindly arrange this, together with any information you may consider it necessary to give him. Please acknowledge receipt of this memo.'[27]

After taking command of the Second Army, Plumer was permitted by Sir John French to carry out exactly the same withdrawal as had been sought by Smith-Dorrien, who discovered on his return to England that French had spread rumours he was too ill to retain his command. When Smith-Dorrien met Kitchener in London on 10 May, the Secretary of State for War 'was surprised to see a robust individual, as he had been informed from France that my health had broken down.'[28]

Haig felt little sympathy for Smith-Dorrien: his dismissal removed yet another competitor for the job of C-in-C, if French departed. Haig's sentiments regarding Smith-Dorrien were contained in another letter to Rothschild, which, given Haig's disgust with British newspapers reporting battlefield developments, was remarkably indiscreet: 'I enclose a typed note of information gained from prisoners after the first days of fighting regarding their lines. [. . .] The enemy has drawn off most of his guns and Infantry from Ypres. Still I hear that our troops there are suffering a great deal. The country is so dirty and smelly – dead horses everywhere! [. . .] The gas too, which the enemy has used on several occasions on that front, has a demoralising effect on troops subjected to it. For all these reasons our troops about Ypres, I am told, are not in really good condition, notwithstanding the departure of Smith Dorrien!'[29]

Beyond this squabbling between the BEF's senior commanders, a more profoundly serious problem was threatening to disrupt efforts to win the war – a growing lack of munitions. Kitchener had already instructed Sir John French to divert 2,000 rounds of 4.5-inch howitzer shells and 20,000 18-pounder shells to the Dardanelles, at a time when French already felt the BEF was being starved of ammunition.[30] The shell shortage was to affect Haig's next planned attack, at Aubers Ridge, which was to be in support of a much bigger offensive by the French Tenth Army in Artois. The land before Aubers Ridge was flat, water-logged and without any natural cover for attacking troops, but the ridge itself, if it could be gained and held, offered the prospect of dominating the important city of Lille. Haig's First Army started a forty-five-minute bombardment at 5am on 9 May but a combination of well-prepared defences, a strong counter-artillery bombardment by the Germans, and many British shells falling short and killing their own men, meant the attack was a complete failure. It was called off by Haig by 6pm that same day, at a cost to the BEF of some 10,000 casualties.

The conclusions Haig drew from this fresh setback were both right and wrong. While he recognized that German defences were now much stronger and better-prepared than at Neuve Chapelle, he still argued that what was required was a longer and more intense bombardment. This tactic was put into practice almost immediately at the Battle of Festubert, which opened in the early hours of 13 May with an even bigger bombardment, scheduled to last thirty-six hours and with much greater use of indirect fire. This battle dragged on for a fortnight before petering out with less than a mile gained; at Festubert the BEF's casualty list was even higher, at 16,000.

In Britain, however, news of this costly failure was completely overshadowed by the publication in *The Times* on 15 May of an article by Repington, which flatly stated that at Aubers Ridge 'the want of an unlimited supply of high explosive shells was a fatal bar to our success.' The British army was indeed facing a severe shell shortage; almost thirty million rounds of 18-pounder ammunition had been ordered since the start of the war but only 1.4 million rounds had been delivered.[31] Yet it is fair to say that even a substantially greater amount of ammunition for this gun – which was suitable for slaughtering infantry in the open, but not for collapsing defensive bunkers – would not have changed matters at Festubert. Haig frequently complained in his diary at this time that the First Army was squeezed between two contradictory demands – to conserve artillery ammunition while also to press home attacks – although this predicament derived as much from Haig's own ambition to swamp the enemy in shells as anything else. By the end of May 1915 the BEF was down to less than one week's supply of all types of artillery shell.[32]

Repington's article caused a furore in Britain, where it was immediately suspected to have derived entirely from information fed to him by Sir John French. It was a political embarrassment for Kitchener, but also a useful means by which the Secretary of State could depict Sir John as an intriguer – never mind that Kitchener himself had resorted to similar manipulation of the press during his battle with Curzon in India. The 'shell scandal,' as it quickly became known, was highly damaging to Asquith, who had, on Kitchener's advice, stated in April 1915 that the BEF had sufficient shells for its needs. Repington's article was ritually burned on the floor of the London Stock Exchange, but it helped topple Asquith's Liberal Government and paved the way for the National Coalition administration, in which Asquith remained Prime Minister and, crucially for Haig's future, Lloyd George's star ascended as he became Minister of Munitions.[33] One of Lloyd George's first actions in his new post was to send to France a committee to investigate Repington's story, a member of which enquired as to how many cannon-balls were used these days.

On 30 May, Haig received word from Robertson, Chief of the General Staff, that General Ferdinand Foch, who then commanded the northern group of French armies, was pressing Sir John French to make an attack on Loos, a small mining town which the French had already tried and failed to capture. The build-up to this battle and the political machinations that preceded it say much about the shifting balance of power between Kitchener and Sir John French, and between the British and French allies; Loos was a battle which neither Haig, nor Sir John, nor – at the outset – Kitchener wished to fight.

At an inter-Allied conference on 6 July at Calais, Kitchener informed the French that, while the BEF would be augmented by twenty-five fresh divisions from Britain by the end of 1915, it was necessary to conserve these and maintain a posture of 'active defence' until they had become fully integrated into the BEF and were ready to go onto the offensive in the spring of 1916. The French high command regarded this as an inordinately protracted delay, particularly as the British were devoting so much effort to the Dardanelles, which the French saw as a sideshow. Furthermore, defeatism was in the air in some influential French political circles: even a former Prime Minister, Joseph Caillaux, was vociferously advocating a negotiated peace settlement with Germany.[34] It is difficult to judge just how deeply rooted French disaffection with the war was at this stage, although Joffre, the French C-in-C, certainly exploited it to press the British into fresh action. On 14 June, Haig had been visited by Captain de Couvreville of Joffre's staff, who told him: '"The French people are getting tired of the war." The tremendous cost of the war, the occupation of a very wealthy part of France by the enemy and the cessation of trade and farming operations were affecting them. Everything was practically at a standstill and the whole of the manhood of the nation was concentrated on this frontier. There was a general wish that a vigorous effort should be made to end the war by the autumn.'[35]

In a visit to France on 16–18 July 1915, Kitchener jettisoned his earlier opposition to any offensive action by the BEF on the Western Front before 1916, and agreed a joint Anglo-French assault there for the autumn of 1915. He then, on 20 August, persuaded the British Cabinet to agree to this remarkable *volte-face*. Kitchener's move was partly inspired by alarm at the unexpectedly rapid collapse of Russia, whose armies were pushed out of Galicia in June 1915, and whose hold on Warsaw collapsed on 4 August. The failure to advance beyond the Gallipoli beachheads in the Dardanelles simply added to Kitchener's sense that events were slipping from his grasp. Any shift of French war-weariness into outright clamour for a peace settlement would have left the BEF – and the British empire – vulnerably exposed to German ambitions. It has also been suggested[36] that Kitchener's change of heart was partly the result of the malign influence of a deeply pessimistic Viscount Esher, who was now resident in Paris and, since April 1915, had been acting as Kitchener's unofficial intelligence-gatherer in the French capital.

Haig gave little credit to the rumours of an imminent collapse of French support for the war, nor did he have any time for the argument that campaigns in other theatres might usefully divert German divisions from the Western Front. He wrote to Rothschild on 25 July: 'It seems to me that those in London who understand the Balkans can't act, and those who can act don't understand the Balkans! [. . .] The French people in this part are making great profits by selling things to our soldiers at 5 times the usual prices. The love of gain attracts them right forward into villages which are sometimes under fire! But they don't seem to mind the loss of their friends, and they come back as soon as the shelling is over.'[37]

But consideration of what to do to break the stalemate was taking place at a level above Haig's. Autocratic and mistrustful, Kitchener insisted that, rather than taking his view of Parisian politics from Bertie, the British ambassador to Paris since 1905, he would henceforth rely on Esher and Lieutenant-Colonel Le Roy-Lewis, British military attaché in Paris. Le Roy-Lewis detested Bertie and was yet another Esher protégé. Major-General Sir Henry Wilson, by now established as British liaison officer with Joffre's staff, and whom Haig believed to be 'more French than the French',[38] supported Esher's gloomy prognostications. Flatly contradicting communiqués sent to London by Bertie, Esher erroneously insisted that Caillaux's pacifism was widely supported, and that to keep France in the war it was vital that the BEF join with the French in mounting a significant offensive on the Western Front. Only that, claimed Esher, would be enough to bolster the will of the French pro-war faction, led by Kitchener's French counterpart, Alexandre Millerand, who in turn backed General Joffre.[39]

According to the historian Rhodri Williams, the reality was somewhat different: 'Bertie was quite correct in trusting the robustness of the *union sacrée* [a condition of French civil and religious unity declared by President Poincaré at the start of the war], but his voice was drowned out by the growing chorus of alarmism in British circles in France in the early summer of 1915. [. . .] The British mistook the instability of French parliamentary life for a symptom of disunity on the issue of the war, whereas in fact it had been a chronic feature of the Third Republic since its foundation.'[40]

The Battle of Loos, which was fought between 25 and 28 September 1915, was therefore originally conceived not as an opportunity for a genuine breakthrough but, as the historian David French has argued, as 'a political gesture designed to reassure the allies of Britain's support for them'.[41] The 61,000 casualties in Haig's First Army that resulted from the battle naturally had no inkling of this, and even Haig may not have been aware of the full background. Instructed by Sir John French to begin planning an assault on Loos, on 20 June 1915 Haig made a distant inspection of the area over which his soldiers were to attack. Generals Horne and Haking also made their own independent observations; none of them liked what they saw. The ground before Loos was a wide, flat, open plateau, over which German observation was totally unimpeded. The area was dominated by a tall, well defended German-held slag heap called the Hohenzollern Redoubt, from whose elevated position German artillery spotters could direct fire across the whole area. Haig got a 'very good view' of two lines of tangled German barbed wire, and feared that the numerous coal pits and houses which dotted the area would provide perfect defensive emplacements for the enemy.

To order men across this plain was to condemn them to almost certain massacre; this much was feared long before the battle. The Germans in addition had considerably reinforced their defences, following the earlier failed French attack. Haig sensibly informed GHQ that all this did not augur well: '[. . .] it would be possible to capture the enemy's first line of trenches (say a length of 1200 yards) opposite Maroc (ie west of Loos), but it would not be possible to advance beyond, because our own artillery could not support us, as ground immediately in front cannot be seen from any part of our front.[42] On the other hand the enemy has excellent observing stations for his artillery. [. . .] The Enemy's defences are now so strong that, sufficient ammunition lacking to destroy them, they can only be taken by siege methods – by using bombs, and by hand-to-hand fighting in the trenches – the ground above is so swept by gun and machine gun and rifle fire that an advance in the open, except by night, is impossible.'[43]

Sir John French, under enormous pressure from Kitchener, who would brook no defiance, was adamant, ordering Haig on Tuesday 22 June to 'submit a project for the attack of the Enemy's front between your right and the La Bassée Canal. It is proposed to make the attack between 10 and 15 July, and in as close cooperation as possible with the French so that each of the Allied Armies may derive the full advantage from the attack of the other.'[44]

The French, however, were unable to prepare their joint attack to their liking by the dates specified and, between 9 and 17 July, Haig took leave in England. Invited to an audience with the king on 14 July, Haig was delighted to have conferred on him the Knight Grand Cross of the Order of the Bath (GCB); but the sub-text of the meeting was George V's desire to learn Haig's current opinion of Sir John French.[45] The king opened the topic by criticizing French's 'dealings with the press'; implied French was not 'fit for his position'; said he 'had lost confidence in French'; and revealed that he had promised Kitchener his full support in 'whatever action he took in the matter of dealing with French'. Placed in such an impossible position, Haig played a very canny game, neither suggesting that French should be removed nor giving the C-in-C his wholehearted endorsement: 'I pointed out that the time to get rid of French was imme-diately after the retreat. [From Mons] Now the Army was stationary and could practically be controlled from London! The King hoped that I would write to Wigram [Major Clive Wigram, George V's assistant private secretary] and said that no one but he and Wigram would know what I had written.'[46]

The king was not the only one that day to encourage Haig to speak his mind about the C-in-C. Later he met Kitchener, who also asked Haig to write to him privately: 'At both my interviews today, I was urged to write regarding the situation and doings of the Army in Flanders to Lord Kitchener. The King quite realised the nature of such conduct on my part, because he told me he had said to Lord Kitchener with reference to it "If anyone acted like that, and told tales out of school, he would at school be called a 'sneak.' Kitchener's reply was that we are beyond the schoolboy's age!" '

The role of George V in the appointment and supervision of senior military officers was ill-defined. Although the king had the right to express his views, military appointments were ultimately a matter for the government. While the suggestion that Haig should write directly to him about the military situation was underhand and opened the way for all manner of crossed wires, it was a long-standing practice for British monarchs, who suspected – with some justice – that politicians did not tell them the whole truth. George V, like his father and grandmother, stubbornly adhered to the notion that senior military appointments were his decision. As Asquith put it: 'By an odd convention all our Sovereigns (I have now had to deal with *three*) believe that in Army and Navy appointments they have a special responsibility and a sort of "divine right of Kings" prerogative. Anyhow they have to be humoured and brought in.'[47]

Haig can only have emerged from his meetings with Kitchener and the king with the certainty that both were completely disenchanted with Sir John French; this knowledge alone would have been enough to strengthen Haig's own growing dissatisfaction with the C-in-C. Haig did not betray French here; George V and Kitchener had already made up their minds and, on 14 July, merely sought to know if Haig approved the final assassination, which he certainly did. This modus operandi should astonish no one; it was custom and practice then and is so today.

What is more surprising than any of this is the fact that Kitchener was prepared to hand control over the BEF to Joffre, who, via Millerand, proposed to Kitchener on 30 July that: 'During the period in which the operations of the British Army take place principally in French territory, and contribute to the liberation of this territory, the initiative on combined action of the French and British forces devolves on the French Commander-in-Chief, notably as concerning the effectives to be engaged, the objectives to be attained, and the dates fixed for the commencement of each operation. The Commander-in-Chief of the

British Forces will of course fully retain the choice of means of execution.'[48]

This would certainly not have received Haig's blessing had he known of it. It also flatly contradicted Kitchener's original, albeit ambiguously worded, instructions to Sir John French at the start of the war, and reduced the role of the BEF's C-in-C to that of an administrative go-between. Joffre's adroit effort to take control of the BEF worked; when Kitchener visited France between 16 and 19 August he accepted without emendation Joffre's proposal. It remains unclear precisely how well-briefed the British Cabinet – and George V – were about this significant concession by Kitchener, who, it seems, consulted none of his colleagues in government before effectively delivering control of the BEF to the French General Staff.[49] It is also unclear whether or not Kitchener, who was to die in June 1916, when the cruiser HMS *Hampshire* sank after hitting a mine while taking him to Russia, and thus was never called to answer for this move, intended the arrangement to be merely temporary.[50]

Haig, however, remained ignorant of this dramatic development and, following instructions from Sir John French, had drawn up his plan for the forthcoming battle. On 7 August, he attended a conference at St Omer with French and Robertson, during which, according to Haig's diary entry for that day, Sir John 'agreed entirely with the views I had expressed in my written report' (suggesting alternative places for an attack) but added: 'Sir John has decided to comply with General Joffre's wishes, even though he disagrees with the plan. I am therefore to work out proposals for giving effect to the decision, but my attack is to be made chiefly with artillery and I am not to launch a large force of infantry to the attack of objectives which are so strongly held as to be liable to result only in the sacrifice of many lives. That is to say, I am to assist the French by neutralising the Enemy's artillery, and by holding the hostile infantry on my front.'[51]

Sir John duly transmitted this scheme to Joffre, who was by now under the impression that he was in a position to command rather than request; Joffre naturally realized that 'holding' was not 'advancing', and insisted upon an all-out attack. Sir John was in an awkward position: as the now very junior partner of the alliance on the Western Front, he had been committed by Kitchener to fall into line with Joffre's plans, even though his most senior general, Haig, had clearly stated that a frontal assault at Loos would result in needless slaughter.

A month later, Haig duly informed his corps commanders and their staffs that 'My orders [to them] are to break the Enemy's front and reach Pont à Vendin.'[52] The town of Pont à Vendin, although a useful ultimate objective, situated as it was on a north-south railway line, was more than four miles beyond Loos, almost five miles beyond the First Army's jump-off line before the battle. Thus Haig appears to have used the instruction to advance, and not merely to hold, to require a much greater advance than was perhaps either sought by the French or strictly feasible. Given his early opposition to *any* attack at Loos, this distant objective was a vain ambition.

By the end of August, neither Haig nor Sir John any longer possessed executive control over the choice of battleground, although, impelled by their own sense of status, they acted as though they did. Their role had actually been reduced to that of obeying the strategic dictates of their French ally. It was a significant moment in the war for both of them but, if it represented any sort of political or ethical crisis, it was not publicly acknowledged by either the British government, French or Haig. Neither French nor Haig considered resigning in protest against orders they had previously strongly opposed. It was a moment, for both, when conscience perhaps wrestled with ambition, and ambition – or, if we feel generous, duty – won. For Haig, a visit to his HQ by Kitchener on 19 August provided at least some degree of exoneration for the catastrophe which lay ahead. Kitchener informed Haig that, such was the pressure on Russia and the fragility of the French, 'he had decided we "must act with all our energy, and do our utmost to help the French, even though, by doing so, we suffered very heavy losses indeed." '[53]

At a meeting of his corps commanders on 6 September, Haig repeated Kitchener's line, that the collapse of Russia necessitated the BEF abandoning its current defensive attitude on the Western Front. All concerned could always comfort themselves later by claiming that they never sought the battle ahead. Churchill, for one, did just that, claiming in 1937 that he had argued in Cabinet against the Battle of Loos: 'But nothing availed against the will-power of Joffre and the outlook of the French staff. [. . .] I warned Sir John French that the new battle would be fatal to him. It could not succeed, and he would be made the scapegoat of insane hopes frustrated. So it all fulfilled itself.'[54] This impression of fruitless resistance to fate needs some qualification. Kitchener, French and Haig all had a choice, and they chose to commit themselves to what became an ill-prepared and frequently chaotic direct frontal infantry assault on Loos.

The main objective to be captured was Hill 70, a substantial waste-dump mound less than a mile to the east of Loos, along with a ridge to the north of Hill 70 which stretched to the village of Hulluch; this ridge was on the left flank of the French Tenth Army, as it assaulted the Vimy plateau. IV and I Corps – commanded by Lieutenant-General Sir Henry Rawlinson and Lieutenant-General Sir Hubert Gough respectively – comprised some 75,000 fighting troops of six divisions (two of which, the 9th and 15th, were raw New Army formations), which were to attack along a seven-and-a-half-mile front between the Grenay-Lens road and the Béthune-La Bassée Canal. They were opposed by just two under-manned German divisions, some 20,000 troops. The attack was scheduled to open on the morning of 21 September with a four-day preliminary bombardment of 110 heavy guns and 841 field guns; this was almost three times the number of guns used at Neuve Chapelle but, alarmingly for Haig and his staff, the guns were more thinly spread across a front that was six times longer than at Neuve Chapelle. The shortage of available artillery and munitions that Repington had pinpointed had yet to be rectified and, to compensate for an obvious insufficiency of fire-power, Haig intended to resort to a weapon previously untried by the BEF – chlorine gas.[55] He had told Sir John French at GHQ as late as 18 September that 'if the 25th [the planned date for the infantry attack] was unfavourable for gas and an attack had to be made notwithstanding, the scope of my offensive would be much curtailed because we only had enough guns to cover the attack of 2 divisions.'[56]

That same day, Haig was irked to learn that the C-in-C had decided to keep the whole of the general reserve for the imminent battle in the neighbourhood of Lillers, more than sixteen miles behind Haig's First Army, and under his own direct command.[57] This reserve comprised the 21st and 24th Divisions, two New Army Divisions which had only been in France for two weeks, and the newly formed Guards Division, which together formed General-Lieutenant Haking's XI Corps. These troops, whom Haig had asked French should be placed under his command before the battle was opened, were scheduled to arrive with him on 25 September: 'This is too late!' Haig wrote in his diary on 19 September.

Haig's hopes for the poison gas at Loos had meanwhile been raised, by a rash commitment from the Ministry of Munitions that it could supply forty tons of gas by 17 July, which it was believed was enough for a thirty-minute release on a 5,000-yard front, and thereafter 150 tons a week, enough for two thirty-minute attacks a week over a five-mile front.[58] In the event, there was an insufficient amount of gas and cylinders to provide a continuous thirty-minute release on the day of the infantry assault, and Lieutenant-Colonel Foulkes, a Royal Engineer in charge of the Gas Brigade, had to settle for a release order of twelve minutes of gas, followed by eight minutes of smoke, followed by another twelve minutes of gas and a final eight minutes of smoke.

On the night of 24 September, as the softening-up artillery bombardment was drawing to its conclusion, Haig held a meeting with Rawlinson and Gough, in which he made it clear that the attack would go ahead regardless, gas or no gas – despite his previous insistence that only the effective use of gas would be able to compensate for the shortage of artillery.[59] The next morning at 5am, when the artillery bombardment was dying away and the wind almost at a standstill, Haig walked outside with his ADC Alan Fletcher to see for himself what the weather was like. Fletcher secured himself a place in history by lighting a cigarette to detect any breeze and, as Haig observed, the smoke 'drifted in puffs towards the NE [northeast]. Staff Officers of Corps were ordered to stand by in case it was necessary to counter order to attack. At one time owing to the calm I feared the gas would simply hang about <u>our</u> trenches! However at 5.15

I said "Carry on". I went to the top of our lookout tower. The wind came gently from southwest and by 5.40 had increased slightly. The leaves of the poplar gently rustled. This seemed satisfactory. But what a risk I must run of gas blowing back upon our dense masses of troops!'[60]

The final sentence of this passage is not in the manuscript version of Haig's diary but is a later addition to the typescript version, as if Haig felt the need to acknowledge, after the event, that this is what actually happened. In some sectors, the chlorine gas drifted across no man's land (which ranged from 100 to 500 yards), creating varying degrees of useful havoc in those parts of the German trenches into which it seeped.[61] In other sectors, such as that of the 2nd Division, the gas blew straight back into the British lines, causing equal but much less useful chaos; the division's attack never got off the ground.

The nature of gas attacks at this stage of the war was always problematic; too much wind and the gas would quickly be dispersed; too little and it would damage the user as much as the enemy. Given the prevailing weakness of the wind on the morning of 25 September 1915, it could be argued that Haig should have ordered a postponement of the attack, but his instructions to Rawlinson and Gough the previous evening show that he was determined to go ahead with it, even if no gas support was available. His mind had been made up, not least because he knew that any postponement would have had serious consequences for himself; he would have had to face the wrath of Sir John French, Kitchener and his French allies. Haig did not recognize this momentous decision, taken on the drift of his ADC's cigarette smoke, as having any moral dimension, but the fact that he permitted the battle to go ahead had terrible consequences for the men under his command. The political and professional repercussions of postponement – his possible sacking – outweighed his military good sense; he had permitted himself to be placed in an impossible position.

Despite the patchy success of the gas dispersal, and the fact that the BEF's artillery bombardment had only cut the wire in a few places, the tenacious courage of those regiments who crossed no man's land ensured that, by midday on 25 September, both Loos and the Hohenzollern

Redoubt had been taken, although the second line of German defences was intact. At 2pm Haig received a message from Haking informing him that XI Corps (minus the Guards) were now, by order of Sir John French, under the command of Haig. Yet during the day of 25 September the 21st and 24th Divisions, after three nights of foot-slogging, travelling by night to avoid aerial observation, exhausted, hungry and sodden by a downpour, had still five miles to go to reach the front line, and were in no condition for the battle that awaited them. By nightfall that same day, Haig learnt that the French Tenth Army's much bigger attack on Vimy Ridge – which the BEF at Loos was intended to support – had collapsed, leaving the German defenders completely dominating the ground the British troops would have to cross, if they attempted to move beyond Loos to try to effect a breakout beyond the positions they had captured so far. On the night of 25 September, the Germans counter-attacked at Loos in force; the next morning, Haig ordered the 21st and 24th Divisions, which had finally reached the front line, to dislodge the Germans from their stubbornly held second line of defences. Haig was still determined to exploit the success of the first wave of the attack. But the men of the 21st and 24th were slaughtered by close-range machine-gun fire, and those left standing quickly fled back to their own lines.

This failure of the 21st and 24th had nothing to do with their New Army status; two other New Army divisions, the 9th and 15th, performed well at Loos. But the fact that sufficient reserves were not readily at hand, and in good time, to exploit the battle's initial success was, in Haig's view, entirely the fault of Sir John French and his inability to grasp, in the weeks prior to the battle, that a break-in at Loos could be turned into a breakout. Against this, it needs to be reiterated that the battle had originally been conceived only as a supportive action for the much larger French attack on Vimy Ridge, the site where the real breakout was supposed to take place. Moreover, the 21st and 24th Divisions, in a wretched condition even before they reached the battlefield, should not have been brutally thrust into a situation where other, much more seasoned troops had fought valiantly but failed to rupture the German second defensive line. None the less, the battle for Loos, which was finally brought to an end on 16 October, had failed.

What did Haig learn from Loos? His distrust of his French allies, who, he felt, had failed to fight sufficiently vigorously at Vimy Ridge, was deepened. The key lesson from Loos should have been a determination never again to fight a battle at a time and place that he felt from the outset made the chance of success almost helpless, yet he was persuaded into precisely the same in 1916 at the Somme. Equally damagingly for the BEF and his own reputation, Haig became obsessed with the highly debatable idea that Loos' initial success could have been widened into a much larger and lasting breakthrough, if only Sir John French had shifted the ill-fated 21st and 24th Divisions much earlier to the vicinity of Loos, and placed them under Haig's authority from the start, or had placed at Haig's control other, more experienced and less physically exhausted divisions.

It is now, of course, impossible to know if three experienced and/or fresh divisions at Loos would have made all the difference on 25 September; more importantly, it was impossible for Haig to know that. He only hoped it might have been so. Much later, in 1921, Robertson said Loos demonstrated that 'More troops, more training, more aeroplanes, more guns, more ammunition, were required before decisive results could be achieved.'[62] This was all true, yet Haig cannot be exonerated from his own mistakes at Loos. He permitted himself to be forced to fight over ground he knew was exposed to German artillery. On the morning of 25 September, he casually started the gas attack on the basis of the smoke from a cigarette, without canvassing the opinion of the professionals manning the gas cylinders as to whether conditions were suitable. He had set his commanders an unrealistic goal by aiming to capture a town, Pont à Vendin, five miles distant, after a battle in which he already knew he would not have sufficient fresh reserves to exploit such a dramatic breakthrough, if it happened. And, when he sensed that the small gains made on the first day might be slipping from his grasp, he recklessly threw in more reserves before confirming whether they were battle-ready. None of these considerations was uppermost in Haig's mind in the messy in-fighting that ensued after Loos concluded. Haig instead focused his own and others' attention entirely on his assertion that the only cause of failure was the dilatory arrival on the battlefield of the reserves.

There are two possible conclusions to be drawn about Haig from this episode, and neither is flattering. One is that Haig may have felt – there is nothing, however, in his diary or letters to support this – that he had to blame Sir John French to deflect attention from his own conduct. This would have been dishonourable. The other is that Haig genuinely did feel the failure at Loos was due to the lack of sufficient reserves. Yet this is to ignore other relevant factors, and brings into question Haig's competence.

In any case, Haig by now thought French was finished. At a meeting between them on 28 September, the C-in-C 'seemed tired of the war, and said that in his opinion we ought to take the first opportunity of concluding peace otherwise England will be ruined! I could not agree, but said we cannot make peace till the Germany military party is beaten.'[63] For Haig, French was now a defeated man.

Taking full advantage of Kitchener's invitation to write frankly, Haig next day sent Kitchener an implicitly damning indictment of French in which, without actually naming Sir John, he stated: 'My attack, as has been reported, was a complete success. The enemy had no troops in his second line which some of my plucky fellows reached and entered without opposition. Prisoners state the enemy was so hard put to it for troops to stem our advance that the Officers' servants, fatigue men, etc. in Lens were pushed forward [. . .].' He went on to remind Kitchener that he had asked GHQ for reserves to be close at hand well before the battle, and concluded, ominously for French, 'We were in a position to make this the turning point in the war, and I still hope we may do so, but naturally I feel annoyed at the lost opportunity.'[64]

Was this a betrayal of Sir John French; merely Haig doing what he considered his duty; or simply his way of fending off criticism he may feared was headed his way? By early October, wounded men of the 21st and 24th Divisions were back in England, complaining publicly that they had been asked to carry out impossible orders and had not been properly fed for several days prior to being flung into battle. Whatever Haig's own hidden thought, he pursued his grudge against Sir John's supposed failure with Lord Haldane, who had been sent by Asquith's government to France on a fact-finding mission to learn what had gone wrong at Loos. Haig's first point to Haldane was that 'Neither the C-in-C, nor his Staff fully realised at the beginning (in spite of my letters and remarks) the necessity for Reserves being close up before the action began'. He ended by saying, 'Many of us felt that if these conditions continued, it would be difficult ever to win!'[65]

Prior to Haldane's visit, Haig had written a letter on 5 October to his brother John, then in Canada, in which, interestingly, he appeared to lay the blame for the failure at Loos more on the quality of the reserves, rather than their race to get to the battle in good time: 'You will have seen in the papers of our success on the 25th Sept & following days. We captured 28 guns, and took the enemy's position on a front of over 5 miles. Two new Divisions were placed behind my attacking troops as a Reserve. They had just landed in the country and the poor d – ls had never seen a shot fired in earnest. Consequently they were not much good. Otherwise I think we would have been right through the Enemy's second line as well as his first. Fighting is still going on hard, and we are causing the Germans heavy losses.'[66]

His opinion had subtly shifted by the time he wrote again to John, on 2 November: 'We actually broke the Enemy's line on the 25th Sept but French insisted on keeping the Reserves under his own hand so long that they did not arrive in time to be of use. And then although other Divisions which had had experience in the war were available, the Reserves consisted of two new arrivals. These when they did come up were worn out with fatigue and fled at the first shelling!'

By mid-October 1915, Sir John French's position had become impossible, and Loos became the justification for his ousting. Haig assisted in delivering the *coup de grâce*, although he would not have seen it as such. According to Haig's diary for 17 October, King George V had instructed Lord Stamfordham, his private secretary, to ask Sir William Robertson, CGS,[67] if 'he did not consider the time had come to replace Sir J. French.

Robertson did not answer. He saw the King afterwards in London, and now he came to discuss the point with me. I told him at once that up to date I had been most loyal to French and did my best to stop all criticisms of him or his methods. Now at last, in view of what had happened in the recent battle over the reserves [. . .] I had come to the conclusion that it was not fair to the Empire to retain French in command. Moreover, none of my Officers Commanding Corps had any opinion of Sir John's military ability or military views; in fact, they <u>find no confidence in him</u>. Robertson quite agreed, and left me saying "he knew now how to act, and would report to Stamfordham." '[68]

This stiletto in French's back – if it is viewed as that and not as the justified removal of an incompetent C-in-C – was not something that Haig initiated. Far more deadly blows had been struck by Robertson who, as French's CGS, might have been expected to have remained loyal, but struggled to do so. Robertson had written to Stamfordham in 1915 that, as far as the British government was concerned, 'he [French] is a discredited nonentity, I take it. He, moreover, has never really sincerely, and honestly concerted with the French, while they regard him as by no means a man of ability or a faithful friend, and therefore they do not confide in him. Joffre and he have never yet been a mile within the heart of each other. Further, he has never fully laid his opinions before the Government. He has too much taken the stand of doing as he wishes, and telling the Government nothing. I have been very concerned about this for a long time past.'[69]

In retrospect, this letter from Robertson is painfully ironic; Robertson himself (and Haig, too) were to do their best, later in the war, to keep the government just as much in the dark as did French. To his nephew Oliver, then a colonel in the County of London Yeomanry, Haig wrote on 31 October 1915: 'As you know I have only one thought and that is how to beat the Germans! I have been most loyal to French from the outset and I don't intrigue. But I have come to the conclusion that it will be difficult to beat the Germans in this area with him in chief command! He does not understand the game at which the Armies are playing!'[70]

On 25 November, Robertson told Haig that a Cabinet decision had been taken to sack Sir John French. By Friday 3 December Haig was at the War Office, where Kitchener told him he had been recommended to Asquith to take over from French, a decision confirmed by a letter dated 8 December 1915 and signed by Asquith. The Prime Minister disingenuously stated that French had resigned, although he had actually been threatened with being given nothing if he did not leave quietly. Haig's appointment as the new C-in-C was formally announced by the War Office on 15 December. One of French's last acts as C-in-C was an attempt to browbeat Asquith into replacing Kitchener as Secretary of State for War, a crude ploy to obtain some personal revenge that was understandably rejected by the Prime Minister. Sir John, before he left, received in Paris the Croix de Guerre from a French high command that was delighted to see him go.[71] Back in England, French was appointed to the military equivalent of the man who brings on refreshments at half-time: C-in-C Home Forces. Later, he was to be used by Lloyd George, when Prime Minister, as an emissary designed to bring down Haig. For French, Haig was the villain responsible for his downfall.

The government hoped that, with Haig as C-in-C, relations with the French high command might improve. Unlike the king – and Sir John – Haig had a good grammatical grasp of the French language and could converse freely, although with a distinct English accent; he took daily French lessons, time and work permitting.[72] Kitchener privately instructed Haig to 'keep friendly with the French. General Joffre should be looked upon as the C-in-C, in France where he knew the country and general situation well. It was different elsewhere, e.g., the Balkans and Egypt, etc. But in France we must do all we can to meet the French C-in-C's wishes whatever may be our personal feelings about the French Army and its Commanders.'[73]

Thirty years since his first commission, Haig, now fifty-four, had been handed the greatest operational task for a British officer. Others who might have vied for the post had fallen by the wayside. Grierson was dead; Smith-Dorrien had been sacked; Hamilton had become mired in the disaster at Gallipoli. In December 1915 Haig was a fairly unfamiliar figure to ordinary British citizens and not much loved by the press, which either knew or suspected he held that trade in contempt. The *Sunday Times* published a generally warm profile of the new C-in-C on 19 December 1915, though it opened with the barbed comment that: 'There are spots on every sun and it must be confessed that the new Commander-in-Chief does not like journalists.'

On 27 December Doris learned from her husband what he thought was expected of him: 'Everything is going very smoothly here, thanks. Indeed I am astonished at the feeling of relief which is manifested at Sir J's [French's] departure. On the other hand all seem to expect success as the result of my arrival, and somehow give one the idea that they think I am "meant to win" by some Superior Power. As you know, while doing my utmost, I feel one's best can go but a short way without help from Above.'

But Haig soon discovered that the pinnacle of power was a windswept, comfortless place, peopled by many unpredictable enemies and few genuine friends. For one thing, the BEF was still starved of sufficient shells; in the final week before Christmas 1915 the BEF's howitzers had been limited to 200 rounds per division, which worked out at less than three rounds per howitzer per day. No sensible offensive action could be planned until this crippling shortage was solved; it would take months. The Germans were almost the least of Haig's worries. His orders from Kitchener were uncannily similar to those handed to Sir John French in August 1914: 'The defeat of the enemy by the combined Allied Armies must always be regarded as the primary object for which the British troops were originally sent to France, and to achieve that end the closest cooperation of French and British as a united Army must be the governing policy; but I wish you distinctly to understand that your command is an independent one, and that you will in no case come under the orders of any Allied General further than the necessary cooperation with our Allies already referred to.'[74]

Thus Haig was saddled with precisely the same ambiguity concerning his command that had caused French endless friction and which, ultimately, had been his undoing. Moreover, Haig failed to anticipate – and never really understood – that his elevation to the post of C-in-C meant he was no longer simply a military officer, but had become a political general, whether he liked it or not. Would Haig prove any better than his old mentor, at understanding the real nature of the game?

# CHAPTER TEN

# The Somme

The situation is never so bad or so good as first reports indicate.

Douglas Haig

What worries me is the making of the peace. I confess that I have anxiety when I think of the day on which we may be seated round the Council Table discussing terms of peace. I am not thinking so much of the enemy as of the Allies.

William Robertson

How Haig conducted the battles of the Somme in 1916, with what was essentially an army dominated by raw volunteers, is critical to our lasting judgement of him as a man and a general. On balance, he emerges from this campaign with his weaknesses and strengths more exposed than ever before. What did Haig see as his task at the Somme? Was it to be a limited battle, with clearly defined and feasible targets? Or was it to be a battle fought in an *ad hoc* fashion, pushing against the German defences to probe for weaknesses that might be exploited? Or both? Haig's aspirations shifted to and fro during the course of the campaign, not so much in response to the behaviour of the German divisions he faced but more according to the fluctuating demands of his French allies and the hectoring of his political masters in London.

The Somme threw the weaknesses of Haig's personality and the army's traditional *modus operandi* into a harsh light. A lifetime's professional indoctrination in such a hidebound organization as the Victorian army had done little to erode Haig's innate conservatism, and during the Somme, which rather than a single battle was a series of overlapping attempts to dislodge the Germans from their frontline defences, Haig's occasionally contradictory personality naturally manifested itself through his managerial style. While on the one hand he was remote, dogmatic, staunchly self-certain and only superficially collegiate, he was also sometimes open to persuasion, willingly embraced new technology (such as the tank), and frequently devolved considerable operational responsibility to his immediate subordinates, the corps commanders.

Haig's strategic method never wavered from the one he first set the BEF at Neuve Chapelle – a probe in strength of supposed weak spots in the German defences, to be followed by an extensive breakthrough on a broad front. Yet he had nothing to offer subordinates by way of suggestions as to what tactics might achieve that goal, other than reiterating the need for urgency, determination and stoicism; in other words, he conducted the Somme, and Third Ypres in 1917, according to the dictates of his character and the tools he had to hand. While he required his corps commanders to develop their own schemes for the offensive, he often rejected, amended or overruled them when they did not tally with his preconceived strategic ambition – which always looked for the chance of a complete breakthrough.

With hindsight, Haig seems to have been remarkably confident throughout the war that the German army on the Western Front was perpetually on the brink of throwing in the towel. This irrepressible optimism led Haig to credit the more encouraging intelligence reports fed to him by Charteris, particularly those that claimed German morale was close to collapse. Nor was Haig's burden of responsibility eased by constant harrying from his French military peers, who remained, for far too long, convinced of the moral superiority of the offensive. And it certainly did not help that Haig, as did Sir John French, found himself fighting a war on two fronts – against the Germans in front of him and hostile British politicians at his back.

The Somme established that Haig's major asset as a commander in the field was an implacable long-term determination not to give up hope, but when this virtue translated into short-term stubbornness, it became a besetting vice. His error was a refusal or inability to recognize that the political, technological and material conditions prevailing in 1916 rendered a swift return to fighting in open ground – a return to mobile warfare – quite impossible. This was compounded by his failure to pose, to himself and others, penetrating questions as to why the Somme offensive, after it drew to an end, simply resulted in a prolongation of the prevailing stalemate. In his final dispatch as C-in-C in 1919, he asserted: 'If the whole operations of the present war are regarded in correct perspective the victories of the summer and autumn of 1918 will be seen to be as directly dependent upon the two years of stubborn fighting that preceded them.'[1] This post-war defence of his conduct of the Somme – that it had been a necessary battle of mutual attrition, the wearing down of the enemy's strength, numbers and will power being an intrinsic part of an inescapable process which, in turn, laid the groundwork for ultimate success – was certainly not how Haig viewed events during the battle itself.

His justification of the Somme (and Third Ypres) in 1919 was a *post hoc ergo propter hoc* fallacy which sought to persuade that, because the war ended in a German agreement to sign an armistice, therefore the bloody battles of 1916 and 1917 were contributory factors in bringing about that armistice. Yet both before and during the Somme campaign Haig shifted his ground, sometimes considering that the BEF was engaged in a battle of attrition with limited territorial aims, while at other times exhorting corps and divisional commanders that a decisive breakthrough was just around the corner. This can be viewed as understandable pragmatism, given changing battlefield conditions; but it was also confusing for his senior commanders, who often received orders from GHQ setting targets they did not believe achievable. When they had sufficient backbone to say so, they were conscious that they risked at worst dismissal or at best a good 'talking to'. Mostly, they preferred to try to interpret Haig's wishes and translate them into concrete instructions as best they could, relying on junior officers all down the line to implement orders that, the closer to the fighting they were, the more hopeless they often seemed. Haig's personality – inarticulate, intimidating, dogged – only painfully adapted to the altered nature of warfare. In one sense, Haig himself had much to learn; that he was a diligent but slow pupil is now indisputable.

Haig started the disheartening year of 1916 by reaffirming on 1 January to Colonel (later General) Jean des Vallières, who had taken over as head of the French mission at GHQ, that he would try to fulfil Kitchener's inherently contradictory general instruction: 'I pointed out that I am <u>not under</u> General Joffre's orders, but that would make no difference, as my intention was to do my utmost to carry out General Joffre's wishes on strategical matters, as if they were orders!'[2]

It seems not to have occurred to Haig at this date, or indeed ever, that the ambiguous instructions he inherited from Sir John French had indirectly led to the debacle at Loos. They left unresolved the vital question of who – if and when a crisis arrived – was actually in overall command of strategy in France and Belgium. Haig would take guidance from Joffre *if* he chose to do so and so long as it was understood they were *not* orders; Joffre was free to make his wishes known to Haig, but could not be certain that they would be met. Overlaying this uncertainty about overall command prevailing between GHQ and its French equivalent, GQG (Grand Quartier Général), was a condition of paralysing bureaucratic confusion in London, where the Committee of Imperial Defence had sunk into abeyance and a succession of advisory committees to the government, all of whose members were variously involved in intrigues against other factions, clogged the machinery of war. Not until December 1916, when Lloyd George as Prime Minister formed his War Cabinet – 'in essence a democratic form of constitutional dictatorship'[3] – did the British government begin to develop a method of implementing executive decisions more quickly. Even then, however heavily the War Cabinet relied on a plethora of sub-committees with overlapping responsibilities, the scope for muddle and shirking controversial decisions never entirely disappeared. One reason why Kitchener behaved with such abrupt authority as Secretary of State for War was because he was determined to avoid being sucked into the quagmire that was the prevailing mode for the War Office.

Robertson, now Chief of the Imperial General Staff (CIGS) at the War Office, began in 1916 a detailed correspondence with Haig, the recurring theme of which was the inability of the government's leading figures to agree on almost anything regarding the conduct of the war. Robertson's hand had been considerably strengthened at the War Office, as he had made it a condition of his appointment that he, not Kitchener, would be chief military adviser to the government. This direct access to the Cabinet was used by Robertson to promote his and Haig's settled opinion that all other theatres but the Western Front were wasteful diversions. After seventeen months of fighting, however, the mutual suspicion between London's politicians and the generals in France was shortly to mutate into outright hostility, making Haig's task inordinately more difficult than it was already.

On 2 January 1916 Haig made a small, yet, given his position, highly symbolic gesture which reinforced the growing view at GHQ that he was a very different type of C-in-C to French; he stepped inside a 'small dingy concert-hall at 116 rue de Dunquerque' in St. Omer, which had been allocated as an 'uninviting' home to the Church of Scotland. Once inside, 'A most earnest young Scotch man, George Duncan, conducted the service. He told us that in our prayers we should be as natural as possible and tell the Almighty exactly what we feel we want. The nation is now learning to pray and that nothing can withstand the prayers of a great united people. The congregation was greatly impressed and one could have heard a pin drop during the service. So different from the coughing and restlessness which goes on in Church in peace time.'[4] Since his childhood, Haig's religious observance had eased into an unostentatious faith; but during the war he increasingly felt need of spiritual reassurance, and frequently expressed this by reiterating that the struggle was not just with the German armies, but evil incarnate.[5]

The Reverend Duncan was a very junior army chaplain and, although his work involved him ministering to units attached to GHQ, high-ranking officers such as Haig had never previously joined his congregation. Of Sir John French 'and the officers on the GHQ staff I saw nothing. They moved in an altogether different realm.'[6] Duncan was gratified but also astonished to see Haig among his congregation, but the C-in-C was clearly touched by Duncan's plain style and unadorned sermons. Haig's instrumentalist view of army chaplains held them to be not just moral and spiritual guardians, but also rear-area soldiers with a vital role in boosting morale.[7] One of his first meetings as C-in-C was with the Bishop of Khartoum, the Right Reverend L. H. Gwynne, Deputy Chaplain General with responsibility for chaplains in France. Haig listened to Gwynne's Christmas Day 1915 sermon and informed the Bishop that 'a good chaplain is as valuable as a good general [. . .] We are fighting for Christ and the freedom of mankind.'[8] He regarded the widely prevalent internal bickering of the Church of England, over the role and functions of its clergy within the BEF, to be pointless time-wasting.[9]

Haig's own faith was not something that he either discussed or agonized over. On the eve of the Somme, he would write to Doris:[10]

> Now you must know that I feel that every step in my plan has been taken with Divine help – and I ask daily for aid, not merely in making the plan, but in carrying it out, and this I hope I shall continue to do until the end of all things which concern me on earth. I think it is this Divine help which gives me tranquillity of mind and enables me to carry on without feeling the strain of responsibility to be too excessive. I try to do no more than 'do my best and trust to God', because of the reasons I give above. Very many thanks for telling me your views on this side of my work, because it has given me the chance of putting my ideas on paper. For otherwise I would not have written them, as you know I don't talk much on religious subjects.[11]

For Haig, God was a palpable if metaphysically ill-defined being, and his worship of the deity was practical and unaffected. As far as it was possible with such an introspective person, Duncan struck up a close relationship with Haig and became a frequent guest at GHQ. He later wrote: 'Haig did not wear his religion on his sleeve. Never once during the war, so far as I recall, did he appeal in any public utterance to the Divine name. On addressing the troops he never invoked the Almighty as an ally. [. . .] If he did not give expression to his religion in public, he showed a similar reticence in private conversation. Had he been disposed to unbosom himself on matters of personal religion, he might presumably have done so to me. Yet he practically never did, either in speech or in writing; the occasions on which he did so might be numbered on the fingers of one hand.'[12]

Shortly after Haig first met Duncan, Henrietta, now in her sixty-fifth year, reminded her brother that spirits other than the Almighty were also keen to make contact. On 6 January she sent him another letter dictated by their dead brother George, who 'asked' her to convey to Haig that '[. . .] Almighty God is his helper and his guide and by the blessing of God a great soldier is allowed to be always near Douglas to advise him in his task. Napoleon is that soldier and his heart and soul are in the work and all the prayers of a great nation are united in asking God to guide His Armies to victory. I see the end of this struggle and how by God's blessing and Guidance our Douglas is the instrument He uses to crush the German invaders in France and Belgium. So tell Douglas with my love and blessing to go on as he is doing trusting to the mighty power above to shew him the way and tell him he will not ask in vain.'[13]

With God – and Napoleon – by his side, it is perhaps no surprise that Haig remained incorrigibly optimistic for all but the very darkest days of spring 1918, even though he faced a range of almost overwhelmingly complex tasks. The BEF expanded rapidly from some 270,000 officers and other ranks in December 1914 to more than one million by February 1916,[14] and the welding together of this greatly enlarged army, now utterly transformed by the influx of Kitchener's volunteers,[15] was comparable to the management of a vast business empire.[16]

The welding together of the new citizen army with the remnants of the old regular contingents was not always well handled. Brigadier-General Crozier, a tough-minded Northern Irish regular officer who fought throughout the war, thought the amalgamation of Kitchener's volunteers with the old regular army was carried out in extremely haphazard fashion: 'Round pegs are shoved into square holes. The old army, which runs the great national army, knows nothing about psychology and cares less. Names, ranks, records and length of service and suchlike things count most. When things and men run right it is purely a matter of luck, because unless the personal factor is taken into account, the formula is incomplete. Personal friendships and ability to tell good stories over a glass of port or to toady to military magnates are made the hidden reasons for recommendations for promotion.'

Promotion remained largely a matter of seniority rather than merit yet, as Crozier immediately pointed out, enlightened regular officers at his level could, if they had backbone, challenge the old nepotistic ways: 'I will have none of it. With us it is leadership, the lives of men and victory. That is why I have to send away a colonel, a charming fellow, a staff college graduate and a one-time instructor of some military subject, at some military establishment, sent to me for a month "to qualify for a brigade." He is unable to kick the Germans out of his line quickly on his own initiative, and prefers to write orders to doing things!'[17]

This was an attitude which Haig *believed* he shared. On taking over as C-in-C he had informed his military secretary, Brigadier-General Lowther – who dealt with the official correspondence of the C-in-C – that '[. . .] in my eyes only those who had proved their fitness for advancement should be promoted. I had no "friends" when it came to military promotion [. . .] He told me Sir John [French] wished to give an infantry brigade to Winston Churchill! I said that was impossible until Winston had shewn that he could bear responsibility in action as CO of a battalion.'[18]

This does not necessarily contradict Haig's appointment of old Aldershot and India associates to key positions on his staff at GHQ for, as far as Haig was concerned, they *had* so proved themselves; but neither was he indifferent to the undoubted benefit to himself of having people he knew around him. There was no objective selection (or dismissal) process in the BEF, and, as at Aldershot, Haig placed a premium on loyalty and determination, and none at all on the kind of creative debate that might sometimes have been more fruitful.[19] While this is how the British army had functioned since time immemorial, the discouragement of dissent at senior army conferences can, retrospectively, be seen as a serious failure within the planning and operational deliberations of

Boer commandos outside Ladysmith, 1899. British army failures in South Africa forced radical reforms, embraced by Haig. (*Imperial War Museum*)

Army manoeuvres in East Anglia in September 1912 saw Haig humiliated by developments in aircraft, such as the BE 3 model, seen here; but he learned a lasting lesson. (*GSL / JMB / Fleet Air Arm Museum*)

Haig (right) at Aldershot with King George V, *c.*1912. Haig's rise to senior rank owed much to his royal connections. (*Museum of Edinburgh*)

British lancers retreat during the Battle of Mons, late August 1914. For Haig, cavalry was always a vital military component. (*Imperial War Museum*)

France 1916: an impassive David Lloyd George (right) appears unmoved by Haig, while Albert Thomas, French Secretary for Munitions, and General Joseph Joffre look on. (*Museum of Edinburgh*)

Haig at GHQ in 1917 with his private secretary, Sir Philip Sassoon, one of the wealthiest men in England. (*Houghton Archives*)

Passchendaele Ridge, October 1917. The BEF's capture of this unimportant position had by this date become an end in itself. (*Imperial War Museum*)

8 August 1918: Overwhelming numbers of BEF Mark V tanks played a crucial part during the Battle of Amiens, the final rout of German troops. (*The Tank Museum*)

GHQ. By the time Haig became C-in-C he did not actively have to ban dissent; his reputation – a glance – was enough.

The BEF's battles of 1916 and 1917 were more bloody than they might have been not just because of deficiencies of *matériel* but because they were conducted under the aegis of the traditional, hierarchical ideology that was intrinsic to the old regular army, whose attitudes dominated what was in effect a new citizen army. At Aldershot, Haig had said he wanted a new generation of officers, trained to think for themselves; in the Great War, when many of the old regular army officers had disappeared by the time Haig took over as C-in-C, he was faced with a new generation of amateur volunteers; he did not feel sufficiently confident to trust that they would not only think, but also act according to what he believed was required.

Haig could not hope to control every aspect of the working of the BEF; he did not even have complete control over his closest staff. He wanted General Butler, who had served him as chief of staff at First Army, as his CGS at GHQ, but the War Office insisted this more senior appointment went to General Sir Launcelot Kiggell, who was senior to Butler, who became Kiggell's deputy.[20]

Despite his shortcomings, both innate and acquired, Haig was nevertheless in many respects a vast improvement over Sir John French. He was physically tough, emotionally stable, and mentally focused. He was capable of long working days, weekends included. The fact that he was careful to eat only plain food, drank little alcohol, and did not smoke ensured that he remained healthy.[21] His childhood asthma was a thing of the past, and the recurrent bouts of malaria and typhoid-related debilitation that peppered his days at the War Office – when he was evidently often bored – did not affect him during the Great War.[22]

GHQ staff found Haig's stability and unassuming personality a refreshing change. To have a C-in-C whose whereabouts were always known, and who perpetually exuded calm was, for GHQ staff, an enormously beneficial contrast to the disorderly and mercurial Sir John French. Major Neville Lytton, attached to GHQ's press bureau and no sycophant, even detected a touch of charisma: 'I fell immediately under the spell of his personal magnetism. [. . .] The common saying is, "Oh! Haig is not a clever man." I don't think he is very clever; personally I have never admired cleverness, it is the attribute of small successful men. Haig's qualities are much more moral than intellectual; what intellectual qualities he has have been used almost entirely within his own profession, but he exhales such an atmosphere of honour, virtue, courage, and sympathy that one feels uplifted as when one enters the Cathedral of Beauvais for the first time.'[23]

As C-in-C Haig held fast to his usual daily routine, any deviation from which he detested. After rising early, he checked the barometer and recorded its reading in his diary. He took a moderate breakfast before going to his office to study reports from the front, read cables from London, and hold meetings with senior staff and visiting officers. Regular briefings from Charteris, his senior artillery commander, General Noel Birch, and the RFC's Major Hugh Trenchard, punctuated the day. He spent most afternoons inspecting units close to the front. He then returned to GHQ, usually on horseback for at least part of the journey, or, in extreme cold, when the ground was too dangerous for riding, walked part of the way before being picked up by car.

Evenings usually saw a handful of guests at dinner, when Haig would leave much of the conversation to others and make his excuses after coffee, generally no later than 9.30pm. Rarely, he would meet privately after dinner with an especially influential guest – such as Asquith or Churchill – over coffee and brandy, but he preferred to retire to his study or bedroom and, after a final consultation with Kiggell, write his diary and personal letters. Before falling asleep he would usually read a few lines from the *Bible* or *The Pilgrim's Progress*, two of the very few non-military books he thought worth devoting time to.

Haig's working life was punctuated by regular meetings, usually weekly, with army commanders, occasional morale-boosting visits to units in rest areas, bestowing medals at regimental bases or meeting subordinates in the field. A mountain of paperwork – official and unofficial letters, memos, battle plans, correspondence with all and sundry – constantly accumulated on his desk. Occasionally, he would be called on to confirm a death sentence served on a British soldier for military crimes such as desertion or refusing to obey an order in the face of the enemy, or even murder. This was the responsibility of the C-in-C and Haig, as French had before him, refused to confirm the vast majority – 89 per cent – of the death sentences that came his way. He always preferred to give a condemned man a second chance – although by today's standards a number of the 306 men executed for specifically military crimes might be judged to have been dealt with harshly.[24]

Haig certainly lived in relative comfort, while an hour's drive away the soldiers he commanded were often in filthy, cramped and dangerous trenches; but each bore their own particular stresses, and Haig had proved his personal courage, if not much interest in roughing it, in both this and earlier conflicts.[25] It would have been of no use to the men in the trenches for Haig to have endured their conditions; it was unthinkable that he should. In any case, Haig signified a greater degree of permanence and purpose in his command by moving GHQ on 31 March 1916 from its hurriedly arranged and crowded accommodation at St Omer to the small, pretty town of Montreuil-sur-mer near the French coast. Two miles outside Montreuil, Haig established his personal base at Château de Beaurepaire, a peaceful mansion in its own woodland set back from the road.

Now thrust into the glare of public attention as never before, Haig responded by becoming even more circumspect as to what he said, and to whom he said it. Through the doors of GHQ flowed an unending stream of Cabinet ministers, trade unionists, journalists, politicians, writers, artists, as well as BEF and French staff officers and commanders, some of whom helped keep him abreast of political machinations in London, Paris and Chantilly, the town where the French GQG was then situated. Most of these guests found Haig willing to listen but rarely ready to speak, his innate taciturnity distilled into almost total distrust of anyone but the king, Doris, Henrietta and his closest aides; given the likelihood of chance remarks being repeated as interesting gossip, this was only wise.[26]

One of Haig's first important guests, in January 1916, was Lloyd

George, in his capacity as Minister of Munitions. He found Lloyd George to be 'astute and cunning, with much energy and push but I should think shifty and unreliable.'[27]

This instant judgement by Haig, so characteristic of the man, would have been picked up by the sensitive politician's antennae – their relationship got off to a bad start, and deteriorated as time passed. This failure to trust and respect each other's merits was highly damaging to Britain's war effort.

Haig assiduously collected military information and personal gossip, but fed little of either to his visitors; his private diaries and letters to Doris and family provided an outlet for the often savage dismissals of those he met.[28] Much of the badgering sycophancy Haig was subject to was handled by Haig's private secretary, the almost equally enigmatic Sir Philip Sassoon MP,[29] whose commission as a second lieutenant in the East Kent Yeomanry had been activated on 5 August 1914.[30]

At twenty-seven, Philip Albert Gustave David Sassoon was one of Britain's richest men, with the vast annual private income of £12,000 until, at the age of thirty, he came into his full inheritance and became wealthier still.[31] Sassoon was superbly equipped for the delicate task, far more so than Haig himself, of handling with great tact both enemies and friends of the C-in-C.[32] Churchill later wrote that Sassoon sat 'like a wakeful spaniel at the front door' of GHQ[33] but he was more akin to Haig's magpie, acquiring useful titbits of information and gossip, some of which he conveyed to the 'Chief', as Haig became universally known.[34]

Sassoon's appointment was Haig's way of repaying a debt, and also meant he kept a finger on the pulse of the establishment back in London; he was a cousin of Haig's old friend Leopold Rothschild, with whom Haig had maintained a warm friendship since their first encounter in a Swiss spa town in 1906. Sir Philip had also been taken up by Esher, who publicly befriended everyone he thought useful, even those whom he privately despised.[35] When Haig arrived at GHQ, the ever generous Rothschild continued to send hampers of game, delectable wines and fine brandy; in return, Sir Philip wrote letters of grateful thanks on behalf of Haig, dropping and passing on titbits of news and gossip, both great and small. These letters betray an insouciant remoteness from the harsher realities of the war. On 20 March 1916, for example, Sassoon informed Rothschild that 'as you are kind enough to say that you would like to know what would please him – might I make a suggestion – namely that occasionally instead of mixed fruits and Foie Gras – a chicken or shoulder of lamb (which the King's Messenger could bring out) would be most gladly and greedily welcomed. He loves good meat and it is rather hard to get out here.'[36]

Rothschild happily obliged. On 27 March 1916 Sassoon thanked him for the 'fowls and meat. [. . .] It was all quite excellent and made the pièce de résistance of our dinner to Caddina[37] who wolfed down your meat and no wonder. He was a very nice simple little man – a great contrast to Son Excellence Porro.[38] He presented Sir D.H with the Grand Cordon of St Maurice and Lazarus – apple green moiré with ornaments of frosted sugar. I saw it first on an empty stomach and it gave me quite a turn!'

It was a rarefied existence compared to that of most front line soldiers. The robust Brigadier-General Crozier took a very dim view of this kind of cosseting when he came across it in his own, rather less cushioned, part of the Western Front. Crozier later wrote: 'I remember one rich brigadier who in 1916 kept a sort of open mess for which he paid, but which was more like a society lunch than a serious effort to establish war hardiness and endurance. Chickens, hams, jellies, wines and various rich and unwholesome foods were posted to this soldier daily by a devoted wife, or consigned from fashionable stores. It was not war.'[39]

Compared to Sassoon, Haig was poor. At the start of the war Haig had slightly more than £5,260 in his bank deposit and current accounts;[40] in August 1916 his pay as C-in-C (including field and other allowances) totalled £447, 8 shillings and 4 pence for the month, on which he paid tax of almost £73.[41] This was, however, a handsome salary compared to the average weekly pay for the humblest private soldier, which was slightly more than eleven shillings, or that of £3 and 10 shillings a week (including field allowances) for a subaltern.[42] Although Haig enjoyed basking in the glow of others' wealth, as did Lloyd George, Sassoon was in some respects an odd choice by Haig for his private secretary. For one thing, Sassoon was distinctly 'sharp', his cleverness placing him well beyond the average competence Haig had once told Henrietta was the attribute he most sought from subordinates. On the other hand, Sassoon's personal fastidiousness[43] (his main delights were gossip, mixing with high society, and interior decor) caused Haig no embarrassment. Doris, considerably more sensitive to social conventions than her husband, intensely disliked Sir Philip, whom the snobbish Virginia Woolf later dismissed as 'an underbred Whitechapel Jew'.[44] Despite their very different natures, Haig and Sassoon's relationship survived all the ups and downs that were to come, with Sassoon at the end of 1918 acting as a useful intermediary between Haig and Lloyd George in the thorny matter of a government gratuity and Haig's peerage.

As Haig was taking over as C-in-C, plans for operations on the Western Front in 1916 were being formulated at a conference of Allied military commanders at GQG at Chantilly, between 6 and 8 December 1915. There, Joffre outlined his wish for a concerted simultaneous attack by all Allied armies on all the main European fronts of the Central Powers. There was little profundity to this scheme; by such simultaneous offensives it was hoped to stretch Germany and Austria–Hungary to breaking point. The Chantilly conference agreed that efforts to under-mine the Central Powers at Gallipoli and Salonika, both conspicuous failures, should be either abandoned (Gallipoli) or reduced to a holding position (Salonika). The Italians would resume their attack at Isonzo, northwards into Austria–Hungary, from which they had already been repulsed on five previous occasions; the Russians would hold their southern front against Austria–Hungary while launching a major onslaught to the north, against Germany; the French and British would focus their efforts around Picardy, on either side of the River Somme, which lay roughly midway in the German line, with the French army taking the leading role. And finally, in order to build up sufficient manpower[45] and material resources, the generals agreed this concerted effort would not be unleashed before the spring of 1916.

This overall plan was duly endorsed by the Allies' political leaderships.

In London, the War Committee,[46] a sub-committee of the Cabinet, had already become disenchanted with the Dardenelles expedition and, not for the last time, switched direction, reverting (to Haig's satisfaction) to the Western Front as its main hope for defeating the Central Powers. The War Committee had recommended on 15 November 1915 that no further British resources should be given to the campaign in Salonika, and on 23 November it had decreed an evacuation at Gallipoli. The Committee also agreed that the actual plan of attack in France and Belgium was to be left to the discretion of the commanders in the field, Joffre and Haig.

All this partially satisfied Haig, who was certainly glad to learn that the waste of resources at Gallipoli would be ended. On the other hand, he was doubtful that some aspects of the general scheme of attack stood much hope of success. In particular, he had no respect for the Italian army, nor much for Italians generally. Following a conference at Joffre's HQ at Chantilly on 12 March 1916, he noted in his diary that 'The Italians seem a wretched people, useless as fighting men, but greedy for money. Moreover, I doubt whether they are really in earnest in this war. Many of them too are German spies.'[47] Haig's xenophobia, if such it was, was hardly exceptional, and he would merely have judged it bad manners, rather than anything else, to air this contempt for the Italians in public. He held much the same low opinion of the Portuguese, the Belgians, the Serbians and other allies, and his feelings in this regard did not moderate as the war proceeded. His greatest suspicions, though, were reserved for the French.

The War Committee was, however, internally divided, and in early January 1916 one of its members, Arthur Balfour, disseminated a memo questioning the strategy of focusing all aggressive efforts on the Western Front at the neglect of other theatres. Another member, Reginald McKenna, Chancellor of the Exchequer, demanded of Kitchener that he guarantee the success of the Western-focused strategy in 1916, otherwise 'he could not accept it.'

Kitchener himself was in two minds. He told the War Committee in January 1916 that he was convinced that 'a violent offensive in the spring, followed up by another in the summer, may bring about the crisis of the war.'[48] Yet by the end of March 1916 Kitchener told Henry Rawlinson, GOC Fourth Army, that he was opposed to a big attack, and that, rather than seek a complete breakthrough, he preferred a number of small offensives 'with a view solely to killing Germans.'[49]

This irresolution was to remain at the heart of British military planning throughout 1916 and 1917, and returns us to our initial question – what was Haig's task to be at the Somme? The political vacillation in London fed through to Haig and Robertson and made their planning for the spring attack on the Western Front more difficult. Everyone hoped, Haig included, that *this* particular battle might succeed in finally breaking the German lines, as well as killing more Germans; when it failed to be so, attention then switched to the next battle. The hope was laudable, but the failure to learn from experience lamentable.

As far as Haig was concerned, Joffre's proposal of December 1915 was placed in further doubt by the French C-in-C's wish that the BEF should conduct, much earlier than the main French offensive, a series of continuous, smaller, wearing-down actions, designed to pull German reserves away from where the main French thrust would occur. Haig was aware that Joffre was anxious about French manpower resources; by the spring of 1916 French casualties amounted to some 1.43 million.[50] Yet Loos ought to have taught Haig the importance of not being drawn into a battle that was presented to him by the French as a *fait accompli*. An uneasy compromise was reached at a meeting at GQG between Haig and Joffre on 14 February, where Joffre agreed with Haig's proposal that the BEF's diversionary attacks would happen almost simultaneously with the French attack, with a delay of at most two weeks. What was clear to both sides at the conclusion of this meeting was that the BEF's strategic aim for 1916 was not a permanent breakthrough, but short-term attrition.

All these plans and counter-proposals were thrown into confusion when, on 21 February 1916, some 1,220 German guns fired two million shells in eight hours across an eight-mile front around the fortified French positions at Verdun, 200 miles south-east of the Somme. The German Chief of the General Staff, Erich von Falkenhayn, wrote in his post-war memoirs that, from the start, he had conceived of the

German attack at Verdun as an attritional battle to bleed France white and force it to its knees. Today, this is regarded as a post-hoc validation by Falkenhayn for his failure to achieve his real ambition to capture Verdun and bring about France's collapse, thereby achieving complete victory. His post-war self-justification in many respects bears a striking similarity to that offered by Haig for his own efforts at the Somme and Third Ypres – that attrition was always the intention, rather than merely an unfortunate by-product of a much grander aim. Falkenhayn was confident that French manpower reserves were on the brink of collapse and that the BEF – which Haig felt at this time was not really an army 'but a collection of divisions untrained for the field' – would be forced to flee Flanders, once the French army was crushed. By December 1916, when the French and Germans had achieved little more than mutual exhaustion around Verdun, French casualties from the battle were well in excess of 350,000 killed and wounded, Germany's almost as many,[51] and seventy out of a total of ninety-six French divisions serving on the Western Front had been rotated through the Verdun mincing machine.

Initially, the French GQG did not regard the attack on Verdun as a grave threat, but, as the struggle persisted through May, Joffre became desperate to put the Europe-wide grand offensive into action, with the important change that the BEF would now constitute the main force, with the aim not just of killing Germans but of relieving the pressure on the French at Verdun. In short, Verdun severely circumscribed Joffre's plans for the Somme; he had originally estimated deploying forty French divisions but by the end of May he reduced this to just twenty-five.[52]

Other disasters had already ensued; on 18 March a Russian attempt to force Germany to withdraw divisions from the west, by an ill-conceived attack at Lake Naroch, the largest lake in what is now the Republic of Belarus, resulted in humiliation and Russian casualties of some 100,000, without a single German division being diverted from the Western Front. On the Italian front, the Fifth Battle of the Isonzo (9–17 March 1916) had been hastily abandoned as an Austro-Hungarian Army attacked through the Trentino mountain passes in the north of Italy. In this context of generally depressing gloom the War Committee authorized Haig on 7 April to go ahead with his part of the Anglo-French offensive at the Somme. Haig and Joffre discussed the finer details of the offensive, established the dividing line between the French and British forces, and deliberated the timing of the attack.

In these discussions, between April and June 1916, Haig and Joffre found one another exasperating. At their meeting on 7 April Haig '[. . .] explained my views but Joffre did not seem capable of seeing beyond the left of the French Army [. . .] or indeed of realising the effect of the shape of the ground on the operations proposed. [. . .] The old man[53] [Joffre was sixty-four, nine years older than Haig] saw, I think, that he was talking about details which he did not really understand, whereas I had been studying this particular problem since last January, and both knew the map and had reconnoitred the ground. The conclusion I arrived at was that Joffre was talking about a tactical operation which he did not understand, and that it was a waste of my time to continue with him. So I took him off to tea. I gather that he signs everything which is put in front of him now and is really past his work, if, indeed, he ever knew anything practical about tactics as distinct from strategy. Joffre was an engineer.'[54]

Haig told Joffre he would bring forward the BEF's attack from its planned mid-August date to 20 June, even though this meant he would not have assembled all the artillery he considered necessary. Joffre replied that 1 July would be soon enough. Haig also began focusing his attention on Rawlinson and his Fourth Army, which Haig had determined would form the centrepiece of the British attack. At the invitation of Haig, Rawlinson had already suggested two possible courses of action. The more ambitious was an attempt to seize control in one rush over all the German lines of defence as far south as the Albert-Bapaume road. The other was 'less ambitious, but in my opinion more certain; to divide the attack into two phases, the first of which would give us possession of the enemy's front system, and all the important tactical points between the front system and the second line. The second phase to follow as soon as possible after the first, so as to give the enemy as little time as possible to construct new defences and bring up guns and reserves. The first alternative, I considered, was a gamble which involved considerable risks.'[55]

This represented an early formulation of the 'bite and hold' tactic, by which limited and more easily achievable objectives would be set for an offensive, rather than, as Haig had hitherto preferred, having a complete breakthrough as an ambition, if not an explicit goal. In early April 1916, however, Haig had already decided that Rawlinson's preferred option literally did not go far enough: 'I studied Sir H. Rawlinson's proposals for attack. His intention is merely to take the Enemy's first and second system of trenches and "kill Germans". He looks upon the gaining of 3 or 4 kilometres more or less of ground as immaterial. I think we can do better than this by aiming at getting as large a combined force of French and British across the Somme and fighting the Enemy in the open!'[56] 'Fighting the enemy in the open' was Haig's entirely worthy aim; less admirable was his failure to consider if such an aim was realistic.

By 30 April Rawlinson was in no doubt about what Haig wanted, although in reality the plan remained alarmingly ill-defined: 'I am quite clear in my mind now, about the plan. The bombardment is to be deliberate, four or five days, according to ammunition supply. The attack is to go for the big thing. I still think we would do better to proceed by shorter steps; but I have told D.H I will carry out his plan with as much enthusiasm as if it were my own.'[57]

The 'big thing' was a generalized breakthrough of all German defensive positions; Haig reiterated this to other senior commanders in the days leading up to the battle. He met General Aylmer Hunter-Weston, GOC VIII Corps (part of Fourth Army under Rawlinson) on 10 May: 'I impressed on him that there must be no halting attacks at each trench in succession for rear lines to pass through! The objective must be as far as our guns can prepare the Enemy's position for attack – and when the attack starts it must be pushed through to the final objective with as little delay as possible.'[58]

Rawlinson's deference to Haig's wishes, and his enforcement of this general instruction on his own subordinate corps and division commanders, was to lead directly to the disasters of the Somme, but the ultimate responsibility was Haig's and it is intellectually and morally dishonest to attempt to exonerate him from this. It is not enough to write, as John Terraine does: 'When one has said that Haig, his Staff and his chief subordinates were all involved together in a vast and tragic mistake, one has said everything.'[59]

The 'tragic mistake' was that Haig failed to think through whether he possessed the means to achieve his end. The British army barely had sufficient artillery for one of Rawlinson's limited, bite-and-hold operations, and to attempt to mount anything more substantial was a stab in the dark. As the historian Ian Malcolm Brown has commented, it was 'a failure in operational planning brought about by a desire to do more than could be attained.'[60] Haig's decision – to widen Rawlinson's task beyond the successively staged and carefully calculated piecemeal capture of the first two German defensive positions to encompass 'the big thing' – has been thoroughly analysed and condemned elsewhere,[61] but the greatest flaw in Haig's grand gesture was not the ambition itself but his failure to take stock of the battle as it proceeded, and to ask himself and his commanders whether or not that bigger aim was, for the time being, unattainable.

Clearly, GHQ staff planned for a major breakthrough right from the start; in May 1916 the Quartermaster General's department pondered how the army would be able to feed a civilian population up to sixty miles behind the German frontline, and requested that transport be reserved specifically for this improbable eventuality.[62] Yet, in partial exoneration of Haig, it must be said that he faced an impossible dilemma. While Rawlinson evidently believed 'the big thing' to be over-ambitious, Haig nevertheless was conscious of the inexorable pressure of great hopes from London; on 14 April Haig met Kitchener and Robertson at the War Office, where they told him he had the full support of the government for the forthcoming attack, and there was confidence that it would result in a 'definite victory over German arms.'[63] The ambiguity of the language – what, precisely, was a 'definite victory'? Complete surrender? – was unhelpful.

Kitchener and Robertson also gave Haig some disappointing news; 150 tanks, a new and untried weapon, yet one on which many hopes rested, would only be provided by 31 July. Haig wrote: 'I said that was too late. 50 were urgently required for 1 June. Swinton[64] is to see what can be done, and will also practise and train "Tanks" and crews over obstacles and wire similar to the ground over which the attack will be made. I gave him a trench map as a guide and impressed on him the necessity for thinking over the system of leadership and control of a group of "Tanks" with a view to manoeuvring into a position of readiness during an action.' Haig has often been criticized for being either unable to grasp the military importance of new technology, or being reluctant to use it, but he readily embraced all new inventions, when they became available and once he had been convinced of their efficacy. In the end, tanks were not available for Haig to use at the Somme until 15 September, and then only in a tiny quantity.[65]

On his return to France Haig again met Joffre, on 2 May. Haig was susceptible to little flatteries and Joffre was inclined to make them when he thought it useful. Haig noted: 'The old man was quite delighted to see me. When I made some ordinary remark about the day clearing up he said, "Il fait toujours beau temps quand vous venez me voir." '[66] On 4 May, Haig met the former French Prime Minister Georges Clemenceau at the latter's invitation. Now chairman of the Senate military committee, Clemenceau wanted to know what plans were in hand, and exhorted Haig to act as a restraining influence on Joffre, whose anxiety over Verdun, Clemenceau feared, might encourage Haig to act prematurely. Once again, the issue of overall command arose, as Clemenceau asked Haig if he was under Joffre's orders: 'I said Certainly NOT – at the same time it must be realised that there can be only one man responsible for the plans. These Joffre and his Staff worked out for France, and I did my best to co-operate with them; but I was responsible for the method of employment of the British Forces, so that if anything unfortunate happened, I am responsible and must bear the blame, not General Joffre!'[67]

Clemenceau's worries were well founded. On 26 May Joffre visited GHQ and brusquely informed Haig that the situation around Verdun was fast deteriorating. If the ranks of the French army were to be depleted at the current rate, then within a few weeks 'the French Army would be ruined! He therefore was of opinion that 1 July was the latest date for the combined offensive of the British and French. I said that before fixing the date I would like to indicate the state of preparedness of the British Army on certain dates and compare its condition. I took 1 and 15 July, and 1 and 15 August. The moment I mentioned 15 August, Joffre at once got very excited and shouted that "The French Army would cease to exist, if we did nothing till then"! The rest of us looked on at this outburst of excitement, and then I pointed out that, in spite of the 15th August being the most favourable date for the British Army to take action, yet, in view of what he had said regarding the unfortunate condition of the French Army, I was prepared to commence operations on the 1st July or thereabouts. This calmed the old man, but I saw that he had come to the meeting prepared to combat a refusal on my part, and was prepared to be very nasty. [. . .] They are, indeed, difficult Allies to deal with!'[68]

This feeling was mutual and also widespread; Haig was not the only British soldier to find the French difficult.[69] Joffre did not want to hear Haig's calm outlining of options; all Joffre really wanted to know was how many British troops could be flung into battle, and how soon. In fact, Joffre was exaggerating, although perhaps not deliberately, the gravity of the situation at Verdun; by 14 July, two weeks after the launch of the Somme offensive, French counter-attacks had pushed the German troops back and their attempt to take Verdun was effectively over, although such was the lack of inter-Allied cooperation that, at the end of May, Haig was unaware of the precise balance of the Verdun battle.

Haig's difficulty was that, while he did not want to be hustled by Joffre into a battle for which the BEF was unready, he was also concerned that, if Joffre's fears were right, the defeat of the French might lead to a general collapse, with himself held to blame because he had not started the BEF's offensive in good time. At the back of Haig's mind on 26 May was his uncertainty as to whether the BEF's New Army divisions would be ready to shoulder the brunt of the fighting at the Somme. Training exercises within the BEF were often unrealistic, and the skill with which new recruits to this citizen's army were handled was highly variable. GHQ's main instructional handbook was *Training of Divisions for Offensive Action*, issued by Kiggell, but it was very general and platitudinous. Rawlinson produced his own booklet, called simply *Tactical Notes*, which was distributed through Fourth Army down to the rank of captain; it at least tackled how new weapons such as Stokes mortars and Lewis guns (lighter, portable automatic guns) should be used in close support during an attack. There was, though, no overall, centrally controlled and administered training scheme, and, by the time the Somme battle started, many of the New Army divisions were already exhausted by laborious pre-battle rehearsals.

More damagingly, there was little or no coordinated artillery training; the high command 'was still thinking in terms of an infantry war.'[70] Although he did not realize it at the time, in his manual Rawlinson had hit upon a tactic that was to become increasingly important in 1917 and 1918 – the use of the creeping artillery barrage: '[. . .] the artillery to keep their fire immediately in front of the infantry as the latter advances, battering down all opposition with a hurricane of projectiles.'[71] But at the Somme this was to be just a suggestion; there was no attempt to impose this concept on any corps or divisional commander.

On 27 May, Haig met the commanders of the First, Second and Third Armies and asked them to finalize their operational plans for 'misleading the Enemy as to the real point of attack', advising them that these schemes should be ready for implementation by the end of June. The BEF's Second Army, commanded by Plumer, was to take the left, holding the line from north of Ypres to south of Armentières. To the immediate right of this was the Fourth Army, under Rawlinson. To the right of this was positioned the BEF's Third Army, commanded by Pulteney. Despite his encouragement to Rawlinson and other subordinate commanders to push the battle as far and as fast as possible, in the days immediately prior to 1 July Haig seemed to acknowledge he had no real hope of defeating Germany in 1916. He wrote to Bertie in Paris on 5 June[72] that:

My policy is briefly to

1. Train my Divisions, and collect as much ammunition and guns as possible.

2. To make arrangements to support the French attacking in order to draw off pressure from Verdun, when the French consider that the military situation demands it–

3. But while attacking to help our Allies not to think that we can for a certainty destroy the power of Germany this year. So in our attacks we must also aim at improving our positions with a view to making sure of the result of the campaign next year.

'Improving our positions' to aim for victory in 1917 was a vague aim and, more relevantly, not what Haig actually asked his subordinates to achieve at the Somme. On Friday 9 June, three days after the death of Kitchener, Haig attended a meeting with Asquith, Sir Edward Grey, Foreign Secretary, and Maurice Hankey, Secretary of the Imperial War Cabinet, at 10 Downing Street, where he told them what to expect from the forthcoming battle, which was to be of, in Joffre's words, 'durée prolongée'. That afternoon, Haig travelled with Doris and their two daughters, who had been once again brought down from North Wales to see their father, from London to Deal for a three-day break. While on the beach and leaning against some rocks, Doris and Douglas were surprised to be getting much more public attention than usual. Then they noticed that the children had scribbled in chalk above their heads THIS IS SIR DOUGLAS HAIG.[73]

On 24 June 1916, a sunny day, the preliminary bombardment of the BEF began over the Somme, reaching a crescendo two days later, whereupon the skies clouded over with rain, preventing RFC aircraft from seeing if the artillery were landing their shells on the right targets, or any targets at all.[74] There was a coordinated discharge of poison gas at 10pm on 24 June across the whole 24,000-yard front, from 20,000 cylinders; but thereafter, when gas was used during the Somme, it was sporadic and *ad hoc*, thus less effective than it might have been. According to Lieutenant-Colonel Foulkes, the engineer in charge of the British Gas Brigade, on 25 June Rawlinson, 'much to my disappointment, left the arrangements for the discharge of the remainder of the gas to his five Corps Commanders, who, in turn, delegated them to the thirteen Division Commanders in the front line, the result being that the one big operation that had been planned was broken up into a number of smaller attacks, thus putting the enemy on the alert after the first had taken place, and enabling him to concentrate the inevitable artillery retaliation on each one in turn.'[75] Foulkes's chagrin was understandable. By this stage of the war the use of poison gas had become immensely more technical, yet the different types of gas, and combinations of gas and smoke discharged at intervals and in varying quantities, were capable of creating, if not significant casualties, at least seriously debilitating nuisance. As it was, numerous divisional commanders simply instructed the gas units attached to them to get rid of the stuff as soon as possible.

On 27 June Haig instructed Rawlinson to prepare for 'a rapid advance': 'In my opinion it is better to prepare to advance beyond the Enemy's last line of trenches, because we are then in a position to take advantage of any breakdown in the Enemy's defence. Whereas if there is a stubborn resistance put up, the matter settles itself! On the other hand if no preparations for an advance are made till next morning, [after the first day of the battle] we might lose a golden opportunity.'[76]

The weather deteriorated further, however, and Rawlinson had to postpone his attack for forty-eight hours. The low cloud cover persisted through 29 and 30 June, again preventing observing aircraft from seeing if the German barbed wire and defensive emplacements had been destroyed; but the attack had to proceed on 1 July, otherwise it was feared the artillery would have insufficient ammunition for any follow-up after the infantry went in.

As the preliminary bombardment drew to an end, Haig wrote to Doris on 30 June:

> I feel that everything possible for us to do to achieve success has been done. But whether or not we are successful lies in the Power above. But I do feel that in my plans I have been helped by a Power that is not my own. So I am easy in my mind and ready to do my best what ever happens tomorrow.[77]

That same evening, Rawlinson noted in his diary: 'That the Boche will break, and that a débâcle will supervene, I do not believe; but if that should take place I am quite ready to take full advantage of it. We have done all that we can, and the rest is in the hands of the good God.'[78]

The failure of the British artillery to destroy the German defensive positions at the Somme needs no retelling here; many of the British shells were duds[79] and accuracy was poor, the result partly of poor spotting of the fall of shells. Out of the 1,500 artillery pieces used by the British in the bombardment, 1,000 of them (and one million out of the 1.6 million shells fired) were dedicated to destroying the thickets of barbed wire in front of the first and second lines of German trenches. But even this weight of explosive was hopelessly inadequate. The pre-battle calculation by Rawlinson's artillery adviser, Major-General Charles Budworth, who has been credited by some with the idea of the creeping barrage, was that the front to be attacked, almost fourteen miles, required 200 heavy how-itzers, one for every 120 yards. This was twice the number of guns used at Loos, but they were required to subdue twice the length of front.[80] Furthermore, the German frontline trench system was not a single line but a series of heavily defended redoubts and deeply dug emplacements, with a strongly defended second line anywhere between 2,000 and 4,000 yards behind the first.

The BEF did not possess enough artillery or shells for the task, nor for that matter, sufficient information about the German defences. Its gunnery was insufficiently accurate, and there was no assessment after the bombardment of the damage caused. There could therefore be no overall certainty that the German defenders had been destroyed before the first divisions left their trenches. As it was, in several parts of the German lines, as soon as the bombardment ceased, machine-gunners emerged from their undamaged dugouts and slaughtered British troops not just in their jumping-off positions in the front line but in reserve trenches far behind. To make matters worse, the failure of the BEF's counter-battery efforts meant that German shells rained down on the attackers, while many of the troops who did manage to reach the German front line discovered that in places the barbed wire was still intact.

On top of all this, the over-stretched transport system failed to guarantee sufficient supplies in the right place at the right time. Logistically, it is now clear that the BEF in mid-1916 'could not properly sustain the Somme. Until a system had been created that could, the BEF's offensives would invariably have the same character as the Somme – a prolonged drive into German lines, using ever-increasing quantities of ammunition and increasingly damaging the transportation infrastructure, until the offensive could no longer be maintained.'[81]

One enduring myth of the Somme should, however, be finally laid to rest; it is not true that the British troops who went over the top on 1 July were commanded not to run but only to walk, heavily laden, across the battlefield. In his *Tactical Notes* Rawlinson laid down no single speed nor any particular formation to be used to cross no man's land; unit commanders were given a wide latitude to conduct the advance as they thought most appropriate, given the particular circumstances of their part of the battlefield. The majority of the eighty battalions which went over the top in the first wave – fifty-three – had in any case crept out into no man's land, close to the German lines before zero hour, and then rushed the German trenches.[82]

At the same time, it is clear where this notion – of serried ranks of men slowly walking to their death – comes from. On 15 June, as he noted in his diary, Haig met his army commanders and instructed them that: 'The advance of isolated detachments should be avoided. They lead to loss of the boldest and best without result: Enemy can concentrate on these detachments. Advance should be uniform. Discipline and the power of subordinate Commanders should be exercised in order to prevent troops getting out of hand.'[83]

Army commanders who took away from this conference the view that a 'uniform advance' was the order of the C-in-C, and who filtered this down through their commands, merely followed instructions. Haig and his staff at GHQ had still not yet grasped the changed nature of the battlefield; they still emphasized above all else the idea that battles were to be won by infantry taking and holding enemy positions, and that the artillery's role was subordinate to that ultimate aim.[84] Yet with 57,000

British casualties (including some 19,000 dead) by the end of 1 July, the harsh lesson already taught the regular army at Neuve Chapelle and Loos – that spirited attacks with rifle and bayonet were no match for the machine-gun – had now been painfully learned by Kitchener's New Army, too. As the historians Robin Prior and Trevor Wilson argue, '[. . .] if the artillery had done their job it mattered little if the infantry walked or ran or executed the Highland fling across no man's land.'[85]

On 2 July, a Sunday, Haig noted in his diary that the casualty figures were more than 40,000: 'This cannot be considered severe in view of the numbers engaged, and the length of front attacked.' Indeed, Haig and others at GHQ regarded the initial attacks at the Somme a success, despite the heavy losses and insignificant gain. In his final dispatch in 1919 Haig, would still insist, against all the evidence, that 'Immense as the influence of mechanical devices might be, they cannot by themselves decide a campaign. Their true role is that of assisting the infantryman, which they have done in a most admirable manner. They cannot replace him. Only by the rifle and the bayonet of the infantryman can the decisive victory be won.'[86] This was almost precisely the same view that Kiggell had expressed at the Staff Conference in 1911. If this passage in his final published view of the war was not a rhetorical flourish – something Haig was not much given to, although it is probable that Sassoon composed much of this dispatch – but genuinely meant, then it demonstrates a radical failure by Haig to understand what had happened in Flanders in the years 1916–18.

On 3 July, when Haig was visited by Joffre, who initially was enraged that the attack was apparently not being pressed home, Henrietta sent him another letter, supposedly dictated by their dead brother George:

My dear Douglas–
God bless and keep you safe because you are going to be the Saviour of your Country. [. . .] I am always going to see you and always there is the great Soldier Napoleon straining every nerve to give you health and a right judgement of the situation – as he can visit also both the camps he is of course in a better position to advise than one who only sees his own side:

at the present time all is going as it ought to do – There will of course be
sets back as a wave recedes to come again with added force so your Armies
will ebb and flow each flow being in advance of the one before – I think
you are so confident of success it is your own magnetism that puts strength
into the soldiers and makes them brave even death itself for their cause.
[sic] and the pride & confidence of the whole Army in you is unsurpassed
and their morale perfect [...] May our Heavenly Father lead you and
guide you in all that you do or undertake is the daily prayer of your
devoted Mother and Geordie.[87]

On 8 July, Haig reluctantly met *The Times*' military correspondent,
who had secured the meeting at GHQ by pulling strings with Esher.
Repington noted that 'Haig explained things on the map. It is staff work
rather than generalship which is necessary for this kind of fighting. [...]
He said that he welcomed criticisms, but when I mentioned the criticisms which I had heard of his misuse of artillery on July 1, he did not
appear to relish it, and denied its truth. As he was not prepared to talk of
things of real interest, I said very little, and left him to do the talking.
[...] I don't know which of us was the most glad to be rid of the other.'[88]
In his own version of the meeting Haig noted that he 'hated meeting such
a dishonest individual, but I felt that it was my duty to the Army do so –
otherwise he would have been an unfriendly critic of its actions.'

The day before, yet another 'dishonest individual' had taken a step
closer to his ultimate ambition, the occupancy of 10 Downing Street. On
7 July Lloyd George handed over the Ministry of Munitions to Edwin
Montagu and took over as Secretary of State for War, in the wake of
Kitchener's death. This meant he acquired civilian authority over Haig
and the generals, a power he was determined to use to rein in what he
regarded as their wastefulness of manpower.

On the Western Front, the weeks succeeding 1 July brought just
enough minor breaches in the German front lines – there was, for example, a relatively successful attack against Bazentin in the dawn of 14 July,
by two divisions of Rawlinson's Fourth Army, formed up under cover of
darkness in no man's land, a plan which Haig initially opposed as being

impossible – for Haig and GHQ to consider the early stage of the Somme an overall success. Ironically, the success at Bazentin merely served to encourage Haig's greater ambition for a significant breakthrough; in their praise of him, his acolytes kept his hopes unrealistically buoyant. On 7 August 1916, by which time the promise of further limited success had evaporated, Esher wrote to Haig:

My dear Douglas,

Your steady but fatalistic progress is wonderful. It must be due to what Northcliffe calls your Fifeshire chin! [. . .] Yesterday I went to Chantilly and saw Clive.[89] He told me privately that Robertson was a bit 'rattled' by the politicians. They actually asked him to '*certify* that the offensive would attain its objects.' This is a demand which I should imagine had never in the whole history of war been made upon a soldier. But the old man responded gallantly, and 'certified' accordingly. [. . .] If the combination of you and Robertson were to fail, no other is possible, and we may as well hand over to Joffre, or make peace. [. . .] You are on top of the plateau, in more senses than one.

Next day George V visited Haig's temporary HQ at Cassel and on 12 August he was guest at a lunch attended by the French President, Raymond Poincaré, and Generals Ferdinand Foch and Joffre, the latter visibly dismayed at being offered a choice of lemonade or ginger beer over lunch; afterwards Kiggell was knighted, while Haig was rewarded by the king with the Knight Grand Cross of the Royal Victorian Order (GCVO) and thanked by him for what he had done for his 'family'. The king had previously informed Haig that both Churchill and Sir John French were busily at work in London, criticizing the Somme offensive. Haig told him these were 'trifles' that should not 'divert our thoughts from our main objective, namely "beating the Germans"! I also expect that Winston's head is gone from taking drugs.'[90] Whether these 'drugs' were medicinal or recreational, Haig sadly did not say.

Sassoon duly echoed his master's voice to Rothschild on 14 August: 'Everything is going very satisfactorily here and the whole outlook is good. If we can, as I hope, keep up combined pressure right into the

Autumn the decision ought not to be far off. I believe everyone is pleased at home except Winston and Sir John! Ever since the offensive began I have heard that Churchill has been crabbing it, saying that it was premature, was far too costly and was turning out a complete failure. He has a personal grievance against Haig.'[91]

Throughout the Somme campaign, Haig received intelligence reports from Charteris that encouraged his incorrigible optimism about the supposed poor morale of the German troops – reports which did not accord with the facts as seen by others at the time: 'The German morale at this time was excellent, in spite of the weekly statements to the contrary issued by the Intelligence Department at G. H. Q. We were constantly being told that "the enemy morale is breaking down under the continuous pressure of our attacks," [. . .] but there were no symptoms of it in the splendid defence which was put up. Whether these statements were issued in order to inspire our men with confidence, I do not know, but they had no foundation in fact, neither at the Battle of the Somme nor, a year later, during the Third Battle of Ypres, when we were informed almost daily, that "the breaking point had been reached." '[92] Indeed, the intelligence Charteris produced sometimes seems entirely irrelevant: on 22 August, for instance, he informed Haig that while a German division was 'worn out' in four and a half days when opposing a British division, 'opposite the French they last very much longer, sometimes 3 weeks! This clearly shows how regular and persistent is the pressure by the British.'[93] This was risible point-scoring stuff, even by army standards of 1916.

By the end of August, Haig began to pin greater hopes on the arrival of the first batch of tanks, and was planning to use them in a fresh attack in early September. On 29 August he once more found Rawlinson's proposals for this attack were deficient: 'In my opinion he is not making enough of the situation and the deterioration of the Enemy's troops. I think we should make our attack as strong and as violent as possible, and go as far as previously possible.' Nothing had altered Haig's mind since 1 July.

He ordered tanks to be used for the first time on 15 September, at the battle of Flers-Courcelette, the biggest operation conducted by the BEF since 1 July. It is another controversial episode in Haig's career, as he has been accused of wasting a rare opportunity for surprise by using this new weapon when it was still only available in small numbers. Yet expectations of what the tank might achieve in September 1916 were too high, and the consequent disappointment that they did not achieve more was too bleak. The reality was that the first tanks were crude machines and their crews were not battle-ready: 'Few, if any, of the officers had had experience in France and that probably was completely out of date. Most of the officers and crew had been suddenly pitch-forked from the calm, almost academic, atmosphere of a training camp in England into the ear-splitting, nerve-wracking tornado of the front line.'[94]

The Mark I tank deployed on this occasion – the much-improved Mark V was not available until 1917 – was noisy, slow, smelly and prone to mechanical breakdown. The Mark I had a range of only twelve miles before it required almost a complete engine overhaul, and was able to move at no more than four miles per hour, even over perfectly flat ground; its crew was usually exhausted after eight hours of combat, if they survived that long.

Suggestions that Haig merely threw away this new weapon in a piece-meal attack are, however, misplaced: '[. . .] whatever tests are carried out under peace conditions, the only true test of efficiency is war, consequently the final test a machine or weapon should get is its first battle, and until this test has been undergone, no guarantee can be given of its real worth, and no certain deductions can be made as to its future improvement.'[95]

Once more, before the actual battle at Flers-Courcelette started, Haig had extended the depth to which the BEF's divisions were expected to penetrate the German lines, this time to the third line and beyond, a distance beyond the range of all but a handful of British artillery. Clearly, he still conceived of a breakthrough that would permit his beloved cavalry to race onwards, in open ground, behind the German front lines. In one sense, this inability of the British artillery to span the depth of German defences paradoxically assisted this attack, as the artillery was inevitably reduced to concentrating its firepower on the first and second line of trench systems, with a weight of shell per yard double that of 1 July.[96]

And by now the creeping barrage technique had been sufficiently developed to provide greater support for the attacking infantry. Yet as it eventually transpired, German machine-gunners were untouched in pockets all along the front of the assault, so Haig's grand ambition for a major breakthrough was once again thwarted. However, this minor engagement at least reaffirmed the value of tanks in the attack. While a portion of the German second line was taken and, as Haig observed, 'some of the Tanks have done marvels!', there was no breakthrough.

Haig was now visited at GHQ by Lloyd George, who was later dismissed by Doris on this occasion for being 'accompanied by a crowd like a lot of Cook's tourists'.[97] Later, on 17 September, Foch came to see Haig and the latter was shocked to learn that, during his stay in France, Lloyd George had asked Foch 'his opinion as to the ability of the British generals. [. . .] Unless I had been told of this conversation personally by Gen. Foch, I would not have believed that a British Minister could have been so ungentlemanly as to go to a foreigner and put such questions regarding his own subordinates.'[98]

Sassoon duly conveyed this information to Lord Northcliffe, whose newspapers quickly published articles in praise of the BEF and Haig in particular. Howell Arthur Gwynne, the rabidly pro-army editor of the *Morning Post* and, according to Esher, a 'vulgar and thick headed fellow',[99] wrote a leader criticizing Lloyd George's supposedly underhand dealings with Haig: 'The Army is perfectly aware of what took place during the recent visit of the WAR MINISTER to France. That particular form of what the French call "gaffe" must not be repeated; and we may mention that in case of its repetition we shall feel it our duty to publish the facts of the occurrence.'[100]

Infuriated at what he saw as a plot between Robertson and the press, Lloyd George in October 1916 raised the stakes by sending French to visit Joffre at GQG, to report on French artillery use and tactics, which, he felt, were vastly superior to those of the BEF. Lloyd George, who during this five-month interregnum at the War Office felt himself to be simply 'the butcher's boy who leads the animals to the slaughter. When I have delivered the men my task in the war is over',[101] clearly agonized over the carnage on the Western Front, but his dispatch of the former C-in-C to France, effectively to tell tales against Haig and his command, was both tactless and regarded by Haig, who duly informed the king of French's visit, as a threat to his authority. Haig was annoyed that he first learned of this visit not by any official communication but through one of his key contacts at the War Office, his friend Lord Derby, then Director of Recruiting. Haig was additionally offended that Robertson had not seen fit to alert him to French's impending visit, a minor infraction of Haig's gentlemanly code that undoubtedly played a part in Haig's gradually cooling view of Robertson.

For Haig, the knowledge that his predecessor was so trusted by the new Secretary of State for War was deeply perturbing, and it cannot have helped his focus on the Somme campaign. Haig nevertheless invited French to visit the battlefront and vowed that 'he will be received with every mark of respect due to a British Field Marshal', even if he privately instructed his senior ADC, Lieutenant-Colonel Alan Fletcher, that he 'would not receive Viscount French in my house. I despise him too much personally for that.'[102] Yet although there was by now no trust between Haig and Lloyd George, this troubled relationship did at least result in one mutual benefit; at the suggestion of Lloyd George, Haig gained the invaluable services of Sir Eric Geddes.[103]

General Manager of the North-Eastern Railway when war broke out, Geddes had taken a wartime post at the Ministry of Munition. He was immediately welcomed by Haig, who took to this highly practical fellow Scot, and asked him during a two-day visit if he would take the job of Director-General of Transportation, as his fourth principal staff officer and with the honorary rank of major-general, one which Haig bestowed to give Geddes some clout at GHQ. Geddes agreed and quickly set about organizing the decidedly chaotic system he found, dividing transportation into five categories of canals, docks, light railways, large railways and roads.

Although the British depended entirely on the goodwill of the French railway network, the BEF itself at this time controlled only thirty-four railway engines. An initial survey by Geddes of the BEF's logistics system led him to conclude that 'no administrative policy existed that was capable of addressing movement, and that such a policy was necessary.'[104] He applied statistical analysis to this crucial aspect of managing the war, replacing the make-do-and-mend approach used till then. By the end of 1916, Geddes, still today a relatively unsung hero of the BEF, had introduced centralized planning to the BEF's systems of transportation. Such were Geddes' achievements that, by the end of 1917, the BEF's railway traffic had increased 50 per cent and the number of imported railway locomotives in France had grown by ten times.[105]

Haig's delight in having Geddes' help in this crucial area provides an important instance of the risk of generalizing about Haig and the way he ran GHQ. Haig has been criticized for failing to subvert and reform the 'traditional officer corps with its public school sense of loyalty, deference and lack of criticism of the traditional hierarchy'. From this perspective, GHQ in France 'rapidly converted to "small-group" decision-making, detached itself from the rest of the army, was reluctant to admit external advice, and under Haig became a virtually isolated operation.'[106] Yet the fact that Haig so welcomed Geddes and recognized his invaluable work contradicts this. Haig sometimes welcomed good advice from the most unlikely quarters; he did not often receive it. Sometimes, too, he was incapable of hearing good advice when given it. More often than not, he was ready to listen to those he considered experts in their own special, technical field. Geddes was one such, and in due course became a godparent to Haig's only son George, who was born in March 1918 after Geddes had left France to return to London.

It is equally true, however, that while Haig embraced Geddes' expertise with mechanized logistical problems, his own blind spot concerning transport – the horse – meant he was unable or unwilling to implement proposals from London that touched an already raw nerve. In early November 1916 Haig was pressed by Robertson, who in turn was under pressure from Lloyd George, to find ways to economise on cross-Channel transport space; as a result of Germany's successful U-boat campaign shipping was becoming scarcer. By this date there were 420,000 horses in service with the BEF, although just 37,000 belonged to the five divisions of the Cavalry Corps. The vast bulk of the horses were required for menial transport tasks, lugging shells, food and equipment. Robertson passed on to Haig the suggestion to ship three cavalry divisions home for the winter. Haig correctly pointed out that this was self-defeating; to do so would require 480,000 tons of shipping capacity (reckoned at 2 tons/man and 8 tons/horse), while simply supplying the fodder and requirements of those divisions in France would require only 75,000 tons.

Robertson then asked Haig if it would not be sensible at least to 'dismount infantry company commanders except for the purposes of training? Would not a Corps pool of chargers for use of infantry officers whose units were withdrawn from the line for training meet the case?' Haig would have none of it:

> There are only about 2,688 [infantry] company commander's horses. Even if two-thirds of these were abolished, only leaving a pool of about 180 horses per Army, the total reduction would only be about 1,782 horses, representing a daily saving of about 16 tons [of fodder]. It is unquestionable that these horses are necessary, except for short periods at a time when the company is actually holding trenches, and it is considered that the dislocation, discomfort and ill-feeling which would be caused throughout the Army [. . .] is out of all proportion to the tonnage saved, which is insignificant compared with the total tonnage requirements of the Army as whole.[107]

He had a point. If all infantry company commanders had been forced to walk rather than ride, the total saving each year would have been perhaps 8,000 tons of shipping space, a negligible amount. Yet if the king could make a largely meaningless symbolic gesture by giving up drink, then why could not Haig, by relinquishing horses used by infantry commanders? He was, however, in no mood to compromise with a government whose Secretary of State for War sought the opinion of French soldiers as to his competence, and who had sent a failed former C-in-C to gather evidence against him.

Despite appearances to the contrary, Haig's public face – of indomitable confidence that all was going according to plan – sometimes crumpled in private. By the end of the first week of November, he belatedly recognised that, in some respects at least, no real progress had been made since the early days of the war: 'The communications are still very bad. In fact we are fighting under the same conditions as in October 1914, i.e with rifle and machine guns only, because bombs and mortar ammunition cannot be carried forward as the roads are so bad.'[108]

Towards the end of 1916, appalling weather set in – heavy rain and chilly temperatures. The area around the Somme had become a morass of shell-pocked swamp. The evidence of his senses and those of others perpetually contradicted Haig's deeply nurtured ambition of a German collapse, yet it was as if he shrugged his shoulders and accepted that the only solution was more of the same, particularly as, by this late in the year, he was increasingly desperate to show some sign of genuine success. In what has been justifiably called a political battle, Haig exerted subtle pressure on Gough, GOC Fifth Army, on 12 November, to try to capture a 'heap of rubble'[109] that was formerly the village of Beaumont Hamel – the taking of which had been a goal for 1 July. Gough, unswervingly loyal to Haig, readily agreed.

The Battle of the Ancre, as this final stage of the Somme became known, resulted in casualties of more than 20,000 BEF and Dominion troops, for the capture of Beaumont Hamel and its neighbouring village, Beaucourt. Despite thick early-morning fog on 13 November, the first day of the battle, and more intelligent use of a creeping barrage, the Fifth Army's divisions rapidly became bogged down in a muddy slime which often reached their waists and rendered their rifles unusable. If the strategic aim was still to achieve a breakthrough, this was a pointless battle; if it simply was a matter of attrition, it was unjustifiably costly. Despite as much artillery ammunition being expended on the Ancre as across the whole battlefield on 1 July, on a front six times shorter, the end result was an advance to a paltry maximum depth of 2,000 yards.

But by this time Haig was in any case working to a different agenda. For in the midst of the Battle of the Ancre, which staggered to a halt on 18 November, Haig was again at Chantilly, at an Anglo-French conference attended by Prime Minister Asquith. Here the key topic was whether or not to send more troops from France and Belgium to Salonika. Uppermost in Haig's mind before Gough's attack at the Ancre was the need, as he confided to his diary and to Gough, to 'appear there [Chantilly] on top of the capture of Beaumont Hamel for instance, and 3000 German prisoners. It would show too that we had no intention of ceasing to press the Enemy on the Somme. But the necessity for success must not blind our eyes to the difficulties of ground and weather. Nothing is so costly as a failure! But I am ready to run reasonable risks.'[110]

Haig's pressure on Gough, the latter's malleability when faced by Haig, and Gough's awareness of his own reputation as a 'thruster', conspired to bring about a battle that in all senses but the political was utterly pointless. Haig got his 3,000 (and more) prisoners and, as he put it, 'the success has come at a most opportune moment.'[111] The Chantilly conference ended with a reassertion of the primacy of the Western Front over all others, and a determination that 'the resources employed in the other theatres [including Salonika] should be reduced to the smallest possible.'[112]

This notion of 'success' does Haig no credit. It is one of the tragedies of the Great War that so many died pointlessly at the Ancre on behalf of preventing the equally pointless waste of yet more lives at Salonika, where the chances of a genuine breakthrough, always remote, were by now utterly extinguished; it is an inescapable criticism of Haig that he believed it necessary to capture a heap of rubble at Beaumont Hamel to achieve this otherwise sensible aim.

Towards the end of the year, despite the lack of any obvious significant advance at the Somme, Haig received yet further assurance of royal backing; the king informed him, when he attended Buckingham Palace on 24 November, that he would warn Sir John French that, unless he ceased his criticisms of Haig and his handling of the BEF, 'it will be necessary to sever his connection with the Army' – a threat that, constitutionally, would have been difficult to carry out, but which nevertheless ensured French adopted a less voluble tone.[113]

Haig's political success at the Battle of the Ancre was in any case shortlived. On 22 November, Haig became aware that Lord Lansdowne, a member of the government, had earlier circulated an internal memo calling for an end to more senseless slaughter, and urged peace negotiations if there was no certainty of victory by autumn 1917. The Northcliffe press (*The Times* and the *Daily Mail*), then entirely pro-army and highly critical of what it regarded as the insufficiently bellicose government under Prime Minister Asquith, ran a rabid campaign against Asquith's twenty-three-member administration, putting out advertising posters carrying the legend 'Wanted! Twenty-three ropes'.[114] Asquith's divided and war-weary coalition government collapsed and, after much closeted conspiring, Lloyd George, now fifty-four, took over as Prime Minister on 5 December, promising the Unionist members of his War Cabinet that neither Winston Churchill nor Lord Northcliffe would be asked to join the government, and that Haig would be retained as C-in-C; in exchange they guaranteed sufficient support to form a cross-party administration.[115]

Lord Derby, a Haig supporter, became Secretary of State for War. One of his first acts was to write frankly to Haig: 'I am not at my own wish on the War Committee. They will settle policy and Wully [Robertson] is the only man from this office who should – or indeed can – give valuable advice. I shall content myself with running the department to the best of my ability. It puts a big responsibility on Wully, but I have told him I will back him up to the full, and his resignation would mean mine for you know me well enough to realise that I am in earnest when I say my one big idea will be to serve the army, and I know you will give me all the assistance in your power.'[116]

While it was useful for Haig to have an ally, albeit one so pliable as Derby, as Secretary of State for War, his most dangerous political enemy was now in the much more powerful position of Prime Minister. One of Lloyd George's first decisions was to dismantle what had been agreed at Chantilly in November; he immediately asked Haig, on 15 December, to make available two divisions from France to go Egypt, for an assault in the direction of Jerusalem, and also to loan 200 heavy guns to Italy. As he left Lloyd George's office that day, Haig felt that the Prime Minister had listened to his explanation why this was a mistake, and that he 'seemed

less determined, I thought, to withdraw troops from France to go elsewhere. I rubbed in that "to obtain great success, we must endure minor
ills." ' Such as, presumably, those incurred at the Ancre. But Haig on this
occasion – and many more to come – completely under-estimated Lloyd
George's determination to wrest control over military affairs from the
generals, himself and Robertson especially.

Of more immediate consequence for Haig than the new Prime Minister
was the appointment of General Robert Nivelle on 17 December 1916 as
C-in-C of the French army, in succession to Joffre, who by now was
tainted with the grisly stagnation at Verdun. In everyone's mind – not least
Lloyd George's – was the knowledge that Haig had promised much but
achieved nothing of consequence. When Haig first met Nivelle, who had
acquired an unjustifiably high reputation for his use of artillery at Verdun,
at Cassel on 19 December, it struck him during their two-hour conversation that here was yet another French general with vaulting ambitions.

Haig found Nivelle to be 'a most straightforward and soldierly man.
[. . .] He is confident of breaking through the Enemy's front, now that the
Enemy's morale is weakened, but the blow must be struck by surprise,
and go through in 24 hours. The necessity for surprise is, after all, our
own conclusion. Our objective on the Somme was the relief of Verdun
and to wear out the Enemy's Forces with a view to striking the decisive
blow later, when the Enemy's reserves are used up. Altogether I was
pleased with my first meeting with Nivelle. He is in his 61st year. Is alert in
mind and has had much practical experience in this war as a gunner, then
in turn a Divisional, Corps and lastly Army Commander. [. . .] Nivelle
also mentioned that Lloyd George had said to him at Verdun that "the
British are not a military people". I said, L.G had never studied our military history.'[117]

Haig met Nivelle once more before the end of 1916, when Nivelle
outlined in general terms his ideas for a fresh offensive in early 1917. Haig,
perhaps mindful of his own recent experience at the Somme, told Nivelle
that, while 'he might be successful', he 'might not get as far as he hoped.'
In fact Nivelle proved disastrous, primarily for the French army but also,
for a time, for Haig.

On 28 December Haig was informed that George V had appointed him field marshal.[118] Haig wrote to thank his most important patron: '[. . .] I must confess that I realise I have attained this great position in the Army, not by my own merits, but thanks to the splendid soldierly qualities of our Officers and men. And I cannot find words to express the pride I feel at having Your Majesty's confidence, and at the privilege which has been given to me to command such Officers and such soldiers.'[119]

The five army commanders of the BEF clubbed together and bought Haig his field marshal's baton. This elevation to the highest rank of the British army was not simply a professional accolade; it was also the monarch's most public endorsement of Haig. That loyalty was to become a useful shield against the man who was to become Haig's most bitter opponent, who was not German, but Welsh.

# CHAPTER ELEVEN

# Passchendaele

Nothing is more discouraged in the Army than a departure from the well-worn path of tradition. The 'good soldier' is one who does what he is told without thinking.

Brigadier-General C. D. Baker-Carr

On the bitterly cold Monday morning of 15 January 1917, with snow lying thick on the ground, Haig was driven from Ascot – where he had been staying at a borrowed house during a brief family holiday with Doris and the children – to 10 Downing Street for a meeting with Lloyd George, at which Sir William Robertson was also present. Haig, who could neither dissemble nor flatter, was congenitally unable to follow perhaps the wisest advice he ever received from Viscount Esher, in mid–1916: 'Please say nice things about the Welsh to L.G. He is a man of sentiment and susceptibility.'[1] On this morning Haig was taken aback by the Prime Minister's open hostility. Gone was Lloyd George's erstwhile façade of respect for his two most senior generals. Instead, he brusquely disparaged the record of the BEF, contrasting it unfavourably with the French army, which, he asserted, had made greater progress with less human cost – although the record did not support this. French casualties had been, proportionately, even worse than the British, and had brought victory no closer.

Lloyd George's abrupt assault momentarily winded Haig and Robertson, accustomed as they were to much gentler handling – and professional respect – from the occasionally inebriated but always supportive Asquith. At this and numerous later, usually equally fraught sessions, Lloyd George purported to speak in the name of the War Cabinet, a group of senior politicians he had assembled around him who shared his distrust of generals. This cabal provided Lloyd George with a useful mechanism to bypass parliamentary oversight of his determination to exercise an increasing control over Britain's conduct – both diplomatic and military – of the war. Indeed, his administration was to evolve into something resembling a prime ministerial autocracy. Arguably, this was justified by the extreme circumstances in which the country found itself. But Lloyd George's lowly upbringing and shady reputation did not endear him to the British establishment, its two most senior army officers included.[2]

Lloyd George, Haig and Robertson resumed their meeting next day, when they were joined in the late morning by Nivelle. Upon being appointed C-in-C of the French army, Nivelle had abandoned the plan elaborated by Joffre and Haig in late 1916. This had envisaged a joint Anglo-French offensive on the Western Front in the spring of 1917, one which would involve a British attack on a line between Vimy-Bapaume and a simultaneous French assault through the valleys of the Oise and the Somme. Under Nivelle's new scheme, the BEF's contribution was to be reduced to a diversionary sideshow to the French assault, which would now be conducted subsequent to, rather than concurrent with, the British attack. It was, in general, very much like the scheme Joffre had conceived of in early 1916. Nivelle also shifted the focus of the attack further south, away from the Belgian coastal areas, which Haig had long been trying to persuade the British Cabinet should be the prime target for BEF attacks, in a search for a way around, and eventually through, the German defences. In order to mount the much larger French attack, Nivelle wanted the BEF to relieve French divisions by taking over more of the front line, occupying by 1 March an additional zone as far south as the Amiens-Ruze road. Nivelle wanted to start his grand offensive, which he affirmed would bring about final victory, no later than 1 April 1917.

Lloyd George was swayed by the French general's plausible self-confidence, and wholeheartedly embraced Nivelle's scheme. Nivelle's fluent

English also enabled Lloyd George, who spoke no French, to feel that at last he had a direct and clear understanding with a French C-in-C. But the most persuasive point in Nivelle's favour – and Lloyd George can be forgiven for clutching at this straw – was the promise that complete success would be secured within forty-eight hours of the start of the new offensive. The Prime Minister was seduced into dropping his guard. As he told his mistress and secretary, Frances Stevenson: 'Nivelle has proved himself to be a Man at Verdun: & when you get a Man against one who has not proved himself, why, you back the Man!'[3]

Haig, Robertson and the other British generals were disappointments; they were not men. Haig naturally did not share this opinion; nor could he comprehend the Prime Minister's trust in Nivelle: almost eighteen months of working in tandem with French officers had merely reinforced his own distrust of foreigners, and refined his belief that working in an alliance was fraught with difficulties. Neither Haig nor Robertson were confident that they understood what the Prime Minister wanted the two of them to do differently. Robertson, who possibly distrusted politicians even more than Haig, wrote to Haig – by now back at GHQ – on 19 January that 'I cannot follow what the Prime Minister has now got in his mind but he seems to have an idea that you and Nivelle are going to do something very effective in the course of three weeks, although he has always hitherto told me that he doubted if we would ever be able to do anything useful on the Western front. He talks a good deal about the value of a partial success, whereas it seems to me that a partial success at this stage will mean nothing less than failure.'[4]

Lloyd George, understandably more acutely conscious of Britain's casualty rate than that of France, considered that, in broad terms, all the British generals had so far achieved was a series of costly failures. So much was true. What this overlooked, however, was that these failures had also brought valuable combat experience; the BEF's ranks of un-trained novices were developing intangible qualities such as resilience and cohesion, as well as painfully acquired fighting skills. The Prime Minister was adamant; such failures could not go on. Yet his solution at the start of 1917 – to place complete confidence in the French – stemmed more from desperation than any strategic insight. He was determined to wrench from Haig and Robertson not just an acknowledgement of his superior political authority, which they in any case accepted, but also his right, as he saw it, to set military strategy and interfere in army organization, which they doggedly resisted. This right he sought to exert in all kinds of ways, including instructing them to pay more attention to the views of junior officers.

Indeed, a few days after the tense January meetings at Downing Street, Lloyd George sent Robertson a note to this affect. This missive, typically, appeared perfectly innocuous to Lloyd George yet, as far as Robertson was concerned, revealed the Prime Minister's profound misunderstanding of the traditional ways of the army: 'When I was at the War Office I put before you a suggestion that the Commander-in-Chief should make a systematic effort to encourage suggestions from his subordinates who had actual experience in carrying out his orders in the field as to the best means of securing success in future operations. I suggested that it would be desirable to invite opinions not merely from Divisional and Brigade Generals, but from Regimental Officers. [. . .] Out of the hundreds of proposals or criticisms that will be forthcoming there will no doubt be a good deal of rubbish; but Field Marshal Haig and General Kiggell will be able to separate the wheat from the chaff.'[5]

This proposition might seem quite sensible today, in an era when the *vox populi* has become synonymous with democracy; yet it implicitly reduced Haig and Kiggell to the status of secretaries. It also revealed the Prime Minister's ignorance of the fact that Haig's office was already inundated with petitioners, civilian and military, each of whom was convinced that their own particular brainchild was the key to complete victory. This kind of political interference, abruptly delivered and without respect for conventional protocols, merely irritated Haig and Robertson.

Forming in Lloyd George's fecund mind was a plot to winkle Haig out or, failing that, at least to tie his hands. The mid-January meetings in Downing Street hinted at this, but a stronger indication came in

February, when a minor imbroglio involving Haig providentially handed to the Prime Minister some useful ammunition. In January 1917 the francophile Major Neville Lytton, Haig's senior press adviser who was in charge of French journalists attached to GHQ, persuaded the C-in-C it would greatly benefit Anglo-French relations if he met a group of French reporters. The precise basis of this meeting was, however, not mutually established from the start; the journalists understood they were free to quote Haig, but, after their account appeared in Britain and was used against him, Haig asserted that he had never intended to be directly quoted. Haig had spoken to the reporters in his grammatically correct, heavily accented French and, according to Lytton, created a good impression, discoursing optimistically about the future course of the war, and generally talked 'in a charming manner of his relations with the French.'[6] Lytton considered Haig had done a good job; the French journalists were pleased and it all seemed entirely innocuous. The French reporters duly presented their copy for censorship before going into print, the draft articles being sent to Charteris – then on leave in England – for his approval, which he gave.[7]

The interview with Haig was well received in France; but, as rendered into English, it opened Haig to accusations of being vainglorious in making, as he had, firm claims that the war would end in 1917 in an Allied victory. In one sense this was precisely the sort of positive propaganda which today might be considered one of the tasks of a British C-in-C. But when the interview appeared in *The Times* – accompanied by an approving editorial, thanks to Northcliffe – questions were raised in the House of Commons, with Philip Snowden, the anti-war Independent Labour Party MP, describing it as demonstrating Haig's 'blazing indiscretion' which had 'shaken the confidence of many people in his judgement and common sense.' There was also concern that, by giving such an interview, Haig had breached King's Regulations, although this was a technicality; Haig infringed these every day, simply by keeping a diary and corresponding with civilians on military affairs. Snowden, who had advised Lloyd George on his controversial 1909 budget, in all likelihood had been put up to his intervention by the Prime Minister.

Haig did his best to shrug off the controversy in a letter to Doris, but he was shaken by how low Lloyd George could stoop:

[. . .] I am doing my best, and have a clear conscience. If they have someone else who can command this great Army better than I am doing, I shall be glad to hand over to him, and will be so happy to come back to my darling wife and play golf and bring up the children. It has not yet come to this. I merely mention it, so that you can see how independent in spirit I feel, and that whatever I do is what I feel and judge to be the best for the country.[8]

Was this indifference feigned? Haig genuinely believed that he was 'doing his best' but he also did what he could, via the king, to protect his position. He was unwilling to hand his head on a plate to the Prime Minister, for whom by now he had developed a deep contempt. Shortly after Lloyd George's death in 1945, Lytton published an article on this incident. In this he claimed that, in early 1917, Lloyd George had sought Northcliffe's influence to help him dislodge Haig. According to Lytton, Northcliffe said: '"The little man" (that was his way of describing the Prime Minister) came to me some weeks ago and told me that he would like to get rid of Haig, but that he could not do so as he was too popular. He made the proposition to me that I should attack him in my group of newspapers and so render him unpopular enough to be dealt with. "You kill him and I will bury him." Those were his very words.'[9] Northcliffe, a monster in many ways but none the less intensely patriotic and deeply loyal to the BEF's high command, declined to join the Prime Minister's intrigue, and the fuss over Haig's interview rapidly dissipated, although Haig would never again submit himself to meeting journalists without first making very clear that he was not to be quoted.

That Lloyd George, a man 'seriously deficient' in physical courage, according to his biographer John Grigg,[10] was determined to render Haig's position impossible is clear from the fact that, on the day that Haig's notorious interview appeared in Britain, 15 February 1917, he held another Downing Street meeting, the thrust of which was to force Haig's subordination to, in Haig's words, 'a junior foreign' general, Nivelle.

Strictly speaking, Haig was right; as a field marshal, he outranked a mere general, but Nivelle was his equal in terms of being in overall command of the French Army on the Western Front. On this day the Prime Minister met Commandant Bertier de Sauvigny, who represented GQG at the War Office in London; also at the meeting was Colonel Maurice Hankey, Cabinet Secretary and a Lloyd George loyalist. According to de Sauvigny, Lloyd George averred: 'There is no doubt that the prestige which Field Marshal Haig enjoys with the public and the British Army will make it impossible to subordinate him purely and simply to the French Command, but if the War Cabinet realises that this measure is indispensable, they will not hesitate to give Field Marshal Haig secret instructions to this effect, and, if need be, to replace him if he will not give the support of all his forces when this may be required, with complete understanding and compliance. It is essential that the two War Cabinets [the French and British] should be in agreement on this principle.'[11] Such underhand behaviour was characteristic of the Prime Minister. He could not easily sack Haig, so he decided to make Haig's position impossible. De Sauvigny was surprised, but dutifully reported this proposal to his superiors in Paris.

The trap for Haig and Robertson was finally sprung at an Anglo-French conference at Calais on 26–27 February 1917. This coincided with the start of a carefully planned German withdrawal, which initially puzzled Haig, although he soon found it expedient to depict it as a retreat,[12] to much stronger defences at the Hindenburg Line, some fifteen miles behind the previous German positions. This re-drawing of the front line gave the German forces the advantage of shortening their front line facing the French and freed additional reserves. The agenda at Calais[13] was nominally concerned with the mundane but vital topic of ironing out transportation bottlenecks in France, as well as a general discussion of Anglo-French operational plans for 1917; its real motive however was to cut Haig and Robertson down to size. At an earlier Allied conference in Rome in January 1917, Lloyd George had already sanctioned the subordination of the British GOC in Salonika, General George Milne, to the French commander, General Sarrail. Milne had reserved the right to appeal to London if he disagreed with Sarrail's plans, but effectively he now had to take his orders from a foreign general. The Salonika arrangement provided a blueprint for what Lloyd George had in mind for Haig.

On the evening of the first day at the Hôtel Gare Maritime, Lloyd George asked the French to draw up before dinner their scheme for a system of command for the forthcoming battle, so that Haig, Robertson and the Prime Minister could discuss it later that evening. Lloyd George claimed to be unwell and did not attend the dinner – although he was well enough to eat in his room, closeted with Hankey – which was a friendly affair at which Haig, Robertson, Nivelle, the French War Minister, General Lyautey, and the French Prime Minister, Aristide Briand, enjoyed, according to Haig, 'quite a cheery talk'.[14] Lloyd George had the French scheme – entitled *Projet d'Organisation de l'Unité de Commandement sur le Front occidental* or, literally, *A Proposal for the organization of a unified command on the Western Front* – delivered to Robertson after dinner. An outraged Robertson and an astonished Haig discovered that it proposed the BEF would, for the forthcoming offensive, be placed under the command of Nivelle; the job of the BEF's C-in-C would be reduced to administering discipline and looking after reinforcements. Robertson would also be bypassed, by having a separate British chief of general staff attached to the French GQG, now based at Beauvais, with the job of reporting to the War Committee in London.[15] Lloyd George had cannily persuaded the French that this scheme would be more likely to receive Haig's and Robertson's reluctant acceptance if it appeared to emanate from the French military, rather than British politicians.

But the consequence of such a manoeuvre would have far greater repercussions than for Haig alone; control over the lives of the hundreds of thousands of soldiers in the BEF was to be casually handed over to the French, simply so that Haig's wings could be clipped. This would signify the end of the original basis on which the BEF had been sent to France – to cooperate with its French ally but as an independent force under British command. Removing Haig by subterfuge was one thing, but the amalgamation by stealth of the BEF with the French army was repugnant not just to Haig and Robertson but many other senior British officers.[16] More than two and a half years of war had revealed many flaws in Anglo-French military cooperation on the Western Front; but ending the BEF's independence in this way would not have improved matters.

On the evening of 26 February, after they saw the supposedly French proposition, Robertson and Haig immediately stormed into Lloyd George's room, where a livid Robertson upbraided the Prime Minister. Lloyd George defended himself by saying that the War Cabinet had already agreed to the proposal – although one member, Lord Derby, as Secretary of State for War, had been absent at the time, his exclusion being deliberate. The Prime Minister had little respect for Derby; nor did Northcliffe, who referred to him as 'that great jellyfish'. Lloyd George tried to rebuff Robertson's bluster by saying that, as this was to be a French battle, it was entirely sensible to place the British C-in-C under French orders and give temporary control of the BEF to the French. Haig, who, unlike the CIGS, held his temper, told Lloyd George it would be 'madness to place the British under the French, and that I did not believe our troops would fight under French leadership.'

It was indeed a mad way of trying to achieve the laudable ambition of a more cohesive Anglo-French command structure; but Lloyd George was willing to sacrifice the BEF's independence in pursuit of his ulterior motive. As they confronted one another across the hotel room, Lloyd George loudly proclaimed, 'I know the private soldier very well. He speaks more freely to me, and there are people he criticises a good deal more strongly than General Nivelle!'[17] Infuriated, Robertson and Haig marched back to their own rooms, vowing privately that they 'would rather be tried by Court Martial than betray the Army by agreeing to its being placed under the French. Robertson agreed that we must resign rather than be partners in this transaction. And so we went to bed, thoroughly disgusted with our Government and the Politicians.'[18]

Yet neither Haig nor Robertson was put to the test of resigning. Lloyd George was clearly shaken by their reaction and overnight he instructed Maurice Hankey to draft a compromise document. Hankey, who like

Lloyd George had a propensity to massage facts to suit circumstances, had by now led Haig to believe that Lloyd George did not have the authority of the War Cabinet for this plan; even today, doubt lingers as to precisely what the War Cabinet thought was intended at Calais. Another of its members, Lord Curzon, evidently supported the subjugation of the BEF to Nivelle. He informed Lord Stamfordham, the king's private secretary, in March 1917 that the War Cabinet – in the presence of Hankey – had concluded, prior to Calais, that 'The War Cabinet did not consider Haig a clever man. Nivelle made a much greater impression on the members of the War Cabinet – of the two in existing circumstances Nivelle was the right man to have supreme command.'[19] But if supreme command was the aim, this was not the way to achieve it amicably. Hankey's revised document stated Nivelle would be in overall command solely for the forthcoming – predominantly French – offensive. The BEF would carry out a subordinate role; and Haig would do his best to conform to Nivelle's wishes.

The following morning – the second day of the conference – the waters were muddied still further, when Haig was invited to a meeting with Lyautey and Nivelle, who 'both spoke of "the insult offered to me and the British Army by the paper which Briand had produced." Indeed, as regards Lyautey, he had not seen or heard of it until he entered the train at Paris to come to Calais today. I understand that the paper was drawn up in Paris with Lloyd George's approval and of course, that of Briand.'[20]

Haig claimed that, when he was presented by Robertson with Hankey's fresh draft on the morning of 27 February, he insisted on inserting a clause to the effect that he had a 'free hand to choose the means and methods of utilising the British troops in that sector of operations allotted by the French C-in-C in the original plan.' This was accepted by Nivelle and Lloyd George, while Haig held that, after the battle, which was 'expected to last about a fortnight, [. . .] the normal state of arrangements will be reverted to.' For Haig, honour had been satisfied; the status quo had been re-established, and he and Robertson signed the document: 'As it stands, the way in which I have worked with the French is not changed. I have always worked on General Joffre's "General Instructions" as if they had been orders, but retained absolute freedom of action as to how I carry them out. This power remains to me. I am however relieved of responsibility for the plan of the battle now being prepared for as well as for the details of the execution of the plan.'

Yet something had indeed irrevocably altered. For while Haig nominally retained the same powers, after Calais he could not fail to have realized that he did not have the confidence of the Prime Minister. The code of the Victorian gentleman should perhaps have dictated to Haig that he offer his resignation. Something prevented that. It may have been self-interest, or possibly Haig's sense of a higher duty (to king, country and empire) outweighed any inclination to offer his resignation to a politician, and such a despised one at that. Lloyd George had proved that he was prepared to cede to a foreign power control over the largest British and Dominion army ever assembled. This alone encouraged Haig and Robertson to resist the Prime Minister. They would not hesitate to recruit others – the press and the monarchy especially – to their cause, which, as they saw it, was now not just to defeat Germany but to protect their beloved army from a British politician prepared to betray its autonomy. Robertson's conclusion, in a note to Haig after Calais, was that Lloyd George 'is an awful liar'. He was right, but naive; such mendacity goes with the job. Ultimately, Calais further confused the Anglo-French military alliance. It misled Nivelle into believing that he had acquired the right to command the BEF to do his bidding.

Haig returned to Château de Beaurepaire, where his by now complete lack of confidence in the French ability and will to fight was reinforced by an aide recently returned from a visit to the French army: 'General Michelère [actually General Joseph Micheler, GOC French Reserve Army Group] incidentally stated that it does not matter what the politicians may decide, the French soldier is not going to fight after the autumn!' This gloomy prognostication was to come to pass rather sooner than Micheler reckoned.

Haig naturally informed George V in a detailed letter dated 28 February 1917 of what had transpired at Calais, reminding the king of

Kitchener's original instructions when he appointed Haig C-in-C: '"To achieve that end (the defeat of the enemy) the closest co-operation of French and British as a united Army must be the governing policy; but I wish you distinctly to understand that your command is an independent one, and that you will in no case come under the orders of any Allied General further than the necessary co-operation with our Allies above referred to."' Haig offered the king an opportunity to replace him, although he couched it in terms which discouraged acceptance:

> Your Majesty will observe that in my dealings with Mr Lloyd George over this question, I have never suggested that I would like to resign my Command, but, on the contrary, I have done my utmost to meet the views of the Government, as any change of Command at this time might be a disadvantage to the Army in the Field. It is possible, however, that the present War Cabinet may think otherwise, and deem it best to replace me by someone else more in their confidence. If this is so, I recommend that the change may be made as soon as possible, because of the proximity of the date fixed for the commencement of offensive operations. At this great crisis in our History, my sole object is to serve my King and Country wherever I can be of most use, and with full confidence I leave myself in Your Majesty's hands to decide what is best for me to do at this juncture.[21]

Haig now adjusted his view of Nivelle, whom he longer regarded as 'a straightforward and soldierly man' but as a 'cad', as he informed Doris in a letter on 3 March. That same day he received a letter from Lord Derby, who pleaded ignorance of what he called the 'Coup de Théâtre' prepared for Haig at Calais. Derby plaintively wrote to Haig again, on 7 March: 'You chose the lesser of two evils, and I in turn, by not resigning, am taking the same course. Robertson is in a terrible state about things – it has quite ruined his nerves. [. . .] How I hate all this intrigue. I wish I could stop it, and I could but only by pulling the house down about our ears. I don't see how we can go back on the agreement – for the *present* offensive – without infuriating the French and risking the alliance.'[22]

Ironically, Lloyd George's plot, once it leaked out, had the unintended consequence of gaining even more support for Haig from the British press. Haig also received from Stamfordham on 5 March a reassuring letter on behalf of the king, who 'begs you to dismiss from your mind any idea of resignation. Such a course would be in His Majesty's opinion disastrous to his Army and to the hopes of success in the coming supreme struggle. You have the absolute confidence of that Army from the highest to the lowest ranks: a confidence which is shared to the full by the King. [. . .] I am to say from His Majesty that you are not to worry: you may be certain that he will do his utmost to protect your interests, and he begs you to continue to work on the most amicable and open terms with General Nivelle, and he feels all will come right.'[23] George V's defence of Haig was not motivated simply by altruism; the king and his closest aides saw Lloyd George's manoeuvrings to place the BEF in French hands as nothing less than the first step towards a republic – a hysterical overreaction, certainly, but given Lloyd George's lack of candour and obvious contempt for the old establishment's ways, it was perhaps understandable.

The messy wrangling at Calais in February necessitated, as far as Nivelle and Briand were concerned, a more precise definition as to what was now the relationship between Haig, the BEF, and the French high command. Thus at their instigation another conference was staged, in London on 12–13 March, at which a new convention was signed. This reiterated that the BEF remained fully under Haig's command – although Nivelle would be in overall command of the spring offensive – and that all communications between Nivelle and the British would travel via Haig at GHQ. Haig took particular care to append to the London conference documentation a statement that the BEF and its C-in-C would be regarded by the French as allies and not subordinates: '[. . .] while I am fully determined to carry out the Calais Agreement in spirit and letter, the British Army and its C-in-C will be regarded by General Nivelle as Allies and not as subordinates, except during the particular operations which he explained at the Calais Conference.'[24] The War Cabinet approved this amendment and the document overall. Thus the Calais plot had seemingly failed to achieve Lloyd George's central ambition – the unseating of Haig – but Haig was irked by the farce he had been put through, telling Robertson '[. . .] we seemed to be always giving in to the French in all their demands, that we trusted in their good faith without any written documents, while they invariably wanted "an agreement in writing" duly signed.'[25]

Objectively, whether he liked it or not, Haig had conceded significant ground, albeit for a limited offensive that was supposed to cease after forty-eight hours if it proved unsuccessful. Nivelle's response to the news of this concession by Haig was unexpected. Rather than regarding it as a triumph, he reportedly burst into tears, remorseful that he had achieved a pyrrhic victory. It struck him that Calais had damaged Anglo-French military goodwill, and that he had been used by Lloyd George. Nivelle tried to heal relations with Haig by asserting that neither he nor French political leaders had sought the Calais and London meetings. The historian Elizabeth Greenhalgh has pointed out that Nivelle tried to make amends, by writing that the two conferences had simply confirmed the pre-existing relationship; that is, the independence-with-cooperation format as originally outlined by Kitchener back in August 1914.[26]

Calais thus brought nothing but frustration for Lloyd George, who, afraid of a collapse in his fragile cross-party government, lacked sufficient courage simply to sack Haig and Robertson. For Haig and Robertson, who would not demean themselves by self-sacrifice to a politician they regarded as a scoundrel, Calais provided conclusive evidence of the Prime Minister's duplicity. All three men shared the conviction that they were motivated not by personal ambition but by patriotism. Lloyd George claimed much later[27] that, while he always wanted to remove Haig, he did not do so because he was the best of an indifferent group; he could not bring himself to admit that he felt impotent in the face of Haig's powerful backers.[28] Wherever one judges the true fault to lie, it was, as Haig wrote on 28 February 1917, 'too sad at this critical time to have to fight with one's Allies and the Home Government, in addition to the Enemy in the field!'

As the date of Nivelle's grand offensive approached, there were widespread leaks in Paris of what was in store. The capture by German raiding parties of French documents gave even more detail of what Nivelle had in mind, but although the offensive became an open secret, the French C-in-C declined to alter his plans or timetable.[29] By mid-April, when Nivelle's scheme was finally put into action, the French armies in the Champagne region faced a much-reinforced German opposition, of forty-three divisions rather than the ten of just two months before. Nivelle's political backing had begun to crumble even before the battle started; in mid-March General Lyautey resigned as France's War Minister, replaced by Paul Painlevé, who was thoroughly opposed to Nivelle's plans, while Alexandre Ribot, who was fearful of the depletion of the French army, replaced Briand as Prime Minister on 19 March.

The part played by the BEF in the offensive of spring 1917 started well enough, with Allenby's Third Army attacking on an eight-mile front astride the River Scarpe, and the Canadian Corps, under the popular Sir Julian Byng, together with some units of General Horne's First Army, assaulting Vimy Ridge, near Arras, on a four-mile front. Vimy Ridge, a relatively low hillock – just 450 feet above sea level – was nevertheless high enough to enable German domination of the surrounding country-side. It was threaded with deep interconnected dugouts, tunnels and trenches, and provided a terrific strongpoint from which the Germans could observe and fire on advancing troops and their front lines. On Easter Monday, 9 April 1917, 'Byng's Boys' (as they liked to call themselves), who had been thoroughly rehearsed, followed up a precisely calibrated creeping barrage, rapidly taking the ridge. For this attack Haig at last had at his disposal a vast array of firepower; 2,817 guns, 863 of them heavy or medium calibre, delivered more than 50,000 tons of shells, mostly armed with the new type 106 fuze, which ensured that the shells exploded on impact. Under this horrendous blitz even the strongest German emplacements withered and, by 14 April, the Canadians had scored a remarkable success, while Allenby's Third Army also made significant progress, with a total of almost 13,000 prisoners and 200 guns captured. This early triumph quickly soured, however; by mid-May, when Haig called a halt to further attacks, the five-week Arras campaign had not scored any success greater than the taking of Vimy Ridge, for an estimated total of 30,000 dead, out of almost 160,000 casualties.

While the British were congratulating themselves on their rare success at Vimy, on 16 April a slightly delayed French offensive started at the River Aisne, south of Vimy Ridge and along a front of twenty-five miles. (Nivelle's original plan had been wrong-footed by the German withdrawal to the Hindenburg line in February 1917.) This was launched in appalling weather, with sleet and rain creating atrocious conditions, through which the French soldiers slogged on regardless. From the ranks of those headed for the front line were heard baa-ing noises – they were convinced they were destined, like sheep, for slaughter. The covering artillery barrage – upon which Nivelle had staked his promise of a swift conclusion – became disconnected from the advancing infantry and, eventually, as at the Somme, the German defenders reappeared from their underground bunkers and, with relative ease, massacred their attackers. The three French armies that rose from their trenches had little to show for their efforts; after three days more than 100,000 were casualties. They captured some 20,000 prisoners and 175 guns, but gained no ground of any importance.

Nivelle's promise of a miraculous breakthrough swiftly collapsed and, given that France was already thoroughly war-weary, this failure was seen by many Frenchmen as a final demonstration that, although the Allies might not face defeat, they certainly could not win this war. On 25 April Bertie presciently informed the War Cabinet in London that Nivelle would soon be replaced by Philippe Pétain, whose overall strategy might be to abandon offensive operations and instead await the American Expeditionary Force, of which great things such as supplies of aircraft and munitions, if not manpower, had been mistakenly expected when the USA declared war on Germany on 2 April 1917. Following a conversation he had with Alexandre Ribot and Painlevé, Haig wrongly informed the War Cabinet that no such change in the French general staff or its policy was about to happen – only to find that Pétain was indeed appointed French Chief of Staff a few days later, on 28 April, with effective control over the French army.

The failure of Nivelle's offensive threw France's army into chaos. Many of its rank and file soldiers were no longer prepared, as they saw it, to carry out attacks that were doomed from the start. Between 20 May and 10 June 1917 some 40,000 French soldiers mutinied and staged protests, disrupting forty-nine divisions, or about half of the French army on the Western Front. The mutineers' spokesmen told senior officers they would defend their own lines, but would not participate in further futile attacks. This despondency struck at the heart of France; in Paris, civilian workers went on strike, while Socialist parliamentary deputies called for a negotiated peace, and self-appointed pacifist leaders were discovered to have been funded by Germany. Haig regarded the collapse of Nivelle's house of cards as yet further confirmation of his long-held assumption that French generals – and most of their soldiers – lacked the necessary grit to finish the job. He bluntly told Robertson that Pétain's declared strategy of an 'aggressive defence' while awaiting American reinforcements would mean 'the British Army will do all the "aggressive" part, while the French remain on the defensive.'[30] For a long time to come, he was right.

At another Anglo-French conference, this time in Paris on 4–5 May, the changed balance in the Anglo-French alliance was palpable. Attention now shifted to how best the BEF could shoulder the main brunt of offensive action for the foreseeable future on the Western Front. On 15 May Nivelle was finally sacked, and Pétain took over as French C-in-C. While Pétain tried to reassure Robertson that he 'never had the least idea of stopping fighting' but only to cease aiming at 'impossible objectives as Nivelle had done', his first general order to French troops, issued on 19 May 1917, set out his doctrine for the future – limited offensives with limited objectives. French colonial troops on leave had previously that month marched through Paris shouting, 'Down with war!' Pétain also imposed military justice; 629 alleged mutineers were condemned to death and seventy-five executed, with almost 3,000 more being sentenced to various terms of imprisonment.[31] As well as wielding a stick, Pétain distributed some carrots, judiciously granting leave and promising that he would not in future demand of French troops the impossible, although what lay ahead of both them, and the BEF and Dominion soldiers, before the war ended was no less ghastly than they had already suffered.

As with Nivelle, Haig was willing to give Pétain a chance at the start. He found the new French C-in-C 'businesslike, knowledgeable, and brief of speech. The latter a rare quality in Frenchmen!'[32] Haig's goodwill – or naivety – was apparently limitless; after all, he had quite taken to Nivelle on their first meeting. Nivelle's failure was, paradoxically, a remarkable fillip for Haig, whose success at Vimy provided unarguable evidence that there was perhaps, after all, something to be said for the quality of British generalship.

Haig's good luck held firm; from being trussed up, ready for sacrifice in early February, he had by the end of April again become the hero of the hour, as Esher informed him on 21 April: 'Yesterday I spent some hours with Lloyd George, and we lunched on the balcony of the Crillon in the sunshine. He has entirely changed his point of view as to the respective merits of the chiefs of the Allied Army, their staffs, and powers of offence. It is almost comic to see how the balance has turned. For the moment I do not think you could do wrong.'[33] Lloyd George's estimation of Haig might have miraculously recovered; but his relations with Robertson did not improve.[34]

With the French in disarray and Lloyd George's hostility deflected, at least for the moment, Haig welcomed the suggestion in Paris that the BEF should take the leading role in any new offensive, and he used Nivelle's failure as justification. He informed Robertson on 28 May that 'our French Allies had already shown that they lacked both the moral qualities and the means for gaining victory.' This view he felt was reinforced after he was visited by General Debeney, Pétain's chief of staff, on 2 June. Debeney told Haig that French morale was low; at another meeting later that week Debeney also revealed that an unspecified number of French mutineers had been shot, although Haig was erroneously led to believe that the mutiny had been confined to just two divisions.

Haig decided to take advantage of an abashed and enfeebled French military command to resurrect his old ambition of pushing hard into northern Belgium, with the aim of forcing the Germans to relinquish their hold on the Belgian Channel ports of Ostend and Zeebrugge. The

first step in this campaign was to be an assault on a low-lying but dominating ridge which stretched between Messines and Wytschaete, and
which formed a small salient into the British line some ten miles to the
south of Ypres. This ridge, which overlooked the British lines for miles
around, had last been attacked – unsuccessfully – by Smith-Dorrien's II
Corps in December 1915, and had since been a cause of steady losses to
the British.

The operation at Messines, spearheaded by Plumer's Second Army,
was thoroughly prepared and utilized overwhelming firepower. It hugely
raised the BEF's morale, proving to be one of the rare British-led attacks
that was entirely successful from start to finish. Precisely at 3.10am on 7
June a vast explosion, loud enough to be heard in London, threw thousands of tons of earth high into the sky, as the ridge was ripped apart by
nineteen mines – two others failed to detonate – that had been dug, over
two years, beneath the German positions on the ridge. Almost a million
pounds of explosives destroyed the ridge, already pummelled into dust
by a preceding eleven-day bombardment consuming three and a half
million shells. Some 80,000 infantry, supported by seventy-six new Mark
IV tanks, achieved their first objective – the taking of the ridge – in just
over half an hour.[35]

Yet paradoxically this mammoth explosion created its own problems,
shattering the landscape and making advances by successive reinforcing
waves much more difficult. It also posed a new logistical problem – how
to support the troops occupying the newly captured ridge? At this stage
the BEF was using six million gallons of petrol each month; supplying
this alone was an enormous undertaking. Reinforcing the precarious
hold on Messines proved very costly,[36] and the initial success of Plumer's
Second Army proved another false dawn. The limited aims and careful
preparation of the assault had shown that it was possible to gain piecemeal victories, albeit at great cost in men's lives, so long as the temptation
to push harder, go further, was resisted.

While the BEF was celebrating its modest success at Messines, Pétain
remained nervous at the condition of French morale; he cancelled a
French offensive due to commence on 10 June, rather than risk tipping

his fractious troops into outright rebellion. The French authorities did their best to hide, both from their own citizens and their Allies, the extent of the disaffection within the French army. In the first week of June the British War Cabinet learned that the pacifist French politician Caillaux was in Geneva, in discussion with Count Mensdorff, former Austrian ambassador to London, over the possibility of peace between France and the Austro-Hungarian empire, one of numerous peace-feelers put out by all sides in 1917. The scale and severity of the French mutinies nevertheless emerged piecemeal, via rumour, and there is no doubt that British politicians and senior BEF officers alike were aware that the situation was very grave. Adding to the tension was internal turmoil in Russia, where in February 1917 the Tsar had abdicated. On 3 June the first all-Russia Congress of Workers and Soldiers' Soviets opened and, within a month, Russian soldiers were being withdrawn from the eastern front to quell domestic upheavals. London and Paris feared a consequent easing of pressure on Germany; the War Cabinet and GHQ firmly believed the BEF might soon be standing alone against the Central Powers, awaiting the painfully slow arrival of American reinforcements.

Henry Wilson, who was being eased out from his liaison role in Paris by Pétain, visited London between 6 and 11 June, where he pessimistically informed Robertson that 'it will be impossible to keep the French in this war for another 12 or 18 months, waiting for America, without a victory of some sort, and that if we can't get a military success, then we *must* get a diplomatic success. We *must*.'[37] Wilson repeated this grim forecast to Lloyd George and the War Cabinet. Esher added to the sombre atmosphere by telling the Prime Minister on 5 June:

> France is feeling overburdened just now by the weight of war, and her armies are languishing with home-sickness [. . .] unless you assert your volition and great authority with the French masses, the word "Alliance" will soon become an inversion of the truth. [. . .] The supreme risk of allowing the people, and the armies that are so subtly interwoven in sentiment with the people, to think that they must "wait for America," is that the soldiers will insist upon returning to their homes – like their "brothers in Russia".[38]

Lloyd George's response was that of a politician; he formed a committee. On 8 June he chaired the newly formed Cabinet War Policy Committee, whose members, besides himself, were Curzon, Milner and the South African Boer War general turned politician, Jan Christian Smuts; it notably excluded Derby, the figure formally in charge of the War Office. This committee met sixteen times between 11 June and 18 July, interviewing military personnel and politicians; at issue were the darkening international perspectives and, more particularly, what strategic military options were left. Haig and Robertson told this committee that the only chance of keeping the French in the war was by renewing the Flanders offensive initiated at Messines. Lloyd George's preference at this stage was similar to that of Pétain – to stay on the defensive on the Western Front – but with the extra ingredient of reinforcing Italian attacks against Austria-Hungary.

On 17 June Haig travelled to London for ten days, partly to see Doris, who had taken out a lease on a new home, Eastcott, on Kingston Hill, near Richmond, which was to remain the family's main residence until March 1923, and partly to attend meetings with the War Policy Committee. The Haigs' new home offended the exquisite taste of Philip Sassoon, who described his first impressions of it in a letter to Esher on 6 May 1917: 'The hall painted in shiny lint-white enamel is stuffed with foxes roaming through artificial grasses. Bitterns under glass domes, and various trophies of the chase and sport, like crossed swords that hang like the sword of Damocles over the nape of the shrinking guest. The whole freely interlarded with Benares work [decorated and beaten brass work from the city of Benares, now known as Varanasi]. You know the rooms are papered with photos of Kings and Queens. His study has a claret coloured wall paper. I didn't know you could get any now: not even a rich Burgundy that would have made one think of booze, but a dull brick, like an old wine stain. One is not even spared the conservatory leading out of the drawing room (never used) in which a few plants languish of the variety that bear a scanty crop of leaves which they wish they had never produced and can never succeed in shedding.'[39] Little wonder that Doris loathed her husband's private secretary.

On 18 June, Haig gave the new committee his opinion, based on erroneous information supplied by Charteris, that 'Germany was within 6 months of the total exhaustion of her available man power <u>if the fighting continues at its present intensity</u>.'[40] This confidently held but mistaken impression of Germany's military position was at the heart of Haig's strategic thinking throughout 1917. It was a view that was completely contradicted by reports fed to Robertson by his own intelligence chief, Major-General Sir George Macdonogh, a contemporary of Haig's at the Staff College and someone Haig distrusted, at least in part because he was a Roman Catholic.[41] Macdonogh, Director of Military Intelligence at the War Office, invariably departed from Charteris's perennially optimistic view that the German army's morale was declining and its numbers steadily falling on the Western Front. Macdonogh's less sanguine analyses were usually right. In mid–1917, for example, he shared Pétain's view, arguing to Robertson that 'It is obvious that offensive operations on our front would offer no chance of success; and our best course would be to remain on the defensive, strengthen our positions, economise our reserves in manpower and material, and hope that the balance would be eventually redressed by American assistance.'[42]

Macdonogh, formerly commander of the Intelligence Corps of the BEF in France, took to the work brilliantly. His attention to detail and his development of independent intelligence gathering networks in Holland and Germany meant that he knew precisely at any time the position and type of German regiments on the Western Front. When he became Director of Military Intelligence at the War Office in December 1915, just as Haig took over as C-in-C, Macdonogh ensured these networks stayed fresh, rivalling Charteris. Was it purely religious prejudice, or did Haig's antagonism towards Macdonogh stem from some now forgotten rivalry while they were both at Staff College? The most likely explanation is that, while Charteris produced intelligence reports that concurred with Haig's own preconceptions, Macdonogh's distance from GHQ enabled him to take a cooler, more independent line. He was also provided with more balanced views about German morale from his agents on the ground. The fact that Haig preferred to hear auspicious news from Charteris that supported his own hopes that the Germans were forever just on the brink of collapse was not lost on Charteris and his own intelligence team.[43] Certainly, Charteris did not lack support in gathering intelligence; he had on his own staff some 200 specialists at GHQ, including two Nobel physics laureates, one of whom was engaged in the increasingly vital task of developing sound-ranging, the science of locating enemy artillery by the sound of its firing.[44]

Whatever the reality, Haig's mind was made up by mid–1917: Germany was on its knees, and he declined to listen to opinions which contradicted what he regarded as a certainty. Haig's complete faith in Charteris is one of several aspects of his conduct of operations during the Great War which cast a shadow over his stature. Charteris had learned over many years, no doubt sometimes painfully, that what Haig most sought in subordinates was unquenchable optimism; that was Haig's style and he had little time for those whom he thought lacked spirit. Yet Haig on occasion failed to keep Charteris fully apprised of what, prima facie, seems intelligence of the most vital importance, such as the seriousness of the French mutinies in mid–1917.

On 5 March 1927, Haig wrote to Charteris from Cannes, where he was staying at the Hotel Bellevue, saying he had received word from Winston Churchill about his book, *The World Crisis*, on the war: '[Churchill] mentioned that he had criticised me over the Passchendaele operations. I replied I did not care what criticisms he made so long as he clearly stated the facts, as far as it was possible to know them. [. . .] It is impossible for Winston to know how the possibility of the French Army breaking up in 1917 <u>compelled</u> us to <u>go on attacking</u>. It was impossible to change sooner from the Ypres front to Cambrai with Pétain coming to beg me not to leave the Germans alone for a week, on account of the <u>awful</u> state of the French troops! You even did not know the facts as Pétain told them to me in confidence.'[45] At this distance in time, it is difficult to credit the suggestion that Haig's intelligence chief was unaware of the depth of despair within the French army in mid–1917. But if Haig's claim of 1927 is true then it is a serious indictment, both of the competence of Charteris, and also of Haig's failure to keep his closest aide fully apprised of vital information.

Be all this as it may, by late June 1917 there was within the War Policy Committee agreement on little, save the indisputable fact that French morale was at its nadir. To the committee, Haig asserted that the French army would hold firm; but he also insisted that if the BEF failed to resume the offensive on the Western Front, or if the government sanctioned a wasteful – in his view – diversionary campaign in Italy, such as that envisaged by Lloyd George, then this policy 'might lead to the collapse of France.' The War Policy Committee was certainly aware of the rapid degeneration of French military morale. Robertson had been briefed by Brigadier-General Edward Spears,[46] who in his capacity as head of the British Military Mission in Paris, responsible to the War Office, had travelled up and down the French lines in June 1917 visiting the French Northern Army Group. Spears concluded that 'the mutiny was more serious than I or any one else thought at the time.'

The historian David French has cast doubt on precisely how well the BEF's senior officers briefed their political masters in London: 'Neither this report [by Spears], the first to give a reasonably accurate account of the extent of the unrest, nor subsequent reports of French troop morale made by Major Rex Benson, the British liaison officer with the Groupe des Armées du Nord, which indicated the unwillingness of the men to take part in further offensives, were ever seen by the committee. [. . .] To that extent Lloyd George could fairly claim that the committee was the victim of a cover-up by Robertson and [others]. However, the committee knew enough not to make any hurried decisions.'[47]

Spears had, however, certainly briefed Lloyd George; they met on the morning of 14 June at 10 Downing Street, with Robertson in attendance. According to Spears, Lloyd George said: 'I understand you have just visited some sections of the French army where there has been serious trouble. This is a very serious situation. The question I am asking you is a grave one, I presume you realise how grave: is the French army going to recover? You should be able to express a positive opinion.'

Spears felt intimidated by Lloyd George's peremptory manner; he had expected only to report on what he knew had so far happened. He later said that he conveyed to the Prime Minister that 'The French soldier was turning out to be in many ways the opposite of what we had believed him to be. Far from being fickle and volatile, he was proving to be stable, staunch and tenacious.'

Lloyd George then asked: 'Will you give me your word as an officer and a gentleman that the French army will recover?' A now infuriated Spears said he would 'stake my life on it', but not his word of honour, before repeating that 'The French army under Pétain will surely recover.'[48]

One can sympathize with Lloyd George at this juncture, trying as he was to piece together from the daily flow of often contradictory reports and rumours some sense of the objective facts of the war – not least the will of the French to endure. On 20 June, Haig returned to the Privy Council Office for another and more startling session of the War Policy Committee, at which Admiral Sir John Jellicoe, the commander of the Grand Fleet at the Battle of Jutland in 1916 and now First Sea Lord, announced without preamble that the German U-boat campaign against British shipping had reached such a pitch that 'it would be impossible for Great Britain to continue the war in 1918.' While 'no one present shared Jellicoe's view, and all seemed satisfied that the food reserves in Great Britain are adequate,' Jellicoe was adamant: '[His] words were, "There is no good discussing plans for next spring. We cannot go on." '[49]

The committee considered Jellicoe's pessimism to be exaggerated, but this warning from the Royal Navy played directly into Haig's hands. He used Jellicoe's lugubrious assessment, together with Lloyd George's reluctant regard for him in the wake of the success at Vimy, to persuade the War Cabinet of the merits of his long-planned offensive around Ypres, aimed at capturing the Channel ports of Belgium. Part of this plan involved an ambitious amphibious assault on the Belgian coast, to be led by Rawlinson. However, at the very moment the War Policy Committee was about to sanction Haig's renewed Flanders offensive, Haig began to receive reports suggesting that perhaps the worst of the troubles in the French ranks had passed. On 30 June 1917, Esher wrote to Haig: 'The French troubles in the Army are quieting down. Pétain seems to have been firm and sensible. Keeping the French soldiers away from Paris has already done good.'[50] Another Paris-based correspondent,

Jefferson Davis Cohn,[51] wrote a series of letters to Haig between January and August 1917. On 13 July, he addressed Haig as 'My dear General', continuing, 'It may not be without interest to you to know that my friends tell me that the "morale" in the French Army has become very much better, and that one hears no more of incidents at the Front such as distressed those who knew of them after the last offensive. [. . .] at the "Back" the "morale" is also completely re-established.'[52]

Of course, coming from such a source – a journalist – this information was inevitably suspect for Haig; but if the likes of Jefferson Cohn knew of both the mutinies *and* the restoration of some order, then this was clearly common gossip and not the type of grand secret that Haig and others then imagined and later depicted it to have been. Precisely what the British political and military hierarchy knew of the shifting dynamics of the French mutinies is not easy to establish; their French allies certainly did not feel it necessary to give clear or regular assessments of the situation. In his *War Memoirs*, Lloyd George claimed that the War Policy Committee had been tricked into the 1917 offensive that culminated in Passchendaele by the French, Robertson, Haig, and Wilson, in his capacity as head of the British Military Mission to the French GQG. He accused them of knowing about the mutinies but keeping their existence secret, in case British politicians vetoed Haig's plans. But given Lloyd George's own good relations with some French officials, including Albert Thomas, Minister of Munitions until he resigned in September 1917, not to mention his briefing with Brigadier-General Spears, this accusation seems spurious.

In its final report written on 18–19 July, drawn up by Hankey, the War Policy Committee concluded: 'We cannot rely on the French army to take the offensive on a scale calculated to draw the German reserves to the French front in a strength commensurate with the numerical strength of the French army. The British army, if it takes the offensive, must, therefore, expect to encounter the bulk of the German reserves.'[53] This left no one in doubt that, even if the precise scale of the French mutinies was unknown, the War Cabinet accepted that the brunt of any Western Front offensive in 1917 would rest squarely on the BEF. On 20

July the War Cabinet finally approved Haig's plans for a fresh offensive in Flanders, although it stipulated that 'it must on no account be allowed to drift into a protracted, costly, and indecisive operation as occurred in the offensive on the Somme.'

Yet another Somme it became, not least because the general selected by Haig to take overall operational command of what became known as Third Ypres, Hubert Gough, was cast in Haig's own incorrigibly optimistic mould. As one of the more openly critical post-war memoirs records, Gough parroted the prevailing optimism of GHQ: 'Not once but many times, at the Fifth Army Conferences, General Sir Hubert Gough, the Army Commander, opened the proceedings with a statement to this effect: "Gentlemen, I have just come from an interview with the Commander-in-Chief and he tells me that everything points to a complete break-down of the enemy morale and that one more hard thrust will crumple up his defences." There is no possible doubt but that General Gough implicitly believed in what he told us, but there was not one other single member of the Conference who did not know how grotesquely inaccurate this statement was in fact.'[54]

The events of Third Ypres have been amply documented.[55] It is difficult to avoid an adverse judgement as to Haig's management of this campaign, where the fundamental mistake he made at the Somme – an over-optimistic assessment of the chances of a lasting breakthrough – was repeated, with apparently little learned from 1916. The original plan for Third Ypres, as developed by Plumer and Rawlinson after the successful limited engagement at Messines, envisaged an initial first-day advance of no more than a mile, to take the second German line of defences. This would be followed by a two-day recuperation and regrouping, allowing field artillery batteries to be pulled forward far enough to direct sufficient firepower onto the next German line. And so, by careful steps, the British would leap-frog to eventual victory. This painstaking method of advance was, however, jettisoned by Gough, whose reputation as a more aggressive commander persuaded Haig that his Fifth Army should spearhead the attack, with Gough in overall command of the offensive.

The lure Gough held out to Haig was a much grander, swifter penetration of the German defences; instead of the piecemeal creep forward suggested by Plumer and Rawlinson, Fifth Army would be expected to advance and capture three successive German lines, a distance of almost three miles from the jump-off point, all on the first day of the attack. However, these German positions – there were at least five successive defensive lines facing the British, and on the Gheluvelt Plateau from Broodseinde to Becelaire there were two more – had been considerably reinforced since Messines. The German front line defences were some seven miles ahead of the rearmost, and the area between was strewn with a multitude of heavily defended concrete emplacements – the low-lying and waterlogged ground made dugouts impossible. These defences were protected by German artillery situated behind the Gheluvelt Plateau and Passchendaele Ridge; the guns were well-hidden from direct British observation, yet their fire could be directed onto British attackers by observers on the German-held ridges. Gough's scheme dictated from the outset that, even if the Fifth Army was completely successful in its ambitious plan, it would by the end of the first day reach a point beyond the range of all but a few of the BEF's guns, and bed down in the captured German positions for up to four more days, within easy range of the concealed German artillery, before resuming the attack by an assault aimed at taking the whole of the Passchendaele-Staden Ridge.

Haig's preference for Gough's proposal over Plumer's went against the advice of at least one of his senior staff officers at GHQ. Brigadier-General John Davidson, Head of the Operations Section at GHQ, informed Haig in a memo prior to the offensive: 'An advance which is essentially deliberate and sustained may not achieve such important results during the first day of operations, but will in the long run be much more likely to obtain a decision. By a deliberate and sustained advance, I refer to a succession of operations each at two or three days' interval, each having as its object the capture of the enemy's defences, strongpoints, or tactical features, to a depth of not less than 1,500 yards and not more than 3,000 yards. It has been proved beyond doubt that with sufficient and efficient artillery preparation we can push our infantry through to a depth of a mile without undue losses or disorganisation.'[56]

To avoid the risk of being labelled a 'defeatist', Davidson naturally left his most serious point – that to push infantry beyond that mile would incur serious losses and chaos – implicit. To Davidson's wisely cautious memo, Lieutenant-General Sir Ivor Maxse, one of Gough's corps commanders and widely recognized at the time and since as a very capable commanding officer, appended the word 'Balls!'[57] 'Balls to caution' is hardly a motto that a Great War general might have sought to have emblazoned on his coat of arms upon accepting his inevitable peerage in 1919, but it would have been appropriate for any number of them.

As the historians Trevor Wilson and Robin Prior have pointed out, by effectively doubling the depth of the intended penetration, against Davidson's suggestion, Gough automatically halved the number of shells falling on the area under attack.[58] As at the Somme, when the assault battalions, roughly 100,000 men in total, assembled in the reserve trenches before zero hour (3.50am) on Tuesday 31 July 1917 they marched heavily laden, each man carrying three days' rations, water bottle, helmet, entrenching tool, rifle, bayonet, four grenades, ammunition pouches and an extra bandolier of 220 rounds – all this weighing more than 100 pounds. Perhaps the only significant difference was that there was no anticipation on this occasion that the cavalry would play a part; they were merely served notice that, if a German rout ensued, they would be called upon to exploit the gap. The ground, prone to flooding and already heavily shelled, meant there were no great expectations of the 120 tanks (plus forty-eight in reserve) Gough had at his disposal.

By zero hour the German lines had been bombarded for the preceding fifteen days, deluged by 4.3 million shells; but even this quantity only effectively silenced the German defences in the left and centre of the assault, and only to a depth of some 3,000 yards. Defences beyond that were largely left unscathed, as was the German artillery nestled behind Passchendaele Ridge. Nevertheless, the first day of Third Ypres was considered a success by Gough and Haig; Pilckem Ridge had been overrun, while in the centre and left of the attack the French and British troops had taken the first two German lines and advanced to a depth of some 3,000 yards. Casualties on both sides were similar, about 27,000 apiece – hardly glorious but better than the Somme. But, crucially, Gheluvelt Plateau, a target for the first day, eluded the British.

As the afternoon of 31 July 1917 drew to its close, the scattered showers of the previous few days turned into a downpour. Rain fell across the Third Ypres battlefield throughout August, with total rainfall throughout the month of 127 millimetres, against an August average of seventy. This was genuine bad luck, although Charteris claimed it was entirely predictable. In his supposedly contemporary record, Charteris wrote in early August 1917: 'Every brook is swollen and the ground is a quagmire. If it were not that all the records of previous years had given us fair warning, it would seem as if Providence had declared war against us. [. . .] the front area now baffles description. I went up again yesterday (8 August) towards dusk. It is just a sea of mud, churned up by shell-fire.'[59] This seems, on the face of it, to point to another failure of intelligence, yet such bad weather was far from typical for the time of year. Lieutenant-Colonel Ernest Gold, in charge of the Meteorological Section of the Royal Engineers at GHQ, was to point out as late as 1958 that such rainfall was actually most unusual: 'The rainfall directly affecting the first month of the offensive was more than double the average; it was over five times the amount for the same period in 1915 and 1916. [. . .] The quite exceptional heavy rain from July 29 to August 4, 1917, was followed by muggy, stagnant weather which prevented the drying by evaporation, normal in the intervals of fair weather at that time of year.'[60]

The rain turned the whole region into a swamp and the low cloud made aerial observation impossible; the soldiers of the BEF thrown into the battle in its later stages began to stumble blindly through an ochre-yellow sticky morass, pock-marked with shell-holes, reeking of gas, fighting desperately for every inch of ground. Brigadier-General Baker-Carr graphically described the scene as he saw it: '[. . .] the whole surface of the ground consisted of nothing but a series of overlapping shell craters, half full of yellow, slimy water. Through falling into these ponds, hundreds upon hundreds of unwounded men, while advancing to the attack, lost their lives by drowning. The mere act of walking over this tortured swamp, unencumbered by the sixty pounds weight [Baker-Carr may have discounted the rifle and bayonet] which the soldier carries in action, was one that entailed considerable effort, though one was able to move at one's own pace and choose the easiest routes . . . Under the most favourable conditions, an attack against such a position as confronted us would have been a task of great difficulty and risk. As things actually were, it was nothing but rank folly.'[61]

The mud did have its benefits: many smaller shells were rendered useless as they plunged into it and exploded harmlessly. Through August, September and October 1917, a series of small but costly engagements – Langemarck, Menin Road Bridge, Polygon Wood, Broodseinde, Poelcapelle – saw successive attempts by the BEF and Dominion troops to capture the elusive and now shattered village of Passchendaele, which lay ahead on a minor ridge that had no strategic significance in itself. In September, Haig faced his own mutiny at the BEF's base camp at Etaples, close to GHQ and just fifteen miles south of Boulogne. Etaples was a notoriously grim place, where both new recruits and experienced soldiers were put through an oppressively harsh training regime. On Sunday 9 September some gunners from ANZAC units, later joined by Scottish soldiers, decided they would no longer tolerate the abusive treatment they received from Military Police; a fight started, swiftly spreading into wider demonstrations over the following week. This was no anti-war rebellion but rather an expression of disgruntlement by weary, battle-hardened troops who bitterly resented the bullying they received. Haig made no mention in his diary of these brief but embarrassing incidents and a veil was drawn across the episode.

As events at Etaples reminded GHQ that it faced its own discipline problems, Haig decided to move Gough and his Fifth Army further to the north, and handed back to Plumer and his Second Army responsibility for a fresh assault on the Gheluvelt Plateau, which was still in German hands. Augmented by the Australians and New Zealanders of I Anzac Corps, the Second Army took the Plateau on 20 September, and Polygon Wood six days later. This, together with yet more hyperbole from

Charteris on supposedly collapsing German morale and diminished reserves, encouraged Haig by early October to consider that Passchendaele Ridge was within his grasp. Plumer's bite-and-hold tactics were indeed apparently working; small advances were made and consolidated, and thousands of prisoners taken. But it was a painfully slow and costly business; by October not only was the normal autumnal rain well established, it had also become bitterly cold. On 9 October, when the Battle of Poelcapelle was launched, Plumer had begun to share Haig's optimism that perhaps they were on the verge, finally, of a generalized German collapse, although by 14 October, as the soldiers under his command failed to make headway through the mud, he began to have doubts; that day the *Times*'s Repington found him 'rather sarcastic about Charteris's optimism.'62

As the first and second battles of Passchendaele – 12 October–6 November – quickly succeeded one another, with the Canadian Corps finally taking the ridge, the frontline soldier had lost all sense of any wider strategy, if he had ever possessed it. He was only concerned to survive and take the next shell-hole. As for Haig, Third Ypres had descended into an increasingly desperate battle of attrition; if the Germans, as Haig convinced himself, were indeed about to collapse, then the larger strategic aim of taking the Belgian coastal ports was a distinct possibility, and Haig saw it as his duty to pile on whatever pressure he could bring to bear, despite the cost. That he was mistaken in this hope can only be judged with hindsight; that he was mistaken to place his trust in Charteris's optimistic reports was, however, becoming increasingly obvious to many in the late autumn of 1917.

Given the human costs and scant gains, it was inevitable that Lloyd George once more began to have doubts about Haig's abilities. The Prime Minister commissioned a paper from Field Marshal Viscount French and Lieutenant-General Sir Henry Wilson – currently under-employed as GOC, Eastern Command in England – to report on the operations of Third Ypres. As part of this task, Wilson received War Office casualty figures purporting to show that between 1 July 1916 and 10 October 1917 'Haig has lost 900,000 killed, wounded and missing, not sick, and of these 80,000 are missing.' On 17 October French, Wilson and Lloyd George met over dinner at French's home where, Wilson realized, 'It became very clear to me tonight that Lloyd George means to get Robertson out, and means to curb the powers of the C-in-C in the field. This is what I have been advising for two and a half years, and this is what the whole of my paper is directed at – not to getting Robertson out, but to forming a Superior Direction over all the C.G.S.s and C-in-C.s.'[63]

French and Wilson duly recommended in late October a return to the defensive, and to await sufficient American reinforcements to push home the attack in 1919, although they declined to back Lloyd George's obsession with diverting Britain's military resources to theatres other than the Western Front, nor did they call for Haig to be replaced. The Prime Minister took their advice on establishing some form of 'Superior Direction', through which he saw the possibility of achieving the ambition that had been thwarted at Calais in February. By now, too, it was becoming much clearer that French military morale was fast recovering. In the autumn of 1917, Pétain was confident enough to inform Repington, who met the French C-in-C at his HQ at Compiègne on 7 October, that French 'moral [sic] was now completely re-established at the front. He only feared the rear and the effect of current scandals and treacheries'. Repington was also reminded on this occasion of the severe limits – as the French saw it – to Anglo-French military cooperation: '[. . .] Pétain's officers at our GHQ did not receive all the information asked for, and Pétain said that he had only a very approximate idea of our numbers. His officers at GHQ were told that the details would not interest the French, though these matters stood at the base of all calculations. He was merely informed that the British would have a difficulty in keeping up their strength after December. He said that Charteris killed off the Germans too quickly, and that he and Davidson egged on Haig to believe that he was winning the war when we were still far from that desirable consummation.'[64]

On 1 November, Lloyd George travelled to Paris, along with Wilson, Smuts, and Hankey. The purpose of their journey was to finalize with the French the establishment of a Supreme War Council, a body which, it was hoped, would bring about more cohesive Anglo-French military cooperation. En route the Prime Minister revealed that he was considering sending Haig to the Italian front to command the British and French in that theatre. Next day Kiggell, Haig's chief of staff, met Wilson. He had been mandated by Haig to try to persuade Wilson to support the continued offensive in Flanders. Wilson wrote in his diary that Kiggell 'pleaded that in another eight days Douglas Haig would take enough of the Paschendaele [sic] Ridge to make himself secure for the winter, and that this operation ought not to be stopped.'[65]

In this is contained the essence of why Haig pushed his soldiers to the edge of human endurance in the final days of Third Ypres; by November 1917 it had nothing to do with relieving pressure on other fronts, either in Italy, Russia or France. If Haig's soldiers failed to gain and hold Passchendaele Ridge before the worst of the winter set in, all the meagre gains made so far would be nullified; they would either have to withdraw to more easily defended positions, beyond the immediate sweep of German artillery, a humiliation in itself, or face the appalling prospect of sitting through the winter under the direct observation of German artillery spotters still in occupation of the height of the ridge. The taking of Passchendaele had collapsed from being one element of a much wider strategy to being an end in itself.

On 4 November, the Prime Minister met Haig in Paris, where he accused the C-in-C of feeding the British press with hostile views about him, which Haig denied. Haig even offered to write a letter of complaint to the editor Lloyd George named, John Alfred Spender[66] of the *Westminster Gazette*, a periodical sympathetic to Asquith; the Prime Minister, who recognized that such a letter would merely add fuel to the fire, replied: 'Oh, please do not do that.' Haig reflected in his diary on this encounter with Lloyd George in Paris: 'I thought LG is like the German, who, whenever he proposes to do anything extra frightful, first of all complains that the British or French have committed the enormity which he is meditating.' Then he added, displaying considerably less insight: 'I gave LG a good talking to on several of the questions he raised, and felt I got the best of the arguments.'

Haig deluded himself. The Prime Minister was a master at rhetoric and, as the relative reputations of each of them today demonstrates, he never lost an argument with Haig. Eight days later Lloyd George was once more in Paris, where he addressed a lunch for public dignitaries and subtly ridiculed Haig's efforts. He told his guests: 'We have won great victories. When I look at the appalling casualty lists I sometimes wish it had not been necessary to win so many. [. . .] When we advance a kilometre into the enemy's lines, snatch a small shattered village out of his cruel grip, capture a few hundreds of his soldiers, we shout with unfeigned joy.'

This was regarded by Haig and Robertson and many of their sympathizers in the British press and Parliament as a slur, not just on them but the whole army. Yet, from the Prime Minister's standpoint, the dispassionate balance sheet of territory gained versus human losses spelled a bankruptcy of military leadership. Surely, after such a public rebuke from his Prime Minister, Haig's days were numbered? On the same day that Lloyd George made his inflammatory speech, the Supreme War Council was established, with the Prime Ministers of France, Italy and Britain and their respective military advisers (Foch, Cadorna and Wilson), charged with the task of 'watching over the general conduct of the war', but without executive power. Its HQ was to be at Versailles. Charteris viewed this development as 'utter rubbish so far as fighting is concerned. It will mean delay in any attack on the Germans and will break down at once if the Germans attack us. But it also means that the Cabinet is going to oust D. H or Robertson, or both.'[67] Haig did not even think it worth recording in his own diary.

The Supreme War Council did not mark a greater step towards unified Allied command but only a half-hearted intention. From its inception, it was regarded as little more than another talking shop; Georges Clemenceau, whose second term as President (and simultaneously War Minister) started on 16 November, told 'Colonel' House, President Woodrow Wilson's roving foreign ambassador, that he would put in a second- or third-rate man as France's permanent military representative 'and let the thing drift where it will.'[68] Sir Henry Wilson asked Robertson on 6 November what he thought of the Supreme Council. Robertson, predictably, opposed it: 'He does not see how it can work without responsibility, nor why it should be given responsibility. [. . .] I asked him if, looking back over two years, he was satisfied with the conduct of the war, and whether he would act in the same way again, and he replied in the affirmative to both questions. Since he has been C.I.G.S we have lost Rumania, Russia and Italy, and have gained Bullecourt, Messines and Pascendaele [sic].'[69] Clearly, the Council was not going to become the means by which the Prime Minister could ensure Robertson and Haig were bypassed.

But the year did not end on the futilities of Passchendaele, the ghastly finale to Third Ypres, where, since Messines, an estimated 70,000 British and Dominion soldiers had died, and more than 200,000 others had become casualties. There was still Cambrai, a battle that produced for Haig, lucky Haig, an undisputed, rapid, and, in terms of lives lost, a relatively cheap victory – one that had church bells ringing across the English countryside for the first time since the start of the war. Cambrai scotched the Prime Minister's plans to assemble sufficient press and political support finally to sack the C-in-C.

The Battle of Cambrai, which commenced on 20 November 1917, has come to be remembered mainly for its apparently successful deployment of massed tank formations, yet the British owed their success here as much to the fact that the Germans were, unusually, taken completely by surprise as to anything else. For Cambrai was the first British attack to be based on the principles of scientific gunnery: there was no preliminary bombardment to alert the enemy; instead there was a carefully calibrated barrage which relied on map references to direct fire at pre-selected targets. The idea of an attack involving serried ranks of tanks had been accepted in principle by both GHQ and the War Office as early as March 1917,[70] but a lack of suitable ground and insufficient quantities of tanks meant it had dropped down the agenda, until the political need for a quick and impressive victory had sent staff officers scurrying off to reconsider all plans and possibilities, however risky.

Haig himself had always supported greater development and use of the tank, informing the War Office on 5 June 1917 that in his opinion '[. . .] events have proved the utility of Tanks, both as a means of over-coming hostile resistance [. . .] and as a means of reducing casualties in the attacking troops and I consider that sufficient experience has now been gained to warrant the adoption of the Tank as a recognised addition to the existing means of conducting offensive operations.'[71] Haig's support for tanks was also bolstered by the fact that the Tank Corps was led by a veritable fire-eater – and another old Cliftonian – in the person of Lieutenant-Colonel Hugh Elles. Elles was by training a Royal Engineer, a Staff College graduate and a staff officer at GHQ for a period after August 1916, and, while a man of great personal courage, he was universally recognized as lacking any great intellectual curiosity. He possessed, in fact, all the qualities that would endear him to Haig.

The basis of the attack at Cambrai was laid before Haig by the clever soldier Julian Byng as early as September 1917, when Haig was still preoccupied with Third Ypres; by late October he had endorsed Byng's proposal. In a matter of days, the senior officers to be involved were briefed to conduct an assault without a preliminary barrage on the German lines between the St Quentin Canal and the Canal du Nord, with the aim of capturing the town of Cambrai. Only two German divisions held the six-mile-front to be attacked, and they were known to be supported by very little artillery. At dawn on 20 November, more than 300 tanks led five infantry divisions from the Third Army through a thick mist and a bank of fog, created by artillery firing smoke shells to mask the attack. By the end of the day, a penetration of almost four miles had been achieved at some points, far more than anything witnessed during the preceding battles of Third Ypres. It created a sizeable salient in the German lines, one that exposed the British troops to flanking attack. Cambrai itself eluded Byng's grasp; German skill at shifting reinforcements to threatened areas once again coincided with British inability to capitalize upon any wedge driven into the enemy's trenches, and over the next few days ferocious counter-attacks by German storm-troopers succeeded in recapturing almost all the lost ground.

Yet Cambrai marked genuine progress in the developing resourcefulness of the BEF; it showed, on a small scale, what could be achieved by a surprise attack mounted by a well-coordinated combination of infantry, artillery, tanks and aircraft, the latter having played a key part in aerial observation and directing repressive gunfire during the battle. Regrettably, this lesson was not learned either rapidly or thoroughly by some senior staff officers at GHQ. Brigadier-General Baker-Carr, himself in command of 1st Brigade of tanks, wrote much later that, after Cambrai, Kiggell informed Elles that the number of tank battalions should be reduced by 50 per cent and that Cambrai had been 'a splendid show, but one that can never be repeated.'[72] It was not a view shared by Haig, for whom the tank had finally proved its worth.

As 1917 drew to a close, Haig's luck held in his struggle to survive the threat posed by Lloyd George, largely thanks to the efforts of Elles, Byng and countless forgotten troops who in late November battled to hold on to a vital ridge extending into Bourlon Wood, west of Cambrai; but the War Cabinet required some sacrifice for the year's costly balance sheet. All – save Haig – joined in selecting the hapless Charteris, who by now, it seems, was loathed by all of Haig's army commanders.

Esher had informed Haig on 28 October 1917: 'Rawly [Rawlinson] came to see me yesterday and in course of a long rigmarole, delivered the usual second-hand criticisms of the Principal Boy! [Charteris's nickname among GHQ staff] I rubbed into his thick head that C had no influence over you, and that you knew perfectly well his merits and demerits. And then I told him what you once told me that in your grave military matters, upon which your operations depended, Charteris' information had never once let you down. All questions of tact, manners etc etc are wholly subsidiary to this crucial test.'[73]

Derby, with his usual loquaciousness, meanwhile urged Haig in a telegram (marked secret and personal) on 7 December to deliver the *coup de grâce*: 'The War Cabinet are constantly saying that the statements and views you have put forward at different times regarding the moral [sic] and numerical weakening of the enemy are not borne out by the opposition your troops encounter, and so it appears to me and to the General

Staff here. As you can imagine, the events of the 30th [the successful German counter-attack at Cambrai] and subsequent days have not reduced the feeling that you had not been as well advised by your Intelligence Staff as you ought to be. It is felt that not only is too much made of indications of the enemy's weakness, but that indications and information regarding his remaining strength are not fully and fairly represented to you. On the whole the Cabinet think that it is essential you should have a more reliable D.M.I [Director Military Intelligence] and have so informed me. [. . .] You will agree that it is very necessary the War Cabinet should have the fullest confidence in the opinions and judgement of officers of your Staff, and this they will not have so long as Charteris remains D.M.I. I naturally should prefer that the initiative should come from you and hope that you will see your way to make a change, and as soon as possible. [. . .]'[74]

Sir Philip Sassoon was, of course, well aware of Derby's telegram and wrote to Esher the same day, distancing himself from Charteris: 'As you know I have never agreed with these foolish optimistic statements which Charteris has been putting in D.H's mouth all the year but what they [the War Cabinet] ought to know is that morale is a fluctuating entity & there is no doubt that events in Russia & Italy have greatly raised the enemy's spirits.'[75]

Haig did not let go of his obedient subordinate without a struggle. He replied to Derby that Charteris's duty 'is to collect, collate and place before me all evidence obtainable in regard to the enemy. [. . .] My judgment is not formed on the information collected by him alone, but on the views of commanders under me, who are in close daily touch with the troops and the situation on the battle fronts, and on my own experience of the German forces from the commencement of the war until now. [. . .] I cannot accept his resignation at present for many reasons. No charge has been made against him beyond that mentioned in your letter which, as I have already said, is based entirely on matters for which, if the charge is justified at all, I am responsible and not Charteris. [. . .] If the War Cabinet desire to leave the Chief Command in this theatre in my hands through the difficult months which lie before us, I am entitled to ask that their confidence may be extended to my capacity to choose my own staff, and I certainly do not desire at the present juncture to change the head of my Intelligence Branch.'[76]

If Haig would not bend to the will of the War Cabinet, then the Cabinet was prepared to resort to pressure from another and potentially much more threatening direction. By no coincidence whatsoever, Northcliffe's *The Times* weighed in against Charteris in a leader on 12 December. Under the sub-heading 'A Case for Inquiry' the newspaper threatened that '[. . .] we can no longer rest satisfied with the fatuous estimates, e.g, of German losses in men and moral, which have inspired too many of the published messages from France. [. . .] Sir Douglas Haig's position cannot but depend in large measure on his choice of subordinates. His weakness, if it be a weakness, is his inveterate devotion to those who have served him longest – some of them perhaps too long, or at least too long without a rest. [. . .] To judge only from our Correspondent's account of its incidents [the reversal at Cambrai] – of Brigade Headquarters raided, of generals fighting in their pyjamas, of doctors interrupted in their dressing stations – we may agree that they are all magnificent, but they should never have occurred. It is here that inquiry is needed – prompt, searching, complete, and free from all suspicion that those responsible, however remotely, are sitting in judgment on their own miscalculations.'

By the standards of the day, *The Times'* depiction in December 1917 of Haig's published reports as 'fatuous', and its suggestion that Haig might have a 'weakness', signified a rebuke of Olympian magnitude. The paper shied away from calling for Haig's departure, but everyone who read the editorial understood that by 'those who have served him longest' was meant Charteris; his head was necessary and if GHQ failed to deliver it promptly, the demanded 'inquiry' might widen to include even Haig himself.[77] Northcliffe threatened as much to Sassoon the very next day, telling him: 'I ought to tell you frankly and plainly, as a friend of the Commander-in-Chief, that dissatisfaction, which easily produces a national outburst of indignation, exists in regard to the Generalship in France. [. . .] Outside of the War Office I doubt whether the High Command has any supporters whatever. Sir Douglas is regarded with affection in the army, but everywhere people remark that he is surrounded by incompetents.'[78]

Two days later, Charteris was gone. When Haig informed 'poor Charteris' that he had to go, both understood, if they did not commit it to paper, that Charteris was being called on to make what was for him the supreme sacrifice. Haig somewhat disingenuously intimated to Doris that it had been his decision, after all – a remarkable *volte-face* from his initially adamant refusal: '[. . .] although he has done his work admirably and his Intelligence Branch is in excellent order, I feel that it would be wrong of me to keep an officer at this time who seems really to have upset so many people and to have put those who ought to work in friendliness with him against him. [. . .] I shall, of course, do my best to find Charteris another good job [. . .]'[79]

This is quintessential Haig; rather than interrogate himself as to precisely why Charteris had become the focus of the Cabinet's hostility, he brushed it aside as some kind of misunderstanding, a view that might not have been shared by many of those who slogged their way through the mud of Passchendaele.[80] While Charteris fully deserved this belated sacking, no one emerges from this incident with any credit. Haig was culpable; his unquestioning replication of the patronage system that had assisted his own career elevated Charteris to a position that, if it was not so at the start, ultimately proved totally beyond his abilities. Moreover, Haig uncritically swallowed Charteris's vainly optimistic assessments of the conditions and strength of the opposing German forces, without subjecting them to cross-checking by those holding divergent opinions, such as the more astute and sceptical Macdonogh. Haig's diaries for 1917 are replete with references to reports from all and sundry, but the only name that crops up in the context of intelligence assessments of German morale and numbers is that of Charteris. It was, for many of the soldiers under Haig's command, a tragically symbiotic master-servant relationship; Charteris fed Haig what he thought was required, while Haig gladly accepted what he wanted to believe was accurate. Lord Derby, as Secretary of State for War, may have informed Haig that the War Cabinet had long distrusted Charteris's reports, yet this pusillanimous and vacillating set of politicians had permitted Haig to cling onto Charteris for far too long.

To the end of his life, Haig held to the belief that Third Ypres had been a success in that it was an inescapable part of the destruction of German morale and had additionally saved the French Army from complete collapse. This view was not shared by Brigadier-General Baker-Carr, who felt that GHQ was 'prone to live in a little world of its own, far removed from the turmoil and filth of battle. [. . .] I am absolutely convinced that the department responsible for the staging of the Ypres offensive had not the remotest conception of the state of affairs existing and, accordingly, formulated their plans on a hopelessly incorrect basis. [. . .] The Third Battle of Ypres, the first full-dress attack by the British to serve their own undivided purpose, will ever remain an example of British stubbornness and British stupidity. The very lack of success seemed to urge the High Command to more and more vigorous efforts.'[81]

Of course, it might be said that such critics of Haig's conduct of Third Ypres failed to see the bigger picture – the precarious state of the French army from April to August 1917, the collapse of the Italian army at Caporetto on 25 October, and the taking of power in Russia by the Bolsheviks, who immediately initiated peace negotiations; all exerted pressure on the British government and, indirectly, on GHQ to produce victories in Flanders. Haig's justification for the perpetuation of this battle, long after the point had been reached when it became a protracted, costly, and indecisive operation was that it was necessary to prevent the Germans from trampling through the supposedly rotten ranks of the French army.

Credence was eventually lent to Haig's view in 1928 with the publication by General Hermann von Kuhl of his *Der Weltkrieg 1914–18*, in which this former chief of staff of Prince Rupprecht of Bavaria's Army Group commented: 'Today, now that we know the circumstances of the situation in which the French Army found itself during the summer of 1917, there can be no doubt that in fact the stubbornness shown by the British bridged the crisis in France. The French Army gained time to restore itself and the German reserves were drawn to Flanders. The casualties which Britain sustained in defence of the Entente were not in vain.'[82]

The key word in Kuhl's passage is 'summer'; by October 1917, order had been restored within the ranks of the mutinous French divisions, as Pétain established an authority and, equally important, a measure of popularity with the *poilus* unknown since the days of Joffre's command in early 1914. Pétain recorded that 'In August [1917] only four cases of indiscipline took place at the front, though unrest still continued to a certain extent at stations and on leave trains. Most important, however, the Paris region was now calm, [...] By September, confidence in the High Command was apparent everywhere. The Intelligence Service of GQG reported in October that the postal censorship produced the following information: "Morale excellent in 24 per cent of units; good in 71 per cent; mediocre in only 5 per cent." '[83]

Haig knew from various informants of this perceptible improvement between May and September within the French Army; that he declined to give it sufficient credence was yet another serious intelligence failure, this time of his own making and not simply Charteris's. As for Lloyd George, he vigorously disputed Haig's argument that Third Ypres had to be prolonged into late November in order to prop up the French Army, writing to *The Times* long after the war: 'I have examined with great care all the records of the War Cabinet and I can find no statement in any of the confidential reports given to us by the C.I.G.S [Robertson] from the Army Headquarters that during the Flanders operations [Third Ypres] the French were urging us to attack without pause. [...] When I was bringing pressure to bear upon Sir William Robertson to take steps to call off this ghastly operation, he never suggested in reply that the French were urging us to continue our attacks in order to save their Army. [...] In Sir Douglas Haig's dispatches there is nothing said about the French entreaties. Most remarkable of all, in the memorandum on the military position and prospect written for the Cabinet in October, 1917, Earl Haig does not inform us that the French Commander-in-Chief is entreating him not to pause. [...] By that time I knew quite well what the opinion of the French military leaders was about the wisdom of the operation.

I heard Marshal Pétain's oft-quoted and striking comment on the Passchendaele fighting: "You cannot fight the *boue* and the *Boche* at the same time." '[84] All of which was true, but begs the question as to why Lloyd George did not force his will on Robertson and Haig, and call a halt to a campaign which his War Cabinet only sanctioned in July 1917 on the basis that it did not deteriorate into a sordid repetition of the Somme.

In the memo Lloyd George referred to, dated 8 October 1917, Haig had accepted that, while grave, the French mutinies did not signify a willingness to surrender:

> Though the French cannot be expected to admit it officially, we know that the state of their armies and of the reserve manpower behind the armies is such that neither the French Government nor the military authorities will venture to call on their troops for any further great and sustained offensive effort, at any rate before it becomes evident that the enemy's strength has been definitely and finally broken. Though they are staunch in defence and will carry out useful local offensives against limited objectives, the French Armies would not respond to a call for more than that, and the authorities are well aware of it.[85]

Haig thus tacitly acknowledged that Macdonogh's suggestion – advanced long before the first gas shells dropped over Pilckem Ridge – to regroup and recover, falling back on the defensive while awaiting American reinforcements, might have had something to be said for it; the French divisions, although demoralized, would still have been 'staunch in the defence'. It will always be debatable as to why, given the paucity of the gains made by the British and Dominion troops up to the end of September, and amid such impossible conditions – conditions of which Haig was well aware – the BEF's C-in-C insisted on pursuing the battle for as long as he did. His rationalization, that the condition of the French army gave him no other choice, was always insubstantial and today seems thoroughly implausible. Moreover, as Basil Liddell Hart pointed out,[86] this contradicted Haig's confident assertion of 19 June to the War Cabinet that Germany was then within six months of 'total exhaustion'. Hubris got the better of Haig at Passchendaele; he was fortunate to get off so lightly. Even he acknowledged, in a memo of 15 December 1917, that 'The whole Army is therefore at present much exhausted and much reduced in strength.' But this was not a sign that he wished to cease future offensives; it was merely an aside in a much longer argument as to why the BEF should not accede to a French request to take over more of the front line. After the war Haig reiterated in various letters that his choice of the Ypres sector as the site of his renewal of the offensive in June 1917 was prompted primarily by his fear that the French were on the brink of collapse. This was another instance of post-hoc justification for a long-nurtured ambition to break out from Ypres and thus ultimately outflank his German opponents.

At almost the end of the year, a terrible one for the Allies, Robertson excused himself from his War Office duties and travelled to Clifton College, where he presented some of the aspirant riflemen of the school with the National Rifle Association's Public School Trophy.[87] Robertson deployed the conventional euphemisms of the day when referring to Clifton's most famous old boy: 'The troubles and difficulties all fetched up sooner or later in the room of the Commander-in-Chief; all the human failings came there – the misunderstandings, the stupidity, the recklessness, the forgetfulness, a thousand and one things all finished up with the Commander-in-Chief, and he had to bear the burden alone simply because no-one could help him.'[88]

Robertson, with complete sincerity, misled his young audience; there were many who wanted to help Haig, and some of them might even have been useful to him. Haig's personality, however, inclined him to prize in subordinates the passive attributes of loyalty, optimism, and certainty, when very different qualities – such as scepticism, caution and self-criticism – would undoubtedly have been more appropriate to the circumstances. Who knows? If Haig and Robertson had followed Lloyd George's instruction of January 1917, and solicited the views of soldiers across all ranks of the BEF, they might have learned something useful.

There were no celebratory Christmas lunches funded by Rothschild at

GHQ in 1917, just a drab sense of the turn of the most miserable year of the war for the Allies so far, with nothing to suggest that 1918 would be any better. Haig left France for London on 29 December. There, a disheartened War Cabinet was conscious that not even the minor victories at Messines and Cambrai could alter the fact that Haig had little to show for the permanent loss of as many as 150,000 troops. His 'Fifeshire chin' remained as stubborn as ever, but that was all. Indeed, the Cabinet was about to spring another unpleasant surprise on Haig: the sacking of his last remaining powerful ally, apart from the king.

# CHAPTER TWELVE

# Victory

He was, I should say, a man of chivalrous and scrupulous character. He made me feel that the war would last for thirty years and that he would carry it on irreproachably until he was super-annuated.

George Bernard Shaw on Haig

Let us not hear of Generals who conquer without bloodshed. If a bloody slaughter is a horrible sight, then that is ground for paying more respect to War, but not for making the sword we wear blunter and blunter by degrees from feelings of humanity, until some one steps in with one that is sharp and lops off the arm from our body.

Clausewitz

Scarcely had Haig got off the boat at Dover at the end of 1917 before he was dealt the blow. Lord Derby travelled through the cold, frosty streets of London in the early morning of Tuesday 1 January 1918, to convey worrying news to Haig at his home at Kingston. When they met at 9.45am, Derby told Haig that Lloyd George was intent on sacking Robertson as CIGS, but had backed down after Derby threatened to resign if either Robertson or Haig were removed.

Haig was by now well aware of his diminished stature in the eyes of Lord Northcliffe, who was almost as powerful a figure in the shaping of national British opinion as the Prime Minister. Although he had nothing but contempt for journalism and its practitioners – in September 1918 Haig wrote to Sir Henry Wilson, by then in possession of the coveted title of CIGS: 'I am not, nor am I likely to be a "*famous* general." For that must we not have pandered to Repington and the Gutter Press?'[1] – he could not fail to recognize the political influence wielded by men such as Northcliffe. What Northcliffe and his ilk wanted, of course, was for Haig to fawn over them, to flatter them by seeking their views as to how best fight the war. This he could not bring himself to do, to his cost in the longer term. At the start of the final year of the war, Haig was thus encircled by intensified political and newspaper hostility. There were exceptions. The *Morning Post* notably backed Haig and Robertson through thick and thin, employing Repington for the task after he left *The Times* following a violent disagreement with Northcliffe over the latter's change of heart concerning the British high command. But even they had difficulty ignoring or disputing the tales told by casualties returned home from the ghastliness of Passchendaele.

On 2 January Haig met George V, who at Buckingham Palace formally presented him with his field marshal's baton. In exchange, Haig lectured his monarch on the real purposes of the war: 'I told the King that it was very desirable to tell the Army in a few unambiguous sentences what we were fighting for. The Army is now composed of representatives of all classes in the nation and many are most intelligent and think things out. They don't care whether France has Alsace & Italy Trieste: they realise that Britain entered the war to free Belgium & save France. [. . .] Few feel that "democratising Germany" is worth the loss of an Englishman! I also pointed out that the removal of the Hohenzollerns from Germany is likely to result in anarchy just as was the case in Russia. This wd. be a serious evil for the rest of Europe. The King was most affable and on my taking leave he said "send my love to Doris". I got back to Eastcott in time to take Doris for a walk. After tea I read "Aladdin" to the children in preparation for our visit to the Pantomime [at the Drury Lane Theatre] on Friday.'[2] The next day, Haig went to Harrods with Doris, where they coincidentally met Henrietta, by now deeply distressed in her marriage. Haig unemotionally noted: 'She seemed rather sad: Willie is still most unkind & has stopped her from signing cheques. He has given her an allowance of only £250 a year.'[3]

On 7 January Haig attended a session of the War Cabinet, where the thorny topic arose of how many fresh troops he wanted in 1918. Haig said he believed the Germans would launch a general offensive against both the British and French in early 1918, and that intelligence reports supported this view; in his opinion, Germany would attempt to bring an end to the war before the trickle of American divisions became a flood. The question of manpower for the Western Front was highly charged for all concerned; Lloyd George, who chaired the Cabinet Committee on Manpower, was determined to give Haig as few reinforcements as possible, convinced they would merely be wasted in fresh futile attacks. Robertson had already lodged a request for 615,000 more men to be sent to Haig's command, but the Manpower Committee was prepared to sanction only 100,000 category A1 (physically fit in all respects) soldiers.[4]

According to Robertson, 'The Committee considered that the lesser number would suffice because a defensive policy was to be pursued on the Western Front, and, in their opinion, that would automatically entail fewer losses than the offensive policy of the past.'[5] For Robertson and Haig, this was anathema. Haig wanted to renew his Flanders offensive in 1918, regarding that as the best way of retaining the initiative, although after Passchendaele it was not clear that the BEF had the upper hand.[6] They also argued that the BEF was already 130,000 men short of full strength by the end of 1917, although they did not raise the obvious point that this was in part a result of the failed offensives of that year.

Robertson later argued that Haig fell into a well-laid trap at the meeting on 7 January, where the C-in-C was asked whether, if he were the German commander, '[. . .] there was a sufficiently good chance of breaking through the Entente defences as to justify accepting the losses which would thereby be incurred. Sir Douglas replied to the effect that, if the Germans were wise, they would think twice before making the attempt, because if they failed their position would be critical.'[7] Haig regarded this response as entirely innocuous but it was seized upon by the Cabinet as supporting the idea that no German offensive should be expected, ergo Haig had no need for the vast number of additional troops he and Robertson sought. As they left the meeting, a crestfallen Robertson ticked off Haig; now it would be 'quite impossible for the War Office to secure for him the drafts he required. [. . .] He denied having said anything that would bear that interpretation, and I could only reply that I was afraid the War Cabinet would think differently.'[8]

Lacking the sophistry that was common currency in the devious relationship obtaining between the War Office and 10 Downing Street, Haig had inadvertently handed to Lloyd George precisely the ammunition he sought; Haig himself had cast doubts on the chances of a German offensive. He would therefore get only the barest minimum of reinforcements. The Manpower Committee's report, in draft form in early January 1918, proposed an accountant's solution to the manpower question; by reducing the size of the divisions in France from twelve battalions to nine, the withdrawn battalions could be used to create a larger and more mobile reserve. On 10 January, the Army Council asked Haig to carry out this measure.

It has become received wisdom that in early 1918 Lloyd George 'starved' Haig of reinforcements, yet it was always a part of the Prime Minister's policy to use his power over recruitment indirectly to control the manpower available for military reinforcements. As early as 18 April 1917, he had Maurice Hankey draft a memo for the War Cabinet stating it should keep 'the War Office short [of men] to compel the soldiers to adopt tactics that will reduce the waste of man-power. [. . .] Further, they desire the War Office to work out their own salvation by a careful substitution of elderly and partially fit men and coloured men for fit men in all services behind the lines.'[9]

This has unjustly been interpreted by Lloyd George's enemies – and Haig's friends – as a foolish risk, one which so weakened the BEF's defences it was forced in the spring of 1918 into a retreat which, had there been sufficient reserves sent to France, might not have occurred. Yet the Prime Minister was given no pressing practical reason in January 1918 by either Haig or Robertson for diverting more men to the trenches, other than the C-in-C's vaguely expressed wish to carry on doing more of the same. Haig failed to make a sufficiently compelling case for the extra men he sought. While Haig did not like seeing the BEF's casualty lists mount remorselessly, he was prepared to accept this scale of losses; it was his view that only through such attrition would the war be won. In contrast, Lloyd George was unconvinced that more men would guarantee a greater chance of victory.[10]

Haig's case cannot have been helped by a lunch at 10 Downing Street on 9 January, when he sat next to the Prime Minister:

> We had a very cheery party. Conversation turned on the length of the war and some betting took place. Derby bet the P.M 100 cigars to 100 cigarettes that war would be over by next new year [that is, New Year 1919]. L.G disagreed. I said I thought the war would be over because of the internal state of Germany. She could not continue after the coming autumn because her population was degenerating so fast that even if she won, there wd. not be the men to exploit & develop the country after the war etc etc.[11]

This was highly prescient and in broad terms shows Haig's sound grasp of the wider perspective. The 'internal state of Germany' indeed played a major part in the war's ending when it did. At the same lunch Haig, despite Robertson's criticism, reiterated that he doubted Germany would try to risk a generalized breakthrough, but he added a warning note: 'All seemed to depend on the struggle now going on in Germany between the military and civil parties. If the military won they would certainly attack & try to deliver a knock out blow against the Western Front, probably against France.'

This is a point where there is an interesting difference between the hand-written (and thus contemporaneous) diary entry, and that of the later typed and corrected diary. In the typed version, Haig added immediately after the last sentence: 'We must be prepared for this. The PM by cunning argument tried to get me to commit myself to an opinion that there would be "no German offensive", that the "German Army was done" but I refused to agree to his suggestions.'[12] Given the later vitriolic dispute as to whether or not Haig seemed to encourage the War Cabinet into thinking there would not be a serious German offensive in early

1918, it must have been tempting for Haig to have later inserted this extra comment, if for no other reason than to reinforce a point he had in fact made earlier.

As for the controversy over the Prime Minister's withholding vital reinforcements, there is little evidence to accuse Lloyd George of doing anything more than carefully husbanding what few reserves Britain possessed by this late stage of the war. In fact, between January and March 1918, Haig received 174,379 men, including 32,384 Dominion troops and 7,359 labour and non-combatants, as well as a division returned from Italy, making a total of almost 190,000 reinforcements. Admittedly, some were designated category B, less than 100 per cent physically fit; but this sizeable quantity nevertheless helped GHQ reassign category A troops out of rear-area posts and into the front line. Germany's first spring offensive in 1918 succeeded not because Haig had insufficient men, but through the skill of the assault and the ineptitude of the commander of Fifth Army, General Hubert Gough.

By Saturday 12 January Haig was back in Montreuil. Next day, he met Sir James McClay, Britain's Controller of Shipping, who did little to dissuade Haig of his entrenched opinions of the duplicity of the French: 'He was most interesting as regards his relations with the French in shipping matters. The French he considered so dishonest, that they could not believe the British meant to be honest, and cd. act (as we do) against our own *mercantile* interests. The French are always scheming to have a better situation after the war: the British do not look beyond winning it!'[13]

That same month, Lloyd George sent Hankey and Smuts to France to find a replacement for Haig. In his *War Memoirs* Lloyd George candidly admitted their failure: 'It is a sad reflection that not one among the visible military leaders would have been any better. There were among them plenty of good soldiers who knew their profession and possessed intelligence but Haig was all that and probably better than others within sight. [...] Had we removed Haig we might have set up in his place a man who had not his mastery of the profession. When I was considering the problem I sent General Smuts and Sir Maurice Hankey around the front [...] and I asked them confidentially to look and see whether amongst the Generals they met, there was one whom they considered might fill the first place.' Haig was well aware of the reason for the three-day tour by Hankey and Smuts, during which they visited the HQs of all five armies and seventeen corps on the Western Front. Although privately fuming, he feigned indifference. But, as the Prime Minister later wrote: 'They came back with a very disappointing report.'[14]

Although the Allies now possessed the semblance of a unified command structure, there was little evidence that this would make much difference to overall strategy for the coming fighting season; the usual ambivalence prevailed. On 1 February, at a meeting of the Supreme War Council, it was agreed that, as far as the Western Front was concerned, the policy for the immediate future would be defensive although, contra-dictorily, 'Commanders-in-Chief should prepare offensive projects suit-able for the forces at their disposal.'[15] It was also agreed that a General Reserve, with unspecified elements from both the BEF and the French army, would be established, under the command of France's General Foch – which, as Haig acknowledged, 'to some extent makes Foch a Generalissimo.' Haig, however, regarded this agreement as having neither constitutional legitimacy – he saw it as yet another backdoor attempt to restrict his authority – nor practical efficacy. He and Pétain instead reached a private understanding to lend one another mutual assistance, should the need arise; although when that need arose, this informal arrangement almost collapsed under the strain.

Shortly after this, Lloyd George finally acted on a desire he had nurtured for many months. On 9 February, Haig arrived back in London at Victoria Station, where he was met by Doris and Derby. The Secretary of State for War took Haig off in a car and drove him round the streets of London, explaining to him the *coup d'état* against Robertson that had been agreed by the War Cabinet. Eventually they arrived at 10 Downing Street, where Lloyd George craftily put it to Haig that Robertson's job was changing, merely so that the Prime Minister would be able to have a closer relationship with Haig. Robertson was to be offered the position of permanent military member at the Supreme War Council in Versailles, which, given Lloyd George's intense dislike of Robertson, spoke volumes as to the Prime Minister's opinion of the importance of the Council. Moreover, Robertson was to report to the new CIGS, Sir Henry Wilson, who would act as the sole adviser to the War Cabinet.

Lloyd George also set another trap for Haig, which on this occasion he spotted in advance: 'The P.M also said that he considered that the best solution of their present difficulties would be to make me "generalissimo" of the [sic] *all* the British Forces. Derby concurred and I was asked what I thought of the proposal. I replied that with a serious attack impending in France, I considered that no change should be made in the command there. I knew every detail of the situation, and it would not be fair to the Army to suddenly put on a new commander such a serious responsibility. P. M agreed & said he "ought to have made me generalissimo" last Sept.'[16]

Had Haig agreed to this tantalizing suggestion, he would, no doubt, have found himself with a grand title but no real authority. As it was, he accepted without demur the abrupt humbling of Robertson, a man who had been his unswervingly loyal defender for more than a year. But Haig consistently defended the constitutional authority of the civilian power over military matters, much though he loathed its current head, and Robertson had begun to overstep the intangible but real dividing line between civilian power and military subordination. On 11 February, Haig noted he had told Robertson it was '[. . .] his duty to go to Versailles if the Govt. wished it. [. . .] I am afraid that in the back of his mind he resents Henry Wilson replacing him in London, and means to embarrass the Govt. to the utmost of his power.'

Robertson declined the offer, however, and another Haig stalwart was gone.[17] Haig was too accustomed to the ways of the world to shed tears over the rise and fall of anyone, and he made no exception for Robertson. He had written to Doris on 4 February, sensing, like many others, that Robertson's days were numbered: 'I, like you, am sorry for Robertson, but then it seems to me (and I can write it to you privately) that he has not resolutely adhered to the policy of "concentration on the Western Front". He has *said* this is his policy, but has allowed all kinds of resources to be diverted to distant theatres at the bidding of his political masters.

So I think he ought to have made a firm stand before. Anyhow don't let the Versailles Conference trouble your little head. The machinery there is so big and clumsy it will take some time before it can work fast enough to trouble me. So I don't mean to be influenced by it against my better conscience.'[18]

Haig could happily see the departure of Robertson because by the end of 1917 Robertson had become convinced that a breakthrough on the Western front was impossible, and would only condone offensives that were limited in scope. This was an anathema to Haig. Furthermore, it was also rather rich of Haig to condemn Robertson for not making a 'firm stand before'. At Calais in February 1917, one moment when a 'firm stand' was appropriate, Robertson had, quite literally, led the way.

Haig spent the rest of February inspecting defensive preparations on his front; he found nothing amiss. Yet the situation of Gough's Fifth Army was far from satisfactory. The force was almost entirely composed of New Army volunteers and second-line Territorials, originally spread thinly along a twenty-five-mile front south of the Flesquières salient. Its front defensive zone was quite well covered by barbed wire but there was no continuous trench system, only a loosely connected network of individual machine-gun nests. The second defence position, dubbed the 'battle zone', had not prepared sufficient defensive emplacements and was largely composed of separate redoubts positioned on slightly higher ground; these housed machine-guns which were intended to cover the spaces that separated them. The most rearward zone, the corps line, was incapable of resisting a committed attack. Fifth Army had recently been ordered to take over an additional twenty-eight miles of front line from the French at the Somme; Gough's twelve divisions therefore found themselves defending forty-two miles of ill-prepared and, in places, unfamiliar front. Haig was prepared to relinquish the lightly held front zone in an attack, imagining that the Germans would be tempted forward into the more heavily defended central battle zone where, as they spent valuable time eradicating pockets of resistance, the BEF would be able to bring up reinforcements, counter-attack and halt any further advance.

In the light of the mutual rancour that followed the German spring offensive that smashed through Gough's Fifth Army on 21 March and succeeding days, Haig's confidence on 2 March seems astonishing, especially considering his own belief that the BEF was desperately undermanned. He noted in his diary: 'I was only afraid that the Enemy would find our front so very strong that he will hesitate to commit his Army to the attack with the almost certainty of losing very heavily.'[19]

And, once more, the BEF was experiencing a shortfall in its requests for artillery ammunition. Before the German offensive, Haig learned from Brigadier General Noel Birch, his chief artillery adviser at GHQ, that, since October 1917, of the 630,000 4.5-inch howitzer shells requested, only 228,000 had been delivered; of the 1.05 million 60-pounder and 6-inch howitzer shells, just 295,000 had been sent; and of the requested 786,000 18-pounder shells, none at all had arrived.[20] On 12 March, Haig was nevertheless in his usual good spirits, eager for the anticipated German attack:

My job is really made fairly simple by the splendid fellows I have to help me, and the grand spirit of loyalty which exists all through the Army [. . .] I have been twice round the Divisions holding the front during the past 3 weeks, and found the spirit splendid and everyone full of confidence and anxious that the Bosche should attack [. . .] The Americans are disappointing. They are so slow, and don't seem to realise the magnitude of the problem. However Old England is able to run the show herself if our Govt. will only give us more men before the Autumn. That may possibly be an anxious time for us.[21]

That the attack was expected by all concerned there is now no doubt. Haig's new intelligence chief, Major-General Herbert Cox,[22] warned of '20 definite signs of an immediate attack'. At an army commanders' conference at Doullens on Saturday 2 March, Cox pinpointed the likelihood of it being against the Fifth and Third Armies. Next day, Haig entertained at GHQ an American journalist 'of name Cobbe [actually Cobb[23]] of the "Noo York Evening News" and many other papers in the USA. I was asked by the Foreign Office to receive him. He is an extraordinary ugly man, big, tall as well as broad, with a bottle nose & prominent lower lip and rubi-cund countenance. A veritable "Mr Bung the Brewer" in the flesh! However he was not such a bad fellow, though it is sad to think that such second rate people should wield such power because of owning a few newspapers! In fact they are the "tyrants" of the present age.'[24]

That same day, Haig reluctantly bowed to another inevitability; in belated recognition of the changed nature of warfare, the Army Council decreed the three Household Cavalry regiments would lose their horses for the duration of the war and be converted into machine-gun battal-ions. Haig returned to London on 12 March and next day saw Lloyd George at an inter-Allied conference, where he warned that 'we must be prepared to meet a very strong attack on a 50 mile front.' Such was the scepticism about intelligence reports from GHQ that it appears the Prime Minister did not believe Haig on this occasion; the conference focused on the rather less pressing issue of creating a general reserve, which Haig continued stubbornly to resist.

Amidst all this, the Haigs were preparing for the arrival of their third child. Haig had arranged for Colonel Ryan, his personal medical officer at GHQ, to return to London – taking with him half a sheep and some butter – to attend to Doris. On the evening of 15 March Doris went to bed early, troubled by what she and Ryan diagnosed as a bad dose of flatu-lence. Her labour started at 10.45pm, and seventeen minutes later their son George was born.[25] Haig returned to England to see him, and on 16 March *The Globe* newspaper trumpeted: 'There is not a man in the great army which the Field Marshal commands, and which now awaits with equal confidence and impatience the attack of which the enemy so loudly boasts, who will not see in this event an omen of victory.'

The following day, Haig paid his usual courtesy visit to the king – who complained that the departure of Robertson meant he heard little 'inside news of what is going on' – at Buckingham Palace, had lunch with Henrietta (roast beef and Yorkshire pudding at Charing Cross), then returned to France, where there were further signs that the German army was about to move. Information from German prisoners captured on 18 March near St Quentin was supported by reports from a night raid by units of General Maxse's XVIII Corps on 20 March, which revealed the German attack would start next day. At 4.30am on the fog-drenched morning of 21 March, the Germans opened with a massive blitz by 8,000 heavy and medium artillery and large trench mortars on the opposing British artillery positions, switching after two hours to the British trench lines. At around 9am the German infantry, preceded by a creeping barrage and covered by low-flying aircraft, swept across no man's land against Gough's Fifth Army and Byng's Third Army[26] on a front that was initially thirty-five miles wide but which, following successive offensives against both the British and French Armies up to July, expanded to cover some 200 miles.

The objective of this first stage of the offensive, called Michael by the German high command, was subsequently rationalised by Erich Ludendorff, First Quartermaster-General of the German army, as intended to sweep up behind the BEF, driving a wedge between it and the French army, and to push the BEF northwards, back to the Channel and thence into the sea. However, this post-war grand strategising played no part in the German plans for the March offensive, seen in tactical terms as probing for weakness, which it found. The British and French high commands had long been expecting an attack, but neither could be certain that this was the main one or if that was about to fall on the French in the Champagne region. This worried Pétain, as Haig urgently called for French reinforcements. The tactics used by the highly trained German assault shock-troops, who were instructed to go around rather than overwhelm defensive emplacements, and to get as far and as fast behind the British lines as possible, had already been tried successfully at Caporetto in October 1917, and they wrought havoc again in Flanders. The poor morale of Fifth Army – noted in London by Macdonogh at the War Office, if not by GHQ – and the skill and ferocity of the German attackers meant that those of Gough's troops who could, fled in disarray.

Derby had cabled Haig in December 1917 expressing his doubts about Gough's leadership, warning Haig that the 'feeling against him [. . .] is very strong, not with civilians – but with both officers and men who have served under him. [. . .] his gallantry is nullified by a lack of confidence in him.' As recently as 5 March 1918, Derby had again communicated to

Haig the serious reservations he had heard expressed, now by civilians as well as military personnel, about Gough's competence as an army commander, and extended to Haig the chance to shunt Gough aside to the sinecure of governor of Gibraltar: 'I know your extraordinary loyalty to your subordinates, and recognising this, I beg you to believe that if you change any Commander, however well he has served you, for one whom you think is perhaps less tired, I will do my best to see that the man you send home is not left on the rocks.'[27] It was a hint Haig ignored.

The C-in-C never liked his sleep disturbed unless there was a crisis; Haig was not aroused by Lawrence, his CGS, until 8am on the morning of 21 March. Given that a major German offensive was expected, this might appear lax but it was entirely consistent with Haig's routine. The next three weeks, the lowest point of the war for Haig personally and the worst days for the BEF since the retreat from Mons in 1914, saw very few get a full night's rest at GHQ or in the front line. The Michael offensive was the first of four German thrusts on the Western Front, the final, the Second Battle of the Marne, beginning on 15 July. It lasted until 5 April and very nearly succeeded in parting the French and British lines.[28] It also laid bare the inadequacies of Gough's defensive preparations and prised open the cracks in the Anglo-French coalition; as something approaching panic swept the British and French high commands, the mutual fears and suspicions which had been simmering for almost four years finally boiled over. As Esher noted in his journal on 19 May 1918, after the worst had passed: 'If one thing is sure about this war, it is that the English and French will be thoroughly sick of each other. I only hope that the war will not last long enough to breed the same feeling of ennui between us and the Americans.'[29]

By the second day of the Michael offensive, Gough had been misled into believing that the Germans had penetrated behind his right flank, which was held by a French division. He therefore ordered – with Haig's approval – a retirement to the Somme, opening up a gap which, fortunately for the Allies, the Germans failed to exploit. In its first four days the German advance gained fourteen miles and some units of the Fifth Army went into headlong retreat. On 23 March, Haig met Pétain and asked him to provide French support to block the gap between the two armies and to help prevent Fifth Army's retreat from turning into a rout. That day Haig, most unusually and in an indication of his alarm at the prospect of a real German breakthrough, issued an order to be read out to all ranks of the BEF next morning. He exhorted the troops that 'I feel that everyone in the Army, fully realising how much depends on the exertions and steadfastness of each one of us, will do his utmost to prevent the enemy from attaining his object.'[30]

This devastation to Fifth Army and, to a lesser extent, Byng's Third Army, prompted a flurry of interchanges between Haig, Pétain, Paris and London. The Michael offensive eventually petered out, as the German supply lines became overstretched and the doggedness of the British defence held the line, partly thanks to support lent by the French divisions which arrived to help close the gap. But the attack had controversial repercussions, resulting on Tuesday 26 March in General Foch being anointed Allied supreme commander, responsible for coordinating both French and British Armies on the Western Front and thus, *in extremis*, bringing about the greater unity of command between the BEF and the French Army that had been resisted by Haig for so many months.

Haig's role in this episode is still the subject of intense debate and represents either a remarkable *volte-face* on his part or a deep humiliation for him, depending on how we interpret the facts. Since the notorious conference at Calais in February 1917, Haig had staunchly opposed any move to subordinate his command to French control but, such was the genuine sense of the threat of defeat in March 1918, he changed his mind. The facts are that on 26 March an inter-Allied conference was held at Doullens to determine what action to take to counter the threat posed by the German offensive. It was agreed that Foch should be appointed 'Generalissimo', with authority over both the French and British armies on the Western Front. Haig claimed that this was at his instigation, but this has been disputed by recent scholarship, based partly on discrepancies between Haig's handwritten diary for Monday 25 and Tuesday 26 March, and the undated but later typed transcript.

The historian Elizabeth Greenhalgh has alleged that Haig amended the record of this crucial turning point to present himself in a better, more magnanimous light.[31] Innocuous changes of all kinds exist between the manuscript and the typed versions of Haig's Great War diary, and certainly the two differ in some respects for these two crucial days. For example, in the typed diary entry for 25 March, the following paragraph, which is absent from the handwritten version, appears: 'Lawrence at once left me to telegraph to Wilson (CIGS London) requesting him and Lord Milner to come to France at once in order to arrange that General Foch or some other determined general, who would fight, should be given supreme control of the operations in France. I knew Foch's strategical ideas were in conformity with the orders given me by Lord Kitchener when I became C-in-C and that he was a man of great courage and decision as shown during the fighting at Ypres in October and November 1914.'

The use of the past tense here suggests it might have been an after-thought; the question is, however, was it a thought that Haig had had on the day itself? If so, there can be no criticism of him. But Greenhalgh accuses Haig of massaging the facts; her reasoning is that, rather than sending for Milner, it would have been more logical if Haig had called for Lord Derby instead, who remained Secretary of State for War until 19 April. The suggestion is that Milner acted independently, or perhaps following a tele-phone conversation with Lloyd George, or even that Clemenceau, the French Premier, sent for him. Yet it was also logical that Haig might send for Milner; it was widely suspected that Milner would become Secretary of State for War, and Milner also acted as Lloyd George's alternate on the Supreme War Council. He carried real authority, while Haig would have recognized that Derby was no man for a crisis such as this. It is also conceivable that the British and French governments decided in advance of the meeting to admit Foch as Generalissimo – and that at the Doullens meeting Haig decided to make a virtue out of necessity.

Whatever the truth, it is quite clear that at the emergency meeting at Doullens Haig supported calls for Foch to be placed in overall charge – unless, that is, Haig's contemporaneous manuscript diary is also to be regarded as a fraudulent record. He recorded in his own handwriting the events at Doullens on that momentous Tuesday 26 March:

About 12 noon I had a meeting (also at Doullens) between Poincaré (President of France), Clemenceau (Premier), Foch, Pétain and Lord Milner, Gen H. Wilson (CIGS), my CGS (Lawrence) and myself. We discussed situation and it was decided that Amiens must be covered at all costs. French troops are being hurried up as rapidly as possible and Gough has been told to hold on with his left at Bray. We also decided [this has been crossed out with downward, right-sloping pen strokes and replaced with] It was proposed that Foch shd be appointed to coordinate the operations at Amiens – I at once recommended that he should coordinate the action of all the allied Armies on the Western Front. Both Govts agreed to this.[32]

The most that can be said concerning this diary entry is that the crossing out of the phrase 'We also decided' contains a hint that perhaps the proposal that Foch be appointed supreme commander of the Anglo-French armies emerged from the meeting generally, and was not simply or solely Haig's idea. The text of the agreement reached at Doullens, signed by Milner and Clemenceau, stated that 'General Foch is charged by the British and French governments with the coordination of the action of the Allied armies on the Western Front. He will arrange to this effect with the Generals-in-Chief [Haig, Pétain] who are invited to supply him with all the necessary information.'[33]

If appointing Foch was indeed Haig's idea, and his hand was not forced by Milner, it signified an astonishing reversal of his previous stubborn opposition to such a subordination of his own powers. Haig neither trusted his French counterparts nor had much respect for their determination to fight. Yet on 26 March he meekly handed authority to the French over both himself and the BEF. Haig never explained this *volte-face* and we can only make reasoned assumptions. The twenty divisions he called on Pétain to provide to bolster Gough's crushed Fifth Army had materialized, as agreed between them before the battle started. All of Gough's troops that remained south of the Somme had by been placed by Haig under the command of the French General Fayolle. But mutual suspicion had not completely dissipated. Haig feared Pétain would retreat to Paris; Pétain was alarmed that Haig might flee for the Channel ports. The threat of the Anglo-French coalition coming apart was very real. What passed through Haig's mind at Doullens was probably no single thought but a combination of many. That he could have been motivated by self-interest is obvious – if the retreat of Fifth Army became a rout, Haig would have been identified as the British commander who presided over the loss of the war. Far better to shuffle the burden of responsibility onto Foch, and thus ensure the French did everything possible not to lose contact with the British right wing. Haig, naturally, wanted to present the gesture as motivated by necessary self-sacrifice – in other words, he was accepting subordination to French command for the greater good of preserving a united Allied determination to fight on. But he may have been given no choice. Certainly, by 29 March Haig was convinced that Foch was showing much more willingness to support the BEF than he felt had been the case with Pétain: 'I think Foch has brought great energy to bear on the present situation, and has instead of permitting French troops to retire back from Amiens, insisted on some of them relieving our troops & on covering Amiens at all costs. He & I are quite in agreement as to the general plan of operations.'[34]

Whatever Haig's real conviction, Doullens represented a turning-point in the war; out of the very depths of their despair, the Allies had painfully fashioned a will to work together in a more coordinated manner than at any time since August 1914. Yet before we favourably judge Haig's willing subordination to Foch, we should consider the distribution of responsibility for the debacle on 21 March. Haig had not made, in his own words, a 'firm stand' against his government's instructions at the end of 1917 to over-stretch Gough's Fifth Army by having it occupy an extra twenty-five miles of French front lines, taking the entire British front to more than 125 miles; Lloyd George's Manpower Committee failed to provide the quality and quantity of additional troops which Haig had called for; and Haig had complacently failed to insist that Gough improve his defences in depth in the weeks before the long-awaited attack. This concatenation of incidents played directly into German hands; but only Gough[35] would pay the price of failure, even though Henry Wilson, the new CIGS, was busily advising the Cabinet that Haig should be sacked.[36] On 4 April, following a stormy War Cabinet meeting at which, according to Wilson, the sentiment 'was I think unanimously agst. Haig & the whole GHQ. There was no question that all confidence is lost', Derby sent Haig a telegram recalling Gough from France, adding in a personal cable that 'among men returned in this country in the various hospitals there is a consensus of opinion [against Gough] which neither this Government or any other Government can afford to ignore.'[37]

By 5 April, the Michael offensive had drawn to a close. British and French losses have been estimated at 240,000 killed, wounded and missing – those of the Germans perhaps 300,000.[38] On 7 April, Haig informed Derby by telegram that he would only remain C-in-C if he retained the confidence of the War Cabinet – the closest Haig ever came to a direct offer of resignation to the government. Wilson believed that Lloyd George wanted to take up the offer, but the Prime Minister's courage failed him at the vital moment when he might finally have been able to force Haig's removal; he inexplicably argued they should wait until Haig's final report.[39] So Lloyd George yet again veered away from removing Haig, a failure of nerve he may have bitterly regretted in years to come.

On 9 April, the second German offensive of that spring, named Georgette, was launched, this time threatening to cut the BEF from its links to the Channel coast, with the ports of Boulogne, Calais and Dunkirk the main targets. Now it was the turn of the Second Army, under Plumer, and the First, under Horne, to be pushed back, and on 11 April, the crucial day of this attack, Haig issued his most famous order to the British army: 'There is no other course open to us but to fight it out! Every position must be held to the last man: there must be no retirement. With our backs to the wall, and believing in the justice of our cause, each one of us must fight on to the end. The safety of our homes and the freedom of mankind alike depend on the conduct of each one of us at this critical moment.' A final, downbeat sentence of the original draft was crossed out by Haig. It read: 'But be of good cheer, the British Empire must win in the End.'[40] Sometimes criticized for being underwhelming, this call to his soldiers to stand their ground was typically Haig in its sober realism. In the days following, until the end of Georgette on 30 April, concerted counter-attacks by British, French, American, Canadian and ANZAC units halted the German advance; but all the territorial gains that the BEF had so laboriously made in 1916 and 1917 were now gone in less than one month. Complete disaster was averted not solely thanks to the physical courage of Allied troops. At long last, the BEF was able to be profligate with artillery ammunition, firing almost five and a half million 18-pounder and some one and a half million 4.5-inch howitzer shells in the three weeks following the launch of the Michael offensive, almost as many 18-pounder shells as possessed by the entire BEF just prior to the Somme. Even with the loss of 859 guns in the first week of the 21 March offensive, the BEF still had a surplus of all types of guns in reserve, apart from 12-inch howitzers, of which it was short by just two.[41]

As Georgette ground to a halt, the German troops again suffering from over-extended supply lines and insufficient firepower to overwhelm British resistance, the German high command switched its attention to the French, battering their lines from Soissons and Rheims between 27 May and 11 June. Again, the German onslaught had considerable initial success, advancing to within forty miles of Paris at Château-Thierry, where, in one of their first major actions of the war, American machine-gunners halted the by now exhausted German assault troops. German hopes of a rapid victory expired; while the British and French were badly bruised, they remained unbroken, with American reinforcements beginning to flow into France in ever greater numbers.

At this stage of the war, although Haig seems from his diary to have been extremely busy visiting his army commanders and receiving guests at GHQ, the usually loyal Sassoon noted in his own diary that 'It is incredible how little work he does & how completely out of touch he is with everything. He never goes near the office . . . He ought to spend the whole day up at the office & get really au fait with the situation – instead of making himself ridiculous by his splendid isolation & his obvious ignorance of existing conditions.'[42] Yet perhaps Haig was simply following advice from the wily Esher, who a few days previously had advised

Sassoon: 'Whatever happens, never permit D.H. to open his mouth. His silence is a tremendous factor.'[43]

As the weight of the German attack switched to the French lines in June, the British front returned to greater calm, easing the pressure on Haig from the War Cabinet. He began to think better of the agreement he had accepted at Doullens on 26 March. Foch was becoming too demanding, too autocratic in the exercise of his authority as supreme commander, at least as far as Haig was concerned. Foch had moved 'many' French and American reserves from behind the British lines, a switch Haig resented, not because he seriously believed it weakened his front but because it affronted his sense of status: 'The effect of the Beauvais Agreement is now becoming clear in practice. This effect I had realised from the beginning, namely, that the responsibility for the safety of the British Army in France could no longer rest with me because the "Generalissimo" can do what he thinks right with my troops. [. . .] This delegation of power to Foch is inevitable, but I intend to ask that the British Government should in a document modify my responsibility for the safety of the British Army under the altered conditions.'[44]

By mid-July Haig felt himself trapped – although, by his own claim, it was a trap he had himself suggested. The rise to dominance of Foch he now felt was '[. . .] a case of "heads you win, & tails I lose!" If things go well the Govt. takes credit to themselves and the Generalissimo: if badly, the Field Marshal [i.e. Haig] will be blamed.'[45] Haig was absolutely right. The petty squabbling that had beset British and French military and civil relations prior to the first phase of the German spring offensive had, by the summer of 1918, insidiously returned and would endure until and beyond the Armistice. As the German attacks went on, Haig struggled to keep his head above a swamp of pettiness, which perpetually threatened to overwhelm him. Hardly a day passed without some courtier begging him for a favour. For example, on Wednesday 29 May, Sir Arthur Sloggett, Director General of Medical Services at HQ, had a farewell dinner with Haig; Sloggett was due next day to retire and return to England, having reached the age of sixty. Over dinner he buttonholed Haig, asking that he should 'get him a decoration on going from France, either a Baronetcy or a G.C.B!! I asked Lord Milner to arrange the Baronetcy if possible. Possibly the Baronetcy may be a source of annoyance to Sloggett's son, unless he is well off.'[46]

But, having survived the spring offensives, the Allies could begin to consider that, perhaps, the beginning of the end was in sight. At the Supreme War Council session on 1 June it was agreed that, by the same date in 1919, the USA should send no less than 100 divisions, some two and a half million men, to fight in France. While all present on that occasion sniffed the probability of ultimate victory, thanks to this promise of millions of young Americans, no earlier date for victory was considered possible than 1919, or perhaps even 1920. Wilson, in his capacity as CIGS, went so far as to publish on 25 July a War Office document called 'British Military Policy 1918–1919', which argued that there was no real hope of breaking the stalemate on the Western Front before mid-1919. On the front cover of his copy, Haig wrote: 'Words! Words! Words! lots of words! and little else! Theoretical rubbish! Whoever drafted this stuff would never win any campaign.'[47]

The German offensives finally ended, inconclusively, in the second week of June. They had not achieved their prime purpose: ground had been regained but the Allied line had not been broken, and German casualties had been heavy. Despite this, none of the political leaders in London, France, Rome or Washington conceived that victory might come in 1918. None recalled the prescient words of Haig to the War Cabinet on 7 January 1918, when he said that 'if the Germans were wise, they would think twice before making the attempt [to break the British lines], because if they failed their position would be critical.' Haig had been absolutely right, of course, but even when the balance of power did shift more favourably towards the Allies, this too went unrecognized by their field commanders, Haig included. For that failure to perceive the turning of the tide they may be forgiven, for the first step was very small indeed.

On 4 July 1918 ten battalions – some 7,500 men – of the Australian Corps, spearheaded by sixty of the latest Mark V tanks, which were more manoeuvrable and less prone to mechanical failure than their predecessors, attacked the village of Hamel on a narrow three-and-a-half-mile front. They were commanded by General Sir John Monash,[48] who was by profession an engineer and lawyer. Monash had taken command of the Australians on 18 May 1918, commanding four very under-strength divisions. Although the opposing twenty-seven German battalions at Hamel were of variable quality, they occupied heavily fortified woods. Monash's well-coordinated plan set the limited task of advancing just one mile, to capture Vaire Wood, Hamel Wood, Pear Trench and Hamel village, all key strong points on a ridge.

The attack was almost aborted just two days beforehand, as confusion over the inclusion of 2,000 American troops, along with a threat to Monash from the Australian Prime Minister, William Hughes, jeopardized the venture. Hughes had visited Monash on 2 July and told him to ensure the Australians were sufficiently rested. Monash replied that he was under the command of Haig and must obey orders. Hughes thundered back: 'So? Well, he may be Commander-in-Chief, but I am the Prime Minister of Australia. This is a command from me. General Monash, you are, as you say, a soldier – and I think you are a great soldier. But you may not be one tomorrow. The time has come to speak plainly. You are a soldier and I am Prime Minister. If I wish, I can have you removed from your Australian command. This I do not wish to do; but I want you to understand that the welfare of Australia's troops is my first concern. Tell General [sic] Haig that unless my request is agreed to, I will withdraw all Australian troops from France.'[49] Fortunately, however, Monash ignored Hughes.

The success of Hamel was due in part to its limited and precisely planned ambition, but it is also now regarded as the first battle fought by the BEF with proper coordination between all arms – infantry, artillery, tanks and aircraft. Monash, who had a keen intellect, argued that 'a modern battle plan is like nothing so much as a score for a musical composition, where the various arms and units are the instruments, and the tasks they perform are their respective musical phrases. Each individual unit must make its entry precisely at the proper moment, and play its phrase in the general harmony.'[50]

The artillery deployed for the assault at Hamel was, for the very limited objectives, overwhelming – more than 600 guns – and there were also four battalions from the Machine-Gun Corps. For two weeks prior to the actual assault, the German positions were drenched with a combination of gas and smoke shells, ensuring that on the actual day of the attack, when only smoke was used, the German troops automatically donned their vision-restricting gas masks. Prior to the battle itself, the noise of the assembling tanks and infantry was disguised by the ceaseless over-flying of RAF Vickers and Handley-Page bombers. A fixed artillery barrage on the morning of the assault allowed the Australians to close to within fifty yards of it, whereupon it was lifted forwards 100 yards every three minutes until halfway to the final objective, where it halted for ten minutes to allow the advancing troops to gather themselves together for the final heave. The artillery plan was, in other words, closely tied to the needs of the infantry. The tanks, too, were used differently. Rather than advancing in front of the infantry, they moved simultaneously behind the barrage and, on arrival at the German trenches, traversed up and down the battlefield parallel to the German defences, creating havoc and dealing with pockets of resistance, rather than seeking to achieve maximum penetration.

The assault started at 03.14 hours; by 04.47 hours all objectives had been taken at the cost of just 800 Australian casualties, almost all walking wounded. Only three of the tanks had broken down or been knocked out. Hamel was a textbook exposition of the symphonic destruction envisaged by Monash. Haig recognized as much, and sanctioned the formalization of Monash's successful tactics: 'Before the month was out they [GHQ] had published a pamphlet which was to be the guidebook to combined arms attacks for the rest of the war. In it was outlined the reasons for the victory: good planning, excellent cooperation between the infantry, the machine guns, the artillery and the RAF, the secrecy maintained, the effectiveness of the barrage, the skill and dash of the tanks – and the fine fighting spirit of the infantry. [ . . . ] it was the triumph of a trained mind over a complex of problems.'[51]

While Haig and GHQ were absorbing the lessons of Hamel, the spirit world was still intent on bothering Haig, except on this occasion it was not his brother George but Lord Kitchener. At least, that is, according to an (alas) unnamed woman, who 'wrote down' a communication from the thoroughly dead Kitchener, concerning German troop dispositions in mid-1918. This small incident was investigated in 1921 by the editor of *Truth*, who had got wind of the story and wrote to Haig to see if it was true: 'She showed [the writing] to her husband, who showed them to a Brigadier-General in London, who showed them to another. The two Brigadiers thought the matter so important that one of them came out to G. H. Q in France and showed the document to your Lordship. You were much interested and asked the Brigadier to get you some more information from the same sources, which I believe was done.'

In his reply – marked 'personal and not for publication': he had learned circumspection when dealing with journalists – Haig agreed:[52] 'That is so, as I felt it my duty to get information likely to aid me in prosecuting the campaign, from any source! I received messages regularly, about one a week, for 3 or 4 months – all quite useless. I kept them carefully for a year after the armistice in case a question on them might be asked – and then had them destroyed.'[53]

By 15 July 1918 the final last-ditch German offensive had petered out. A much restored French army, inspired partly by evident German disappointment but also by the arrival in France of increasing numbers of confident, fresh young American reinforcements, swiftly took advantage by launching a surprise attack on 18 July in what became known as the Second Battle of the Marne. Utilising improved technology and more flexible tactics, and deploying vast numbers of light Renault tanks, artillery and aircraft, this combined French and American attack convinced Germany that the opportunity for victory had finally disappeared.

By 20 July, Haig felt sufficiently free of anxiety to play a round of golf at Le Touquet with his ADC, Captain Fletcher, the first time in the war he had played golf in France. Already in preparation was an attack by the Australian and Canadian Corps of Rawlinson's Fourth Army, with French and British divisions, east of the city of Amiens. A scaled-up version of the procedure at Hamel, the Battle of Amiens took the Germans by complete surprise; on a single day, 8 August, the soldiers of

Fourth Army, supported by 552 Mark V tanks, advanced up to eight miles. It was the greatest one-day advance by the British on the Western Front with relatively few casualties of approximately 9,000. New techniques of pre-registered counter-battery firing by the artillery meant that 504 out of the 530 defending German guns had been identified before the attack, and silenced.

General Ludendorff, the German C-in-C, referred to 8 August as the 'black day' of the German army. He immediately offered his resignation to the Kaiser – who rejected it – and appears to have suffered a breakdown. The collapse in German morale was finally occurring, and it became increasingly clear to Haig and his senior commanders. As a result, pressure was sustained all along the line with other, similarly constructed attacks, until the end of September when all the ground taken in the German spring offensives had been recovered, an advance by the BEF alone of twenty-five miles across a forty-mile front.

The BEF's and Dominion battalions' casualties in these final hundred days were high, at 180,000, but there was a new spirit of optimism among the attacking troops, now confident in their new tactics, and also at GHQ. The BEF now also had all the shells it could wish for. For the assault on the Hindenburg Line, which started on on 27 September, the Fourth Army under Rawlinson expended 27.5 million pounds of shells, more than double the quantity fired on 8 August.[54] October saw a massive assault by the American Expeditionary Force in the Ardennes Forest and supportive French attacks aimed at taking Brussels: both convincingly demonstrated to the broken-spirited German soldier and high command, now beset by simmering social revolution back in Germany, that there was no longer any hope.

Haig's defenders frequently refer to the 100 days following the Battle of Amiens as evidence of his ultimate vindication, yet in truth he bore little responsibility for the changes of this period, which enabled the steady progress towards victory. The brunt of the fighting was borne by Dominion soldiers from the single New Zealand division, the four from Canada, the five from Australia, and the single brigade from South Africa. They were commanded by officers subordinate to Haig but with great latitude over tactics. One of them, the commander of the Canadian Expeditionary Force, Lieutenant-General Arthur Currie, had substantially revised offensive training following the miseries at Passchendaele. Their troops, who had largely escaped the onslaughts of the Germans in the spring offensives, proved tough and resourceful.

By mid-1918 the Allies were also able to intercept and decode most German radio messages about plans and morale. British artillery losses in March 1918 were more than compensated for, and the British and French commanders running the post-July 1918 attacks wisely did not aim to try to extend tactical successes beyond what they could immediately support; to that extent, Rawlinson's old idea of 'bite and hold' tactics now fully came into their own. Above all, success bred greater confidence among Allied troops and, conversely, diminished German hopes. In all this, Haig's role was largely that of a figurehead; he now had little choice but to watch as his branch managers pushed ahead on their own momentum. On top of which deteriorating German morale – poor and declining rations, a widening sense of impending defeat, and a degree of awe in the face of overwhelming military hardware all played their part – convinced all concerned that the tide had turned.

On 3 October, Germany appealed to President Woodrow Wilson for an armistice, and twenty-four days later Ludendorff resigned. On 4 November, the final major British offensive of the war, the Battle of the Sambre, commenced; both Byng and Rawlinson politely declined Haig's offer of delivering to their command the remnants of the Cavalry Corps – their mounts, they argued, could neither get through the congested roads nor be reliably fed if they succeeded. On 11 November, the Armistice, the formal signing of which Haig attended in a railway carriage in the Compiègne forest, came into force at 11am; Haig recorded in his diary, *inter alia*, that the Kaiser had fled to Holland: 'If the war had gone against us no doubt our King would have had to go, and probably our Army would have become insubordinate like the German Army! cf. John Bunyan's remark on seeing a man on his way to be hanged, "But for the Grace of God, John Bunyan would have been in that man's place!" '[55]

What was the key to victory? Was it even a victory? If it is judged one, it must be accepted that it was very narrow. Haig learned from Macdonogh – now adjutant-general at the War Office – on 21 October that, at the prevailing level of recruitment, the BEF would have been reduced to thirty-six divisions in 1919, against the sixty-one then in place. Relative to the size of the British population, the statistics were appalling: the army's casualty rate was running at some 13 per cent, and one in every three households in the UK had lost a member, either dead, wounded or taken prisoner. Britain suffered sixteen deaths per thousand of its wartime population; this was not as severe as Germany's thirty deaths per thousand, France's thirty-four or Serbia's fifty-seven, but it was bad enough.[56] Of the tens of thousands who died, 578 came from Haig's old school, Clifton, which had sent 3,100 of its boys to the war.

Explanations abound as to why the final hundred days of the war should have seen such a remarkable shift in the balance of fortunes on the Western Front, but no one answer suffices. According to historians such as Ian Malcolm Brown, success was achieved through vastly improved logistical expertise and the rise of the professional administrative officer – the product of the creation by Haldane, Esher and Haig of the General Staff – combined with the pragmatic approach of Haig, who was ever willing to take on talent such as Geddes' when it made itself available: 'The BEF had not been prepared in 1914 for the difficulties of modern warfare. By 1918, however [. . .] Haig had at his fingertips a truly superb fighting and administrative organisation.'[57] But there were other factors. The naval blockade against Germany had severely reduced the country's food and other essential supplies, fomenting social discord. The German spring offensives were, was as Haig put it, a 'gambler's last throw', and with their failure the morale of the German army rapidly deteriorated. New technologies, completely unknown to the army in which Haig had grown up, also played their part. Haig would have us believe that it was the superior morale of the BEF and its strength in depth across the empire that made the final difference. None of these in themselves won the war, but all of them enabled the infantry to do so.

Haig sought no acknowledgement that he somehow had been personally responsible. The Reverend Duncan recalled that, on 13 November

1918, 'When I attempted to express congratulations his immediate reaction was: "Oh! You mustn't congratulate me; we have all been in this together, all trying our different ways to do our part." After a time he added, pointing to a piper: "Come and speak to this fine fellow over here. He came out in 1914; and in the early days was through some of the worst of it. It is fellows like him who deserve congratulations." '[58] In his final dispatch, Haig was to take pains to show how fully his army represented the whole of British life, citing the examples of one brigadier who had driven a taxi before the war, of a former railway worker and an ex-coal miner who were now in command of battalions, of cooks and clerks who were now staff officers. This of course ignored the fact that the most senior appointments within the BEF were closed to any but former regular army officers.

Accusations have been made ever since the end of the war that Haig lobbied hard to be rewarded with honours and money, but the reality once again seems more complex. Less than a month after the Armistice, he wrote to one of his relatives: 'I am amused at your meeting people in the road talking about <u>my</u> reward! As a matter of fact I have told the authorities that I will accept nothing until proper provision has been made for Disabled Officers. The Pensions Minister has asked for <u>charity</u> to support those who have fought for their country! [. . .] I consider that everyone has a right to be reinstated, or recompensed to the full, who has suffered in the country's cause. But as regards myself, all I want is to be left alone, and to be able to lead my own life in peace and quietness. I despise the Politicians, or Statesmen as they would like to be called! They wd have lost the war if it had been possible to do so. It was the soundness of the British people which saved the situation.'[59] The nobility of such sentiments is somewhat undermined by a letter Sassoon wrote to Esher on 14 September 1918, in which he declared, 'D.H has not been offered a Peerage again & I know he wouldn't accept it. What he wants is a Grant. "What's the use of being a peer & having to live in hotels" he says.'[60]

Following past precedents, Haig, as a victorious general, would be rewarded by Parliament, both financially and with honours.[61] The Duke of Cumberland had been richly rewarded for his victory over the Jacobite clans at Culloden, while the Duke of Wellington had received grants of £100,000 for winning the Battle of Salamanca, his dukedom and £400,000 upon the defeat and abdication of Napoleon Bonaparte, and a further £200,000 from Parliament after Waterloo. These were all considerable sums of money. More recently, Kitchener had been created a peer for his victory at Omdurman and had received a £30,000 gratuity. Financial rewards and honours were duly scattered among the British army's most senior generals at the end of the Great War. Allenby was given £50,000 and created a viscount in October 1919; Byng and Rawlinson were both created barons and given £30,000, while Horne, Plumer and Birdwood were each given a baronetcy and £10,000. By contrast, the Australian government declined to promote Monash, whom at one stage Lloyd George contemplated as a replacement for Haig, to full general, and he received neither financial reward nor honours.

What, however, was no doubt uppermost in Haig's mind were two simple things: he had been at the head of the largest army Britain had put into the field and one that had, moreover, just won an astonishing victory; and he had three young children, whom he was determined to see remained in the social position that he had achieved for himself. In the days following the Armistice, there was an increasingly frantic correspondence[62] between Haig and Lloyd George, initially conducted by telegram, concerning what Haig might be awarded. On 18 November 1918, he received this telegram from Lloyd George: 'I have the honour to inform you that His Majesty, on my recommendation, has been pleased to approve that the dignity of a Viscountcy of the United Kingdom be conferred upon you in recognition of the signal services which you have rendered to the Empire as Commander-in-Chief of the British Armies in France and Flanders.'

Haig was extremely sensitive to the hierarchical system of British honours; he was well aware that accepting a viscountcy would place him on the same level as Sir John French, who had been forced out as C-in-C. Understandably, he found the implied comparison insulting, and responded by cannily linking his own reward to that of consideration for the men under his command: 'Please express my very grateful thanks to the Prime Minister for the signal honour for which he has been kind enough to recommend me. I hope however that he will allow all question of reward for me to stand over until he has been able to fix the allowances for disabled officers and men as well as batta [an Anglo-Indian military term for financial reward for serving in the field of combat] for all ranks of the Armies under my orders.'

On 20 November, Lloyd George sent Haig another telegram on the same question: 'Private and personal. I quite appreciate the reason for which you wish to defer the honour offered you by the king but I sincerely hope you will reconsider your refusal. Sir David Beatty [Jellicoe's successor as commander of the Grand Fleet] to whom a similar honour was offered has accepted unconditionally. It would be a wholly false situation, generally misunderstood by the public and distressing to the king, if only Beatty was honoured at this moment, indeed, until you assent, I do not see how his name can be put forward alone. As far as the questions of allowances batta etc, about which you are very rightly concerned, goes, I think you may take it from me, that the government will deal with them in no niggardly spirit, though it may take a little time to get everything settled.' Haig replied on 21 November: 'I have written to General Wilson on this matter. Until definite assurance is given that our disabled and the widows and children will receive adequate help I regret I cannot accept any reward of any sort.'

This threatened to become a serious embarrassment for Lloyd George, who was using one of his favoured instruments of power – the bestowing of honours – as a means to inflict a final humiliation on Haig. Relations between Haig and Lloyd George were further soured when, on 30 November, Haig received a telephone call from Lloyd George's office asking him to be in London for the following day, a Sunday, when he was expected to attend a ceremonial procession in which numerous Allied dignitaries were to drive through the streets to attend a reception at the French embassy, one to which Haig was not invited. When Haig discovered that he was to be placed in the fifth carriage along with Henry Wilson, he declined to participate, calling it a 'political stunt', as indeed it was; but it was also wounded pride and affronted dignity that led him to refuse. He could not tolerate being asked to take his place in line after carriages occupied by Foch and Clemenceau; being expected to sit in the same carriage as Wilson added insult to injury.

On 4 December 1918, Haig vented his ill temper with Lloyd George in a letter to a relative, Rose Haig Thomas: 'I may tell you <u>privately</u> that I considered it an insult to be asked by your [sic] P.M to return to London with a pack of foreigners, and on a Sunday too! [. . .] So I said "I would not come unless I was ordered." The whole thing was got up for Election purposes I imagine. As regards "rewards", there too I am "agin the Govt", and have declined their proffered Viscountcy (twice). Ten days ago I told the War Office that I wd accept no reward until adequate provisions have been made for disabled <u>officers</u>. I think it disgraceful that the Pensions' Minister shd appeal for charity to support those who have fought & given everything for their Country. All who have suffered must be <u>adequately</u> recompensed. Up to date the Govt has neglected the unfortunate disabled Officer.'[63]

The mutual loathing between Haig's supporters in the army and Lloyd George's administration spilled out into the press shortly afterwards. On 18 December, the British newspapers carried an anonymous statement put out by the government's Press Bureau, defending the government's decision not to issue a formal vote of thanks to the army. On Thursday 19 December Haig, his army commanders[64] and assorted staff officers sailed from Boulogne at 8.30am in the destroyer HMS *Termagant*, bound for Dover. As he crossed the Channel, Haig gave no hint of being anything other than his usual outwardly imperturbable self. He certainly gave no indication of his private fury with what he regarded as the vainglorious self-aggrandisement of Lloyd George, who was already orchestrating a press campaign to dub himself 'the man who won the war'. Haig's happiness at returning to his family, his pride in his army and its victories, his sense of vindication and success were none the less tainted by the bitterness he felt at the struggles he had been forced to engage in with the War Cabinet since early 1917, and the snubs he was now receiving. At Dover, Haig and his senior officers dutifully listened to the first of hundreds of tedious civic speeches in their praise, before cheering crowds swept them onto a special train bound for London.

At a Charing Cross festooned with pennants and flags, crowds which had been gathering since the previous evening gave raucous cheers as the generals were met by Lloyd George and, on behalf of King George V, the Duke of Connaught. Among the crowd Haig spotted the ever faithful Henrietta, to whom he gave a kiss before inspecting a guard of honour from the Grenadier Guards. To the left of the Guards were a host of dignitaries, members of the War Cabinet, the Admiralty, the Army Council, Asquith and the elderly Sir Evelyn Wood VC. Haig was deeply moved by the spontaneous public acclamation as his party's five carriages drove through Trafalgar Square[65] and along Pall Mall before arriving at Buckingham Palace: 'The route was not lined with troops. The reception was essentially a <u>welcome by the people</u>, without any official interference, and I could not help feeling how the cheering from great masses of all classes came from their hearts. As ADC to King Edward, I have taken part in many functions, but never before have I seen such crowds, or such wholehearted enthusiasm.'[66]

At the palace, the generals were given a lunch reception by the king, who was seated between Plumer and Dorothy Haig, while the two bitter enemies, Haig and Lloyd George, sat on either side of Queen Mary. Haig thanked the king for the 'splendid welcome which had been given me' before being once more buttonholed by Lord Stamfordham, who tried to press Haig into accepting an earldom. Haig was cross and in no mood for compromise. Stamfordham argued that Admiral Beatty was to be made an earl and General Plumer a viscount, and that it would be publicly embarrassing if Haig was not simultaneously announced as being awarded something. Haig was blunt: '[...] why not state the truth and say I wished no reward until the Army had been provided for. I then told him that Government had neglected its duty to the <u>Disabled</u>, and outlined some of the reports of hard cases which had reached my ears.'

There the matter languished, occasionally picked over by an increasingly curious press, which wanted to know precisely how the field marshal was to be rewarded. On 18 February 1919, while Haig was back at GHQ in France, Sassoon was sent to London to discuss terms with Lloyd George. Sassoon floated the idea that, while Haig would not decline a peerage, because that would appear 'ungracious' to the king, 'he must receive a sufficient grant to enable him to maintain a suitable position, otherwise he would have to decline.' Lloyd George opened the bidding at £100,000, Sassoon suggested £250,000, and eventually – although not at that meeting – a compromise was struck: an earldom and £100,000.[67] Lloyd George gave an assurance to Sassoon that, within two months, the matter of suitable pensions for ex-servicemen would be sorted out, an undertaking that he failed to fulfil until much later than promised.

The day of his victorious return to England, 19 December 1918, had been a long one for Haig and Doris; they did not arrive at their home, Eastcott, until 5pm. Later that evening a large crowd, estimated by Haig at 10,000, including three bands, gathered outside their home in an impromptu torchlight procession to cheer and welcome him. He summed up the mixed feelings of the day: 'Today was indeed a red letter one in my life. To receive such a spontaneous welcome all the way from the coast to my house at Kingston Hill shows how the people of England realise what has been accomplished by the Army and myself. This more than compensates me for the difficulties put in my way and the coldness towards me by the Prime Minister (Lloyd George).'[68] Yet on reading this, and his later correspondence, it is hard to ignore a lingering suspicion that Haig felt increasingly estranged, isolated and, ultimately, bitter.

Between the end of 1918 and April 1919, when he retired from his post as C-in-C of the BEF and took up the command of the Home Forces in England, Haig was engaged in a mixture of celebratory social occasions and overseeing the gradual dismemberment of his beloved army in Flanders. When he finally came home for good, he returned in a small craft to Dover, where this time there were no crowds awaiting him. According to Churchill, Haig then 'disappeared into private life. There was an interlude of pageantry, of martial celebrations, the Freedom of

Cities, of banquets and the like; but in fact the Commander-in-Chief of the British Armies in France passed, as he left the gangway and set foot on the pier, from a position of almost supreme responsibility and glorious power to the ordinary life of a country gentleman. Titles, grants, honours of every kind, all the symbols of public gratitude were showered upon him; but he was given no work. He did not join in the counsels of the nation; he was not invited to reorganize its army; he was not consulted upon the Treaties; no sphere of public activity was opened to him. [. . .] he was full of energy and experience, and apparently at the moment when he was most successful, there was nothing for him to do; he was not wanted any more. He must just go home and sit by the fire and fight his battles over again. He became one of the permanent unemployed.'[69]

This is only partly true. It creates the impression that Haig nurtured hopes of an influential quasi-governmental post in the years after the Great War, whereas he was not the slightest bit interested in participating in political life; his early contempt for politicians had been thoroughly reinforced by his experience of their untrustworthiness during the Great War. And while he was certainly fêted at innumerable civic dinners and similarly tedious functions, he was far from being permanently unemployed. Instead, he threw his remaining energies into campaigning for the welfare of the soldiers who had stood in his army.

# CHAPTER THIRTEEN

# Of Politics and Poppies

Pride and reserve are not the only things in life; perhaps they are
not even the best things. But if they happen to be your particular
virtues you will go all to pieces if you let them go.

Ford Madox Ford

The Armistice put an end to the slaughter in Flanders, but in one respect
merely opened the way for a new phase of recriminations back in Britain,
as the leading generals and politicians began their struggle to accumulate
praise and allocate blame. These tensions had been largely hidden from the
public gaze during the war, but they quickly surfaced once the guns fell
silent. Rather as on the Western Front, there would be a minor offensive
here and there – often conducted in the letters pages of *The Times* – with
the occasional 'great push', such as the publication of memoirs by Viscount
French and Winston Churchill. But for those who treasured the memory of
Field Marshal Earl Haig, it was the publication of Lloyd George's *War
Memoirs* in the 1930s that, with its sheer magnitude, demolished Haig's
reputation with a deluge of Lloyd George's favourite armament: words.

This battle of the books, one conducted on the Churchillian principle
that 'history will be kind to me because I intend to write it', was not
publicly joined by Haig, whose own post-war strategy was largely defensive; he published no memoirs but occasionally intervened when he
thought his own ramparts were threatened. He took a close interest in the
construction of Britain's official history of the war, written by his old
Staff College compatriot, Brigadier-General Sir John Edmonds, and was

OF POLITICS AND POPPIES

naturally closely involved in the compilation and publication of his collected dispatches.[1] Charteris may have written after Haig's death that he 'never publicly gave expression to any extenuation or defence of his policy, nor did he ever authorise one word to be written in contradiction of accusations and criticisms levelled against him in the post-war flood of controversial literature,'[2] but this does not entirely accord with the facts. Every post-war speech Haig made – and there were many – was a *de facto* defence of his 'policy', which was that victory had been achieved in the primary theatre, the Western Front, by means not just of improved technology but of superior character.

Haig also made efforts to have his own view of events recorded in print, by asking Lieutenant-General Sir Launcelot Kiggell and General Sir Herbert Lawrence, his two former chiefs of staff, to write a 'Memorandum on Operations on the Western Front, 1916–18'. Copies of this were sent to both Edmonds and King George V.[3] He also cooperated with Lieutenant-Colonel J. H. Boraston and the journalist G. A. B. Dewar in their 1922 book, *Sir Douglas Haig's Command, December 19 1915 to November 11 1918*, in which the authors charged Lloyd George with almost losing the war through his plots against the British high command. This book, which, according to Repington, laid into the former Prime Minister 'with a whip which seems to be composed of barbed wire and scorpions',[4] further goaded Lloyd George into seeking his own written revenge against the generals, and Haig especially.

With the war over, Haig publicly gave every appearance of remaining implacably aloof to political machinations, yet privately he was still passionately consumed with loathing for Lloyd George. Immediately following the Armistice, the friction between the two men was exacerbated by the messy demobilization plans of the BEF, which in theory were based on the entirely sensible need to rebuild the country's economic strength. Instead of demobilizing whole units, it was intended to release pre-selected individuals from the army on the basis of the contribution they would supposedly make to the most urgent needs of British industry. The demobilization scheme envisaged five categories of service personnel who were to be released in sequence. The first to go –

the 'demobilizers' – were those deemed essential to ensure the smooth demobilization of everyone following. The second – and most contentious – category was that of so-called 'pivotal men'; these were to be selected according to the degree to which their return to economic productivity would create employment for others.[5] The third class were the so-called 'slip men', to be released after general demobilization orders if they could produce a slip from an employer testifying that there was a job waiting for them. The fourth category comprised men who did not possess a slip but whose pre-war employment showed them to have been engaged in a sector of high national importance. The fifth and final group comprised all the rest, in an ill-defined order related to the importance of their previous civilian employment. This order of release was further complicated by undertakings that married men, men with long service records, and those who had been in battle for lengthy periods would take preference within the five categories. These plans had been drawn up and gradually refined by a Cabinet committee within the Ministry of Reconstruction.

Long before the war ended Haig had given considerable thought to the difficult question of dismantling the BEF and he showed a remarkable foresight in calling attention to the problems that might ensue if demobilization was mishandled. On 3 October 1917 he had sent a detailed memo to Lord Derby, then still Secretary of State for War, in which he predicted that the end of the fighting would produce 'a general relaxation of the standards of discipline; men's minds, energies and thoughts will no longer be occupied by the task of defeating and destroying the enemy, but will trend naturally towards early return home. [. . .] Hence as soon as demobilisation commences a feeling of jealousy will arise, men will only watch the dates of departures of others and will institute comparisons as to their respective claims, there will be generally an unsettled state, and as the natural consequences of a prolonged and arduous war, nerves will be in an irritable and unstable condition.'[6]

The demobilization plan was administered by no fewer than fourteen separate government departments, and it was a typically bureaucratic scheme; fine in theory, hopeless in practice, wide open to corruption and, most dangerous for social stability, regarded by serving soldiers as flawed in terms of simple equity: '[. . .] a nonslip man with three years of front-line service and with a wife and child at home had no priority over the slip or pivotal man who had served only a year, possibly in England, and who possessed no dependents [sic].'[7]

Haig had consistently counselled against this scheme. Quite correctly, he anticipated that it would cause untold damage to the maintenance of the spirit of post-war comradeship, which he felt was vital to prevent a slide into social disunity. Like many conservatives at the time, he was deeply concerned that his adored country and its empire would, under the pressure of economic strain, fall prey to the kind of revolutionary self-destruction that had torn apart Russia. Haig's advocacy of demobilization by units and complete formations was, however, ignored by the government, and his worst fears in 1917 were duly confirmed in late 1918 and early 1919 by regular secret reports from the BEF's postal censors, which contained remarkably frank insights into the discontented mood of the rank and file, following the limbo that prevailed between the Armistice and the start of demobilization. The censors reported to Haig in December 1918 the troops' view of the demobilization scheme: 'The most striking feature is a very general mistrust of the Government, and consequently of all authorities. The official scheme is evidently too complicated for the men to grasp; failing to understand it they generally have little belief in it and are inclined to regard it as "something to keep the public quiet." In this state of mind they are apt to jump at any grievance, real or imagined; many grievances of both kinds are stated but not, as a rule, intelligently discussed.'

Lloyd George claimed he would build a land fit for heroes, but his greater preoccupation in early December 1918 was his own political career rather than supervising the efficient and equitable dismantling of the BEF. Shortly after the Armistice he called a general election, intent on capitalizing upon the domestic post-war euphoria. Demobilization in any case did not begin until 9 December, a delay which seemed inordinate to many British soldiers, who mistakenly but understandably conflated the Armistice with a peace treaty which was not, in fact, signed until 28 June

1919. The British press took a unanimously dim view of the demobilization delays, the response of London's *The Herald* being typical: 'Send the
boys home. Why in the world the delay? The war is not officially over, but
everybody knows that in fact it is over. Munition-making has stopped;
motorists can joy-ride; the King has had a drink; society has had its victory ball and is settling down to its old job of pleasure-making [. . .]
Danger of too rapid demobilisation? Bunkum! There are thousands of
men for whom jobs are waiting, but the Army won't let them go. And –
even if a man hasn't got a job – why not let him go home at once?'[8]

Such pressure in the newspapers helped whip up wider public protest
against the dilatory and unjust manner of demobilization, and threatened to damage Lloyd George's electoral hopes. On 13 December, the
government therefore hurriedly adjusted the demobilization scheme; in
future, a serviceman on leave in the UK would be released if he could
prove to the military's satisfaction that he had a firm job offer from a pre-
war employer, and if he was not deemed indispensable to the forces. On
14 December, Lloyd George's coalition of Conservatives and some
Liberals – for which Haig voted, despite his detestation of Lloyd George,
as being the least bad alternative – returned to power with 459 seats,
more than 59 per cent of the popular vote, while Asquith's Liberals were
smashed, losing 235 seats and being reduced to a rump of just 36 MPs.

Meanwhile, discipline within the BEF was rapidly falling apart, just as
Haig had predicted. A postal censor's report of 23 December 1918
captured the ugly mood: 'Large numbers of men state that they have
refused to vote either on account of ignorance of the candidates and their
views, or as a protest against the election taking place at the present time.
[. . .] In individual cases at any rate men's feelings appear to be little short
of mutinous, and there is evidence of organised insubordination in some
units. [. . .] Short rations, bad billets, and, at the Bases, long working
hours are the commonest complaints. The comparative comfort of
officers' billets is not infrequently remarked upon.'[9]

Matters had not improved by early January 1919: 'It appears probable
that in many units officers have made no attempt to understand the
regulations or to explain them to the men. An instance of lack of tact,

which it is hoped is not common, is seen in the following from Calais:-
"We had a rare shock last night. The Adjt. [adjutant] called a meeting and
told us that we need not expect to get demobilised yet and that it would
take at least three months even if a man was applied for. You can imagine
our feelings. The fellows are nearly mad. They threw over the tables and
created h—." . . . generally speaking there is much unrest throughout the
army.'[10] Indeed, on 3 and 4 January 1919, 10,000 soldiers at Folkestone and
as many as 2,000 in Dover refused to board ships returning to France;
sympathetic demonstrators took to the streets of Bradford, Birmingham,
Bristol, Leeds, Manchester, Newcastle, Northampton and Sheffield. On 7
January, soldiers drove lorries up and down Whitehall in London, holding aloft banners proclaiming: 'We won the war. Give us our tickets' and
'No more red tape – we want civvies suits'.[11]

This demoralization might have been avoidable if Haig's counsels had
prevailed, as Winston Churchill, Secretary of State for War in Lloyd
George's newly formed government and no uncritical supporter of Haig,
pointed out in a Cabinet memo: 'It will be of interest to the Cabinet to
read Sir Douglas Haig's letter, written more than a year before the
Armistice. It will be seen that he forecasted accurately the state of indiscipline and disorganisation which would arise in the Army if pivotalism, ie
favouritism were to rule in regard to the discharge of men. [. . .] It is
surprising that the Commander-in-Chief's prescient warnings were
utterly ignored, and the Army left to be irritated and almost convulsed by
a complicated artificial system open at every point to suspicion of
jobbery and humbug.'[12] It was, naturally, impossible to send all BEF
soldiers home immediately after the Armistice. An Army of Occupation
on the Rhine was needed, as well as a force to remove the detritus of
battle from France and Belgium – as late as April 1919, the 'Clearing Up
Army', as it was called, amounted to more than a million personnel.[13] But
Churchill helped ease the demobilization crisis by sending thirty-eight
battalions of conscripted eighteen-year-olds as an occupying force, to
replace battalions of the Second Army.

On 13 March 1919, shortly before he was due to visit Ypres and Flanders
in the company of Doris and other family members, Haig received a

telegram from Winston Churchill offering him the post of C-in-C Home Forces, replacing Sir William Robertson, who had been appointed to the command of the Army of the Rhine. By April 1919, Haig's GHQ was itself being demobilized and dismantled, with Lieutenant-General John Asser, formerly GOC Lines of Communication, supervising the process.[14] Haig's new appointment in charge of Home Forces was abruptly abolished by the government on 31 January 1920, thus removing Haig's last vestige of official military authority. Just thirteen years before, Haig had been considered so able that he was at the centre of Lord Haldane's profound reorganization of the army. Now his military career was over, a sotto voce ending.

The government commissioned no official study of the conduct and management of the war, but it seems today an extraordinary oversight not to have have utilized Haig's experience – and that of other senior commanders – in some capacity. Such was the loathing Lloyd George felt for the generals by the war's end, however, that his new administration did not consider that they might have anything further to contribute. Haig nurtured neither political nor other grand ambitions, but the several organizations of ex-servicemen which had sprung up during and after the war inevitably looked to him as a figurehead, in their effort to achieve what they considered to be just compensation for having saved the country. He thus took up a new fight, one he conducted with the same resolution he had shown in Flanders. As he said in one post-war speech: 'During the war, and even more frequently since, the words "dogged", "determined" have on more than one occasion been used to describe my character. At certain periods of the war the words used to be "obstinate" and "pig-headed", but the qualities of character remained the same. So far as they merited the words applied to them, I may say that my characteristics have not changed, and that I am determined to see this thing through, even though it takes longer than the war – if it is humanly possible.'[15]

All that a Lloyd George administration required of Haig by the end of 1918 was that he drift away into silent retirement, trudging the country, collecting worthy baubles and making dutifully dull speeches. Some of this Haig did. For much of 1919 and 1920 he traversed Britain, attending as guest of honour a flurry of public events at which he would make a sonorously uncontroversial speech, usually concluding with his being granted the freedom of the city or town.[16] Between 23 January and 1 October 1919 he gave at least fifty forgettable speeches at different venues. He also began writing more openly to relatives about his feelings for his former French allies. On 15 April 1919, he told Rose Haig: 'How few realise that 1917 was the most critical period of the war for the Allies, because the French Army was then in such a very bad state of discipline that it was useless for defence, and of course for attack. There were "200,000 mutineers" at one time! [. . .] Indeed the truth about the worthlessness of the French will not be told until our next war with them! They are an ungrateful pack!'[17]

On 14 May 1919, Haig was inaugurated as Rector of St Andrews University. In his Rectorial Address[18] to the students, he gave a speech that offers perhaps the clearest statement of his beliefs and values. Haig wrote his own speeches, which were typed up for his delivery, whereupon he would laboriously go through them with a pencil, underlining points he wished to emphasize and crossing out phrases or words of which, on reflection, he thought better.

The sentiments and ideas he expressed at St Andrews seem almost unbearably remote today; Haig's Olympian view of the Great War was not that of the average Tommy. Yet his idealism remains above mockery:

> We have won, and if my reading of history and current events is correct, we have won because our national character is sound; because it is founded in honesty and love of justice, inspired by comradeship and self-sacrifice, secured by a great capacity for common action in pursuit of high ideals. Let us do our utmost to keep it so and to hand it on strengthened to our children. So long as our national character remains unchanged we shall always win in all we undertake. It is the sword and buckler of our Empire.

He told his audience that 'the mainspring of our political development has been the liberty of the individual' and talked of his sense of a world-wide mission for Britain: 'It has been given to us to develop for ourselves and others free institutions, to provide a pattern upon which other nations aspiring to a like freedom may model their own institutions, and, in the case of communities whose civilisation has not yet reached our standard, to assist and train them so that in the course of time they too may become fitted to take their place in the ranks of free nations.'

The early twenty-first century does not favour such views, regarding them as intensely patronizing, yet they evince both a genuine sense of duty on Haig's part and, on occasion, an astonishing prescience, as for example in the following passage: 'The unequal standards of living and wide differences of civilisation existing today in different parts of the globe, the economic pressure which must result therefrom and the racial and colour antipathies likely to accompany the development of the latter, all force me to the conclusion that struggles still more terrible are in store for this earth, unless wise and decisive action is taken to remove the causes.'

Haig went on to remark on the move by newspapers and novelists to use the term 'Yellow Peril' in their attempt to sensationalize the looming issue of Asian competitiveness, before shifting to draw a more universal conclusion from the recent conflict in Europe: 'Another great lesson of the war has been the restatement, in terms that everyone who wishes can understand, of the old political axiom that every right carries a corresponding duty. [. . .] It is well to have been reminded of it, for in the development of modern social ideas there has been an increasing tendency to look to the state as a universal provider, from whom everything is to be expected, to whom as little as possible is to be given. Such a tendency is in direct conflict with our old national ideals and our old national character. It is subversive of discipline both in private and public life. It opens the way to political corruption and to all the social evils which have led to the decay of former Empires. It is destructive of that power to combine for the common good and for the maintenance of an ideal above self which alone brought us safely through the war.'

This is no less true now than it was almost a century ago. Finally, at St Andrews, Haig drew for his audience what was, for him, the key lesson of the Great War:

In the first place, success in war depends more on moral than physical abilities, and only what is simple will obtain success. [. . .] Success in war cannot be gained by intelligence alone, but by intelligence ripened by experience of the human feelings and emotions by which men's minds are swayed. [. . .] Knowledge of war and of its science will not bring success, unless it is combined with self-sacrificing courage, tenacity and confidence; for the foe is really conquered, not by his physical destruction, but by the annihilation of his hopes of victory.[19]

Such views, too, are out of kilter with current opinion, which places much greater emphasis on technological innovation than the intangibles of human psychology; but the annihilation of German hopes of victory was surely what ultimately caused the Kaiser's armies to collapse so rapidly in the late summer of 1918.

On 26 June 1919, Haig was at Oxford University,[20] where this non-graduate of BNC was awarded the honorary degree of DCL (Doctor of Comparative Law). Two nights previously, he had been guest of honour at a lavish thirty shillings a head dinner – including 1912 Chateau Y'quem Sauternes and 'bombe victoire' – for 300 in Oxford's town hall, where the largely ex-service male diners toasted his health and victory while, from a gallery above, an assembly of invited ladies looked down. Haig's speech that evening reiterated his belief that victory had been secured by strength of character: 'I do not deny the great value of the constant growth of the material resources at the disposal of our Armies, the accumulated masses of artillery, the tanks, and the aeroplanes, or of the reinforcements sent out to us, after the great and deadly peril of the German spring [1918] attacks. All these things, too, were essential. Yet they do not suffice wholly to account for the wonderful events of 1918. [. . .] In order fully to comprehend the wonderful performances of our Armies last year, one must seek in other directions than merely the material. The decisive factor which held up at last the enemy's attacks, and then which carried our troops forward to victory, was British stubborn determination, British comradeship, British spirit, British moral [sic].'[21]

Haig attended so many of these functions that, in the draft of a speech to the Worshipful Company of Skinners, in London on 29 March 1920, he considered saying: 'I am become a Freeman now of so many Companies, and of many towns and Cities – so that there have been periods during the past twelve months when it has almost happened to me to experience a sense of pleasing novelty to be asked to pay for my own meals.' But Haig had second thoughts and struck out the remark about paying for his own meals. A speech delivered to Bangor University College on 15 July 1920, following yet another honorary doctorate, originally contained the following: '[...] the Englishman, Welshman and Scotsman who were returning together from a holiday at Brighton, each of them taking with him a present for his family. The Englishman had a useful jug, inscribed "A present from Brighton". The Welshman had a pretty watch for his wife, also inscribed "A present from Brighton"; and the Scotsman was carrying back with him a very excellent knife and fork, upon which were neatly engraved the words "London Brighton and South Coast Railway." ' Again, he struck it out, although, as a Scot himself, he might as well have left it in.

Haig's deliberate avoidance of controversy gradually eroded, however, as he warmed to the public issue now closest to his heart, the welfare of ex-servicemen and the failure of government to award proper compensation. Central to this was the formation of the British Legion, established in 1921.[22] It is widely, although mistakenly, believed that Haig was the Legion's founder,[23] but his much greater contribution was that of providing a rallying point for ex-servicemen and assisting in the unification of the disparate ex-servicemen organizations which had sprung up during and after the Great War.

The history of the various ex-servicemen societies is complicated. The first to be formed, the National Association of Discharged Sailors and Soldiers (the 'Association'), grew out of a public meeting in Blackburn in September 1916, and was from the start closely connected to the Trade Unions and Labour Party. The National Federation of Discharged and Demobilised Sailors and Soldiers (the 'Federation') was formed in April 1917 and was linked to the Liberal Party. The Association was strongly anti-officer, while the Federation initially barred officers from its membership, other than those commissioned from the ranks. Both the Association and the Federation contained within them politically radical activists; alarmed by this, Conservative MPs, along with press barons and some senior former army officers, formed a third entity, the Comrades of the Great War, in August 1917, which opened its membership to both officers and other ranks. In 1919 yet another, much more radical organization was created, the National Union of Ex-Service Men, one of the founders of which, John Beckett, later became a Labour MP before he joined Oswald Mosley's British Union of Fascists in 1934.

Haig's position concerning this plethora of ex-servicemen organizations was avowedly anti-factional; he early on pushed for unification of the disparate assortment of ex-officers' associations and in August 1919 he presided over a London meeting which achieved this, giving rise to another entity, the Officers' Association, publicly launched on 30 January 1920. The Officers' Association was granted its legal existence by a Royal Charter which came into effect on 30 June 1921, just one day before the formal establishment of the British Legion. Haig had been asked by Colonel George Crosfield, a leading activist in the Comrades of the Great War, to become the Legion's first President in 1919, but he declined, instead urging Crosfield to bring about a unified ex-service organization for all ranks.[24] Instead, Haig accepted an invitation to become the first life member of the Comrades, it being the only entity which then opened its membership to both officers and men.

What rankled most with Haig in the days after the war ended was that Lloyd George's new administration had signally failed to make sufficient pension and welfare provisions for former officers. In his address to the Mansion House on 30 January 1920 – the day before his final official military appointment was abolished – Haig implicitly attacked the Prime Minister: 'Undoubtedly the main cause of distress among officers is want of generosity on the part of the Government.' Haig also berated employers for not doing enough for ex-servicemen. That same day, he wrote to Rose Haig Thomas: 'Today I took part in a great meeting at the Mansion House to launch the scheme & raise funds.[. . .] I spent last week visiting Manchester, Leeds, Sheffield and Hull. Each place gave me a great reception and I duly rubbed in the shortcomings of many of the Employers in not taking on more ex-service men. Some of course have done more than their share, & have 20%, whereas we only want them all to take 5%. In the West Riding 25 p.cent of the Employers have taken on 9000 ex-servicemen. There are still 4000 in that area out of work, and 75 p.cent of the Employers still available to do it! Nearly all of them in that part have made great fortunes, so we are not asking very much really.'[25]

Haig's irritation was that, while other ranks had been given a state allowance of £2 a week to cover the gap between their discharge and receiving a pension, former officers received next to nothing. The government had created a fund of £104,000,000 to provide financial assistance for ex-servicemen, but only £2,000,000 of this was for the relief of ex-officers, the majority of whom, by the end of the war, had in any case been commissioned from the ranks. Haig asserted in January 1920 that 20,000 ex-officers were out of work and 33,000 disabled former officers were trying to survive on an average pension of £70 a year, which was about half the average wage of an agricultural labourer. Haig exhorted his Mansion House audience '[. . .] to set an example to every town and village in the land and to every household that can spare anything from its necessities. It is my considered opinion that we owe it to these men that we are not today the poor despoiled vassals of a foreign State. But for the unselfish bravery of those for whom I plead, our mighty Empire would have crumbled, and this great city and all the wealth and grandeur in it would have suffered the fate that overtook great imperial cities in the past.'[26]

It was a message he repeated in succeeding weeks. By the time he addressed the Worshipful Company of Skinners on 29 March 1920, he was more outspoken: 'In the past the reputation of this country as regards the treatment accorded to ex-servicemen, officers and other ranks broken in the country's battles, has scarcely been worthy of our reputation in other things. On this occasion, the problem has been almost inconceivably larger than any corresponding problem of former wars. It was obvious, that the chief burden of solving a problem so immense could only be undertaken by the State, and my first object was to see that the State faced its obligations in a spirit as generous as the condition of the national finances permitted. And I don't mind telling you, that in a matter of this kind I would not pay any unduly fastidious regard to the state of the nation's finances. I say to myself, the war was costing us 8 millions a day, and these men, and others like them, ended the war for you, ended it successfully. Though we were on the verge of bankruptcy we must be generous to these men. So we kept on badgering the State, as represented by His Majesty's Government.'[27]

Haig was rightly concerned that the alarmingly high unemployment levels among ex-servicemen were not conducive to the greater public good. Welfare organizations for former servicemen that entrenched divisions between officers and men would only exacerbate social tensions in British society. He felt that, just as the Great War had been won by national and imperial unity, so too could a lasting and happier domestic stability be achieved only if class and other divisions were dissolved into a single ex-servicemen's organization. He wrote to Colonel Crosfield in March 1922 on the topic of rank in the Legion: 'Really there ought to be no question of "rank" in the Legion, we are all "comrades"! That however is not possible and so we must legislate to ensure that the "other ranks" are adequately represented.'[28]

The Legion was regarded by Haig as the place where it was possible to replicate the spirit of national unity that he felt had existed within the BEF, as he outlined in a speech in 1926: 'Subversive tendencies are still at work in our midst, short cuts to anarchy are still the fools-talk of unstable intellectuals and the over-paid outpourings of the street corner agitator. There is all the greater need for men of all ranks who are determined by steady, patient and self-sacrificing work, to bring comfort and happiness to this sore stricken nation, to stand stoutly and solidly together. The Legion offers a rallying ground for such men. It appeals today to all who have worn the King's Uniform, who therefore realise the nobility of service to enrol themselves to win the Peace even as they won the War.'[29]

This kind of language, and Haig's undeviating hostility towards working-class political activism, whether from the left – as in Russia – or the right – as in post-war Germany with the growth of the Freikorps –

encouraged some to refer to the Legion as 'Haig's White Guard', a description first used by the *Daily Herald* in 1924. Yet the Legion was never regarded in this light by Haig, nor by its leading officials, and he resisted all attempts by the government to look to the army to act against striking civilians. In January 1919, Winston Churchill had instructed the army's GHQ in London to 'prepare a complete scheme and organisation of Military Forces throughout the United Kingdom to act in aid of the Civil Power in the event of a national strike of a revolutionary character.'[30] The government was deeply afraid that the 'triple alliance' of railway, transport and coal-mining unions would bring about a Socialist revolution, but, while Haig had no sympathy for trade unions, his conservatism also dictated that he resisted any attempt to draw his beloved army into what he saw as work for the police. The army was to be used only in the direst of circumstances. As he spelled out to his subordinates in the Home Force, in the event of being called upon to act against civilians, 'Troops should be kept concealed as long as possible, and should only appear when the civil authorities require their help. As soon as the necessity for action is over the troops must at once be withdrawn out of sight.'[31]

The possibility that the government might need to call on the resources of the army to quell civil unrest was real. A strike that broke out at the end of September 1919 threatened to stretch to breaking point the under-manned and demoralized police force of England and Wales, which had previously gone on strike briefly in August 1918 and again in August 1919; the police force did not recover its pre-war strength of some 54,000 officers until March 1920. As it was, a general strike in September 1919 fizzled out with little disturbance and, by November, the War Office, never much enamoured of using soldiers to break strikes, was reassured by the government that the army's civil role would revert to what it had been before the war: it would only be deployed on the streets in the last resort.

Haig's dislike of trade unions and political agitators was reinforced after the war by the refusal of some unions to assist in the retraining of disabled ex-soldiers, for fear of job losses and cheaper competitive

London, 1919: When he returned to Britain, Haig was acclaimed for his role as the victorious commander of the BEF. (*Museum of Edinburgh*)

Berlin, 1918: German troops returned home with a sense of betrayal but their heads held high. (*Imperial War Museum*)

PEACE MARCH.

Haig in field marshal's uniform, *c*.1920. His senior commanders during the Great War had clubbed together to buy his baton. (*Museum of Edinburgh*)

The Haigs with their two eldest daughters, Alexandra and Victoria, after the Armistice in November 1918. (*Museum of Edinburgh*)

Douglas Haig and his wife Dorothy, *c.*1920. (*Museum of Edinburgh*)

Richmond, January 1928: The day before he died, Haig visited a poppy-making factory and spoke to Boy Scouts there. (*Museum of Edinburgh*)

Haig's coffin and guard of honour, which was open for two days from 1–2 February, 1928, at St Columba's in Knightsbridge. His death invoked a national sense of mourning, his loss symbolizing that of countless others. (*Thompson & Co., Ltd / Museum of Edinburgh*)

labour, at a time when wage levels, which for industrial skilled workers had soared during the war, remained relatively high. Workers in the metal and electrical industries voted by ballot against retraining disabled ex-soldiers. Haig did not – could not – comprehend the reasoning behind the unions' behaviour – that they regarded their function as being to defend the interests of their members, not to re-absorb ex-soldiers into the national workforce. The first issue (May 1920) of the *Comrades Gazette*, published by the Comrades of the Great War, West of Scotland Division, included an extract from an address Haig gave to the annual meeting of the Comrades on 27 February 1920. Under the heading 'Neither Political, Sectarian, Nor Extreme', he instructed the Comrades to 'have nothing to do with political parties'. For Haig, this had become a personal creed through bitter personal experience; that it was perhaps unrealistic and impractical was of no concern to him. His training and experience had induced in him an enduring and paternalistic view of the soldiers under his command. His duty, as he saw it, was to marshal them into a situation in which they would be able to do their best; their duty, he took for granted, was to respond wholeheartedly in the knowledge or at least the belief that they were all pulling together in the same direction.

Such paternalism also meant that, although Haig was by nature very careful with his money, he could also be generous to ex-servicemen when he felt it was deserved. In a letter[32] to his nephew Oliver Haig in early 1919 he wrote: 'When does Bee [Haig's brother, John] go into residence on this farm you mention? It is a bad time to start is it not, as prices of everything are so high? I'll see what I can do to help him if required. But I feel the Disabled bears a prior claim – I have just given £1000 to help our Officers Fund. I'll do what I can to get you a decoration. I was delighted to see that you had been made a Colonel.'

Although Haig was now fully occupied with touring the country and chivvying the government to be more magnanimous towards ex-officers, he had managed to reach a settlement with it concerning his *ex gratia* payment. His retirement in 1920 had not entailed financial loss; as a field marshal, he was entitled to remain on the army's active list, on full salary of some £3,500 annually, an income that was, by the standards of the day, ample.[33] To give some comparison, the novelist Henry Williamson, who had served as a Territorial in France, ultimately as an officer in the Machine-Gun Corps, rented for himself and his young family a cottage near Barnstaple, Devon, in 1929, for £60 a year.[34] In 1920, Parliament finally agreed a gratuity for Haig of £100,000; it was indeed a vast sum of money, but he did not benefit from it directly.[35] Haig's gratuity was administered by the Public Trustee and invested on behalf of his four children, who stood to inherit an equal portion when they came of age or married. The range of investments recommended by the Public Trustee's office were suitably cautious, consisting of government War Loan stock, Canadian Pacific Railway debentures, Investment Trust debentures and various Latin American debentures,[36] yielding an average 4.25 per cent per annum. These investments would have augmented the trust's income by some £4,250 annually, about £500,000 in 2007 terms. He also held a handful of company directorships,[37] together with a few shares in those companies, as well as in ICI and rubber plantations.

Haig's private income and his salary meant that he could enjoy a very comfortable retirement and, unlike some of his senior colleagues, he had no need of government sinecures. He was free, if he chose, to revenge himself in print on his old enemy, Lloyd George, for whom Haig's contempt did not abate with the passing years. But while Haig delighted at the demise of Lloyd George, who was by now badly tarnished through his widely alleged involvement in the sale of honours, and whose National Liberal Party was crushed in the general election on 15 November 1922, Haig had no interest in writing his own account of the war. He contented himself with private sniping, usually to wartime comrades, such as in this letter of 4 January 1923: 'It's interesting to see how quickly LL. George has disappeared from the public gaze & popular favour. His fall has indeed been a crushing one! [. . .] Well, the Welshman who had begun to think himself "a strategist" (as Dewar puts it) has been beaten in the political arena just as he was in the strategical one during the War! It will be a long time before the country will trust itself to him & his kidney again. He had become a real danger to the State, and his disappearance is a Godsend.'[38]

Yet Lloyd George's own consequently increased spare time was to cost Haig dearly, as the former Prime Minister knuckled down in earnest to writing his memoirs, both to earn money and also to tweak the noses of his wartime enemies, whose regular attacks were a great source of irritation: 'Every volume of memoirs, or every biography, of a leading politician or soldier that appeared was anxiously scanned by Lloyd George's assistants for any derogatory references to their chief [. . .]'[39]

After his electoral defeat, Lloyd George took to complaining that his seventeen years in government had left him short of money, a suggestion no more true than the one that Haig was poor. It was not widely known but, in addition to his MP's annual salary of some £400, Lloyd George had been left an annuity of £2,000 by the millionaire Andrew Carnegie in August 1918. He had also as Prime Minister enjoyed until quite recently an annual salary of £5,000. His party's fortunes in the November general election had not been helped by a storm of protest over his apparent financial greed, which broke on 12 August 1922, when the *London Evening Standard* revealed that the Prime Minister was about to sign a contract to publish his memoirs. Curtis Brown, Lloyd George's literary agent, had sold the rights for the unprecedented sum of £90,000.[40] This aroused a storm of protest from Lloyd George's enemies, and the *Manchester Guardian* called for his resignation as Prime Minister if publication went ahead. In the resulting furore, Lloyd George declared he would donate all profits to war charities.[41] He additionally signed a deal with the United Press Association (UPA) to write thirty newspaper articles on politics and the war, for a fee of £500 per article – a total of £15,000. The UPA deal, which naturally undermined the potential for the book, so annoyed the book publishers that they revoked their contract. In his first year of journalism Lloyd George earned a staggering £30,000.

Haig himself regarded with admiration those empire service personnel who had worn uniform and fought in the Great War, and was largely contemptuous of those who had not. For Haig, 11 November 1918 symbolized the strength of the empire, subsuming divisions of class, creed and nationality into a grand unity, in which the only hierarchy was one defined by loyalty, duty and honour; it was his ideal that this wartime spirit should be extended into the peace. Haig was not a profound thinker, however; he never precisely formulated what he meant by this yearning, beyond rather superficial exhortations, such as that he made just two days before he died, in his last public speech. On that occasion, when addressing a group of Scouts and Cubs, sons of disabled ex-servicemen employed at the British Legion Poppy Factory at Richmond, he alluded to a phrase from his fellow Cliftonian, Sir Henry Newbolt. The boys, said Haig, should always '[. . .]play the game and to try and realise what citizenship and public spirit really mean. When you grow up, always remember that you belong to the great Empire, and when people speak disrespectfully of England always stand up and defend your country.'[42]

It was an exhortation from thirty years before, when Newbolt first produced his cricketing metaphor, but it hearkened back to a mythic age of chivalry. For Haig and many of his contemporaries such words spoke of axiomatic truths. The difficulty for us now is the associated odour of narrow nationalism; as for the empire, the very concept is today redolent of racial prejudice, oppression and cruelty. It was not so for Haig, who held fast to an idealized notion of empire as a unity of peoples working for common ends.[43]

In his final years, Haig was still physically vigorous and mentally alert, although some contemporary photographs show him walking with a stick, perhaps as a result of the gout he occasionally endured. As well as his work on behalf of the British Legion – which Doris continued after his death, not always tactfully[44] – he maintained his daily ritual of physical exercise, normally taking a long walk, playing golf or riding, and, when at Bemersyde, the one place he felt truly settled, he spent time supervising and working on the creation of a flower garden out of its rough, infertile ground. The Haigs did not move to Bemersyde until 15 March 1924, ten months after it was vacated by the previous tenant; the old house had gradually fallen into serious disrepair and, according to Doris, Haig spent some £40,000 on putting it in a 'satisfactory state'.[45]

The preparations for Haig's return to the family seat certainly occupied some of his thoughts during 1921 and 1922. He and Doris visited Bemersyde in February 1922 to see what needed doing. The field marshal, who had been given a free railway pass by the LM & S (London Midland & Scottish) Railway after the war, could even arrange for the Carlisle-Edinburgh express train to make an unscheduled stop at Melrose, near Bemersyde, to drop them off.[46]

Haig maintained his usual parsimonious ways in recruiting servants, writing to his local Melrose factotum, James Curle, who was overseeing the repairs and other work at Bemersyde, in response to Curle's suggestion that Haig take on a man called George Allan as head gardener: 'As he is to be the head man I am inclined to pay him well if he is a good servant to me; but £2. 6/- [a week] seems enough to start on at this time, together with his cottage and 4 tons of coals. If he suits me, he will have a permanent place for his life of course.'

George Allan, however, was not taken on; he offended Haig with his request for modern conveniences. In November 1922 Haig informed Curle that: '[. . .] as regards George Allan, please tell him that I decline to give any definite undertaking regarding doing up the Lodge specially to meet his requirements; so I do not need his services. At the same time I intend that all cottages on my part of the Bemersyde property be brought up to the usual standard of modern requirements in similar dwellings, and I should be much obliged if you will kindly ask Mr Alison to look round all my cottages, and advise as to what should be done in each case.' But at the beginning of December, Haig had engaged a man named Wightman as head gardener and informed Curle that 'Wightman only has "Parafin" lamps where he is, and there are only "Parafin" lamps in the "big house" [Bemersyde itself] also! So he is quite pleased to fall in with our simple ways, unlike the gentleman I saw last time [. . .] who wished for water closets and electricity!'[47]

Haig felt real affection for Bemersyde, Spartan though it was, and had nurtured his love for this quarter of Scotland while in France; he had written to his niece, Ruth De Pree, that 'I want to live in Scotland and the east coast of Scotland for the few remaining years I have left after the War. I want my children brought up in Scotland, the Scotch are the best and most patriotic people.'[48] Old acquaintances visited him at Bemersyde, some of whom, such as Philip Sassoon and John Charteris, Doris did little to encourage, and Haig seemed to take more pleasure than ever before in social events; he appeared finally to have relaxed, somewhat, his rather stiff formal demeanour. He took his two younger children trout fishing and organized family picnics. His son recalled him as a gentle, kindly parent, who 'rather took a back seat leaving it to my mother when discipline was needed.'[49]

In due course, Haig lost the service of his faithful Secrett, who fell out with him over the question of money. Secrett wrote later that he had left the army at the end of the Great War, following twenty-eight years in uniform, with a pension of nineteen shillings and sixpence a week; Haig would have been well aware of Secrett's pension and gave him a salary of £65 a year – slightly more than half what he was prepared to pay a head gardener. For Secrett this was not enough, for he had plans to marry, having been engaged for several years. He told Haig he could not marry on £65 a year. According to Secrett, Haig 'was most difficult to approach on the matter. To him I was always Secrett, always there and always reliable, and he could not conceive of one being so unreasonable as to seek any change from that position. [. . .] It was impossible to marry on that. I had hoped he would have seen my point, but he was essentially conservative in his arrangements and I believe he thought in his heart I could never break away. Finally, I knew that it was a question of giving up all my life for ever and breaking with my future wife, or breaking with the Earl. What I felt about it is too deep to put into print. [. . .] I know he was on the point of offering something that would have made the break unnecessary, but he could not bring himself to do it. I, on my part, could not bring myself to beg or even to suggest.'[50]

Secrett was aware of Haig's penny-pinching ways, and also of how Haig would have viewed this step as the ultimate in disloyalty; it must have been a painful encounter for both of them.[51] Secrett left Haig's employ on 27 September 1925, armed with a testimonial from his employer, which says as much about what Haig valued as Secrett's own virtues as an employee: 'He is hardworking, civil, and obliging. Honest and sober; an early riser, punctual and reliable, and gets on well with his equals and superiors in life.'[52]

Haig and Doris also spent time travelling, visiting Canada and South Africa. In February and March 1926, they visited Rome, Florence and Venice on a Thomas Cook tour. In 1927, he wrote a pamphlet on his old love, the cavalry, where – despite all the evidence to the contrary from the Great War – Haig insisted it would always be an essential part of the British army: 'I judge the large reduction in our cavalry cadres since the War to have been unwise and ill-timed. Unwise, because, given thoughtful reorganisation and methodical training the role of the Cavalry in modern War is as important now as ever: and ill-timed because it is well known that "Cavalry cannot be improvised" and that once that splendid Cavalry spirit – the result of years of tradition and loyal service to the Country – is lost it cannot be reproduced the moment War breaks out and the Country's safety <u>again</u> depends (as in 1914) on the immediate mobilisation of trained Cavalry regiments.'[53]

In December 1927, Haig chaired a large formal Brasenose College dinner at the Hyde Park Hotel in London at which, across the expansive tables decorated with large yellow chrysanthemums draped with thin black ribbons, and to familiar tunes played by the band of the Grenadier Guards, he 'looked the picture of health; in fact years younger than he had done at the dinner in Oxford in 1919. He seemed in the best of spirits, and as jolly as a schoolboy when he rose at the end of dinner to propose the "Principal and Fellows of Brasnose".'[54]

Yet in a little more than a month he was dead.

## CHAPTER FOURTEEN

# 'Cause to Reverence His Name'

A SHORT POEM ABOUT LLOYD GEORGE

Lloyd George no doubt when his time is out,
Will ride in a fiery Chariot,
And sit in state on a red hot plate,
Between Annanias and Judas Iscariot.

The devil will say to Annanias that day,
Your title as President fails,
Shift up a bit higher, away from the fire,
And make way for the lawyer from Wales.[1]

Anon.

D.H. is a rum cove, but he always was.

Sir Philip Sassoon

At midnight on Sunday 29 January 1928, loud groans were heard from Haig's room at 21 Prince's Gate, Henrietta's London home in Kensington, where Haig was staying. Doris was elsewhere that night, which she later explained by saying that Henrietta '*always* kept a little single room for her brother so that he could stay there any time he went to London, but as her house was otherwise full on this occasion I had decided to stay with some friends quite near.' Henrietta, now seventy-six, was, according to Doris, herself too far gone to realize that Douglas had died. According to one reverential biography, published later the same year, it was his brother John who found Douglas in his death throes, and there were no others present save for Henrietta and her husband Willie Jameson.[2]

Doris was due to speak to a group of Girl Guides and Brownies on 1 February at the same Richmond poppy factory that Haig had visited on 28 January, when she had been at his side. The separation between Doris and Douglas that evening seems remarkable, given that she had noticed 'for a second or two' how he looked 'deadly pale' while addressing the Boy Scouts, and that only shortly before Haig had had a riding accident while out hunting in Scotland, suffering several broken teeth and, possibly, a fractured jaw. But relations between Doris and Henrietta had never been close, while between Henrietta and Haig there existed to the end a strong tie. What seems likely is that while staying in London Haig enjoyed the familiar comfort of his surrogate maternal home, while Doris chose to stay where she felt more welcome.

Doris claimed that she tried to speak to her husband by telephone twice on Sunday 29 January but that he was unavailable; Haig never spoke on the telephone if he could avoid it, but he seems to have spent the day quietly at home, playing cards and resting, and it is odd that he and Doris did not speak at some point during his final day. Doris wrote later that, on the morning following his death, when she arrived at Prince's Gate, 'there were dense crowds outside and I was attacked by many reporters.' A post-mortem examination revealed Haig had suffered a massive heart attack; there was no inquest. Doris attributed his death to the stresses and strains of the Great War, and yet Haig, who was sixty-six when he died, had nevertheless managed to live twenty-six years longer than the average life expectancy for a man born in Scotland in 1861, which was just 40.3 years, although this statistic is distorted by the high rate of infant mortality at the time of Haig's birth.[3]

Doris abandoned her planned visit to the Girl Guides but sent the girls a message, which appeared in *The Times*: 'His last act was to preside at the enrolment of Scouts and Cubs, his own troop – your brothers. He did not complain of being ill, but when he was making his speech I was not happy about him. [...] He felt very strongly that a young girl's first duty should be "playing the game" and helping mother at home, and by so doing gaining the knowledge that will make her a good wife. In your cases, oh! How one realizes what your fathers and mothers have been through. You know better than I how much. Oh! help them, and let that solemn oath of yours, "Lend a hand," be first carried out at home. There is much around you outside to be done, and if you trust God, He will show you the way and help you.'[4]

As aspirations go, that of being 'a good wife' was stiflingly narrow, even in 1928; Doris's words have echoes of Haig's adored mother Rachel. Both Doris and Haig privately knew that 'playing the game' was not unambiguous, that there were moments when that public refusal to flinch under adversity was privately inadvisable; indeed, the course of Haig's military career had been peppered with episodes which contradicted this apparently high-minded morality. Haig was no different from any of his contemporaries, in that he had always conducted a private game alongside the public, using surreptitious means – in his case, Henrietta's royal connections, the substantial loan to Sir John French, direct communications with the monarchy and influential mentors – to lubricate the upward thrust of his career. In this respect, the battle over Haig's reputation has been more difficult for his defenders, not least because of an understandable reluctance on their part to be entirely frank about this aspect of how the socially powerful permitted themselves to be condemned to an insidious hypocrisy.

Doris's sense of loss was overwhelming and irreparable. The rest of her life was dedicated to an increasingly frantic defence of her dead husband's prestige and reputation. One of her first acts after his death was quintessentially Victorian – she commissioned a plaster death mask of Haig, and the sculptor C. d'O. Pilkington Jackson used it to make a bronze version.[5] The sculptor wrote to the Duke of Atholl, a friend of the Haigs, on 23 July 1928: 'I think I told you that I had persuaded Lady Haig to allow me to make a permanent bronze cast of the Death Mask, in the interests of posterity. She, however, does not like it or wish to have it and is much attached to the original plaster, which has some of the actual hair still upon it. I am making an oak casket lined with grey velvet to hold this original, the top opening in two halves and it is simple but looks precious. As you may know Lady Haig is somewhat alarmed about her finances. As she does not like the bronze (I must say I think it more beautiful than the plaster), and as it ought to belong to the Nation, do you think your Museum[6] could take it for £15. For a few pounds I could make a similar casket to hold it.' Atholl took both the bronze and the casket.

Doris's efforts to burnish Douglas's image became increasingly unbalanced as the years went by and, by refusing to admit the possibility that he was not flawless, she inadvertently eroded sympathy for her cause. For Haig's young son George, who remembered his father with 'enormous love, we adored him', the loss was not just that of a parent, but of a solid, trustworthy model: 'He was a rock-like man. He talked quietly and intently. When he actually made the effort to discuss anything it was to the point, he didn't waste words. I remember him coming to say goodnight to us, dressed to the nines, and giving a loving kiss. We were relaxation for him. Only when he died did we realise he didn't just belong to us.'[7]

News of Haig's death spread rapidly, prompting an empire-wide wave of spontaneous and, given his lowly reputation today, astonishingly powerful public grief, almost as if it exorcised some long pent-up trauma. The mass demonstrations of mourning before, during and after his state funeral, although focused on Haig himself, spoke of a need to come to terms with a war whose complexities still, more than ninety years later, resist easy comprehension. The *Daily Mirror* tried to capture the mood on 31 January 1928: 'A ticket collector at Baker Street yesterday asked me: "Can it be true?" and a porter said: "Is there another Lord Haig?" These men had served in the Army, and had never actually seen Lord Haig, yet they seemed to feel his death as a personal loss. London generally was shocked to hear the news. For a moment it seemed as if the war had come back again and presented us with a stunning casualty.'[8]

We have now become inured to displays of public grief, but the mass demonstration of sadness following the death of Haig was unusual, both in its scale and also its evocation of loss. Many people were prompted to speak or write of their sense of a genuine grief, as if they had personally known this utterly enigmatic man. In 1928 there was no question of any adverse press coverage on the death of a figure of such clear national significance; even Lloyd George obeyed the social convention of *de mortuis nil nisi bonum. The Times* on 31 January 1928 published several fulsome tributes, including this artfully worded encomium from the former Prime Minister: 'Earl Haig was a man of unfailing courage and tenacity of purpose, and he never lost heart during the worst moments in our military fortunes. [. . .] My personal relations with him were always of the very best, and whatever arrangements were made, whether he liked them or not, he very faithfully carried out the policy that had been laid down. [. . .] He behaved not merely like a great patriot, but like a great gentleman.' Another erstwhile opponent, Winston Churchill, suggested Haig stood out as 'incomparably the finest British soldier of this fateful age.'[9] Which perhaps was not saying much, given the available choice.

Doris was immediately inundated with condolences from Haig's social milieu, which, although following a well-established ritual, were nevertheless sincere. King George V and Queen Mary sent a telegram: 'Deeply distressed and shocked at the overwhelming sorrow which has befallen you our hearts go out to you in warmest sympathy at your grief May God help you and your children to bear this heavy blow.' The king followed that with a handwritten letter on 5 February, which contained an endorsement of what later became an axiom for the Haig family, the personalization of Haig as the Great War's 'winner': 'You know how fond I have always been of Douglas & I had absolute confidence in him & knew that if he was given the chance & not interfered with, that he would win.'[10]

The Prime Minister, Stanley Baldwin, who had served as a minister in Lloyd's George's wartime government, wrote on 30 January: 'Whatever consolation it may be that a whole nation mourns with you, you have. I think in his case the country had come to realise the man as well as the great soldier, and to many like myself who had only known him for a few years and not intimately, there is the sense of loss of his calm strength, his perfect integrity and his lofty sense of honour [. . .] you are in my mind so much, and my admiration for him so deep and sincere.' Sir Eric Geddes, J. M. Barrie and John Buchan were among those who wrote personal letters, as did Haig's fellow Scot Sir Arthur Conan Doyle, whose son had died in the trenches of the Western Front, and who in 1916 had publicly declared that he had positive proof of life after death. On 4 February 1928, Conan Doyle wrote to express his 'deepest sympathy': 'I hesitate to intrude and have waited some days. On Friday I had a long message from a source which should be reliable. It professed to be from the Earl and some of it is directly addressed to you. I know that some people are averse from such messages. I therefore will not forward it until I receive your acquiescence.'[11]

H. A. Gwynne, editor of the ultra-conservative *Morning Post*, always a staunch defender of Haig and a ferocious critic of the government during 1917–1918, wrote Doris a very warm letter: 'No one except those who had pierced the triple armour of reticence and shyness ever realised the greatness of the man behind it. It was my greatest good fortune to know the man beneath the Commander-in-Chief and I revered him and loved him. These simply vainglorious politicians never knew him but the great British public that seems to have a woman's instinct for sizing up these public men had no doubt about his greatness, his unselfishness and his burning patriotism.' When he wrote his condolences, Gwynne was naturally ignorant as to how Haig had regarded *him* during the war. Haig had noted in his diary a visit by Gwynne to GHQ on 30 September 1916: 'He is anxious to do the right thing, but, like most newspaper men, is very self-satisfied and talks as if he rules the universe. He has a commendable dislike of the politicians.'[12]

Some were less tactful than Gwynne. Major-General Hugo De Pree, Haig's nephew and co-trustee of the Haig estate, wrote to Doris with an odd request. Sir George Milne[13] had just been promoted field marshal and had approached De Pree to ask Doris 'as to whether there would be any possibility of his taking over any of Uncle Douglas's Field Marshal's uniform or equipment. He was very diffident about asking you, but I said that it might be possible that you would like to have it put to a useful purpose.'[14]

As well as sympathies from the socially prominent, Doris received over the coming weeks hundreds of letters, telegrams, memories and poems, written by people from all social classes and all ages; few had met Haig but all wrote of feeling a personal loss, indicating how tremendously popular a symbol of national pride and dignity Haig had become since the end of the war, and also how his death provided a focus for a generalized mourning. School children sent verses they had composed about his death and a couple of Tommies sent a poppy 'picked from the battlefields of France'. Typical of this correspondence was a letter from Frank Wilson, an ex-private of the Middlesex Regiment:

> Your ladyship,
>
> I hope you will allow me as one of the great Army of unemployed ex-Soldiers to offer you my deepest sympathy in your great sorrow. As one who would many a time have seen his children hungry, but for the Winter Relief of the late Earl's beloved Legion, I have cause to reverence his name. I was in the late War, and though only a Private, I like many others am deeply sorry to hear of our late Commander's death. Your ladyship's loss is also the Empire's loss. Perhaps this little effort of mine, will help to convey to you, how we ex-Service men, esteemed our Leader.

Many eulogies depicted Haig as a chivalrous figure, a knight of ancient lineage. His work for the British Legion no doubt helps explain this immediate posthumous veneration; it had won him the respectful admiration not just of former soldiers but the nation generally. The historian Daniel Todman has suggested, with a degree of no doubt intentional bathos, that: 'By the time of his death Haig had less the status of a conquering general and more that of a sort of moustachioed military Queen Mother.'[15]

Immediately following the post-mortem, Haig's coffin lay for the next two days in St Columba's, on Pont Street in Knightsbridge, the Presbyterian church in London where Haig was an elder. An estimated 25,000 mourners each day lined up to pay their respects. His coffin had a guard of honour from the King's Own Scottish Borderers; the pews were stacked high with wreaths. *The Bulletin* on 3 February published a photograph of a group of mourners, including Lady Haig. Beneath the story of the funeral was a small general knowledge competition, the first item of which was a photograph, with the question: 'Whose portrait is this?' The photograph showed a young-looking Hubert Gough, by then evidently obscure enough to challenge the memories of the newspaper's readers. On 3 February, following a short service at St Columba's, the coffin was carried through streets brimful with people wanting to see Haig's final parade. It was estimated that at least one million people turned out on the streets of London to watch the funeral procession. According to contemporary accounts, the dominant spirit of the crowd was one of comradeship, such as had suffused the trenches at the worst moments of the war.

The coffin was borne on a Union Flag-draped gun carriage, one that had carried the gun that fired the first shot of the war, at Binche, and which had, in 1920, carried the Unknown Soldier to Westminster Abbey. The pall bearers included Marshals Foch and Pétain, and General Deceuninck of the Belgian Army, which, given what later became known of Haig's private views of some of the French generals, was more than ironic. The king was represented by his three sons, and there were representatives of the British Legion and the 'Old Contemptibles'. Detachments of Haig's old regiments, the 17th/21st Lancers and the 7th Hussars, as well as battalions of the Guards, Belgian Grenadiers and French Chasseurs, lined the route. Immediately behind the gun-carriage came Haig's old charger,[16] led by his former man-servant, Secrett. At the Abbey, where the coffin passed the Tomb of the Unknown Soldier, the order of service – broadcast by the BBC in one of the first such 'live' events – and which had been drawn up by Doris, included the hymn 'Abide With Me' and the Lord's Prayer. A piper played the Scottish lament, 'The Flowers o' the Forest', followed by the 'Last Post', 'Reveille', one verse of the National Anthem and, to conclude, 'Onward Christian Soldiers'.

After the service at the Abbey, the coffin was taken across Waterloo Bridge to Waterloo station, where occurred the only notable incident of the funeral. Clive Wigram, assistant private secretary to the king, wrote to Doris later that 'There was one touching incident. "Haig" the charger went splendidly but as the Blues were taking the coffin off the gun carriage to place it in the van, the old horse suddenly became restless –

Secrett and the two men had to hold him tight by the bridle. As the coffin was lifted he cocked his head and neighed – wasn't that an extraordinary coincidence? I am sure the old horse wished to pay his last respects to his great Chief. I know the horse well and constantly ride him on parade. He has the most perfect manners for ceremonial and I have never known him do this.'[17]

The coffin was then transported to Edinburgh and spent the weekend at St Giles Cathedral, where the crowds were even greater than in London; the queue to pass the coffin stretched for a mile, despite driving sleet. From St Giles, the coffin was taken by train to the station of St Boswells and thence carried on an unadorned farm cart drawn by four farm horses, to the ruined abbey at Dryburgh, close to Bemersyde, where Haig had expressed a wish to be buried. The same graveyard contains the remains of Sir Walter Scott, perhaps the single individual who had done most to revive the nineteenth century's interest in the creed of the modest chivalrous gentleman, a creed in which Haig consciously participated and which, during the public commentaries surrounding his death and funeral, was widely resorted to in characterizing his life and deeds. At a memorial service in Cape Town, General Smuts delivered a panegyric in which he described Haig as the most outstanding example he had ever met of the 'strong, silent man. [. . .] He was shy, reserved, and a gentleman in every sense of the word. He refused to play to the gallery.' Had he played a little more to that gallery, Haig's reputation today might be rather higher than it is.

Doris never fully recovered her equilibrium following Douglas's death. Her fragility was exacerbated by anxieties over money, fretfulness over her children's health, and her sense that she had to defend Haig's reputation, which went into remarkably swift decline following his funeral. The family was left without an immediate regular source of income; Haig's field marshal's salary immediately disappeared (to be substituted by the much smaller widow's pension), as did the income from his company directorships. Yet Doris was far from destitute. Haig had originally drawn up a trust disposition – his last will and testament – on 11 March 1920, nominating Doris and Neil Wolseley Haig as his executors, along with his solicitor, James Ogilvy Shepherd. Under this he made two annuities, to be paid quarterly: £400 for his brother John, and £52 to 'my servant Sergeant Thomas Secrett, in recognition of his long and faithful service to me [. . .]' The two witnesses to this were Secrett himself and Lieutenant-General Alex H. Gordon. This will also instructed the trustees to pay Doris an income of £3,000 a year, 'free of all deductions in respect of Income Tax and Super Tax.' The seventh condition of his disposition made George, his only son, the sole inheritor of all his property, subject to the financial arrangements for John, Doris and Secrett, upon George reaching twenty-one years of age; any remaining income from the inheritance was to be added to the capital sum or used for Haig's surviving family, as the trustees deemed appropriate.

So it might be imagined that, although the emotional shock was terrible, once the estate was sorted out the family should at least have been comfortable. Haig had in fact revised his will in September 1926, withdrawing the annuity from Secrett[18] and appointing new trustees, Wolseley Haig and James Ogilvy Shepherd having died; the two new trustees were Colonel Bertie D. Fisher, Commandant of the Cavalry Brigade, and Haig's nephew, Major-General Hugo Douglas De Pree, then Commandant of the Royal Military Academy at Woolwich.[19] The inventory of Haig's personal estate, recorded at Duns in Scotland on 23 July 1928, showed he left more than £18,853 in cash, shares and realized value on sold items such as two vehicles, from which had to be deducted almost £6,605 for debts and funeral expenses. Land and buildings were valued at another £12,110. The inventory also contains a reference to an 'account no. 4' – there are no other details – which was valued at more than £146,675 and on which, according to the solicitors who drew up the inventory, Messrs W. & J. Ogilvy Shepherd of Leven, 'duty is not now paid', giving a total estate of £171,033. His estate was liable for 23 per cent death duty on almost £24,659, (amounting to £5,671, rounded down), suggesting a total final inheritance of more than £165,000, excluding the £100,000 war gratuity.

In today's money, this estate would be worth more than £28 million. Conservatively invested in government bonds, it would perhaps have yielded almost £5,000 in annual income at the time. Not all the estate could be so invested – Bemersyde and the land, for instance – but even a lesser sum of perhaps £100,000, cautiously invested, would have given an annual income of some £3,000 a year.[20] This was not inordinate riches but neither was it penury, and it was, coincidentally, the sum Haig had in mind for Doris when he first drew up his will. Yet his death appears to have thrown the family into not just emotional but also financial turmoil, as recalled by his son: 'My mother wasn't very well afterwards, and she had a lot of strains and stresses, including financial difficulties. None of my father's directorships came any more, nor indeed any of his pay, and we were saddled with a large house and lots of servants and inadequate money to pay them with. So most of the servants had to go, and we really had to cut down. It was a cold wind that started blowing.'[21] While it is possible that the collapse of stock markets in 1929 affected some of the family's investments, it seems more plausible that, rather than facing serious financial distress, Lady Haig was so distraught in her bereavement that she suffered an entirely understandable emotional collapse. Haig also unintentionally left his widow a poisoned chalice, in the sixth provision of his will: 'I have written certain Diaries in connection with the recent Great War. I hereby authorise my Trustees to publish the same and any other writings or papers which I may leave, and that at such time or times and on such terms and conditions as they, in their uncontrolled discretion may think fit; and until such publication the said Diaries and other writings and papers shall remain in the custody of my said wife [. . .]'

This left a certain ambiguity concerning the legal rights over Haig's diaries, especially those from the Great War. Haig may have considered that his diaries, if properly handled, would be potentially lucrative for his family; given his position and the diaries' contents – acerbic criticisms of his French, American and other allies, as well as barbed references to politicians, journalists and other individuals – they would have been a publishing sensation had they appeared quickly after his death. Doris certainly thought the handwritten version was for the trustees, her included, to use as they saw fit. In a letter from June 1928 to a South

African friend, she wrote: 'You ask me about the publishing of the diary. I am in a curious position about it. The big diary which I typed for Douglas and has official papers attached, is only to be published if I get the leave of Trustees. But it has so many letters, and the leave of so many would have to be asked that I cannot do that during my life time or even perhaps the boy will not be able to. But the original diary in Douglas's own handwriting, is my own property and I can do anything that I like with it. It is at times very tempting because I am terribly poor, living here [Bemersyde]. As yet not had a penny and debts just piling up. But I must pause and realise what is best to do and meanwhile suffer [. . .]'[22]

Doris contemplated publishing the diaries soon after Haig's death but she was blocked by the very institution that had done so much to elevate Haig during his lifetime, and which he had served so dutifully – the monarchy. On 21 February 1928, Major-General Hugo De Pree informed her: 'Clive Wigram [George V's private secretary] tells me that he has written to you about the Diaries. The King told him to send for me the day the Will was published in the papers, & told him to let me know that he felt very strongly about their publication, and how averse he was to it. I do not know what you think about the matter, but without having consulted you, my opinion is that it would be a great mistake to publish them at the present time. The reasons are too long to give in a letter like this . . .'[23]

Brushing off Doris with the suggestion that the reasons 'were too long' to explain was disingenuous of De Pree. King George V would not, of course, have possessed any detailed knowledge of the contents of the diaries, but he was fully aware of Haig's prickly relations with Lloyd George and many others, and undoubtedly feared embarrassing revelations; his 'aversion' was a politely couched but nevertheless firm instruction not to publish. This was not what Doris wished to hear but, in deference to the king's wishes, the trustees, including Doris, agreed to withhold publication. This censorship inadvertently left the field free to be occupied by others who swiftly went into print with their own views of Haig and his role in the Great War.

Thomas Secrett's memoir of his master, a peculiar blend of the reverential and the personally damaging, appeared in late 1928, and while purportedly the testimony of a devoted servant, it nevertheless showed Haig to be occasionally gullible, obstinate and tight-fisted, as well as courageous, caring of his soldiers and staunchly determined. Haig's arch-enemy, Lloyd George, had no compunction about raking over old feuds, nor would he have permitted himself to be so hamstrung by the sovereign's sensitivities. The intense publicity which greeted each new instalment of his *War Memoirs*,[24] publication of which began in April 1933, included full-page and sometimes front-page write-ups in the *Daily Express* and *Daily Mail.* Lloyd George's sensationalist rhetoric received maximum attention at a time of extreme anti-war sentiment, and was to be largely responsible for the animus regarding Haig that has endured ever since. As the historian George Egerton has put it, the former Prime Minister ' "worked incessantly" to marshal the evidence behind his indictment of Haig and the Passchendaele campaign. He saw these chapters as the heart of the *War Memoirs*, and they went through many, many drafts. At stake was nothing less than the British people's memory of the Great War and their assessment of the nation's military and political leadership in directing the war effort and bringing ultimate victory [. . .] Lloyd George hinged his indictment of the British military elite on the case he builds against Haig.'[25] Lloyd George told his secretary in October 1934 he was 'very sick that Haig and Robertson were not alive. He intended to blow their ashes to smithereens in his fifth volume.'[26]

The *War Memoirs'* voluminous index entries on Haig alone are evidence of Lloyd George's lack of balance when it came to Haig, but his triumphal destruction of Haig's reputation rapidly became received wisdom. The *War Memoirs* 'were a success judged by all criteria of their intentional functions: they sold well and brought handsome financial rewards; they were reviewed widely and won literary praise; they helped keep the author in the front ranks of British politics through the thirties, although return to office eluded him; they settled old scores with deadly effect; and they powerfully vindicated his war leadership before contemporaries and posterity [. . .] what was at stake in the reception and impact of Lloyd George's *War Memoirs* was nothing less than the British memory and interpretation of the Great War.'[27]

Unsurprisingly, the *War Memoirs* contained no satisfactory explanation as to why their author, as Prime Minister and therefore in overall charge, had not sacked all the alleged blunderers. The society in which Lady Haig moved regarded Lloyd George as a scoundrel, both as a person and a politician, and, although he was a dangerous man to cross, she could not permit his view of her husband to go unchallenged. If she could not easily publish Haig's diaries verbatim (they would have amounted to several volumes), Doris could at least commission an authorized biography, whose author would be granted full access to the diaries, and so accomplish two purposes in one stroke – reinstate her husband's reputation and also earn some royalties for her and the children. She thus informed her fellow trustees that she wanted a biographer capable of doing full justice to the memory of her husband.

The diplomat, politician and popular author Alfred Duff Cooper, who was to become first Viscount Norwich in 1952, was eventually selected. His credentials were sound: an old Etonian, Duff Cooper had served with the Grenadier Guards in the final year of the Great War, winning the DSO. He had also published in 1932 a critically acclaimed biography of the French diplomat Talleyrand. He knew, however, that he had not been the first choice: 'On Thursday morning, March 23 [1933], I was told that General Fisher, Director of Recruiting, wished to speak to me. I imagined it was some small matter of routine. [Duff Cooper was then Financial Secretary to the War Office.] He seemed nervous and began by telling me he was one of Lord Haig's executors. I thought it had to do with the long dispute that has been going on about his equestrian statue.[28] He then told me that he wanted me to write Haig's life. I was astonished and immediately thought of all my disqualifications [. . .] They had offered the job first to John Buchan, who had accepted but Lady Haig had taken strong exception and had written him an insulting letter. The matter was dropped for the time and later George Trevelyan was approached. He had at first liked the idea but had finally refused on the ground that he had done nothing of the kind before and that it would interfere with his other work. Then, having over-persuaded Lady Haig, they had gone back to Buchan but he refused to reconsider it. [. . .] I shall insist on being given a completely free hand to put in or leave out what I like and to make the book whatever length I please.'[29]

Duff Cooper's is an elegantly written biography, distributing deference and generosity towards Haig in equal portion without in the least pleasing Doris, although, by excluding any quotations from Haig's diary that betrayed his subject's lofty contempt for his French allies, it did enormous disservice to historical accuracy. Duff Cooper raised no uncomfortable questions concerning Haig's rise to the top; he delicately hinted at the political back-stabbing Haig had endured during the Great War; he amply demonstrated the nightmarish complexities involved in the management of the BEF. But for Lady Haig only a secular canonization of her late husband and a simultaneous verbal destruction of Lloyd George would have sufficed. Duff Cooper was too judicious a politician and too intelligent a writer for either task. The entry for 30 April 1933 of his published diary gives a flavour of the problems he had with Haig's widow: 'All is now settled with regard to the life of Haig. The great difficulty that was expected to arise in connection with Lady Haig has been overcome. It was thought that she would not agree to my writing it. She is hardly sane and impossible to deal with. [. . .] Lady Haig lives alone in a flat in Edinburgh and will see nobody. [. . .] Lady Haig made very little objection and has signed a letter which will commit her.'[30]

Almost immediately following the commissioning of Duff Cooper to write his account, Doris decided to write her own biography, one that would truly vindicate her dead husband. The unintended consequence of this was that she progressively alienated those few remaining allies and friends she (and Haig himself) possessed, as Haig's son later recognized: 'My mother alienated some people because of her protectiveness of my father's reputation. Among them was Duff Cooper who wrote the official and excellent biography. My mother felt that, because of his different make-up, Duff Cooper could not understand my father. She, as a Trustee, had been responsible for his appointment and she was ill-advised to go against him. [. . .] Sadly she must have been lacking in sound advisers who might have helped her to resolve the difficulties with Duff Cooper.'[31]

But Doris did not lack for sound advisers; her fellow trustees, who had been carefully chosen by Haig, should have been permitted to sign up Buchan, who would have produced the kind of resounding riposte to Lloyd George that Doris sought. Duff Cooper, who throughout acted with complete scrupulousness, meanwhile had to contend with her increasingly bizarre behaviour. Faber & Faber contracted to pay £10,000 for Duff Cooper's biography, while Sunday Pictorial Newspapers agreed a further £10,000 for serial rights. Duff Cooper in turn contracted to pay 50 per cent of profits to the Haig Trust, of which Haig's children were the beneficiaries. Doris's decision to publish her own biography, which inevitably would compete against Duff Cooper's, was hubristic in the extreme as well as financially naive. Absurdly, she claimed to have been deceived by Duff Cooper into thinking that he would write a biography without any quotations from Haig's diaries or letters, which she had loaned him as source materials for his book. She wrote: 'You will remember that I very kindly sent you this material only to help you with a Biography, namely a Life written and not actual quotations from the diary, unless permission is given, and certainly not actual material written by me in preparation for publication. During our second or third interview [. . .] you mentioned that you were using my description of our marriage and engagement, but of course you had no right to do this, and I have never granted you permission.'[32]

When Duff Cooper learned in 1934 that Doris had embarked on a competing biography, he understandably became anxious that sales of his book would be damaged. Doris failed to see this, writing: 'I cannot agree with you that the publication of this material [her book] should in any way damage the sale of your Biography. After all I presume that your work will not contain more of my husband's own writings than is necessary to bear out your own personal views on the subject, thus it is difficult to see where the two volumes overlap.'[33] Her real problem, sadly, was that Haig's death had left her permanently distraught. As she acknowledged in a letter to Duff Cooper on 20 September 1934: 'I feel myself the Custodian of my husband's memory.'[34]

Doris even quarrelled with her two fellow trustees, who tried to persuade her to drop her own book idea. She declined to listen and, in a letter to De Pree on 18 January 1935, wrote: 'I wish to point out to you too; that the responsibility of the choice of Mr Duff Cooper as Biographer lies on yourself and General Fisher (remembering the state of my health at the time, which my Doctor can confirm.) That the amount of money brought into the Estate by this Publication is also only the responsibility of you two Trustees.'[35] She added that she intended 'to claim on Mr Duff Cooper's book the income due to me, as per my husband's will, namely £3,000 per year free of all taxes, etc etc and any other monies that are legally due to me [...]', as well as the hopelessly over-optimistic claim that she would stand to gain from her own version of Haig's life 'at least £80,000 (including royalties) [almost £14 million in today's terms] and perhaps much more.'

This was a complete fantasy, based upon her misconception as to the importance of her husband and the public's estimation of him which, seven years after his death, was already in decline, partly as a result of Lloyd George's publishing success. Even the former Prime Minister's phenomenally successful *War Memoirs* did not earn as much as Doris expected to gain from her book. Major-General De Pree exasperatedly replied on 25 January 1935: 'His [Duff Cooper's] choice was the best we could make after years of enquiry and effort, and has been approved on all sides. It is ridiculous for you now to say that you did not agree to the choice, or that you did not approve of it afterwards. You told me you thought he was an excellent man for the work – you got on very well with him and yourself helped him and lent him the papers at Bemersyde. A letter of yours is extant to show that you thoroughly approved of him. [...] I have told you several times that the sum of £80,000 for your publication is considered fantastic by the best authorities. Whatever you may have been promised you would never get it. As regards Gen. Fisher and myself taking action about the damage or loss which you say Mr Duff Cooper did to the papers, I do not see what action we can take. You lent him the papers, we do not know which they were, or what state they were in before and after he had them – he strenuously denies that he damaged them, and we know that the chief one which he was supposed to have lost, the Atbara print [a print of the skirmish in the Sudan], was found in your own possession. In the circumstances I personally am not prepared to fall out with Mr Duff Cooper over this matter. [. . .] I do wish we could get to understand one another's views instead of going on working at cross purposes.'

Despite this plea, Doris pressed ahead; her solicitor – appropriately, in the circumstances, named Ralph Risk – of the firm Maclay, Murray & Spens of Glasgow, sent her a letter dated 12 July 1935 with a publishing contract attached. She received no advance, itself an indication of the publisher's fear of poor sales, instead contenting herself with the promise of a large royalty of 20 per cent for all copies above 15,000 sold. Risk covered himself by informing her: '[. . .] it may be said that having regard to your original approval of Mr Duff Cooper as your husband's biographer, you are not acting in good faith in publishing a biography of your own prior to or contemporaneously with his.'

By now, Doris was uninterested in questions of good faith. She instructed her solicitors to send to her fellow trustees a letter, dated 17 August 1935, claiming that Duff Cooper had broken a promise he had made to her to show his book in manuscript, although no written evidence exists that such a promise had been made. The other trustees, Generals De Pree and Fisher, replied by appealing to her to permit Duff Cooper's book (the first volume of which appeared in 1935, the second the following year) to enjoy six months in the public domain before the appearance of her own; she refused, leaving them little choice but to take legal action against her on behalf of the Haig Trust, to try to prevent her book appearing simultaneously to Duff Cooper's, an action which she decided to defend. It was a suicidal case, as her solicitor stated in a letter dated 25 November 1935: 'One has also to bear in mind the expenses of the case, and the fact that you have said that of course you do not wish your son to be any worse off as a result of the case. If you were to win and recover your costs from the other side, as well as possibly recover damages in consequence of the publication having been delayed through the interdict which is granted at the risk of the other side, then such costs and damages would normally come out of the trust estate. I do not think it would be possible to make the Trustees themselves personally liable.'

Nevertheless, Doris obdurately persisted until the end of October 1936, when, in the Edinburgh Court of Session, Lord Carmont, the presiding judge, ruled that the petitioners (De Pree and Fisher), 'had made a prima facie case that Chapter 9 of her [Doris's] work had infringed copy right in a substantial part of her husband's war diaries'[36] and had thus caused loss to the estate. Carmont granted the petitioners an interim interdict against the publication of Lady Haig's competing book. With the odds now so obviously stacked against her, a deeply embittered Doris settled out of court, meanwhile conducting a private campaign of vilification against Duff Cooper. Her heavily edited book, which lawyers had crawled over to ensure did not directly compete with the authorized biography, was finally published on 4 December 1936,[37] soon after Duff Cooper's, and the same year as Lloyd George's final volume of *War Memoirs* appeared to overwhelming acclaim and which also saw the publication of *French Replies to Haig*, written by the former C-in-C's second son Gerald, which openly accused Haig of having been treacherous to his father.[38]

While Duff Cooper's biography received praise, Doris's disappeared, almost unnoticed. She lacked the public profile and political clout of the Welsh wizard; and while Duff Cooper fenced, Lloyd George pounded away with a mace, and to great effect. Churchill astutely adjusted his judgement on Haig after Duff Cooper's biography appeared, arguing almost a decade after his acclamation of Haig on his death that: 'Haig's mind [...] was thoroughly orthodox and conventional. He does not appear to have had any original ideas; no one can discern a spark of that mysterious, visionary, often sinister genius which has enabled the great captains of history to dominate the material factors, save slaughter, and confront their foes with the triumph of novel apparitions. [...] If Haig's mind was conventional, his character also displayed the qualities of the average, decent man concentrated and magnified. [...] He was rarely capable of rising to great heights; he was always incapable of falling below his standards.'[39]

Churchill's reassessment of Haig owed much to Duff Cooper's cool conclusion, one that infuriated Lady Haig: 'Genius, if it were, as it was once defined, an infinite capacity for taking pains, Haig might lay claim to; but not according to any other definition. There is no action that he took, no sentence that he wrote nor one recorded utterance bearing the hallmark of that rare quality which puts certain men in a separate category, dividing them by a thin but unmistakable line from those who possess the highest talents.'[40]

Haig was certainly no genius, but to suggest, rather romantically, that greatness is synonymous with genius, and that genius is the only quality to be strived for, does a disservice to Haig and the men he commanded. Haig's greatness ultimately was cut from the same cloth as that of the millions of men who served under him in the trenches, and it took the form of a gritty determination to stay put and not crack under the strain. Jan Smuts, against whom Haig had fought in the South African war and who had served in Lloyd George's Imperial War Cabinet, judiciously compared Haig with William of Orange: 'Of William of Orange it was said that he never won a victory, but in the end he won the war. [. . .] Haig had not the personal magnetism of many of the great personages of Europe. He was shy, reserved, and had a deep personal quality. There was no charlatanism in his nature. I suppose to be a great leader, you must to a certain extent be a charlatan – an actor, able to impress the unthinking world. Napoleon, Alexander, Hannibal, and the outstanding war leaders of the world were men who had not only supreme genius and supreme human qualities, but had this element to appeal to people. [. . .] In all these points of personal magnetism, Haig was wanting. He was much too solid and too Scotch for that sort of thing.'[41] Smuts was right; for the characteristic both Duff Cooper and Churchill found lacking in Haig was precisely the charlatanism that was the staple of Lloyd George.

Dorothy Haig's defeat in the courts, her publishing flop, the roaringly successful self-publicity of Lloyd George, all helped foster within her an increasingly unbalanced obsession with her husband's reputation. In

December 1938, she first cajoled and then threatened with legal action Leslie Hore-Belisha – who was, by coincidence, another Old Cliftonian had replaced Duff Cooper in 1937 as Secretary of State for War under Prime Minister Neville Chamberlain – in her efforts to revenge herself on Duff Cooper. No more was heard of the matter.[42] Almost her final public act, one that revealed how completely out of touch she was with the new world, was to insert in the Court Circular of *The Times* on 5 January 1939 the following: 'Countess Haig, who has been unwell for a very long time, is anxious to finish a book that she is writing, and therefore asks to be spared all unnecessary correspondence.'[43]

In a final humiliation, it was made evident that public interest in the life of Haig was, by the mid-1930s, almost extinguished. In an obscure court case in Edinburgh on 13 July 1939, which considered whether or not the Haig Trust should be liable for income tax on its portion (£10,000) of the advances received by Duff Cooper for his biography, it was ruled that the estate was not liable. Furthermore the court learned that 'royalties due on publisher's sales had not come up to the sum of £10,000 and it was unlikely that they ever would.' In other words, Duff Cooper's book had failed to earn out its advance, a failure as far as the publisher's commercial interest was concerned.

In recent years, many historians of the Great War have tried to shift the focus of attention away from personalities to technology, social forces, or the respective underlying economic strength of the powers involved, all of which are relevant but, ultimately, are controlled by human hands and guided by human minds; personality inevitably reasserts itself, despite the understandable desire to focus on matters open to more rational examination. Those who take against Haig have done everything to destroy his reputation, while his uncritical admirers, whose ranks have inevitably been thinned by the passage of time, have lost no opportunity to assert his unique, personal contribution to winning that appalling war. The truth is that Field Marshal Haig, or someone equally resolute, was necessary. The British and French Allies, together with their American associates, did not purposefully march to victory in the final one hundred days of war with a clearly elaborated or carefully constructed plan; they stumbled along in their advance, sometimes blindly, sometimes mistakenly, occasionally cleverly and always courageously, often surprised to find that first pockets, then whole swathes of the German army crumbled, burdened as they were by a growing sense that all was utterly lost. It was in a very real sense a victory; but one that took everyone, including Haig, by surprise. Haig's greatest contribution in mid-1918 was, finally, to delegate, and let others get on with their specific tasks. His contribution prior to that had been his own unflappable character – leadership, of a sort.

Haig's career is both more impressive, and the man less profound, than his enemies and friends have credited. His is an archetypal Victorian story of dogged upward progress, a progress initially funded by private wealth and later occasionally boosted by useful and cleverly exploited social connections. He rose through a series of hierarchies in the British army, an organization in which the need to conform sat uneasily alongside the pressure, which Haig recognized and to which he responded, to adapt and change. The evolution of Haig the soldier sometimes saw him reach beyond the ability of the army to change – for example, with Haldane at the War Office his vision as to how best prepare for a land war was both accurate and yet ultimately thwarted. Sometimes that evolution lagged behind the technological inventiveness of more creative spirits, such as that displayed at the Battle of Hamel in 1918. Had Haig been in Monash's place, it is likely that he might have planned that battle, a crucial step in the progress to the defeat of the Germans in November 1918, very differently; yet once he had glimpsed the possibilities of such a properly orchestrated attack, Haig immediately sanctioned their further development.

But what, finally, did Haig stand for? One of the last actions of his life was to sign a joint letter addressed to the boys of Clifton College, prompted by a visit of the Prince of Wales to Clifton. Haig, together with three other Old Cliftonians – Sir Herbert Warren, former Vice-Chancellor of Oxford University, J. H. Whitley, the former Speaker of the House of Commons and the third chairman of the BBC, and Sir Francis

Younghusband, the Tibetan adventurer – all put their names to an open letter composed by Sir Henry Newbolt.

In its high-minded, vague, but broadly inclusive way, the letter very well sums up what Haig took as his fundamental credo: '[. . .] Life has become more controversial; controversy is more violent; the unintelligent are perverting science into a new form of superstition; religion is in danger of being crushed out between the materialistic selfishness of the rich and luxurious and the materialistic hopes of the overworked and underpaid. [. . .] In the last forty or fifty years we have lived through times of great national prosperity and still greater danger and anxiety. These years have convinced us that no kind of life is complete, no kind of life can make the world intelligible or give us any lasting satisfaction unless there enters into it the element which is called Religion. We are not speaking of this or that form of religion, but of the impulse which is expressed in all such forms; the desire to find God in the universe and to understand our relation to Him. [. . .] Guidance and lasting satisfaction are, as we believe, to be found only in faith – in the assurance that the life of man progresses by conformity with a Universal Spirit and a divine beauty of character; so that every act and preference of every one of us is of immortal consequence, because it either helps or hinders the realization of the order which God is perpetually designing for the world.'[44]

The hero of what is perhaps one of the twentieth century's most reward-ing novels, Ford Madox Ford's *Parade's End*, also attended Clifton.[45] Through its central character, Christopher Tietjens, can be detected a subtle account of the code of honour aspired to by a man who wished to lead the virtuous life. While nominally *Parade's End* shares the same preoc-cupation of Newbolt's 'Vitaï Lampada', an exploration of what constitutes the highest moral behaviour for a late Victorian or early Edwardian, they are otherwise utterly divided, Newbolt's poem being a preaching, simplistic tract and Ford's novel a psychologically complex, hesitant exploration.

Douglas Haig was neither a creatively glib, morally hypocritical Newbolt,[46] nor an impossibly honourable, morally heroic Tietjens. The many millions of words left behind by Haig are almost entirely lacking in introspection, as if he were solely concerned with externals, with action or the lack of it; he was Laertes, not Hamlet. Indeed, had he been more self-analytical, he would perhaps have been less able to act. If nothing else, his subordinates and colleagues always took heart from being under the control of a commander who was unflinching, unbending, and who rarely floundered. His very lack of passion was, for some of his contemporaries, his most important characteristic, as identified by Esher, when he wrote: 'The noblest characters among our politicians and soldiers were Edward Grey, D. H. [Haig], Robertson [Field Marshal Sir William Robertson] and Kitchener. None of them were actuated ever by any but unselfish motives. [...] There were abler men, perhaps, than any of these, but they were many of them, consciously some and unconsciously others, moved by passion, and so do not show crystal clear.'[47]

While it is impossible to swallow Esher's claim that Haig, and still less Kitchener, was never selfishly motivated, it is nevertheless true that Haig's virtues of loyalty, dedication and determination, together with a willingness to delegate and an open-minded approach to technological innovation on the battlefield, were of critical importance in ensuring that the British army was able, in the end, to capitalize on Germany's internal collapse. Yet Haig lacked the creative spark of some of the Allied generals, most obviously Monash. He was not an initiator but an administrator. He was less intellectually gifted than some of his peers, such as Grierson. He was less passionate and spirited than others, such as Wilson, whose sense of the absurdity of human affairs the humourless Haig could never have shared.

In January 1915, Henry Wilson found that he had been completely ignored in the first New Year's honours list of the Great War. There was much adverse gossip at GHQ about this omission and Wilson felt wounded, but told a young officer that he was now 'going up in his balloon'. The young officer asked what he meant and Wilson replied: 'When I was young, my father [...] used to say – "Now, whenever you are a bit down and things don't seem to be quite what they should be, just go up in your balloon. As the world recedes, you will look over the side and will note how all objects, which bulked so large, and all the funny little men who seemed so prominent when you were on the earth, gradually diminish and diminish till they matter not at all. You will regain your sense of proportion, and a true perspective of the things that really matter." So I am now going up in my balloon.'[48]

There is something admirable about Wilson's ready wit and jocularity, even if he was forever scheming, and though his prognostications about the war were nearly always wrong. In contrast, Haig was no schemer in Wilson's mould, and he was consistently right in his overall judgement as to how the war would develop, despite his proclivity for grasping at straws at Loos, the Somme and Third Ypres. Of the two, Haig certainly made a better manager of the BEF, yet Wilson would no doubt have made a better companion in all other circumstances. The abiding wonder of Haig's life is not that he was in any way an exceptional man, but that this very conventional Victorian so typifies, for good and ill, the age in which he was raised and came to prominence. As Wilfred Bion, a junior officer in command of a small section of tanks in 1917–18 who went on to become a psychoanalyst, later wrote: 'Why a man with the defects common to all men became and remained Commander-in-Chief is a question which can only be answered, if ever, when it is known why an ordinary man comes to recognised be as "great" while all other ordinary men remain ordinary.'[49]

For many of his contemporaries, for whom the errors of the Somme and Passchendaele had hardly begun to be explored, Haig had, by his activities in his final decade, partially redeemed himself for having been the man who commanded so many to march to their death. A Doncaster clergyman, the Reverend Roy Machon, wrote to Doris on 2 September 1930 and enclosed a cutting from a local newspaper, detailing a service he had organized to commemorate what he referred to as 'Haig Day', on Sunday 2 February 1930. The cutting read: 'Canon Brook, in his address, said that they were there that day to honour the memory of a great man, a man who was great because he was good. Whether Douglas Haig was a great general was not for him to say. [. . .] Whatever might be the verdict of history on his services in the field it would not be chiefly for this he would hold an honoured place in the memory and affection of the English people. The services which Douglas Haig had rendered to the country since the war were greater than those he rendered during the war. [...] The British Legion was the great and abiding memorial to Douglas Haig, that great organisation which existed to keep alive among those who had served in the war, and to pass on to others that spirit of comradeship which the war created.'[50]

Haig himself never sought to be recognized as great, least of all as a genius; his modest ambition was to perform his duty – something he saw as being the responsibility of all citizens – as a loyal soldier to his king and country, and, through a fortunate blend of luck, opportunism, judgement and resilience, that is what he achieved. That the means he adopted to achieve this goal were often riddled with contradictions; that he was of his time and did not transcend the limitations of it and his own character; that his greatest flaw was to fail to understand, on the battlefields of Flanders in 1916 and 1917, the impossibility of achieving a lasting breakthrough – all these things are certainly true. But, rather than condemning Douglas Haig to lasting opprobrium, they should instead serve to remind us of his, and our own, human fallibility. Would the Allies have won the Great War without Haig? Almost certainly yes. Does that diminish his contribution? Arguably not.

# Afterword

War hath no fury like a non-combatant.

Charles Edward Montague

Vilify! Vilify! Some of it will always stick.

Pierre-Augustin Caron de Beaumarchais

Some of my most vivid childhood memories are those associated with the annual rituals around Armistice Day, which has now become conflated in our minds with Remembrance Day, a name lacking in any resonance or identifiable focus.[1] The televised Armistice Day service in the Royal Albert Hall was for me and my family as much a fixture in the calendar as Christmas or Easter. I remember my incredulity when my parents first told me that each of the poppies that fell from the rafters in the final, solemn stillness of the service represented a life lost in the Great War and the Second World War. Could, I wondered, so many have died?

I recall, too, the poppies sold during my childhood; they seem huge in my memory, with a deep red hue, and silken to the fingers. The poppy was fixed to one's buttonhole by means of a metal spike, which could be twisted to ensure that it stayed firmly in place. In each poppy's centre was a hard, black, deep button, made from bakelite or some similarly durable material, on which was a raised inscription – for me then very obscure – which simply read 'Haig Fund'. The 'Haig Fund' motto has disappeared from the mass-produced paper poppies which are today available in England, with their ugly bright green but child-friendly plastic stems, that refuse to attach the flower to a lapel with any reliability. When I last bought a Remembrance Day poppy, it was in 2005 in Edinburgh – where the charity established in 1921 by Douglas Haig, the Earl Haig Fund, still

exists, supplied with its poppies by an Edinburgh factory established by
his widow in 1926 – and I was pleasantly surprised to see it still had 'Haig
Fund' inscribed on its black centre. Elsewhere, however, the field marshal
whose name was once carried by poppies everywhere in Britain, in
recognition of his and his wife's charitable efforts, has disappeared,
symbolizing the slump in Haig's reputation, outside Scotland at least.[2]

Esteem for Britain's generals of the Great War has, by and large, been
in uninterrupted decline since the end of that conflict, and Haig's
posthumous reputation has suffered more than most. When, at the age
of fifteen, I prepared for the GCE English literature examination, my
class was introduced to a selection of Great War poets – Owen, Sassoon,
Sorley and others – and I drank deeply of their sombre depictions of
horror, anguish and death. From them I, like thousands of others,
learned that it was not difficult to understand who the real enemy was –
not the German army, but the British generals. This immature
judgement was not the fault of the poets; yet it is an interpretation of
their work that lingers in the recesses of the minds of all those who, as
fifteen-year-olds, have been introduced to the poetry and novels of
post–1918 disillusionment.

Those of us living in Britain in the first decade of the twenty-first
century cannot really appreciate that the euphoria in London, Paris and
Washington which greeted news of the Armistice on 11 November 1918
was not inspired simply by relief that the war was, finally, all over, but also
by a genuine sense of victory. Haig was an enormously popular figure in
the days and months that followed, and his steely imperviousness – his
defining characteristic – was the very quality most admired. The popular
joy that greeted a victorious conclusion to the Great War inevitably
soured, as the British and Dominion soldiers who returned home
gradually gave their graphic eyewitness accounts, not just of heroism but
also of manifest incompetence and, from their inevitably very narrow
individual perspectives, waste and futility. The agglomeration of this mass
personal experience inescapably engendered a sense of bitterness, as well
as a growing need to identify and blame those responsible. As it became
increasingly clear that they had returned to a land very far from one fit for

heroes, a questioning of all authority – including that of the BEF's military leadership – took firmer hold.

There was no single moment when Britain's generals slipped from their pedestals and became acceptable targets of public vilification. Lloyd George's *War Memoirs*, although widely known through their newspaper serialization, were so voluminous that they probably were read in full only by very few. The rash of angry and disillusioned post-war novels made a much greater and longer-lasting impact, even though, as Douglas Jerrold pointed out in 1930, one unifying factor of these novels was that they falsely depicted the tragedy of the war as 'the death of so many men whose duty it was to live, whereas the real tragedy was that duty offered no alternative but death.'[3] Jerrold's revisionist efforts failed; six years later, C. S. Forester published *The General*, which built on preceding anti-war novels and devastated the reputation of Britain's Great War generals.

Forester was fourteen when that war broke out and thus did not serve. *The General* proved so popular that, or so rumour has it, Adolf Hitler made it required reading for the Wehrmacht's general staff in the Second World War. Forester depicted Britain's Great War generals as unintelligent, complacent and unimaginative, deeply suspicious of creative thought, and quiescent in the face of stupid orders from above, for fear of being sacked. Most damagingly of all, his novel suggested that they were uninterested in innovation – in doing things better. Forester depicted their planning conferences as 'like the debate of a group of savages as to how to extract a screw from a piece of wood. Accustomed only to nails, they had made one effort to pull the screw out by main force [. . .] They could hardly be blamed for not guessing that by rotating the screw it would come out after the exertion of far less effort; it would be a notion so different from anything they had ever encountered that they would laugh at the man who suggested it.'[4]

This image succeeds not only because it is memorable but because it has a grain of truth. When war broke out, Haig and other senior officers could do nothing more than use the tools they had to hand. Haig recognized from the start that those tools were inadequate for the task confronting the BEF. As the war progressed, the existing tools were refined through experience, and new tools – the tank and better techniques of artillery spotting especially – became, often with painful slowness, more widely available. Some senior officers on Haig's staff at GHQ, such as Kiggell, clearly failed to comprehend the potential of these new tools and, worse, discouraged others from the hope that they could be improved or used more creatively. But others, Haig included, endorsed and promoted new technology and refinements whenever available and practical.

As it was, the inevitable delays in gearing up British industry to produce more and better tanks, aircraft, range-spotting devices for artillery, a better fuze for shells, and other improvements to essential weapons, all played their part in what now seems an unendurable crawl towards creating the optimal circumstances for the eventual victory of November 1918. Yet if Britain and its allies progressed only by harsh experience, their opponents in many respects failed to learn critical lessons, even when these were painfully administered. What is rarely remembered today is that, for all its repute as an efficient and sophisticated military machine, the German army resolutely turned its face against the tank in the Great War, never possessing more than fifteen of their own design and production as well as a few Mark IV tanks captured from the BEF.[4] All armies on the Western Front in August 1914 – ignoring the ideas of Ivan Bloch – had trained and prepared for a war of movement, and such was the relative primitiveness of the military technology available that neither the Germans nor the British or French could envisage any means of lasting success other than more artillery and shells – an only slightly more sophisticated version of a battering-ram – to try to break through and return to open warfare.

The innovation which truly worked – a combined assault involving infantry, armour, artillery and aircraft – took time and harsh experience to evolve and had numerous authors, and while Haig was not one of them, he early on recognized the importance of technological advances on the battlefield and did his best to promote them.

Technological improvements (to tanks and aircraft and wireless communication) had finally, by August 1918, caught up with the needs of the battlefield. In these circumstances, to blame Haig is therefore to blame all his peers, too. Ultimately, Haig possessed one priceless quality lacking in many of his contemporaries (and which ultimately deserted his opponents): a determination never to budge an inch.

After his death, Haig's widow – with occasionally unbalanced ardour – pursued a campaign to have her husband acclaimed as one of the greatest British generals in history. Her struggle to achieve this end has been continued, with much greater pragmatism but no less vigour, by their son, George, the second Earl Haig, whom I met at Bemersyde when I was researching this book, and who retains an enormous pride in his father and a deep affection for both his parents. Walking the grounds at Bemersyde I could finally understand the deep affection the field marshal had for the place, and why he always longed to return to its tranquillity and natural beauty. The second Earl Haig has the impecc-able manners and generously trusting nature of a bygone age. But he brooks no criticism of his father and mother. Prickly on the subject of the family's financial position following his father's death, and fiercely dismissive of a recent less than reverential biography of his father – the biographer in question, Gerard de Groot, 'didn't understand anything', according to Earl Haig, although it may be fairer to say that de Groot understood a great deal but was utterly unsympathetic – even at his advanced age, the field marshal's son has not tired of defending his father's reputation. As I left Bemersyde, Earl Haig grasped my hand and, ensuring that he had my complete attention, emphatically said: 'He won the war, you know.' It is very difficult to spend a day as the guest of a hospitable, intelligent person and then openly dispute something that has been one of their principal missions in life. I think that in response I demurred, saying what I genuinely believe to be the case: 'Well, he certainly *helped* to win it.'

Before starting this book, I shared in what I presumed was received wisdom concerning Haig's professional qualities – at best unimaginative, at worst utterly incompetent and out of his depth. He is a hard character to like, not least because 'being liked' was never very high on his list of ambitions. In life, Douglas Haig sharply divided opinion and that gulf has endured to this day, but in the course of writing this book I have, almost without realizing it, moved from grudging respect to something close to admiration for his virtues, which superficially appear to be minor but which, on closer consideration, are actually rather important. Among them, I most respect his sheer tenacity, his refusal ever to give up, whether it be over his entry to Staff College or his struggles with Lloyd George or his refusal to consider the possibility of defeat by Germany. Of course, the obverse of this virtue is the vice of stubbornness, from which Haig often suffered, to the cost of the men he commanded in the latter stages of the Somme and Third Ypres.

The way in which Haig early grasped the manner in which power and influence can be acquired through the making and cultivation of the right connections also provides a salutary object lesson, and one that I suspect has not lost any of its relevance today. I do not admire the fact that this is how power is won or exercised; but I do respect Haig's instinctive ability to make the system he lived within work to his own benefit. More profoundly, Haig's unwavering belief that there are higher duties than obedience to the transient whims of politicians and public acclaim is an aspect of his character that was unknown to me and which, as I grow older myself, becomes increasingly compelling. Haig's steeliness when he stood at the pinnacle of the BEF, his unshakeable sense that duty transcends the reach of any mere politician, even his insensitivities and imperviousness to the swirl of rumours and gossip which surrounded him – and which might have drowned someone given to greater introspection – were vital qualities that enabled him to hold himself and his army together in the most desperate of circumstances. The Finns have an almost untranslatable word for it – *sisu*, which might be defined as an innately courageous determination to see something through to the end, bitter or not.

My own view of Haig is that, while he was just a man, with any man's petty frailties, he nevertheless embodied some moral absolutes that we have lost, and greatly to our detriment. Of course, he ordered men – many thousands of men – to march to their death; and, like all generals throughout history, he sometimes commanded his soldiers' personal ultimate sacrifice when it should have been evident, even to Haig himself, that such a sacrifice was futile. His stoicism, self-discipline, courage and unshakeable determination to defend the inviolability of British interests are anachronisms in today's society, one in which public figures, at the drop of a hat, lay bare their souls, beat their breasts, thump tubs, even if they have very little to say.

Haig would have regarded such emoting as deeply vulgar and destructive of human dignity. He would have loathed contemporary society, not for the dramatic changes technology has wrought, nor even for its flattening out of social distinctions, but for its having forgotten that we not only all have rights but that we also all have duties. He may not have been a general fortunate to have been born with innate military genius – although we tend to forget that even the greatest of such supposed geniuses were largely indifferent to the slaughter of their own soldiers – but paradoxically he acquires greater moral stature as time passes. The time should be at an end when Haig is pilloried, even if there will never be a time when he is worthy of canonization. One of the obligations imposed on historical biographies is to try to remember the dead without fear or favour, but with respect for all the known facts. That has been the aim of this book.

# NOTES

## Introduction

1 *Queen Victoria*: Lytton Strachey (Penguin edition, 1978), page 240.

2 The slogan was invented in 1934, six years after Douglas Haig's death, for a print advertising campaign created by the advertising agency Lord & Thomas.

3 Vitriolic expressions of anti-Haig sentiment take their inspiration from David Lloyd George's *War Memoirs*. Later exemplars are *British Butchers and Bunglers of World War One*: John Laffin (Sutton, 1988), and *Haig's Command*: Denis Winter (Viking, 1991). Winter's numerous factual errors have been pinpointed by scholars; see especially John Hussey, 'The Case Against Haig: Mr Denis Winter's Evidence', published in *Stand To!*, the magazine of the Western Front Association.

4 Hansard, 5 May 1921.

5 *Afterthoughts*: Frances, Countess of Warwick (Cassell, 1931), pp 222–3. It seems she did not spot the joke.

6 *The Times*, 31 January 1928.

7 *Curzon*: David Gilmour (John Murray, paperback edition, 2003), page 492.

8 *Great Britain and the War of 1914–1918*: Sir Llewellyn Woodward (Methuen, 1972), page 140.

9 John Terraine, The Douglas Haig Fellowship Records, Issue No 3, 1996.

10 The moustache is easily explained; at the time Haig joined the army in 1885 it was Queen's Regulations that officers were not permitted to shave their upper lip. This was still King's Regulations during the Great War.

11 De Groot, in *Haig – A Reappraisal 70 Years On*: ed. Brian Bond and Nigel Cave (Leo Cooper, 1999), page 39.

12 *The First World War, An Illustrated History*: A. J. P. Taylor (Penguin Books, 1966), pp 105–6.

13 *The Unquiet Western Front*: Brian Bond (Cambridge University Press, 2002), page 61. Bond reminds readers that Raymond Fletcher, a Labour MP who

acted as the military adviser to Joan Littlewood's Theatre Workshop Group for its production of *Oh! What a Lovely War*, worked as a Soviet agent during the Cold War.

14 NLS Acc 3155 No 64: letter from Montgomery, dated 7 August 1969, to Colonel Sir Henry Abel Smith.

15 General Sir Launcelot Kiggell served Haig for a period as his Chief of General Staff at General Headquarters in France.

16 Haig and other GHQ staff paid regular visits to the front lines throughout the war and while some cosseted staff officers probably had no direct experience of conditions at the front, this was not true of Haig nor of most of his senior commanders.

17 There are comparatively few statues of Haig. Apart from the one in Whitehall, there is another at Clifton College, the public school he attended in Bristol, another in Edinburgh, and one in Montreuil, near where he had his GHQ during the Great War. The Montreuil statue was his wife's favourite, although it currently (2007) is in a state of some neglect, vandals having broken the scabbard in half.

18 6 November 1998. With delicious irony, sitting beneath the headline was a large red poppy, symbol of the fund that Haig and his wife established after the war to assist disabled ex-servicemen and their families.

19 *Sunday Telegraph*, 7 May 2000.

20 *The History Boys*: Alan Bennett (Faber and Faber, 2004), pp 23–4.

21 Academic historians have been redressing the balance. See Dan Todman's book *The First World War: Myth and Memory* (Hambledon Continuum, 2005) and Ian Beckett and Steven Corvi's book *Haig's Generals* (Leo Cooper, 2006), for a sample of the changing perspective.

22 *Love and the Loveless*: Henry Williamson (Sutton, 1997), page 314.

23 Quoted in *Haig: A Reappraisal 70 Years On*: ed. Brian Bond and Nigel Cave, op. cit., page 256.

24 John Bourne, in *Haig: A Reappraisal 70 Years On*, op. cit., pp 2–3.

25 *The Spectator*, 21 January 2006, 'Will Haig end up as a cuddly toy?'.

26 See, for example, a pamphlet designed for use in secondary school history classes in the UK, *General Haig: Butcher or War Winner?*, Josh Brooman (Longman, 1998): 'The more that people came to know about the horrors and the costs of the war, the more they looked for someone to blame. They looked especially at the generals who had sent their men into battle. Who was more obvious to blame than the Commander-in-Chief, Sir Douglas Haig?' page 46.

27 Robin Prior and Trevor Wilson, *Australian War Memorial Journal*, October 1993, page 57.

28  Foreword to *Field Marshal Haig*: Brigadier-General John Charteris, (Cassell, 1929).

29  J. M. Bourne, in 'Haig and the Historians', in *Haig: A Reappraisal 70 Years On*, op. cit.

30  *The Man I Knew*: The Countess Haig (Moray Press, 1936), page vii.

31  Douglas Scott published an edition of Haig's diaries and letters between 1861–1914, *The Preparatory Prologue* (Pen & Sword, 2006), a virtuous homage by a dutiful grandson of Haig.

32  Perhaps the most egregious example of this is to be found in Norman Dixon's *On The Psychology of Military Incompetence* (Pimlico, 1994).

33  *Haig*: Duff Cooper (Faber & Faber, 1935).

34  *The Man I Knew*: The Countess Haig, op. cit.

35  *Douglas Haig, The Educated Soldier*: John Terraine (Hutchinson, 1963).

36  *Field Marshal Haig*: Philip Warner, The Bodley Head, 1991; Cassell reprint, 2003.

37  *Douglas Haig, 1861–1928*: Gerald De Groot, Unwin Hyman, 1988.

38  *Architect of Victory*: Walter Reid (Birlinn, 2006).

39  There are various methods of measuring the relative value of money across time. The most appropriate in this case is to compare average earnings, which is the average of all workers of weekly wages, non-cash (in-kind) payments, bonuses, commissions, and piece-rate payments. This measure is arguably the best to obtain relative value for income or wealth, which is what we are most concerned with in the case of Haig. This can yield some startling results. They reflect, however, not just the income or wealth of the class from which Haig derived, but also the *relative position* of that class and individuals within it. I have used the on-line calculator at http://measuringworth.com developed by two economists – Professor Lawrence H. Officer (University of Illinois) and Professor Samuel H. Williamson (Miami University) – in estimating Haig's income and wealth at various stages of his career. This is a fairly broad-brush statistical approach, but it is useful for demonstrating the relative financial position Haig occupied in his society.

40  *The Pound in Your Pocket*: Peter Wilsher (Cassell, 1970), page 30.

# Chapter One

1  The distillery is still working although it now produces Gordon's gin and is owned by United Distillers and Vintners (UDV), part of the Diageo drinks conglomerate.

2  Equivalent to almost £7 million in contemporary terms.

3 Douglas Haig also became a Freemason. It appears his interest was rather passive but it is striking that many of his later influential friends and supporters were, too.

4 Douglas Haig joined the board of DCL (Distillers Company Ltd) in 1894. Although the distilleries were part of DCL, the blending company John Haig & Co only became part of DCL in 1919.

5 *The Rise and Fall of Class in Britain*: David Cannadine (Columbia University Press, 1999), page 108.

6 *Winnowed Memories*: Field Marshal Sir Evelyn Wood VC (Cassell, 1918), page 378.

7 NLS Acc 3155 No 322.

8 *A New England? Peace and War, 1886–1918*: G. R. Searle (Oxford University Press, 2004), page 2.

9 The Haig children sometimes spelled her name 'Rachael'; on Douglas's birth certificate it is spelled 'Rachel' and that version is adopted here.

10 Despite his strong will Haig was also modest and this trait was as genuine as his others. It appears to have extended even to the family name. His niece Ruth De Pree wrote to congratulate him on his appointment as C-in-C of the BEF in December 1915 and told him: 'You have made the name of Haig illustrious – hitherto it has been celebrated merely by reproducing its species and keeping Thomas the Rhymer's prophesy true!' To which he replied: 'There has been no celebrated man in the family, and the quicker it dies out the better.'

11 *The Haigs of Bemersyde*: John Russell (William Blackwood, 1881), pp 393–5.

12 NLS Acc 3155 No 346.

13 William Henry, the first child, was born in February 1841. He died in June 1884, when Douglas was 25. The second, Mary Elizabeth, was born 1 April 1843. She married Lieutenant-Colonel George De Pree, and died in December 1918. The third was Hugh ('Hugo') Veitch, born February 1845. He married his cousin Anne Fraser, and died in February 1902. Janet ('Jenty') was born in 1847. She too married a cousin, Charles Edwin Haig, and died in February 1924. A fifth child, a daughter named Alicia (Lally), was born in 1849 but died in 1857. Henrietta Frances was born 17 April 1851 and died 25 April 1928, three months after Douglas. Another son was born in 1853 but died the same year, while in 1855, Dorothea was born, only to die two years later. The ninth child, John ('Bee'), was born on 5 April 1857. George ('Georgie' and 'Geordie') was born in July 1859; he married Augusta, and died in 1905.

14 Of married women born between 1851–5 in England and Wales, 15 per cent had ten or more confinements. *Changing Family Size in England & Wales: Place, Class & Demography 1891–1911*: edited by Eilidh Garratt, Alice Reid, Kevin Schurer and Simon Szreter (Cambridge University Press, 2001).

15 She was 59 when she died.

16 NLS Acc 3155 No 3a.

17 Even at the height of the Great War in January 1917, by which time the British army had no choice but to admit to its officer class many who previously would not have been considered 'gentlemen', Lord Northcliffe, the irascibly overbearing press baron and certainly no gentleman, abruptly stopped during a visit to Haig's GHQ in France and remarked, apropos of nothing, to John Charteris: 'What an enormous advantage it must be to be a gentleman, like Sir Douglas.' [*At G.H.Q.*: Brig-Gen John Charteris, 1931, page 189.] Northcliffe's long-standing support of Haig owed much to this sense of social status.

18 *The Rise and Fall of Class in Britain*, op. cit., page 95.

19 *My Father's Son: The Memoir of Dawyck Haig*: The Earl Haig (Leo Cooper, 2000), page 1.

20 Letter from his mother to DH dated 15 July 1875: NLS ACC 3155 No 3a.

21 NLS Acc 3155 No 322.

22 In a letter dated 8 March 1920, when Henrietta was in her sixty-ninth year, she sought Douglas's advice in trying to resolve an emotional battle over an unnamed woman who had latched onto her husband:

> Darling Docky,
>
> Yours of the 5th came yesterday – all you say is most sensible and I will gladly meet Willie half way & try to make this place a Home for him, but I fear there is not likely to be a 'half way'. He wants everything to be <u>his</u> way. On Saturday he told me he is anxious the girl should go home to Australia, but sometimes she says she won't go – He thinks she is mad, and asked me to look on her as not normal & make allowances. She is very rude to me & he says she is the same to him – she certainly is not making his life happy – If he is even civil to me it makes her angry – I said to Willie if he considers she is off her head we better get Maurice Craig* to see her & he agreed.
>
> It is so good of you to say you will try & get her a passage – I told Willie, & he said 'she refuses to leave me' so there it is – a deadlock–
>
> Willie says they are going to London on Thursday – I don't think I will go as he refuses to pay my allowance – & I am not going to stay with them until he does. Do you not think I am right? [. . .] Willie told me the cause of her anger against me just now is because of some letters of mine she read before she came here.
>
> It turns out she ransacked my private writing table and read all she could find – among others a [spirit-world] letter from Geordie which was not complimentary to her & has caused offence! I asked Willie if he

did not tell her she had done a dishonourable thing – & he said he did – but she has no feeling whatsoever. I am wondering if Willie is speaking truthfully when he told me he wants her to go home?

I want to see you Docky – & think I shall go over the beginning of next week.

best love to Doris and <u>thank you</u>.

yr loving sister

Henrietta.

(*The great mental specialist, Percy's man)

23  Conversation with author, February 2005.
24  *Field-Marshal Earl Haig*: Charteris, op. cit., page 3.
25  *The Man I Knew*: The Countess Haig, op. cit., page 10.
26  NLS 3155 No 322, memoir by John Haig.
27  De Groot, in *Haig: A Reappraisal 70 Years On*: ed. Bond and Cave, op. cit., page 38.
28  Douglas's elder brother Hugo, who clearly *was* a hypochondriac, showed what even a supposedly sick Victorian male could pack away at one dinner on Easter Sunday 1883 in France, when he gobbled up '12 oysters, a whole chicken, a rice pudding besides a glass of strong gravy from our own mutton, spinach and potatoes, No wonder he had a little discomfort.' (Haig diary, 1883, entry for Sunday 25 March: NLS Acc 3155 No 1.)
29  De Pree, *Memoirs of her Uncle Douglas Haig*, NLS, Haig Papers.
30  *On The Psychology of Military Incompetence*: Norman Dixon, op. cit., page 376.
31  NLS 3155 No 3a.
32  NLS MS 28001.
33  *The Mid-Victorian Generation 1846–1886*: K. Theodore Hoppen (Oxford University Press, 1998), pp 501–2.
34  NLS 3155 No 1.
35  *The Rise of Respectable Society*: F. M. L. Thompson (Fontana, 1988), page 66.
36  *Haig*, Vol.I: Duff Cooper (Faber & Faber, 1935), page 18.
37  NLS Acc 3155 No 251.
38  In *War, Economy and the Military Mind*: ed. Geoffrey Best and Alexander Wheatcroft (Croom Helm, 1976), page 9.
39  NLS 3155 No 3a.
40  NLS 3155 No 3a.
41  The first, Charles Evans, was appointed at the start of 1861 but resigned in August 1862 to become head of King Edward's School in Birmingham.
42  Established in 1878, shortly before Haig left, Polack's House closed in July 2005, after 127 years.

43 *Centenary Essays on Clifton College*: ed. N. G. L. Hammond (J. W. Arrowsmith, 1962), page 1.

44 Ibid., page 13.

45 *Classes and Cultures, England 1918–1951*: Ross McKibbin (Oxford University Press, 1998), page 244.

46 The family could easily afford such foreign travel: 'a six weeks' Cooks package tour for two people, starting from London and taking in the Rhine, Switzerland, and France, cost about £85 in the early 1870s, three to four months' salary of a senior clerk at the height of his career.' *The Rise of Respectable Society*: F. M. L. Thompson, op. cit., pp 262–3.

47 NLS 3155 No 3a.

48 Letter to Dorothy Haig dated 5 February 1929; NLS 3155.

49 *Field-Marshal Earl Haig*: Charteris op. cit., page 5.

50 The death certificate tentatively offers as cause of death, 'Cirrhosis of liver?'

51 *My Father's Son: The Memoirs of Dawyck Haig*: The Earl Haig (Leo Cooper, 2000), page 2.

52 *On the Psychology of Military Incompetence*: Dixon op. cit., page 376.

53 Ibid., page 381.

## Chapter Two

1 *The Brazen Nose*, Vol.III Number 3, November 1920 (College Magazine).

2 From *The Brazen Nose* in 1969: 'The only casualty in the operation [the refurbishment] was the plaque commemorating Field Marshal Haig (1880) as the first among Brasenose warriors of 1914–18. Its legend [. . .] was often regarded as being not wholly in the happiest of taste. Its removal, to make room for the Senior Tutor's enlarged notice board, may or may not demonstrate the superiority of the pen over the sword, but is unlikely to cause a widespread sense of loss.' This wrongly implies that Haig had been elevated above others, whereas obviously his name was singled out as, in 1920, simply the most famous of the BNC soldiers.

3 Negotiations to join forces, later abandoned, went on throughout 1877–8. See *The History of the University of Oxford*: eds. M. G. Brock and M. C. Curthoys (Oxford University Press, 2000), page 124.

4 *The History of the University of Oxford*, ibid., page 423.

5 As an indication of his scholarly status, Cradock merits not a single mention in *The History of the University of Oxford* published by the university in 2000.

6 *The Oxford Magazine*, 23 February 1928, Lord Askwith, and BNC College Records.

7 Charteris, op. cit., page 7.

8 The derivation of this story, often repeated but rarely identified, stems from Lord Askwith, the same undergraduate who was advised by Dr Cradock to drink lots of port, in his memoir in *The Oxford Magazine* 23 February 1928. There he wrote that 'Mr Sampson, the present Principal, tells me that Haig said Pater taught him how to write English.'

9 From *The Brazen Nose*, Vol.IV, Number 8, May 1928.

10 'Pater and Wilde: aestheticism and homosexuality', *The New Criterion*: Louis Auchincloss, October 1991.

11 *Brasenose Monographs*, Part II, 1909, page 24.

12 Proctors' duties included ensuring undergraduates obeyed college rules, not least those related to moral standards.

13 See *Inventing the Victorians*: Matthew Sweet (Faber & Faber, 2001), page 196.

14 The instance of Reginald Brett, Viscount Esher, who became an inveterate promoter of Haig in later life and who conducted lifelong affairs with younger men while maintaining an apparently happy marriage, shows how sexual ambiguity was no bar to social elevation so long as it was not publicly paraded.

15 See *The Woeful Victorian: A Biography of John Addington Symonds*: Phyllis Grosskurth (Holt, Rinehart and Winston, 1964).

16 *The Bourgeois Experience, Victoria to Freud*: Peter Gay (Oxford University Press, 1984), page 298.

17 Patrick Shaw-Stewart, elected to an All Souls fellowship in 1910, wrote to a friend of Namier's blackballing that 'We elected three miserable specimens, but no one jolly was in; and anyhow, by the strenuous efforts of me and one or two others, the election of a Polish Jew from Balliol, much the strongest candidate really, was prevented.' *The History of the University of Oxford*: eds. M. G. Brock and M. C. Curthoys, op. cit., page 802.

18 In 1915 Haig's wife received 'a very generous cheque' from Cassel in donation to a fund she was beginning to establish for disabled officers: 'all those whom he had helped so liberally and entertained so lavishly in the past had quite deserted him on account of his nationality.' [*The Man I Knew*: The Countess Haig, op. cit., page 137.]

19 *Afterthoughts*: Frances, Countess of Warwick (Cassell, 1931), page 40.

20 'Lord Northcliffe came to luncheon today. [He said] The Anglo-German Jew firms in England and Cassel and such like people are endeavouring to create an atmosphere of peace, and in the Cabinet there are several such short-sighted persons.' *The Diary of Lord Bertie*, volume II, 1924, page 10. Bertie was British ambassador to Paris during most of the Great War. According to the *British Jewry Book of Honour*, published in 1922, some 60,000 British Jews fought in the war: 2,324 were killed and 6,350 were casualties.

21 The barrier against professing Jews taking seats in Parliament had been lifted only in 1860; prior to 1871, Jewish students had been barred from taking degrees at Oxford and Cambridge Universities.

22 *Journals and Letters of Viscount Esher*, Vol. 2, 1903–1910 (Ivor Nicholson & Watson, 1934), page 255.

23 NLS 3155 Acc 6.

24 NLS Acc 3155 No 328.

25 *The Press and the General Staff*: Neville Lytton (Collins, 1920), page 138.

26 *Ethical Studies*: F. H. Bradley (Oxford University Press, 1962), pp 193–202.

27 *F. H. Bradley*: Richard Wollheim (Peregrine Books, 1969) page 243.

28 Frances, Countess of Warwick, op. cit., page 42.

29 26 November 1914: *War Diaries and Letters 1914–1918*: ed. Gary Sheffield & John Bourne (Weidenfeld & Nicolson, 2005), page 83.

30 'The House': more familiar name for Christ Church college. At this date Christ Church was academically weak but a magnet for the aristocracy; in 1861 half of all the old Etonians at Oxford were to be found at Christ Church.

31 Hitchcock was one of Haig's oldest and closest friends, to whom he paid public tribute as late as December 1927, calling him 'one of the best type of Americans [. . .] we ought to make the most of fellows like Tommy, a true friend. I am all for a good understanding with the USA but *the Americans must meet us half-way*. I believe they would understand and appreciate us if we told them straight what our views are; and left it at that.' (*The Brazen Nose*, May 1928, original emphasis).

32 *Oxford Magazine*, ibid.

33 *Haig*: Duff Cooper, Vol.1, op. cit., page 22.

34 There are a couple of surviving charcoal/pencil landscapes by Douglas Haig in the NLS.

35 Among the Fish's habits were riding an orange bicycle to avoid confusion of ownership and feeding crumpets to rats. His pet name for his wife was 'Fluffy'.

36 Haig never entirely lost his distrust of Roman Catholicism; his wife converted to Catholicism shortly before her death in 1939.

37 Haig was always predisposed to take on trust the assertions of those who occupied a higher rung on the ladder of British society. It is unlikely that one of the children of the Duke of Westminster, whose extensive properties in Belgravia, Mayfair and Pimlico made the family the wealthiest in Britain upon his elevation to the Dukedom in 1874, was really forced to gamble to eke out his allowances from his father.

38 Almost £140,000 in today's money.

39 About £700 in today's money: *Oxford and Oxford Life*: Joseph Wells (Methuen, 1892), page 52.

40 NLS Acc 3155 No 324: letter from Leeson Marshall to Lady Haig 9 October 1929.

41 There are no entries for Haig in the college's Buttery Book, the record of meals taken and bills accrued, for the whole of the summer term of 1881.

42 On Haig's death the BNC Principal gave an address in the college chapel in which he said: 'He missed the Summer Term of 1881 owing to an illness which (as he himself told me) we should now call Influenza [. . .] He passed all the examinations for the B.A degree, but was never fully qualified by residence.'

43 Although he left Oxford without a degree, his name was reinstated on the College books in 1908, when BNC revived for him and two others the status of Gentleman Commoner, an eighteenth-century category, and he was elected an Honorary Fellow by BNC in 1915.

44 NLS Acc 3155 No 251.

45 *Douglas Haig*: Gerard De Groot (Unwin Hyman, 1988), page 28.

46 *The Army in Victorian Society*: Gwyn Harries-Jenkins (Routledge, 1977), page 96.

47 *Field Marshal Earl Haig*: Charteris, op. cit., page 9.

48 S. J. Anglim in the *British Army Review* (No 101, August 1992) records that Haig's intake contained other later eminent soldiers, including the future General Sir Walter Congreve, who passed out in fifth place and was to win the VC at Colenso in the Second Boer War in 1899 and was to command the 15th Corps at the Somme and Cambrai in the Great War. Another was the future Lieutenant-General Sir Sydney Lawford, who commanded the 41st Division at Passchendaele.

49 The Anson Memorial Sword was at that time awarded to the cadet who passed out top of his intake at Christmas. At the time Haig was a cadet, the course lasted one year divided into two terms, with cadets being admitted in May and September, the former passing out in December. For the latter, who passed out in midsummer, the General Proficiency Sword was awarded to the intake's first-placed cadet. In 1892 the course was extended to eighteen months divided into three terms.

50 *Douglas Haig*: De Groot, op. cit., page 29.

51 Academic merit at Sandhurst was no guide to future success as a practical soldier. Major-General George Pomeroy-Colley passed top of his class at Sandhurst aged just sixteen; he passed first at the Staff College after sitting the final exam after one year and not two. By 1880 he was Governor of Natal, a well-respected and highly intelligent soldier. But in the first South African War he was defeated at Laing's Nek and then killed at Majuba Hill, after foolishly taking his seven infantry companies and a naval detachment to the top of the hill.

52 *From Private to Field-Marshal*: Field-Marshal Sir William Robertson (Constable, 1921), pp 4–5.

53 *Professional Men: The Rise of the Professional Classes in Nineteenth-Century England*: W. J. Reader (Weidenfeld & Nicolson, 1966); quoted in *The Victorian Army and the Staff College, 1854–1914*: Bond, 1972, page 26.

54 Robertson, op. cit., pp 30–31.

55 The Duke of Cambridge became C-in-C of the Army in 1887 and held onto the post until he resigned in 1895, when he was unable to accept that his position should be subordinated to that of the Minister of War.

56 About £900,000 in today's money.

57 *From Midshipman to Field Marshal*: Wood (Methuen, 1906).

58 G. R. Searle, op. cit., page 255.

59 *Soldier True*: Victor Bonham-Carter (Muller, 1963), page 5.

60 *The War Office At War*: Sir Sam Fay (Hutchinson, 1937), pp 15–16.

# Chapter Three

1 *Earl Haig*: Ernest Protheroe (Hutchinson, 1928), page 16. Whether the epithet 'von' was entirely 'friendly' at a time of growing Anglo-German rivalry is open to doubt.

2 NLS Acc 3155 No 1 b.

3 Figures from Haig's diary; John Hussey gives the total as twenty-one officers, 587 NCOs and men, fifty women and forty-seven children ('Douglas Haig, Adjutant: Recollections of Veterans of the 7th Hussars', *Journal of the Society for Army Historical Research*, No 73 (1995).

4 NLS Acc 3155 No 1 b.

5 *Soldier True*: Victor Bonham-Carter, op. cit., page 34.

6 Haig did not have a natural flair for languages. William Robertson, without the benefit of public school and Oxford, landed in India in December 1888, two years after Haig. By the end of 1890 Robertson had qualified as an interpreter in five Indian languages (*Soldier True*, op. cit., page 33), while Hamilton learned Hindustani.

7 Haig probably carried the bacterium *Salmonella typhi* for the rest of his life. Without antibiotics, the infection can seriously damage the digestive system; Haig's later fastidiousness about his diet was simply a sensible precaution to avoid exacerbating this chronic affliction.

8 Most of all he relished occasional local expeditions, when he would compile rations' lists; this is one from this period:

*all quantities in lbs*

| | | |
|---|---|---|
| 2 corn flour | 1 pea flour | 5 flour |
| 6 oatmeal | 2 shredded oats | rice |
| 2 dried apples | 2 coffee and milk | 1 Van Houten (2 small tins) |

| | | |
|---|---|---|
| 1½ Swiss rusk (2 tins) | ½ essence of coffee | 1 treacle |
| 4 sugar | 2 tea | 3 marmalade |
| 2 apricot jam | Holloways ointment | Vaseline |
| ½ Epsom Salts | ¼ essence of ginger | 4 candles in tin |
| axe | padlocks | oil for rifles |
| arsenical soap | corrosive sublimate | measuring tape |
| thermos | laces | string |
| rope | small flash | whistle |
| lime juice | 24 butter | 4 Oxford sausages |
| 6 Corned Beef | 4 beef & vegetable | 4 bacon in tins |
| 6 Hotch Potch | 3 Mulligatawny | 3 Oxtail |
| 3 Mock turtle | 2 sardines | 3 salmon |
| ½ caviare | 2 brown biscuits | 2 captains biscuits |
| 2 albert biscuits | 1 extra toast biscuit | 2 ginger nuts |
| 2 Sucotash | 2 petit pois | 2 haricots verts |
| 4 Chollet's compound | 2 tomatoes | 1½ Worcester sauce |
| ½ ketchup | 1½ rd cabbage | ½ mixed |
| ¾ curry powder | ½ cayenne and black pepper | 2 salt |
| 2½ bicarb soda | 1 vinegar | ½ mustard |
| ½ castor oil, capers | essence of rennet | |

9  NLS Acc 3155 No 324 a.

10  Harrison's claim to this rank has been disputed by the military historian John Hussey, who asserts that regimental records of the 7th Hussars show Harrison to have achieved no more than the rank of Sergeant.

11  NLS Acc 3155 No 324 a.

12  The home of his nephew, Oliver Haig.

13  Late Victorian ditties of this sort were published in great quantities; there is no evidence to suggest this was Haig's own creation, not least because there is no reliable evidence of his having written any other poetry, other than a piece of doggerel attributed to him by his army servant, Sergeant Secrett. He claimed Haig wrote and dedicated to his South African War mount, Red Hussar, 'A Toast to My Sweetheart of Yesterday, A Health to My Pal of To-Day'. *Twenty-Five Years With Earl Haig*: Thomas Secrett (Jarrolds 1928), pp 68–9.

14  Horace Smith-Dorrien, who attended the Staff College in 1887–8, recalled that he 'enjoyed every minute of my two years there. I do not think we were taught as much as we might have been, but there was plenty of sport and not too much work.' According to legend, after he had been there three months he was found wandering the corridors asking to be directed to the library. *The Victorian Army and the Staff College*: Brian Bond (Methuen, 1972), page 141.

15  It was impossible, however, to change overnight the encrusted pedantry of decades, and some of Haig's contemporaries found the work rather undemanding. (Brigadier-General Sir) James Edmonds used his time at Camberley to begin work on a large history of the US Civil War, while (Lieutenant-General Sir) George Macdonogh, Director of Military Intelligence at the War Office in London 1916–18, managed to read for the Bar in London. (Bond, 1972 op. cit., pp 159–160.)

16  *Haig*: Duff Cooper, op. cit., Vol.1, page 37.

17  When he was at Staff College a few years later, Haig's health was noted by his fellow students as being 'far from robust, and the hearty lunches of cheese, pickles and new bread we used to pick up at the local "pubs" were not to his taste, and sometimes made him ill.' (Brigadier-General James Edmonds, 'An Instructor's Forecast', *British Legion Magazine*, March 1928.

18  John Hussey's scholarship in his '"A Very Substantial Grievance", said the Secretary of State: Douglas Haig's Examination Troubles, 1893', *Journal of Army Historical Research*, Vol. 74, 1996, provides the background for this episode.

19  NLS Acc 3155 No 6e.

20  NLS Acc 3155 No 6e.

21  In the House of Commons on 9 September 1893 Henry Campbell-Bannerman, Secretary of State for War, acknowledged that the maths paper had been set 'a good deal higher' than in previous years and that he was satisfied that 'there was a very substantial grievance on the part of those who entered as candidates [. . .]'

22  '"A Very Substantial Grievance"': Hussey, op. cit.

23  The subject of Haig's alleged colour-blindness crops up in some of the source materials. Duff Cooper wrote that one day in Flanders Haig was out riding and pointed out to an aide-de-camp 'the beauty of the scarlet poppies that were growing there. The discreet aide-de-camp murmured his agreement, but looking where the Commander-in-Chief was pointing, he could see nothing but the rich brown earth recently turned by the plough.' Haig's niece, Ruth De Pree, daughter of Haig's sister Mary Elizabeth, recalled in 1931 that when she was a child she once wore a green dress 'and when I asked him the colour of it he said it was yellow. Next night I tried him with another colour, but he was not pleased': NLS, Haig Papers.

24  Almost 100 years later, little had changed. In 1962 'Gustavus' wrote a guide to studying for Staff College exams: 'Another idea which may be worth some research is to indulge in the dangerous game of question spotting. Analyse the questions in old Staff College papers, going back six or so years, and then concentrate on revising those questions which are thought most likely to reappear. It is extraordinary how accurate predictions can turn out to be [. . .]' (*British Army Review*, No 10, 1962.)

25 Dorothy Haig wrote that this 'was the first serious check in his career. Douglas felt it very keenly [. . .]'. (The Countess Haig, op. cit, page 25.)

26 *Haig*: Duff Cooper, Vol.1, op. cit., pp 38–9.

27 NLS Acc 3155 No 6.

28 French, another cavalryman, gave a lecture following these manoeuvres, in which he said the role of cavalry was not 'to cut and hack and to thrust at your enemy wherever and however he may be found. The real business of cavalry is so to manoeuvre your enemy as to bring him within effective range of the corps artillery of your own side [. . .]': *The Tragedy of Sir John French*: George H. Cassar (University of Delaware Press, 1985), page 29.

29 The manner in which British army career fortunes depended as much on *who* you knew as *what* you knew is carefully delineated in Tim Travers' book *The Killing Ground* (HarperCollins, 1987).

30 *The Army in Victorian Society*: Gwyn Harries-Jenkins, op. cit., pp 3–4.

31 NLS Acc 3155 No 6. Letter to Henrietta dated 4 May 1895.

32 *Caligula: Eine Studie über römischen Caesarenwahnsinn* (Caligula: A Study of Imperial Insanity).

33 His stay resulted in a War Office publication of 1896, Notes on German Cavalry: NLS 3155 Acc 74.

34 NLS Acc 3155 No 1.

35 Duff Cooper wrote there were eight officers (Vol.1, page 43) but this seems an error; the names were (in order of precedence according to the size of the present): Rittmeister von Arnim, 1st Guard Dragoons; Major von Schmidt-Pauli, 1st Guard Uhlans; Carl von Bulow, General Staff; Major von Blumenthal, Staff Officer, Guard Cavalry Division; Graf von Moutgelas, Guard Hussars; Graf von Kageneck, Adjutant of the Guard Hussars; Rittmeister von Esebeck, 3rd Guard Uhlans; Rittmeister von Reibnitz, Gardes du Corps; and Major von Goszler, Guard Hussars.

36 NLS Acc 3155 No 6.

37 NLS Acc 3155 No 6. Letter to Henrietta.

38 '"A Very Substantial Grievance"': Hussey, op. cit.

39 The Staff College regulations had been amended by Army Order 72 of 1894, permitting the C-in-C to nominate eight officers each year instead of as previously four; he could nominate more if the competitive positions were unfilled.

40 '"A Very Substantial Grievance"': Hussey, op. cit.

41 *The Victorian Army and The Staff College*: Bond, op. cit., page 162.

42 It was by any standards an exceptional year for Staff College entrants. Allenby (1861–1936) commanded the Cavalry Division, the Cavalry Corps, V Corps and the Third Army on the Western Front and from June 1918 was GOC-in-C of the Egyptian Expeditionary Force, and ended up Field Marshal Viscount Allenby.

Edmonds (1861–1956) made his name as the Official Historian of the Great War; an exceptionally intelligent man, he acquired the nickname 'Archimedes' at Camberley for his outstanding intellect but the strain of the early days of the war saw him replaced as GSO1 4th Division in September 1914; he spent the rest of the war at GHQ, ultimately as Deputy Chief Engineer, ending as Brigadier-General Sir James. Major-General Thompson Capper (1863–1915), an 1882 Sandhurst graduate who was one of three young Captains (Haig included) sent by Sir Evelyn Wood to assist Kitchener in Sudan, won the DSO in South Africa, and became Commandant of the Indian Staff College at Quetta. While GOC 7th Division, Capper died of wounds at the Battle of Loos in 1915. Brigadier-General Richard Haking (1862–1945), GOC 5th Division on the Western Front, fought in the South African war during 1899–1901 and became a professor at the Staff College 1901–1906; he was wounded on 16th September 1914 but rose through the war to command the XI Corps. Lieutenant-General Sir George Macdonogh (1865–1942) ultimately became Adjutant-General; during the Great War he was intelligence chief at the War Office in London, from where he acquired a deserved reputation for remarkably accurate, reliable assessments of German strength and morale, reports which frequently clashed with those of Charteris, Haig's intelligence chief at GHQ. As C-in-C BEF, Haig distrusted Macdonogh's reports and, rather dishonourably, cast doubt on them partly because of their author's Roman Catholicism.

43 Quoted in *The Victorian Army and the Staff College*: Bond, op. cit., page 161.

44 *From Private to Field Marshal*: Robertson, op. cit., page 88.

45 Harries-Jenkins, op. cit., page 28.

46 'An Instructor's Forecast': Edmonds, op. cit.

47 Edmonds, op. cit.

48 Edmonds, op. cit.

## Chapter Four

1 'They Pass On The Torch of Life'.

2 *Kitchener*: Philip Magnus (Penguin Books, 1968), page 89.

3 Debate still rages over Kitchener's sexuality. Philip Magnus strongly hinted he thought Kitchener was homosexual; John Pollock, in *Kitchener: Saviour of the Realm* (Constable and Robinson, 2001), rebuts the suggestion.

4 Magnus, op. cit., page 100.

5 Gerard De Groot, op. cit., page 54.

6 *The River War*: W. S. Churchill (Four Square Books, 1960) pp 174–5.

7 Churchill, ibid., page 92.

8 NLS Acc 3155 No 1, diary for 1898.

9 Khalifa is an Arabic word which literally translates as 'one who succeeds some-one who died', but in this context the Khalifa was deemed the prophet Mohammed's successor as the political, military and administrative leader of the Muslims.

10 *The Man I Knew*: The Countess Haig, op. cit., pp 26–7. It is this kind of odd reticence which has encouraged some to re-title her book as 'The Man I Never Knew'. She never published the promised Sudan book.

11 *Blood Brothers*: Iain McCallum (Chatham Publishing, 1999), page 48.

12 According to the Countess Warwick, Prince Edward 'would impose no restraint upon those who came to visit him in his capacity as a country gentle-man.' *Afterthoughts*: Frances Countess of Warwick, op. cit., page 256.

13 Quoted in *King Edward the Seventh*: Philip Magnus (Murray, 1964), page 268.

14 *Architect of Victory: Douglas Haig*: Walter Reid (Birlinn, 2006), page 118.

15 See Peter Brent, *The Edwardians* (BBC publications, 1972), page 224, and Margaret Blunden, pp 129–130 of *The Countess of Warwick* (Cassell, 1967), who wrote: 'Only a few of the "many men" [whom she acknowledged sleeping with] can now be identified, and more only guessed at. Probably amongst their number was Douglas Haig, who as a young and serious-minded Captain in the Seventh Hussars was a frequent visitor to Warwick Castle ["Daisy's" country residence].'

16 Reid cited as the source for his assertion 'Family tradition, communicated to the author by the present Earl Haig [Douglas Haig's only son]'. Yet something does not add up here. Reid pinpoints the affair to a date in Haig's career by when he was a general; however, Haig was not appointed a general until November 1903, by which time he was in India, where he stayed until 5 May 1905, when he arrived back in England on leave. Two months after that he was married to Doris. It must either have been a very brief fling with Daisy; or it pre-dated his appointment as general; or possibly it did not happen. To add further confusion, the current Earl Haig informed me by letter in January 2007 that 'Walter Reid's assertion is not based on anything I told him nor on any family tradition . . . I do remember my elder sister mentioning the possibility but without any real knowledge.' It is unlikely that this puzzle will ever really be satisfactorily cleared up.

17 In her name-dropping autobiography Daisy pointedly omitted any mention of Haig's wife. Dorothy Haig, strait-laced and proper, and Daisy, an upper-class baggage who metamorphosed into a slightly batty socialist in the 1890s, would not have hit it off.

18 *Life's Ebb & Flow*: Frances, Countess of Warwick (Hutchinson 1929), pp 209–210.

19 NLS Acc 3155 No 6 b–d.

20  *The River War*: Churchill, op. cit., pp 195–6.

21  NLS Acc 3155 No 1.

22  *The Educated Soldier*: John Terraine (Cassell, 2000 edition), page 17.

23  Letter to Sir Evelyn Wood, quoted in *Haig*: Duff Cooper, op. cit., Vol.1, page 54.

24  NLS Acc 3155 No 1.

25  Churchill gave different casualty figures: one British officer wounded; six Egyptian troopers killed and ten wounded; and about thirty horses lost or disabled.

26  Haig later discussed the awarding of the VC for rescuing wounded men with King George V in December 1914. The king 'expressed the opinion that the grant of the Victoria Cross for carrying a wounded man out of action was justified and beneficial. I replied that each case must be judged on its merits but, as a rule in *civilised* war such efforts did the wounded man harm and also tended to increase loss of valuable lives.' (*War Diaries & Letters 1914–1918*: ed. Gary Sheffield and John Bourne, op. cit., page 84).

27  NLS Acc 3155 No 6.

28  Philip Warner, in *Field Marshal Earl Haig*, op. cit., page 49, gives the total casualties as 568, including 125 British.

29  More than £400,000 in today's money.

30  The 21st Lancers, which had been reformed from the 21st Hussars in Cairo in 1897, were the only regular cavalry to serve with the Anglo-Egyptian army.

31  Another soldier who occasionally supplemented his miserly regular army's pay by writing journalism was Ian Hamilton, whose successful military career foundered at Gallipoli. In 1883 Hamilton was writing as 'Correspondent from Army Headquarters' for the *Madras Mail* in India, with the approval of the C-in-C of the Madras Presidency, then Sir Frederick (later Earl) Roberts.

32  Churchill's column was titled 'From a Young Officer'.

33  One of the best accounts of this charge is in *A History of the British Cavalry*: The Marquess of Anglesey (Leo Cooper, 1982) Vol.3: 1872–1898, pp 378–386.

34  News of this scandalized public opinion in England and Queen Victoria protested to Kitchener; the Mahdi's head was later quietly buried in a Moslem cemetery, under Kitchener's orders.

35  More than £12 million in today's money.

36  About £161 million in 2005 terms; figures taken from *Kitchener*: Philip Magnus, op. cit., page 168.

# Chapter Five

1 *Field Marshal Earl Haig*: Charteris, op. cit., pp 17–18.

2 See *The Little Field Marshal*: Richard Holmes (Weidenfeld & Nicolson, 1981).

3 *The Tragedy of Sir John French*: George H. Cassar (University of Delaware Press, 1985), page 21.

4 Known as 'The Dumpies' because the regiment seemed to attract shorter and stouter men than other cavalry regiments.

5 *The Tragedy of Sir John French*, op. cit., pp 182–3.

6 *The Tragedy of Sir John French*, op. cit., page 32.

7 In today's money, more than £1 million.

8 NLS 3155 No 334 c: this contains a letter from William Shepherd of Wallace & Shepherd, bank agents and solicitor & notary, Royal Bank Building, Leven, 14 September 1899, confirming that the loan had been made to French on Haig's instructions and that a life insurance policy (number 3576) on the life of French had been taken out for the sum of £2,500. The letter was addressed to Major Douglas Haig, Cavalry Brigade, Aldershot. The suggestion it was £2,000 seems to derive from Blake's edition of Haig's private papers (Blake, op. cit., page 37) and that figure has been unquestioned ever since. The authorized biography by Duff Cooper draws a veil over the episode, merely stating that 'Haig had lent a considerable sum of money to a senior officer who would otherwise have been compelled to leave the service. He had done so, as he explained to his sister at the time, not only out of friendship for the officer concerned, but also in the belief that his retirement would be a loss to the army.' That Duff Cooper should decline to name French indicates the potential embarrassment, not just to French, who had died in May 1925, but also possibly to Haig's reputation, as it would have provoked accusations that Haig used his wealth to boost his career by making a loan not just to a 'senior' but a *superior* officer.

9 Haig's military servant, Thomas Secrett, recalled that after the Great War indigent ex-officers asked Haig for handouts 'but never a penny did they get from Lord Haig! That was one thing he would not do; he would never part with money to them.' Secrett said Haig refused to make such gifts partly because they would only have encouraged others and he could not afford them all, and that Haig in any case used his post-war influence to try to obtain jobs for genuine hardship cases. Haig did make donations to ex-servicemen organizations – just not to individuals. *Twenty Five Years With Earl Haig*: Thomas Secrett (Jarrolds, 1929), op. cit., page 279.

10 French's daughter, Essex, recalled Haig's conversation as very limited outside military affairs. She found him 'desperately dull. Sometimes he would break a painful silence by saying, "very nice tea today, Essex" while on other occasions

he would gaze at the mongrel Daphne and mutter, "Daphne, poor old dog."'
*The Little Field Marshal*, op. cit., page 51.

11  NLS Acc 3100 No 347/10: a letter from R. Stryben, in Constantia, South Africa, dated November 1969.

12  The discovery of diamonds and gold in the nineteenth century in regions where the Boer farmers lived created considerable tension. The British annexed Transvaal in 1877; in 1880 the Boers staged a revolt against British rule and an uneasy peace settlement was reached in 1881. Paul Kruger used the new mineral wealth of his Transvaal republic to purchase guns and weapons from Germany, which under Kaiser Wilhelm II delighted in Britain's South African difficulties. In 1896 Dr Starr Jameson led an independent and unofficial raid from Mafeking into the Transvaal in an attempt to recapture the Boer Republic for Britain. Jameson's Raid was an embarrassing failure. Britain nevertheless steadily reinforced its Cape Colony garrisons in 1899, and round two of the Anglo-Boer War was a consequence of intense mutual suspicion and determination by Britain not to be humiliated again.

13  *The Army in Victorian Society*: Gwyn Harries-Jenkins, op. cit.

14  NLS Acc 3155 No 6.

15  NLS Acc 3155 No 2.

16  The original 'Express Train' rifles were manufactured and so named by Purdey in 1856. They were high-velocity, long-range and accurate rifles which were powerful enough for tackling game in the bush. It is revealing that Haig justifies here the spearing of fleeing Boer commandos partly because of their use of a rifle which was, for them, their usual weapon, as if somehow the Boers were being 'unsporting'.

17  NLS Acc 3155 No 6 b–d.

18  British cavalry in South Africa were largely equipped with the Lee-Enfield cavalry carbine, which, although an improvement on earlier rifles, was accurate only up to about 1,200 yards. This gave the Boers, using rifles with accurate ranges of some 2,000 yards, a distinct advantage.

19  By the time the cavalry of the British Expeditionary Force sailed for France in August 1914, they were indeed Haig's ideal, fully trained for dismounted action, armed with the short magazine Lee Enfield rifle, one of the best rifles then available, and the Hotchkiss machine-gun Mk 1, and, for mounted action, carrying the 1908 design cavalry sword and the lance.

20  Rudyard Kipling, 'The Lesson', from *The Five Nations* (Methuen, 1903).

21  Haig followed the convention of his day and used the word 'moral' where we use 'morale'.

22  In Cape Town he also became a supporter of conscription. In a letter (16th November) to his brother Hugo he wrote: 'I fancy some modified form of

conscription will be necessary after this war, for there is no doubt that our infantry do not represent the nation. We must have men of 25 to 30 years of age, and if they won't enlist voluntarily, then they must be compelled to join for a limited period.'

23  A more intellectually analytical officer, Henry Rawlinson, born in 1864, who also became a general in the Great War, served as an infantry lieutenant-colonel, first on Kitchener's staff and later in command of a column of mounted infantry in South Africa. On the boat home to England in 1902 he committed some of his thoughts to paper:

I have jotted down what I consider to be the military lessons of the war. Here they are:

1.  The volunteer soldier fights, in my opinion, far better than the conscript, and I think that we ought to stick to voluntary enlistment, provided that we can obtain the necessary number of men.
2.  We must have means of expansion, and should take much more trouble with the training of the Militia and Volunteers.
3.  We must have a properly organized staff system.
4.  Military education is essential to all commanders. Our theoretical education must have more practical aims than it has had in the past, and must be available for Militia and Volunteer commanders.
5.  Mounted riflemen and cavalry trained to fight on foot will become more and more valuable as weapons increase in range and power; but infantry remains the only arm that can decide the issue of battle.
6.  We must train our infantry to shoot better and faster, and should give them well-equipped machine-gun companies.
7.  We must have better co-operation between our infantry and artillery.
8.  The control of battle by a commander is becoming more and more difficult. Therefore subordinates must be trained to accept responsibility and use it properly. Study of ground is of prime importance.
9.  The moment when a battle seems to be lost is the moment to refuse to accept defeat and to attack with every available man and gun.

Some of these ideas were extremely prescient and had, sadly, to be re-learned all over again just twelve years later. *The Life of General Lord Rawlinson of Trent*: Major-General Sir Frederick Maurice (Cassell, 1928), pp 77–8.

24  NLS Acc 3155 No 6; dated 23rd December 1899.
25  Letter to Dorothy Haig from J. F. Laycock who served in SA with Haig: NLS 3155 No 34.
26  Quoted in *Haig*: Duff Cooper, Vol.1, op. cit., page 83.

27 NLS Acc 3155 No 6.

28 NLS 3155 No 334.

29 De Groot, op. cit., page 81.

30 Douglas Scott, Douglas Haig's grandson, wrote a brief memoir of Secrett for the July 2005 edition of the online *First World War Studies Journal*, produced by the Centre for First World War Studies at the University of Birmingham (http:www.js-ww1.bham.ac.uk).

31 *Twenty-Five Years with Earl Haig*: Thomas Secrett (Jarrolds, 1928), pp 22–3.

32 De Groot, op. cit., page 89.

33 NLS Acc 3155 No 6. Today this sort of transaction would be regarded as insider trading; then it was seen as just canny.

34 *A Soldier's Life: General Sir Ian Hamilton 1853–1947*: John Lee (Macmillan, 2000), page 66.

35 *Haig*: Duff Cooper, Vol.1, op. cit., page 89.

# Chapter Six

1 More than £19 million in today's money.

2 Quoted in *Defence and Diplomacy*: Alfred Vagts (Kings Crown Press, 1956), page 119.

3 Esher, born to an English father and French mother, had after Eton and Oxford created for himself a role close to the Royal Family as a bustling courtier. A former MP with fingers in many pies, in 1903 he was serving as Deputy Governor of Windsor Castle, having previously turned down Balfour's offer of the job of Secretary of State for War.

4 See *The Enigmatic Edwardian*: James Lees-Milne (Sidgwick & Jackson, 1986). Though he married and fathered four children, Esher's central emotional outlet was an idealized homosexuality which, like many of the time (such as Pater), he could rationalize by reference to classical Greek art and philosophy. Esher's *Collected Journals and Letters* (Ivor Nicholson & Watson, 1934) are a bowdlerized version of his massive 400-volume bound collection of private papers, removing all reference to his homoerotic romanticising.

5 *Collected Journals and Letters of Viscount Esher*, Vol.2, ibid., page 183.

6 Lees-Milne, op. cit., page 142.

7 When Henry Rawlinson became assistant adjutant-general in the newly created Department of Military Education in April 1903 at the War Office, he found it 'a terrible place. There are far too many cooks concerned with every brew of broth, and it takes an unconscionable time to get anything through. Even when the bigwigs here are at length induced to approve a plan, it is ten to one, if any money is involved, that the Treasury knocks it on the head. I have

never worked harder for six months with less result than I have here.' He joyfully departed after just eight months to become Commandant at the Staff College. *The Life of General Lord Rawlinson of Trent*: Major-General Sir Frederick Maurice (Cassell, 1928), op. cit., page 83.

8  NLS Acc 3155 No 254.

9  'Twenty thousand bullets were fired for each casualty in Manchuria. The statistic was the modern equivalent of the aphorism that it took a ton of lead to kill a man.' *Fire-Power: British Army Weapons and Theories of War 1904–1945*: Shelford Bidwell and Dominick Graham (George Allen & Unwin, 1982), page 22.

10  See *The Cavalry Journal*, Vol.III (January–October 1908), page 271: a précis by Colonel W. H. Birkbeck of a translation of a two-volume work on Japanese cavalry training regulations following the Russo-Japanese war: 'As a general rule, Cavalry will fight mounted, but when there is little hope of success by mounted action alone, the rifle will be used to supplement it [. . .]'.

11  General (as he became) Sir Ian Hamilton was an altogether wittier and more outspoken soldier than Haig, but these qualities were not treasured by some of the most senior commanders. As an infantryman in an army dominated by the social snobberies attached to the cavalry, his caustic dismissals of the future role of the cavalry make it even more remarkable that he rose as far as he did.

12  Supplementary Report by Sir Ian Hamilton, 8th September 1904, attached to Captain J. B. Jardine's report of 30th July 1904, 'Action of Cavalry – Fire Action versus Shock Tactics, with Special Reference to the Trans-Baikal Cossacks', in General Staff – War Office: *The Russo-Japanese War: Reports from Officers Attached to the Japanese Forces in the Field*, Vol. I (Revised Edition, HMSO, 1906), page 323.

13  It was also not merely a question of learning lessons from the Russo-Japanese war but also providing enough funds to train soldiers in the new weaponry. Field Marshal Sir William Robertson later recorded how, in light of experience of the Manchurian conflict, it was considered important to train British infantry in the use of hand grenades. As Director of Military Training at the War Office, he asked for a supply of dummy bombs and a small quantity of live grenades. Because dummy bombs cost two pence each and live grenades £1 a piece he was only allowed 2,000 dummy grenades; no live grenades were sanctioned. Instead, battalions were permitted to watch engineers throw some. *From Private to Field-Marshal*, op. cit., page 192.

14  *A Soldier's Life: General Sir Ian Hamilton 1853–1947*: John Lee, op. cit., page 22.

15  'Tomorrow's Army: The Challenge of Nonlinear Change' by Lt. Colonel Antulio J. Echavarria II, in *Parameters*, autumn 1998.

16  *The Cavalry Journal*: op. cit., pp 146–7.

17  *Collected Journals & Letters of Viscount Esher*, Vol.2, op. cit., page 33.

18  *Memories of Forty Eight Years' Service*: General Sir Horace Smith-Dorrien (John Murray, 1925), pages 327–8.

19  *Field-Marshal Sir Henry Wilson*: Major–General Sir C. E. Callwell (Cassell, 1927), page 55.

20  *Collected Journals and Letters of Viscount Esher*, ibid., Vol.2, pp 50–51.

21  *Curzon*: David Gilmour (John Murray, 1994), page 248.

22  At Oxford Curzon – heir to an old peerage – had been written of thus: 'My name is George Nathaniel Curzon, I am a most superior person'; as the grandson of a tea merchant, Kitchener was no doubt painfully aware of their differing antecedents.

23  *Great Contemporaries*: Winston Churchill (Thornton Butterworth, 1937), page 279.

24  The Viceroy was advised and assisted by a small cabinet of councillors; the Military Member during Curzon's time as Viceroy was a now long-forgotten general, Sir Edwin Collen, whom Curzon regarded as an 'obsolete amiable old footler, the concentrated quintessence of a quarter of a century of departmental life.'

25  Repington, an incorrigible snob, was forced to leave the army following a scandal involving the wife of a fellow officer, sufficient dishonour for Haig to dislike him. Gwynne and Repington resurfaced in Haig's life during the Great War, when their rabidly pro-army stance was objectively supportive of Haig in his battle with Lloyd George, though Haig loathed them, their work and personal lives rendering them definitely not gentlemen.

26  *Curzon*: David Gilmour, op. cit., page 249.

27  *Curzon*: David Gilmour, ibid., page 340.

28  *Collected Journals and Letters of Viscount Esher*, op. cit., Vol.2, pp 68–70. Curzon in fact returned to India and did not resign until August 1905.

29  The result of these Indian staff rides was Haig's 1907 publication *Cavalry Studies* (London, Hugh Rees). In this he foretold his own predicament in France during the Great War: 'Military history teaches us that the whole question of cooperation with an ally is fraught with difficulties and danger. When the theatre of operation lies in the country of the ally, these difficulties increase, for war can rarely benefit the inhabitants on the spot, and ill feeling is certain to arise.'

30  Dorothy Vivian was born on 9 July 1879 in London.

31  Their four children were Alexandra Henrietta Louisa (born on 9 March 1907); Victoria Doris Rachel (7 November 1908); George Alexander Eugene Douglas (15 March 1918); and Irene Violet Freesia Janet Augusta (7 October 1919).

32 His niece, Ruth De Pree, said Dorothy's mother told him that 'my daughter cannot possibly be ready [for the marriage] in three weeks' to which Haig replied: 'It will be then or not at all.' (De Pree memoir, NLS archive).

33 'At signs [sighs?] and murmurs from her such as "Do look at the love-birds" he [Douglas] became annoyed and remarked "Hold your tongue Henrietta." ' De Pree memoir, op. cit.

34 Louisa Alice Duff died on 3 April 1926. In 1908 Viscount Esher found Munthe, by that time personal physician to Queen Victoria of Sweden, to be a 'clever, pushing, rather pretentious man.'

35 The fourth Baron Vivian won the DSO, the Légion d'Honneur and the Croix de Guerre in the First War; he died in 1940, aged 60.

36 *The Man I Knew*. op.cit., pp 32–3. Haig's niece, Ruth De Pree, recalled Henrietta once told her: 'Douglas says very few women know when a kettle is actively boiling.'

37 *The Man I Knew*. op.cit., page 33.

38 Ibid, page 34. Ruth De Pree, in 1930, put the episode slightly differently. According to her, Haig proposed to Doris on the terrace of Windsor Castle early Friday morning and then went off to play golf at Sunningdale with his nephew Hugo. Doris informed the queen (who was in her bath) loudly through the door that she was engaged: 'The Queen got out of her bath quickly and congratulated the Maid of Honour, and told her she would have to send and get Douglas back to receive the King's consent, so the game of golf was stopped and my Uncle sent for his knee breeches and valet. The King gave his consent and said to Doris "I am losing my best girl." That night in the drawing room the Queen shook her fan at Doris.' (From an unedited version of Ruth De Pree's memories of Douglas Haig, at the NLS; an edited version was published in the Douglas Haig Fellowship Records, issue no 8, December 2002.

39 NLS Acc 3155 No 254.

40 NLS Acc 3155 No 254.

41 NLS Acc 3155 No 347: passport issued to The Honourable Dorothy Maud Haig, née Vivian, on 13 March 1919.

42 NLS Acc 3155 No 91.

43 July 16 1905: NLS Acc 3155 No 91.

44 NLS 3155 No 334.

45 There is a persistent myth that Haig was hard up. Kenneth Rose (in his biography of George V) wrote: 'by Edwardian standards Haig was a poor man – he held no shares in the family whisky business and had been left only £500 by his father.' (*King George V*, Weidenfeld & Nicolson, 1983, page 192.) This is incorrect. Haig had been left £6,000 by his father; he did have shares in the family firm; he was far from poor by Edwardian standards.

46  *The Pound In Your Pocket 1870–1970*: Peter Wilsher, op.cit., pp 96–7. For comparison, King Edward VII, when he came to the throne, was granted by Parliament an annual income of £470,000, £85,000 more than Queen Victoria had received.

47  *The Man I Knew*: The Countess Haig, op.cit., page 41.

48  The old duties of the Military Member of the Viceroy's Council were redistributed between a new official, the Military Supply Member (MSM), and the C-in-C, who officially became the sole expert of the government on purely military questions. The MSM's duties were nominally important but actually limited to questions only of supply.

49  *The Man I Knew*: op.cit., pp 43–4. Kitchener thought himself a sophisticated collector of antiquities, but Dorothy cast doubt on his expertise. While the Haigs were in India, Kitchener asked an American expert to value his collection of Japanese and Chinese bowls, which he thought was 'priceless'. 'Douglas told me that he had been much upset because after going through them the guest remarked that only a few were genuine.'

50  NLS Acc 3155 No 25. Letter to Haig from Viscount Esher (on Buckingham Palace notepaper), 15 February 1906.

51  General Sir Neville Gerald Lyttelton (1845–1931) commanded a brigade during the River War in Sudan and was C-in-C in South Africa during 1902–04 and thus knew Haig; at this date he was CGS and first military member of the Army Council (1904–08).

52  NLS Acc 3155 No 25.

53  From 9 December 1907 they rented Trunk House at Cove, also near Farnborough.

54  Letter dated 8 February 1937; NLS Acc 3155 No 327.

55  The previous year, 1905, Esher used his influence with King Edward VII to secure a secondment for his favoured son, Maurice, from the Coldstream Guards to the staff of Sir John French, thus adding to the network of mutual grooming which surrounded Haig. By 1904 'all appointments to the War Office, which had to be approved by the King, were first agreed to and often suggested by Regy [Viscount Esher].' *The Enigmatic Edwardian*, op.cit., page 150.

56  *Collected Journals and Letters of Viscount Esher*, Vol.2, op.cit., page 401.

57  *Haig*: Duff Cooper, op.cit., Vol.1, page 106.

58  Seely (later Baron Mottistone, 1896–1947) was a Liberal MP and later Secretary of State for War 1912–14. He commanded the Canadian Cavalry Brigade during most of the Great War. Of his memoirs *Fear and Be Slain* (1931) it was quipped by Churchill that it caused the printers difficulty because they ran out of capital 'I's. Yet Seely was also brave. Charteris wrote that at First Ypres in

1914 Seely 'seems determined to get killed, and is always going where the fighting is most fierce.' *At G.H.Q.*: Charteris (Cassell, 1931), page 50.

59  Prior to the Haldane reforms, the British army comprised three types of non-regular unit available for Home Defence: the Militia, mainly recruited from unskilled workers; Volunteers, normally drawn from the richer classes; and the Yeomanry Cavalry, usually drawn from the landed gentry.

60  *Collected Journals and Letters of Viscount Esher*, Vol.2, op.cit., pp 195–7.

61  Ellison (later Lieutenant-General), born the same year as Haig, was at this time Military Secretary to Haldane. He later served as Deputy Quartermaster General at Gallipoli in 1915; he died in 1947.

62  The original purpose of the Territorial Army was defence of the British mainland but in 1910 its members were invited to accept the additional liability of service abroad in the event of mobilization. Some units did accept and thus on the outbreak of war in August 1914 went to France; the Oxfordshire Hussars were the first Territorial unit in action, on 5 October 1914. The first major action fought by the Territorials was at Messines on 30 October 1914, when the London Scottish were in action. By the end of 1914, twenty-three Territorial battalions were in the field.

63  Leopold de Rothschild (1845–1917) was youngest of three sons of Baron Lionel de Rothschild and a grandson of the famous banker Nathan Rothschild. He had no real political interests; on his death *The Times* obituary was headed 'Philanthropist and Sportsman', though his sporting interests were limited to horse racing. Haig's genuine friendship with Leopold is yet another example of how the conventional anti-Semitism of Haig's class and generation resists easy generalization.

64  Interestingly, given their subsequent enmity, Lloyd George in 1910 also advocated that Britain adopt the Swiss compulsory militia system.

65  NLS Acc 3155 No 254.

66  'Of the Indian Rope Trick, the Paranormal, and Captain Shearer's Ray': John Hussey, *British Army Review* No 112, pages 78–87, April 1996. Hussey is not strictly correct, however, in asserting that 'nothing in Haig's diaries and letters has prepared us for this séance' – as we have seen, his mother wrote to the adolescent Haig of her and his sisters' efforts to contact the spirits of the dead.

67  *The Man I Knew*: The Countess Haig, op.cit., page 63.

68  Dorothy Haig claimed that the idea of an Imperial General Staff was Haig's: see *The Man I Knew*, page 60, although once the Committee of Imperial Defence was created it was an obvious further step.

69  *British Legion Magazine*, op.cit., March 1928.

# Chapter Seven

1 Brigadier-General Archibald Murray (contemporaries nicknamed him 'Old Archie', although he was just a year older than Haig) took over from Haig as Director of Military Training. Murray was later to serve unhappily as chief of staff to John French in France in 1914 before being appointed GOC/Egypt in 1916–17.

2 The play, produced by J. M. Barrie, was written by Captain (later Lieutenant-Colonel) Guy du Maurier, older brother of Gerald, who coincidentally attended Sandhurst (passed out forty-eighth of 129) the same time as Haig; Guy du Maurier was killed in action in 1915 while commanding a battalion of the Royal Fusiliers.

3 *An Englishman's Home* represented the high tide of a new genre, the invasion fantasy, which played on fears posed by foreign threats to Britain's shores. It originated in 1871 when George Tomkins Chesney's *The Battle of Dorking*, in which Dorking is besieged by German invaders, was published in Blackwood's magazine. Perhaps the most lasting contribution to the genre was Erskine Childers' *The Riddle of the Sands* (1903), which features two British adventurers discovering German barges assembled ready to invade Britain.

4 NLS Acc 3155 No 334, diary entry.

5 NLS Acc 3155 No 82.

6 Brigadier-General Sir James Edmonds recalled Haig told him 'it was a good thing to see the inside of the War Office for a short time, as it prevented one from having any respect for an official letter, but that it was a mistake to make a career there.' *British Legion Magazine*, op. cit., March 1928.

7 'Patronage and social connections, the seniority promotion system, the lack of a general staff and of socially acceptable staff college training, leadership of the Volunteer and Militia system, colonial "small war" heroes and personalities – all tended to "personalize" the late Victorian and Edwardian army – and to produce an army that acted as an instrument in preserving traditional attitudes.': 'The Hidden Army: Structural Problems in the British Officer Corps, 1900–1918', Tim Travers, *Journal of Contemporary History*, Vol. 17, No 3 (July 1982), pp 523–544. Travers elaborates this theme in his book *The Killing Ground* (Allen & Unwin, 1987).

8 *Kitchener*: Pollock, op. cit., page 341.

9 *The Man I Knew*, op. cit., page 71. When King George V travelled to India in December 1911 for the Delhi Durbar, among his party were a cowherd from Windsor Castle and three cows, to ensure regular supplies of fresh milk.

10 See, for example, *The Bovine Scourge: Meat, Tuberculosis and Public Health, 1850–1914*: Keir Waddington (The Boydell Press, 2006). Only in 1909 did the

Board of Agriculture issue a Tuberculosis Order to limit sales of milk from those herds that were *obviously* infected with TB, and the Order was never fully implemented, as being too expensive. There was a real risk of TB infection from British milk in 1909, even for people such as the Haigs.

11  During the general staff conference in 1911 Kiggell 'intervened to say that he envisaged a [future] battlefield with lines of infantry pressing forward, bayonets fixed, to close with the enemy. This vision of the future was so much at variance with the events in Manchuria that two Royal Artillery members of the directing staff at the Staff College, Colonel John du Cane and Lieutenant-Colonel William Furse, took him to task.' *Fire Power*, Bidwell and Graham, op. cit., page 11.

12  *Collected Journals and Letters of Viscount Esher*, op. cit., Vol.2, page 417.

13  *The Man I Knew*, op. cit., page 73.

14  Were Maida Hill's mediums below average, and thus not to be trusted?

15  *The Man I Knew*, op. cit., page 77.

16  Thomas Secrett tells of another occasion when Haig encountered an Indian fakir, who performed the 'rope trick', sending a boy up a perpendicular rope. Secrett claimed to have seen through the trick immediately but 'it was quite a long time before Haig would really believe that his eyes had deceived him.' *Twenty-Five Years With Earl Haig*, op. cit., page 47.

17  *The Man I Knew*, op. cit., page 80.

18  General Hamilton Gordon, whose Army nicknames were 'Merry and Bright' and 'Sunny Jim' because of his prevailing aura of despondency, had worked with Haig at the War Office when Haig was Director of Military Training. Haig promoted him in the Great War to GOC IX Corps from June 1916, which position he held until General Rawlinson managed to have him removed, prior to the September 1918 attack on the Hindenburg line. Others failed to understand Haig's support for Hamilton Gordon: General Edward Bulfin said his appointment to command IX Corps was 'Haig's idea of a joke.'

19  *Haig*: Duff Cooper, op. cit., Vol.1, pp 118–19.

20  Letter to Ellison dated 14 April 1910: NLS Acc 3155 No 256.

21  NLS Acc 3155 No 334. £3,000 in 1910 equates to more than £1 million in today's money.

22  Robertson served at Aldershot as Assistant Quartermaster General under Smith-Dorrien, of whom he had the highest opinion: 'Full of energy himself, [Smith-Dorrien] expected every one in his command to be equally zealous and to take his profession seriously. He held strongly that the utmost should be done for the welfare of the men and their families, and that they should be trusted not to abuse the increased privileges granted to them.' *From Private to Field-Marshal*: Robertson, op. cit., page 157.

23 *Memories of Forty-Eight Years' Service*: Smith-Dorrien, op. cit., pp 358–9.

24 This was an example of preparing to fight the next war by learning a lesson from the previous; quality of marksmanship was of no real consequence in the Great War, when rapidity of concentrated unaimed rifle fire, as during the retreat from Mons in 1914, proved to be more important than the ability of an individual soldier to hit a distant target.

25 *Memories of Forty-Eight Years' Service*, op. cit., page 361. Smith-Dorrien dates this meeting as happening in 1909; however the Vickers Mark I was not introduced by the British Army until 1912.

26 Ibid., page 346.

27 Ibid., page 346.

28 More than £19 million in today's money.

29 On 21 December 1911, a week after the king and queen left India for Nepal, a bomb was thrown at the elephant carrying Lord Hardinge, the Viceroy, as he made his first State entry into the newly designated capital, Delhi, seriously wounding him and killing his personal servant.

30 More than £1.5 million in today's money.

31 The Haigs were unable to recoup their costs of fitting out Government House by selling on fixtures and fittings after they left because the war intervened, and Aldershot became more of a staging post than a garrison.

32 *King George V*: Kenneth Rose, op. cit., page 135.

33 General Lake, then aged fifty-six, served in London at the start of the Great War and in April 1916 was appointed to GOC in Mesopotamia; having failed to relieve the siege at Kut-al-Amara in July 1916, he was sacked and replaced by Major-General Sir Stanley Maude.

34 *The Man I Knew*, op. cit., page 102.

35 NLS Acc 3155 No 334.

36 NLS Acc 3155 No. 334.

37 Acc 3155 No 334 d.

38 *Douglas Haig: The Educated Soldier*: John Terraine, op cit., page 53.

39 Grierson, a Scot, was a corpulent man who once said he fought his best battles when armed with a knife and fork. His girth belied his intellectual ability; he was the British army's leading authority on the German, Japanese and Russian armies, and spoke several languages. On this occasion his success owed much to the advice of one of his senior officers, Colonel (later Lieutenant-General Sir) Charles Briggs, GOC of the South East Mounted Brigade. Briggs persuaded Grierson to give the Blue Force RFC detachment, commanded by Major H. R. M. Brooke-Popham, permission to carry out independent reconnaissance, catching Haig's Red Force unawares. In the Great War Briggs was passed over for the highest command, to the surprise of his contemporaries;

some have suggested his career suffered because Haig may have borne a lengthy grudge against the man responsible for his humiliation in the Cambridge fens, though in the absence of conclusive evidence this may just be the kind of malicious gossip which has dogged Haig. Briggs ended up in the miserable backwater of Salonika, first commanding a division and later a corps. Brooke-Popham had a very successful career with the RFC in the Great War and ended up Air Chief Marshal Sir Brooke-Popham.

40  Peter Wright in *Cross & Cockade*, Vol. 23 No. 4 (1992), discusses the 1912 manoeuvres from the viewpoint of the aircraft involved.

41  *Field Marshal Earl Haig*: John Charteris, op. cit., pp 65–6.

42  *The Man I Knew*, op. cit., page 108.

43  *Field Marshal Earl Haig*: John Charteris, op. cit., 1929, page 64.

44  *A New England?*: G. R. Searle, op. cit., page 496.

45  *The Times*, 22 July 1911.

46  *Die große Politik der europäischen Kabinette, 1871–1914: Sammlung der diplomatis-chen Akten des Auswärtigen Amtes*: ed. Johannes Lepsius, Albrecht Mendelssohn-Bartholdy, and Friedrich Thimme, Berlin, 1922–26, Vol.XXXI, 98.

47  NLS Acc 3155 No 91.

48  NLS Acc 3155 No 334 d. Letter dated 8 May 1913.

49  NLS Acc 3155 No 334 d. Letters dated 25 and 31 January 1914.

50  There are many books devoted to the Curragh incident; an excellent overview of the military aspects of this episode is in *A History of the British Cavalry* Vol. 7: The Marquess of Anglesey (Leo Cooper, 1996).

51  He was replaced by General Sir Charles Whittingham Horsley Douglas.

52  *Great Contemporaries*: Winston Churchill, op. cit., page 83.

53  Ibid., op. cit., page 84.

## Chapter Eight

1  *Twenty-Five Years With Earl Haig*: Thomas Secrett, op. cit., pp 75–6.

2  NLS Acc 3155 No 347/25. This file is inscribed 'Letters written by his sister Henrietta under the spirit influence of her brother George.'

3  Letter to Haldane 4 August 1914: Haldane Papers, NLS, no. 5910.

4  *Memories and Reflections*: H. H. Asquith, (Little, Brown, 1928), Vol.2, page 24.

5  *The First World War*: Hew Strachan (Oxford University Press, 2001), page 109. Some scholars now question whether the Schlieffen Plan as originally proposed was anything more than a mechanism by which the German military sought to press their government into devoting more resources to the army. See *Inventing the Schlieffen Plan: German War Planning 1871–1914*: Terence Zuber (Oxford University Press, 2002).

6 Also in attendance were Sir Edward Grey, Foreign Secretary; Winston
 Churchill, First Lord of the Admiralty; Lord Roberts; Lord Kitchener; Prince
 Louis of Battenberg, First Sea Lord; Sir John French, C-in-C BEF; Sir Ian
 Hamilton, GOC Home Forces; Sir Henry Wilson, sub-Chief of General Staff,
 BEF; Sir John Cowans, Quartermaster General; Sir Stanley von Donop, Master
 of the Ordnance; Sir James Grierson; Sir Archibald Murray, Chief of General
 Staff, BEF; Colonel Hankey, Secretary to the Cabinet; and Colonel St G.
 Gorton. Kitchener was already on bad terms with not just French but also
 Wilson and Churchill (who pointedly did not include Kitchener in his 1937
 book *Great Contemporaries*).

7 Notes of the War Council meeting held at 10 Downing Street, 5 August 1914,
 Public Record Office London, CAB 42/1/2.

8 NLS Acc 3155 No 98. This passage is obviously crucial for our opinion of Haig's
 strategic thinking. The difficulty is that Haig's manuscript diary, in his handwriting, does not start until 13 August; the period of 29 July–13 August exists in
 a typed version only, one that Doris suggested she typed contemporaneously,
 as she received copies of the manuscript diary from Haig at the Front. It is
 therefore open to question as to whether Haig actually said these words, in this
 form, on the day in question. Given his dislike of extemporization and the
 carefully constructed phrasing of this passage, Haig would probably have written out his contribution to this first session of the War Council beforehand;
 but there is no handwritten document containing these thoughts in the Haig
 archive, which unfortunately adds to the mystery. It is obvious that the passage
 was written by Haig after the meeting – the parenthetical comment regarding
 Sir John French's opposition makes that clear. But this is not to concede to
 Haig's critics that this passage was designed by Haig to show him as possessing
 a greater prescience than he may have had on the day. Given that Haig argued
 very much along the same lines in a handwritten letter to Haldane just the day
 before, it is reasonable to suggest that this was indeed the line Haig took at this
 important Downing Street assembly.

9 *Field Marshal Sir Henry Wilson: His Life and Diaries*: ed. Major-General Sir C.
 E. Callwell, op. cit., page 159.

10 Major-General R. C. Money, quoted in *A Nation In Arms*: eds. Ian Beckett and
 Keith Simpson (Manchester University Press, 1985), page 68.

11 The Maxim had a maximum fire rate of 500 rounds per minute. The irrevoca-
 ble change to the battlefield wrought by machine-guns ought to have been
 well-known to the BEF's high command before August 1914, if the experience
 and views of progressively minded but unfortunately rather junior-ranking
 officers the School of Musketry at Hythe had filtered through to them. By 1910
 Hythe instructors were aware that two Maxim guns fired by men with only two

weeks' training were capable of inflicting 60 per cent casualties on an enemy 'advancing at two paces interval between 800 and 600 yards in one minute.' Bidwell and Graham, op. cit., page 29.

12  There is an entrenched myth that Haig was a congenital opponent of the machine-gun. It is – along with some other myths about Haig – deeply unfair. Its origination can be traced to the military historian and mischief-maker Basil Liddell Hart, whose early admiration of Haig expired in the 1930s, when it became fashionable to disparage the reputation of Britain's (long-dead) generals. Liddell Hart wrote in 1930 (*The Real War*, Faber & Faber, page 143) that Haig 'declared that it [the machine-gun] was "a much overrated weapon" and that this scale [two per battalion] "was more than sufficient".' Liddell Hart irritatingly did not provide a source for this allegation. John Terraine (*History Today*, August and November 1958) suggested the source was James Edmonds, and that Edmonds's original source was Brigadier-General C. D. Baker-Carr, who formed the first Machine-Gun School in France in late 1914. Baker-Carr had a grudge against Haig, who, he alleged, twice refused to give him command of the newly formed Tank Corps (Haig promoted another Old Cliftonian, Hugh Elles, to the role), on the grounds that Baker-Carr was not a Staff College graduate and was not a regular soldier (*From Chauffeur to Brigadier*: Brigadier-General C. D. Baker-Carr [Ernest Benn, 1930] page 202). Baker-Carr in his memoir does not attribute the anti-machine-gun comment to any named individual, although he criticized Haig on other grounds. In early 1915 Baker-Carr 'tentatively' put forward the proposal to GHQ that battalions should have four machine-guns, doubling the original number, and 'had been promptly told to mind my own business' (page 85). Baker-Carr then added: 'In the front line my suggestion was received with enthusiastic acclamation, but, as I progressed in a westerly direction towards St Omer French's GHQ, the enthusiasm gradually wilted until, at last, at GHQ, it expired completely and was replaced by a cold hostility' (page 86). Baker-Carr then wrote a memo on why he wanted to double the number of machine-guns per battalion and sent this to GHQ. The memo was eventually returned to him with the comments of army and corps commanders: 'Not a single individual had had the courage openly to support our suggestion, not even those who had privately given it their cordial approbation; many had "hedged" badly; others were frankly hostile. One Army Commander gave his opinion that "the machine-gun was a much over-rated weapon and two per battalion were more than sufficient." Another half-heartedly approved of the idea, but doubted if it could be carried out' (page 87). Yet by late 1914 Haig clearly believed machine-guns were vital, and, given his later call for more tanks, guns, aircraft and all forms of advanced weaponry, it is unlikely that he would have opposed an

extra couple of machine-guns per battalion. He wrote to his nephew Oliver Haig on 6 November 1914 (NLS Acc 3155 No 337): 'You must not fret because you are not out here. There is a great want of troops, and numbers are wanted. So I expect you will all soon be in the field. Meantime train your machine guns. It will repay you.' The Machine-Gun School was set up on 22 November 1914, ten days after the end of the first battle of Ypres; by November 1918 the Machine-Gun Corps had 6,432 officers and 124,920 other ranks. Perhaps Haig *was* the original source of Baker-Carr's story (we may never know for certain) but, even if he was, he certainly changed his mind after early 1915, when Baker-Carr began lobbying for more machine-guns.

13 *From Private to Field-Marshal*: Robertson, op. cit., page 214. Robertson added that by the Armistice of 11 November 1918 the BEF had more than 40,000 machine-guns and almost 6,500 artillery pieces, more than a third of which were medium and heavy calibre.

14 'The British Army and Conduct of Warfare, 1914–1918': Ian F. W. Beckett (MIT Securities Studies Program Seminar, 9 October 2002).

15 *The Great War 1914–18*: I. F. Beckett, (Longman, 2001), page 46.

16 Comments in *Some Lessons from the Russo-Japanese War*: J. A. L. Haldane (Hugh Rees, 1906), page 20.

17 Also known as Jean de Bloch and Johann von Bloch.

18 Published in an abbreviated English version in 1899 – *Is War Now Impossible? Being an Abridgement of 'The War of the Future in its Technical, Economic and Political Relations'* – by the English left-wing journalist W. T. Stead who, coincidentally, was also the political mentor of 'Daisy', Countess of Warwick, in her Socialist middle age.

19 *Is War Now Impossible?*: Ivan Bloch (Grant Richards, 1899).

20 For an analysis of Bloch's ideas and their impact on British military thinking of the time, see 'The Centenary of the British Publication of Jean de Bloch's *Is War Now Impossible?*' by Michael Welch, *War In History* 2000/7 (3) pp 273–94.

21 *Paths of Glory: The French Army 1914–1918*: Anthony Clayton (Weidenfeld & Nicolson, 2003), pp 36–7. Bidwell and Graham (op. cit., page 52) assert that at a Staff Conference in 1910, the first which Kiggell attended in his new function of Director of Staff after Haig had left for India, he summed up proceedings: 'After the Boer War the general opinion was that the result of the battle would for the future depend on fire-arms alone, and that the sword and thus bayonet were played out. But this idea is erroneous and was proved to be so in the late war in Manchuria. Everyone admits that. Victory is won actually by the bayonet, or by the fear of it, which amounts to the same thing as far as the actual conduct of the attack is concerned.'

22 General Herr, commander of the French VI Corps' artillery at the start of the war, described the French view of the coming conflict: 'The battle will be primarily the struggle between two infantries [. . .] the army must be an army of personnel and not of material. The artillery will only be an accessory arm.' (Quoted in Bidwell and Graham, op. cit., page 15.)

23 'German infantry field instructions, issued in 1906, make this very clear: "The actions of the infantry must be dominated by this one thought; forward on the enemy, cost what it may . . . an uninterrupted forward movement and the desire to get ahead of its neighbours should animate all units in the attack."' *The Old Contemptibles*: Robin Neillands (John Murray, 2004), page 135.

24 *The First World War*: Hew Strachan (Oxford University Press, 2001), page 230.

25 Ibid., page 241.

26 Each corps had two divisions; each division, three brigades; each brigade, four battalions. The full strength of a division was about 18,000 men.

27 *Douglas Haig: War Diaries and Letters*: ed. Sheffield & Bourne, op. cit., page 56. This extract is from the typed version of Haig's diary covering the Great War. That this entry for 11 August exists in the typed version only leaves room (for those inclined to see Haig in a bad light) for speculation that it was a *much* later addition, enabling Haig to lay claim to a foresight about Sir John's not being up to the job that he did not in fact possess at the time. To which the only answer is: in that case he rather understated the case against Sir John.

28 On 1 November 1914, at a meeting in Dunkirk, Kitchener proposed to Raymond Poincaré, the French President, and General Joffre that Sir John French be replaced by Hamilton. However, the French supported Sir John on this occasion, who, thanks to Henry Wilson, immediately learned of Kitchener's action – which naturally exacerbated their mutual antagonism.

29 The degree of the personal friction between politicians and senior army officers, and within their own ranks, is documented by Ian Beckett in his essay 'Frocks and Brasshats' in *The First World War and British Military History*: ed. Brian Bond (Clarendon Press, 1991).

30 Grierson died of an aortic aneurysm, en route to France, on 17 August 1914, robbing history of a tantalizing alternative. He had served as Director of Military Operations at the War Office in 1904–6, when he had travelled extensively through the region where the BEF was to fight. In his diary of the Great War (*At G.H.Q.*, 1931) Charteris wrote at the start of the war that Grierson 'knows Germany better than any soldier I have yet met' (page 10).

31 Secrett, op. cit., page 72.

32 *The Man I Knew*, op. cit., page 116. Doris said 'at the time I missed them bitterly, but it was all for the best, because I soon received news that I must vacate Government House [their official residence at Aldershot].'

33 Ibid., page 58.

34 There are many examples but one must suffice. On 26 February 1915 Haig visited Brigadier-General Herbert Henry Watts, commanding 21st Brigade, part of Haig's First Army. He found Watts to be 'a plucky hard little man, with no great brains, I should judge from his doings at Ypres last November.' This lack of brains did not prevent Haig (when C-in-C) approving Watts' promotion to lieutenant-general in command of XIX Corps in 1917. As an example of how Haig's career was meteorically successful by comparison with some of his peers, that same day he encountered Brigadier-General (later Major-General Sir) Sidney Lawford, then in command of 22nd Brigade. Lawford had been at Sandhurst with Haig and was commissioned into the 7th Fusiliers. Haig judged Lawford to be 'endowed with no great ability' but thought him nevertheless 'a hard-fighting, plucky soldier.'

35 Army Field Regulations, as laid out in the Field Service Pocket Book of the time, stated: 'In no circumstances is specific reference to be made on post cards, in letters, on matter posted in parcels, or in private diaries sent from the theatre of operations, to the place from which they are written or despatched; to plans of future operations, whether rumoured, surmised or known; to organization, numbers and movements of troops; to the armament of troops or fortresses; to defensive works; to the moral or physical condition of the troops; to casualties previous to the publication of official lists; to the service of maintenance; or in case the writer is one of the garrison of a besieged fortress, to the effects of hostile fire. Criticism of operations is forbidden, as are statements calculated to bring the army or individuals into disrepute.' (HMSO, 1914.)

36 *The Tragedy of Sir John French*: Cassar, op. cit., page 185.

37 King's Messengers (now Queen's Messengers) provided a diplomatic courier service, carrying all manner of items in sealed bags. Possessing diplomatic passports, they were and are protected from customs' inspections. Haig and his wife used these not just to transport official documents but also personal items, which, later in the war, included rationed food items and delicacies.

38 In the early days of the war Doris was informed by Sir Clive Wigram, the king's private secretary, that Haig's diaries would go direct to Buckingham Palace and then be passed to her. She told Douglas of this and he wrote back to her 'a very forcible reply' saying he would be sending dictated reports to the king but that his diaries were for her alone and she would continue getting them. When Doris visited Windsor Castle as the guest of the king in May 1917 'the war was not discussed, but Sir Clive Wigram was very anxious to see Douglas's diaries, which arrived for me each day, and he was much interested in the parts I showed to him.' (*The Man I Knew*, op. cit., page 196.) Clearly the

diaries were by that stage of the war seen by Haig as a vital part of his daily routine; that he troubled to see they were taken personally to Doris *each day* is indicative both of his habitual nature and also his concern that his version of events was safely in the hands of the one person apart from Henrietta he completely trusted.

39 For one example of many, Haig wrote to Leopold Rothschild on 2 November 1915, when Haig was GOC First Army, that he had sent Charteris to him, armed with 'some of our photos and maps that you may get an idea of what we are doing here.'

40 *Comrie Castle* served as a troopship throughout the war and ended its days in 1940 in the waters of Folkestone harbour, scuttled to provide a block against possible enemy entry. In his book *At G.H.Q.* (op. cit., page 9), Charteris wrote of this first crossing that there were only two available cabins and 'These were seized by D.H and Jimmy Grierson and their senior Staff officers. The rest of us bivouacked on deck. [. . .] It was very uncomfortable. There were no arrangements for feeding us on board, but fortunately [. . .] D. H. produced a well-stocked lunch basket. I was one of the lucky ones who were invited to share it.'

41 A good analysis of the relations between the French and British general staffs is in *Anglo-French Relations and Strategy on the Western Front, 1914–18*, by William James Philpott (Macmillan, 1996). This asserts that the initial ambiguity in the relationship created a situation in which the BEF was *de facto* forced into a subordinate role. Against this, Elizabeth Greenhalgh in *Victory Through Coalition* (Cambridge University Press, 2005) argues that the balance of power within the coalition shifted to and fro throughout the war, until Marshal Foch became overall supreme commander after the German spring offensives in 1918.

42 Command and Control in the 'Great Retreat' of 1914: The Disintegration of the British Cavalry Division: Nikolas Gardner, *Journal of Military History* Vol.63, No 1 (January 1999) pp 29–54.

43 *At G.H.Q.*: Charteris, op. cit., page 18.

44 Richard Holmes, in *The First World War and British Military History*: ed. Bond, op. cit., page 120.

45 *1914*: Sir John French (Constable, 1919), page 95.

46 NLS Acc 3155 No 98, diary entry for 25 September 1914.

47 Ibid.

48 4 December 1914, *Douglas Haig: War Diaries and Letters 1914–1918*, ed. Sheffield and Bourne, op. cit., page 84.

49 Sheffield and Bourne, ibid., pp 84–5.

50 Ibid., page 84.

51 Ibid., page 87.

# Chapter Nine

1 NLS Acc 3155 No 257.
2 Now called Bayer, the company still uses the Sanatogen brand name for a variety of vitamin supplements.
3 NLS Acc 3155 No 257.
4 Ibid.
5 Ibid.
6 Ibid.
7 NLS Acc 3155 No 214: 23 January 1915.
8 Sir John French wanted Henry Wilson as his chief of staff but Asquith and Kitchener blocked this over Wilson's involvement in the Curragh Incident. In his diary Wilson wrote that he learned the news from Sir John who 'hinted that the less work I did the better. I might go to Russia and see what they were doing there. How funny!' (Calwell, op. cit., page 194). Instead, Wilson was given another key appointment, that of chief liaison officer between Sir John and General Joffre. Haig's suspicions of Wilson were not alleviated by his being informed by the incorrigible gossip Repington (on 22 January) that Wilson had asked Victor Huguet, French liaison officer at the British GHQ, to request that Joffre and the French government be pushed for Wilson to be appointed Sir John's chief of staff.
9 Murray after the war wrote frankly to General Sir Ian Hamilton on his brief stint at the War Office with Kitchener: 'I cannot describe to you, working with him day after day, how impossible I found him. He never had his CIGS, AG, and QMG in his room together and told them what he wanted. No, he sent for them in turn and gave his instructions, telling each of them as little as possible, whilst he kept the threads in his own hands. There was only one branch of the work that I got on well with him and that was the "K" [New] Armies. Here it was "hands off my own troops, they must have every chance". For the Territorials, their history, organisation, and customs he cared nothing. He would at any time break them up and send them anywhere poorly armed and trained, and inadequately equipped. No "K" Division left the country incomplete.' (From *Soldier True*: Victor Bonham-Carter, op. cit., pp 132–3.) Kitchener's ego, fuelled by his paranoid contempt for others, helps explain why Britain conducted itself so poorly in the early years of the Great War; but his popular reputation today, thanks almost entirely to that single iconic poster, remains high.
10 *From Chauffeur to Brigadier*: Baker-Carr, op. cit., page 89.
11 Diary entry for 4 January 1915.
12 The RFC overall was commanded by Major-General (later Lieutenant-General Sir) David Henderson, Director-General of Military Aeronautics before the war.

13 Part of the 'donkeys' myth is the notion that British generals lived a comfortably danger-free existence. Yet of the 1,257 British generals who served in the Great War, 232 were killed and wounded, a casualty rate of 18.5 per cent. (Centre for First World War Studies, University of Birmingham: *http://www.firstworldwar.bham.ac.uk/biogs.htm*, and *Bloody Red Tabs*: Frank Davies and Graham Maddox [Leo Cooper, 1995], page xii.)

14 Brigadier-General Richard Butler, another old Aldershot associate, replaced Gough as Haig's chief of staff.

15 NLS Acc 3155, No 214: diary entry for 22 February 1915.

16 *Fire Power*: Bidwell and Graham, op. cit., page 57.

17 Rawlinson's nickname among his contemporaries, according to Brigadier General James Edmonds, was 'The Cad': *The First World War and British Military History*: ed. Brian Bond, (Clarendon Press, 1991), page 73.

18 NLS Acc 3155 No 214: diary entry for 2 March 1915.

19 NLS Acc 3155 No 214: diary entry for 19 March 1915. This was naive and more a reflection of Haig's congenital loathing of newspapers; German commanders would have been only too well aware of the duration of the bombardment.

20 *The Great War 1914–1918*: Ian Beckett (Longman, 2001), page 166.

21 *The Man I Knew*, op. cit., pp 127–8.

22 Sheffield & Bourne, op. cit., page 112, diary entry for 27 March 1915.

23 Ibid., page 115, diary entry for 12 April 1915. Robertson in his autobiography (*From Private to Field-Marshal*, 1921), said Lambton 'was a pleasant and practical officer to do business with.' (page 225).

24 Haig's First Army took no part in Second Ypres save for sending reinforcements when called upon.

25 Bennet Burleigh had covered a number of earlier wars in sensationalist but shallow style, including the Sudan.

26 *Memories of Forty-Eight Years Service*: Smith-Dorrien, op. cit., page 479.

27 Ibid., page 479. It is worth noting here that Smith-Dorrien's close relationship with King George V did not save him from this humiliation. The king was, ultimately, powerless when it came to military appointments – a fact worth bearing in mind when we come to David Lloyd George's explanation in his *War Memoirs* that he could not sack Haig because he enjoyed the king's backing.

28 Ibid., page 479.

29 NLS Acc 3155 No 214: 30 May 1915. This kind of indiscretion was sometimes carried to extremes by Haig in his correspondence with Rothschild and others who occupied no official posts. On 25 October 1915 Haig sent Rothschild a copy (marked 'secret') of a criticism by Robertson of a proposal to transfer British troops to the Balkans, with the comment: 'I thought possibly the

soldiers' view of this question might interest you!!! Robertson is a good sound practical fellow. In my opinion he is most wanted at the head of the General Staff in London. The present man (Sir A. Murray) seems to modify his views to suit Lord K's orders!! The war will be won or lost in <u>London</u>.' Haig evidently suspected that Rothschild, a substantial figure, might use his own backdoor influence to help scupper this scheme. Duff Cooper in his biography asserts that Haig first learned of his appointment as C-in-C from a letter from Rothschild (7 December 1915) which enigmatically said 'all had been satisfactorily arranged' (*Haig*, op. cit., Vol.1, page 278).

30  Richard Holmes, in *The First World War and British Military History*: ed. Bond (Clarendon Press, 1991), page 126.

31  *The Great War*: Beckett, op. cit., page 46.

32  *British Logistics on the Western Front*: Ian Malcolm Brown (Praeger, 1998), pp 90–92.

33  Asquith excluded Haldane, by now falsely tarnished as a German sympathizer, from his National Coalition government, but in a courageous public gesture of his own esteem for Haldane, George V conferred on him the Order of Merit.

34  Caillaux was a focus for French pacifist activities throughout the Great War. He was imprisoned on 4 January 1918 on a charge of treason, although the case was so politically fraught that his trial was delayed until February 1920, when he was acquitted of the main accusation but found guilty of 'damaging the external security of the state' and sentenced to three years. Amnestied in 1924, he returned to parliament where, in 1938, he backed Edouard Daladier's attempts to negotiate with the Nazis. He declined an invitation to join the Vichy government and died in 1944.

35  *The Private Papers of Douglas Haig*: Robert Blake (Eyre & Spottiswoode, 1952), page 95.

36  'Lord Kitchener and the Battle of Loos' by Rhodri Williams, in *War, Strategy, and International Politics*: ed. Lawrence Freedman, Paul Hayes and Robert O'Neill (Clarendon Press, 1992).

37  NLS Acc 3155 No 214.

38  Henry Wilson's close relations with the French high command date from his visit in December 1909 to the École Supérieure de Guerre in Paris, where he struck up a close and lasting friendship with General Foch, its commandant. In a second meeting in Paris in January 1910 Wilson asked Foch what was the smallest British military force that would be useful in a fight with Germany. 'One single private soldier, and we would take good care that he was killed,' replied Foch. (*Field-Marshal Sir Henry Wilson, His Life and Diaries*: ed. Callwell [Cassell, 1927,] Vol.1, page 79.)

39 At the Ritz, in Paris, Esher was one evening spotted sporting his own personal uniform (he held no rank save that of honorary colonel): 'His lordship was gorgeously caparisoned; round his neck hung a cross, and his breast was so covered with medals that I came to the conclusion that not only must he be at least a Commander-in-Chief, but must also have played a prominent part in the Hundred Years War.' (*The Enigmatic Edwardian*: James Lees-Milne, op. cit., page 264.) That a maverick such as Esher was permitted to undermine the established ambassador while employed by the Secretary of State for War was itself symptomatic of the inherent flaws of the British wartime establishment. Millerand, regarded as so vital a presence in June 1915, was in any case pushed from office in October 1915; his departure saw no collapse of French commitment to the war. Being so badly wrong in his judgement of French morale neither perturbed Esher nor caused his star to wane back in London.

40 Rhodri Williams, op. cit., pp. 126 and 131.

41 *British Strategy and War Aims 1914–1916*: David French (Allen & Unwin, 1986), page 112.

42 Haig implicitly here reveals his ignorance of the possibilities of indirect fire by artillery.

43 *Haig*: Duff Cooper, op. cit., Vol.2, pp 254–5 and *Douglas Haig: The War Diaries and Letters 1914–1918*: ed. Sheffield and Bourne, op. cit., pp 128–9.

44 Sheffield and Bourne, ibid., page 128.

45 Duff Cooper drew a discreet veil over this episode, despite being fully aware of Haig's diary entries, which told the unvarnished version, writing simply: 'At his interview with His Majesty the war in all its phases was discussed, and the two found themselves in substantial agreement both as regards principles and personalities.' (*Haig*, Vol.1, page 253.) Nor did Doris mention this aspect of the conversation in her biography.

46 Diary entry for 14 July 1915: Sheffield and Bourne, ibid., page 130. Wigram, commissioned into the Royal Artillery (like Stamfordham), later transferred to the Indian Cavalry before joining the royal household staff. King George V found him a 'glutton for work' (*King George V*: Rose, page 144), though a fellow equerry, Sir Frederick Ponsonby, thought Wigram had 'the true British contempt for all foreigners which is now rather out of date, and his political views are those of the ordinary officer at Aldershot.' Which undoubtedly made him all the more useful an intermediary between George V and Haig.

47 *King George V*, Kenneth Rose, op. cit., page 186.

48 English translation in *Military Operations France and Belgium, 1915*: Brigadier-General Sir James Edmonds (HMSO, 1928), Vol.2, page 125.

49 As Elizabeth Greenhalgh has pointed out, this deal between Kitchener and Joffre in July-August 1915 could be interpreted as implying French control of

the BEF would endure as long as the war lasted: 'The wording of the formula states specifically that so long as the fighting is taking place on French soil in order to liberate French territory the initiative belongs to Joffre.' ( *Victory Through Coalition*, op. cit., page 30.)

50 After the war much of the controversy over Anglo-Allied command and control focused on the episode in the spring of 1918 when, under tremendous pressure from the German offensives, Foch was anointed supreme commander of the Allied armies in France and Belgium. This much earlier concession by Kitchener has been largely overlooked and in memoirs by leading figures is not mentioned. Robertson, for example, (*From Private to Field-Marshal*, 1921) merely records that by December 1915: 'Any suggestion at this time of introducing the same system of centralised command as that which the prospect of stark defeat compelled the Allies to adopt in 1918 would have been peremptorily turned down as too impossible for any self-respecting country to entertain.'

51 *Haig*: Duff Cooper, op. cit., Vol.1, page 257.

52 Sheffield and Bourne, op. cit., page 144. Diary entry for 6 September 1915.

53 Sheffield and Bourne, op. cit., page 137.

54 *Great Contemporaries*: Winston Churchill, op. cit., pp 88–9.

55 In *British Logistics on the Western Front* (Praeger, 1998), pp 100–2. Ian Malcolm Brown argues that this insufficient quantity of artillery condemned the attack to failure even before it started. Yet had the quantity of gas been greater and its delivery not so botched, it might have been more successful.

56 Sheffield and Bourne, op. cit., page 149, diary entry for 18 September 1915.

57 *The Tragedy of Sir John French*: Cassar, op. cit., page 263.

58 *Chemical Soldiers*: Donald Richter (Leo Cooper, 1992), page 31. The point of thirty minutes was that the BEF's intelligence understood that German gas masks at the time were not effective after twenty minutes.

59 Sheffield and Bourne, op. cit., page 152.

60 Sheffield and Bourne, op. cit., page 153.

61 Later in the war, poison gas was delivered more accurately by shells fired from artillery and mortars; but by that time both sides had developed more effective gas masks, and the shock impact of gas attacks, potentially so important in this first British use at Loos, had been reduced almost to zero.

62 *From Private to Field-Marshal*, op. cit., page 233.

63 Sheffield and Bourne, op. cit., page 159, diary entry for 28 September 1915.

64 *Haig*: Duff Cooper, op. cit., Vol.1, pp 271–2.

65 Sheffield and Bourne, op. cit., page 163; diary entry for 9 October 1915.

66 NLS Acc 3155 No 214.

67 Robertson's role as an intermediary between the king, the government, Sir John French and Haig in this episode is indicative of how a nominal role – in

his case French's Chief of General Staff at GHQ – did not necessarily reflect the actual and often more influential backroom functions that senior officers performed. In his autobiography *From Private to Field Marshal*, published in 1921, Robertson makes no mention of this episode, nor of the sacking of French, who for anyone reading Robertson's book in isolation, mysteriously just disappears from France at the end of 1915.

68 Diary entry for 17 October. Sheffield & Bourne, op. cit., pp 165–6; *The Private Papers of Douglas Haig 1914–1919*: ed. Robert Blake, op. cit., page 108.

69 *Soldier True*: Victor Bonham-Carter, op. cit., page 125. This letter is undated according to the author but is clearly from late 1915.

70 NLS 3155 No 334.

71 Cassar, op. cit., pages 285 and 287.

72 'Like most other senior French generals, Joffre absolutely refused to converse in any language except his own, but he was quick to grasp the sense of what was said to him, no matter how quaint the words or vile the pronunciation.' *From Private to Field-Marshal*: Robertson, op. cit., page 286.

73 Sheffield & Bourne, op. cit., page 171.

74 *Victory Through Coalition*: Elizabeth Greenhalgh, op. cit., page 44.

# Chapter Ten

1 Dated 20 March 1919, Haig's final dispatch was published on 10 April 1919 in a fourth supplement to the *London Gazette* of 8 April 1919.

2 Diary entry 1 January 1916. According to Haig, des Vallières regarded Joffre as an 'underbred individual': NLS Acc 3155 No 96.

3 *Soldier True*: Bonham-Carter, op. cit., page 147.

4 NLS Acc 3155 No 104. The hush of the congregation probably resulted from a shocked silence at Haig's arrival rather than anything to do with the service.

5 Ruth De Pree, Haig's niece, had a distinct memory of Haig's religious faith, as filtered through Grierson, just before war broke out in August 1914: 'General Grierson went to visit him [at Aldershot]. One Sunday coming back from an Episcopalian church service, General Grierson remarked, "That is not the kind of service Douglas likes – the sort of thing he cares for is more like this – Oh Lord come doon and help us, come doon and help us in oor need, and if ye dinna come doon and help us ye'll hear mair aboot it."' NLS, Haig Papers, De Pree Memoir.

6 *Douglas Haig As I Knew Him*: G. S. Duncan (George Allen & Unwin), page 19.

7 Haig sometimes invited some of his staff to accompany him to Duncan's church. Charteris noted on 29 April 1917 that 'the sermon was to the effect that we all had to believe that God is working in us for a definite purpose; all very

cheering if you are quite certain that that purpose is our victory. But it is difficult to see why a German preacher could not preach just such a sermon to Hindenburg and Ludendorff. All the same, D.H. seems to derive an extraordinary amount of moral strength from these sermons.' *At G.H.Q.*, op. cit., page 219.

8 There was also a political edge to Haig's religion. On 22 July 1917 he told the Archbishop of York, visiting GHQ, that 'we ought to aim at organising a great Imperial Church to which all honest citizens of the Empire could belong. In my opinion Church and State must advance together and hold together against those forces of revolution which threaten to destroy our State.'

9 'The clergy of the Church of England are squabbling terribly amongst themselves over High Church and Low Church methods.' (Diary entry 30 March 1916). When Randall Davidson, Archbishop of Canterbury, on 21 May 1916, asked Haig what he wished for from the Church, he was explicit: 'The Chaplains should preach to the troops about the objects of Great Britain in carrying on this war. We have no selfish motive, but are fighting for the good of humanity. [The Church of England] must cease quarrelling amongst themselves. In the Field we cannot tolerate any narrow sectarian ideas. We must all be united whether we are clerics or ordinary troops.' *The Private Papers of Douglas Haig*. ed. Blake, op. cit., page 143.

10 On 29 June 1916, as the preliminary bombardment for the Battle of the Somme was raging, Haig's dinner guest at his Advanced GHQ was the Reverend George Duncan, by now Haig's *de facto* personal spiritual adviser.

11 *Haig*: Duff Cooper, op. cit., Vol.1, pp 327–8.

12 *Douglas Haig As I Knew Him*: G. S. Duncan, op. cit., pp 119–120.

13 NLS Acc 3155 No 347/25.

14 This figure rose to more than 1.36m by 1 July, the opening disastrous day of the Somme. The BEF's peak was achieved on 1 August 1917 with an estimated 2,044,627 officers and other ranks, including Dominion units. *Statistics of the Military Effort of the British Empire, 1914–1920* (HMSO, 1922), page 64.

15 Henry Wilson on 17 September 1914 had privately mocked the idea that Kitchener could raise such a large army so quickly: 'His ridiculous and preposterous army of 25 Corps is the laughing-stock of every soldier in Europe. It took the Germans 40 years of incessant work to make an army of 25 Corps with the aid of conscription; it will take us to all eternity to do the same by voluntary effort.' (*Field Marshal Sir Henry Wilson: His Life and Diaries*, ed. Callwell, op. cit., page 178.) Wilson's extravagant language and wayward judgement was wrong on this occasion, as it had been in October 1914, when he was convinced that the war would be 'over in February or March [1915].' (Ibid., page 181.)

16 The American journalist Isaac F. Marcosson in 1917 wrote: 'The Commander-in-Chief bears the same relation to the carrying on of war that a Master Sales Manager bears to the dissemination of a product. His task is to deploy his output where it can hit the hardest, and on the success of this alignment his Cause stands or falls.' ('A Visit to Sir Douglas Haig', The Avenue Press, 1917.) John Hussey has described Haig as 'principal director of Britain's newest and greatest corporate enterprise' (*Haig: A Reappraisal 70 Years On*: ed. Bond and Cave, op. cit., 1999, page 19). Shifting from command of the First Army to C-in-C of the BEF was akin to moving from running an individual supermarket to becoming chief executive of Wal-Mart.

17 *A Brass Hat in No Man's Land*: Brigadier-General F. P. Crozier (Jonathan Cape, 1930), page 144. Crozier later commanded the Auxiliary Division of the Royal Irish Constabulary, fighting the IRA, although he resigned in protest at the brutality of the Black and Tans.

18 Diary entry 14 December 1915 (Sheffield and Bourne, op. cit., page 173.) The old antagonism with Churchill had been deepened by Churchill's promotion of the Dardanelles campaign, which Haig considered a terrible waste of manpower and resources; so it was, but, had it been better planned and executed, Churchill might have been considered a war leader of genius long before 1940.

19 There are numerous cases of senior BEF officers being abruptly sacked with litle obvious justification. On 8 August 1916, for example, Haig sacked Lieutenant-General Sir John Keir, GOC VI Corps, on the basis of a report by General Allenby (GOC Third Army at the time) that Keir's 'defensive arrangements were unsatisfactory, and that he had no real plans worked out for offensive action.' (NLS Acc 3155 No 96, diary entry for 8 August 1916.) Keir, just two years older than Haig, was livid at being pushed out simply because he and Allenby did not get on.

20 Before this appointment Kiggell had not served in France and was resented by some at GHQ as an inexperienced interloper. Kiggell embodied the old attitudes of the regular army's emphasis on fighting spirit, and adhered throughout the war to the view that it was men with bayonets rather than guns and shells that won wars.

21 Colonel 'Micky' Ryan, attached to Haig's staff throughout the war as medical officer, was, according to Charteris, 'the only man who can bully D.H. He sends him to bed like a naughty child if he tries to stay up too late at night, but as a matter of fact D.H.'s day is mapped out with the regularity of a public school [. . .] He is very upset if anything interferes with it, and distinguished visitors have to conform.' (*At G.H.Q.*, op. cit., page 169.)

22 For those who credit the possibility of psychosomatic disorders, it is salutary that the splenetic Sir John French was frequently in bed with bouts of flu when

C-in-C, while the phlegmatic Haig, who relished the job even at times of intense crisis, usually enjoyed better health.

23 *The Press and The General Staff*: Nevill Lytton (Collins, 1920), page 66–7.

24 *Blindfold and Alone*: Cathryn Corns & John Hughes-Wilson (Cassell, 2001), page 450.

25 Moreover, Haig's expectations and those of the ordinary Tommy were inevitably different. 'For many, [of the New Army recruits] army food was more substantial, and probably more nutritious, than what they had been able to buy on pre-war wages. [. . .] Away from the front line, their accommodation was often no more overcrowded than what they had been used to at home.' Jay Winter, 'Army and Society' in *A Nation At Arms*, eds. Ian F. W. Beckett and Keith Simpson (Manchester University Press, 1985), page 196.

26 Among the literary guests were Conan Doyle, H. G. Wells, and George Bernard Shaw, the latter being at the behest of Haig himself, according to Charteris (*At G.H.Q.*, op. cit., page 221). With some difficulty, the vegetarian Shaw was provided with two poached eggs, spinach and macaroni for lunch. Later on he took a drive in a tank, and tried to tip the driver upon leaving.

27 NLS Acc 3155 No 104.

28 A small selection: General Galliéni, French Minister of War, looked like 'an old rag and bone man, gaunt and thin' (29 December 1915); Colonel des Vallières, who took over as head of the French mission at GHQ, was 'So quiet and silent for a Frenchman – and such a retiring gentlemanly man' (1 January 1916).

29 Sassoon was an MP for the Unionist Party with a constituency in Kent, inherited from his father in 1912, when he was just twenty-three. As was expected of a gentleman, Sassoon waived his MP's annual salary.

30 This regiment of volunteers remained at Canterbury until 8 October 1915, when it arrived at Gallipoli and was attached to the 42nd Division. Sassoon had been seconded to the staff at GHQ in February 1915 and later that year joined the staff of Rawlinson's IV Corps as an ADC. He ended the war with the rank of major.

31 Peter Stansky (in *Sassoon: The Worlds of Philip and Sybil*, Yale University Press, 2003, page 48) wrote that Sassoon's wedding present in August 1913 to his adored sister Sybil was a white Rolls-Royce, which she and her husband drove round India on their honeymoon. They called it '*la vièrge*' or 'the virgin'. Sir Philip had a more famous cousin, the poet and war hero Siegfried Sassoon, but their relationship was very distant.

32 Such were Sassoon's diplomatic gifts that after the war he was taken on by Haig's greatest enemy, Lloyd George, as his private secretary.

33 Quoted in Stansky, op. cit., page 56.

34 Sassoon would casually call upon key figures working behind the scenes in Paris and London, simply to gauge the mood. A typical task for which Sassoon was perfectly adapted was described by Bertie in Paris on 3 October 1916: 'I had an unexpected visit this afternoon from Philip Sassoon accompanied by one of Haig's staff: they brought civilities but no particular message from him; everything is going on satisfactorily. They asked whether here there is contentment with what the British are doing, and what the feeling in the public is; I said that notwithstanding the croakings of some ignorant busybodies [by which he intended Esher] everything is going well.' *Diaries*, Lord Bertie of Thame, op. cit. Vol.II, page 38.

35 Esher carried on in his old self-important way. As the Somme dragged on he wrote to Haig from Paris on 17 August 1916: 'I cannot understand why *Joffre* has a liaison office with London: and *you* have none with Paris! Why is this? If it were not for me, you would be shut off from all knowledge of what goes on here.' (NLS Acc 3155 No 214 [f].) Given Esher's previous promotion of Haig's career, Haig no doubt paid attention to this unreliable informant.

36 NLS Acc 3155 No 214.

37 Ibid. Sassoon meant General Luigi Cadorna, chief of staff of the Italian Army, who had visited GHQ on 25 March. Italy was initially neutral but declared war on Austria–Hungary on 23 May 1915. Haig's belief that the Italian front was not a sector where the war would be won or lost can be gauged from the fact that, when over dinner Cadorna suggested Haig visit it, 'Douglas politely declined the invitation, pointing out that he was really too busy at the moment but that after the war he would be delighted to accept!' [*The Man I Knew*, op. cit., pp 151–2].

38 Cadorna's deputy.

39 *A Brass Hat in No Man's Land*: Brigadier-General F. P. Crozier, op. cit., page 154.

40 About £1.3m in today's money.

41 NLS 3155 Acc No 347/41: Details from Haig's bank book, on the front of which is inscribed Lieut. Gen (crossed out and Field Marshal substituted) 'Sir Douglas Haig. Royal Bank of Scotland, from 2nd June 1914 to 1918.' Income tax had risen to 3 shillings and sixpence per £1 in September 1915.

42 *A Nation In Arms*: eds. Ian Beckett and Keith Simpson (Manchester University Press, 1985), pp 46 and 77.

43 Many suspected Sassoon to be homosexual but there is no conclusive evidence of his having had intimate relations with anyone or anything.

44 When Sassoon visited Haig at Bemersyde after the war, Doris would 'make him wait in the hall', according to Dawyck Haig (conversation with the author, February 2005).

45 By 1916, recruitment to the BEF was beginning to dry up, as initial euphoria soured. The January 1916 Military Service Act, which hoped to coerce where

encouragement was failing, introduced conscription in the UK (excluding Ireland) for single men age 18–41, with numerous exemptions. Monthly enlistments nevertheless continued to run at less than half those under the previous voluntary enlistment and in May 1916 the government passed a second Military Service Act, which included married men of the same age range. Time-expired regular soldiers were still permitted to leave the Army, and as late as the summer of 1916, 5,000 a month on average were doing so. During the Great War 2.4 million British men volunteered for military service; another 2.5 million were conscripted. (*The Great War*, Beckett, op. cit., page 210.)

46 The War Council evolved from the Dardanelles Committee in June 1915 and became the War Committee in December 1915.

47 Blake, op. cit., page 136; diary entry for Sunday 12 March 1916.

48 *Journals and Letters*, Esher, op. cit., pp 1–12.

49 *The Life of General Lord Rawlinson*: Maurice, op. cit., page 152.

50 *The Somme*: Peter Hart (Weidenfeld & Nicolson, 2005), page 35.

51 *1914–1918, The History of the First World War*: David Stevenson (Allen Lane, 2004), page 162.

52 Perversely, Joffre insisted that, despite Verdun, the Allied contingents at Salonika should be reinforced with 100 heavy artillery pieces and more troops, further sapping the firepower for the Somme.

53 Doris toned this down in her biography, saying Haig referred to Joffre as 'a dear old boy'. (*The Man I Knew*, op. cit., page 142.)

54 *Haig*: Duff Cooper, op. cit., Vol. I, pp 311–12. For Haig, engineers were by definition incapable of organizing battles.

55 *The Life of General Rowlinson of Trent*: Maurice, op. cit., page 158.

56 Diary entry for 5 April 1916. This, of course, is reminiscent of Haig's riposte to Rawlinson's limited aims at Neuve Chapelle, when Rawlinson was GOC IV Corps.

57 Maurice, op. cit., page 158.

58 Diary entry 10 May 1916.

59 *Douglas Haig: The Educated Soldier*: Terraine, op. cit., page 204.

60 *British Logistics on the Western Front*: Brown, op. cit.

61 *The Somme*: Robin Prior and Trevor Wilson (Yale University Press, 2005); *The Killing Ground*: Travers, op. cit.

62 *British Logistics on the Western Front*: Brown, op. cit., page 125.

63 *The Somme*: Prior and Wilson, op. cit., page 28.

64 Lieutenant-Colonel Ernest Swinton DSO had served in the Boer War and spent the early days of the Great War as an official war correspondent. During December 1914 he spotted a Holt's tractor at work in Britain and from that

developed the idea of what became the tank, gaining the support of Winston Churchill (who thereafter always claimed to have been its 'inventor').

65 'This attack on September 15, from the point of view of tank operations, was not a great success. Of the forty-nine tanks employed, only thirty-two reached their starting-points; nine pushed ahead of the infantry and caused considerable loss to the enemy, and nine others, though they never caught up with the infantry, did good work in clearing up points where the enemy was still holding out. Of the remaining fourteen, nine broke down from mechanical trouble, and five became ditched.' *Tanks in the Great War*: Col. J. F. C. Fuller (John Murray, 1920), page 56.

66 *Haig*: Duff Cooper, op. cit., Vol. I, page 313.

67 *Haig*: Duff Cooper, op. cit., Vol. I, pp 314–15; Sheffield & Bourne op. cit., page 186.

68 Sheffield & Bourne, op. cit., page 188.

69 One of the resentments that developed on the British side was the suspicion that ordinary soldiers and the British authorities generally were made to pay an exorbitant price for everything they purchased. 'The shopkeepers in the towns had never known such prosperity. For example, the owner of a sporting-goods establishment in St Omer told me that he had made more money in the eighteen months during which G. H. Q. was there, than he had made in the previous twenty-five years he had been in business.' (Baker-Carr, op. cit., pp 92–3.)

70 *The Somme*, Prior and Wilson, op. cit., page 58.

71 Prior and Wilson, ibid., page 60.

72 NLS Acc 3155 No 214.

73 *The Man I Knew*, op. cit., page 156.

74 For the battle itself Haig moved his Advanced GHQ to Beauquesne, about twenty miles north-east of Amiens.

75 *Gas! The Story of the Special Brigade*: Major-General C. H. Foulkes (William Blackwood & Sons, 1934), page 123.

76 NLS Acc 3155 No 97, diary entry for 27 June 1916.

77 NLS Acc 3155 No 144.

78 Maurice, op. cit., page 161.

79 The Ministry of Munitions had been shaken up by Lloyd George following the shell scandal of the previous year; but greater quantity of output was not accompanied by notable improvements in the quality of fuzes.

80 And with 150,000 more yards of defences behind the front, according to Prior and Wilson, op. cit., page 53.

81 *British Logistics on the Western Front*: Brown, op. cit., page 134.

82 *The Somme*, Prior and Wilson, op. cit., page 115.

83 NLS Acc 3155 No 96, diary entry for 15 June 1916.

84 The British army's conception of the battlefield prior to and through much of the Great War has been rightly castigated by many writers; Shelford Bidwell and Dominick Graham (op. cit., pp 26–7) argue that British military training at the time did not lay down as a fundamental tenet that 'the positive purpose of taking an objective was to establish a new fire base on it from which to continue the fire-fight with advantage. That ought to have been the shared aim of the infantry and the artillery. [. . .] The existing doctrine [which prevailed at the Somme] encouraged the infantry to attack ground for no better reason than that the enemy was occupying it and firing at them. The artillery became an accessory to this directionless motivation when it bombarded the enemy to enable the infantry to "push on" regardless of the consequences.' While this is true in general, it neglects the fact that, at the Somme, the quantity of artillery and shells was in any case insufficient for the purposes Haig had to attempt to implement in a hurry.

85 *The Somme*, Prior and Wilson, op. cit., page 115.

86 Fourth supplement to the *London Gazette*, 10 April 1919.

87 NLS Acc 3155 No. 347/25: 'Letters written by his sister Henrietta under the spirit influence of her brother George.'

88 *The First World War 1914–1918*: Charles À Court Repington (Constable, 1921), pp 265–6.

89 Brigadier-General George Stanley Clive, head of the British Mission at the French GQG and later Haig's intelligence chief at GHQ after the forced removal of Brigadier-General John Charteris.

90 NLS Acc 3155 No 97, diary entry for 8 August 1916.

91 NLS Acc 3155 No 214.

92 *From Chauffeur to Brigadier*, Baker-Carr, op. cit., page 196.

93 NLS Acc 3155 No 96, diary entry for 22 August 1916.

94 *From Chauffeur to Brigadier*, Baker-Carr, op. cit., pp 192–3.

95 *Tanks in the Great War*, J. F. C. Fuller, op. cit., page 59.

96 *The Somme*: Prior and Wilson, op. cit., page 226.

97 *The Man I Knew*: The Countess Haig, op. cit., page 170.

98 NLS Acc 3155 No 108.

99 NLS Acc 3155 No 214 (f): Letter from Esher to Haig, 13 October 1916.

100 *Morning Post*, 28 September 1916.

101 Quoted in *Lloyd George*: Peter Rowland (Barrie and Jenkins, 1975), page 343.

102 NLS Acc 3155 No 108.

103 Geddes lives on in popular memory for his statement at the end of the war that 'we will get everything out of her [Germany] that you can squeeze out of a lemon and a bit more. We will squeeze her till the pips squeak.' He had come to the notice of Lloyd George through his success as a deputy director

of munitions supply, after Lloyd George became Secretary of State for War in July 1916.

104 *British Logistics on the Western Front*: Brown, op. cit., p 140.

105 *Sir Douglas Haig's Despatches*: ed. J. H. Boraston (J. M. Dent & Sons, 1919), dispatch dated 25 December 1917, pp 142–3.

106 'The Hidden Army: Structural Problems in the British Officer Corps, 1900–1918': Tim Travers, *Journal of Contemporary History*, Vol.17, No 3 (July 1982), pp 523–544.

107 NLS Acc 3155 No 214 (h).

108 NLS Acc 3155 No 97, diary entry for 8 November 1916.

109 *The Somme*, Prior and Wilson, op. cit., page 294.

110 NLS Acc 3155 No 97, diary entry for 12 November 1916.

111 NLS Acc 3155 No 97, diary entry for 13 November 1916.

112 NLS Acc 3155 No 97, diary entry for 16 November 1916.

113 NLS Acc 3155 No 97, diary entry for 24 November 1916.

114 *Haig*: Duff Cooper, op. cit., Vol, II page 8. Northcliffe was a dangerously fickle ally. When he visited GHQ on 21 July 1916, he took to Haig but, as Charteris realized, this meant little: '[. . .] we can count on his support until some new maggot enters into his brain.' (*At G.H.Q.*, op. cit., page 157.)

115 *Lloyd George*: Peter Rowland, op. cit., page 373. Lloyd George's Cabinet on taking office consisted of 8 Liberals, 2 Labour Party members, and 14 Unionists.

116 NLS Acc 3155 347/46.

117 Sheffield and Bourne, op. cit., page 261.

118 The rank of Field Marshal, the highest in the British army, was created by King George II in 1736; the first holder was George Hamilton, Earl of Orkney.

119 Sheffield and Bourne, op. cit., page 261.

# Chapter Eleven

1 NLS Acc 3155 No 214 (f): Letter from Esher to Haig, 1 August 1916.

2 The War Cabinet initially comprised (as well as Lloyd George) a series of individuals who each had their reasons for distrusting army officers. They were Andrew Bonar Law, the Conservative MP and Chancellor of the Exchequer; Lord Milner; Lord Curzon; and Arthur Henderson, leader of the Labour Party.

3 *Lloyd George: A Diary*: Frances Stevenson, Hutchinson, 1971; entry for 15 January 1917, page 139.

4 NLS Acc 3155 No 110.

5 *The Military Correspondence of Field Marshal Sir William Robertson*: ed. David Woodward, Army Records Society (Bodley Head, 1989), pp 144–5.

6  *The Press and The General Staff*: Lytton, op. cit., pp 66–71.

7  Charteris's reputation never recovered from this incident; he was blamed in London for giving Haig bad advice. Lord Derby, uncomfortable with the atmosphere of closeted intrigue that prevailed in the War Cabinet, wrote to Haig on 20 February 1917 (NLS Acc 3155 347/46): 'You will get an official letter on the subject, but I cannot help saying that I think Charteris's action in passing this interview for publication without first submitting it to you is absolutely unjustifiable. He has let you down very badly, and let you down in a respect which you in France can hardly realise at the present moment. He has destroyed in this country all confidence in his judgement, and everything which passes through his hands as having been approved by him will be subject of suspicion.'

8  *Haig*: Duff Cooper, op. cit., Vol.II, page 38.

9  NLS Acc 3100 No 347/26: Article from *Blackwood's Magazine*, July 1945, 'Some Episodes in the Life of David Lloyd George' by the Hon Neville Lytton.

10  *Lloyd George: War Leader, 1916–1918*: John Grigg (Penguin, 2003), page 35.

11  *Prelude to Victory*: Major-General Sir E. L Spears, Cape, 1939: Dispatch by de Sauvigny dated 16 February 1917, in translation as Appendix IX.

12  On 1 March 1917 Haig wrote to Rothschild on the German withdrawal: 'It is difficult to say what they mean by this retirement. Possibly it may be to draw us on until our Reserves are exhausted and then they will counter attack at Ypres or elsewhere on the West, or perhaps they mean to attack Russia and want some more reserves in the West in case of need. Time will show; the main thing is to be ready for any emergency and not to make up our mind too soon what the enemy is about to do.' By 25 March he had made up his mind, writing again to Rothschild: 'The papers give you all the news regarding the German retreat. I am surprised that so few papers have recognised the truth, viz. that the enemy would have remained in his old original positions if he could have done so without risking a defeat! He wisely decided to withdraw *before* he became seriously involved!' (NLS Acc 3155 No 214 [a]).

13  British representatives were Lloyd George, Hankey, Robertson, Haig, and their advisers; French delegates were President Aristide Briand, Minister of War General Hubert Lyautey, Nivelle and their staff.

14  Lyautey was to resign on 14 March 1917 in protest against Nivelle's forthcoming offensive, correctly believing it doomed from the outset; Briand's government collapsed two days later, but the offensive went ahead.

15  John Grigg (*Lloyd George: War Leader 1916–1918*, op. cit., page 34) inexplicably considered Robertson should have helped the Prime Minister ('less of a humbug than most successful public figures') to find a new C-in-C, and suggested Robertson's working-class roots made him blindly deferential to 'the

traditional officer class that Haig epitomized.' But Robertson put an even higher value on doing what he thought was right; as we have seen, Robertson willingly connived at the removal of another C-in-C (Sir John French) when convinced that it was right for the army and the country.

16 The British and French proposed in 1917 exactly the same amalgamation within their own ranks for the American Expeditionary Force – and were vigorously rebuffed by the Americans.

17 *Lloyd George*: Peter Rowland, op. cit., page 391.

18 Sheffield & Bourne, op. cit., page 272.

19 Cited in *Lloyd George and The Generals*: David R. Woodward (University of Delaware Press, 1983), page 146.

20 NLS Acc 3155 No 97, diary entry for 27 February 1917.

21 *The Private Papers of Douglas Haig*: ed Blake, op. cit., pp 204–5.

22 NLS Acc 3155 No 347/46.

23 *The Private Papers of Douglas Haig*: Blake, op. cit., pp 205–6.

24 NLS Acc 3155 No 97, diary entry for 14 March 1917.

25 Ibid.

26 *Victory Through Coalition*: Elizabeth Greenhalgh (Cambridge University Press, 2005), page 146.

27 *War Memoirs*: D. Lloyd George, (Vol. IV, Ivor Nicholson & Watson, 1934–6), page 2267.

28 'No one better was found to take his place.' Lloyd George, op. cit., page 3424.

29 'It seems Enemy captured during his successful attack near Sapingneul [on 4 April] (when he took 800 French prisoners) the whole plan of attack of three French Corps! Information from GQG states that a division had published a written order which had gone down to battalions indicating the whole plan of operation! With such carelessness it seems difficult to avoid information from reaching the Enemy.' (NLS Acc 3155 no 112, Haig diary entry for 17 April 1917.)

30 Quoted by David French, in *War, Strategy, and International Politics*: ed. Lawrence Freeman, Paul Hayes and Robert O'Neill (Clarendon Press, 1992).

31 *Les Mutineries de 1917*: Guy Pedroncini (Presses Universitaires de France, 1967).

32 NLS Acc 3155 No 97: diary entry for 18 May 1917. This was a fairly standard locution of Haig's when dealing with foreigners. When he first met General John Pershing, C-in-C of the American Expeditionary Force, on 20 July 1917, he was 'much struck with his quiet gentlemanly bearing – so unusual for an American.' Pershing, he thought, 'has already begun to realise that the French are a broken reed.' (NLS Acc 3155 No 97.) Haig liked people like himself – especially those who did not talk too much.

33 NLS Acc 3155 No 214 (f).

34 On 7 May the Prime Minister visited GHQ and, in Haig's absence but before the assembled senior officers over dinner, gave a remarkably good imitation of Robertson at a Cabinet meeting, 'as good, or better, than any music-hall turn.' (*At G.H.Q.*: Charteris, op. cit., page 223–4.)

35 At Messines the tanks once again failed to lived up to expectations; only 27 reached the first objective, the ridge line itself. (*Tanks in the Great War*, Fuller, op. cit., page 110.)

36 *British Logistics on the Western Front*: Brown, op. cit., pp 166–7.

37 *Field Marshal Sir Henry Wilson: His Life and Diaries*: Callwell, op. cit., Vol.I, page 361.

38 *Journals and Letters of Viscount Esher*, op. cit., Vol.4, pp 122–3.

39 Quoted in *The Enigmatic Edwardian*: James Lees-Milne, op. cit., page 313.

40 NLS Acc 3155 No 97, diary entry for 19 June 1917.

41 In October 1917 Charteris submitted to Haig yet another report claiming the opposing German divisions at Third Ypres were losing their fighting spirit. Haig noted in his diary for 15 October: 'Yet it is stated in a note by the DMI [Macdonogh] War Office dated 1 October [. . .] "The moral of the troops in the field gives no anxiety to the German High Command". I cannot think why the War Office Intelligence Department gives such a wrong picture of the situation except that General Macdonogh is a Roman Catholic and is (unconsciously) influenced by information which doubtless reaches him from tainted (i.e Catholic) sources.' (NLS Acc 3155 No 97.) Underlying this view of Haig's was the widespread suggestion that, because Pope Benedict XV issued a peace note in August 1917 – which was completely ignored, save by Austria–Hungary – the Roman Catholic church was undermining the resolve to fight.

42 Quoted in *Military Operations: France and Belgium, 1917*: Brigadier-General James Edmonds, Vol.II (HMSO, 1948), page 98.

43 (For information on other sources of intelligence, see chapter 4 of *Secret Service*: Christopher Andrew, Heinemann, 1985.) Charteris was not the only incorrigible optimist at GHQ; Trenchard (in command of the RFC) and others also regularly fed Haig with bullish reports. From Haig's diaries it is evident that there was a culture at GHQ which prioritized the bearing of good tidings to the C-in-C, encouraged by the awareness that Haig's character always tended to look on the bright side, and that he preferred the company of similarly minded officers. There was no need for Haig to make this explicit; it was an attitude that he daily exemplified.

44 As recorded by Reverend George Duncan in his diary entry for Thursday 22 June 1916: *Military Miscellany I*: eds. A. J. Guy, R. N. W. Thomas and G. J. De Groot (Army Records Society, 1996), pp 291–2.

45 NLS 3155 No 337/l.

46 Born Edward Louis Spiers (1886–1974) he changed the spelling of his surname to Spears in 1918.

47 'Who Knew What and When?': David French, in *War, Strategy, and International Politics*: eds. Lawrence Freeman, Paul Hayes and Robert O'Neill (Clarendon Press, 1992), page 149.

48 *Two Men Who Saved France*: Major-General Edward Spears (Eyre & Spottiswoode, 1966), pp 44–7.

49 NLS Acc 3155 No 97 (manuscript) and 114 (typed) diary entries for 20 June 1917.

50 NLS Acc 3155 No 214 (a).

51 Cohn is one of the period's minor colourful characters who futilely imagined he enjoyed a relationship with Haig. A godson of the US President Jefferson Davis, Cohn traded in race horses and for a time was private secretary to Lord Michelham. Cohn is alleged to have had an affair with Michelham's wife, and fathered the Lord's second son. Cohn married Florence Bottomley, daughter of the British swindler and self-publicist Horatio Bottomley (whom Haig found to be 'a true friend of the soldier, and imbued with sound patriotic ideas' when Bottomley visited GHQ on 12 September 1917), and later married Marcelle Jenny Favrel, a French cinema actress; they divorced in 1931. At this period Cohn was working as a journalist for a Paris-based newspaper.

52 NLS Acc 3155 No 214 (i).

53 David French, in *War, Strategy and International Politics*, op. cit., pp 150–1.

54 Baker-Carr, op. cit., page 228.

55 See for instance two recent works: *Passchendaele: The Sacrificial Ground*: Nigel Steel and Peter Hart (Cassell, 2000), an excellent study from the perspective of many of the ordinary BEF soldiers who fought, while *Passchendaele: The Untold Story*: Robin Prior and Trevor Wilson (Yale University Press, 1996) considers the campaign from a more strategic level.

56 *Haig: Master of the Field*: Major-General Sir John Davidson (Peter Nevill, 1953), pp 26–9.

57 Ibid., page 68.

58 *Passchendaele*, Prior and Wilson, op. cit., page 76.

59 *At G. H. Q.*, op. cit., pp 241 and 243.

60 Quoted in *Passchendaele: The Sacrificial Ground*: Steel and Hart, op. cit., page 141.

61 *From Chauffeur to Brigadier*: C. D. Baker-Carr (Ernest Benn, 1930), pp 229–30.

62 *The First World War 1914–1918*: Repington, op. cit., page 99.

63 *Field Marshal Sir Henry Wilson: His Life and Diaries*: Callwell (Cassell, 1927), Vol.II, page 18.

64 *The First World War 1914–1918*: Lieutenant-Colonel C. À Court Repington, op. cit., Vol.II, pp 83–4.

65  Callwell, op. cit., page 20.

66  An uncle of the poet Stephen Spender.

67  *At G.H.Q.*, op. cit., page 267.

68  *The Intimate Papers of Colonel House*: ed. Charles Seymour (Houghton Mifflin, 1926–8), Vol.III, page 268.

69  Callwell, op. cit., page 22. This was a typical piece of Wilsonian rhetoric. Romania and Russia had 'lost' themselves, while Italy had not been 'lost' at all. But if Robertson genuinely would not with hindsight have done things differently, that is an indictment.

70  *Men, Ideas and Tanks*: J. P. Harris (Manchester University Press, 1995), page 95.

71  Ibid., page 97.

72  Baker-Carr, op. cit., page 294. Baker-Carr claimed that as soon as he learned this from Elles he contacted a friend on the newly-formed Supreme War Council, who in turn contacted Foch who, allegedly, requested from the British a speeding up of new tank deliveries and the formation of new tank units as soon as possible.

73  NLS Acc 3155 No 214 (f). Such gossip was no doubt responsible for Haig's own scepticism about Rawlinson's merits.

74  NLS Acc 3155 No 347/46.

75  Quoted in *The Worlds of Philip and Sybil*: Peter Stansky, op. cit., page 71.

76  *Haig*: Duff Cooper, op. cit., Vol. II, pp 199–200.

77  By this stage Northcliffe's erstwhile admiration of Haig had slumped. Northcliffe had been in the USA in November 1917 and visited Haig at GHQ on his return, where he regaled an uninterested Haig with his great deeds in encouraging American war efforts. Northcliffe's pride was wounded by what he felt was a snub from Haig – who intended no insult, but was simply preoccupied and bored with Northcliffe's preening. *The Times* had run exaggerated headlines on the early news of the success at Cambrai, proclaiming a decisive victory. When it turned out to be nothing of the sort, the newspaper (and its proprietor) looked rather foolish. Haig's lack of interest in flattering Northcliffe's ego thus lost him a vital ally, at precisely the point he most needed one. Lloyd George had by now cleverly bought the services of some of the most influential newspaper owners of the day. Lord Rothermere (owner of the *Daily Mirror*, the most popular newspaper among the troops on the Western Front) was given the Air Ministry. Max Aitken – who had a controlling interest in the *Daily Express* as well as owning the *London Evening Standard* – was given a peerage and appointed Minister of Information. Northcliffe harboured hopes of the even greater position of Secretary of State for War. Lloyd George repaid Northcliffe for his greater loyalty by ensuring he received a Viscountcy in the 1918 New Year's honours list.

78 Quoted in Stansky, op. cit., page 71.

79 NLS Acc 3155 No 149; letter dated 14 December 1917.

80 Charteris was replaced initially by the much more capable Sir Herbert Lawrence, GOC/66th Division, who was sufficiently wealthy to be completely indifferent to the opinion (and patronage) of anyone in the army, Haig included. The quality of GHQ intelligence reports improved rapidly. A few weeks later Lawrence was appointed Chief of Staff at GHQ, when Kiggell, reported as unwell, was eased out (again at the behest of the War Cabinet). Kiggell was diagnosed by Haig's medical officer, Colonel 'Micky' Ryan, as suffering from 'nervous exhaustion'; Derby secured for Kiggell the comfortable sinecure of Governor of Jersey, a seven-year appointment, on a stipend of £1,600 per annum. The post also carried with it a resplendently comfortable house.

81 Baker-Carr, op. cit., pp 246–7.

82 Quoted in 'The Battles in Flanders During the Summer and Autumn of 1917': *British Army Review*, August 1997.

83 *Two Men Who Saved France*: Spears, op. cit., page 125. In his book, published almost five decades after the events he described, Spears revealed that before the Second World War he had been given detailed notes by Pétain, on the mutinies and how the crisis was handled, before the Second World War, but that Pétain's collaboration with the Nazis had made it impossible to publish. In 1966 he felt able to do justice to the man who had brought the French army back from the brink of collapse in early summer 1917.

84 *The Times*, 15 November 1934, letters, page 15, column E.

85 NLS Acc 3155 No 216 (d).

86 'How Myths Grow – Passchendaele': Basil Liddell Hart, *Military Affairs*, Vol.28, No 4 (Winter 1964–5), pp 184–6.

87 This competition was the NRA's 'Sniping Competition for Public Schools', open to one team of eight from the school contingent of the Junior Division of the OTC of each school which entered a team for the Ashburton Shield Competition in 1914 or any preceding year. Twenty-two schools entered in 1917.

88 *Centenary Essays on Clifton College*: ed. N. G. L. Hammond (J.W. Arrowsmith, 1962), page 79.

# Chapter Twelve

1 Letter to Wilson, 20 September 1918: quoted in Sheffield & Bourne, op. cit., page 462.

2 NLS Acc No 97, diary entry for Wednesday 2 January 1918. They 'all enjoyed it greatly', Haig noted in his diary on 4 January, adding: 'Butter & milk is now very difficult to obtain in London.'

3 Ibid., diary entry for 3 January.

4 David R. Woodward ('Did Lloyd George Starve the British Army of Men Prior to the German Offensive of 21 March 1918?', *The Historical Journal*, Vol.27 No 1 (March, 1984), pp 214–252, basing his argument on *Statistics of the Military Effort of the British Empire during the Great War, 1914–1920*, pp 371–4, has pointed out that this demand for 615,000 Category A men to be drafted by November 1918 was in any case unrealistic: 'When the massive German attacks in 1918 compelled the government to increase dramatically its recruiting, combing out men from the vital occupations, only 372,330 category "A" men could be found from all sources from January to November 1918.'

5 *Soldiers and Statesmen*: Field Marshal Sir William Robertson (Cassell, 1926), pp 317–19.

6 NLS Acc 3155 No 97, Haig diary entry for 7 January 1918.

7 *Soldiers and Statesmen*: Robertson, op. cit., Vol. I, page 320.

8 Ibid., page 322.

9 David R. Woodward, op. cit.

10 No clearer expression of this divide can be had, perhaps, than in a letter to the *Spectator* (10 January 1958) by E. A. Osborne, who was a GSO II at GHQ in 1917. It was Osborne's job to visit forward armies five days a week and report back on them. Osborne had 'a clear recollection of one day during the battle of Passchendaele. It was in the last part of October, 1917. The 34th Division was in action at Poelcapelle. I went up and spent some hours at brigade and battalion HQs. I could see, and heard much about, the awful conditions. I felt very bad about it all, probably to an increased extent as so many valued friends were involved. On return that evening I dictated and signed what could only be described as a violent report. After dinner I was sent for by the CGS, General Sir Launcelot Kiggell. He took me straight to the C-in-C's room. There was nobody else there. Sir Douglas took me across the room to a big wall map and told me to elaborate my report. I did this at considerable length and with great emphasis. As far as I remember, though very attentive, he made no little or no comment. At he end he said, "Thank you, Major Osborne. Good night." I left with a great feeling of relief. [. . .] I had unburdened my soul to a great man and a real commander.' Osborne also thereby should have laid to rest the enduring myth that GHQ did not understand the conditions in which it was expecting soldiers to fight.

11 NLS Acc 3155 No 97, diary entry for 9 January 1918. Also in attendance were Lord Reading, Lord Cecil, Winston Churchill, the Labour politician George Barnes, and Hankey.

12 NLS Acc 3155 No 123.

13 NLS Acc 3155 No 97, diary entry for 13 January 1918.

14 *War Memoirs*: Lloyd George, op. cit., Vol. IV, pp 2266–7.

15 NLS Acc 3155 No 123, diary entry for 1 February 1918.

16 Ibid., diary entry for 9 February.

17 Robertson was offered a choice by the Prime Minister; either go to Versailles or, if he wished to remain CIGS, accept that the main military adviser to the Cabinet would be the Secretary of State for War, a restoration of the status quo prior to Kitchener's own demotion and loss of power in early 1916. Robertson resigned with bad grace and the matter was hotly debated in the House of Commons, where Lloyd George was a master of persuasion, on 19 February. As Haig laconically noted in his diary on 20 February: 'Opposition statesmen shed crocodile tears over R's departure but human nature being what it is, the latter is well nigh forgotten already.' Henry Rawlinson was appointed in place of Wilson at Versailles at the Supreme War Council. Robertson later that year took over as GOC Eastern Command (he needed an income, despite his injured pride) and then, in 1919, as commander of the British Army of Occupation in Germany.

18 NLS Acc 3155 No 163: letter to Lady Haig dated 4 February 1918.

19 NLS Acc 3155 No 97, diary entry for 2 March 1918.

20 Ibid., diary entry for 11 March 1918.

21 Letter to Sir George Greaves, NLS 3155 no 337/l.

22 Macdonogh had a high regard for Cox, writing in the *Royal Engineers Journal* XXIX, 2 February 1919, that Cox's 'appreciations of the situation, given at the Army Commanders' Meetings in February and March [1918], marked him out as an officer of the highest ability, with an unrivalled knowledge of the German Army, of the mentality of the German commanders.'

23 Irvin S. Cobb was by this date a highly experienced war correspondent, having covered the war on the Western Front since the start, initially for the *Sunday Evening Post*.

24 NLS Acc 3155 No 97, diary entry for Sunday 3 March 1918.

25 For George Haig's baptism there was a glittering array of fourteen godparents: 'The King, Lords Cambridge, Derby and French, an Indian Maharajah Sir Pratap Singh, Sir Eric Geddes who had been in charge of the railways in France, my cousin General Neil Haig and my great uncle Walter Vivian, who referred to me in a letter to my mother as the War Warrior. The list of godmothers was no less imposing, consisting of Queen Alexandra, The Empress Eugénie, widow of Napoleon III, and three of my mother's friends Mrs Cazalet, Mrs Max Wood and Mrs Fox Pitt and finally my aunt Violet Vivian.' *My Father's Son*: The Earl Haig, page 11. The only oddity in this list is French, given the bad blood that existed between him and Haig at this date.

26 Third Army, which had occupied its stretch of the line for a year, had spent much more time on preparing its defences; as a consequence, it resisted the attack much better.

27 Both quotes from NLS Acc 3155 No 47.

28 In his *The German Offensives of 1918* (Tempus, 2001), Martin Kitchen provides a good operational level view of the assaults, largely from the German perspective.

29 *Journals and Letters*, op. cit., Vol.4, page 201.

30 Published in *The Times* 28 March 1918.

31 Elizabeth Greenhalgh in 'Myth and Memory: Sir Douglas Haig and the Imposition of Allied Unified Command in March 1918' (*Journal of Military History*, June 2004, pp 771–820) argues that Haig amended his diary record of the events around the first few days of the Michael offensive.

32 NLS Acc 3155 No 97, diary entry for 26 March 1918. It is not true that Haig despised all politicians nor all Frenchmen; sometimes, as with Clemenceau, he formed a good and lasting mutual respect with a politician who was also French. On 1 April Clemenceau visited Haig and gave him forty pounds of chocolate from Marquis, a famous Parisian chocolatier. 'In reply to my asking how he had got it, he said that he had sent the Commissaire of Police to seize the best quality for me in Marquis' shop.' NLS Acc 3155 No 375, typed diary, entry for 1 April 1918.

33 This agreement was later ratified by the Belgians, Italians and Americans at a further conference at Beauvais on 3 April. Significantly, this also expanded Foch's jurisdiction to encompass 'all powers necessary' to create a coherent Allied military strategy. Beauvais gave tactical control to Haig and Pétain over their respective armies, and each had the right to appeal to their government if they were requested by Foch to carry out a strategic movement they disagreed with.

34 NLS Acc 3155 No 97, diary entry for Friday 29 March 1918.

35 Haig had replaced Gough with Rawlinson after Doullens; Rawlinson was given the task of re-constructing Fifth Army, which was re-designated Fourth Army.

36 Wilson confided to his diary on 11 May 1918 that he advised the Cabinet that Haig should be 'brought home. But Lloyd George and Milner would not decide.' *Field Marshal Sir Henry Wilson, His Life And Diaries*: C. E. Callwell, op. cit., Vol. II, page 99. Wilson travelled to France on 20 May and informed Haig that 'I had suggested to Lloyd George that he should bring him (D.H) home to succeed Johnnie (French) [as C-in-C Home Forces], because of the altered status of the Commander-in-Chief here. He did not say anything, but said the way I was being criticized was hateful' (page 101). Haig's diary entry for this meeting was equally bland: 'He [Wilson]

seems anxious to do the right thing. [. . .] Nor did the Cabinet desire to replace me in France and give me the Home Command. So no one has been chosen yet!' (NLS Acc 3155 No 97, diary entry for 20 May 1918). While it was clearly vexatious for Haig to know he was being so seriously undermined by his CIGS in London, he could not really complain; he had done exactly the same to his predecessor.

37 NLS Acc 3155 No 347/46.

38 *The Kaiser's Battle*: Martin Middlebrook (Penguin, 1983), page 348.

39 Callwell, op. cit., Vol.II, page 88, Wilson diary entry for 8 April 1918.

40 Sassoon was given the original handwritten version of this document by Haig. Much later, after Haig's death, Doris asked Sassoon if he would give it to her; Sassoon unceremoniously refused, as, he said, it had already been promised to the British Library on his own death.

41 *British Logistics on the Western Front*: Brown, op. cit., pp 189–90.

42 *Sassoon: The Worlds of Philip and Sybil*: Peter Stansky, op. cit., pp 74–5.

43 Ibid., page 74. Esher of course was right, but it is remarkable that this and Sassoon's comments derive from persons supposedly supportive of Haig.

44 NLS Acc 3155 No 97, diary entry for 11 June 1918.

45 NLS Acc 3155 No 97, diary entry for Monday 15 July 1918.

46 NLS Acc 3155 No 97, diary entry for 29 May 1918. Sloggett got the baronetcy.

47 Quoted in Duff Cooper, op. cit., Vol.II, page 328. Haig naturally knew who the author was.

48 The relationship between Monash, a Jew, and Haig was mutually warm, and warns us against regarding Haig as simply a composite of conventional prejudices. Monash regarded Haig's views on discipline as 'peculiar' but after the war wrote about Haig with affection: 'Haig was, technically speaking, quite out of his depth in regard to the minutiae of the immense resources which were placed in his hands to wield. I was, at first, quite dismayed to find that he obviously did not know the composition in detail of his own formations. [. . .] But I learned to appreciate that it was not indispensable for a Commander, placed as he was, to have a detailed knowledge of such matters, and that it was his personality and his influence upon his environment that counted so heavily. It was [. . .] a source of immeasurable relief and consolation to find him calm, resolute, hopeful and buoyant, in the face of apparently irretrievable chaos and disaster.' *John Monash*: Geoffrey Serle (Melbourne University Press, 1982), page 388.] Similarly, few chief executives of major corporations know the precise operational details of individual subsidiaries.

49 *William Morris Hughes*: William Farmer Whyte (Sydney, 1957), page 370.

50 *Forgotten Victory*: Gary Sheffield (Headline, 2001), page 197.

51 'Hamel, 1918: A Study in Military-Political Interaction': R. A. Beaumont, *Military Affairs*, Vol.31, Spring 1967, pp 10–16.

52 NLS Acc 8900.

53 This, of course, neither confirms nor finally refutes the possibility that Haig gave some credence to spiritualism. It does, however, establish that Haig's connection to spiritualism, albeit remote, extended late into his time as C-in-C.

54 *Command on the Western Front: The Military Career of Sir Henry Rawlinson, 1914–1918*: Robin Prior and Trevor Wilson (Blackwell, 1992), page 350.

55 NLS Acc 3155 No 97, diary entry for 11 November 1918.

56 *The Great War and the British People*: J. M. Winter (Harvard University Press, 1985), pp 66–75.

57 *British Logistics on the Western Front*: Brown, op. cit., page 239.

58 *Haig As I Knew Him*: G. S. Duncan, op. cit., page 90.

59 NLS Acc 3155/347 No 69. Letter to Mrs C. E. Haig, 4 December 1918.

60 *Sassoon: The Worlds of Philip and Sybil*: Stansky, op. cit., page 85.

61 By the end of his life Haig had accumulated an array of foreign honours including: Knight Grand Cross, St Maurice & St Lazarus (Italy); Order of Rama (Siam); Danilo 1st Class (Montenegro); Karageorge 1st Cls (Serbia); Order of the Rising Sun (Japan); Croix de Guerre (France); Croix de Guerre (Belgium); Order of Chia-Ho (Excellent Crop) (China); St Michael the Brave, 2nd class (Roumania); Cross of Honour (USA); Gold Medal (Montenegro); Medaille Militaire (France); Distinguished Service Medal (USA); Order of Leopold (Belgium); Cross of St George (Russia); Towers & Sword, Grand Cordon (Portugal); Gold Medal (France); St Anne, 3rd Class, with swords (Russia). He had also been awarded the British distinctions of the Order of Merit, GCB, KT, KCIE and GCVO.

62 NLS Acc 3155 No 216.

63 NLS Acc 12263.

64 Among the entourage were Henry Horne, GOC First Army; Herbert Plumer, GOC Second Army; Julian Byng, GOC Third Army; Henry Rawlinson, GOC Fourth Army; General Sir William Birdwood, GOC Fifth Army.

65 Haig had wanted to ride on horseback from Charing Cross to Buckingham Palace and not sit in carriages 'like a party of politicians or old women' but the government vetoed this, which he regarded as yet another attempt to humiliate.

66 *Douglas Haig: War Letters and Diaries*: Sheffield & Bourne, op. cit., page 491.

67 *The Private Papers of Douglas Haig*: Blake, op. cit., page 358.

68 Sheffield & Bourne, op. cit., page 492.

69 *Great Contemporaries*: Winston Churchill, op. cit., page 223.

# Chapter Thirteen

1 There has been considerable debate concerning Edmonds' role in the creation of a supposedly sanitized version of the BEF's high command in the Official History, not least because Edmonds himself in the 1930s gave rise to this belief in conversations he had with Basil Liddell Hart. After Haig's death, Edmonds continued to borrow Haig's diaries from Doris, to whom he ambiguously wrote (on 17 February 1928): 'You may be quite sure that I shall endeavour to write the history of his command as he would have wished it.' NLS Acc 3155 No 328.

2 *Field Marshal Earl Haig*: Charteris, op. cit., page 374.

3 'Sir Douglas Haig's Reputation, 1918–1928': David French, *The Historical Journal*, Vol.28 No. 4 December 1985, pp 953–960.

4 Advertising blurb from *Publisher's Weekly*, Vol.CIII No. 1, 6 January 1923.

5 The army censor's report of 20 January 1919 contained a typical extract from a disgruntled soldier's letter: 'One of our chaps is a "pivotal man!!!" He joined up 2. Jan. 1918, arrived in France April, 1918, and goes back tomorrow. Now what do you think of that! The rest of the section, which includes 6 1914 men, are absolutely on the verge of mutiny.'

6 NLS 3155 No 220.

7 'Military Demobilisation in Great Britain Following the First World War': Stephen Richards Graubard, *The Journal of Modern History*, Vol.19, No 4 (December 1947).

8 Editorial in the *Herald*, London, 7 December 1918.

9 NLS 3155 No 220.

10 Ibid.

11 *The Times*, 8 January 1919.

12 NLS 3155 No 220, dated 21 February 1919.

13 This included more than 650,000 officers and men of the BEF, as well as women of the WAAC, 100,000 Indians, 80,000 Chinese labourers and about 193,000 German POWs. (*The Occupation of the Rhineland*, HMSO, 1987 edition, pp 151–2.)

14 At the end of 1919 Asser, who was in command of the clear-up and disposal of surplus stores, handed over to Brigadier-General Evan Gibb, by which time the number of British troops in France and Belgium was down to 38,000.

15 NLS 3155 No 349 (b).

16 These included the freedom of the cities of Glasgow, Edinburgh, St Andrews, Liverpool, Chester, Southport, Newcastle, Wolverhampton, Bournemouth, Canterbury, and the City of London, as well as numerous City guilds and livery companies. Twelve universities bestowed honorary degrees and Haig was asked

to become President of Clifton College. He had been chosen as Rector of St Andrews in 1916, after the Battle of the Somme; the same university chose him as its Chancellor in 1922. He also served as the Colonel of four regiments, and as Honorary Colonel of a fifth.

17 NLS Acc 12263.

18 NLS Acc 3155 No 337.

19 This was an axiom for Haig, one he returned to in speech after speech. He told his audience at Clifton College on Friday 30 June 1922: 'Tanks, guns and aeroplanes would not have sufficed to bring us victory in the Great War if the character of our people had been other than it was.'

20 Other dignatories receiving honorary degrees were General John Pershing (C-in-C of the American Expeditionary Force), Marshal Joffre, Field Marshal Sir William Robertson, General Sir Henry Wilson, Lieutenant-General Sir John Monash, Herbert Hoover, Victor Orlando (former prime minister of Italy) and Admiral Sir David Beatty.

21 *The Brazen Nose*, Vol.III, No 1, November 1919. (BNC archives.)

22 For a complete overview of the early days of the British Legion see *The Official History of the British Legion*: Graham Wootton (MacDonald & Evans, 1956).

23 The myth that Haig founded the Legion was created shortly after his death, when George Crosfield, chairman of the Legion, paid tribute to Haig: 'Lord Haig has been rightly called the Founder of the British Legion, for, although he did not initiate the steps which the Association, Comrades and Federation took to come together, it was his far sighted action which made those steps necessary.' The Legion's official historian wrote: 'The Legion has no founder, only founders. It is a monument to a number of men not one.' (Wootton, op. cit., page 107.) On the formation of the British Legion Haig was its first choice as National President and was annually re-elected to that position by the Legion's members until his death.

24 *The Official History of the British Legion*: Graham Wootton, op. cit., page 15.

25 NLS Acc 12263.

26 NLS Acc 3155 No 349 (2).

27 NLS Acc 3155 No 349 (2).

28 Wootton, op. cit., page 109.

29 Presidential Address, British Legion Scotland Annual Conference 1926.

30 'The British Army And Internal Security 1919–1939': Keith Jeffrey, *The Historical Journal*, Vol.24, No 2 (June 1981), pp 377–97.

31 NLS Acc 3155 No 2, diary entry for 2 September 1919.

32 NLS Acc 3155, 2 Feb 1919.

33 Worth more than £400,000 in 2007 terms.

34 *A Shadowed Man*: Lois Lamplugh (Exmoor Press, 1990), page 52.

35 Gratuities for lower ranks were much less: a private got £5 (about £150 in 2007 terms) with an additional ten shillings paid for each month of overseas service after the first year and an additional five shillings per month after the first year for home service.

36 NLS Acc 3155 No 346 (d).

37 On his death they included the Royal Bank of Scotland; the Royal Insurance Company; the Distillers Company; John Haig & Co.; and the Fife Coal Company. Inventory of the personal estate of Haig, dated 23 July 1928, NLS.

38 Letter to Major Piet Van der Byl, DSO MC, in South Africa: NLS 11317.

39 *Lloyd George*: Peter Rowland, op. cit., page 640.

40 'The Lloyd George "War Memoirs" ', by George W. Egerton, *Journal of Modern History*, Vol.60, No 1 (March 1988). This was a stupendous sum, more than £14 million in 2007 terms.

41 In the 1930s, when he eventually did publish his *War Memoirs*, Lloyd George received approximately £65,000 in book royalties and newspaper serialization rights, about £11 million in 2007 terms. His charitable donation promise of 1922 was quietly forgotten. 'The Lloyd George "War Memoirs" ', by George W. Egerton, Journal of Modern History, Vol.60, No. 1 (March 1988).

42 *Earl Haig*: Ernest Protheroe (Hutchinson, 1928), page 111.

43 Some argue that Haig's call for national and imperial unity was 'far from apolitical' (see for example 'Sans peur et sans reproche': Daniel Todman, *Journal of Military History* 67, October 2003, pp 1083–1106) but that misses the point. Haig's yearning for social unity above political factionalism was obviously innately conservative, but for Haig conservatism was synonymous with Christianity, and thus, metaphysically, with universal order itself. For him, all other world views spelled not just political but universal chaos.

44 Doris was Patron of the British Legion's Poppy Appeal and in August 1930 she wrote to Colonel Brown, then chairman of the Legion, complaining that the 'printing for Poppy Day appeals was being carried out by a cheap Jewish Firm.' She asked Brown to transfer the printing to disabled ex-servicemen. (NLS Acc 3155 No 330). Poppy Day receipts in 1928 and 1929 were staggeringly high, well above £500,000 each year, more than £82m in 2007 terms. By 1932 annual Poppy Day receipts had slumped below £100,000, about £17m in 2007 terms.

45 *The Man I Knew*, op. cit., page 315. The place was full of woodworm and other defects that needed repair before it was suitable as a family home, but this was a large sum for the day and quite implausible. Thomas Secrett said that Bemersyde was in a 'state of dilapidation' when Haig took it over but that 'it cost him nearly six thousand pounds to make it habitable'. (*Twenty-Five Years With Earl Haig*, Secrett, op. cit., page 283.) Doris also disingenuously implied that a good portion of Haig's apparently generous government gratuity had

been substantially swallowed by putting the family home right: 'No doubt it must have caused him considerable anxiety having to spend such a large sum of money on the building, almost half the grant voted him by Parliament, but he could not bear to think of the place going to ruin [. . .]' (page 315).

46  NLS Acc 9431, letter dated 4 February 1922. Doris, whose name was also on the free rail pass, scrupulously returned the pass to the L M & S after Haig's death; they sent it back and asked her to carry on using it, which she did until she died.

47  NLS Acc 9431, letters dated 22 October, 18 November and 7 December 1922.

48  Ruth De Pree, unedited memoir, NLS.

49  *The Douglas Haig Fellowship Records*, Issue No 3, 1996, page 9.

50  Secrett, op. cit., pp 287–8.

51  This was not the end of Secrett's involvement with the Haigs. In 1930 he approached Doris, looking for work. She wrote a hostile reply on 17 November (NLS Acc 3155 No 330) in which she said she was 'very angry with you, because of book [sic] which came out, supposed to be written by you, just one mass of lies. [. . .] I am trying just to remember the services that you rendered to my husband and [. . .] trying not to think of those hurtful remarks in the last chapter of that scurrilous book. I expect that you were got hold of, because, I know that you have not the education to write anything. You were thoroughly warned, by my Uncle, when you were staying with me at Bemersyde for the funeral at Dryburgh.' Secrett responded to this with a brief self-pitying letter which contained not a single piece of punctuation – thus strongly supporting Doris's contention that Secrett's book was ghosted.

52  NLS Acc 3155 No 330.

53  NLS 3155 No 346 (h): 'The Future Uses of Cavalry'.

54  *The Brazen Nose*, Volume IV, No 8, May 1928.

## Chapter Fourteen

1  NLS 3155 Acc No 325. The (unattributed) poem is contained in the materials Doris collected for her biography of Haig.

2  *Earl Haig*: Ernest Protheroe, op. cit., pp 111–12.

3  Data from the General Register Office for Scotland: http://www.gro-scotland.gov.uk/files/04t5–4.pdf

4  *The Times*, 1 February 1928, page 16.

5  NLS Acc 4714 No 21. The mask was apparently 'considerably distorted and drawn, owing to the fact it was taken after the post mortem and not before.'

6  The Scottish National War Memorial, for which the Duke of Atholl was a leading campaigner and fund-raiser, opened in 1927.

7  Conversation with author, February 2005.

8 The same issue of the *Daily Mirror* also valiantly struggled to find something light-hearted by which to recall the field marshal. In another story it carried the following: 'He never failed to be amused when relating what he facetiously termed "an example of consummate tact." That occurred when he was reviewing one of the colonial battalions behind the lines. In the ranks he found a coloured man. "What are you?" he asked. "A niggah, sah," was the rather disconcerting reply. But the General rose to the occasion, and said: "Then see that you remain so, my man!"'

9 *The Times*, 31 January 1928.

10 NLS Acc 3155 No 248.

11 NLS Acc 3155 No 330 [c]. There is something unnerving in the realization that, even when he was dead, Haig continued to be pestered in this manner by the 'spirit world'. There is nothing in the Haig archive to suggest that Doris acquiesced to Conan Doyle's entreaty.

12 *The Private Papers of Douglas Haig*: ed. Blake, op. cit., page 168. Haig's opinion of Gwynne did not improve. On Saturday 8 September 1917, when Gwynne again visited GHQ, Haig commented in his diary: 'His only redeeming quality is that he is "out to help". But he is very self-satisfied and highly conceited.'

13 From January 1916 until the end of the war Milne commanded the British forces in the ill-fated Salonika expedition. He was appointed CIGS in 1926.

14 In November 1928 Doris distributed some of Haig's personal effects: Sassoon received a compass, Charteris a gold pencil, Kiggell and Edmonds each got a silver box, Allenby the lunch hamper, Gough a hunting crop, Secrett cuff links, and Byng a magnifying glass.

15 'Sans peur et sans reproche': Daniel Todman, *Journal of Military History* 67, October 2003, pp 1083–1106.

16 This horse – called 'Haig' – was destroyed in November 1929 at Buckingham Palace after lung trouble; three of its preserved hooves were sent to Doris at Bemersyde, one was retained and is kept at the museum at the Palace.

17 NLS Acc 3155 No 248, letter dated 5 February 1928. This story also appeared almost verbatim in *The Times* the day after the funeral, suggesting that Wigram thought it so interesting that he fed it to the newspaper. The *Daily Mail* published a photograph of the funeral in which it claimed could be detected a wraith-like figure hovering above the gun carriage, an obvious allusion to the myth of the angels at Mons.

18 Haig's decision to cut Secrett from his will was a rather petty response to Secrett's decision to leave his service, which in turn no doubt encouraged Secrett to cash in on his knowledge of the field marshal by writing his ghosted memoir. Lady Haig never really forgave Secrett for what she

regarded as his disloyalty; as late as January 1939 she wrote to a Mr Rowe, Haig's personal standard bearer between December 1914-October 1915 that 'I am glad you and Secrett met after so many years – he is a great character. The lunch I gave was in his honour as my chief guest. I am afraid – privately to you – I do not think much of his wife, so beware of her.' Secrett had been on at least one previous occasion the beneficiary of Haig's limited generosity: Haig's wartime bank book (NLS 3155 Acc 347/41) shows he gave Secrett £50 on June 10 1916.

19 *My Father's Son*, op. cit., page 34. Fisher also acted as a guardian to George Haig, whom he advised Doris against sending to Stowe public school 'because of its progressiveness and lack of austerity.' Haig had wanted George to attend Winchester rather than Eton, which he had 'vetoed [. . .] for its snobbery.'

20 The Public Trustee's office contacted Doris on 28 November 1929 in regard to the marriage settlement trust (number M.3262/S) on her daughter, Lady Victoria; this reveals that Doris was at that time receiving some £300/month, or £49,000 in 2007 terms, from the trust. (NLS Acc 3155 No 330.)

21 *My Father's Son*, op. cit., page 28. George, then just ten years old, would, arguably, have been more aware of the personal devastation than precisely how much money the household now had.

22 Dated 15 June 1928, to Piet van der Byl: NLS 11317.

23 NLS Acc 3155 No. 248.

24 The six volumes appeared in two-volume stages in 1933, 1934 and 1936.

25 The Lloyd George 'War Memoirs', George W. Egerton, *The Journal of Modern History*, Vol.60, No. 1 (March 1988).

26 *Life With Lloyd George: Diary of A. J. Sylvester*: ed. C. Cross (Macmillan, 1975), page 111.

27 Egerton, op. cit., 1998, pp 86–7 and page 90.

28 Parliament voted to erect a statue of Haig in February 1928 but by October that year there was still no agreement over where it should be positioned. At one point it was proposed to place it in Trafalgar Square. A very public row then broke out over the design, by Alfred Hardiman, a relatively young sculptor for whom the project became a political nightmare and a financial drain. An excellent survey of this episode is provided by 'A "matter for artists, and not soldiers"? The Cultural Politics of the Earl Haig National Memorial, 1927–1937', by Stephen Heathorn, in the *Journal of British Studies* 44 (July 2005), pp 536–561. Doris could not abide Hardiman's first design (it made Haig look 'too fat' she said) and she loathed the second and final design, now standing in Whitehall near the Cenotaph. She refused to attend its public unveiling on Wednesday 10 November 1937.

29 *Old Men Forget*: Duff Cooper (Hart-Davies, 1953), pp 179–80.

30  *The Duff Cooper Diaries*: ed. John Julius Norwich (Weidenfeld & Nicolson, 2005), page 224.

31  *My Father's Son*, op.cit., page 52.

32  NLS Acc 3155 No 312. This file contains the correspondence with her solicitors and the Haig trustees about Dorothy Haig's biography of her husband and is the source for the material on this topic in this chapter.

33  Letter dated 7 September 1934.

34  In her biography, Doris wrote that Haig had consigned to her the job of writing his life: 'He insisted that one day I would write it because he was quite sure that he would be so tired of the whole war and the difficulties that were put in his way, that he would be quite unable to write sufficiently tolerantly of some of the members of the Government who had made his task so irksome.' (*The Man I Knew*, op.cit., page 203.) This was undoubtedly true on one level, but Haig never lost his obsession with the events of the Great War, and it is unclear why he felt it imperative to write tolerantly of the government. His diaries, in any case, express his thorough contempt for his political masters.

35  Doris seems to have been perpetually prone to imprecise ill health after her husband's death. She agreed to Duff Cooper as the authorized biographer and her attempt to disavow this in this letter is undignified.

36  *The Times*, 31 October 1936.

37  She spoke at a Foyle's Literary Lunch to launch her book where, as well as disparaging Duff Cooper's book, she announced (rather surprisingly, given what we now know about her earlier hopes to maximise the proceeds from her book for her family's future financial security), that 'any royalties in respect of the sale of this book are being handed over by me to the ex-service man.' The ex-serviceman saw little benefit, if any. She also intriguingly told her audience that, after the war was over and while Haig was out one day, she burned all the letters she had ever sent him, all of which he had kept. What inspired this action we can only guess at.

38  *French Replies to Haig*: Gerald French (Hutchinson, 1936). Lloyd George wrote an introduction. As late as 1960 Gerald French returned to the fray in his *The Kitchener-French Dispute: A Last Word*, in which he said the communications between Haig and Kitchener were 'shameless duplicity.'

39  *Great Contemporaries*: Winston Churchill, op.cit., pp 230–33. Haig's relationship with Churchill started badly in the Sudan, while Churchill's early position as a committed 'easterner' in the Great War caused a further division with Haig. Yet they developed a mutual respect, particularly after Churchill's courageous resignation from the Cabinet in protest against the failure to prosecute the Dardanelles campaign more stubbornly. Churchill's decision to lead a battalion on the Western Front impressed Haig, and later, after the war,

Churchill was one of a number of individuals who put together the money to buy Bemersyde for Haig.

40  *Haig*: Duff Cooper, op.cit., Vol.II, page 435.

41  General Jan Smuts: 'The Strong, Silent Man', *British Legion Magazine*, March 1928.

42  When a selection of about 20 per cent of Haig's war diaries was first published (by Robert Blake in 1952), their vitriolic comments on the French high command and French fighting spirit further damaged Haig's reputation. One British reviewer commented that Haig had thus committed posthumous suicide; surviving French generals claimed to be so shocked by their contents (one wonders how genuine was their surprise) that they initially refused to believe Haig was their author. Marshal Alphonse Juin, who had fought on the Western Front (where he lost an arm), commented to *Le Figaro*: 'I am convinced that such texts are apocryphal. Marshal [sic] Haig could not have written them, for he was not only a great soldier but also a perfect gentleman.' (Quoted in *The Times*, 24 November 1952).

43  *The Times*, 5 January 1939. She died at Glyn, Bangor, on 18 October 1939.

44  *Field Marshal Earl Haig*: Charteris (Cassell and Company, 1929), pp 5–6.

45  *Parade's End* was published in four parts between 1924 and 1928, the year Haig died.

46  While Newbolt superficially lived the life of an upright Victorian he also enjoyed a *ménage à trois* with two Sapphically inclined women, Margaret Duckworth and Ella Coltman.

47  *Journals and Letters of Reginald, Viscount Esher*: Vol.4 (1916–1930), op.cit., page 265.

48  *Field-Marshal Sir Henry Wilson: His Life and Diaries*: ed. Callwell, op.cit., Vol.1, page 208.

49  *The Long Weekend*: Wilfred R. Bion (Free Association Books, 1986), page 270.

50  NLS Acc 3155 No 328.

# Afterword

1  The two are separate however. Armistice Day falls on 11 November, Remembrance Day on the Sunday nearest to 11 November.

2  In September 2006 the Earl Haig Fund Scotland – the charity established by Haig and which raises money for former service personnel in Scotland – changed its name to Poppyscotland, which sounds like an Enid Blyton character. Poppyscotland's chief executive justified the change: 'We discovered that too few people recognised the link between the Earl Haig Fund Scotland and the Scottish Poppy Appeal. A new identity will not only help solve that

problem but help integrate our various activities.' Perhaps Haig's name will
shortly disappear from the poppies sold in Scotland, too.

3  *The Lie About The War*: Douglas Jerrold, Criterion Miscellany No 9 (Faber &
Faber, 1930), page 19. The British Legion in Scotland remains a distinct entity
from that in England.

4  *The General*: C. S. Forester (Michael Joseph, 1936), page 210.

5  *Tanks in the Great War*: Colonel J. F. C. Fuller (John Murray, 1920), page 212.

# HAIG: BIBLIOGRAPHY

## Primary Sources

Asquith, H. H.: *Memories and Reflections*, Little, Brown, 1928.

Baker-Carr, Brigadier-General C. D.: *From Chauffeur to Brigadier*, Ernest Benn, 1930.

Bertie, Francis Leveson (Lord Bertie of Thame): *Diaries* (two volumes), Hodder and Stoughton, 1924.

Blake, Robert: *The Private Papers of Douglas Haig, 1914–1919*, Eyre & Spottiswoode, 1952.

Boraston, J.H.: *Sir Douglas Haig's Despatches*, Dent, 1919.

Brett, Reginald (Viscount Esher): *Journals and Letters* (four volumes), Ivor Nicholson & Watson, 1934–38.

British Legion Journal, *Earl Haig Memorial Issue*, March 1928.

Calwell, Major-General Sir C. E.: *Field Marshal Sir Henry Wilson: His Life and Diaries*, Cassell, 1927.

Charteris, Brigadier-General John: *Field Marshal Earl Haig*, Cassell, 1929.

Charteris, –: *At G.H.Q.*, Cassell, 1931.

Charteris, –: *Haig*, Duckworth, 1933.

Churchill, Winston Spencer: *The River War*, Four Square Books, 1960.

Crozier, Brigadier-General F. P.: *A Brass Hat in No Man's Land*, Jonathan Cape, 1930.

De Pree, Ruth: *Her Memories of Her Uncle Douglas Haig*, National Library of Scotland.

Duff Cooper, Alfred: *Haig* (two volumes), Faber & Faber, 1935.

Duff Cooper –: *Old Men Forget*, Hart-Davis, 1953.

Duncan, G. S.: *Douglas Haig As I Knew Him*, George Allen and Unwin, 1966.

Edmonds, Brigadier-General Sir John: *Military Operations: France and Belgium*, 14 volumes, HMSO 1922–1949.

Fay, Sir Sam: *The War Office At War*, Hutchinson, 1937.

Foch, Marshal Ferdinand: *Memoirs*, William Heinemann, 1931.

Foulkes, Brigadier-General Charles Howard: *Gas! The Story of the Special Brigade*, William Blackwood, 1934.

Fox, Sir Frank: *GHQ*, Philip Allan, 1920.

French, J. D. P (Viscount French): *1914*, Constable, 1919.

Fuller, Colonel. J. F. C.: *Tanks in the Great War*, John Murray, 1920.

Gough, General Sir Hubert: *The Fifth Army*, Hodder & Stoughton, 1931.

Haig, Douglas: *Papers* at the National Library of Scotland, Manuscripts Division.

Haig, –: *Cavalry Studies*, Hugh Rees, 1907.

Haig, the Countess Dorothy: *A Scottish Tour*, The Moray Press, 1935.

Haig, –: *The Man I Knew*, The Moray Press, 1936.

Haig, the Earl: *My Father's Son*, Leo Cooper, 2000.

Haldane, J. A. L.: *Some Lessons from the Russo-Japanese War*, London, 1906.

Harmsworth, Alfred (Lord Northcliffe): *At The War*, Hodder and Stoughton, 1916.

Lloyd George, David: *War Memoirs*, Ivor Nicholson & Watson, 1934–6.

Lytton, Neville: *The Press and the General Staff*, Collins, 1920.

Maurice, Major-General Sir Frederick: *The Life of General Lord Rawlinson of Trent, from his journals and letters*, Cassell, 1928.

Monash, Lieutenant-General Sir John: *The Australian Victories in France in 1918*, Lothian, Melbourne, 1923.

Repington, Lieutenant-Colonel Charles À Court: *The First World War 1914–1918*, (two volumes), Constable, 1920.

Robertson, Field Marshal Sir William: *From Private to Field Marshal*, Constable, 1921.

Robertson –: *Soldiers and Statesmen 1914–1918*, Cassell (two volumes), 1926.

Secrett, Thomas: *Twenty-Five Years With Earl Haig*, Jarrolds, 1928.

Sheffield, Gary, and Bourne, John (eds.): *Douglas Haig: War Diaries and Letters 1914–1918*, Weidenfeld & Nicolson, 2005.

Smith-Dorrien, General Sir Horace: *Memories of Forty-Eight Years' Service*, John Murray, 1925.

Stevenson, Francis: *Lloyd George, A Diary*, Hutchinson, 1971.

Warwick, Frances, Countess of: *Life's Ebb & Flow*, Hutchinson, 1929.

Warwick, –: *Afterthoughts*, Cassell, 1931.

Wood, Field Marshal Sir Evelyn VC: *Winnowed Memories*, Cassell, 1918.

Wood –: *From Midshipman to Field Marshal*, Methuen, 1906.

Woodward, David R. (ed.): *The Military Correspondence of Field Marshal Sir William Robertson*, Army Records Society, Bodley Head, 1989.

## Secondary Sources: Books

Andrew, Christopher: *Secret Service*, Heinemann, 1985.

Anglesey, Marquess of: *A History of the British Cavalry*, Leo Cooper, volumes 3 (1982), 7 (1996), and 8 (1997).

Arthur, G.: *Lord Haig*, Heinemann, 1933.

Barnett, Corelli: *The Swordbearers*, Eyre & Spottiswoode, 1963.

Barr, Niall: '*Service Not Self: The British Legion 1921–1929*' (Ph.D Thesis), St Andrews University, 1994.

Beaverbrook, W. M. A.: *Politicians and the War 1914–16*, Thornton Butterworth, 1928.

Beckett, Ian F. W. and Simpson, Keith (eds.): *A Nation in Arms*, Manchester University Press, 1985.

Beckett, Ian F. W.: *The Great War 1914–18*, Longman, 2001.

Beckett, Ian F. W. and Corvi, Steven J. (eds.): *Haig's Generals*, Pen & Sword, 2006.

Bennett, Alan: *The History Boys*, Faber & Faber, 2004.

Bernhardi, General Friedrich von: *Germany and the Next War*, Longmans, Green, 1912.

Best, Geoffrey and Wheatcroft, Andrew: *War, Economy and the Military Mind*, Croom Helm, 1976.

Bidwell, Shelford and Graham, Dominick: *Fire Power: British Army Weapons and Theories 1904–1945*, Allen & Unwin, 1982.

Bion, Wilfred R.: *The Long Weekend, 1897–1919*, Free Association Books, 1986.

Bloch, I. S.: *Is War Now Impossible*, Grant Richards, 1899.

Blunden, Margaret: *The Countess of Warwick*, Cassell, 1967.

Bond, Brian: *The Victorian Army and the Staff College, 1854–1914*, Eyre Methuen, 1972.

Bond, Brian (ed.): *The First World War and British Military History*, Clarendon Press, 1991.

Bond, Brian and Cave, Nigel (eds.): *Haig: A Reappraisal 70 Years On*, Leo Cooper, 1999.

Bond, Brian: *The Unquiet Western Front: Britain's Role in Literature and History*, Cambridge University Press, 2002.

Bonham-Carter, Victor: *Soldier True*, Muller, 1963.

Bradley, F. H.: *Ethical Studies*, Oxford University Press, 1962.

Brent, Peter: *The Edwardians*, BBC Publications, 1972.

Brock, M. G. and Curthoys, M. C (eds.): *The History of the University of Oxford*, Oxford University Press, 2000.

Brooman, Josh: *General Haig: Butcher or War Winner?* Longman, 1998.

Brown, Ian Malcolm: *British Logistics on the Western Front*, Praeger, 1998.

Bruce, Anthony: *The Purchase System in the British Army 1660–1871*, Royal Historical Society, 1980.

Burk, Kathleen (ed.): *War and the State*, HarperCollins, 1982.

Burnett, John: *Liquid Pleasures: A Social History of Drinks in Modern Britain*, Routledge, 1999.

Cannadine, David: *The Rise and Fall of Class in Britain*, Columbia University Press, 1999.

Carrington, Charles E.: *Soldier from the Wars Returning*, Hutchinson, 1965.

Cassar, George H.: *Kitchener, Architect of Victory*, Kimber, 1977.

Cassar, –: *The Tragedy of Sir John French*, University of Delaware Press, 1985.

Cecil, H and Liddle, P.: *Facing Armageddon: The First World War Experienced*, Leo Cooper, 1996.

Churchill, Winston Spencer: *The World Crisis, 1911–18*, Thornton Butterworth, 1931.

Churchill, –: *Great Contemporaries*, Thornton Butterworth, 1937.

Clark, Alan: *The Donkeys*, Hutchinson, 1963.

Clayton, Anthony: *Paths of Glory: The French Army 1914–18*, Weidenfeld & Nicolson, 2003.

Corns, Cathryn & Hughes-Wilson, John: *Blindfold and Alone, British Military Executions in the Great War*, Cassell, 2001.

Corrigan, Gordon: *Mud, Blood and Poppycock*, Cassell, 2003.

Cross, C. (ed.): *Life With Lloyd George: Diary of A. J. Sylvester*, Macmillan, 1975.

Davenport-Hines, Richard: *Letters from Oxford: Hugh Trevor-Roper and Bernard Berenson*, Weidenfeld & Nicolson, 2006.

Davidson, J.: *Haig, Master of the Field*, Peter Nevill, 1953.

Davies, Frank and Maddox, Graham: *Bloody Red Tabs*, Leo Cooper, 1995.

De Groot, Gerard J.: *Douglas Haig 1861–1928*, Unwin-Hyman, 1988.

De Groot, –: *Blighty – British Society in the Era of the Great War*, Longman, 1996.

Dewar, G. A. B. and Boraston, J. H.: *Sir Douglas Haig's Command 1915–1918* (two volumes), Constable, 1922.

Dixon, Norman F.: *On the Psychology of Military Incompetence*, Cape, 1976.

Duffy, Christopher: *Through German Eyes: the British & the Somme 1916*, Weidenfeld & Nicolson, 2006.

Edmonds, Brigadier-General James: *The Occupation of the Rhineland 1918–1929*, HMSO, 1987.

Ferguson, Niall: *The Pity of War*, Allen Lane, 1998.

Forester, C. S.: *The General*, Michael Joseph, 1936.

Freedman, Lawrence, Hayes, Paul; and O'Neill, Robert (eds.): *War, Strategy, and International Politics*, Clarendon Press, 1992.

French, D.: *British Strategy and War Aims 1914–1916*, Allen & Unwin, 1986.

French, –: *The Strategy of the Lloyd George Coalition 1916–18*, Clarendon Press, 1995.

French, Gerald: *French Replies to Haig*, Hutchinson, 1936.

Fussell, Paul: *The Great War and Modern Memory*, Oxford University Press (USA), 1977.

Garratt, Eilidh, Reid, Alice, Schurer, Kevin and Szreter, Simon (eds.): *Changing*

*Family Size in England & Wales: Place, Class & Demography 1891–1911*, Cambridge University Press, 2001.

Gay, Peter: *The Bourgeois Experience: Victoria to Freud*, Oxford University Press, 1984.

Gibbs, Philip: *Realities of War*, Heinemann, 1920.

Gilbert, Bentley Brinkerhoff: *David Lloyd George: Organizer of Victory 1912–1916*, Batsford, 1992.

Gilmour, David: *Curzon*, John Murray, 2003 edition.

Girouard, Mark: *The Return to Camelot: Chivalry and the English Gentleman*, Yale University Press, 1981.

Gooch, John: *The Plans of War: the General Staff and British Military Strategy, 1900–1916*, Routledge and Kegan Paul, 1974.

Greenhalgh, Elizabeth: *Victory Through Coalition: Britain and France during the First World War*, Cambridge University Press, 2005.

Grieves, Keith: *The Politics of Manpower, 1914–1918*, Manchester University Press, 1988.

Griffith, Paddy: *Battle Tactics of the Western Front*, Yale University Press, 1994.

Grigg, John: *Lloyd George: War Leader 1916–1918*, Penguin, 2003.

Grosskurth, Phyllis: *The Woeful Victorian: A Biography of John Addington Symonds*, Holt, Rinehart and Wilson, 1964.

Gudmundsson, Bruce I: *Stormtroop Tactics: Innovation in the German Army, 1914–18*, Westport, 1995.

Guy, A. J., Thomas, R. N. W. and De Groot, G. J.: *Military Miscellany I*, Army Records Society, 1996.

Haber, Ludwig F.: *The Poisonous Cloud: Chemical Warfare in the First World War*, Oxford University Press, 1986.

Haldane, R. B.: *Autobiography*, Hodder and Stoughton, 1929.

Hammond, N. G. L (ed.): *Centenary Essays on Clifton College*, J. W. Arrowsmith, 1962.

Hankey, Maurice: *The Supreme Command 1914–1918*, Allen & Unwin, 1961.

Harries-Jenkins, Gwyn: *The Army in Victorian Society*, Routledge and Kegan Paul, 1977.

Harris, J.: *Private Lives, Public Spirit: A Social History of Britain 1870–1914*, Oxford University Press, 1993.

Harris, J. P.: *Men, ideas and tanks: British military thought and armoured forces, 1903–1939*, Manchester University Press, 1995.

Harris J. P. and Barr, Niall: *Amiens to Armistice: The BEF in the Hundred Days' Campaign, 8 August–11 November 1918*, Brassey's, 1998.

Hart, Peter: *The Somme*, Weidenfeld & Nicolson, 2005.

Holmes, Richard: *The Little Field Marshal: A Life of Sir John French*, Weidenfeld & Nicolson, 1981.

Holmes, –: *Tommy: The British Soldier on the Western Front 1914–1918*: HarperCollins, 2004.

Hoppen, K. Theodore: *The Mid-Victorian Generation*, Clarendon Press, 1998.

Hume, John R. and Moss, Michael S.: *The Making of Scotch Whisky: A History of the Scotch Whisky Distilling Industry*, Canongate, 2000.

Johnston, Paul Barton: *Land Fit For Heroes*, University of Chicago Press, 1968.

Kennedy, Paul: *The Rise of Anglo-German Antagonism*, Routledge, 1982.

Kitchen, Martin: *The German Offensives of 1918*, Tempus, 2001.

Lamplugh, Lois: *A Shadowed Man*, Exmoor Press, 1990.

Lang, Theo: *My Darling Daisy*, Michael Joseph, 1965.

Laslett, Peter: *The World We Have Lost*, Methuen, 1965.

Lee, John: *A Soldier's Life: General Sir Ian Hamilton 1853–1947*, Macmillan, 2000.

Lees-Milne, James: *The Enigmatic Edwardian*, Sidgwick & Jackson, 1986.

Liddell Hart, Basil: *The Real War 1914–1918*, Faber & Faber, 1930.

Lowry, D. (ed.): *The South African War Reappraised*, Manchester University Press, 2000.

Luvaas, Jay: *The Education of an Army*, Cassell, 1965.

Mackenzie, J. M. (ed.): *Imperialism and Popular Culture*, Manchester University Press, 1986.

Macmillan, Margaret: *The Peacemakers*, John Murray, 2001.

Magnus, Philip: *King Edward the Seventh*, John Murray, 1964.

Mangan, J. A.: *Athleticism in the Victorian and Edwardian Public School*, Routledge Falmer, 1986.

Mangan, –: and Walvin, James (eds.): *Manliness and Morality*, Manchester University Press, 1987.

Marshall-Cornwall, General Sir James: *Haig As Military Commander*, Batsford, 1973.

Mason, M.: *The Making of Victorian Sexuality*, Oxford University Press, 1994.

McCallum, Iain: *Blood Brothers*, Chatham Publishing, 1999.

McKibbin, Ross: *The Ideologies of Class: Social Relations in Britain 1880–1950*, Oxford University Press, 1990.

McKibbin, –: *Classes and Cultures: England 1918–1951*, Oxford University Press, 1998.

Middlebrook, Martin: *The First Day on the Somme*, Allen Lane, 1971.

Middlebrook, –: *The Kaiser's Battle*, Allen Lane, 1978.

Moyer, Laurence V.: *Victory Must Be Ours: Germany in the Great War, 1914–1918*, Hippocrene, 1995.

Neillands, Robin: *The Old Contemptibles*, John Murray, 2004.

Norwich, John Julius (ed.): *The Duff Cooper Diaries*, Weidenfeld & Nicolson, 2005.

Pakenham, Thomas: *The Boer War*, Macdonald, 1982.

Parker, P.: *The Old Lie: The Great War and the Public School Ethos*, Constable, 1987.

Pedersen, P. A.: *Monash as Military Commander*, Melbourne University Press, 1992.

Pedroncini, Guy: *Les Mutineries de 1917*, Presses Universitaires de France, 1967.

Philpott, W. J.: *Anglo-French Relations and Strategy on the Western Front, 1914–18*, Macmillan, 1996.

Pollock, John: *Kitchener: Architect of Victory, Artisan of Peace*, Constable, 2001.

Porter, A. (ed.): *The Oxford History of the British Empire: The Nineteenth Century*, Oxford University Press, 1999.

Prior, Robin and Wilson, Trevor: *Command on the Western Front: The Military Career of Sir Henry Rawlinson*, Blackwell, 1992.

Prior, –: and Wilson, –: *Passchendaele, The Untold Story*, Yale University Press, 1996.

Prior, –: and Wilson, –: *The Somme*, Yale University Press, 2005.

Protheroe, Ernest: *Earl Haig*, Hutchinson, 1928.

Reid, Walter: *Architect of Victory: Douglas Haig*, Birlinn, 2006.

Richter, Donald: *Chemical Soldiers*, Leo Cooper, 1994.

Rose, Kenneth: *King George V*, Weidenfeld & Nicolson, 1983.

Rout, Guy: *Occupation and Pay in Great Britain 1906–79*, Macmillan, 1980.

Rowland, Peter: *Lloyd George*, Barrie and Jenkins, 1975.

Russell, J.: *The Haigs of Bemersyde*, Blackwood, 1881.

Samuels, Martin: *Command or Control? Command, Training and Tactics in the British and German Armies, 1888–1918*, Frank Cass, 1995.

Scott, Douglas (ed.): *Douglas Haig: The Preparatory Prologue 1861–1914*, Pen & Sword, 2006.

Searle, G. R.: *A New England? Peace and War, 1886–1918*, Oxford University Press, 2004.

Serle, Geoffrey: *John Monash*, Melbourne University Press, 1982.

Seymour, Charles: *The Intimate Papers of Colonel House*, Houghton Mifflin, 1926–8.

Sheffield, Gary: *Forgotten Victory: The First World War – Myths and Realities*, Headline, 2001.

Sheffield, Gary and Todman, Dan (eds.): *Command and Control on the Western Front*, Spellmount, 2004.

Simkins, Peter: *Kitchener's Army*, Manchester University Press, 1988.

Sixsmith, Major-General E. K. G.: *Douglas Haig*, Weidenfeld & Nicolson, 1976.

Smith, Iain R.: *The Origins of the South African War 1899–1902*, Longmans, 1995.

Sommer, D.: *Haldane of Cloane, His Life and Times, 1856–1928*, Allen & Unwin, 1960.

Spears, Major-General Sir Edward: *Two Men who saved France – Pétain and de Gaulle*, Eyre & Spottiswoode, 1966.

Spears, –: *Prelude to Victory*, Cape, 1939.

Spears, –: *Liaison 1914 – a narrative of the great retreat*, Eyre & Spottiswoode, 1968.

Spiers, Edward M.: *Haldane: an Army Reformer*, Edinburgh University Press, 1980.

Spiers, –: *The Late Victorian Army, 1868–1902*, Manchester University Press, 1992.

Stansky, Peter: *Sassoon: The Worlds of Philip and Sybil*, Yale University Press, 2003.

*Statistics of the Military Effort of the British Empire, 1914–1920*, War Office, 1922.

Steel, Nigel and Hart, Peter: *Passchendaele: The Sacrificial Ground*, Cassell, 2000.

Stevenson, David: *1914–1918, The History of the First World War*, Allen Lane, 2004.

Strachan, Hew: *The Politics of the British Army*, Clarendon Press, 1997.

Strachan, –: *The First World War, Volume I: To Arms*, Oxford University Press, 2001.

Strachey, Lytton: *Queen Victoria*, Penguin, 1978.

Sweet, Matthew: *Inventing the Victorians*, Faber & Faber, 2001.

Taylor, A. J. P.: *English History 1914–1945*, Clarendon Press, 1965.

Taylor, –: *The First World War, An Illustrated History*, Penguin, 1966.

Terraine, John: *Douglas Haig: The Educated Soldier*, Cassell, 2000 (first published by Hutchinson, 1963).

Thompson, F.M.: *The Rise of Respectable Society*, Fontana, 1988.

Todman, Dan: *The Great War: Myth and Memory*, Hambledon Continuum, 2005.

Tombs, Robert and Isabelle: *That Sweet Enemy*, Heinemann, 2006.

Tosh, J.: *A Man's Place: Masculinity and the Middle-Class Home in Victorian England*, Yale University Press, 1999.

Travers, Tim: *The Killing Ground*, Allen & Unwin, 1987.

Travers, –: *How The War Was Won*, Routledge, 1992.

Tuchman, Barbara W.: *The Guns of August*, Macmillan, 1962.

Vagts, Alfred: *Defence and Diplomacy*, Kings Crown Press, 1956.

Waites, Bernard: *A Class Society at War*, Berg, 1992.

Warner, Philip: *Field Marshal Earl Haig*, Cassell, 2003 (first published by Bodley Head, 1991).

Wells, Joseph: *Oxford and Oxford Life*, Methuen, 1892.

Williamson, Henry: *Love And The Loveless*, Sutton, 1997.

Wilsher, Peter: *The Pound in Your Pocket*, Cassell, 1970.

Wilson, Trevor: *The Myriad Faces of War*, Cambridge University Press, 1988.

Winter, Denis: *Haig's Command: A Reassessment*, Penguin, 1992.

Winter, J. M.: *The Great War and the British People*, Harvard University Press, 1985.

Winter, –: and Robert, Jean-Louis (eds.): *Capital Cities at War – Paris, London, Berlin 1914–1919*, Cambridge University Press, 1997.

Wollheim, Richard: *F. H. Bradley*, Peregrine, 1969.

Woodward, David R.: *Lloyd George and the Generals*, University of Delaware Press, 1983.

Woodward, Sir Llewellyn: *Great Britain and the War of 1914–1918*, Methuen, 1967.

Wootton, Graham: *The Official History of the British Legion*, MacDonald & Evans, 1956.

Zuber, Terence: *Inventing the Schlieffen Plan: German War Planning 1871–1914*, Oxford University Press, 2002.

# Secondary Sources: Articles

Anglim, S. J.: Haig's Cadetship – a Reassessment, *British Army Review*, 101 (August 1992).

Beaumont, R. A.: Hamel, 1918: A Study in Military-Political Interaction, *Military Affairs, 31, No 1* (Spring 1967).

Bond, Brian: Soldiers and Statesmen: British Civil-Military Relations in 1917, *Military Affairs, 32, No 2* (October 1968).

Brodick, George: A Nation of Amateurs, *The Nineteenth Century 48* (1900).

Brown, Ian M.: Not Glamorous, But Effective: The Canadian Corps and the Set-Piece Attack, 1917–1918, *The Journal of Military History, 58, No 3* (July 1994).

De Groot, Gerard: Educated Soldier or Cavalry Officer? Contradictions in the pre–1914 career of Douglas Haig, *War and Society 4* (1986).

Egerton, George W.: The Lloyd George 'War Memoirs': A Study in the Politics of Memory, *The Journal of Modern History, 60, No 1* (March 1988).

Englander, David and Osborne, James: Jack, Tommy, and Henry Dubb: The Armed Forces and the Working Class, *The Historical Journal, 21, No 3* (September 1978).

French, David: The Meaning of Attrition, 1914–1916, *English Historical Review 103* (April 1988).

French, –: Sir Douglas Haig's Reputation, 1918–1928: A Note, *The Historical Journal, 28, No 4* (December 1985).

Gardner, Nikolas: Commnd and Control in the 'Great Retreat' of 1914: The Disintegration of the British Cavalry Division, *Journal of Military History 63 No 1* (January 1999).

Gill, Douglas and Dallas, Gloden: Mutiny at Etaples Base in 1917, *Past and Present 69* (November 1975).

Graubard, Stephen Richards: Military Demobilization in Great Britain Following the First World War, *Journal of Modern History 19 No 4* (December 1947).

Greenhalgh, Elizabeth: 'Parade Ground Soldiers': French Army Assessments of the British on the Somme in 1916, *Journal of Military History, 63, No 2* (April 1999).

Greenhalgh, –: Why the British Were on the Somme in 1916, *War in History 6, No 2* (1999).

Greenhalgh, –: Myth and Memory: Sir Douglas Haig and the Imposition of Allied Unified Command in March 1918, *Journal of Military History, 68, No 3* (July 2004).

Grieves, Keith: C. E. Montague and the Making of Disenchantment, 1914–1921, *War in History, 4, No 1* (1997).

Harris, Bernard: The Demographic Impact of the First World War: An Anthropometric Perspective, *Journal of the Society for the Social History of Medicine 6* (1993).

Heathorn, Stephen: A 'matter for artists, and not for soldiers'? The Cultural Politics of the Earl Haig National Memorial, 1928–1937, *Journal of British Studies 44* (July 2005).

Hussey, John: John Fortescue, James Edmonds, and the History of the Great War, *Journal of the Society for Army Historical Research Vol.70* (1992).

Hussey, –: A Hard Day at First Ypres, *British Army Review 107* (August 1994).

Hussey, –: Without an Army and Without any Preparation to Equip One – the Financial and Industrial Background to 1914, *British Army Review No 109, 4* (1995).

Hussey, –: Douglas Haig, Adjutant: Recollections of Veterans of the 7th Hussars, *Journal of the Society for Army Historical Research 73* (1995).

Hussey, –: Of the Indian Rope Trick, the Paranormal, and Captain Shearer's Ray – Sidelights on Douglas Haig, *British Army Review No 112, 4* (1996).

Hussey, –: 'A Very Substantial Grievance', Said The Secretary of State: Douglas Haig's Examination Troubles, 1893, *Journal of the Society for Army Historical Research, 74* (1996).

Hussey, –: The Movement of German Divisions to the Western Front, Winter 1917–1918, *War in History 4, No 2* (1997).

Jeffrey, Keith: The British Army and Internal Security 1919–1939, *The Historical Journal, 24, No 2* (June 1981).

Liddell Hart, Basil: How Myths Grow – Passchendaele, *Military Affairs, 28, No 4* (Winter 1964–1965).

London Gazette, Fourth Supplement, 10th April 1919 (final dispatch of Field Marshal Sir Douglas Haig).

McEwen, J. M.: Northcliffe and Lloyd George at War, 1914–1918, *The Historical Journal, 24, No 3* (September 1981).

Palazzo, Albert P.: The British Army's Counter-Battery Staff Office and Control of the Enemy in World War 1, *Journal of Military History, 63, No 1* (January 1999).

Petter, Martin: Temporary Gentlemen in the Aftermath of the Great War: Rank, Status and the Ex-Officer Problem, *Historical Journal 37 No 1* (March 1994).

Phillips, Gervase: The Obsolescence of the *Arme Blanche* and Technological Determinism in British Military History, *War in History 9, No 1* (2002).

Razzell, P. E.: Social Origins of Officers in the Indian and British Home Army, 1758–1962, *British Journal of Sociology 14* (1963).

Samuels, Martin: British Tactical Experiments in 1915, *British Army Review 105* (December 1993).

Singleton, John: Britain's Military Use of Horses 1914–1918, *Past and Present, No 139* (May 1993).

Strachan, Hew: The British Way in Warfare Revisited, *The Historical Journal, 26, No 2* (June 1983).

Taylor, William L.: The Debate over Changing Cavalry Tactics and Weapons, 1900–1914, *Military Affairs, 28, No 4* (Winter 1964–1965).

Todman, Daniel: 'Sans peur et sans reproche', *Journal of Military History 67*, October 2003.

Travers, Tim: Technology, Tactics and Morale: Jean de Bloch, the Boer War, and British Military Theory, 1900–1914: *Journal of Modern History 51* (1979).

Travers, Tim: The Hidden Army: Structural Problems in the British Officer Corps, 1900–1918, *Journal of Contemporary History 17 No 3* (1982).

Travers, Tim: Could the Tanks of 1918 Have Been War-Winners for the British Expeditionary Force? *Journal of Contemporary History, 27, No 3* (July 1992).

Travers, –: Reply to John Hussey: The Movement of German Divisions to the Western Front, Winter 1917–1918, *War in History 5, No 3* (1998).

Ward, Stephen R.: Intelligence Surveillance of British Ex-Servicemen, 1918–1920, *The Historical Journal, 16, No 1* (March 1973).

Welch, Michael: The Centenary of the British Publication of Jean de Bloch's *Is War Now Impossible?* (1899–1999), *War in History 7, No 3* (2000).

Woodward, David: Did Lloyd George Starve the British Army of British Men Prior to the German Offensive of March 1918? *Historical Journal 27* (1984).

Wright, Peter: The 1912 Manoeuvres, *Cross & Cockade International Journal, 23, No 4* (1992).

# INDEX

Abbreviations are used as follows: Sir Douglas Haig is referred to as DH and Lady Haig as DMH; David Lloyd George as DLG and Sir John French as SJF.

Ranks are generally those finally achieved.